URBAN POLITICS

PAST, PRESENT, & FUTURE

Harlan Hahn
University of Southern California

&

Charles Levine
University of Maryland

Longman
New York & London

URBAN POLITICS
Past, Present, and Future

Longman Inc., New York
Associated companies, branches, and
representatives throughout the world.

Copyright © 1980 by Longman Inc.

Developmental Editor: Irving E. Rockwood
Editorial and Design Supervisor: Joan Matthews
Interior Design: Pencils Portfolio, Inc.
Cover Design: Dan Serrano
Manufacturing and Production Supervisor: Louis Gaber
Composition: A&S Graphics
Printing and Binding: Book Press

Library of Congress Cataloging in Publication Data

Main entry under title:

Urban politics.

1. Municipal government—United States—Addresses,
essays, lectures.   I. Hahn, Harlan, 1939–
II. Levine, Charles H.
JS331.U7   1980   352′.008′0973   80-471

Manufactured in the United States of America

9 8 7 6 5 4 3 2 1

JS
331
.U7
c.2

Acknowledgments

The editors wish to thank the following authors and publishers for their kind permission to reprint:

"The Politics of Reform in Municipal Government in the Progressive Era" by Samuel P. Hays. From *Pacific Northwest Quarterly*, Vol. 55, October 1964, pp. 157–189. Copyright © 1964 by Samuel P. Hays. Reprinted by permission of the author and the publisher.

"Why Political Machines Have Not Withered Away and Other Revisionist Thoughts" by Raymond E. Wolfinger. From *The Journal of Politics*, 34-2 (May 1972), pp. 365–398. Copyright ©1972 by *The Journal of Politics*. Reprinted by permission of the publisher and the author.

"Machine Politics: Old and New" by Theodore Lowi. From THE PUBLIC INTEREST, No. 9, Fall 1967, pp. 83–92. Copyright © 1967 by National Affairs, Inc. Reprinted by permission of the author and the publisher.

"The Local Community as an Ecology of Games" by Norton Long. From *American Journal of Sociology*, Vol. 64, November 1958, pp. 251–261. Copyright © 1962 by *American Journal of Sociology*. Reprinted by permission of the author and the publisher.

"Two Faces of Power" by Peter Bachrach and Morton S. Baratz. From *American Political Science Review*, Vol. 56, December 1962, pp. 947–952. Copyright © 1962 by *American Political Science Review*. Reprinted by permission of the author and the publisher.

"The City as a Growth Machine" by Harvey Molotch. From *American Journal of Sociology*, September 1976, pp. 309–332. Copyright © 1976 by *American Journal of Sociology*. Reprinted by permission of the author and the publisher.

"Cleavages, Coalitions, and the Black Candidate: The Los Angeles Mayoralty Elections of 1969 and 1973" by Harlan Hahn, David Klingman, and Harry Pachon. From *Western Political Quarterly*, December 1976, pp. 507–520. Copyright © 1976 *Western Political Quarterly*. Reprinted by permission of the publisher.

"Mandating Urban Equality: The Distribution of Municipal Public Services" by Robert L. Lineberry. From *Texas Law Review*, Vol. 53, No. 26, December 1974. Copyright © 1974 by Texas Law Review. Reprinted by permission of the publisher.

"Life-Style Values and Political Decentralization in Metropolitan Areas" by Oliver Williams. From *Social Science Quarterly*, Vol. 48, No. 3, December 1967, pp. 299–310. Copyright © 1967 by Oliver Williams. Reprinted by permission of the author.

"Service Delivery Rules and the Distribution of Local Government Services: Three Detroit Bureaucracies" by Bryan D. Jones, Saadia R. Greenberg, Clifford Kaufman, and Joseph Drew. From *The Journal of Politics*, Vol. 40, 1978, pp. 332–368. Copyright © 1978 by *The Journal of Politics*. Reprinted by permission of the publisher and the authors.

"New York City's Fiscal Crisis: The Politics of Inflation and Retrenchment" by Martin Shefter. From THE PUBLIC INTEREST, No. 48, Summer 1977, pp. 98–127. Copyright © 1977 by National Affairs, Inc. Reprinted by permission of the author and the publisher.

"Intergovernmental Relations: An Analytical Overview" by Deil S. Wright. From THE ANNALS of The American Academy of Political and Social Science, Vol. 416, November 1974, pp. 1–16. Copyright © 1974 by Deil S. Wright. Reprinted by permission of the publisher.

"The New System of Intergovernmental Relations: More Fiscal Relief and More Governmental Intrusions," by David B. Walker. From *Governmental Finance*, Vol. 7, No. 4, November 1978, pp. 17–22. Copyright © by the Municipal Finance Officers Association of the United States and Canada. Reprinted by permission of the publisher.

"Metropolitan Reform: Propositions Derived from Two Traditions" by Elinor Ostrom. From *Social Science Quarterly*, Vol. 53, No. 3, December 1972, pp. 474–493. Copyright © 1972 by Elinor Ostrom. Reprinted by permission of the author and the publisher.

"The City in the Future of Democracy" by Robert A. Dahl. From the *American Political Science Review*, December 1967, pp. 953–970. Copyright © 1967 by Robert A. Dahl and American Political Science Review. Reprinted by permission of the author and the publisher.

"The Future of Urban Government" by Douglas Yates. From *New York Affairs*, Vol. 3, No. 2, Winter 1976, pp. 8–19. Copyright © 1976 *New York Affairs*. Reprinted by permission of the publisher.

"The Future of Community Control" Norman I. Fainstein and Susan S. Fainstein. From *American Political Science Review*, September 1976, pp. 905–923. Copyright © 1976, *American Political Science Review*. Reprinted by permission of the publisher and the author.

CONTENTS

URBAN POLITICS

The Politics of Urban America and the Study of Urban Politics

In order to know where American cities are heading, it is necessary to know where they have been. History does not always repeat itself precisely, but the major trends which emerge from the past often have a profound and continuing impact upon the present and the future. Just as individuals frequently discover that their earlier experiences may mold and shape their lives, so it is with the aggregations of people who live in geographically defined areas known as cities. The effort to understand the present and assess the future of urban government and politics—which is the principal goal of this book and the primary concern of most urban scholars—must be based upon a thorough appreciation of the sources from which cities have evolved and the dominant concerns that have guided the study of urban problems and politics.

In order to understand the present and speculate on the future, we must consider four aspects of the past and present that are likely to have a continuing importance for urban politics: the conflict between political machines and reformers; the debate over the structure of political power and democracy in American cities; the disputes about the responsiveness of municipal governments, bureaucracies, and services; and the difficulties involved in ordering relationships between neighborhoods, cities, counties, states, and the federal government. Since local government and politics are only two of the many forces that have helped to shape America's urban areas, this perspective enables urban politics to be framed against a background that incorporates the demographic, economic, and national political changes that have occurred throughout America's urbanization. Taken together, these concerns provide a rich mosaic of the forces that bind the future to the past, constrain public policy choices, and shape the capacity of city governments to solve the problems of their citizens.

MACHINES AND REFORMERS

Perhaps the most important influence upon the origins of U.S. cities was the fact that America began—and has, to some extent, remained—a predominantly agrarian country.

The authors gratefully acknowledge the assistance of Richard F. Lewis in the preparation of this essay.

Until the end of the nineteenth century, the vast majority of Americans lived on farms or in small villages and towns. The general growth of large population concentrations—and giant metropolitan areas—did not occur until later in the twentieth century.

If the sometimes overly romanticized accounts of the early nineteenth century can be believed, life in the small communities of America at that time was relatively tranquil. Most local problems were handled by the common and voluntary efforts of a homogeneous group of citizens. There were no municipal police departments, for example, and, in general, government activities were kept to a minimum. Under a peculiarly American legal doctrine commonly known as "Dillon's Rule," cities were considered creatures of the state; and they could undertake only those projects and programs which were specifically authorized for them by state legislatures. Many city charters at the time were almost direct imitations of the U.S. Constitution. They included the separation of powers into distinct executive, legislative, and judicial branches. Some city councils were even bicameral, that is, they were divided into separate upper and lower bodies.[1]

As increasing numbers of immigrants began to arrive from foreign shores during the middle and latter nineteenth century, however, both the nature of urban populations and the characteristics of local governments underwent a dramatic change. Surrounded by newcomers from diverse ethnic backgrounds, who often spoke a different language, the established residents of American communities discovered that they could no longer solve their problems through a consensus based upon mutually shared values. Those residents often mounted a determined effort to resist the growing political power of the immigrants; and ethnic conflict, occasionally accompanied by violence, erupted in many cities during this period.[2] American cities were being introduced to the idea that community affairs could not be handled without disagreement and that politics was an essential component of decision-making at the local or grass-roots level.

The late nineteenth century in America was also a period of rapid economic growth and industrialization. Cities were under intense pressure to pass laws and provide services needed by factories and the growing number of people who came to work in them. But they were often hampered by legal restrictions and by their own governmental institutions which had been carefully designed—as had the American Constitution—to prevent the centralization or the accumulation of power by any major political leaders.

Gradually, to overcome the legal fragmentation built into city charters and the resistance of established residents, ethnic groups began to develop a political style—and a form of political organization—that was distinctively their own. The new form of political organization which emerged in American cities during the late nineteenth century was the political machine. Since power was so diffuse and dispersed in the formal structure of government, leaders relied upon an informal, extralegal organization, usually a political party, as a means of centralizing or concentrating influence. The head of the machine was the so-called "boss" who sat at the top of an informal hierarchical organization which encompassed elected officials, government employees, district or ward party leaders, and precinct workers. The underlying dynamic of the machine consisted of a system of patronage through which government jobs, franchises, contracts, and nominations for major elective or party positions were distributed primarily on the basis of a person's record of service and loyalty to the party machine. Since public officials were dependent upon the machine for their jobs, they could ignore the directives of the boss only at their peril. At that time, there was little doubt about who ran the cities: it was the party machine and the boss.[3]

There is still a great deal of historical debate about the value of the old-style party-based political machines. In most evaluations, the city machine has been linked to ethnic politics and the attraction it had for ambitious new arrivals eager for the upward social and economic mobility otherwise denied to them by established private businesses. From this perspective, the machine provided immigrants a rare opportunity for full-fledged involvement in the mainstream of American life. The machines also performed a number of community organization and welfare functions; they may have been responsible for the growth of neighborhood unity and cohesion, while also dispensing many needed social services.[4] A bucket of coal or a turkey during the holidays hardly compares with contemporary welfare programs, but the benefits and favors provided by the machine seemed to play an indispensable role in the lives of many immigrant families. On the other hand, there is little doubt that some machines were corrupt. Petty favoritism, bribes, kickbacks, and graft permeated the machines in many cities. Some writers felt that the corruption may have been caused by the entrepreneurs and businessmen who were seeking municipal franchises and contracts that were essential for the development of urban industrialism at the time.[5] Other commentators simply ascribed the graft and corruption of city government under machine rule to the blind ambition and venality of the boss and his "wardhealers."

The battle between the defenders of the machine and the proponents of reform raged for decades. Underlying the antagonism was a basic conflict of political values. This conflict was perhaps best expressed by Richard Hofstadter when he drew a distinction between what he called the "Yankee-Protestant" and the "immigrant" political ethos.[6] According to Hofstadter, the Yankee-Protestant political ethos "assumed and demanded the constant, disinterested activity of the citizen in public affairs, argued that political life ought to be run . . . in accordance with general principles and abstract laws apart from and superior to personal needs, and expressed a common feeling that government should be in good part an effort to moralize the lives of individuals," while the economic system would provide an outlet for their baser and more aggressive instincts. On the other hand, the immigrant ethic "took for granted that the political life of the individual would arise out of family needs, interpreted political and civic relations chiefly in terms of personal obligations, and placed strong personal loyalties above allegiances to abstract codes of laws or morals."[7]

Although the struggle over these opposing values continued for decades, public attitudes—and much of the research on urban politics—appear to have been strongly influenced by the values of the dominant Yankee-Protestant ethos of political participation in the absence of self-interest.[8] Students were often told that they should analyze public issues and participate in politics primarily on the basis of altruistic concerns about the "public interest" or "the general good of the community" rather than their personal advantage or the impact of a policy upon a particular group of which they may be a member. While those sentiments represent noble goals, many scholars have also noted that the machine performed important functions by providing a basis for community organization, by "humanizing" government services, and by distributing welfare and jobs to a dependent clientele. Perhaps the best defense of the machine was provided by Martin Lomansey, the political boss of Boston, when he was confronted by the muckraker Lincoln

Steffens's audacious proposal that he ought to destroy his own machine. Lomansey seemed to capture the distinction between the Yankee-Protestant and the immigrant ethos when he replied, "I think there's got to be in every ward somebody that any bloke can come to—no matter what he's done—and get help. Help, you understand; none of your law and your justice, but help."[9]

Despite such appeals, the municipal reform movement was generally successful in realizing many of its goals. Even though the issue of corruption ultimately was the key to their triumph, and the ethnic machines survived in some cities longer than in others, the reformers also managed to produce a series of changes in the form or structure of urban government which have had a continuing and fundamental impact upon city politics and the type of policies that they adopt.

Since the basic objective of the reform movement was to destroy machine politics, a system of local government needed to be devised that would eliminate the connection between party-controlled votes and government jobs, contracts, and services. Although there were originally many other proposals in the reform movement such as proportional representation and the "short ballot," the major planks of the reform platform to accomplish this goal included nonpartisan at-large elections, the merit-based civil service system, and the city manager plan.

The adoption of nonpartisan elections, which removed party labels from the ballots, proved to be the most direct and effective means of reform. During the machine era, the concept of "politics" had changed from a conflict between competing interests and values to "partisan political"—a denotation which still continues today to designate electoral contests between organized political parties. Because the latter use of the word "politics" conjures up the unattractive image of the fat, cigar-smoking corrupt politician or party boss, the reformers argued that nonpartisan elections would offer the best means of eliminating such characters from local politics. Since political parties exist principally for the purpose of nominating and electing candidates, the adoption of nonpartisan elections produced a gradual weakening of party organizations at the local level, a decline in voter interest and turnout in local elections, and a decline in accountability because voters often found party labels useful clues in guiding their electoral choices.

In a few ostensibly nonpartisan cities, voluntary citizens groups sprang up to fill this void; in some communities, parties continued to be active, even though their names did not appear on the ballot; but, in other places, elections reflected a free-for-all in which candidates with the greatest name recognition or money often emerged victorious. With the advent of nonpartisan local elections, political activism declined—especially among the low-income ethnic groups that had been the primary base of the machine.[10]

Perhaps most significantly, however, the gradual decay of the party machine removed an important centralizing influence from the formal structure of local government. Political parties were disentangled from the apparatus of government, and the centralizing leverage of the machine was gone. Power or influence in urban politics during the reform era was just as diffuse and as fragmented as it had been before the machine emerged.

A second major element in the "reform" platform was the innovation of at-large elections. During the machine era, members of city councils and other representatives were usually elected by wards, districts, or neighborhoods within the city. In this way, the link between the demands and needs of citizens and city council votes were tightly forged. The reformers charged that ward politics permitted narrow neighborhood-based interests to dominate the agenda of local politics at the expense of broader city-wide issues and the "public interest." The reformers proposed that representatives be elected at large so that they would be chosen by the city as a whole rather than by specific electoral districts. But the elimination of ward or district representation removed a crucial personal link between the voters and elected officials. Moreover, the difficulty of identifying to whom at-large representatives were responsible seemed to complicate, rather than to simplify, the search for leadership in the city.

Thirdly, the reformers sought the abolition of patronage and the introduction of merit-based civil service systems.[11] Since patronage was the foundation of the power of the old-style machines, the desire of the reformers to eliminate patronage was clearly related to their efforts to destroy the machine. But the acceptance of "merit systems," through which municipal jobs were filled by competitive examinations rather than by personal appointments, had far-ranging implications for the implementation of local policies. Under civil service procedures, the qualifications acquired by training and occupational experience became more important prerequisites for obtaining a government job than the skills developed by "party work"—that is, organizing and serving local residents in exchange for their vote.

A final major proposal of the reform movement was the city manager plan. In some respects, this feature of the reform platform was anomalous.[12] Unlike the other major aspects of the reform program, which sought to decentralize authority and to prevent power from concentrating again in the hands of a single political leader, the city manager was designed to serve as the sole head of a vast administrative structure that would control the day-to-day operations of local government. In designing the "city manager plan," the reformers gave implicit recognition to the need for some centralizing influence in city politics.

A more crucial rationale for the city manager plan probably can be traced to the widespread acceptance of a distinction between "politics" and "administration." The reformers—and most experts of urban government at that time—accepted the idea that political issues would continue to exist in American cities and should be resolved by elected officials such as a mayor and a city council, whereas purely administrative problems could be handled by the city manager and the civil servants. The elected representatives of the people would continue to be responsible for designing policy and for making basic political decisions, while the administrators would simply have the task of putting those decisions into effect. Therefore, even though the reformers were not prepared to permit the centralization of political influence, they were willing to allow administrative duties to become concentrated in a bureaucratic hierarchy led by a city manager. Unlike political questions, to the reformers, administrative matters seemed relatively routine and innocuous. The reformers argued successfully and with conviction: "There is no Republican or Democratic way to clean the streets."

For a time, this division of labor between "politics" and "administration" appeared to be working. City governments facilitated the industrial expansion which had begun in the nineteenth century; and they continued to provide seemingly mundane services needed to support this economic growth, such as electricity, water, streets, and sewer systems. The violence which accompanied the migration of black Americans from the rural South to the urban North at the end of World War I was an ominous sign of events which were yet to unfold; but the dominant themes in municipal government during the early twentieth century were economy and efficiency in municipal services.

This perspective was badly shaken with the advent of the Great Depression and the New Deal. These developments made it clear that massive national social and economic problems required the resources and legal authority of the federal government and that the social and economic consequences of the Depression impacted on cities in ways that could not be solved by local governments acting alone. In the struggle to end the Depression and to win World War II, the problems of governing cities appeared to be temporarily forgotten. Even the accelerating phenomenon of suburbanization, which was largely subsidized by national mortgage insurance programs and by federal highway funds, seemed to arouse more interest among novelists than among public officials or urban scholars. Even late into the 1950s, Lawrence Herson could describe the study of municipal politics as a "lost world."[13]

POWER AND DEMOCRACY

Power

The calm was finally broken by the publication of an important book in 1953. A sociologist named Floyd Hunter conducted an intensive study of Atlanta, Georgia, in an effort to determine who really ran the city.[14] In his book, *Community Power Structure*, he reported that a small interacting group—an elite consisting primarily of local businessmen and wealthy families—which operated outside of electoral politics, dominated most of the major decisions made by the city government.

Hunter's study had massive reverberations among political activists, public officials, and urban researchers. It stimulated interest again on the crucial effort to identify power and leadership in American cities. Although political scientists always have had a great deal of difficulty in defining the concept of "power," which is basic to their discipline, they were at least forced to grapple with the issue. Many students of urban politics began to ask themselves some fundamental questions: Where was power lodged? Could it be found among political organizations, interest groups, or elected officials? Was it located in the bureaucracies which had developed to administer the everyday operations of local government? Or did it reside in members of the social and economic elite, who usually did not occupy any public offices and who were not accountable to the voters for their decisions?

The latter possibility appeared especially disturbing. For a long period of time, the primary concerns of the cities seemed to be focused on economic expansion and on the provision of municipal services which urban areas required for their continued growth. While some observers, such as Lincoln Steffens, strongly suspected that businesses were responsible for the corruption of the old-style political machines, other commentators were highly suspicious of the economic interest of the reformers. They speculated that the reformers may have been motivated by the desire to overthrow the ethnic politicians and to replace them with business leaders who were more interested in economic prosperity than in "good government" or the plight of the ethnic poor. Although the reform movement had dispersed power and influence in much the same way that it had been fragmented prior to the growth of the machine, Hunter's study focused attention on the fact that the centralization of power had not disappeared in city politics. Could it be that the machine had been destroyed only to be replaced by another powerful group which existed outside—or apart from—the formal institutions of local government and which imposed its will on most crucial decisions? Had American cities substituted an economic elite for a political boss?

Perhaps the most important aspects of the research on community elites and power structures involved its implications for the theory and practice of democracy. Many people began to ask, if politics at the grass-roots level is dominated by an oligarchical elite, are there similar elites which control the states or the country? In America, governments which are closest to the people are usually considered the most democratic and the most susceptible to public influence. People often feel that they have a better chance to shape the decisions that are made at city hall than those that are made in state capitols or in Washington, D.C. But perhaps the real decisions are not made at city hall. What if the choices that determine the fate of a city—and the people who live in it—are actually made by a shadowy clique of business leaders who may simply allow elected officials to legitimize the decisions which they already have agreed upon? Under these conditions, it not only becomes difficult to "fight city hall," but it may be impossible to fight back at all. The ramifications of such reasoning had a stimulating and a constructive effect. For several years, increased emphasis was directed at the study of power and leadership in urban politics; and the question—who really runs American cities?—became a predominant concern of social scientists.[15]

Pluralism

Hunter's research on "elites" was answered in a 1960 study of decision-making on several major issues in New Haven, Connecticut, by a political scientist, Robert Dahl. In his classic book, *Who Governs?*, Dahl used several methods to reconstruct the decision-making process on those issues and to identify the person or persons who exerted critical or decisive influence in shaping the outcome of the issues.[16]

Dahl believed that the results of his study of local politics in New Haven were consistent with the concept of "pluralism." His findings indicated that citizens were not necessarily barred from effective participation in the local government decision-making process if they did not belong to a single, long-established, small elite. From his perspective, the support of the so-called "community power structure" was not indispensable to the success of city projects or innovations. All community decisions were not made by an elite. Instead, Dahl argued that the decision-making process was open to different people who had the ability to exert a critical impact upon policies in which they were interested, and in which they were willing to invest their time, talents, and expertise. Influence was not confined to a selected few; and, even though it did tend to concentrate within separate issue areas, Dahl and his followers became convinced that power at the local level had not been captured by an exclusive unchanging clique. Power was sufficiently dispersed both within the formal structure of government—and within the general community—to allow different configurations of interests to sway the outcome of separate local policy issues.

For several years, the debate between the so-called "elitists" and "pluralists" became the dominant controversy not only in the study of urban politics but also in the discipline of political science as a whole.[17] In some respects, the viability of democracy as an ideal and a reality seemed to be at stake.[18] The evidence that local decisions were dominated by an oligarchical elite raised serious doubt about the capacity of democracy to survive as a workable ideal, not only in American cities but also in the country as a whole and in other societies of the world. On the other hand, the findings of the pluralists suggested that democracy could function—albeit perhaps imperfectly—by allowing different groups with specific interests to emerge and to have a crucial effect upon various local decisions.

Despite the obvious importance of the issue, unfortunately, the question was never fully answered and the debate never fully resolved. Several studies were conducted to examine elitist and pluralist theories within the same city.[19] A few attempts were made to compare elitist and pluralist models in various communities.[20] But, in large measure, the controversy became bogged down in a methodological quagmire.[21] The principal method used was to ask people who were knowledgeable about local affairs a question like "Who really runs things in this community?" This technique, called the "reputational approach," usually elicited a relatively small list of people who had contact with each other and who corresponded with the highest social and economic stratum of the city. But the pluralists charged that this approach did not really measure power or influence; it simply measured a *reputation* for power or influence.[22]

By contrast, the pluralists felt that it was necessary to study actual decisions, often by reconstructing the decision-making process, to identify those individuals who exerted key influence at crucial times during the development of an issue. This technique, called the "decisional approach," was, in turn, criticized as being more subjective than the reputational method. Whereas the reputational technique could be replicated indefinitely to see if other scholars arrived at the same list of names, there was no assurance that two independent researchers would choose similar issues as significant or that they would reconstruct the same decision in a way that would necessarily identify similar persons as having a crucial impact upon the outcome of the issue.[23] Perhaps more importantly, the emphasis of the pluralists upon actual decisions was criticized by another group of writers who argued that perhaps the most important phenomena in urban politics were the "nondecisions" of community politics, that is, the issues that had never been placed upon the political agenda, and the persistent needs and concerns of urban residents that had never been translated into policy proposals—perhaps due to the resistance or the dominating influence of local elites.[24]

Although the "elitist-pluralist controversy" was never settled in a definitive or satisfactory manner, it at least succeeded in injecting an important focus and a renewed vigor into the study of urban politics. Not since the days of the old-style political machine had the question of identifying major centers of leadership and power been a predominant concern of urban researchers. With the emergence of the elitist-pluralist debate, however, the concerns of both urban researchers and public officials were again focused on the crucial effort to discover the real sources of power and influence in the city.

Polarization

Before the argument between elitists and pluralists could be settled, however, a new and even more important set of forces emerged in American communities to raise questions about American urban democracy. During the 1960s, as a result of the migration which had begun during World War I, it was clear that many major cities were becoming either predominantly or in large part black. Although the movement for civil rights began in the South, it quickly spread to the North; and the cities became the primary battlefields for the struggle between blacks demanding equal rights and white residents and city officials who resisted these changes.

The rise of blacks and other minority groups presented new problems. In the days of the old-style party machine, European white ethnic groups had managed to develop mechanisms to overcome the diffusion of influence in the formal institutions of government. But the reform movement had changed all that.

Even though elitists and pluralists were unable to agree as to where power was located in American cities, one thing was certain: it was not to be found among urban minorities. During the 1960s the rise of black political power and white resistance caused American cities to enter a new period of *polarized* racial and ethnic relations that required new political strategies and that forced urban researchers to turn their attention in different directions.

The persistent needs and demands of minorities confronted urban America with its most severe challenge. According to pluralist assumptions and to the classic tenets of American politics, a small segment of the population could combine with other groups in coalitions to promote their mutual objectives. In this way, the major needs of all portions of society could be served through the formal governmental system. But blacks and other non-European ethnic groups constituted a visible and persistent minority. At least at the state or national level, they had little hope of ever achieving majority status; and as they looked for white groups with whom they might form coalitions, they were often met with indifference and rebuffs.[25]

Some members of minority groups responded to their plight by railing against the "white power structure." Others attempted litigation in the courts to test the constitutionality of local as well as national policies, often with notable and striking success. But the basic problem of forming alliances and coalitions with the white electorate remained. Although black voters were becoming highly mobilized and activated, they still needed at least a measure of support from the dominant white population in order to meet their needs and to fulfill their goals.

One method of approaching this problem involved the widespread use of demonstrations and protests. Out of the civil rights movement in the South, many minority leaders learned that they could focus attention upon their cause and attract a certain measure of external support by amassing a substantial number of people who would march or picket or sit in at the site of the institutions against which the demonstrations were directed. These actions were not taken in the belief that the target of protest would necessarily capitulate. In most cases, the protestors sought the intervention of outside forces. The first target was the mass media, which sometimes regarded the protest as an unusually dramatic news event, worthy of extensive coverage and exposure. This publicity, in turn, occasionally aroused the sympathies of a liberal white audience, including the federal government, which was capable of generating the political pressure necessary to produce important changes in public policies.[26] In this way, local protests such as the famous Montgomery bus boycott and the civil rights marches in Birmingham, Alabama, were undoubtedly responsible for the passage of much important civil rights legislation. But gradually, by the late 1960s, the attention of the white public began to diminish; and the political strategy of protests, marches, and demonstrations no longer seemed able to produce the fundamental policy changes desired by minorities in urban America.

At the same time, however, another important demographic trend was changing the face of American cities. The white movement to the suburbs, which had escalated after World War II, had continued unabated throughout the 1950s and 1960s. During the same period, the migration of minority groups from rural areas to central cities and from south to north was also increasing steadily. Blacks, and in some cities Latin Americans, began to foresee another possibility: they might actually become a majority, or at least a dominant minority, within the core of some of America's largest cities.

The growth of black and brown urban populations and civil rights activity produced three important sets of events during the late sixties. First, in 1964 President Lyndon Johnson launched a "War on Poverty" that included legislation guaranteeing the poor "maximum feasible participation," thereby spawning experiments with community action and control. Second, rioting by blacks, beginning in the New York City ghettos of Harlem and Bedford-Stuyvesant in 1964 and in the Los Angeles ghetto of Watts in 1965 and then spreading to over 100 cities by 1968, immobilized city governments and terrified whites. Third, at the close of the decade, a number of central cities elected black mayors over white opponents after racially divisive campaigns. All of these events reflected and contributed to a heightened level of racial division and polarization between American blacks and whites during the 1960s.

The Community Action Program of the War on Poverty was a brief and significant experiment in "community control" or neighborhood government in cities.[27] The basic purpose of community control was to establish a grass-roots forum in which neighborhood residents would be free to discuss and to decide policies that had a major effect upon the areas in which they lived. The central thrust of community control was intended to increase participation in local decisions, especially among those segments of the population that had not previously been active in the policy-making process.

The results of various community control experiments around the country, however, were not altogether encouraging. Participation in neighborhood bodies usually remained at a low ebb; and most of the people who did become involved tended to be the same individuals who were already active in voluntary associations, political parties, and similar organizations.[28] Perhaps part of the problem was that major city officials often were reluctant to delegate real decision-making authority—rather than advice and consultation—to neighborhood groups. Or perhaps many urban residents were simply so preoccupied with the everyday problems of maintaining a job, keeping a roof over their heads, putting food on the table, and raising their families that they just could not afford the luxury of engaging in collective political action, even about policies which could conceivably contribute to the solution of their daily problems.

The brave experiment with "maximum feasible participation" came to a quiet end in 1967 after the passage of an amendment to the Economic Opportunity Act of 1964 which limited the authority of the Community Action agencies. More often than its designers would have liked or had anticipated, the Community Action programs at the neighborhood level had used federal funds for organizing opposition to city government and its officials. In subsequent legislation, the relevant clause was modified simply to require "*widespread* citizen participation" and shifted decision-making power over federally funded antipoverty programs to elected officials and to city hall.[29]

The War on Poverty turned out largely to be wishful thinking. The program never called for poverty to be attacked by seeking a redistribution of income either through direct payments or changes in the tax laws. Instead, a large part of the antipoverty program rested on the hope that Community Action programs and education would provide the basis for sustained improvements in ghetto neighborhoods. A similar logic permeated other federal urban programs: education was to be enhanced by improved facilities and highly qualified teachers; housing was to be provided by increased construction and rent subsidy programs; and crime was to be reduced by additional equipment and trained manpower. But most of these hopes for solving urban poverty-related problems proved to be futile and short-lived. The escalation of the Vietnam War drained critical resources; and many seemingly simple problems turned out to be complex and unresponsive to government intervention. For example, the massive studies of the Coleman Report indicated that influences in the home might have a greater impact upon a child's level of educational attainment than school facilities; and some subsequent research has even suggested that a teacher's subjective impression of a student could have a greater effect upon his or her scholastic attainments than either the home or school environments.[30] Similarly, massive urban renewal programs and low-cost housing not only failed to meet the needs of central-city residents, but also seemingly provided greater advantages for business and commercial interests in the city than for the urban poor.

The raising—and then the dashing—of the hopes of America's ghettoized blacks contributed to widespread discontent and alienation. In the mid-1960s, urban America suddenly erupted in flames. New York in 1964, Watts in 1965, Detroit and Newark in 1967, the upheavals after the assassination of Martin Luther King, Jr., in 1968, and a number of other incidents of violence throughout the country produced the highest levels of death and property destruction in the history of American urbanization. The polarization which had surfaced during civil rights protests was also evident during the rioting. The National Advisory Commission on Civil Disorders documented the trend gravely when it noted that "America is moving toward two societies: one white, one black; separate and unequal."[31]

Despite the dramatic nature of the urban violence of the 1960s, there was considerable confusion about its meaning.[32] Some observers simply viewed the violence as another form of protest. Although massive violence never was triggered or precipitated directly by protest demonstrations, that interpretation may have been partially accurate. When ghetto residents were asked what had caused the violence, they responded with the familiar litany of pressing urban problems—high unemployment, inadequate housing, poverty, poor schools, insufficient transportation, increasing crimes and a host of similar problems that have plagued the cities.[33] But the violence also may have represented something more. During the period of time when the violence was in progress, the effective authority which controlled the neighborhood could not be found in city hall, the state capitol, or in Washington, D.C. It resided in the crowds on the streets; and, even though the violence bore no evidence of rebellion or insurrection, it may have represented an effort by rioters to take control of their own destinies in the ultimate and only manner that was available to them.[34]

A more conventional outlet for urban racial turbulance and black discontent during the late 1960s was the electoral campaigns of black mayoral candidates. The struggle and eventual elections of Carl Stokes in Cleveland, Ohio; Richard Hatcher in Gary, Indiana; Kenneth Gibson in Newark, New Jersey; Coleman Young in Detroit, Michigan; Maynard Jackson in Atlanta, Georgia; and Thomas Bradley in Los Angeles, California, heartened blacks everywhere and helped to increase the credibility of the black vote as a well-disciplined political weapon.

Many people hoped that the electoral base provided by black mayors in the central cities would permit the emergence of minority leadership with the power to solve many pressing urban problems. But this optimism was clouded by three important realizations. First, the office of the mayor is usually relatively powerless to institute major policy changes. Although black mayors may have important symbolic value, mayors in general are often frustrated by their inability to overcome the division of influence in local government and to accomplish the policy changes that they—and their supporters—want to achieve. Second, the results of city elections indicated that the campaigns of black mayoral candidates tended to reinforce debilitating racial cleavages between blacks and whites; none of the early black candidates for mayor, with the exception of Thomas Bradley, received more than 25 percent of the total white vote.[35] Finally, and perhaps most importantly, most of the black mayors elected in bigger cities found that they had won, if not exactly a "hollow prize," leadership in cities that were beset by financial and economic trouble.[36] In these cities—Cleveland, Newark, Gary, and Detroit, for example—declining economic bases combined with swelling dependent minority populations to force black mayors to pursue federal and other outside funding to keep services running. This dependency on outside funding limited the scope of policy issues over which black leaders could exert influence and minimized the extent to which black political power could accomplish urban social change.[37]

The frustration of black voters that came from the realization that voting power was not easily converted into "policy power" was to some extent shared by political scientists. By the end of the decade of the 1960s scholarly interest had shifted from a nearly exclusive focus on political stratification and the search for community power toward more policy-related concerns.[38] In order to explore the link between power and policy, political scientists no longer just asked, "Who governs?" but also asked, "What difference does it make?"[39] Increasingly, the answers were found in the structures of urban government, city bureaucracies, and in the distribution of public services.

THE RESPONSIVENESS OF URBAN GOVERNMENTS AND BUREAUCRACIES

Comparative Policy Studies

A number of developments contributed to the growth of research on the relationship between politics and policy over the last half of the 1960s and through the 1970s. First, changes in cities during the period brought a host of new policy problems to public attention, providing new topics for political science research. Second, the introduction of new methodologies and technologies in social science research facilitated the analysis of large bodies of data and gave rise to the use of carefully designed interview procedures, survey and evaluation instruments, and new methods of measuring, modeling, and analyzing. Third, the growth of policy research reflected a public and scholarly awareness that city governments and their bureaucracies distribute social benefits or services that produce inequalities between regions, between cities, between cities and suburbs, between neighborhoods, and between people of different racial, class, and age groups.[40]

The first studies of public policy outputs sought to explain why "reformed" and "unreformed" governmental structures affected outputs differently, and why certain types of city social environments were more conducive to the adoption of one or the other of the different governmental forms.[41] The basic aim of these studies was to determine if reformed and unreformed cities significantly varied in social and economic composition, whether types of political institutions play an important role in the political process, and whether reformed institutions are more or less responsive to political cleavages than unreformed institutions. These studies characteristically treated aggregate taxation and expenditure levels as the variables to be explained; and the presence or absence of at-large elections, council-manager government, and nonpartisanship were considered the explanatory variables.[42]

Results generally indicated that population size and growth rates are related to governmental structure; that the homogeneity or heterogeneity of the population is somewhat associated with structure; that spending and taxing are related to the presence or absence of reform institutions; and that reform cities are less responsive to political cleavages in the population than unreformed cities.[43]

Socioeconomic characteristics of cities were also analyzed to determine if they affected policy outputs. Research on this subject touched off a heated debate among political scientists because the studies sought to test whether or not the city environment—especially socioeconomic heterogeneity—directly influenced policy actions without the intervening effect of political structure. The general thesis of this research is that political institutions have a negligible effect on policy outcomes, whereas the major forces shaping policy lie outside the formal political system.

Findings from this research generally indicate that variables such as population size, density and growth, proportion of high- and low-income residents in the city, and the size of nonwhite and ethnic populations all substantially affect the level and nature of government outputs. Interpretations of these findings generally suggest that these variables are the major forces which determine the level of demand for services and pressure exerted upon local governments. Governments will generally respond favorably to these pressures, no matter what the political system structure is like. Thus, advocates of this position suggest that it is the type and level of demand rather than political structures that influences policy, and it is ultimately the city environmental characteristics that influence demand. This debate, although later overshadowed by other issues, has never been resolved.

Studies of policy outcomes across a large number of cities also stimulated work in comparative research on community power and the extension of the elitist-pluralist conflict to issues of policy consequence. These comparative power structure studies—relating community power structure with community characteristics and policy outputs—extended the questions of "who governs?" to "who governs where, when, and with what effects?" and moved power structure analysis from studies involving one or a few cities in depth to larger numbers of communities. This new line of research allowed questions to be addressed that involved the analysis of what characteristics of communities are likely to encourage different patterns of power and leadership and what policy consequences emerge from different types of power structures.[44] Specifically, the new comparative power structure research focused on determining what encourages decentralized and centralized power structures to emerge and survive and how these structures convert power into policy.

This research also examined the characteristics of the central actors in the power and decision-making structure, and how these actors gain and use resources to create influence, that is, the relationships between potential political resources and actual political influence. The major difference between these studies and the previous case studies of community power was the "shift away from the *process* of decision-making toward the *policy consequences*" of decision-making.[45] The policy focus of these community power studies coincided and overlapped with the studies considering governmental and community structure and policy outputs. Like other research, the comparative analysis of community power and policy outcomes usually employed fiscal indicators and aggregate expenditures as policy data. While the results of these policy-oriented power studies have often been inconclusive and sometimes contradictory, they generally conclude that "the greater the horizontal differentiation (between economic, social and political activities) in a social system, the greater the differentiation between potential elites, and the more decentralized the power and decision-making structure."[46] The major finding of this research about policy was that centralized decision-making structures are associated with increased output of collectively shared public goods (goods widely shared by community residents, such as air pollution control), while decentralized decision-making structures tend to be associated with increased output of separable goods (goods which can be allocated discreetly to specific groups and neighborhoods, such as street repair).[47]

The Power of Bureaucracies

The scholarly interest in policy outputs coincided with a renewal of interest in the role of bureaucracies as formulators and producers of public policy. Although the reformers had sought to bring rationality and professionalism to government by dispersing much of the power over public services to the service agencies themselves, it became increasingly clear during the 1960s that these supposedly neutral service agencies were rarely neutral at all. Instead, the agencies of city government—police, fire, schools, sanitation, recreation, and the rest—usually made service decisions according to their own criteria, autonomous from any effective public control or participation. The evidence suggested that these agencies, originally designed to deliver services equitably and efficiently, actually were in many cases inequitable and inefficient. To make matters worse, these bureaucracies were steadily gaining power from the outpouring of program-specific federal aid while local political parties were declining in influence, thereby weakening citizen access and public accountability. During the late 1960s and continuing through the 1970s, these changes stimulated political scientists to look into the workings of these bureaucracies and to analyze the changes they were producing.

Interestingly, professionalized urban service bureaucracies—one of the institutions which the reformers thought would eliminate the machine—have been characterized as machines themselves. In a pathbreaking analysis, Theodore Lowi described bureaucracies as the new machines in urban government, and pointed out many similarities between party-based and bureaucracy-based machines. Lowi contended that the reformers' dream of abolishing politics from local government was not realized. Politics remained in local government; only its form was altered. Instead of the party organization constituting the base of power, today the bureaucratic agencies form independent bases of power.[48]

These new bureaucracy-based machines are functional instead of geographic in scope, relying on formal and professional authority rather than the cooperation of voters. The influence of bureaucracies is augmented by their cohesiveness in a setting otherwise characterized by widely dispersed power.[49] Like the old machines, these agencies are nearly autonomous structures of power with self-perpetuating leadership that allows them to shape public policy with little accountability to higher authorities.

The result is the formation of insular islands of functional power nested in city government with limited overarching central coordination. The new machine bosses are loyal only to their specific agency and professional norms. Consequently, elected officials are left relatively powerless to formulate new policies or to change agency routines.

This pattern of bureaucratic autonomy has suggested the need for additional investigation into the relationship between bureaucracies and their clients. Critics argue that most urban service bureaucracies exhibit distinct anti-client behavior. The reasons for this behavior are threefold. First, it can be attributed to the professional norms, biases, and aspirations of bureaucrats. Professionals generally are career and self-development oriented, which leads them to want to serve those clients who will respond most successfully to agency services. This bias often leaves clients who are in the most need of help with relatively little attention.[50]

Secondly, professionals also seem to be dominated by a middle-class bias which leads them to design services to appeal to middle-class clients. Consequently, they often ignore the culture of the clients they are supposed to be serving. The instructions they give and the techniques they use are often inappropriate for their clients, bringing frustration to both parties in the service relationship.

Thirdly, there tends to be conflict between the wants and needs of professionals and the wants and needs of clients. A typical clash is between the desire of professionals to have conventional nine-to-five hours in a convenient and pleasant location, and the needs of clients for services at unconventional hours—nights and weekends—in neighborhoods that are unattractive and inconvenient to middle-class professionals.[51]

Professionalism is not the only cause, however, of anticlient attitudes. Bureaucratic structures, particularly specialization, also contribute to client dissatisfaction.[52] Labor and functional specialization in large bureaucracies breeds impersonality and routinization. Narrow productivity norms encourage bureaucrats to find ways to simplify, control, and ration services. They develop routine actions and standard operating procedures rather than tailoring services to fit the unique needs of each particular client. Since specialization also increases the need for coordination, a strong emphasis on rules and rigidly defined procedures tends to develop in professionalized agencies. Attempts by professionals to improve the way their agency handles clients are stifled as professionals learn that following the rules has many rewards. In many rigidly "bureaucratized" agencies, professionals are discouraged from becoming committed and involved with the clients; instead, they learn to "process" only a part of a person's problem.

Complementing the study of the pathologies of bureaucratic structure, some political scientists have analyzed those people who actually provide services to clients—what Michael Lipsky has called "street-level bureaucrats."[53] The work of street-level bureaucrats is characterized by regular interaction with clients; wide discretion in terms of decisions and approaches to citizens; an extensive impact on the citizens with whom they deal, many of whom, like criminals, come into contact with bureaucracies on a nonvoluntary basis; and extremely difficult problems incurred in measuring work performance and accounting for productivity.

The main focus of Lipsky's analysis has been on the mechanisms street-level bureaucrats develop to contend with complexity as well as limited organizational and personal resources; physical and psychological threats; and conflicting and ambiguous role expectations. To cope with complexity and limited organizational and personal resources, street-level bureaucrats develop routines, stereotypes, and simplifications that produce short cuts for decisions, that is, categorical attitudes toward clients. Routines and simplifications are also developed to cope with threats to authority and physical well-being. Policemen, for example, are instructed to be tough and are taught to look for clues to identify potential troublemakers quickly and deal with touchy situations selectively. To cope with ambiguous role expectations, street-level bureaucrats try either to change the definitions of their clientele or to alter job expectations. For example, street-level bureaucrats may try to get clients to equate the quality of their job performance with the difficulties they encounter. By emphasizing these difficulties, the bureaucrats increase client dependency and simultaneously lower client expectations.

The attempts by street-level bureaucrats to struggle with complex social problems and role ambiguity has led to the increasing professionalization of public employees. Initially, the increase in the number of professionalized municipal employees was the result of reformist efforts to substitute administrative competence and impartiality for the corruption that occurred during the machine era. To accomplish this, the reformers introduced the "merit system" so that municipal employee selection would be on the basis of ability and academic qualifications rather than on the basis of patronage. "Professionalism" meant that agency emphasis would be placed on meeting generalized rules and regulations, rather than directly on client satisfaction—familiarity with rules came to overshadow familiarity with the needs of clients.

Eventually, professionalization involved the development of standards of conduct for occupational roles which were used as the basis for the education of future employees.[54] Professionalization stressed autonomy and self-regulation which helped to insulate public employees from the oversight of the general public and elected officials. Furthermore, because the training and professional norms of bureaucrats determined the "approved" methods for administering government programs, professionalism came to dominate many government agencies and programs. As a result, administrators were able to dismiss policy and administrative failures by arguing that failures only indicate the need for more professionalism and more "properly" trained employees.

Clearly, professionalization has not solved urban problems. To some observers, it has made matters worse. In fact, one outgrowth of professionalization—the growth of unionization during the 1960s—has helped to turn urban government and management into an almost hopelessly complex tangle of constraints and counterpressures.

Unionization has produced major changes in local political power and governmental practices. In addition to the substantial power of unionized public employees in local elections, unionization has altered the basic operations of municipal bureaucracies; that is, unions have managed to gain influence over compensation patterns, merit system rules, supervisory authority, and even service delivery procedures.

Professionalism and unionism are reinforcing because unions help their members achieve professional goals. For example, unionization is consistent with the desire of professionals to share in management functions that concern their specializations. In this way, unions seek to reinforce the professional principle of sharing power and authority equally among colleagues.[55]

The growth in the number and strength of municipal unions has made them a topic of great interest for social scientists.[56] Research into this subject was initially fragmentary, but, increasingly, as in the study of other urban policy areas, research has begun to coalesce around a systems framework. This framework identifies and defines major components of collective bargaining and their interrelationships.[57] These systems-oriented studies use the public organization as the main unit of analysis and contract change as the major policy output of collective bargaining. Municipal collective bargaining is considered to be different than private-sector collective bargaining. Unlike two-party private-sector collective bargaining, the negotiation episodes are more open to a variety of outside influences—making municipal collective bargaining more multilateral than bilateral.[58]

The multilateral character of municipal collective bargaining stems from the political power of unions.[59] They are able to control effectively a large block of voters and to influence other voters. Thus, elected officials avoid making enemies of the unions and are often divided in their loyalties between taxpayers and unions. Elected public officials always fear that when a union strikes or stages a work slowdown, the public will turn its anger and frustration towards them and demand the quick restoration of public services— often at any cost.

It would be incorrect, however, to assume that unions have unbridled power. In most states, tax limitation laws constrain the size of city budgets and thereby limit the size of municipal salaries. Also, in recent years, some elected officials have been able to mobilize citizen support to help them resist union demands.[60]

One aspect of unionization—its effect on financial management—has stirred perhaps the most uneasiness among city officials and citizens.[61] While it is true that unions have raised public payrolls, in most cases salaries have not been raised above what comparable occupations receive in the private sector. A more important adverse effect of unionization on financial management is the loss of control over tax decisions when binding arbitration is used.[62] If binding arbitration is required, and a settlement is made in favor of a union pay increase, local officials have no choice but to raise taxes or to lay off low-seniority employees in order to pay for the raises. If the latter course is chosen, service delivery usually suffers.

Unionization transformed both public personnel management and urban politics in the 1970s. By driving up public payrolls, unionization helped to alert public officials and taxpayers to the costs of urban services. This concern and the related interest in the quality, efficiency, and equity of government, served to reawaken the interest of political scientists in the delivery and distribution of public services.

Urban Service Delivery

While bureaucracies and their influence in local politics continue to attract scholarly attention, the major focus of academic research seems to be shifting to the actual delivery and distribution of urban services. Research on service delivery has centered mainly around three questions: (1) what are the actual patterns of benefits, costs, and sanctions? (2) how are distributional decisions made? and (3) how *should* services be distributed?

The dominant approach to studying urban services has sought to answer questions about service distribution and equality—looking precisely at which groups are getting what; why is it that they are getting (or not getting) them; and how they are getting (or not getting) them.

The distribution of services is important because the quality of urban life is so closely tied to government services. This relationship was highlighted by the riots of the mid-1960s and subsequent analysis which attributed black discontent to the poor and unequal quality of education and police and recreational services. Additionally, in recent years, a number of notable court decisions have focused on service equalization cases, the most notable of which—Hawkins vs. Town of Shaw—ended with the town of Shaw, Mississippi, being ordered to provide services to blacks which are equal to those provided whites.[63] Furthermore, recent studies have shown that few cities allocate services equally to all areas of the city and to all groups of citizens.[64]

Despite the importance of service delivery analysis, there are many obstacles to the valid study of service distribution patterns. Measurement of services is difficult because public goods cannot be evaluated by market pricing mechanisms. Also, because many public services are neither tangible nor marketable, it becomes difficult to define an output unit for measurement. Furthermore, since the output from a service agency is usually only one of many factors contributing to the *impact* of a service, an agency's direct effect on clients is difficult to account for. Finally, other approximate measures of service delivery, such as money spent, are also not very accurate indexes of service quality because high expenditures may only reflect high labor costs or inefficient services.[65]

Because of the difficulties involved in measuring service delivery, few studies have focused explicitly on the outcomes of urban services. A notable exception, *Urban Outcomes*, by Frank S. Levy, Arnold J. Meltzner, and Aaron Wildavsky, assessed the distribution of government services for different socioeconomic groups in Oakland, California, and attempted to gauge the importance of this distributional pattern for the different groups.[66]

They found that the distribution of services varied according to the type of service and the decision rules used in distributing different services. To account for different patterns of service distribution, each particular service agency had to be considered separately. From their analysis, it is incorrect to state in sweeping terms that urban services consistently are provided at higher levels to the wealthy and at lower levels to the poor. In some cases, this was true; in others, just the opposite was true; and, in still other cases, neither group benefited disproportionately.

One service which Levy, Meltzner and Wildavsky studied in depth provides an example of their approach. In their analysis of libraries, they attempted to identify whether predominantly rich neighborhoods or predominantly poor neighborhoods received the bulk of money for new books, new personnel, and new multimedia services. They found that library resources generally went where the most people were using the library and where circulation volume was highest. Since this usage pattern tended to coincide with wealthier neighborhoods, the consequences of this distribution pattern were that the people who were already heavy readers received larger selections of books, news media services, and more staff, while those who needed encouragement to read received fewer books and services. Related to this distribution practice was the fact that, in most cases, the books in the libraries located in poor neighborhoods were selected to appeal to middle-class readers and tended to discourage the poor from using the libraries.[67]

A second stream of service delivery research has attempted to discern what decision-making models best account for certain patterns of service distribution. Three kinds of decision-making models—based on politics, rational choice, and bureaucratic decision rules—have been used. The political decision-making models assume that distributional patterns of services are attributable to the reactions of elected officials toward demands produced by the electorate. Differences in the distribution pattern among neighborhoods are attributed to variations in the power and demands of separate neighborhoods. The rational choice models, on the other hand, assume that distributional decisions will be made on the basis of maximizing criteria such as equity, efficiency, or the need for services.[68] In most cases, however, the models fall far short of predicting actual service delivery patterns. Their inaccuracy suggests the need for the development of a third explanation for service distribution patterns—bureaucratic decision rule models—which seem to hold great promise for the analysis of service delivery.

The bureaucratic decision rule models suggest that distribution patterns are the result of traditional, profession-supported norms which are used by bureaucracies to determine service distribution.[69] Many of the consequences of these rules are unintended, since the rules are devised mainly to simplify complex organization tasks. In many cases, therefore, inequitable and perverse distributional patterns are the result of spillovers from rule-based decisions designed to resolve other problems. For example, the decision to collect garbage once a week in all neighborhoods has the effect of allowing garbage to mount up in high-density neighborhoods, attracting rats and other vermin, while low-density neighborhoods with small populations remain relatively well off.

The concepts of incrementalism and routine are crucial to understanding bureaucratic behavior. *Incrementalism* (making changes in small steps) and *routine* (maintaining regular activity patterns) dominate bureaucracies because they stabilize and simplify administration. But incrementalism and routine also tend to perpetuate decision rules even though they may no longer serve the purposes for which they were created.[70]

Besides "equity," decision rules take four different forms: depending on demand, professional norms, need, and political pressure.[71] The bureaucratic rule for response based on *demand* is "if a customer makes a request, take care of him in a professional manner, otherwise leave him alone."[72] Thus, allocations are based upon past allocations, and recent consumption patterns. The bureaucratic response based on *professional norms* involves making use of national criteria, usually promulgated by professional associations, outlining how a service should be provided. An example of these standards would be the criteria for locating firefighting equipment so that no home or business is less than three minutes from a department.[73]

Decision rules also are based upon *need* in the sense that services may be clustered in such areas as high crime districts, high fire-risk areas, and high poverty areas. Finally, decision rules are also based upon *political pressure*. Since bureaucracies are sensitive to their need for political support, decision rules are frequently based on the old adage "the squeaky wheel gets the grease."[74]

The strong correlation between bureaucratic decison rules and actual service delivery patterns highlights the dominant role of government agencies in urban politics. Furthermore, decision rule models suggest that any change in service delivery patterns will require fundamental changes in the agencies themselves.

The third area of service delivery research—determining how services *should* be distributed—is perhaps the most complex. In order to make judgments about service delivery standards, an evaluation criteria must be selected. But choosing a standard to evaluate service distribution is never value free; and choosing among the three standards that are generally discussed as possibilities—input equality, output equality, and efficiency—requires making difficult value judgments.[75] Satisfying standards of *input equality* would mean equal resources allocated to neighborhoods or clients in quantity or quality. Standards of *output equality* would require rendering service until all neighborhoods or clients attain an equal condition after receipt of the service. *Efficiency* standards would require agencies to allocate resources so that the most service could be delivered at the least cost. Since each of these criteria conflict to some extent with the others, making service delivery choices is very complicated. For example, when input equality is used, the wants and needs of clients are not considered. Because neighborhoods are rarely equal in condition, attaining maximum efficiency is very unlikely. Also, different costs are incurred in producing the same service to various neighborhoods and clients. This means that to achieve equality of condition, many services require unequal input distribution. Clearly, this practice will clash with the standard of input equality.

The standard of efficiency also presents many difficulties. First, the assumption that a certain optimal combination of inputs will produce a desired level of outputs has been shown to be tenuous at best. Because there is no "one best way" to produce services, a single prescribed model for a service will probably be inappropriate in some places. Secondly, efficiency measurement is confounded by the unavailability and inadequacy of city records, the difficulty involved in using census data to infer conclusions about individuals, and problems involved in defining appropriate units of analysis.[76]

Despite the obvious difficulties faced by students of service delivery, in recent years they have made great progress toward building a conceptual base for analyzing urban service delivery patterns. In the years ahead, this area of scholarship should grow in activity and significance as court mandates and political realignments require more equitable city services, and, at the same time, the fiscal strains on cities' budgets force city officials to search for new and more efficient ways of providing services. These concerns will complement and add to the long-standing interest in the appropriate design and functional alignment of services within the federal system of government.

FROM METROPOLITICS TO INTERGOVERNMENTAL RELATIONS

During the 1970s the search for the most appropriate structure for urban governance shifted from a horizontal to a vertical axis, that is, from the politics of metropolitan reorganization to the politics of intergovernmental financial aid and federal program implementation. Both of these concerns—which address the fundamental relationships between neighborhoods, cities, suburbs, counties, states, and the federal government—are responses to the problems that arise from urbanization and suburbanization, metropolitan and regional governmental fragmentation or overlap, the intergovernmental system of taxation, and the division of functional responsibilities between levels of government. Taken together, political action and scholarly activity in this area represents a continued commitment to search for the most accountable, responsive, equitable, and efficient means for solving local problems within our federal system.

Metropolitics: The Horizontal Axis

Metropolitan areas have unique problems of governance that stem from the historic economic and demographic processes which formed metropolitan activity patterns. Most fundamentally, metropolitan areas suffer from mismatches between wealth and service need caused by twentieth-century shifts in business and residential location patterns and preferences. In this century, particularly after World War II, the suburbanization of industry and the residences of the upper and middle classes combined with the legal and practical limits on annexation and the migration of the rural poor into central cities to produce a fiscal disparity of crisis proportions.[77] As the economic base of the central city declined throughout the 1950s, 1960s, and 1970s, and the demand to serve growing dependent populations continued to rise, the metropolitan core became an area of high needs and low resources. By contrast, the suburban fringe became an area of relatively low needs and high resources.[78] Efforts to reconcile these disparities sparked a variety of proposals to equalize local services by requiring suburban communities to shoulder some responsibility for central city expenses. These proposals and their accompanying politics—often called "metropolitics"—pitted central cities against their suburbs and dominated much of urban reform politics from the mid-1950s to the early 1970s.[79]

The decentralization of population and the desire by groups with similar values to protect favorable locations also had the effect of stimulating the creation of thousands of local governments and special district authorities. This trend made the metropolitan governmental structure extremely fragmented, which in turn made interlocal coordination and cooperation difficult, and effective citizen participation in policymaking unlikely.

In order to solve these metropolitan problems, reformers—many of whom were associated with reform efforts during the machine era—concluded that the structure of metropolitan government needed to be changed. To overcome the problems of fragmentation, overlap, resource disparities, and limited citizen participation, the metropolitan reformers promulgated a series of proposals to consolidate and centralize metropolitan government.[80]

Two main types of consolidation models were proposed: metropolitan federation and city-county consolidation. Metropolitan federation, or two-tier government as it is sometimes called, involves the creation of an area-wide governmental unit to share political responsibilities with local governments. The two tiers have a concurrent power relationship. The upper tier determines priorities among regional functions, coordinates local decision-making concerning matters below the area-wide level, and provides a forum for conflict resolution between local units. The two tiers also share power over the different services provided in the metropolitan area. The upper tier usually is concerned primarily with regional services, and the local units generally focus on services which are best administered at the local level. The goal of this type of structure is to promote greater equity in the region, greater representativeness, and greater responsiveness to citizens.[81]

There are presently no examples of federated metropolitan governments in the United States which fully conform to this model. The theoretical model is best demonstrated in the Toronto metropolitan area. In Toronto, a major structural change was implemented which involved the creation of a new metropolitan-wide body to govern the metropolitan area concurrently with six local governments. The second-tier government possessed certain exclusive metropolitan powers and shared other powers with the six localities which completely blanketed the metro area.[82]

In the United States the only systems which are close to the Toronto example are the Miami-Dade County metro area and the Minneapolis-St. Paul metro area. Instead of creating a new second-tier government in the Miami-Dade County metro area, the state simply vested more power in the existing county government. The county government became responsible for providing services which are metropolitan in scope, as well as some other services to unincorporated rural areas.[83] The differences between Miami-Dade County and Toronto revolve around the fact that the first-tier governments in Dade County do not completely blanket the metropolitan area—there are some unincorporated rural areas—

and the fact that power is not really shared in Miami-Dade; it is more or less divided between the two tiers. The Minneapolis-St. Paul system is also different from the Toronto example in that the second tier for this region is a metropolitan council with state-appointed members. This council, which is autonomous from the localities, prepares regional development guides, reviews local comprehensive plans, and reviews grant proposals to the federal government for the region. Again, the second tier does not function as a comprehensive unit of metropolitan government as the second tier in Toronto does.[84]

City-county consolidation involves a much more drastic change in the existing political structure of a metropolitan area than federation. Consolidation generally involves creating one large governmental structure which replaces the previous county and local governments. If the metropolitan area is contained within one county, then the consolidation may involve a reorganization of the county government, enabling it to assume the responsibilities of a single government for the entire metropolitan region. Thus, the new governmental structure would be responsible for providing local as well as region-wide services. In this type of structure, all service provision—education, law enforcement, fire protection, garbage collection, recreation, etc.—and all revenue collection would be centralized.

Consolidationists argue that centralizing services allows the attainment of economies of scale in the production of urban services (by lowering their per-unit costs), facilitates the equitable delivery of services (by reducing fiscal disparities between units of local government), and removes the externalities or "spillover effects" caused by many units making independent and self-centered decisions in policy areas like transportation and economic development which produce problems and costs for one another. Regional development issues—which are sometimes indifferently treated by state governments or were ignored altogether—such as managing peripheral growth, optimizing land-use decisions to benefit the entire region, and coordinating policies to reduce the impact of decay on one location—become among the central concerns addressed by a consolidated government.[85]

To date, city-county consolidations have successfully been carried out in Baton Rouge-East Baton Rouge, Louisiana; Nashville-Davidson County, Tennessee; Jacksonville-Duval County, Florida; Indianapolis-Marion County, Indiana; Columbus-Muskogee County, Georgia; Lexington-Fayette County, Kentucky; and Anchorage-Greater Anchorage Area Borough, Alaska.[86] However, in dozens of other metropolitan areas such as Cleveland, St. Louis, and Memphis, voters have resoundingly rejected consolidation proposals. Moreover, in those places where consolidation has been accepted, compromises with existing boards and localities have been made which precluded complete consolidation.

Despite the advantages claimed by proponents of the local government consolidation model, its desirability and the validity of the evidence offered in its support have been challenged by both the voting public and academic researchers. Voters have resisted consolidation for a number of reasons. Suburbanites have been disinclined to assume the high taxation rates and service delivery problems of central city residents. Suburbanites have also not wanted to surrender their local autonomy over matters such as zoning, planning, police services, and education. Finally, many suburban officials resist consolidation because it promises to reduce their authority or eliminate their jobs altogether.[87]

Surprisingly, central city blacks have also opposed consolidation proposals in many areas. Many blacks have feared that consolidation will dilute their voting strength at a time when they are becoming a majority voice in the central city. At the heart of this issue are the questions of representation and resources. Under a ward-based system, homogeneous black communities can be guaranteed substantial representation; in an at-large system, these kinds of guarantees are more difficult to make. On the other hand, if blacks resist consolidation in the hope of becoming dominant politically in the central city, they may be wasting their efforts only to win a "hollow prize." This conclusion is especially persuasive when one surveys the almost bankrupt fiscal condition of many central cities with black majorities or near majorities.[88]

Criticism of the consolidationist proposals has also come from the academic community. Theorists associated with the "public choice school" have argued that metropolitan consolidation severely restricts service and taxation options for citizens. Under a consolidation scheme, if citizens are dissatisfied with centrally determined mixes of services and taxes, they will have little hope of moving within the metropolitan area to find a more suitable mix.[89] This criticism of the consolidationist model is buttressed by related research into the consolidationist's claims of service cost reductions that stem from larger scale production of urban services. This research shows that for most services including police, fire, education, and the delivery of welfare services, the local level (that is, individual small community level) is the most efficient size for the production of labor-intensive face-to-face public services.[90] Given this optimal size, the anticonsolidationists argue that service costs are lowered under fragmented arrangements because of competition between localities to provide services as inexpensively as possible. Moreover, for services that are not most efficiently produced at the small community level, the best alternative is for these communities to contract with larger cities to purchase their services.[91] These services would similarly become more efficient and higher in quality as competition forces the producing cities to make improvements in order to sell services. Thus, these theorists argue, the monopolistic tendencies of a centralized government would be countered by fragmentation, much as the existence of many producers counters monopolistic tendencies in the free market economy.[92]

A compromise between the federation and consolidation models has produced an institution in metropolitan areas known as the Council of Governments (COG). COGs are multifunctional voluntary regional associations of local governments with the chief officeholders from each locality forming the official body of the COG.[93] COGs do not possess any formal power or any means of enforcing policy that is formulated by the governing body of the COG. COGs are financed primarily by voluntary assessments from the local constituent governments. Since COGs are dependent on the consensus of member governments, they tend to avoid controversial social issues. Typically, they deal with noncontroversial regional issues such as comprehensive regional land-use planning, transportation planning, air and water quality planning, solid waste disposal, and projects funded with federal funds such as airports, water supply projects, and hospitals.[94]

The first COG was the Supervisors Inter-County Committee formed in the Detroit region in 1954. Other COGs were later formed in Washington, D.C.; San Francisco; Salem, Oregon; Seattle; Los Angeles; Philadelphia; and New York. Until the early 1960s, only these few COGs existed. However, during the 1960s—due to encouragement by the federal government—COGs emerged in most large metropolitan regions, so that by 1970 there were over 300.[95]

The effectiveness of Councils of Governments as a solution to the problems of metropolitan fragmentation has also been questioned. Municipalities often bicker over policy, and small suburban jurisdictions frequently veto policies that would benefit a large proportion of the metropolitan area population. Moreover, COGs are highly fragile arrangements since they are voluntary associations. Municipalities are able to withdraw whenever policy developments are not satisfactory to them. Critics argue that COGs are also ineffective because they cannot deal with the important social issues that exist in metropolitan areas. They are dependent on local support, and they are only able to review (as opposed to reject, amend, or initiate) projects.[96]

From the criticisms of proposals to concentrate and centralize metropolitan government, an alternative approach to metropolitan governance problems has arisen—the decentralist or neighborhood movement. The neighborhood movement shares a logic similar to the community control experiments of the War on Poverty years; that is, small decentralized governments provide a better opportunity for citizen access to government, for preferences to be expressed, and for citizens to participate in making policy on issues that affect them. The neighborhood government movement differs from the earlier community control experience in that it involves middle-class neighborhoods as well as lower-class areas and is dominated by cooperative relationships between neighborhood groups and city hall as opposed to the antagonistic relationships which dominated some of the earlier community control experiments.[97]

There are essentially two main types of decentralized metropolitan government structures: neighborhood models and polycentric models. The neighborhood models propose a governmental structure with decision-making decentralized to the grass-roots level. The ultimate goal of this decentalization is to make government more responsive to the people by letting citizens make policy choices in matters that affect them. Advocates of these models suggest that there should be both administrative and political decentralization. Administrative decentralization entails the processes of managing institutions and programs. Political decentralization refers to policymaking.[98] Thus, neighborhood government advocates suggest a transfer of power and responsibility that would have the ultimate effect of providing neighborhood-size population clusters with the control of important services.[99]

For the neighborhood movement to be meaningful, both types of decentralization must take place. If only the administrative aspects of services are decentralized without accompanying control over these services, the result will be an increasingly independent and unresponsive system. Since most local government administrative bureaucracies are relatively autonomous from central political direction, further decentralization that does not give policy-making control to neighborhood residents will leave citizens without control over the mechanisms that most affect their daily lives.[100] Therefore, advocates of the neighborhood model are in favor of more decentralization and fragmentation of government, provided control over service bureaucracies is decentralized to the geographic areas served.

One manifestation of the neighborhood movement has been the formation of "little city halls'' in New York, Atlanta, Houston, Boston, Baltimore, and Columbus, Ohio. Most little city halls do not furnish actual services. Instead, they serve as branch offices of the mayor's office, with the purpose of improving communication, promoting neighborhood ties, expediting city services to neighborhoods, and serving as an ombudsman. The most advanced little city hall program is in Boston, where 14 little city halls combine a service function with their communications responsibilities. Generally, however, the little city halls have tended to be ineffective since they are usually regarded by local officials as an experiment in *administrative* decentralization without an equivalent degree of political decentralization.[101]

Other manifestations of the neighborhood movement have been community action agencies, community corporations, community school boards, district service cabinets (tried in New York to coordinate service management at the district level), and neighborhood councils.[102] In all of these decentralization experiments, there has been either political or administrative decentralization, but seldom both at the same time. Thus, while some citizen involvement has been provided by these experiments, they have not had much impact on solving the problems of metropolitan areas.

The other decentralized models are the polycentric models associated with the "public choice school." These polycentric models are primarily concerned with maximizing the options of citizens to satisfy their preferences for public goods by making residential choices from a selection of governments with different combinations of services and taxes. The polycentric models involve multiple overlapping jurisdictions of differing size. Advocates of polycentric models argue that jurisdictions of different sizes are needed because different public services have different economies of scale. Services requiring large expenditures for physical equipment are provided more efficiently by large units, serving large areas and populations. On the other hand, services such as the police, being difficult to manage and highly sensitive to individual preferences, are best provided by small units. Thus, a metropolitan area composed of multiple overlapping jurisdictions would be able to take advantage of the different economies of scale in urban services and, at the same time, provide more efficient, responsive service to citizens.[103]

Polycentric models have been primarily theoretical because no formal experiment has been conducted to test the argument. In one sense, however, their logic has been applied; that is, polycentric models essentially advocate maintaining the status quo of metropolitan governmental fragmentation and overlap.

The decentralization models also have been challenged by citizens and scholars who charge that they do not offer a viable alternative to solve pressing metropolitan problems. Critics argue that a decentralized structure does not allow the equitable aggregation and allocation of scarce resources and does not help settle conflicts involving separate jurisdictions.[104] Moreover, the multiplicity of policymaking units with independent legal powers tends to perpetuate the racial and economic segregation of metropolitan areas because housing costs, exclusionary zoning, and racial discrimination limit the mobility of minorities and other low-income groups. The continuation of metropolitan governmental fragmentation, critics charge, will perpetuate neighborhood enclaves segregated by class and race.[105] Finally, many local officials and most public service agencies oppose radical neighborhood decentralization proposals because they fear that their power over budgeting and policymaking will be diminished and turned over to local community activists with little expertise and little understanding of the day-to-day workings of government agencies.[106]

On the whole, however, while consolidation schemes have attracted the most attention from citizens and scholars alike, some of the more interesting urban government innovations have involved the decentralization of government to the neighborhood level. Nevertheless, both movements have failed to make widespread changes in the structure and functioning of metropolitan government. Indeed, while the debates over the proper assignment of functional responsibility among levels of local and metropolitan government have yielded more academic heat than political action—at least in the 1970s—the growing financial distress of central city governments (and their poor inhabitants) has increasingly brought federal government efforts and resources to bear on solving local problems. Concommitantly, during the 1970s, the search for remedies to urban governance problems shifted radically from the horizontal to the vertical axis, that is, from interlocal to intergovernmental relations.

Intergovernmental Relations: The Vertical Axis

The failure of metropolitan areas to develop inter- and intra-local relationships and mechanisms that are capable of solving large-scale urban problems has led to the development of bonds between the city, the state, and the federal government in a complex pattern of vertical relationships. These vertical relationships began at the turn of the century as problems caused by urbanization, industrialization, and unprecedented levels of foreign immigration began to raise serious doubts as to whether the simple division of functions between the national and state government was actually workable. Cities, which by state charter had a limited ability to tax, began searching for ways to increase their revenues in order to cope with the growing public service demands being made by the large concentrations of the urban poor. Initially, the cities turned to the states which responded to localities with certain "emergency" loans of money, and assumed an increased role in local affairs. The "emergency" label for the state's actions, however, characterizes the belief of the times that the problems were temporary in nature.[107]

Even state assistance was insufficient for the problems that came with the Great Depression in the 1930s. The Depression forced federal involvement in local problems in a variety of policy areas. At first, the national government became a bank for the states, granting and lending matched funds. Later, this federal role was increased dramatically by the programs of the New Deal, which, in many cases, were relief programs for cities.[108] The involvement of the federal government in local programs, however, was not regarded as a departure from traditional practices or an infringement on the separation of federal, state, and local government, since once again aid was viewed as a temporary emergency measure. Yet, these initial links were only the beginning of a permanent set of relationships which would grow to enormous proportions and become highly complex by the 1970s.

The large increase in suburbanization after World War II only aggravated the already strained conditions of older central cities by furthering the imbalance between their tax bases and service costs.[109] Local public officials were quickly learning that it was easier to look to Washington for aid than to bear the brunt of local opposition to tax increases.[110]

During the postwar era, substantial changes were taking place in American federalism. The new form of federalism was characterized by direct national-local relationships, state-local relationships, national-state relationships, and national-state-local relationships.[111] Not only was the system becoming more complex, but it was also becoming more expensive. The accelerated movement of population to the cities provided urban areas with a larger share of the nation's political base which enabled them to make effective demands on the national government for urban programs. The growing financial importance of this political change can be seen by the fact that from 1932 to 1963, national payments to local governments multiplied by 94 times.[112]

Thus, the new system of American federalism which emerged during this century involved the increasing centralization of government at the national level; "the reassigning of functions to higher governmental levels, and the change in level at which control or decision-making for a functional area takes place."[113]

The term which best captures this new system of government is *intergovernmental relations* (IGR). As an approach to understanding government, IGR places emphasis on the informal, continuous, day-to-day interactions among officials at all levels of government. The prime focus of IGR is on how policy is developed and implemented. The central policy issues which IGR addresses are fiscal policy issues.[114]

The intergovernmental system is characterized by an increase in the number of governments and by a growth in the size of government at all levels. Many areas of domestic policy and programming today involve all three levels of government simultaneously. Because of their interdependence, the areas of autonomy and discretion for each governmental unit have become comparatively small.[115]

IGR also involves intense, regular contacts among public officials. Thus, the actions and attitudes of individual officials involved in IGR become important. Since the power and influence which one unit possesses is limited, these interactions take on a pattern of bargaining, involving the exchange of agreements. As a result of these exchanges, resources and influence are transformed across government boundaries constantly altering authority relations among officials. Thus, IGR creates interdependence among governmental units, a blurring of governmental levels, and a system which is moving more and more toward the centralization of domestic policymaking in Washington.

The new linkages have caused a tremendous growth in intergovernmental fiscal aid. This growth in intergovernmental aid has been substantial. In 1961, metropolitan areas received 3.89 billion dollars in federal aid, whereas in 1974 the figure was 31.42 billion.[116] In addition, total federal outlays have doubled in constant dollars since 1965 and increased sevenfold since 1957.[117]

One major reason for this tremendous growth in fiscal assistance is the nationalization of urban problems, especially for the concern for inequities between regions and jurisdictions. The use of national aid to reduce inequities and aid local governments has had varied and pronounced consequences for local areas. Localities have become more dependent on the federal government; and with this dependency, they have surrendered decision-making control over many local problems.[118] In many cases the main intent of federal assistance is to alter the behavior, output, programs, or decisions of the local governments by prescribing and limiting the choices available to city officials. The dependency that federal aid had produced in the localities has given the national government a club—that of withdrawing money—which can be used to alter local policy.[119] This system, according to David Walker of the Advisory Commission on Intergovernmental Relations, causes centralization of real decision-making at the federal level, local fiscal dependence on the federal government, federal intrusion into the operation of state and local governments, and an undermining of the essential meaning of state and local elections.[120] Thus, quite often the local role in this new system is only to be the local agent of the national government, carrying out policy which is formulated and designed in Washington.

Recognition of this increased control over local affairs, which the federal government exercises through grants, has led to a number of pleas for reform of the federal grant system. Specifically, proponents of reform have argued for greater reliance on condition-free funds such as general revenue sharing. Replacing existing categorical grants with general revenue sharing money, they contend, will return control over local affairs to local elected officials, and will enable those officeholders to set priorities for funds in accordance with local needs and preferences.

The idea behind President Nixon's New Federalism was to remove the federal impact on local affairs. However, this goal is far from being reached. Categorical grants still make up the bulk of federal assistance to localities. In addition, more restrictions have been attached to the use of general revenue sharing—and all other federal assistance—in the form of national policies which must be complied with as a condition for receiving funds. Even in the case of block grants—which have less strings than categorical grants, but more than revenue sharing—increasing restrictions have been added, eroding the decision-making scope of local officials.

Recent activity by the Carter administration requires that any new federal program involvement in local communities be accompanied by an Urban Impact Analysis. These studies are designed to detail any adverse impacts that may arise as a result of a federal program.

The federal government cannot force localities to accept grants and the baggage of restrictions that accompanies them. However, even though localities do not have to accept federal aid, most communities cannot afford to refuse it. Moreover, while it is also true that local officials can disrupt and change the intent of federal programs, this behavior rarely solves the problem of not being able to control the setting of local priorities or the problem of budget shifts that result from restrictive federal money.

At least one additional aspect of federal policymaking seems beyond local influence for now and the near future. The national orientation towards urban problems has come to involve the judiciary, as cases have been decided at the national level which have a pronounced impact upon the activities of local governments. Judges have contributed to the changing relationships among levels of government by being the arbiters of inter-governmental conflict and settling disputes which directly influence intergovernmental relations.

For example, federal courts have taken action to force cities to discontinue racially motivated unequal service distribution patterns and to institute appropriate corrective measures. In these cases, the decisions are taken out of local hands, and the remedies require the establishment of intergovernmental fiscal linkages because the only possible way that these cities can radically improve service to long-neglected neighborhoods is with federal aid. Thus, the judiciary has become both an actor in, and a motivating force behind, the growth of vertical intergovernmental linkages.

As implied earlier in the discussion of intergovernmental fiscal links, the new vertical relationships also involve substantial political linkages with other levels of government. Local officials must now spend a great deal of their time establishing external relationships with their counterparts elsewhere. Furthermore, these contacts with other officials must be made on a continuing basis, to build positive constructive relationships. As a result, local officials are often more attentive to what is happening in Washington than to what is happening in their immediate environment.[121]

In this new vertical system, at the local level, mayors and managers generally occupy the key positions as IGR actors. Also, department heads, budget and finance staffs, personnel administrators, and other program specialists are involved. For local officials, grant programs have produced a long list of decision rules on how to get aid, what to do with the aid, and how to establish relationships and rules for grant searching and grant acquisition. The growing importance of these rules and the time devoted to these activities by local officials underscore and strengthen these vertical relationships.

The vertical relationships have also produced changes in the organization and activities of local staffs. Most local governments have set up offices of financial aid coordination, and they have allocated substantial amounts of manpower and resources to them. The task of these offices is to get as much federal or state money as possible into the local system to ease the burden on local taxpayers. These offices are also responsible for active participation in lobbying efforts in Washington either individually or through the so called "public interest groups"[122] (PIGS or SLIGS—State and Local Interest Groups—as they are called in Washington).

The establishment and growth of the PIGS as exemplified by the "Big 7" [International City Management Association (ICMA), National League of Cities (NLC), United States Conference of Mayors (USCM), Council of State Governments (CSG), National Governors Association (NGA), National Conference of State Legislatures (NCSL), and the National Association of Counties (NACO)] is also an indication of the ascendency of vertical relations in local government. The PIGS provide a channel for information and political pressure to flow from elected officials in one level of government to officials in other levels, as well as to focus local and state pressure on federal policymakers.[123]

As might be expected, these vertical relationships have had a disruptive influence on local government that has produced conflict between elected general officials and program-specific bureaucrats. This tension has its roots in the propensity of federal programs to stimulate strong professional connections between specialists in Washington and kindred experts in the cities.

In many cases, the day-to-day intergovernmental contact among program professionals in one policy area tends to be greater than the intragovernmental contact among professionals involved in different functions in the same city government. The result is that the intergovernmental networks of specialists in welfare, education, and urban renewal, for example, become relatively self-contained decision-making structures for their particular policy domain. These vertical functional alliances effectively thwart the efforts of general local officials to exercise control over their agencies and tend to eliminate citizen representation in the delivery of services. Thus, there is a constant and growing source of conflict in the new system between local elected policymakers and professionals in these relatively autonomous alliances of functional bureaucracies.

The struggle between these two sets of actors is conditioned by the different types of federal aid available. Broadly speaking, these types are: categorical grants, which are transfer payments from the federal government to state and local functional agencies for specific federally defined objectives; block grants, which are federal transfer payments for use in broad functional areas such as crime control, housing, and community development; and revenue sharing which is a federal transfer of money to general purpose local governments with no restrictions on its use.

The impact of these different types of federal aid on urban politics has been substantial. Categorical grants have increased the fragmentation of executive control by weakening the mayor's and manager's control over local services. Top executives and elected officials lose discretion in local programming to the functional specialists because the categorical grants have a functional focus. Moreover, federal officials rather than local officeholders gain the power of review, oversight, and approval. Block grants give local elected officials much more discretion than categorical grants—because these officials determine what projects will be undertaken within a broad functional area. But block grants also give substantial power to the functional specialists, since they require local expertise to be used in applying for federal grants. In contrast, revenue sharing provides for the automatic transfer of money to a locality irrespective of the involvement of functional specialists. Revenue sharing, therefore, gives local elected officials maximum discretion, since allocation decisions are left almost completely in their hands.[124]

The existence of these troublesome problems of intergovernmental relations has brought new importance to the process of federal program implementation. Implementation involves substantial problems of coordination, control, and cooperation because each level of government contains actors with different goals and constituencies. Many implementation problems arise simply because federal government agencies cannot unilaterally order the other levels of government to do anything. Thus, to carry out its domestic programs the federal government must use incentives in the form of aid to local governments with conditions attached.[125]

In most intergovernmental programs it is the local officials who have control over the program elements, and the national agencies who design the programs and are trying to implement them.[126] Federal agencies are therefore up against formidable problems because the dispersion of power and control in the system enables officials at other levels of government to evade and dilute federal regulations.[127] This causes programs to go adrift, break down, or become hopelessly complicated by red tape and regulations.

These joint ventures between levels of government have a number of recurring problems which social scientists are just beginning to explore, such as: contradictory program criteria; antagonistic relationships between actors; delays; problems caused by different interpretations of agreements or dissolution of agreements; and problems of interdependent negotiations and decisions. Difficulties may also center around the difficulty of obtaining clearance from a wide range of participants. Furthermore, in trying to implement a federal program, one is not dealing with an integrated horizontal entity called the city. Rather, one is dealing with an entity which has been sliced up by vertically integrated and professional-dominated subgovernments. Thus, problems that at first seem to involve one federal agency and one city may eventually come to involve many other participants and a more complicated series of decisions than was originally planned.[128]

The rapid growth of intergovernmental relations and the fiscal dependence of local governments on the federal government has produced—and will continue to produce—profound changes in local government and politics. For the most part, political scientists have been caught napping by what Walker has called the "intergovernmentalizing" of the federal system. By and large, they have failed to elaborate upon, refute, or amend his assertion that federal intervention in local-level problems has produced a muddling of appropriate fiscal, administrative, and servicing roles and a fractured concept of public responsibility which has obliterated lines of accountability and eliminated the responsibility of elected local officials to do little more than act as agents of the national government in implementing programs designed in Washington.

THE FUTURE

Forecasting is always hazardous, but in the case of urban government and politics some trends are so strong and so likely to continue that forecasting loses some of its risks. Over the next decade, we expect five trends to dominate American urban politics: (1) austerity and fiscal stress; (2) local dependency and the further "federalization" of local services; (3) the functional restructuring of service delivery systems; (4) the redistribution of power among local interest groups; and (5) a shift in the relationship between city government and neighborhood groups. These five trends may not only dominate the 1980s, but they might also establish patterns for the next several decades as well.

Austerity and Fiscal Stress

Even though the well-publicized fiscal problems of New York City and Cleveland in the 1970s stem from unique local circumstances, they nevertheless point the way to similar problems troubling other cities.[129] New York City had unusually generous public services and civil service salaries, fringe benefits, and pension obligations; and Cleveland's default grew from local squabbling and leadership problems as much as from financial hardship. Despite these peculiarities, there can be little doubt that the fiscal condition of the governments of many central cities—particularly in the "frostbelt" states of the Northeast and Midwest—deteriorated steadily throughout the 1970s.[130]

The litany of problems in our older cities and in the Northeast in general since World War II emphasize the problems of governing under conditions of financial stress. The growth of dependent populations, the suburbanization of business and industry, and the shift in economic activities to the "sunbelt" have put some cities in the impossible position of needing to do more but being forced by declining tax bases to do less.[131]

In addition to the erosion of central city economic bases, inflation has placed an enormous hardship on taxpayers that is likely to continue. During the 1970s, the cost of government doubled and rose at a faster rate over the last half of the decade. Much of the rise in costs was the result of improved salaries and working conditions for public employees; but the cost of all items—and especially those that were energy related—also shot upward during the decade.[132] Cutting costs has not been easy because most local government costs are incurred by personnel salaries, fringes, and pensions (70% to 80% in most cities). Since any appreciable savings in local budgets means making cuts in personnel and subsequent cuts in services, serious austerity will be likely to produce a new politics of cutbacks involving organized employees and neighborhood groups in a struggle to deflect cuts and their impact.[133]

During the 1970s, a special type of financial stress arose with major implications for central cities. Taxpayer revolts, spurred by the success of California's Proposition 13 movement to rollback property taxes, focused the resentment of largely suburban taxpayers on the cost of government. A number of explanations have been offered for taxpayer alienation from government such as the difficulty of tracing the well-being of individual taxpayers to specific government services, the desire of voters to alleviate the impact of inflation on their personal disposable incomes, the backlash of taxpayers against the salary increases of unionized public employees, and the cumbersome nature of financing local services through the mechanism of the property tax.[134] Individually and in combination, all these explanations make sense—especially when linked to assessment increases due to inflation in the price of housing. These increases have made tax limitation and rollback initiatives the only alternatives available to the financially pressed homeowner (irrespective of their future implications for service delivery).

National economic recovery in the middle and late 1970s and increased direct state and federal assistance (Anti-Recession Fiscal Assistance—ARFA, Local Public Works—LPW, and the Comprehensive Employment and Training Act—CETA) mitigated some of the most harmful possible effects of financial stress. Yet, in many cities, local officials had to cut employees, reduce services, raise taxes (where possible within state limits), and defer capital expenditures and maintenance.[135] These developments underscore a major change in local government nationally since resource scarcity and austerity—once regarded as atypical—will probably come to be regarded as commonplace in the decade or two ahead.

Dependency and Federalization

The heavy reliance by local governments on the property tax as their principal source of revenues has rigid constraints (as Proposition 13 clearly demonstrated). Cities with declining tax bases or revenues which cannot keep pace with service costs will need to look to the federal government for help. States may play a role, but, in the Northeast and Midwest, they too have been financially stressed; and in the South and West, state governments have tended to be indifferent to urban financial problems.[136]

The dependence of local governments on federal revenue sources will further erode local autonomy. In many places, local governments will be reduced to land use, zoning, licensing, and inspection decisions and to managing traditional city services—police, fire, sanitation, education, and recreation—under court mandates that guarantee minimum levels and equal distribution by neighborhood.[137] At the same time, we can expect federal programs to become carefully designed so that the influence of local elected officials will be minimized in all but the application stages of the federal grant process.

It has been said that local governments have become "fiscal junkies" permanently dependent on the federal largess. It could hardly be otherwise, given the limited utility of the property tax, inflation, and the need of urban areas for expensive social services and community development projects. This dependency, which built up during the late 1960s and throughout the 1970s, will continue and become so complete that it will not be unusual to find mayors and department heads spending more working days in Washington than in their home towns.

Functional Restructuring

Austerity, dependency, federalization, and the subsequent loss of local autonomy may produce a restructuring of service delivery systems on a multitiered basis (neighborhoods, service districts, regions, etc.) that will have the effect of further weakening multiservice municipal governments. The restructuring could take two directions. The first might be to find new arrangements to finance services like user charges, voluntary workers, contracting out, and joint public-private service provision arrangements. The second will be to find governmental units appropriate for attaining economies of scale while facilitating citizen participation and neighborhood participation. Unlike previous attempts at comprehensive consolidation of metropolitan-wide services, this new system may develop on a service-by-service basis as political opportunities and economic realities develop. The result could be a more polycentric and complex system of special purpose governments overlapping one another—and the city's legal boundaries.[138] Coordination between services will likely occur through the day-to-day self-linking of service agencies on an ad hoc basis, loosely guided by some long-range regional planning body and a broadly articulated and targeted national urban policy.[139]

Power Redistribution

If expanding demand for services and new opportunities caused city politics in the late 1960s to be dominated by the rise of black political power and in the early and mid-1970s by the rise of public employee unions, then the austerity of the 1980s will likely produce another realignment of power. There may be a resurgence of the power of service professionals with ties to Washington and to banks and other financial institutions who hold the cities' debt and control their credit ratings.[140]

The financial plight of urban America has obvious racial overtones. If present trends continue, most U.S. cities will be populated overwhelmingly by blacks, minorities, and the poor, while the suburbs will remain predominantly white and middle class. White suburbanites have consistently refused to pay for their use of central cities, and there are few indications that their resistence is diminishing. Perhaps the greatest fear among some minority groups is that the trend toward austerity in the cities will peak at about the same time that minority politicians will begin to use their local power to redistribute city services. Since citizens often tend to blame elected officials for current problems, regardless of their actual cause, such a convergence of events could have a decisively negative effect upon the emergence of minority political leadership in this country. And even if minority leaders are successful in averting this particular danger, they may face such an impossible set of demands to fulfill the expectations of their constituents—while mollifying white residents—that they may not be able to stem off the intense factionalism and disunity that may develop as neighborhoods struggle for the few slack resources that local governments have available.

There are some, of course, who hope that the problems of polarization—and inadequate policies to meet the needs of low-income urban residents—will simply disappear. Yet, ironically, it seems unlikely in the next decade either that the cities will experience a repetition of the massive violence of the 1960s or that the problems which caused that violence will diminish. The forces for repressing collective violence have increased markedly since that time; so a resurgence of dramatic or spectacular violence in the immediate future seems improbable.[141] On the other hand, the continuance of pressing social problems, especially among minority groups, may produce levels of alienation and resentment which could eventually undermine the political system even more than overt violence.

Unionized public employees also appear to be the big losers of financial stress.[142] During the period of municipal budget growth of the 1960s and 1970s, critics leveled the charge that because public organizations operate in a nonmarket context, there was no incentive for management to deny unions increased benefits in collective bargaining agreements.[143] But the model of unrestrained union power was always more theory than reality since taxpayer resistance and state tax ceilings quickly placed boundaries around the discretion of local officials to grant unions large concessions.[144] By the late 1970s, unions in many places were faced by layoffs, raises that failed to cover increases in the cost of living, less overtime pay, and other indicators that the power of public employee unions had been greatly diminished.

In the next decade, program professionals with ties to Washington funds will be more important than ever in city politics and will be able to operate with minimum consultation with locally elected officials. In addition, bankers, many of whom carefully avoided *direct* involvement with city politics, will be drawn into decision-making councils on a reasonably permanent basis as the credit ratings of city governments become a major element of their public image and an important indicator of a city administration's effectiveness.[145]

City Governments and Neighborhood Groups

Since the 1960s, relationships between city governments and neighborhood groups have often been dominated by confrontational protest politics over such matters as the location of roads, zoning decisions, and most recently, the closing of neighborhood schools. On many issues, neighborhood groups have exercised veto power and have been very successful at preventing local government action. Overall, their influence has been more oriented toward maintaining the neighborhood life style by protecting the status quo than toward creating a better neighborhood environment, that is, more negative than positive.[146]

In the 1980s, we expect this orientation to shift toward a more positive relationship with city government through collaborative planning and implementation of local services and federally funded projects and programs.[147] The logic of this shift is based in large part on the realities of austerity and the nature of service delivery relationships: that is, the cooperation of clients is critically important in order to deliver services with the maximum effect and the minimum cost. Since it is in the interest of both clients and city governments to maintain effective levels of services like police, fire, recreation, education, health, and sanitation, harnessing the volunteer energy of neighborhood groups can allow high levels of services to be maintained even when costs must be reduced. To achieve the political benefits and the economies of service provision that come with neighborhood involvement, in the next decade local governments could move to promote greater neighborhood involvement at all stages of the planning and service delivery process.

Research Directions

Political analysis has always followed political events. Therefore, if these five trends come to dominate urban political life, the study of urban politics will shift emphasis and adopt approaches to analyze them. First, political scientists will likely take a much greater interest in the economic and financial aspects of urban politics, and especially in the linkages between economic health, financial management, private financial institutions (banks, for example), and local policy and services.[148] Secondly, there will likely be a renewed interest by political scientists in the design and evaluation of alternative service delivery mechanisms which will include investigations of the relationships between space, population characteristics, and services. There will also probably be greater effort aimed at exploring the feasibility of user charges, "privatizing" public services through contracting-out and other joint public-private service provision arrangements.[149] Thirdly, there probably will develop even greater interest in intergovernmental relations, such as the role of federal and state influence in local policymaking and, contrariwise, the role of local governments in federal and state policymaking. Fourthly, a number of previously ignored or underused theoretical approaches will probably gain wider currency. Particularly salient may be theories drawn from the fields of political geography,[150] political economy (including Marxist analysis),[151] and organization theory,[152] as political scientists focus more directly on explaining public policy in urban areas by taking account of a region's economic activity, its major business interests, its governmental structure, and its fiscal health. In other words, in the decade ahead political scientists are likely to begin to explore new theoretical paths to answer the discipline's core question: Who gets what, when, how?[153]

Learning from the Past

This somewhat pessimistic view of the future of the cities should not be interpreted as implying that their problems are insoluble. Cities are simply too important to the life of society to be abandoned. Given limited financial reserves, important attempts must be made to allocate those resources as wisely and as effectively as possible.

But in seeking new solutions to urban problems, it is important to learn from the past.

The era of the old-style "machine," for example, not only taught the importance of political organizations as a means of overcoming the decentralization inherent in city governments, but it also demonstrated the value of personalized services in meeting human needs. The plight of the desperate masses who live in the anonymity of contemporary cities may not be alleviated by technology or by "professionalized" civil servants; but it might be ameliorated by personal qualities such as empathy and rapport which may help to rekindle a genuine sense of community in urban areas.

Similarly, the question of power must never be ignored in the analysis of urban life. Although the "elitist-pluralist" debate contributed life and vitality to the study of urban politics at a critical stage of its development, the issue today seems somewhat moot. Since the rise of the modern administrative state, perhaps the most logical candidate for the major concentration of influence, either in the city or in national politics, is the bureaucracy itself. The bureaucrats who run the day-to-day operations of the city may have more impact upon local residents than elected officials. This domination of public affairs by bureaucrats suggests that we might profitably devote much more attention than we have to the question of how administrators can be held accountable and responsible to the public for their actions.

Finally, social and economic inequality and racial and class polarization cannot be neglected. Attempts must be made to design policies which might alleviate or solve these problems. Above all else, to achieve equity and to promote harmony, some method must be found to overcome the inertia of public policy which has enabled "the rich to become richer" and forced the "poor to become poorer." Some method must be found to distribute resources in relation to need rather than to political influence. This is a monumental task; but the future of the cities may depend upon meeting its challenge.

NOTES

1. There are some excellent histories and analyses of early American urban government and politics. See, for example, Charles R. Adrian and Ernest S. Griffith, *History of American City Government: The Formation of Traditions, 1775–1870* (New York: Praeger, 1976); Anwar Syed, *The Political Theory of American Local Government* (New York: Random House, 1966); York Willbern, *The Withering Away of the City* (Bloomington: Indiana University Press, 1964).

2. See Samuel P. Hays, "The Politics of Reform in Municipal Government in the Progressive Era," *Pacific Northwest Quarterly* (October 1964), pp. 157–166; Richard Hofstadter, *The Age of Reform: From Bryan to F. D. R.* (New York: Knopf, 1935); and Daniel N. Gordon, "Immigrants and Urban Governmental Form in American Cities, 1933–1960," *American Journal of Sociology* (September 1968), pp. 158–171.

3. For extensive descriptions and analyses of urban political machines see: Lincoln Steffens, *The Autobiography of Lincoln Steffens* (New York: Harcourt Brace Jovanovich, 1931); Elmer E. Cornwell, Jr., "Bosses, Machines and Ethnic Groups," *The Annals of the American Academy of Political and Social Science* (May 1964), pp. 27–39; William L. Riordan, *Plunkitt of Tammany Hall* (New York: Dutton, 1963); and Edward C. Banfield and James Q. Wilson, *City Politics* (Cambridge, Mass.: Harvard and MIT Press, 1963).

4. See Robert K. Merton, *Social Theory and Social Structure*, rev. ed. (New York: Free Press, 1957), chapter 7, especially pp. 60–82. For other valuable reinterpretations of machine politics see Raymond E. Wolfinger, "Why Political Machines Have Not Withered Away and Other Revisionist Thoughts," *Journal of Politics* (May 1972), pp. 365–398; Martin Shefter, "The Emergence of the Political Machine: An Alternative View," in Willis D. Hawley, Michael Lipsky et al., *Theoretical Perspectives on Urban Politics* (Englewood Cliffs, N.J.: Prentice-Hall, 1976), pp. 14–44.

5. See Steffens, *The Autobiography of Lincoln Steffens*, especially p. 596.

6. See Hofstadter, *The Age of Reform*, pp. 257–271.

7. Ibid., p. 260.

8. The effect of the struggle between immigrant and "Yankee-Protestant ethos" is still felt in urban politics. For discussions and research, see Banfield and Wilson, *City Politics*, pp. 95–96, 101–107, 110–111. See also James Q. Wilson and Edward C. Banfield, "Public Regardingness as a Value Premise in Voting Behavior," *American Political Science Review* (December 1964), pp. 876–887; James Q. Wilson and Edward C. Banfield, "Political Ethos Revisited," *American Political Science Review* (December 1971), pp. 1048–1062; Raymond Wolfinger and John O. Field, "Political Ethos and the Structure of City Government," *American Political Science Review* (June 1966), pp. 306–326; Timothy M. Hennessey, "Problems in Concept Formation: The Ethos Theory and the Comparative Study of Urban Politics," *Midwest Journal of Political Science* (November 1970), pp. 537–564; and Brett W. Hawkins and James E. Prather, "Measuring Components of the Ethos Theory," *Journal of Politics* (August 1971), pp. 642–658.

9. Steffens, *The Autobiography of Lincoln Steffens*, p. 618.

10. See Willis D. Hawley, *Nonpartisan Elections and the Case for Party Politics* (New York: Wiley, 1973); Eugene C. Lee, *The Politics of Nonpartisanship* (Berkeley: University of California Press, 1960); Robert Salisbury and Gordon Black, "Classes and Party in Partisan and Nonpartisan Elections: The Case of Des Moines," *American Political Science Review* (September 1963), pp. 584–592; Oliver P. Williams and Charles R. Adrian, "The Insulation of Local Politics Under the Nonpartisan Ballot," *American Political Science Review* (September 1963), p. 589.

11. See William D. Foulke, *Fighting the Spoilsmen: Reminiscences of the Civil Service Reform Movement* (New York: Putnam, 1919); Frederick C. Mosher, *Democracy and the Public Service* (New York: Oxford University Press, 1968); Winston W. Crouch (ed.), *Local Government Personnel Administration* (Washington, D.C.: International City Management Association, 1976); and Charles H. Levine (ed.), *Managing Human Resources: A Challenge to Urban Governments* (Beverly Hills, Ca.: Sage, 1977).

12. For the philosophy behind the council-manager plan, see Richard S. Childs, *Civic*

Victories (New York: Harper & Row, 1952), especially chapters 14 and 15; John P. East, *Council-Manager Government: The Political Thought of Its Founder, Richard S. Childs* (Chapel Hill: University of North Carolina Press, 1965); Richard S. Childs, *The First 50 Years of the Council-Manager Plan of Municipal Government* (New York: National Municipal League, 1965); and Richard J. Stillman, *The Rise of the City Manager* (Albuquerque: University of New Mexico Press, 1974).

13. Lawrence J.R. Herson, "The Lost World of Municipal Government," *American Political Science Review* (June 1957), pp. 330–345.

14. Floyd Hunter, *Community Power Structure: A Study of Decision Makers* (Chapel Hill: University of North Carolina Press, 1953).

15. The literature produced by the students of urban power structures is enormous. Two of the most comprehensive collections of this literature are: Willis D. Hawley and Frederick M. Wirt (eds.), *The Search for Community Power* (Englewood Cliffs, N.J.: Prentice-Hall, 1968); and Michael Aiken and Paul E. Mott (eds.), *The Structure of Community Power* (New York: Random House, 1970); for an excellent recent review of the issue and the literature, see: John Walton, "Community Power and the Retreat from Politics," *Social Problems* (February 1976), pp. 292–303.

16. See Robert A. Dahl, *Who Governs?: Democracy and Power in an American City* (New Haven: Yale University Press, 1960).

17. For some of this literature that critiques the methodologies of the "elitists" and "pluralists" see Aiken and Mott, *The Structure of Community Power*, especially pp. 193–360.

18. For discussions of this theme, see: Nelson W. Polsby, *Community Power and Political Theory* (New Haven, Conn.: Yale University Press, 1963); David M. Ricci, *Community Power and Democratic Theory* (New York: Random House, 1971); Robert Agger, Daniel Goldrich, and Bert E. Swanson, *The Rulers and the Ruled* (New York: Wiley, 1964); and Wallace S. Sayre and Nelson W. Polsby, "American Political Science and the Study of Urbanization," in Philip M. Hausner and Leo P. Schnore (eds.), *The Study of Urbanization* (New York: Wiley, 1965), pp. 115–156.

19. See, for example, Linton C. Freeman, Thomas J. Fararo, Warner J. Bloomberg, Jr., and Morris H. Sunshine, "Locating Leaders in Local Communities: A Comparison of Some Alternative Approaches," *American Sociological Review* (October 1963), pp. 791–798.

20. See Agger, Goldrich, and Swanson, *The Rulers and the Ruled*; Robert Presthus, *Men at the Top* (New York: Oxford University Press, 1964); and some of the contributions in Terry N. Clark (ed.), *Community Structure and Decision-Making: Comparative Analysis* (San Francisco: Chandler, 1968).

21. See Terry N. Clark, William Kornhauser, Harold Bloom, and Susan Tobias, "Discipline, Method, Community Structure, and Decision-Making: The Role and Limitations of the Sociology of Knowledge," *American Sociologist* (August 1968) pp. 214–217; and Terry N. Clark, "The Structure of Community Influence," in Harlan Hahn (ed.), *People and Politics in Urban Society* (Beverly Hills, Ca.: Sage, 1972), pp. 283–314.

22. See Raymond E. Wolfinger, "Reputation and Reality in the Study of Community

Power," *American Sociological Review* (October 1960), pp. 636–644; and Herbert Kaufman and Victor Jones, "The Mystery of Power," *Public Administration Review* (Summer 1954), pp. 205–212.

23. See Thomas J. Anton, "Power, Pluralism, and Local Politics," *Administrative Science Quarterly* (March 1963), pp. 425–457.

24. See Peter Bachrach and Morton S. Baratz, "Two Faces of Power," *American Political Science Review* (December 1962), pp. 947–952 and "Decisions and Nondecisions: An Analytical Framework," *American Political Science Review* (September 1963), pp. 632–642. See also, Matthew A. Crenson, *The Un-Politics of Air Pollution* (Baltimore: Johns Hopkins Press, 1971).

25. See Stokely Carmichael and Charles V. Hamilton, *Black Power* (New York: Random House, 1967).

26. See Michael Lipsky, *Protest in City Politics: Rent Strikes, Housing and the Power of the Poor* (Chicago: Rand McNally, 1970).

27. For some excellent and somewhat divergent analyses of the "community control" experience, see Daniel P. Moynihan, *Maximum Feasible Misunderstanding* (New York: Free Press, 1969); Alan Altshuler, *Community Control* (New York: Pegasus, 1970); J. David Greenstone and Paul E. Peterson, *Race and Authority in Urban Politics* (New York: Russell Sage Foundation, 1973); Sar Levitan, *The Great Society's Poor Law: A New Approach to Poverty* (Baltimore: Johns Hopkins Press, 1969); and Norman I. Fainstein and Susan S. Fainstein, *Urban Political Movements: The Search for Power by Minority Groups in American Cities* (Englewood Cliffs, N.J.: Prentice-Hall, 1974).

28. See Jon Van Til and Sally Bould Van Til, "Citizen Participation and Social Policy: The End of the Cycle?" *Social Problems* (Winter 1970), pp. 313–323.

29. See Stephen M. Rose, *The Betrayal of the Poor: The Transformation of Community Action* (Cambridge, Mass.: Schenkman, 1972); and Francis Fox Piven, "The Urban Crisis: Who Got What and Why?" in Robert Paul Wolff (ed.), *1984 Revisited* (New York: Knopf, 1973).

30. The literature on the relationships between race, family structure, educational achievement, and educational policy is immense. Two seminal works are James S. Coleman et al., *Equality of Educational Opportunity* (Washington, D.C.: U.S. Government Printing Office, 1966); and Christopher Jencks et al., *Inequality* (New York: Basic Books, 1972).

31. National Advisory Commission on Civil Disorders, *Report* (Washington, D.C.: U.S. Government Printing Office, 1967), p. 1.

32. For an extensive analysis of alternative interpretations of black ghetto rioting, see Joe R. Feagin and Harlan Hahn, *Ghetto Revolts: The Politics of Violence in American Cities* (New York: MacMillan, 1973).

33. See Peter H. Rossi, Richard A. Berk, and Bettye K. Edison, *The Roots of Urban Discontent* (New York: Wiley, 1974); and National Advisory Commission on Civil Disorders, *Supplementary Studies* (Washington, D.C.: U.S. Government Printing Office, 1968).

34. See Feagin and Hahn, *Ghetto Revolts,* chapters 4 and 7; and Robert M. Fogelson, *Violence as Protest* (Garden City, N.Y.: Doubleday, 1971).

35. See Charles H. Levine, *Racial Conflict and the American Mayor* (Lexington, Mass.: Heath, 1974); and Harlan Hahn, David Klingman, and Harry Pachon, "Cleavages, Coali-

tions, and the Black Candidate: The Los Angeles Mayoral Elections of 1969 and 1973,'' *Western Political Science Quarterly* (December 1976), pp. 507–520.

36. See H. Paul Friesema, ''Black Control of Central Cities: The Hollow Prize,'' *Journal of the American Institute of Planners* (March 1969), pp. 75–79.

37. See Michael Preston, ''Limitations of Black Urban Power: The Case of Black Mayors,'' in Louis H. Masotti and Robert L. Lineberry (eds.), *The New Urban Politics* (Cambridge, Mass.: Ballinger, 1976); and Richard Child Hill, ''Fiscal Collapse and Political Struggle in Decaying Cities in the United States,'' in William K. Tabb and Larry Sawers (eds.), *Marxism and the Metropolis* (New York: Oxford University Press, 1978), pp. 213–240.

38. Contrast the first and second editions of Hawley and Wirt, *The Search for Community Power,* 1968 and 1973.

39. See James Q. Wilson, ''Introduction,'' in James Q. Wilson (ed.), *City Politics and Public Policy* (New York: Wiley, 1968), p. 67.

40. See Brett W. Hawkins, *Politics and Urban Policies* (New York: Bobbs Merrill, 1971), pp. 6–7.

41. See, for example, Robert A. Alford and Harry M. Scoble, ''Political and Socioeconomic Characteristics of American Cities,'' *Municipal Year Book 1965* (Washington, D.C.: International City Managers Association: 1965), pp. 82–97; Robert L. Lineberry and Edmund P. Fowler, ''Reformism and Public Policies in American Cities,'' *American Political Science Review* (September 1967), pp. 701–17; Wolfinger and Field, ''Political Ethos and the Structure of City Government;'' and James W. Clarke, ''Environment, Process, and Policy: A Reconsideration,'' *American Political Science Review* (December 1969), pp. 1172–82. Perhaps the best collection of this literature is James Q. Wilson (ed.), *City Politics and Public Policy.*

42. For two excellent overviews of this literature see Philip B. Coulter, ''Comparative Community Politics and Public Policy,'' *Polity* (Fall 1970), pp. 22–43; and Charles O. Jones, ''State and Local Public Policy Analysis: A Review of Progress'' in *Political Science and State and Local Government* (Washington, D.C.: American Political Science Association, 1973), pp. 27–354.

43. See Lineberry and Fowler, ''Reformism and Public Policies in American Cities.'' See also the overview essay on the extensive research program of Michael Aiken and Robert R. Alford, ''Community Structure and Innovation: Public Housing, Urban Renewal, and the War on Poverty'' in Terry Nichols Clark (ed.), *Comparative Community Politics* (Beverly Hills, Ca.: Sage, 1974), pp. 231–287; and the summary volume of ''The Bay Area Project,'' Heinz Eulau and Kenneth Prewitt, *Labyrinths of Democracy: Adaptation, Linkages, Representation, and Policies in Urban Politics* (Indianapolis, Ind.: Bobbs-Merrill, 1973).

44. See Clark (ed.), *Community Structure and Decision-Making: Comparative Analyses; Community Power and Policy Outputs* (Beverly Hills, Ca.: Sage, 1973); and ''Community Structure, Decision-Making, and Public Policy in 51 American Communities,'' *American Sociological Review* (August 1968), pp. 576–593. See also John Walton, ''A Systematic Survey of Community Power Research'' in Aiken and Mott (eds.), *The Structure of Community Power,* pp. 443–464.

45. Clark, *Community Power and Policy Outputs*, p. 53.

46. Ibid., p. 32.

47. Ibid., p. 61. One characteristic feature of these studies—which sets them apart from the earlier power structure studies of Hunter and Dahl—is that they all aggregate data for a large sample of cities. Thus, they were all comparative studies, reflecting the recognition by social scientists that comparative analysis offers a much stronger basis for generalization than case analysis. Furthermore, most of the comparative studies investigating linkages between environment, structure, and output were grounded in the systems approach. One of the most important aspects of this methodological approach is the fact that it provided researchers with a common language and framework for all the disciplines involved and it enabled previous research to be replicated, extended, and accumulated.

48. See Theodore J. Lowi, "Machine Politics—Old and New," *The Public Interest* (Fall 1967), pp. 83–92.

49. Ibid., p. 87.

50. See Clarence N. Stone, Robert K. Whelan, and William J. Murin, *Urban Policy and Politics in a Bureaucratic Age* (Englewood Cliffs, N.J.: Prentice-Hall, 1979), p. 320; see also Peter H. Ross, Richard A. Berk, Bettye K. Edison, *The Roots of Urban Discontent: Public Policy, Municipal Institutions, and the Ghetto* (New York: Wiley, 1974).

51. Ibid.

52. For a classic statement of this problem see Robert K. Merton, "Bureaucratic Structure and Personality," in Merton (ed.), *Social Theory and Social Structure*. See also Harlan Hahn, "Alternative Paths to 'Professionalization': The Development of Municipal Personnel," in Levine (ed.), *Managing Human Resources,* pp. 37–56.

53. See Michael Lipsky, "Toward a Theory of Street-Level Bureaucracy," in Hawley and Lipsky (eds.), *Theoretical Perspectives on Urban Politics*, pp. 196–213.

54. See Hahn, "Alternative Paths to 'Professionalization';" see also J. K. Lieberman, *The Tyranny of the Experts* (New York: Walker, 1970); and Harold L. Wilensky, "Professionalization of Everyone?" *American Journal of Sociology* (September 1964), pp. 137–152.

55. See Felix A. Nigro and Lloyd G. Nigro, "Public Sector Unionism" in Levine (ed.), *Managing Human Resources,* pp. 141–157.

56. Some of the best of this research is contained in David Lewin, Peter Feuville, and Thomas A. Kochan (eds.), *Public Sector Labor Relations: Analysis and Readings* (New York: Thomas Horton and Daughters, 1977).

57. For an overview of this literature see Charles H. Levine, James L. Perry, and John J. DeMarco, "Collective Bargaining in Municipal Governments: An Interorganizational Perspective," in Levine (ed.), *Managing Human Resources,* pp. 159–199; also David Lewin, "Public Sector Labor Relations: A Review Essay," *Labor History* (Winter 1977), pp. 133–144.

58. See Thomas Kochan, "A Theory of Multilateral Collective Bargaining in City Governments," *Industrial and Labor Relations Review* (July 1974), pp. 525–542.

59. Ibid.

60. See Raymond D. Horton, David Lewin, and James E. Kuhn, "Some Impacts of Collective Bargaining on Local Government: A Diversity Thesis," *Administration and Society* (February 1976), pp. 497–516.

61. See Nigro and Nigro, "Public Sector Unionism," pp. 142–154.

62. See Peter Feuille, "Final Offer Arbitration and the Chilling Effect," *Industrial Relations* (October 1975), pp. 302–10; and Raymond D. Horton, "Arbitration, Arbitrators, and the Public Interest," *Industrial and Labor Relations Review* (July 1975), pp. 497–507.

63. Hawkins v. Shaw, 437F. 2d 1286, 1287 (5th Cir. 1971).

64. See Robert L. Lineberry, *Equality and Urban Policy: The Distribution of Municipal Public Services* (Beverly Hills, Ca.: Sage, 1977). Besides specialized questions of equity, responsiveness, and efficiency, there have been few attempts to use service delivery analysis to test and build theories of general urban governance and politics. However, three notable exceptions are Douglas Yates, "Service Delivery and the Urban Political Order," in Willis D. Hawley and David Rogers (eds.), *Improving Urban Management* (Beverly Hills, Ca.: Sage, 1976), pp. 146–174; Elinor Ostrom, "Metropolitan Reform: Propositions Derived from Two Traditions," *Social Science Quarterly* (December 1972), pp. 474–493; and George Antunes and Kenneth Mladenka, "The Politics of Local Services and Service Distribution" in Masotti and Lineberry (eds.), *The New Urban Politics*, chapter 7.

65. See Robert L. Lineberry and Robert E. Welch, Jr., "Who Gets What?: Measuring the Distribution of Urban Services," *Social Science Quarterly* (March 1974), pp. 700–712; Elinor Ostrom, "Exclusion, Choice, and Divisibility: Factors Affecting the Measurement of Urban Agency Output and Input," *Social Science Quarterly* (March 1974), pp. 691–699; Harry P. Hatry, "Measuring the Quality of Public Services," in Hawley and Rogers, *Improving Urban Management*, pp. 3–27; and Robert L. Lineberry (ed.), *The Politics and Economics of Urban Services* (Beverly Hills, Ca.: Sage, 1978).

66. Frank S. Levy, Arnold J. Meltsner, and Aaron Wildavsky, *Urban Outcomes: Schools, Streets, and Libraries* (Berkeley: University of California Press, 1974).

67. See Levy, Meltsner, and Wildavsky, *Urban Outcomes*, chapter 4, pp. 165–218.

68. See Bryan D. Jones, "Urban Policy and the Distribution of Public Services: Problems and Prospects," paper prepared for the Annual Meeting of the Midwest Political Science Association, Chicago, Illinois, April 20–22, 1978, pp. 13–16.

69. See for examples of "decision rule analysis," Bryan D. Jones, Saadia R. Greenberg, Clifford Kaufman, and Joseph Drew, "Service Delivery Rules and the Distribution of Local Government Services: Three Detroit Bureaucracies," *Journal of Politics* (May 1978), pp. 332–368; "Bureaucratic Response to Citizen Initiated Contacts: Environmental Enforcement in Detroit," *American Political Science Review* (March 1977), pp. 291–312; Levy, Meltsner, and Wildavsky, *Urban Outcomes;* and Lineberry, *Equality and Urban Policy*.

70. See Jones, et al., "Service Delivery Rules and the Distribution of Local Government Services," pp. 339–340.

71. See Lineberry, *Equality and Urban Policy,* p. 156; also Levy, Meltsner, and Wildavsky, *Urban Outcomes,* pp. 229–237.

72. Ibid.

73. Lineberry, *Equality and Urban Policy,* p. 157.

74. Ibid., p. 158.

75. See Lineberry and Welch, "Who Gets What?," pp. 704–708; also Lester C. Thurow, "Equity versus Efficiency in Law Enforcement," *Public Policy* (Summer 1970), pp. 451–562.

76. Lineberry and Welch, "Who Gets What?," pp. 708–711.

77. Raymond Vernon, *The Changing Economic Function of the Central City* (New York: Committee for Economic Development, 1959). See also David L. Birch, "The Changing Economic Function," in Alan Shank (ed.), *Political Power and the Urban Crisis,* 2d ed., (Boston: Holbrook Press, 1973), pp. 91–101; and Advisory Commission on Intergovernmental Relations, *Metropolitan Social and Economic Disparities: Implications for Intergovernmental Relations in Central Cities and Suburbs* (Washington, D.C.: U.S. Government Printing Office, 1965).

78. Advisory Commission on Intergovernmental Relations, *Fiscal Balance in the American Federal System,* vol. 2 (Washington, D.C.: U.S. Government Printing Office, 1967), p. 6.

79. See for an extensive treatment of the politics of cities vs. suburbs, Michael N. Danielson (ed.), *Metropolitan Politics,* 2d ed. (Boston: Little, Brown, 1971); see also Scott Greer, *Governing the Metropolis* (New York: Wiley, 1962).

80. Alan Shank and Ralph W. Conant, *Urban Perspectives* (Boston: Holbrook Press, 1975), p. 103–104; see also Committee on Economic Development, *Modernizing Local Government* (New York: Committee on Economic Development, 1966).

81. Advisory Commission on Intergovernmental Relations, *Governmental Functions and Processes: Local and Area Wide,* vol. 4, *Substate Regionalism and the Federal System* (Washington, D.C.: U.S. Government Printing Office, 1974). See also Committee for Economic Development, *Reshaping Government in Metropolitan Areas* (New York: Committee for Economic Development, 1970); and Alan K. Campbell, *Centralization or Decentralization: The Metropolitan Government Dilemma* (Detroit: The Metropolitan Fund, 1972).

82. Advisory Commission on Intergovernmental Relations, *The Challenge of Local Governmental Reorganization,* vol. 3, *Substate Regionalism and the Federal System* (Washington, D.C.: U.S. Government Printing Office, 1974). For further discussion concerning the Toronto experience, see Albert Rose, *Governing Metropolitan Toronto* (Berkeley: University of California Press, 1972).

83. Howard W. Hallman, *Small and Large Together* (Beverly Hills, Ca.: Sage, 1977), p. 104; see also, Aileen Lotz, "Metropolitan Dade County," in Advisory Commission on Intergovernmental Relations (1973B) *Regional Governance Promise and Performance*, Vol. 2, *Substate Regionalism and the Federal System* (Washington, D.C.: U.S. Government Printing Office, 1973).

84. Hallman, *Small and Large Together,* pp. 106–109; see also Joseph F. Zimmerman, "Metropolitan Governance and the Twin Cities Model," paper delivered at the Annual Conference of the National Municipal League, Minneapolis, 1972; and Stanley Baldinger, *Planning and Governing the Metropolis: The Twin Cities Experience* (New York: Praeger, 1971).

85. Robert L. Lineberry and Ira Sharkansky, *Urban Politics and Public Policy,* 3d ed. (New York: Harper & Row, 1978), pp. 155–156.

86. Hallman, *Small and Large Together,* p. 83; for a further discussion on consolidation failures and an analysis of these failures see Vincent L. Marando and Carl Reggie Whitley, "City-County Consolidation: An Overview of Voter Response," *Urban Affairs Quarterly,* (December 1972), pp. 181–203.

87. Shank and Conant, *Urban Perspectives,* p. 109.

88. See Francis Fox Piven and Richard A. Cloward, "Black Control of Cities," *The New Republic* (September 30 and October 7, 1967), pp. 19–21, 15–19; Willis Hawley, *Blacks and Metropolitan Governance: The Stakes of Reform* (Berkeley: Institute of Governmental Studies, University of California, 1972); Tobe Johnson, *Metropolitan Government: A Black Analytical Perspective* (Washington, D.C.: Joint Center for Political Studies, 1972); and H. Paul Friesema, "Black Control of Central Cities: The Hollow Prize."

89. Lineberry and Sharkansky, *Urban Politics and Public Policy,* p. 169.

90. See Vincent Ostrom, Charles M. Tiebout, and Robert Warren, "The Organization of Government in Metropolitan Areas: A Theoretical Inquiry," *The American Political Science Review* (December 1961), pp.831–842; Robert Warren, "A Municipal Services Market Model of Metropolitan Organization," *Journal of the American Institute of Planners* (August 1964), pp. 193–204; Charles Tiebout, "A Pure Theory of Local Expenditures," *Journal of Political Economy* (October 1956), pp. 416–424; and Advisory Commission on Intergovernmental Relations, *Governmental Functions and Processes: Local and Area Wide,* vol. 4.

91. Ostrom et al., "The Organization of Government in Metropolitan Areas."

92. Ibid.

93. Hallman, *Small and Large Together,* p. 69.

94. John J. Harrigan, *Political Change in the Metropolis* (Boston: Little, Brown, 1976), p. 285.

95. Ibid., p. 284.

96. Ibid., pp. 287–288; see also Vincent L. Marando, "Metropolitan Research and Councils of Governments," *Midwest Review of Public Administration* (February 1971), pp. 3–15; and B. Douglas Harmon, "Councils of Governments: Trends and Issues," *Urban Data Service,* vol. 1, no. 8, (Washington, D.C.: International City Manager's Association, August 1969).

97. For further discussion on the neighborhood movement and the concept of government by the people see: Milton Kotler, *Neighborhood Government: The Local Foundations of Political Life* (Indianapolis, Ind.: Bobbs-Merrill, 1969); a slightly different theory for decentralization is offered in Oliver Williams, "Life-Style Values and Political Decentralization in Metropolitan Areas," (Southwestern) *Social Science Quarterly* (June 1967), pp. 299–310; an analysis of two decentralization experiences is offered in Douglas Yates, *Neighborhood Democracy* (Lexington, Mass.: Heath, 1973).

98. Herbert Kaufman, "Administrative Decentralization and Political Power," *Public Administration Review* (January/February 1969), pp. 3–15.

99. See Robert K. Yin and Douglas Yates, *Street-Level Governments* (Lexington, Mass.: Heath, 1975).

100. Ibid.

101. Harrigan, *Political Change in the Metropolis,* pp. 161–162; see also Eric Nordlinger, *Decentralizing The City: A Study of Boston's Little City Halls* (Boston: Boston Observatory, 1972); and George J. Washnis, *Municipal Decentralization and Neighborhood Resources: Case Studies of Twelve Cities* (New York: Praeger, 1973).

102. Hallman, *Small and Large Together,* pp. 116–124.

103. Robert Bish and Vincent Ostrom, *Understanding Urban Government: Metropolitan Reform Reconsidered* (Washington, D.C.: American Enterprise Institute for Public Policy Research, 1973).

104. Advisory Commission on Intergovernmental Relations, *Governmental Functions and Processes: Local and Area Wide*, vol. 4, p. 113; see also Luther H. Gulick, *The Metropolitan Problem and American Ideas* (New York: Knopf, 1962); and M. Neiman, *Metropology: Toward a More Constructive Research Agenda* (Beverly Hills, Ca.: Sage, 1975).

105. Jay S. Goodman, *The Dynamics of Urban Government and Politics* (New York: Macmillan, 1975), p. 277; for a more complete critique of neighborhood government, see Joseph F. Zimmerman, *The Federated City: Community Control in Large Cities* (New York: St. Martin's Press, 1972).

106. Lineberry and Sharkansky, *Urban Politics and Public Policy*, p. 159; see also Alan Altshuler, *Community Control*.

107. Edward K. Hamilton, "On Nonconstitutional Management of a Constitutional Problem," *Daedalus* (Winter 1978), pp. 111–128; see also Morton Grodzins, *The American System: A New View of Government in the United States*, ed. Daniel J. Elazar (Chicago: Rand McNally, 1966).

108. Hamilton, "On Nonconstitutional Management of a Constitutional Problem," p. 115–118.

109. Ibid.

110. Paris N. Glendening and Mavis Mann Reeves, *Pragmatic Federalism* (Pacific Palisades, Ca.: Palisades Publishers, 1977), p. 257.

111. Deil S. Wright, *Understanding Intergovernmental Relations* (Belmont, Ca.: Wadsworth, 1978), p. 8; see also Roscoe C. Martin, *The Cities and the Federal System* (New York: Atherton Press, 1965); and Terry Sanford, *Storm Over the States* (New York: McGraw Hill, 1967).

112. Glendening and Reeves, *Pragmatic Federalism*, pp. 256–257.

113. See Samuel H. Beer, "The Modernization of American Federalism," *Publius* (Fall 1973), p. 49–95; and "The Adoption of General Revenue Sharing," *Public Policy* (Spring 1976), pp. 127–195.

114. Wright, *Understanding Intergovernmental Relations*, pp. 9–14.

115. Ibid., pp. 8–14, 28–29.

116. Glendening and Reeves, *Pragmatic Federalism*, p. 152.

117. John J. Kirlin, "Adapting the Intergovernmental Fiscal System to the Demands of an Advanced Economy," paper prepared for the 1978 meetings of the American Political Science Association, New York, August 1978, p. 6.

118. For a discussion on the effects of federal fiscal transfers, see Michael D. Reagan, *The New Federalism* (New York: Oxford University Press, 1972); Deil S. Wright, *Federal Grants-in-Aid: Perspectives and Alternatives* (Washington, D.C.: American Enterprise Institute, 1968); and for a case study of how federal aid affected one city, see Jeffrey L. Pressman, *Federal Programs and City Politics: The Dynamics of the Aid Process in Oakland* (Berkeley: University of California Press, 1975).

119. For a further discussion of the effects of intergovernmental aid, see Advisory

Commission on Intergovernmental Relations, *The Intergovernmental Grant System as Seen by Local, State, and Federal Officials* (Washington, D.C.: U.S. Government Printing Office, March 1977, A-54).

120. David B. Walker, "A New Intergovernmental System in 1977," *Publius* (Winter 1978), pp. 101–116; see also for a similar treatment of the changes in federalism up until the late sixties, James Sundquist, *Making Federalism Work: A Study of Program Coordination at the Community Level* (Washington, D.C.: The Brookings Institution, 1969).

121. Wright, *Understanding Intergovernmental Relations*, pp. 185–191; see also David J. Kennedy, "The Law of Appropriateness: An Approach to a General Theory of Intergovernmental Relations," *Public Administration Review* (March/April 1972), pp. 135–143.

122. Suzanne Farkas, *Urban Lobbying: Mayors in the Federal Arena* (New York: New York University Press, 1971); and Donald H. Haider, *When Governments Come to Washington: Governors, Mayors and Intergovernmental Lobbying* (New York: Free Press, 1974).

123. Douglas Yates, "The Mayor's Eight-Ring Circus: The Shape of Urban Politics in Its Evolving Policy Arenas," paper delivered at the August 1978 Annual Meeting of the American Political Science Association, New York, p. 23; see also Morton Grodzins, "The Federal System," in *Goals for Americans: Report of the President's Commission on National Goals and Chapters Submitted for the Consideration of the Commission* (Englewood Cliffs, N.J.: Prentice-Hall, 1960); Deil S. Wright, "Revenue Sharing and Structural Features of American Federalism," *The Annals* (May 1975), pp. 115–118.

124. For further discussion on the impact of GRS, see F. Thomas Juster (ed.), *The Economic and Political Impact of General Revenue Sharing* (Washington, D.C.: National Science Foundation/Research Applied to National Needs, April 1976); for more focused case study research see: Richard P. Nathan et al., *Monitoring Revenue Sharing* (Washington, D.C.: The Brookings Institution, 1975); and Nathan et al., *Revenue Sharing: The Second Round* (Washington, D.C.: The Brookings Institution, 1977).

125. Eugene Bardach, *The Implementation Game* (Cambridge, Mass.: MIT Press, 1977), p. 48; for examples and analyses of how the federal government must use incentives to accomplish its purposes, see Martha Derthick, *New Towns in Town* (Washington, D.C.: The Urban Institute, 1972); Martha Derthick and Gary Bombardier, *Between State and Nation: Regional Organizations of the United States* (Washington, D.C.: The Brookings Institution, 1974); Sundquist, *Making Federalism Work*; and Pressman, *Federal Programs and City Politics*.

126. Implementation involves the maneuvering of many semiautonomous actors who exert pressure on and receive pressure from other parties that control some, but not all, of the elements necessary to successfully implement a program. For a discussion of how this process affects the final program, see Walter Williams, "Special Issue on Implementation: Editor's Comments," *Policy Analysis* (Summer 1975), pp. 451–458.

127. For an identification of the parties involved in this process, and further discussion concerning the impact diverse parties have on implementation, see Carl E. Van Horn and Donald S. Van Meter, "The Implementation of Intergovernmental Policy," in Charles O. Jones and Robert D. Thomas (eds.), *Public Policy Making in a Federal System* (Beverly Hills, Ca.: Sage, 1976), pp. 39–62.

128. Jeffrey L. Pressman and Aaron Wildavsky, *Implementation* (Berkeley: University of California Press, 1973), p. 87–124; for further elaboration on the problem of coordinating actors with various interpretations of the program, and varying goals, see Anthony Downs, *Inside Bureaucracy* (Boston: Little, Brown, 1967); and Naomi Caiden and Aaron Wildavsky, *Planning and Budgeting in Poor Countries* (New York: Wiley, 1974).

129. See Richard P. Nathan and Charles Adams, "Understanding Central City Hardship," *Political Science Quarterly* (Spring 1976), pp. 47–62; Terry N. Clark, Irene S. Rubin, Lynne C. Pettler, and Erwin Zimmerman, "How Many New Yorks? The New York Fiscal Crisis in Comparative Perspective" (Report no. 72 of *Comparative Study of Community Decision Making*, University of Chicago, April 1976); David T. Stanley, "The Most Troubled Cities," a discussion draft prepared for a meeting of the National Urban Policy Roundtable, Academy for Contemporary Problems, Summer 1976); and Advisory Commission on Intergovernmental Relations, *City Financial Emergencies: The Intergovernmental Dimension* (Washington, D.C.: U.S. Government Printing Office, 1973).

130. See Roy Bahl (ed.), *The Fiscal Outlook for Cities: Implications of a National Urban Policy* (Syracuse, N.Y.: Syracuse University Press, 1978).

131. See *The President's National Urban Policy Report* (Washington, D.C.: The U.S. Department of Housing and Urban Development, 1978); and Thomas Muller, *Growing and Declining Urban Areas: A Fiscal Comparison* (Washington, D.C.: The Urban Institute, 1976).

132. See "Municipal Cost Index Shows 10 Year Rise of 99.5%," *The American City and County* (September 1978), pp. 61–63.

133. For a fuller discussion of these issues, see Charles H. Levine, "Organizational Decline and Cutback Management," *Public Administration Review* (July/August 1978), pp. 316–325; and "Cutback Management in an Era of Scarcity: Hard Questions for Hard Times," *International Personnel Notes* (January/February 1979), pp. 1–11; see also Andrew Glassberg, "Organizational Responses to Municipal Budget Decreases," *Public Administration Review* (July/August 1978), pp. 325–332; Martin Shefter, "New York City's Fiscal Crisis: The Politics of Inflation and Retrenchment," *The Public Interest* (Summer 1977), pp. 98–127; and Stephen M. David and Paul Kantor, "Policy Theory, Political Change and the City Budgetary Process: The Case of New York City," paper prepared for the Annual Meeting of the American Political Science Association, New York City, September 1, 1978.

134. For a discussion of the cumbersome aspects of the property tax, see Wayland D. Gardner, *Government Finance* (Englewood Cliffs, N.J.: Prentice-Hall, 1978), pp. 361–371.

135. See Roy Bahl, Bernard Jump, Jr., and Larry Schroeder, "The Outlook for City Fiscal Performance in Declining Regions," in Bahl, *The Fiscal Outlook for Cities*, pp. 1–47.

136. See *The President's National Urban Policy Report*, pp. 86–90.

137. For a discussion of limited local government, see Lester M. Salamon's discussion of "The Private City" in "Urban Politics, Urban Policy, Case Studies, and Political Theory," *Public Administration Review* (July/August 1977), pp. 418–429. For a discussion of mandates, see Robert L. Lineberry, "Mandating Urban Equality: The Distribution of Municipal Public Services," *Texas Law Review* (December 1974), pp. 26–59.

138. This model is extensively discussed in Robert A. Dahl, "The City in the Future of

Democracy," *American Political Service Review* (December 1967), pp. 953–970.

139. For a discussion of "self-linking" among public agencies, see Catherine Lovell, "Coordinating Federal Grants From Below," mimeo.

140. For detailed analyses of the politics of fiscal crisis in New York, with implications elsewhere, see Shefter, "New York City's Fiscal Crisis: The Politics of Inflation and Retrenchment"; Jack Newfield and Paul Dubrul, *The Abuse of Power* (New York: Viking Press, 1977); Fred Ferretti, *The Year the Big Apple Went Bust* (New York: Putnam, 1976); and William K. Tabb, "The New York City Fiscal Crisis," in Tabb and Sawers (eds.), *Marxism and the Metropolis,* pp. 241–266.

141. See Feagin and Hahn, *Ghetto Revolts.*

142. See Shefter, "New York City's Fiscal Crisis."

143. For the most complete statement of this critique, see Harry H. Wellington and Ralph K. Winter, Jr., *The Unions and the Cities* (Washington, D.C.: The Brookings Institution, 1971).

144. For analyses of these constraints, see James L. Perry and Charles H. Levine, "An Interorganizational Analysis of Power, Conflict, and Settlements in Public Sector Collective Bargaining," *American Political Science Review* (December 1976), pp. 1185–2101; Levine, Perry, and DeMarco, "Collective Bargaining in Municipal Governments: An Interorganizational Perspective," pp. 159–200; and Raymond D. Horton, "Economics, Politics, and Collective Bargaining: The Case of New York City," in A. L. Chickering (ed.), *Public Employee Unions: A Study of the Crisis in Public Sector Labor Relations* (San Francisco: Institute for Contemporary Studies, 1976), pp. 183–201.

145. See Shefter, "New York City's Fiscal Crisis"; Tabb, "The New York City Fiscal Crisis"; David and Kantor, "Political Theory, Political Change, and the City Budgetary Process."

146. See Williams, "Life Style Values and Political Decentralization in Metropolitan Areas."

147. This idea stems from an interview with Milton Kotler, December 23, 1978.

148. One example of this integrated approach is the work of Terry N. Clark and Lorna C. Ferguson, "Political Leadership and Urban Fiscal Policy," mimeo.

149. For an extensive examination of one form of "privatization," see Annmarie Hauck Walsh, *The Public's Business: The Politics and Practices of Government Corporations* (Cambridge, Mass.: MIT Press, 1978).

150. See, for example, Lineberry, *Equality and Urban Policy: The Distribution of Municipal Public Services*; Oliver P. Williams, *Metropolitan Political Analysis* (New York: Free Press, 1971); Kevin R. Cox, *Conflict, Power, and Politics in the City* (New York: McGraw-Hill, 1973); and Clifford Kaufman, "Political Urbanism: Urban Spatial Organization, Policy, and Politics," *Urban Affairs Quarterly* (June 1974), pp. 421–436.

151. For examples of Marxian analysis, see David Harvey, *Social Justice and the City*; (Baltimore: Johns Hopkins, 1973); Tabb and Sawers (eds.), *Marxism and the Metropolis*; Ira Katznelson, "The Crisis of the Capitalist City: Urban Politics and Social Control" in Hawley and Lipsky, *Theoretical Perspectives on Urban Politics*, pp. 214–229; and Manuel Castels, *The Urban Question* (Cambridge, Mass.: MIT Press, 1977).

152. See for examples of this approach, Herman Turk, *Interorganizational Activation in*

Urban Communities (Washington, D.C.: American Sociological Association, 1973); Roland L. Warren, Stephen M. Rose, and Ann F. Bergunder, *The Structure of Urban Reform: Community Decision Organizations in Stability and Change* (Lexington, Mass.: Heath, 1974); Bardach, *The Implementation Game;* and the collection of essays in Hawley and Rogers (eds.), *Improving Urban Management.*

153. This is the title of Harold D. Lasswell's important formulation for the scope of the discipline of political science. See *Politics: Who Gets What, When, How?* (New York: McGraw-Hill, 1936).

PART 1

Municipal Reform and the Machine

The history of urban politics often has been divided into two periods and two corresponding models of government power—the machine era and the reform era. These two episodes have usually been perceived as sequential; that is, the machine era dominated for awhile only to be rejected and replaced by the reform era. In addition, the machine and reform models have been portrayed as encompassing two distinct and opposing ideologies and methods of political organization.

The articles in Part 1 present a different perspective, namely, that machine politics has *not* died, and that the political actions of the reformers were often not consistent with either their stated ideology or the reform model. In fact, the actions of the reformers were in many respects similar to the actions of those involved in machine politics.

This is the issue that Samuel P. Hays addresses in ''The Politics of Reform in Municipal Government in the Progressive Era.'' Hays criticizes traditional analyses of the reform movement for relying on ideological prescription rather than empirical analysis. Studies, he argues, ''which tend to divide political groups into the moral and the immoral, the rational and the irrational, the efficient and the inefficient, do not square with political practice.''

In order to evaluate the reform movement accurately, it is necessary to determine who the reformers actually were and what they did. Was the reform movement really a movement of the public masses demanding honest government, or was it the effort of a few interest groups disguising their own self-interest and trying to project the image of a mass movement?

In assessing the reformers, Hays looks at three areas: the source of reform, the target of reform, and the political innovations the reformers brought about. Hays argues that the reformers were upper-class business and professional groups who attacked the ''machine'' because it embodied the particularistic interests of lower- and middle-income residents. The reformers opposed more than just the corruption of the machine; they opposed the social and economic status of those in political power.

Hays concludes that the reformers' political innovations shifted power away from a decentralized representative form of local government and centralized government and power in the hands of an elite. The municipal reform movement, therefore, produced the paradoxical situation of an ideology committed to the diffusion of political control and the reality of its concentration.

The article by Raymond E. Wolfinger, "Why Political Machines Have Not Withered Away and Other Revisionist Thoughts," examines whether or not machine politics has died and whether or not the traditional reasons given for its death are accurate. Wolfinger asserts that the disappearance of the organizational form of the "machine"—the strong centralized local political party—has not produced the elimination of "machine politics." Wolfinger draws a distinction between "machines" and "machine politics" by arguing that the essence of machine politics is the active manipulation of incentives such as favoritism in personnel decisions, contracting, and the administration of the law. Although he does not deny that the traditional machine reflected a hierarchical centralized form, he contends that machine politics involves more than a form of organization. According to Wolfinger, the machine has vanished, but machine politics has not.

From an analysis of New York, New Haven, and Chicago, Wolfinger indicates that one of the features essential to machine politics—the existence of patronage—has not disappeared in these cities. In fact, there seems to be more patronage available due to the increasing size of government, the growth of discretionary powers, and the expansion of jobs exempt from civil service regulations.

The incentives in machine politics are tangible, divisible, issue-free rewards. These characteristics make the incentives allocatable to specific individuals as well as impervious to changes in policy. In sum, Wolfinger argues that the fundamental characteristics of machine politics still exist. While the characteristics of cities have changed and political parties have become fragmented, the dynamics of machine politics have remained because the conditions that gave rise to them are still present.

The article by Theodore J. Lowi, "Machine Politics—Old and New," evaluates machine politics by comparing the machine style of organization in Chicago with New York's reform style of organization. Lowi identifies two strains of ideology that guided the reform movement: populism and efficiency. Populism had as its goal the elimination of party politics and the standard of greater efficiency in government was a criteria designed to fill the decision-making void left by the removal of party machinery.

Lowi contends, however, that politics under reform was not abolished; only its form was altered. Old machines were replaced by new machines consisting of autonomous municipal bureaucracies. These institutions are relatively unresponsive structures of power. Each agency shapes policy as though it were insulated from higher levels of elected authority. Lowi concludes that the major goals of the old machines and the new machines of organized civil servants are not basically different; they just approach the aggrandizement of political power differently.

The Politics of Reform in Municipal Government in the Progressive Era

SAMUEL P. HAYS

In order to achieve a more complete understanding of social change in the Progressive Era, historians must now undertake a deeper analysis of the practices of economic, political, and social groups. Political ideology alone is no longer satisfactory evidence to describe social patterns because generalizations based upon it, which tend to divide political groups into the moral and the immoral, the rational and the irrational, the efficient and the inefficient, do not square with political practice. Behind this contemporary rhetoric concerning the nature of reform lay patterns of political behavior which were at variance with it. Since an extensive gap separated ideology and practice, we can no longer take the former as an accurate description of the latter, but must reconstruct social behavior from other types of evidence.

Reform in urban government provides one of the most striking examples of this problem of analysis. The demand for change in municipal affairs, whether in terms of over-all reform, such as the commission and city-manager plans, or of more piecemeal modifications, such as the development of city-wide school boards, deeply involved reform ideology. Reformers loudly proclaimed a new structure of municipal government as more moral, more rational, and more efficient and, because it was so, self-evidently more desirable. But precisely because of this emphasis, there seemed to be no need to analyze the political forces behind change. Because the goals of reform were good, its causes were obvious; rather than being the product of particular people and particular ideas in particular situations, they were deeply imbedded in the universal impulses and truths of "progress." Consequently, historians have rarely tried to determine precisely who the municipal reformers were or what they did, but instead have relied on reform ideology as an accurate description of reform practice.

The reform ideology which became the basis of historical analysis is well known. It appears in classic form in Lincoln Steffens' *Shame of the Cities*. The urban political struggle of the Progressive Era, so the argument goes, involved a conflict between public impulses for "good government" against a corrupt alliance of "machine politicians" and "special interests."

During the rapid urbanization of the late 19th century, the latter had been free to aggrandize themselves, especially through franchise grants, at the expense of the public. Their power lay primarily in their ability to manipulate the political process, by bribery and

53

corruption, for their own ends. Against such arrangements there gradually arose a public protest, a demand by the public for honest government, for officials who would act for the public rather than for themselves. To accomplish their goals, reformers sought basic modifications in the political system, both in the structure of government and in the manner of selecting public officials. These changes, successful in city after city, enabled the "public interest" to triumph.[1]

Recently, George Mowry, Alfred Chandler, Jr., and Richard Hofstadter have modified this analysis by emphasizing the fact that the impulse for reform did not come from the working class.[2] This might have been suspected from the rather strained efforts of National Municipal League writers in the "Era of Reform" to go out of their way to demonstrate working-class support for commission and city-manager governments.[3] We now know that they clutched at straws, and often erroneously, in order to prove to themselves as well as to the public that municipal reform was a mass movement.

The Mowry-Chandler-Hofstadter writings have further modified older views by asserting that reform in general and municipal reform in particular sprang from a distinctively middle-class movement. This has now become the prevailing view. Its popularity is surprising not only because it is based upon faulty logic and extremely limited evidence, but also because it, too, emphasizes the analysis of ideology rather than practice and fails to contribute much to the understanding of who distinctively were involved in reform and why.

Ostensibly, the "middle class" theory of reform is based upon a new type of behavioral evidence, the collective biography, in studies by Mowry of California Progressive party leaders, by Chandler of a nationwide group of that party's leading figures, and by Hofstadter of four professions—ministers, lawyers, teachers, editors. These studies demonstrate the middle-class nature of reform, but they fail to determine if reformers were distinctively middle class, specifically if they differed from their opponents. One study of 300 political leaders in the state of Iowa, for example, discovered that Progressive party, Old Guard, and Cummins Republicans were all substantially alike, the Progressives differing only in that they were slightly younger than the others and had less political experience.[4] If its opponents were also middle class, then one cannot describe Progressive reform as a phenomenon, the special nature of which can be explained in terms of middle-class characteristics. One cannot explain the distinctive behavior of people in terms of characteristics which are not distinctive to them.

Hofstadter's evidence concerning professional men fails in yet another way to determine the peculiar characteristics of reformers. For he describes ministers, lawyers, teachers, and editors without determining who within these professions became reformers and who did not. Two analytical distinctions might be made. Ministers involved in municipal reform, it appears, came not from all segments of religion, but peculiarly from upper-class churches. They enjoyed the highest prestige and salaries in the religious community and had no reason to feel a loss of "status," as Hofstadter argues. Their role in reform arose from the class character of their religious organizations rather than from the mere fact of their occupation as ministers.[5] Professional men involved in reform (many of whom—engineers, architects, and doctors—Hofstadter did not examine at all) seem to have come especially from the more advanced segments of their professions, from those who sought to apply their specialized knowledge to a wider range of public affairs.[6] Their role in reform is related not to their attempt to defend earlier patterns of culture, but to the working out of the inner dynamics of professionalization in modern society.

The weakness of the "middle class" theory of reform stems from the fact that it rests primarily upon ideological evidence, not on a thorough-going description of political practice. Although the studies of Mowry, Chandler, and Hofstadter ostensibly derive from behavioral evidence, they actually derive largely from the extensive expressions of middle-ground ideological position, of the reformers' own descriptions of their contemporary society, and of their expressed fear of both the lower and the upper classes, of the fright of being ground between the millstone of labor and capital.[7]

Such evidence, though it accurately portrays what people thought, does not accurately describe what they did. The great majority of Americans look upon themselves as "middle class" and subscribe to a middle-ground ideology even though in practice they belong to a great variety of distinct social classes. Such ideologies are not rationalizations or deliberate attempts to deceive. They are natural phenomena of human behavior. But the historian should be especially sensitive to their role so that he will not take evidence of political ideology as an accurate representation of political practice.

In the following account I will summarize evidence in both secondary and primary works concerning the political practices in which municipal reformers were involved. Such an analysis logically can be broken down into three parts, each one corresponding to a step in the traditional argument. First, what was the source of reform? Did it lie in the general public rather than in particular groups? Was it middle class, working class, or perhaps of other composition? Second, what was the reform target of attack? Were reformers primarily interested in ousting the corrupt individual, the political or business leader who made private arrangements at the expense of the public, or were they interested in something else? Third, what political innovations did reformers bring about? Did they seek to expand popular participation in the government process?

There is now sufficient evidence to determine the validity of these specific elements of the more general argument. Some of it has been available for several decades; some has appeared more recently; some is presented here for the first time. All of it adds up to the conclusion that reform in municipal government involved a political development far different from what we have assumed in the past.

Available evidence indicates that the source of support for reform in municipal government did not come from the lower or middle classes, but from the upper class. The leading business groups in each city and professional men closely allied with them initiated and dominated municipal movements. Leonard White, in his study of the city manager published in 1927, wrote:

> The opposition to bad government usually comes to a head in the local chamber of commerce. Business men finally acquire the conviction that the growth of their city is being seriously impaired by the failures of city officials to perform their duties efficiently. Looking about for a remedy, they are captivated by the resemblance of the city-manager plan to their corporate form of business organization.[8]

In the 1930's White directed a number of studies of the origin of city-manager government. The resulting reports invariably begin with such statements as, "the Chamber of Commerce spearheaded the movement," or commission government in this city was a "businessmen's government."[9] Of thirty-two cases of city-manager government in Oklahoma examined by Jewell C. Phillips, twenty-nine were initiated either by chambers of commerce or by community committees dominated by businessmen.[10] More recently James Weinstein has presented almost irrefutable evidence that the business community, represented largely by chambers of commerce, was the overwhelming force behind both commission and city-manager movements.[11]

Dominant elements of the business community played a prominent role in another crucial aspect of municipal reform: the Municipal Research Bureau movement.[12] Especially in the larger cities, where they had less success in shaping the structure of government, reformers established centers to conduct research in municipal affairs as a springboard for influence.

The first such organization, the Bureau of Municipal Research of New York City, was founded in 1906; it was financed largely through the efforts of Andrew Carnegie and John D. Rockefeller. An investment banker provided the crucial support in Philadelphia, where a Bureau was founded in 1908. A group of wealthy Chicagoans in 1910 established the Bureau of Public Efficiency, a research agency. John H. Patterson of the National Cash Register Company, the leading figure in Dayton municipal reform, financed the Dayton Bureau, founded in 1912. And George Eastman was the driving force behind both the Bureau of Municipal Research and city-manager government in Rochester. In smaller cities data about city government was collected by interested individuals in a more informal way or by chambers of commerce, but in larger cities the task required special support, and prominent businessmen supplied it.

The character of municipal reform is demonstrated more precisely by a brief examination of the movements in Des Moines and Pittsburgh. The Des Moines Commercial Club inaugurated and carefully controlled the drive for the commission form of government.[13] In January, 1906, the Club held a so-called "mass meeting" of business and professional men to secure an enabling act from the state legislature. P. C. Kenyon, president of the Club, selected a Committee of 300, composed principally of business and professional men, to draw up a specific proposal. After the legislature approved their plan, the same committee managed the campaign which persuaded the electorate to accept the commission form of government by a narrow margin in June, 1907.

In this election the lower-income wards of the city opposed the change, the upper-income wards supported it strongly, and the middle-income wards were more evenly divided. In order to control the new government, the Committee of 300, now expanded to 530, sought to determine the nomination and election of the five new commissioners, and to this end they selected an avowedly businessman's slate. Their plans backfired when the voters swept into office a slate of anticommission candidates who now controlled the new commission government.

Proponents of the commission form of government in Des Moines spoke frequently in the name of the "people." But their more explicit statements emphasized their intent that the new plan be a "business system" of government, run by businessmen. The slate of candidates for commissioner endorsed by advocates of the plan was known as the "businessman's ticket." J. W. Hill, president of the committees of 300 and 530, bluntly declared: "The professional politician must be ousted and in his place capable business men chosen to conduct the affairs of the city." I. M. Earle, general counsel of the Bankers Life Association and a prominent figure in the movement, put the point more precisely: "When the plan was adopted it was the intention to get businessmen to run it."

Although reformers used the ideology of popular government, they in no sense meant that all segments of society should be involved equally in municipal decision-making. They meant that their concept of the city's welfare would be best achieved if the business community controlled city government. As one businessman told a labor audience, the businessman's slate represented labor "better than you do yourself."

The composition of the municipal reform movement in Pittsburgh demonstrates its upper-class and professional as well as its business sources.[14] Here the two principal reform organizations were the Civic Club and the Voters' League. The 745 members of these two organizations came primarily from the upper class. Sixty-five per cent appeared in upper-class directories which contained the names of only 2 per cent of the city's families. Furthermore, many who were not listed in these directories lived in upper-class areas. These reformers, it should be stressed, comprised not an old but a new upper class. Few came from earlier industrial and mercantile families. Most of them had risen to social position from wealth created after 1870 in the iron, steel, electrical equipment, and other industries and they lived in the newer rather than the older fashionable areas.

Almost half (48 per cent) of the reformers were professional men: doctors, lawyers, ministers, directors of libraries and museums, engineers, architects, private and public school teachers, and college professors. Some of these belonged to the upper class as well, especially the lawyers, ministers, and private school teachers. But for the most part their interest in reform stemmed from the inherent dynamics of their professions rather than from their class connections. They came from the more advanced segments of their organizations, from those in the forefront of the acquisition and application of knowledge. They were not the older professional men, seeking to preserve the past against change: they were in the vanguard of professional life, actively seeking to apply expertise more widely to public affairs.

Pittsburgh reformers included a large segment of businessmen; 52 per cent were bankers and corporation officials or their wives. Among them were the presidents of fourteen large banks and officials of Westinghouse, Pittsburgh Plate Glass, U.S. Steel and its component parts (such as Carnegie Steel, American Bridge, and National Tube), Jones and Laughlin, lesser steel companies (such as Crucible, Pittsburgh, Superior, Lockhart, and H. K. Porter), the H. J. Heinz Company, and the Pittsburgh Coal Company, as well as officials of the Pennsylvania Railroad and the Pittsburgh and Lake Erie. These men were not small businessmen; they directed the most powerful banking and industrial organizations of the city. They represented not the old business community, but industries which had developed and grown primarily within the past fifty years and which had come to dominate the city's economic life.

These business, professional, and upper-class groups who dominated municipal reform movements were all involved in the rationalization and systematization of modern life; they wished a form of government which would be more consistent with the objectives inherent in those developments. The most important single feature of their perspective was the rapid expansion of the geographical scope of affairs which they wished to influence and manipulate, a scope which was no longer limited and narrow, no longer within the confines of pedestrian communities, but was now broad and city-wide, covering the whole range of activities of the metropolitan area.

The migration of the upper class from central to outlying areas created a geographical distance between its residential communities and its economic institutions. To protect the latter required involvement both in local ward affairs and in the larger city government as well. Moreover, upper-class cultural institutions, such as museums, libraries, and symphony orchestras, required an active interest in the larger municipal context from which these institutions drew much of their clientele.

Professional groups, broadening the scope of affairs which they sought to study, measure, or manipulate, also sought to influence the public health, the educational system, or the physical arrangements of the entire city. Their concerns were limitless, not bounded by geography, but as expansive as the professional imagination. Finally, the new industrial community greatly broadened its perspective in governmental affairs because of its new recognition of the way in which factors throughout the city affected business growth. The increasing size and scope of industry, the greater stake in more varied and geographically dispersed facets of city life, the effect of floods on many business concerns, the need to promote traffic flows to and from work for both blue-collar and managerial employees—all contributed to this larger interest. The geographically larger private perspectives of upper-class, professional, and business groups gave rise to a geographically larger public perspective.

These reformers were dissatisfied with existing systems of municipal government. They did not oppose corruption per se—although there was plenty of that. They objected to the structure of government which enabled local and particularistic interests to dominate. Prior to the reforms of the Progressive Era, city government consisted primarily of confederations of local wards, each of which was represented on the city's legislative body. Each ward frequently had its own elementary schools and ward-elected school boards which administered them.

These particularistic interests were the focus of a decentralized political life. City councilmen were local leaders. They spoke for their local areas, the economic interests of their inhabitants, their residential concerns, their educational, recreational, and religious interests—i.e., for those aspects of community life which mattered most to those they represented. They rolled logs in the city council to provide streets, sewers, and other public works for their local areas. They defended the community's cultural practices, its distinctive languages or national customs, its liberal attitude toward liquor, and its saloons and dance halls which served as centers of community life. One observer described this process of representation in Seattle:

> The residents of the hill-tops and the suburbs may not fully appreciate the faithfulness of certain downtown ward councilmen to the interests of their constituents. . . . The people of a state would rise in arms against a senator or

representative in Congress who deliberately misrepresented their wishes and imperilled their interests, though he might plead a higher regard for national good. Yet people in other parts of the city seem to forget that under the old system the ward elected councilmen with the idea of procuring service of special benefit to that ward.[15]

In short, pre-reform officials spoke for their constituencies, inevitably their own wards which had elected them, rather than for other sections or groups of the city.

The ward system of government especially gave representation in city affairs to lower- and middle-class groups. Most elected ward officials were from these groups, and they, in turn, constituted the major opposition to reforms in municipal government. In Pittsburgh, for example, immediately prior to the changes in both the city council and the school board in 1911 in which city-wide representation replaced ward representation, only 24 per cent of the 387 members of those bodies represented the same managerial, professional, and banker occupations which dominated the membership of the Civic Club and the Voters' League. The great majority (67 per cent) were small businessmen—grocers, saloonkeepers, livery-stable proprietors, owners of small hotels, druggists—white-collar workers such as clerks and bookkeepers, and skilled and unskilled workmen.[16]

This decentralized system of urban growth and the institutions which arose from it reformers now opposed. Social, professional, and economic life had developed not only in the local wards in a small community context, but also on a larger scale had become highly integrated and organized, giving rise to a superstructure of social organization which lay far above that of ward life and which was sharply divorced from it in both personal contacts and perspective.

By the late 19th century, those involved in these larger institutions found that the decentralized system of political life limited their larger objectives. The movement for reform in municipal government, therefore, constituted an attempt by upper-class, advanced professional, and large business groups to take formal political power from the previously dominant lower- and middle-class elements so that they might advance their own conceptions of desirable public policy. These two groups came from entirely different urban worlds, and the political system fashioned by one was no longer acceptable to the other.

Lower- and middle-class groups not only dominated the pre-reform governments, but vigorously opposed reform. It is significant that none of the occupational groups among them, for example, small businessmen or white-collar workers, skilled or unskilled artisans, had important representation in reform organizations thus far examined. The case studies of city-manager government undertaken in the 1930's under the direction of Leonard White detailed in city after city the particular opposition of labor. In their analysis of Jackson, Michigan, the authors of these studies wrote:

> The *Square Deal,* oldest Labor paper in the state, has been consistently against manager government, perhaps largely because labor has felt that with a decentralized government elected on a ward basis it was more likely to have some voice and to receive its share of privileges.[17]

In Janesville, Wisconsin, the small shopkeepers and workingmen on the west and south sides, heavily Catholic and often Irish, opposed the commission plan in 1911 and in 1912 and the city-manager plan when adopted in 1923.[18] "In Dallas there is hardly a trace of class consciousness in the Marxian sense," one investigator declared, "yet in city elections the division had been to a great extent along class lines."[19] The commission and city-manager elections were no exceptions. To these authors it seemed a logical reaction, rather than an embarrassing fact that had to be swept away, that workingmen should have opposed municipal reform.[20]

In Des Moines working-class representatives who in previous years might have been council members, were conspicuously absent from the "businessman's slate." Workingmen acceptable to reformers could not be found. A workingman's slate of candidates, therefore, appeared to challenge the reform slate. Organized labor, and especially the mineworkers, took the lead; one of their number, Wesley Ash, a deputy sheriff and union member, made "an astonishing run" in the primary, coming in second among a field of more than twenty candidates.[21] In fact, the strength of anticommission candidates in the primary so alarmed reformers that they frantically sought to appease labor.

The day before the final election they modified their platform to pledge both an eight-hour day and an "American standard of wages." They attempted to persuade the voters that their slate consisted of men who represented labor because they had "begun at the bottom of the ladder and made a good climb toward success by their own unaided efforts."[22] But their tactics failed. In the election on March 30, 1908, voters swept into office the entire "opposition" slate. The business and professional community had succeeded in changing the form of government, but not in securing its control. A cartoon in the leading reform newspaper illustrated their disappointment; John Q. Public sat dejectedly and muttered, "Aw, What's the Use?"

The most visible opposition to reform and the most readily available target of reform attack was the so-called "machine," for through the "machine" many different ward communities as well as lower- and middle-income groups joined effectively to influence the central city government. Their private occupational and social life did not naturally involve these groups in larger city-wide activities in the same way as the upper class was involved; hence they lacked access to privately organized economic and social power on which they could construct political power. The "machine" filled this organizational gap.

Yet it should never be forgotten that the social and economic institutions in the wards themselves provided the "machine's" sustaining support and gave it larger significance. When reformers attacked the "machine" as the most visible institutional element of the ward system, they attacked the entire ward form of political organization and the political power of lower-and middle-income groups which lay behind it.

Reformers often gave the impression that they opposed merely the corrupt politician and his "machine." But in a more fundamental way they looked upon the deficiencies of pre-reform political leaders in terms not of their personal shortcomings, but of the limitations inherent in their occupational, institutional, and class positions. In 1911 the Voters' League of Pittsburgh wrote in its pamphlet analyzing the qualifications of candidates that "a man's occupation ought to give a strong indication of his qualifications for membership on a school board.'[23] Certain occupations inherently disqualified a man from serving:

Employment as ordinary laborer and in the lowest class of mill work would naturally lead to the conclusion that such men did not have sufficient education or business training to act as school directors. . . . Objection might also be made to small shopkeepers, clerks, workmen at many trades, who by lack of educational advantages and business training, could not, no matter how honest, be expected to administer properly the affairs of an educational system, requiring special knowledge, and where millions are spent each year.

These, of course, were precisely the groups which did dominate Pittsburgh government prior to reform. The League deplored the fact that school boards contained only a small number of "men prominent throughout the city in business life . . . in professional occupations . . . holding positions as managers, secretaries, auditors, superintendents and foremen" and exhorted these classes to participate more actively as candidates for office.

Reformers, therefore, wished not simply to replace bad men with good; they proposed to change the occupational and class origins of decision-makers. Toward this end they sought innovations in the formal machinery of government which would concentrate political power by sharply centralizing the processes of decision-making rather than distribute it through more popular participation in public affairs. According to the liberal view of the Progressive Era, the major political innovations of reform involved the equalization of political power through the primary, the direct election of public officials, and the initiative, referendum, and recall. These measures played a large role in the political ideology of the time and were frequently incorporated into new municipal charters. But they provided at best only an occasional and often incidental process of decision-making. Far more important in continuous, sustained, day-to-day processes of government were those innovations which centralized decision-making in the hands of fewer and fewer people.

The systematization of municipal government took place on both the executive and the legislative levels. The strong-mayor and city-manager types became the most widely used examples of the former. In the first decade of the 20th century, the commission plan had considerable appeal, but its distribution of administrative responsibility among five people gave rise to a demand for a form with more centralized executive power; consequently, the city-manager or the commission-manager variant often replaced it.[24]

A far more pervasive and significant change, however, lay in the centralization of the system of representation, the shift from ward to city-wide election of councils and school boards. Governing bodies so selected, reformers argued, would give less attention to local and particularistic matters and more to affairs of city-wide scope. This shift, an invariable feature of both commission and city-manager plans, was often adopted by itself. In Pittsburgh, for example, the new charter of 1911 provided as the major innovation that a council of twenty-seven, each member elected from a separate ward, be replaced by a council of nine, each elected by the city as a whole.

Cities displayed wide variations in this innovation. Some regrouped wards into larger units but kept the principle of areas of representation smaller than the entire city. Some combined a majority of councilmen elected by wards with additional ones elected at large. All such innovations, however, constituted steps toward the centralization of the system of representation.

Liberal historians have not appreciated the extent to which municipal reform in the Progressive Era involved a debate over the system of representation. The ward form of representation was universally condemned on the grounds that it gave too much influence to the separate units and not enough attention to the larger problems of the city. Harry A. Toulmin, whose book, *The City Manager,* was published by the National Municipal League, stated the case:

> The spirit of sectionalism had dominated the political life of every city. Ward pitted against ward, alderman against alderman, and legislation only effected by "log-rolling" extravagant measures into operation, mulcting the city, but gratifying the greed of constituents, has too long stung the conscience of decent citizenship. This constant treaty-making of factionalism has been no less than a curse. The city manager plan proposes the commendable thing of abolishing wards. The plan is not unique in this for it has been common to many forms of commission government. . . .[25]

Such a system should be supplanted, the argument usually went, with city-wide representation in which elected officials could consider the city "as a unit." "The new officers are elected," wrote Toulmin, "each to represent all the people. Their duties so are defined that they must administer the corporate business in its entirety, not as a hodge-podge of associated localities."

Behind the debate over the method of representation, however, lay a debate over who should be represented, over whose views of public policy should prevail. Many reform leaders often explicitly, if not implicitly, expressed fear that lower- and middle-income groups had too much influence in decision-making. One Galveston leader, for example, complained about the movement for initiative, referendum, and recall:

> We have in our city a very large number of negroes employed on the docks; we also have a very large number of unskilled white laborers; this city also has more barrooms, according to its population, than any other city in Texas. Under these circumstances it would be extremely difficult to maintain a satisfactory city government where all ordinances must be submitted back to the voters of the city for their ratification and approval.[26]

At the National Municipal League convention of 1907, Rear Admiral F. E. Chadwick (USN Ret.), a leader in the Newport, Rhode Island, movement for municipal reform, spoke to this question even more directly:

> Our present system has excluded in large degree the representation of those who have the city's well-being most at heart. It has brought, in municipalities . . . a government established by the least educated, the least interested class of citizens.
>
> It stands to reason that a man paying $5,000 taxes in a town is more interested in the well-being and development of his town than the man who pays

no taxes. . . . It equally stands to reason that the man of the $5,000 tax should be assured a representation in the committee which lays the tax and spends the money which he contributes. . . . Shall we be truly democratic and give the property owner a fair show or shall we develop a tyranny of ignorance which shall crush him.[27]

Municipal reformers thus debated frequently the question of who should be represented as well as the question of what method of representation should be employed.

That these two questions were intimately connected was revealed in other reform proposals to representation, proposals which were rarely taken seriously. One suggestion was that a class system of representation be substituted for ward representation. For example, in 1908 one of the prominent candidates for commissioner in Des Moines proposed that the city council be composed of representatives of five classes: educational and ministerial organizations, manufacturers and jobbers, public utility corporations, retail merchants including liquor men, and the Des Moines Trades and Labor Assembly. Such a system would have greatly reduced the influence in the council of both middle- and lower-class groups. The proposal revealed the basic problem confronting business and professional leaders: how to reduce the influence in government of the majority of voters among middle- and lower-income groups.[28]

A growing imbalance between population and representation sharpened the desire of reformers to change from ward to city-wide elections. Despite shifts in population within most cities neither ward district lines nor the appointment of city council and school board seats changed frequently. Consequently, older areas of the city with wards that were small in geographical size and held declining populations (usually lower and middle class in composition), continued to be overrepresented, and newer upper-class areas, where population was growing, became increasingly underrepresented. This intensified the reformers' conviction that the structure of government must be changed to give them the voice they needed to make their views on public policy prevail.[29]

It is not insignificant that in some cities (by no means a majority) municipal reform came about outside of the urban electoral process. The original commission government in Galveston was appointed rather than elected. "The failure of previous attempts to secure an efficient city government through the local electorate made the business men of Galveston willing to put the conduct of the city's affairs in the hands of a commission dominated by state-appointed officials."[30] Only in 1903 did the courts force Galveston to elect the members of the commission, an innovation which one writer described as "an abandonment of the commission idea," and which led to the decline of the influence of the business community in the commission government.[31]

In 1911 Pittsburgh voters were not permitted to approve either the new city charter or the new school board plan, both of which provided for city-wide representation; they were a result of state legislative enactment. The governor appointed the first members of the new city council, but thereafter they were elected. The judges of the court of common pleas, however, and not the voters, selected members of the new school board.

The composition of the new city council and new school board in Pittsburgh, both of which were inaugurated in 1911, revealed the degree to which the shift from ward to city-wide representation produced a change in group representation.[32] Members of the upper class, the advanced professional men, and the large business groups dominated both. Of the fifteen members of the Pittsburgh Board of Education appointed in 1911 and the nine members of the new city council, none were small businessmen or white-collar workers. Each body contained only one person who could remotely be classified as a blue-collar worker; each of these men filled a position specifically but unofficially designed as reserved for a "representative of labor," and each was an official of the Amalgamated Association of Iron, Steel, and Tin Workers. Six of the nine members of the new city council were prominent businessmen, and all six were listed in upper-class directories. Two others were doctors closely associated with the upper class in both professional and social life. The fifteen members of the Board of Education included ten businessmen with city-wide interests, one doctor associated with the upper class, and three women previously active in upper-class public welfare.

Lower- and middle-class elements felt that the new city governments did not represent them.[33] The studies carried out under the direction of Leonard White contain numerous expressions of the way in which the change in the structure of government produced not only a change in the geographical scope of representation, but also in the groups represented. "It is not the policies of the manager or the council they oppose," one researcher declared, "as much as the lack of representation for their economic level and social groups."[34] And another wrote:

> There had been nothing unapproachable about the old ward aldermen. Every voter had a neighbor on the common council who was interested in serving him. The new councilmen, however, made an unfavorable impression on the less well-to-do voters. . . . Election at large made a change that, however desirable in other ways, left the voters in the poorer wards with a feeling that they had been deprived of their share of political importance.[35]

The success of the drive for centralization of administration and representation varied with the size of the city. In the smaller cities, business, professional, and elite groups could easily exercise a dominant influence. Their close ties readily enabled them to shape informal political power which they could transform into formal political power. After the mid-1890's the widespread organization of chambers of commerce provided a base for political action to reform municipal government, resulting in a host of small-city commission and city-manager innovations. In the larger, more heterogeneous cities, whose subcommunities were more dispersed, such community-wide action was extremely difficult. Few commission or city-manager proposals materialized here. Mayors became stronger, and steps were taken toward centralization of representation, but the ward system or some modified version usually persisted. Reformers in large cities often had to rest content with their Municipal Research Bureaus through which they could exert political influence from outside the municipal government.

A central element in the analysis of municipal reform in the Progressive Era is governmental corruption. Should it be understood in moral or political terms? Was it a product of evil men or of particular socio-political circumstances? Reform historians have adopted the former view. Selfish and evil men arose to take advantage of a political arrangement whereby unsystematic government offered many opportunities for personal gain at public expense. The system thrived until the "better elements," "men of intelligence and civic responsibility," or "right-thinking people" ousted the culprits and fashioned a political force which produced decisions in the "public interest." In this scheme of things, corruption in public affairs grew out of individual personal failings and a deficient governmental structure which could not hold those predispositions in check, rather than from the peculiar nature of social forces. The contestants involved were morally defined: evil men who must be driven from power, and good men who must be activated politically to secure control of municipal affairs.

Public corruption, however, involves political even more than moral considerations. It arises more out of the particular distribution of political power than of personal morality. For corruption is a device to exercise control and influence outside the legal channels of decision-making when those channels are not readily responsive. Most generally, corruption stems from an inconsistency between control of the instruments of formal governmental power and the exercise of informal influence in the community. If powerful groups are denied access to formal power in legitimate ways, they seek access through procedures which the community considers illegitimate. Corrupt government, therefore, does not reflect the genius of evil men, but rather the lack of acceptable means for those who exercise power in the private community to wield the same influence in governmental affairs. It can be understood in the Progressive Era not simply by the preponderance of evil men over good, but by the peculiar nature of the distribution of political power.

The political corruption of the "Era of Reform" arose from the inaccessibility of municipal government to those who were rising in power and influence. Municipal government in the United States developed in the 19th century within a context of universal manhood suffrage which decentralized political control. Because all men, whatever their economic, social, or cultural conditions, could vote, leaders who reflected a wide variety of community interests and who represented the views of people of every circumstance arose to guide and direct municipal affairs. Since the majority of urban voters were workingmen or immigrants, the views of those groups carried great and often decisive weight in governmental affairs. Thus, as Herbert Gutman has shown, during strikes in the 1870's city officials were usually friendly to workingmen and refused to use police power to protect strikebreakers.[36]

Ward representation on city councils was an integral part of grass-roots influence, for it enabled diverse urban communities, invariably identified with particular geographical areas of the city, to express their views more clearly through councilmen peculiarly receptive to their concerns. There was a direct, reciprocal flow of power between wards and the center of city affairs in which voters felt a relatively close connection with public matters and city leaders gave special attention to their needs.

Within this political system the community's business leaders grew in influence and power as industrialism advanced, only to find that their economic position did not readily admit them to the formal machinery of government. Thus, during strikes, they had to rely on either their own private police, Pinkertons, or the state militia to enforce their use of strikebreakers. They frequently found that city officials did not accept their views of what was best for the city and what direction municipal policies should take. They had developed a common outlook, closely related to their economic activities, that the city's economic expansion should become the prime concern of municipal government, and yet they found that this view had to compete with even more influential views of public policy. They found that political tendencies which arose from universal manhood suffrage and ward representation were not always friendly to their political conceptions and goals and had produced a political system over which they had little control, despite the fact that their economic ventures were the core of the city's prosperity and the hope for future urban growth.

Under such circumstances, businessmen sought other methods of influencing municipal affairs. They did not restrict themselves to the channels of popular election and representation, but frequently applied direct influence—if not verbal persuasion, then bribery and corruption. Thereby arose the graft which Lincoln Steffens recounted in his *Shame of the Cities*. Utilities were only the largest of those business groups and individuals who requested special favors, and the franchises they sought were only the most sensational of the prizes which included such items as favorable tax assessments and rates, the vacating of streets wanted for factory expansion, or permission to operate amid antiliquor and other laws regulating personal behavior. The relationships between business and formal government became a maze of accommodations, a set of political arrangements which grew up because effective power had few legitimate means of accomplishing its ends.

Steffens and subsequent liberal historians, however, misread the significance of these arrangements, emphasizing their personal rather than their more fundamental institutional elements. To them corruption involved personal arrangements between powerful business leaders and powerful "machine" politicians. Just as they did not fully appreciate the significance of the search for political influence by the rising business community as a whole, so they did not see fully the role of the "ward politician." They stressed the argument that the political leader manipulated voters to his own pesonal ends, that he used constituents rather than reflected their views.

A different approach is now taking root, namely, that the urban political organization was an integral part of community life, expressing its needs and its goals. As Oscar Handlin has said, for example, the "machine" not only fulfilled specific wants, but provided one of the few avenues to success and public recognition available to the immigrant.[37] The political leader's arrangements with businessmen, therefore, were not simply personal agreements between conniving individuals; they were far-reaching accommodations between powerful sets of institutions in industrial America.

These accommodations, however, proved to be burdensome and unsatisfactory to the business community and to the upper third of socio-economic groups in general. They were expensive; they were wasteful; they were uncertain. Toward the end of the 19th century, therefore, business and professional men sought more direct control over municipal government in order to exercise political influence more effectively. They realized their goals in the early 20th century in the new commission and city-manager forms of government and in the shift from ward to city-wide representation.

These innovations did not always accomplish the objectives that the business community desired because other forces could and often did adjust to the change in governmental structure and reëstablish their influence. But businessmen hoped that reform would enable them to increase their political power, and most frequently it did. In most cases the innovations which were introduced between 1901, when Galveston adopted a commission form of government, and the Great Depression, and especially the city-manager form which reached a height of popularity in the mid-1920's, served as vehicles whereby business and professional leaders moved directly into the inner circles of government, brought into one political system their own power and the formal machinery of government, and dominated municipal affairs for two decades.

Municipal reform in the early 20th century involves a paradox: the ideology of an extension of political control and the practice of its concentration. While reformers maintained that their movement rested on a wave of popular demands, called their gatherings of business and professional leaders "mass meetings," described their reforms as "part of a world-wide trend toward popular government," and proclaimed an ideology of a popular upheaval against a selfish few, they were in practice shaping the structure of municipal government so that political power would no longer be broadly distributed, but would in fact be more centralized in the hands of a relatively small segment of the population. The paradox became even sharper when new city charters included provisions for the initiative, referendum, and recall. How does the historian cope with this paradox? Does it represent deliberate deception or simply political strategy? Or does it reflect a phenomenon which should be understood rather than explained away?

The expansion of popular involvement in decision-making was frequently a political tactic, not a political system to be established permanently, but a device to secure immediate political victory. The prohibitionist advocacy of the referendum, one of the most extensive sources of support for such a measure, came from the belief that the referendum would provide the opportunity to outlaw liquor more rapidly. The Anti-Saloon League, therefore, urged local option. But the League was not consistent. Towns which were wet, when faced with a county-wide local-option decision to outlaw liquor, demanded town or township local option to reinstate it. The League objected to this as not the proper application of the referendum idea.

Again, "Progressive" reformers often espoused the direct primary when fighting for nominations for their candidates within the party, but once in control they often became cool to it because it might result in their own defeat. By the same token, many municipal reformers attached the initiative, referendum, and recall to municipal charters often as a device to appease voters who opposed the centralization of representation and executive authority. But, by requiring a high percentage of voters to sign petitions—often 25 to 30 per cent—these innovations could be and were rendered relatively harmless.

More fundamentally, however, the distinction between ideology and practice in municipal reform arose from the different roles which each played. The ideology of democratization of decision-making was negative rather than positive; it served as an instrument of attack against the existing political system rather than as a guide to alternative action. Those who wished to destroy the "machine" and to eliminate party competition in local government widely utilized the theory that these political instruments thwarted public impulses, and thereby shaped the tone of their attack.

But there is little evidence that the ideology represented a faith in a purely democratic system of decision-making or that reformers actually wished, in practice, to substitute direct democracy as a continuing system of sustained decision-making in place of the old. It was used to destroy the political institutions of the lower and middle classes and the political power which those institutions gave rise to, rather than to provide a clear-cut guide for alternative action.[38]

The guide to alternative action lay in the model of the business enterprise. In describing new conditions which they wished to create, reformers drew on the analogy of the "efficient business enterprise," criticizing current practices with the argument that "no business could conduct its affairs that way and remain in business," and calling upon business practices as the guides to improvement. As one student remarked:

> The folklore of the business elite came by gradual transition to be the symbols of governmental reformers. Efficiency, system, orderliness, budgets, economy, saving, were all injected into the efforts of reformers who sought to remodel municipal government in terms of the great impersonality of corporate enterprise.[39]

Clinton Rodgers Woodruff of the National Municipal League explained that the commission form was "a simple, direct, businesslike way of administering the business affairs of the city . . . an application to city administration of that type of business organization which has been so common and so successful in the field of commerce and industry."[40] The centralization of decision-making which developed in the business corporation was now applied in municipal reform.

The model of the efficient business enterprise, then, rather than the New England town meeting, provided the positive inspiration for the municipal reformer. In giving concrete shape to this model in the strong-mayor, commission, and city-manager plans, reformers engaged in the elaboration of the processes of rationalization and systematization inherent in modern science and technology. For in many areas of society, industrialization brought a gradual shift upward in the location of decision-making and the geographical extension of the scope of the area affected by decisions.

Experts in business, in government, and in the professions measured, studied, analyzed, and manipulated ever wider realms of human life, and devices which they used to control such affairs constituted the most fundamental and far-reaching innovations in decision-making in modern America, whether in formal government or in the informal exercise of power in private life. Reformers in the Progressive Era played a major role in shaping this new system. While they expressed an ideology of restoring a previous order, they in fact helped to bring forth a system drastically new.[41]

The drama of reform lay in the competition for supremacy between two systems of decision-making. One system, based upon ward representation and growing out of the practices and ideas of representative government, involved wide latitude for the expression of grass-roots impulses and their involvement in the political process. The other grew out of the rationalization of life which came with science and technology, in which decisions arose from expert analysis and flowed from fewer and smaller centers outward to the rest of society. Those who espoused the former looked with fear upon the loss of influence which the latter involved, and those who espoused the latter looked only with disdain upon the wastefulness and inefficiency of the former.

The Progressive Era witnessed rapid strides toward a more centralized system and a relative decline for a more decentralized system. This development constituted an accommodation of forces outside the business community to the political trends within business and professional life rather than vice versa. It involved a tendency for the decision-making processes inherent in science and technology to prevail over those inherent in representative government.

Reformers in the Progressive Era and liberal historians since then misread the nature of the movement to change municipal government because they concentrated upon dramatic and sensational episodes and ignored the analysis of more fundamental political structure, of the persistent relationships of influence and power which grew out of the community's social, ideological, economic, and cultural activities. The reconstruction of these patterns of human relationships and of the changes in them is the historian's most crucial task, for they constitute the central context of historical development. History consists not of erratic and spasmodic fluctuations, of a series of random thoughts and actions, but of patterns of activity and change in which people hold thoughts and actions in common and in which there are close connections between sequences of events. These contexts give rise to a structure of human relationships which pervade all areas of life; for the political historian the most important of these is the structure of the distribution of power and influence.

The structure of political relationships, however, cannot be adequately understood if we concentrate on evidence concerning ideology rather than practice. For it is becoming increasingly clear that ideological evidence is no safe guide to the understanding of practice, that what people thought and said about their society is not necessarily an accurate representation of what they did. The current task of the historian of the Progressive Era is to quit taking the reformers' own description of political practice at its face value and to utilize a wide variety of new types of evidence to reconstruct political practice in its own terms. This is not to argue that ideology is either important or unimportant. It is merely to state that ideological evidence is not appropriate to the discovery of the nature of political practice.

Only by maintaining this clear distinction can the historian successfully investigate the structure of political life in the Progressive Era. And only then can he begin to cope with the most fundamental problem of all: the relationship between political ideology and political practice. For each of these facets of political life must be understood in its own terms, through its own historical record. Each involves a distinct set of historical phenomena. The relationship between them for the Progressive Era is not now clear; it has not been investigated. But it cannot be explored until the conceptual distinction is made clear and evidence tapped which is pertinent to each. Because the nature of political practice has so long been distorted by the use of ideological evidence, the most pressing task is for its investigation through new types of evidence appropriate to it. The reconstruction of the movement for municipal reform can constitute a major step forward toward that goal.

NOTES

1. See, for example, Clifford W. Patton, *Battle for Municipal Reform* (Washington, D.C., 1940); and Frank Mann Stewart, *A Half-Century of Municipal Reform* (Berkeley, 1950).

2. George E. Mowry, *The California Progressives* (Berkeley and Los Angeles, 1951), pp. 86–104; Richard Hofstadter, *The Age of Reform* (New York, 1955), 131–269; Alfred D. Chandler, Jr., "The Origins of Progressive Leadership," in Elting Morrison *et al.,* ed., *Letters of Theodore Roosevelt* (Cambridge, 1951–54), VIII, Appendix III, 1462–64.

3. Harry A. Toulmin, *The City Manager* (New York, 1915), 156–68; Clinton R. Woodruff, *City Government by Commission* (New York, 1911), 243–53.

4. Eli Daniel Potts, "A Comparative Study of the Leadership of Republican Factions in Iowa, 1904–1914." M.A. thesis (State University of Iowa, 1956). Another satisfactory comparative analysis is contained in William T. Kerr, Jr., "The Progressives of Washington, 1910–12." *PNQ*, Vol. 5 (1964), 16–27.

5. Based upon a study of eleven ministers involved in municipal reform in Pittsburgh, who represented exclusively the upper-class Presbyterian and Episcopal churches.

6. Based upon a study of professional men involved in municipal reform in Pittsburgh, comprising eighty-three doctors, twelve architects, twenty-five educators, and thirteen engineers.

7. See especially Mowry, *The California Progressives.*

8. Leonard White, *The City Manager* (Chicago, 1927), ix–x.

9. Harold A. Stone *et al., City Manager Government in Nine Cities* (Chicago, 1940); Frederick C. Mosher *et al., City Manager Government in Seven Cities* (Chicago, 1940); Harold A. Stone *et al., City Manager Government in the United States* (Chicago, 1940). Cities covered by these studies include: Austin, Texas; Charlotte, North Carolina; Dallas, Texas; Dayton, Ohio; Fredericksburg, Virginia; Jackson, Michigan; Janesville, Wisconsin; Kingsport, Tennessee; Lynchburg, Virginia; Rochester,New York; San Diego, California.

10. Jewell Cass Phillips, *Operation of the Council-Manager Plan of Government in Oklahoma Cities* (Philadelpia, 1935), 31–39.

11. James Weinstein, "Organized Business and the City Commission and Manager Movements," *Journal of Southern History,* XXVIII (1962), 166–82.

12. Norman N. Gill, *Municipal Research Bureaus* (Washington, 1944).

13. This account of the movement for commission government in Des Moines is derived from items in the Des Moines *Register* during the years from 1905 through 1908.

14. Biographical data constitutes the main source of evidence for this study of Pittsburgh reform leaders. It was found in city directories, social registers, directories of corporate directors, biographical compilations, reports of boards of education, settlement houses, welfare organizations, and similar types of material. Especially valuable was the clipping file maintained at the Carnegie Library of Pittsburgh.

15. *Town Crier* (Seattle), Feb. 18, 1911, p. 13.

16. Information derived from same sources as cited in footnote 14.

17. Stone *et al., Nine Cities*, 212.

18. *Ibid.*, 3–13.

19. *Ibid.*, 329.

20. Stone *et al., City Manager Government*, 26, 237–41, for analysis of opposition to city-manager government.

21. Des Moines *Register and Leader*, March 17, 1908.

22. *Ibid.*, March 30, March 28, 1908.

23. Voters' Civic League of Allegheny County. "Bulletin of the Voters' Civic League of Allegheny County Concerning the Public School System of Pittsburgh," Feb. 14, 1911, pp. 2–3.

24. In the decade 1911 to 1920, 43 per cent of the municipal charters adopted in eleven home rule states involved the commission form and 35 per cent the city-manager form; in the following decade the figures stood at 6 per cent and 71 percent respectively. The adoption of city-manager charters reached a peak in the years 1918 through 1923 and declined sharply after 1933. See Leonard D. White, "The Future of Public Administration." *Public Management*, XV (1933), 12.

25. Toulmin, *The City Manager*, 42.

26. Woodruff, *City Government*, 315. The Galveston commission plan did not contain provisions for the initiative, referendum, or recall, and Galveston commercial groups which had fathered the commission plan opposed movements to include them. In 1911 Governor Colquitt of Texas vetoed a charter bill for Texarkana because it contained such provisions; he maintained that they were "undemocratic" and unnecessary to the success of commission government. *Ibid.*, 314–15.

27. *Ibid.*, 207–208.

28. Des Moines *Register and Leader*, Jan. 15, 1908.

29. Voters' Civic League of Allegheny County. "Report on the Voters' League in the Redistricting of the Wards of the City of Pittsburgh" (Pittsburgh, n.d.).

30. Horace E. Deming, "The Government of American Cities," in Woodruff, *City Government*, 167.

31. *Ibid.*, 168.

32. Information derived from same sources as cited in footnote 14.

33. W. R. Hopkins, city manager of Cleveland, indicated the degree to which the new type of government was more responsive to the business community: "It is undoubtedly easier for a city manager to insist upon acting in accordance with the business interests of the city than it is for a mayor to do the same thing." Quoted in White, *The City Manager*, 13.

34. Stone *et al., Nine Cities*, 20.

35. *Ibid.*, 225.

36. Herbert Gutman, "An Iron Workers' Strike in the Ohio Valley 1873–74," *Ohio Historical Quarterly*, LXVIII (1959), 353–70; "Trouble on the Railroads, 1873–1874: Prelude to the 1877 Crisis," *Labor History*, II (Spring, 1961), 215–36.

37. Oscar Handlin, *The Uprooted* (Boston, 1951), 209–17.

38. Clinton Rodgers Woodruff of the National Municipal League even argued that the initiative, referendum, and recall were rarely used. "Their value lies in their existence

rather than in their use.'' Woodruff, *City Government,* 314. It seems apparent that the most widely used of these devices, the referendum, was popularized by legislative bodies when they could not agree or did not want to take responsibility for a decision and sought to pass that responsibility to the general public, rather than because of a faith in the wisdom of popular will.

39. J. B. Shannon, "County Consolidation," *Annals of the American Academy of Political and Social Science,* Vol. 207 (January, 1940), 168.

40. Woodruff, *City Government,* 29–30.

41. Several recent studies emphasize various aspects of this movement. See, for example, Loren Baritz, *Servants of Power* (Middletown, 1960); Raymond E. Callahan, *Education and the Cult of Efficiency* (Chicago, 1962); Samuel P. Hays, *Conservation and the Gospel of Efficiency* (Cambridge, 1959); Dwight Waldo, *The Administrative State* (New York, 1948), 3–61.

Why Political Machines Have Not Withered Away and Other Revisionist Thoughts

RAYMOND E. WOLFINGER

Machine politics is always said to be on the point of disappearing, but nevertheless seems to endure. Scholarly analyses of machines usually explain why they have dwindled almost to the vanishing point. Since machine politics is still alive and well in many places, this conventional wisdom starts from a false premise. More important, it has several logical and definitional confusions that impede clear understanding of American local politics. This article shows that machine politics still flourishes, presents a clarified definition of "machine politics" as part of a typology of incentives for political participation, and argues that the familiar explanations both for the existence of machine politics and for its putative decline are inadequate.

THE PERSISTENCE OF MACHINE POLITICS

My first-hand experience with machine politics is limited to the city of New Haven.[1] Both parties there had what journalists like to call "old fashioned machines," of the type whose disappearance has been heralded for most of the twentieth century. Some people in New Haven were moved to participation in local election campaigns by such civic-minded concerns as public spirit, ideological enthusiasm, or a desire to influence governmental policy on a particular issue. For hundreds of the city's residents, however, politics was not a matter of issues or civic duty, but of bread and butter. There were (and are) a variety of material rewards for political activity. Service to the party or influential connections were prerequisites to appointment to hundreds of municipal jobs, and the placement of government contracts was often affected by political considerations. Thus the stimuli for political participation in local politics were, for most activists, wholly external.

I am grateful to Ann Sale Barber, Lawrence M. Friedman, Fred I. Greenstein, Herbert Kaufman, Charles E. Lindblom, Nelson W. Polsby, Adelle R. Rosenzweig, Frank J. Sorauf, and my wife, Barbara Kaye Wolfinger, for their attempts to improve the factual, logical, and stylistic qualities of this article. At the same time, I do not wish to suggest that all of them are in complete agreement with what I have written. A more detailed description of machine politics in New Haven and discussion of other aspects of this general subject may be found in my *The Politics of Progress* (Englewood Cliffs, N.J.: Prentice-Hall, Inc., 1972).

A new administration taking over New Haven's city hall had at its immediate disposal about 75 politically-appointed policy-making positions, about 300 lower-level patronage jobs, and about the same number of appointments to boards and commissions. Summer employment provided around 150 additional patronage jobs. In the winter, snow removal required the immediate attention of hundreds of men and dozens of pieces of equipment.

A hundred or more jobs in field offices of the state government were filled with the advice of the party's local leaders. The City Court, appointed by the governor with the advice of the local dispensers of his patronage, had room for two or three dozen deserving people. The New Haven Probate Court had a considerable payroll, but its real political significance was the Judge of Probate's power to appoint appraisers and trustees of estates. Except in difficult cases, little technical knowledge was necessary for appraising, for which the fee was $1 per $1,000 of appraised worth.

A great deal of the city's business was done with men active in organization politics, particularly in such "political" businesses as printing, building, and playground supplies, construction, and insurance. Competitive bidding did not seriously increase the uncertainty of the outcome if the administration wanted a certain bidder to win.[2] As in many places, it was commonplace for city or party officials to "advise" a prime contractor about which local subcontractors, suppliers, and insurance agencies to patronize. Many government purchases were exempt from competitive bidding for one reason or another. The prices of some things, like insurance, are fixed. Thus the city's insurance business could be (and was) given to politically deserving agencies. Other kinds of services, particularly those supplied by professional men, are inherently unsuited to competitive bidding. Architects, for instance, are not chosen by cost. Indeed, some professional societies forbid price competition by their members.

The income that some party leaders received directly from the public treasury was dwarfed by trade from people who hoped to do business with the city or wanted friendly treatment at city hall, or in the courts, or at the state capitol, and thus sought to ingratiate themselves with party leaders. For example, a contractor hoping to build a school would be likely to buy his performance bonds from the bond and insurance agency headed by the Democratic National Committeeman. Similar considerations applied to "political" attorneys with part-time public jobs. Their real rewards came from clients who wanted to maximize their chances of favorable consideration in the courts or by public agencies.

Control of city and state government, then, provided either local party with a formidable array of resources that, by law, custom, and public acceptance, could be exploited for money and labor. Holders of the 75 policy-making jobs were assessed five percent of their annual salaries in municipal election years and three percent in other years. At the lower patronage levels, employees and board members gave from $25 to $100 and up. Politically-appointed employees were also expected to contribute their time during campaigns and were threatened with dismissal if they did not do enough electioneering.

Business and professional men who sold to the city, or who might want favors from it, were another important source of funds. Both sides in any public contractual relation usually assumed that a contribution would be forthcoming, but firms doing business with the city were often approached directly and bluntly. During one mayoralty campaign a party official asked a reluctant businessman, "Look, you son of a bitch, do you want a snow-removal contract or don't you?'' In the 1957 mayoralty election the biggest individual contributor, who gave $1,500 to the ruling Democratic party, was a partner in the architectural firm that designed two new high schools. A contractor closely associated with a top-ranking Democratic politician gave $1,000. A partner in the firm that built the new high schools and an apartment house in a redevelopment project gave $900. Dozens of city, court, and party officials were listed as contributors of sums ranging from $250 to $1,000.[3]

In addition to jobs and politically influenced selecton of contractors, the third sign of machine politics is ''favors'': for parents of school children, owners of houses with code violations, people wanting zoning changes, taxpayers wanting lower assessments, and so on. In these and numerous other categories of citizen relations with government, machine politicians were prepared to be obligingly flexible about the laws, but a *quid pro quo* was implicit in such requests.

Political spoils in New Haven came from several jurisdictions, chiefly the municipal government, the probate court, and the state government. The more numerous the sources of patronage, the lower the probability that all would be held by the same party, and hence the easier it was for both parties to maintain their organizations through hard times. When one party was triumphant everywhere in the state, as the Democrats were in the 1960s, there was considerable potential for intraparty disunity because the availability of more than one source of rewards for political activity made it difficult to establish wholly unified local party organizations. Inevitably state leaders would deal with one or more local figures in dispensing state patronage. This local representative need not be the same man who controlled probate or municipal patronage. Although the mayor had the power to give out city patronage, either directly or by telling his appointees what to do, he found it prudent to exercise this power in concert with those leaders who could control campaign organizations in New Haven through their access to state and probate patronage. In good measure because of the diverse sources of patronage, the loyalties of Democratic party workers went to different leaders. All this was true also of the Republican party. Thus neither local party organization was monolithic. The Republicans were badly split for much of the post-war generation. The Democrats maintained a working coalition, but not without a good deal of competition and constant vigilance on the part of the mayor and the two principal party leaders. Multiple sources of patronage are commonplace with machine politics and have important consequences, which will be explored in the next section.

A second typical feature of machine politics was that the elections most important to organization politicians were obscure primaries held on the ward level. Issue-oriented ''amateurs'' seldom could muster sufficient strength in these elections. The amateurs seemed to be interested chiefly in national and international affairs, and thus were most active and successful in presidential primaries and elections, where their policy concerns were salient. While the stakes in presidential contests may be global, they seldom include the topic of prime interest to machine politicians—control of patronage—and hence the regulars exert less than their maximum effort in them. Conveniently for both amateurs and regulars, the two sorts of elections are held at different times and usually in different years. When the amateurs' enthusiasm is at its peak, the professionals will be less interested; when the machine's spoils are at stake, the amateurs are less involved.

Participation in election campaigns is not the only form of political action. It is important to distinguish between electioneering and other types of political activity. In New Haven there was a major divergence between campaign and non-campaign activities. The likelihood that richer people would engage in non-campaign activity was far greater than the corresponding probability for campaigns.[4] This divergence reflected the probability that participation in a campaign is less autonomously motivated, for in New Haven the discipline of patronage compels campaign work. There are no such external inducements for most non-campaign political action. Indeed, because such activity usually consists of trying to exert pressure on public officials, it is likely to be viewed with apprehension or disfavor by those machine politicians who dispense patronage. A sense of political efficacy, education, a white-collar job, and higher income—all are thought to be associated with those personal qualities that lead people to try to influence the outcome of government decisions. In many parts of the country, these traits are also associated with electioneering. Some people participate in New Haven elections—particularly for national office—from such motives, but most activists, including party regulars, do not. The essentially involuntary character of much political participation in cities dominated by machine politics has received scant attention from students of participation, who customarily treat the phenomenon they study as the product of solely internal stimuli.

How typical is New Haven? Systematic trend data about the persistence of machine politics are scarce. Ideally, one would develop various measures of the incidence of machine politics and then compare these indicators, both over time and from city to city. One such index might be the proportion of city employees covered by civil-service regulations, a figure that is reported annually for all cities in *The Municipal Year Book*.[5] As this source reveals, formal civil-service coverage is fairly widespread in cities of over 50,000 population. The states of Iowa, New York, and Ohio require their cities to use merit systems, and in Massachusetts local employees come under the jurisdiction of the state civil-service commission. In 1963, 51 percent of cities in the other states had complete civil-service coverage for their employees, 6 percent covered all but manual workers, 27 percent covered only policemen and firemen, and 16 percent (mostly in the South) did not have merit systems.[6] One might assume that in places where formal civil-service coverage is low, patronage is more abundant. The reverse probably is true also, but only in a very general way, for there are many cities where political realities or administrative loopholes weaken the effect of the regulations. Cities in New York, for example, can keep jobs from being covered by civil service by classifying them as "provisional," i.e., temporary, or "noncompetitive," which means that satisfactory tests cannot be devised. In Chicago all municipal workers except those in public utilities are "covered" by civil service, but as a matter of political reality, a great many city jobs can be used for patronage purposes with little difficulty.

Information on other kinds of patronage is also elusive. Two students of the subject in New York report that judicial patronage (receiverships, refereeships, and the like) is "almost impossible even to research," and for this reason "its value as political gifts is unquestionably priceless."[7] Because of the moral and legal delicacy of the subject, systematic and realistic data on machine politics are elusive, and thus comparisons are difficult. Nevertheless, some journalists and scholars have turned up useful information.

A *New York Times* survey of city and state government in New York concluded that "patronage has vastly expanded in the last several decades because of the tremendous growth of government, spiraling government spending, and the expansion of government's discretionary powers to regulate, control, and supervise private industry."[8] The same story reported that the annual payroll in city jobs exempt from civil-service regulations, which had been $10 million in the Wagner administration, soared to $32.8 million under Mayor Lindsay in poverty-program jobs alone. During the first three years of Mayor Lindsay's regime the number of "provisional" employees increased from 1,500 to 12,800. Under Mayor Wagner the City of New York also had 50,000 "noncompetitive" jobs; 24,000 more "noncompetitive" positions were added after Lindsay took office.[9] In the last year of the Wagner administration the city let $8 million in consulting contracts without competitive bidding. By 1969, the city's annual expenditure for outside consultants had risen to $75 million, with many indications that Lindsay was using these contracts as a form of patronage.[10] In addition to the jobs and contracts at his disposal, the Mayor of New York also can wield tremendous patronage power through his control of the municipal agencies that grant zoning variances. Lindsay has made good use of this power for political purposes.[11]

The patronage resources of the New York mayor's office are not much greater than those of the Manhattan Surrogates' Court, which does about $1 billion worth of estate work each year, appointing attorneys to administer estates. These appointments, which are often both undemanding and lucrative, generally are made on the basis of political considerations.[12] Other courts in New York City name referees, trustees, guardians, and receivers in a variety of situations. These appointments also are both rewarding and politically determined.[13] Trustees, in turn, decide where to bank the funds for which they are responsible, and their power in this respect constitutes another form of patronage if decisions are made politically—as they seem to be.

Cities other than New Haven and New York have political systems in which patronage plays a crucial part. Mayor Richard Daley of Chicago is also chairman of the Cook County Democratic Committee. These two positions together give him control of about 35,000 patronage jobs.[14] It is reported that Daley personally scrutinizes each job application. Since there are 3,412 voting precincts in Chicago, the Democratic organization can deploy an average of ten workers to each precinct just on the basis of job patronage.

Over 8,000 state employees in Indiana owe their jobs to patronage and are assessed two percent of their salaries for the coffers of the ruling party's state committee.[15] "Macing" public employees is not uncommon in some locales, including New Haven, but the Indiana method of issuing automobile and drivers licenses and automobile titles is unique. These matters are handled by a franchise system, rather like service stations or Kentucky Fried Chicken outlets. Local "license branches" are "awarded to the county chairman of the Governor's party, or the persons they designate."[16] The branch pays the state party committee four cents for each license sold; otherwise, it retains all fees up to $10,000. Above that figure, half the take must be returned to the state Bureau of Motor Vehicles.

This brief survey shows that formidable patronage resources are available as rewards for political participation in various cities, and thus that New Haven's political practices are not an anachronistic freak. To put it another way, the dependent variable—machine politics—is still a common phenomenon. In the next section I will explore some of the definitional problems that have impeded clear understanding of machine politics, before turning directly to examination of the independent variables said to be associated with its rise and fall.

MACHINE POLITICS DEFINED

The terms "machine politics" and "political machine" are commonly used so as to confuse two quite different phenomena. "Machine politics" is the manipulation of certain *incentives* to partisan political participation: favoritism based on political criteria in personnel decisions, contracting, and administration of the laws. A "political machine" is an organization that practices machine politics, i.e., that attracts and directs its members primarily by means of these incentives. Unfortunately, the term "machine" is also used in a quite different and less useful sense to refer to the *centralization* of power in a party in a major political jurisdiction: a "machine" is a united and hierarchical party organization in a state, city, or county. Now there is no necessary relation between the two dimensions of incentives and centralization: machine politics (patronage incentives) need not produce centralized organization *at the city level or higher*.

The availability of patronage probably makes it easier to centralize influence in a cohesive party organization, since these resources can be distributed so as to discipline and reward the organization's workers. Quite often, however, all patronage is not controlled by the same people. There may be competing organizations or factions within each party in the same area, for where patronage is plentiful, it usually is available from more than one jurisdiction. In New Haven the municipal government had no monopoly on the spoils of government, which were also dispensed by the probate court and the state government. Thus the existence of a cohesive local organization in either party did not follow from the use of patronage to motivate party workers.

This distinction between machine politics and centralized local machines is far from academic, for the former is found many places where the latter is not. Chicago presently exhibits both machine politics and a very strong Democratic machine. Forty years ago it had the former but not the latter.[17] In Boston and New York there are the same kinds of incentives to political activity as in Chicago, but no cohesive citywide organizations. Instead, these cities have several contending party factions. In New York "the party" includes reform clubs with considerable influence as well as a variety of "regular" organizations. The frequently celebrated "decline" of Tammany Hall was not so much the subjugation of the regulars by the reformers, nor the disappearance of patronage and corruption (neither has happened yet), as the decentralization of the city's old-line Democratic organization. As Sayre and Kaufman describe the situation, "Party organizations in New York City are not monolithic in character. Each Assembly District is virtually an independent principality. . . . The parties are aggregations of segments rather than organic entities. They are decentralized and fragmented and undisciplined, but they achieve sufficient unity of purpose and action and leadership to identify them as organizations."[18]

Multiple sources of patronage are one of the factors maintaining this organizational fragmentation. In the 1930s, when hostile organizations controlled city, state, and federal government, Tammany Hall was sustained by patronage from the Manhattan Surrogates' Court, which is thought to have about as much patronage as the Mayor of New York.[19]

While the distinction between *incentives* and *centralization* is useful for accurate description and definitional clarity, it also has important theoretical ramifications. Robert K. Merton's influential explanation of the persistence of machine politics (patronage) points to the presumed coordinating function of centralized political machines:

> The key structural function of the Boss is to organize, centralize and maintain in good working condition the "scattered fragments of power" which are at present dispersed through our political organization. By the centralized organization of political power, the Boss and his apparatus can satisfy the needs of diverse sub groups in a larger community which are not politically satisfied by legally devised and culturally approved social structures.[20]

Yet machine politics exists many places where, as in New York, the party "organization" is a congeries of competing factions.[21] In fact, cohesive organizations like Chicago's may be fairly uncommon, while pervasive favoritism and patronage—machine politics—are much less so. Hence Merton explained the persistence of the incentive system by referring to functions allegedly performed by an institution (a centralized, city-wide party organization) that may or may not be found where machine politics flourishes.

The rewards that create the incentives in machine politics are not only tangible but divisible, that is, they are "allocated by dividing the benefits piecemeal and allocating various pieces to specific individuals."[22] Moreover, they typically result from the routine operation of government, not from particular substantive policy outcomes. Any regime in a courthouse or city hall will hire roughly the same number of people, contract for roughly the same amounts of goods and services, and enforce (or fail to enforce) the same laws, irrespective of the differences in policies advocated by one party or the other. The measures adopted by an activist, enterprising administration will generate a higher level of public employment and contracting than the output of a caretaker government. Yet the differences are not enough to change the generalization that the rewards of machine politics are essentially issue-free in that they will flow regardless of what policies are followed. This excepts, of course, reform of personnel and contracting practices.

One can thus distinguish two kinds of tangible incentives to political participation. The incentives that fuel machine politics are inevitable concomitants of government activity, available irrespective of the policies chosen by a particular regime. A second kind of tangible incentive results from a desire to influence the outcome of particular policy decisions. This second type includes those considerations that induce political participation by interest groups that do not want patronage, but do want the government to follow a particular line of action in a substantive policy area: lower tax rates, anti-discrimination legislation, minimum-wage laws, conservation of natural resources, and the like. A particularly pure example of a political organization animated by substantive incentives would be a taxpayers' group that acted as a political party—naming candidates, getting out the vote, etc.—in order to capture city hall for the purpose of enacting a policy of minimal expenditure. As an ideal type, such a group would not care *who* was hired or awarded contracts, so long as a policy of economy was followed.

Incentives to political activity can be classified along two dimensions: tangible/intangible and routine/substantive. The matrix in Figure 1 shows the possible combinations, and examples of organizations in which each incentive system predominates. These categories are ideal types, of course; in any city people will be drawn to party activity by each kind of incentive, and therefore few cities will display only one incentive system. But cities do vary enormously in the prevailing type of incentive system, which is determined by the resources available, the stakes of electoral outcomes, and the attitudes of the citizens. A kind of Gresham's Law also applies here: in cities with ample patronage resources, ideologically motivated people tend not to participate as actively in local elections, except perhaps in enclaves where they are numerous.

A word should be said about Category III, routine intangible incentives. This category includes several different motivations, all of which have in common certain negative characteristics: they do not involve material rewards for political action nor do they depend on the anticipation of preferred policy outcomes. Among these are "solidary" rewards for party work: personal gratification from membership in an organization or from social contact with other party workers. In principle, there is no reason why such pleasures could not be enjoyed by members of any sort of party organization. In practice, it may be that patronage-based organizations are more likely than other kinds to provide solidary rewards.

FIGURE 1
Incentives to Political Participation

	Routine	Substantive
Tangible	I Patronage —— Machine Politics	II Favorable Policy —— "Main Street"
Intangible	III Sociability Intrinsic Enjoyment of Politics Loyalty to a Leader —— Any Kind of Organization	IV Ideology —— "Amateur"

This has led some observers to suggest that at present machines are sustained as much by these nonmaterial returns as by monetary considerations.[23] It is more plausible, however, that the solidary gratifications are essentially a by-product of a material incentive system that produces more stable and frequent interactions than is the case with amateur politics. One would expect that these interactions would not be wholly instrumental in character, that they would have emotional and social dimensions, and that these would provide a framework of relations that could be satisfying to many of the participants. Since these politically-based social relations seldom exclude the "right kind of people," i.e., people who are not reformers, one might also expect that political clubhouses would offer social pleasures to people who were not at the patronage trough. Some of these people may work for the machine. It would, however, be a serious error to confuse this incidental *effect* with the tangible rewards that *cause* the machine to exist. Consider an analogy: many people get important emotional sustenance from the social relations at their jobs. These rewards, as "morale," may contribute to efficiency, easy recruitment, and low employee turnover. It does not appear useful, however, to argue that the firm exists because of the social benefits that may be a by-product of work.

Substantive policy issues are not normally among the incentives animating machine politics. They are irrelevant to this political style and more an irritant than anything else to its practitioners. One student of Chicago politics said that for the Democratic organization there, "Issues are obstacles to be overcome, not opportunities to be sought."[24] Daniel Patrick Moynihan observed that in New York, "In the regular party, conferences on issues are regarded as women's work."[25] In California, on the other hand, conferences and resolutions about issues are meat and drink to the earnest middle-class activists who man both political parties. By the same token, local campaigns feature debate about issues in inverse ratio to the prevalence of machine politics, as James Q. Wilson noted: "In Chicago, issues in city elections are conspicuous by their rarity. In New York, they are somewhat more common. In Detroit and Los Angeles, candidates often must go to considerable lengths to *generate* issues in order to attract interest to their campaigns for public office."[26]

In New Haven, also, the party organizations did not play an important role in developing alternative courses of municipal governmental action. Indeed, since machine politicians drew their resources from the routine operations of government, they did not concern themselves with policy formation. The party's two top leaders were seldom present at meetings where decisions about municipal policy were made, nor did they play an active part in those matters. On strictly party topics like nominations they formed, with Mayor Lee, a triumvirate. Appointments, contracts, and the like were negotiated among the three.[27] But substantive city affairs were another matter; here the organization leaders were neither interested nor consulted on the outlines of policy. They were not excluded against their will; they were largely indifferent. This does not seem to be an unusual situation. In New York, for example, Sayre and Kaufman report that "the most distinctive characteristic of the party leaders as participants in the city's political process is their relative neutrality toward the content of public policy."[28]

The concerns of machine politicians are not irrelevant to substantive policy formation, for while the politicians are neutral "toward the content of public policy," they are very interested indeed in the details of its execution; and in many policy areas the aggregate of their influence on all the details can be important. In Newark the politicians were not concerned about general policy in the city's urban renewal program, but they did scrutinize "with great care all actions of the staff involving hiring, classification, and compensation of [Newark Housing] Authority personnel, the appraisal and acquisition of properties, the awarding of contracts, the maintenance of NHA-owned property, the selection of public housing tenants . . ."[29]

Sayre and Kaufman explain the considerations that lead to party interest in the execution of policy: "The interest of party leaders in public policy seems to vary directly with its possible effect upon their role in choosing officials. In fact, this perception of their relation to public policy impels party leaders to be most concerned with discrete aspects of policy and its application rather than its range and content."[30]

There are two interesting aspects of this tendency for machine politicians to be interested in the details of public policy rather than its basic outlines. One implication concerns Dahl's portrait of the ideal type politician, whom he called *"homo politicus."* In Dahl's view, "Political man . . . deliberately allocates a very sizable share of his resources to the process of gaining and maintaining control over the policies of government."[31] This may be an accurate characterization of many political leaders, but it is not suitable for machine politicians, who are relatively indifferent to public policy, do not consider issue appeals important or desirable elements of electoral strategies, and are primarily interested in control over the sources of patronage. Thus a political taxonomist could identify two subspecies of *homo politicus.* One of these fits Dahl's description and might be called *h. politicus substantus.* The other, the machine politician, is *h. politicus boodelus.* Forerunners of this classification can be found in the literature. In his autobiography, the late "Boss" Flynn, the famous Democratic leader in the Bronx, persistently distinguished between "Democrats," whom he admired, and "New Dealers," whom he scorned as impractical, rigid meddlers.[32]

A second implication of this tendency for machine politics to slight issues concerns theorizing and research on relations between the level of interparty competition and the character of public policy. The classic position on this topic, generally associated with the work of V. O. Key, was that policies beneficial to the lower classes were more likely with evenly matched parties, while one-party domination tended to benefit the rich.[33] Early quantitative research showed that competition and per-capita spending for various welfare measures were very weakly related at the state level, and thus seemed to disconfirm the old belief about policy consequences of party competition.[34] Both the original proposition and the subsequent research assumed that electoral competition would be "programmatic," i.e., based on alternative policy platforms. But where machine politicians regard issues as "women's work" and "obstacles to be overcome," campaign appeals are likely to include far less issue content. Thus a fair test of Key's proposition would separate "policy competition" from "patronage competition."[35]

WHY POLITICAL MACHINES HAVE NOT WITHERED AWAY

The conventional wisdom in American social science interprets machine politics as a product of the social needs and political techniques of a bygone era. Advocates of this position attempt to explain both the past existence of machines and their suposed current demise in terms of the functions that the machines performed.[36] In analyzing the functions—now supposedly obsolete—that machine politics served, it is useful to consider four questions:

(1) Did the political machines actually perform these functions in the past?
(2) Do machines still perform them?
(3) Has the need for the functions diminished?
(4) Is machine politics found wherever these needs exist?

It is commonly argued that various historical trends have crucially diminished the natural constituencies of machines—people who provided votes or other political support in return for the machine's services. The essential machine constituency is thought to have been the poor in general and immigrants in particular. The decline of machine politics then is due to rising prosperity and education, which have reduced the number of people to whom the rewards of machine politics are attractive or necessary. These trends have also, as Thomas R. Dye puts it, spread "middle class values about honesty, efficiency, and good government, which inhibit party organizations in purchases, contracts, and vote-buying, and other cruder forms of municipal corruption. The more successful machine [sic] today, like Daley's in Chicago, have had to reform themselves in order to maintain a good public image."[37]

One function that machines performed was furnishing needy people with food, clothing, and other *direct material assistance*—those legendary Christmas turkeys, buckets of coal, summer outings, and so on. There is no way of knowing just how much of this kind of help machines gave, but it seems to have been an important means of gleaning votes. From the time of the New Deal, government has assumed the burden of providing for the minimal physical needs of the poor, thus supposedly preempting a major source of the machines' appeal. The growth of the welfare state undeniably has limited politicians' opportunities to use charity as a means of incurring obligations that could be discharged by political support. Some political clubs still carry on the old traditions, however, including the distribution of free turkeys to needy families at Christmas time.[38]

Machines supposedly provided other tangible rewards, and the need for these has not been met by alternative institutions. The most obvious of these benefits is employment. The welfare state does not guarantee everyone a job and so the power to hire is still an important power resource. It has been argued, most ably by Frank J. Sorauf, that patronage jobs, mainly at the bottom of the pay scale, are not very attractive to most people.[39] But these positions are attractive to enough people to maintain an ample demand for them, and thus they still are a useful incentive.

A second major constituent service supplied by machine politics was *helping poor and unacculturated people deal with the bureaucratic demands of urban government.* Describing this function, some writers emphasized its affective dimension. Robert K. Merton put it this way: "the precinct captain is ever a friend in need. In our increasingly impersonal society, the machine, through its local agents, performs the important social *function of humanizing and personalizing all manner of assistance* to those in need."[40] In Dye's view, the machine "personalized government. With keen social intuition, the machine recognized the voter as a man, generally living in a neighborhood, who had specific personal problems and wants."[41] William F. Whyte saw a more cognitive element in politicians' services to the common man: "the uninitiated do not understand the complex organization of government and do not know how to find the channels through which they can obtain action."[42] Whyte's view of the relation between the citizen and his "friend in need" the precinct captain is a great deal less innocent than Merton's: "Everyone recognizes that when a politician does a favor for a constituent, the constituent becomes obligated to the politician."[43]

If machine politics were a response to "our increasingly impersonal society," it would seem to follow that continuing growth in the scope, complexity, and impersonality of institutional life would produce *greater* need for politicians to mediate between individuals and their government. The growth of the welfare state therefore has not diminished this need but increased it and presumably offers the machine politician new opportunities for helping citizens get what they want from the government. Describing the advent of the New Deal social services in a poor Boston neighborhood, Whyte made it clear that the new welfare policies did not so much subvert machine politics as rearrange the channels of access while presenting some politicians with a new opportunity to accumulate obligations. Whyte quotes the wife of a state senator: "If you're qualified, you can get on [WPA] without going to a politician. But it will be four weeks before you get certified, and I can push things through so that you get on in a week. And I can see that you get a better job . . ."[44]

As far as local politicians are concerned, new public services may be new prizes that covetous or needy citizens can more easily obtain with political help. Writing a generation after Whyte, Harold Kaplan reported that in Newark "a public housing tenant, therefore, may find it easier to secure a public housing unit, prevent eviction from a project, secure a unit in a better project, or have NHA [Newark Housing Authority] reconsider his rent, if he has the right sponsor at City Hall."[45] There is no necessary connection, then, between expanded public services and a decline in the advantages of political help or in the number of people who want to use it. While the expansion and institutionalization of welfare may have ended "the party's monopoly of welfare services,"[46] they have vastly expanded the need for information, guidance, and emotional support in relations between citizens and government officials, and thus there is no shortage of services that machines can provide the poor and unassimilated, who are still with us.[47]

There is no doubt that in the past 50 years income levels have risen and the flow of foreign immigrants has dwindled considerably. But there are plenty of poor people in the cities, the middle classes have been moving to the suburbs for the past two generations, and the European immigrants have been succeeded by blacks, Puerto Ricans, Mexicans, and poor rural whites.[48] Moreover, about two and a half million people came to this country as immigrants in the decade from 1950 to 1960. The argument that affluence and assimilation have choked machine politics at the roots, one familiar to scholars for decades, may now look a bit more threadbare. Yet the recent rediscovery of poverty and cultural deprivation has not had a major effect on thinking about trends in the viability of machine politics.

Along with the new interest in the urban poor has come a realization that existing institutions do not meet their needs. Among these inadequate institutions is the political machine, which, in the traditional view, should be expected to do for today's blacks, Chicanos, Puerto Ricans, and poor whites just what it is supposed to have done for yesterday's immigrants. But even in cities with flourishing machine politics there has been a tremendous development of all kinds of community action groups for advice, information exchange, and the representation of individual and neighborhood interests—precisely the functions that the machines are said to have performed. The gap between the disoriented poor and the public institutions serving them seems to be present equally in cities like Chicago, generally thought to be political anachronisms, and in places like Los Angeles that have never experienced machine politics. This leads to an important point: most American cities have had the social conditions that are said to give rise to machine politics, but many of these cities have not had machine politics for a generation or more.

This fact and the evident failure of existing machines to perform their functions cast doubt on the conventional ways of explaining both the functions of machines in their supposed heyday and the causes of their "decline." One conclusion is that the decline is real, but that the principal causes of the decline do not lie in affluence and assimilation. A second possibility is that the machines persist, but have abandoned the beneficent functions they used to perform. A third is that they are still "humanizing and personalizing all manner of assistance to those in need," but cannot cope with a massive increase in the needs of their clienteles. And a fourth alternative is that the extent to which they ever performed these functions has been exaggerated.

It does seem that a whole generation of scholarship has been adversely affected by overreaction to the older judgmental style of describing machine politics. Until a decade or two ago most work on machines was moralistic and pejorative, dwelling on the seamy side of the subject and concerning itself largely with exposure and denunciation.[49] More contemporary social scientists have diverged from this tradition in two respects. One, apparently a reaction to the highly normative style of the old reformers, is a tendency to gloss over the very real evils they described. The other, addressed to the major problem of explaining the durability of machine politics, is the search for "functions": acculturating immigrants and giving them a channel of social mobility, providing a link between citizen and city hall, and coordinating formally fragmented government agencies. Some writers suggest that urban political organizations were a rudimentary form of the welfare state. While the tone of these later works has been realistic, some of them leaned toward idealizing their subject, perhaps in reaction to the earlier moralism or because functionalism has not been accompanied by an inclination to confront the sordid details. Thus the development of a more dispassionate social science has produced, on the descriptive level, a retreat from realism. The functionalists seem to have been somewhat overcredulous: "the precinct captain is ever a friend in need."

This innocence may explain the popularity in recent textbooks of a pious declaration by a celebrated and unsavory ward boss in Boston: "'I think,' said Martin Lomasny [sic], 'that there's got to be in every ward somebody that any bloke can come to—no matter what he's done—and get help. Help, you understand; none of your law and your justice, but help.'"[50] The kind of "help" that could be expected is suggested by the remarks of another local leader in Boston that convey, I think, a more realistic sense of the priorities in machine politics:

When people wanted help from the organization, they would come right up here to the office [of the political club]. Matt [the boss] would be in here every morning from nine to eleven, and if you couldn't see him then, you could find him in the ward almost any other time. If a man came in to ask Matt for a job, Matt would listen to him and then tell him he'd see what he could do; he should come back in a couple of days. That would give Matt time to get in touch with the precinct captain and find out all about the man. If he didn't vote in the last election, he was out. Matt wouldn't do anything for him—that is, unless he could show that he was so sick he couldn't get to the polls.[51]

"Helping" citizens deal with government is, in this context, usually thought to be a matter of advice about where to go, whom to see, and what to say. The poor undeniably need this service more than people whose schooling and experience equip them to cope with bureaucratic institutions and procedures. But in some local political cultures advice to citizens is often accompanied by pressure on officials. The machine politician's goal is to incur the maximum obligation from his constituents, and merely providing information is not as big a favor as helping bring about the desired outcome. Thus *"help" shades into "pull."*

Now there is no reason why the advantages of political influence appeal only to the poor. In places where the political culture supports expectations that official discretion will be exercised in accordance with political considerations, the constituency for machine politics extends across the socio-economic spectrum. People whose interests are affected by governmental decisions can include those who want to sell to the government, as well as those whose economic or social activities may be subject to public regulation.

Favoritism animates machine politics, favoritism not just in filling pick-and-shovel jobs, but in a vast array of public decisions. The welfare state has little to do with the potential demand for favoritism, except to expand opportunities for its exercise. The New Deal did not abolish the contractor's natural desire to minimize the risks of competitive bidding, or the landlord's equally natural desire to avoid the burdens of the housing code. It is all very well to talk about "middle-class values of efficiency and honesty," but the thousands of lawyers whose political connections enable them to benefit from the billion-dollar-a-year case load of the Manhattan Surrogates' Court are surely not members of the working class.

While "help" in dealing with the government may be primarily appealing to people baffled by the complexities of modern society and too poor to hire lawyers, "pull" is useful in proportion to the size of one's dealing with government. Certain kinds of business and professional men are *more* likely to have interests requiring repeated and complicated relations with public agencies, and thus are potentially a *stronger* constituency for machine politics than the working classes. The conventional wisdom that the middle classes are hostile to machine politics rests on several types of evidence: (1) The undeniable fact that reform candidates almost always run better in well-to-do neighborhoods. (2) The equally undeniable fact that machine politics provides, in patronage and petty favors, a kind of reward for political participation that is not available in other incentive systems. (3) The less validated proposition that middle-class people think that governments should be run with impartial, impersonal honesty in accordance with abstract principles, while the working classes are more sympathetic to favoritism and particularistic criteria. These characterizations may be true in the aggregate for two diverse such categories as "the middle class" and "the working class" (although that has not yet been established), but even if these generalizations are true, they would still leave room for the existence of a sizable subcategory of the middle class who, in some political cultures, benefits from and endorses machine politics.

Textbook interpretations recognize these middle-class interests in machine politics, but generally relegate them to an hypothesized earlier stage in urban history. This was the era when America changed from a rural to an urban society, a shift that created a vast need in the new cities for municipal facilities and services: streetcars, electricity, paved streets, and so on. These needs were met by businessmen who corrupted officials wholesale in their eagerness to get franchises. Since the businessmen wanted action, they profited from political machines that could organize power to get things done by centralizing the formally fragmented agencies of government. Thus machine politics served the needs not just of poor immigrants, but also of the generation of businessmen who exploited the foundation of urban America. But after the first great rush of city building, the essential facilities and utilities had been supplied and business interest in local government declined. Machine politics no longer performed a coordinating function for the franchise seekers and hence lost an important constituency.

While this may be an accurate description of relations between business greed and governmental corruption in the Gilded Age, it has a number of deficiencies as an explanation of the rise and fall of machine politics. Three of these flaws have already been discussed in other contexts: (1) Like poverty, urban growth is not a bygone phenomenon, but continues to this day. (2) Machine politics does not occur wherever cities have experienced sudden and massive needs for municipal services. (3) This explanation confuses patronage and centralization of party organizations at the city level, two phenomena that may not be found together.

There are other difficulties with this line of thought. First, uncoordinated public agencies and jurisdictions continue to proliferate. If machine politics were a response to the formal decentralization of government, one would think that it, too, would increase, and that party organizations would grow stronger rather than weaker. It may be that one or more unstated intermediary conditions are preventing these latter trends from occurring; if so, no writer has, to my knowledge, shown what this interactive relation is.

If it were true that "the key structural function of the Boss is to organize, centralize, and maintain in good working condition the 'scattered fragments of power'" typical of American local government, one would expect to find a positive relation between the prevalence of machine politics and municipal institutions that maximize fragmentation. "Strong-mayor" cities should be least ridden by patronage, and commission and council-manager cities should have the most. There is no systematic evidence available about these relations, but what data there are do not support the propositions. (They are also not supported by another piece of conventional wisdom, which associates city managers with reformism.)

Machine politics seems to be far more common on the East Coast than in the West, but so are cities with elected mayors. Cities with mayors and cities with managers are equally likely to have merit systems for their employees, which could be considered an index of the weakness of machine politics.[52]

Finally, political centralization may not be conducive to the interests of businessmen who want prompt and affirmative action from local government. Whether centralized power is preferable depends on what the businessman wants. If he wants a license or franchise to sell goods or services, or to buy something belonging to the government, it may be in his interests to deal with an autonomous official or agency, not with a government-wide hierarchy. John A. Gardiner's study of the notoriously corrupt city of "Wincanton" provides evidence for the proposition that decentralized political systems are *more* corruptible, because the potential corrupter needs to influence only a segment of the government, and because in a fragmented system there are fewer centralized forces and agencies to enforce honesty. The "Wincanton" political system is formally and informally fragmented; neither parties nor interest groups (including the criminal syndicate) exercise overall coordination. The ample patronage and outright graft in "Wincanton" are not used as a means of centralization.[53] Indeed, governmental coordination clearly would not be in the interests of the private citizens there who benefit from corruption, or of the officials who take bribes. Attempts by reformers to stop graft or patronage often founder on the city's commission form of government, which is both the apotheosis of local governmental fragmentation and an hospitable environment for machine politics.

The conventional wisdom also holds that the machines' electioneering techniques are as obsolete as the social functions they used to perform. According to this interpretation, "the old politics" based its campaigns on divisible promises and interpersonal persuasion, and these methods have been outdated by the mass media—particularly television, the growing importance of candidates' personalities, and the electorate's craving for ideological or at least programmatic promises.[54]

Like the other explanations of the machines' demise, this argument has serious factual and logical deficiencies. As we have seen, machine politics is an effective way of raising money for political purposes. There is no reason why the money "maced" from public employees or extracted from government contractors cannot be spent on motivational research, advertising copywriters, television spots, and all the other manifestations of mass media campaigns.

Similarly, there is no inconsistency between machine politics and outstanding candidates. Just as machine politicians can spend their money on public relations, so can they bestow their support on inspirational leaders who exude integrity and vitality. Many of the most famous "idealistic" politicians in American history owe their success to the sponsorship of machine politicians. Woodrow Wilson made his first venture into electoral politics as the gubernatorial candidate of an unsavory Democratic organization in New Jersey. (Once elected governor, Wilson promptly betrayed his sponsors.) In more recent times, such exemplars of dedicated public spirit as the elder Adlai Stevenson, Paul H. Douglas, and Chester Bowles were nominated for office as the candidates of the patronage-based party organizations in their several states.[55]

Sayre and Kaufman explain this organization willingness to support blue-ribbon candidates: "They [machine politicians] have also learned the lesson of what retailers call the loss leader—that is, the item that may lose money for the storekeeper but which lures customers in and thereby leads to increases in purchases of profitable merchandise."[56] Generally, party regulars turn to blue-ribbon "loss leaders" when they think that their popularity is necessary to carry the ticket to victory. Otherwise, machine politicians eschew candidates with independent popular appeal, since popularity is an important bargaining resource in intraparty negotiating. Without it, an elected official is more dependent on organization politicians.

"The new politics" is an ambiguous term. It is used to describe increasing campaign emphasis on the mass media and professional public relations, and also is applied to popular participation in party affairs and direct contact with the voters by campaign workers. In the 1968 election "the new politics" was associated with peace advocates and the young enthusiasts who gave so much tone to Eugene McCarthy's presidential bid. Except for the age of the activists, there was little to distinguish this aspect of McCarthy's campaign from the idealistic appeal of such previous and diverse presidential candidates as Adlai Stevenson and Barry Goldwater, both of whom projected to some people an image of altruism and reform that attracted legions of dedicated workers. "The new politics" seems to be one of those recurring features of American politics that political writers are always rediscovering. The trademark of "the new politics" is intense precinct work, one-to-one conversations with citizens, the same interpersonal style that machines have relied on for generations. As a Democratic organization politician in New York observed: "If the new politics teaches anything, it's that the old politics was pretty good. The McCarthy kids in New Hampshire rang doorbells, made the telephone calls, made the personal contact that people associate with the old-style machine."[57]

Both kinds of "new politics" have at least one thing in common: they tend to be found in elections that draw a great deal of attention and arouse strong emotions. State and local elections and party primaries (except presidential ones) rarely attain much visibility. Candidates for the city council, the state legislature, or the city or state under-ticket seldom attract much public attention. Even paid media advertising in such elections is not feasible because the voting jurisdiction for a single candidacy generally includes only a fraction of the reading or viewing audience of the most widely used media. An occasional mayoral or gubernatorial race may get a good deal of media space and arouse popular enthusiasm, but otherwise these elections do not present a high profile in most voters' perspectives. This is particularly true for local elections, which generally are not concurrent with national campaigns, as well as for party primaries and campaigns for any state office except the governorship. These low-salience contests are particularly amenable to the resources typical of machine politics. A New York state senator explained this point bluntly: "My best captains, in the primary, are the ones who are on the payroll. You can't get the average voter excited about who's going to be an Assemblyman or State Senator. I've got two dozen people who are going to work so much harder, because if I lose, they lose."[58] It is in elections of this type, where neither the mass media nor idealistic amateurs are likely to participate, that most of the spoils of machine politics are at stake. Since precinct work is effective in inverse relation to the salience of the election,[59] "old fashioned machines" do not seem very seriously threatened by either form of "the new politics."

CONCLUSIONS AND SUGGESTIONS

To sum up my argument: Since an increasing proportion of urban populations is poor and uneducated, it is not persuasive to argue that growing prosperity and education are diminishing the constituency for machine politics. While governments now assume responsibility for a minimal level of welfare, other contemporary trends are not so inhospitable to machine politics. Various kinds of patronage still seem to be in reasonable supply, and are as attractive as ever to those people—by no means all poor—who benefit from them. The proliferation of government programs provides more opportunities for the exercise of favoritism. The continuing bureaucratization of modern government gives more scope for the machine's putative function of serving as a link between the citizen and the state.

These trends would seem to have expanded the need for the services the machines supposedly performed for the poor. Yet surviving machines apparently are not performing these functions, and machine politics has not flourished in many cities where the alleged need for these functions is just as great.

The potential constituency for political favoritism is not limited to the poor; many kinds of business and professional men can benefit from machine politics. They do in some cities but not in others. Again, it appears that the hypothesized conditions for machine politics are found in many places where machines are enfeebled or absent.

Real and imaginary changes in campaign techniques are not inconsistent with machines' capacities. In short, machines have not withered away because the conditions that supposedly gave rise to them are still present. The problem with this answer is that the conditions are found in many places where machine politics does not exist.

Attempts to explain the growth and alleged decline of machine politics usually emphasize the importance of immigrants as a constituency for machines.[60] Yet many cities with large immigrant populations have never been dominated by machine politics, or were freed of this dominance generations ago.[61] Machine politics continues to flourish in some states like Indiana, where foreign-stock voters are relatively scarce. In other states, like Pennsylvania and Connecticut, machines seem to have been as successful with old stock American constituents as with immigrants.[62]

Far more interesting than differences in ethnicity or social class are regional or subregional variations in the practices of machine politics and in attitudes toward them.[63] Public acceptance of patronage, for example, appears to vary a good deal from place to place in patterns that are not explained by differences in population characteristics such as education, occupation, and ethnicity. Although systematic data on this subject are not available, it does seem that voters in parts of the East, the Ohio Valley, and the South are tolerant of practices that would scandalize most people in, say, the Pacific Coast states or the Upper Midwest. The residents of Indiana, for example, seem to accept calmly the remarkable mingling of public business and party profits in that state. One researcher notes that these practices have "not been an issue in recent campaigns."[64] Another student of midwestern politics reports that "Indiana is the only state studied where the governor and other important state officials described quite frankly and in detail the sources of the campaign funds. They were disarmingly frank because they saw nothing wrong in the techniques employed to raise funds, and neither did the opposing political party nor the press nor, presumably, the citizenry."[65]

California provides a particularly useful contrast to the East Coast states and Indiana. While California has a cosmopolitan population and an urban, industrial economy, it also displays virtually no signs of machine politics. The Governor has about as many patronage jobs at his disposal as the Mayor of New Haven. Californians who worked in John F. Kennedy's presidential campaign report the bemusement of Kennedy organizers from the East who came to the state with thoughts of building their campaign organization around public employees. These and other practices that are widely accepted in the East are abhorred on the West Coast. Paying precinct workers is commonplace in eastern cities. But when Jess Unruh, a prominent California Democratic leader, hired some canvassers in the 1962 election, he was roundly denounced from all points of the political spectrum for importing such a sordid practice. The president of the California Democratic Council said that Unruh's action "smacked of ward politics" ("ward politics" is a common pejorative in California) and sternly announced, "I am firmly convinced that the expansion and development of the use of paid workers is unhealthy for the Democratic party in California."[66]

The reasons for these marked geographical variations in political style are not easily found, but looking for them is a more promising approach to explaining the incidence of machine politics than the search for functions supposedly rooted in the socioeconomic composition of urban populations.[67]

 **NOTES**

1. Data on New Haven are from an intensive study of that city's politics conducted primarily by Robert A. Dahl, William H. Flanigan, Nelson W. Polsby, and me. Our research is described most fully in Dahl's *Who Governs?* (New Haven: Yale University Press, 1961), 330–340.

2. The most important source of my information about New Haven politics was a year of participant-observation in city hall. Some years after my stay there Mayor Richard C. Lee denied that political considerations affected the placement of government contracts. That is not consistent with information we gathered during our study, or with the large campaign contributions made by these contractors.

3. The Democratic report on campaign expenses and contributions was summarized in the *New Haven Journal-Courier,* December 4, 1957.

4. The tendency for the better-off to participate less in campaigns than in other arenas is discussed at length in Dahl, *Who Governs?* 284–293. Dahl attributes it to the plebeian dominance of the city's political parties, and says that the affluent can influence city officials through channels other than the parties. This assumes that political participation

reflects primarily a desire to influence public policy, a proposition I consider insufficient for New Haven and cities like it.

5. Published in Chicago by the International City Managers' Association.

6. Raymond E. Wolfinger and John Osgood Field, "Political Ethos and the Structure of City Government," *American Political Science Review,* 60 (June, 1966), 314–315.

7. Martin and Susan Tolchin, "How Judgeships Get Bought," *New York Magazine,* March 15, 1971, 34.

8. *New York Times,* June 17, 1968, 1, 30.

9. Martin and Susan Tolchin, "How Lindsay Learned the Patronage Lesson," *New York Magazine,* March 29, 1971, 48.

10. *Ibid,* 47–48.

11. *Ibid.,* 43–46. Lindsay's expansion of patronage is in dramatic contrast to his image as a reformer, and to the widespread interpretation that his election was yet another sign of the decline of machine politics. Since the 19th century genuine and bogus reformers have been elected Mayor of New York over the opposition of various political organizations, to the accompaniment of public death rites for Tammany Hall and the less celebrated but more potent machines in the other boroughs. Yet just as regularly those mayors have been succeeded by organization politicians. Indeed, often the incumbent himself is recast in this role, so that his departure from city hall as well as his entry can be hailed as a symptom of the demise of the machine. Thus when Mayor Robert Wagner won renomination in 1961 by defeating the "organization candidate," this signalled "the machine's" decline. The same interpretation was offered four years later when Wagner, reading the portents as unfavorable to his reelection, withdrew and was succeeded by Lindsay. It appears that one of the reasons why we know Tammany is dead is that it has been killed so many times.

12. *New York Times,* June 17, 1968, 30; and Wallace S. Sayre and Herbert Kaufman, *Governing New York City* (New York: Russell Sage Foundation, 1960), 540–541.

13. Tolchin and Tolchin, "How Judgeships Get Bought," 33. Presumably because of the very large amounts of money involved in numerous cases where judges appoint referees, trustees, guardians, etc., and the custom of making these appointments politically, judgeships of all sorts in New York are highly prized. Although most judges are elected rather than appointed, the parties effectively control the selection process. A man who wants to be a judge usually must have connections in one party or the other, and must also make a sizable payment to the appropriate party leader. Sayre and Kaufman estimated that a minimum payment for the lowest level court was $20,000 (542). Tolchin and Tolchin suggest that the payments usually are higher than this ("How Judgeships Get Bought," 29, 31).

14. *Newsweek,* April 5, 1971, 82.

15. Robert J. McNeill, *Democratic Campaign Financing in Indiana, 1964* (Bloomington, Ind. and Princeton, N. J.: Institute of Public Administration, Indiana University and Citizens' Research Foundation, 1966), 15–16.

16. *Ibid.,* 19.

17. See, e.g., Donald S. Bradley and Mayer N. Zald, "From Commercial Elite to Political Administrator: The Recruitment of the Mayors of Chicago," in *The Structure of Community Power,* ed. by Michael Aiken and Paul E. Mott (New York: Random House, Inc., 1970), 53–60.

18. Sayre and Kaufman, *Governing New York City,* 140, 141.

19. *Ibid.,* 541 n; Tolchin and Tolchin, "How Judgeships Get Bought," 32.

20. Robert K. Merton, *Social Theory and Social Structure* (revised edition; Glencoe, Ill.: The Free Press, 1957), 73. This view of the "functions of the machine" has been expressed by a number of writers.

21. For a description of a city with decentralized governmental institutions, fragmented party organizations, ample patronage, and major corruption, see John A. Gardiner, *The Politics of Corruption* (New York: Russell Sage Foundation, 1970).

22. Dahl, *Who Governs?* 52.

23. Edward C. Banfield and James Q. Wilson, *City Politics* (Cambridge: Harvard University Press and the MIT Press, 1963), 120.

24. James Q. Wilson, *Negro Politics* (Glencoe, Ill.: The Free Press, 1960), 117.

25. Daniel P. Moynihan, "'Bosses' and 'Reformers': A Profile of the New York Democrats," *Commentary,* June 1961, 464.

26. Wilson, *Negro Politics,* 37 (emphasis in original).

27. Most appointments in urban renewal and related fields were made by Lee without accommodating the Democratic organization's interests.

28. Sayre and Kaufman, *Governing New York City,* 474.

29. Harold Kaplan, *Urban Renewal Politics* (New York: Columbia University Press, 1963), 47–48.

30. Sayre and Kaufman, *Governing New York City,* 452.

31. Dahl, *Who Governs?* 225.

32. Edward J. Flynn, *You're the Boss* (New York: The Viking Press, 1947).

33. See especially V.O.Key, Jr., *Southern Politics* (New York: Alfred A. Knopf, Inc., 1949), ch. 14.

34. Research of this kind was published by economists as early as 1952, but the first such study that attracted much attention from political scientists was Richard E. Dawson and James A. Robinson, "Inter-Party Competition, Economic Variables and Welfare Policies in the American States," *Journal of Politics,* 25 (May 1963), 265–289. For a review and critique of the ensuing literature, more sophisticated measures, and different findings, see Brian R. Fry and Richard F. Winters, "The Politics of Redistribution," *American Political Science Review,* 64 (June 1970), 508–522.

35. For one example of such a distinction, see John H. Fenton, *Midwest Politics* (New York: Holt, Rinehart and Winston, 1966).

36. For a cautious, qualified synthesis of the orthodox position, see Fred I. Greenstein, "The Changing Pattern of Urban Party Politics," *The Annals,* 353 (May 1964), 2–13. Another presentation of the conventional wisdom, with fewer caveats, may be found in Thomas R. Dye, *Politics in States and Communities* (Englewood Cliffs, N.J.: Prentice-Hall, Inc., 1969), 256–272.

37. Dye, *Politics,* 276.

38. Tolchin and Tolchin, "'Honest Graft'—Playing the Patronage Game," *New York Magazine,* March 22, 1971, 42.

39. See especially his "Patronage and Party," *Midwest Journal of Political Science,* 3 (May 1959), 115–126. In this and other articles Sorauf has argued not only that patronage is unattractive, but that it is inefficiently exploited by party leaders. His direct observations

are limited to his study of the consequences of the 1954 Democratic gubernatorial victory for the highway maintenance crew in one rural county in Pennsylvania. Sorauf is more persuasive about the ineffectuality of Democratic leaders in Centre County than about the generalizability of his findings. He concludes, moreover, that "the parties need the strength of patronage, however minor and irregular it may be . . ." (ibid., 126).

40. Merton, Social Theory, 74 (emphasis in original).

41. Dye, Politics, 257.

42. William F. Whyte, Street Corner Society (englarged edition; Chicago: University of Chicago Press, 1955), 241.

43. Ibid., 240.

44. Ibid., 197.

45. Kaplan, Urban Renewal, 42–43.

46. Dye, Politics, 271.

47. Some contemporary political organizations do give advice and legal aid, mediate disputes, and serve as clearinghouses for information. See James Q. Wilson, The Amateur Democrat (Chicago: University of Chicago Press, 1962), 176; and Tolchin and Tolchin, "'Honest Graft,'" 42.

48. As many writers are now beginning to realize, the acculturation and assimilation of the European immigrants is far from complete. See my "The Development and Persistence of Ethnic Voting," American Political Science Review, 59 (December 1965), 896–908; and The Politics of Progress, chap. 3.

49. For a description of trends in the study of city politics see Wallace S. Sayre and Nelson W. Polsby, "American Political Science and the Study of Urbanization," in The Study of Urbanization, ed. by Philip M. Hauser and Leo F. Schnore (New York: John Wiley & Sons, Inc., 1965), 115–156.

50. Originally quoted in The Autobiography of Lincoln Steffens (New York: Harcourt, Brace and Company, 1931), 618.

51. Quoted in Whyte, Street Corner Society, 194.

52. Wolfinger and Field, "Political Ethos," 314–316.

53. Gardiner, The Politics of Corruption, 8–12.

54. Interviewing a number of party officials in New Jersey, Richard T. Frost found that "old-fashioned" techniques like door-to-door canvassing were considered more effective, and used more frequently, than newer methods like television advertising. See his "Stability and Change in Local Party Politics," Public Opinion Quarterly, 25 (Summer 1961), 221–235.

55. Bowles is sometimes depicted as a high-minded victim of crasser and smaller men in the Connecticut Democratic party. The principal event presented as evidence for this viewpoint is his defeat by Thomas J. Dodd for the senatorial nomination at the 1958 state Democratic convention. Dodd had long been an opponent of the regular Democratic organization headed by then-Governor Abraham A. Ribicoff and state chairman John Bailey. Bowles, on the other hand, had been the organization's winning gubernatorial candidate in 1950. After his defeat for the senatorial nomination in 1958, he accepted the organization's offer of a congressional nomination and was elected to Congress in the fall. Ribicoff and Bailey thought that Bowles's popularity would help win the seat, then held by a Republi-

can, and brushed aside the claims of the announced candidates for the Democratic nomination, who "voluntarily" withdrew their names from consideration by the convention.

One of the seconding speeches in support of Bowles's unsuccessful try for the senatorial nomination was by Arthur T. Barbieri, the New Haven town chairman (and later a close ally of Dodd's). It was devoted to praising Bowles's willingness, when governor, to accede to the party's wishes in matters involving patronage. The disciplined New Haven delegation voted unanimously for Bowles, a Yankee patrician. Dodd, an Irish Catholic, was the sentimental favorite of many delegates, but almost all of them were city employees or otherwise financially dependent on city hall.

56. Sayre and Kaufman, *Governing New York City,* 155.

57. Quoted in the *New York Times,* June 1, 1970, 27.

58. Quoted in the *New York Times,* June 17, 1968, 30.

59. Raymond E. Wolfinger, "The Influence of Precinct Work on Voting Behavior," *Public Opinion Quarterly,* 27 (Fall 1963), 387–398. Turnout in the primary to select the Democratic candidate for the Manhattan Surrogates' Court rarely reaches 100,000 voters and thus the outcome is more easily influenced by party organizations.

60. For a good statement of this position see Elmer E. Cornwell, Jr., "Bosses, Machines, and Ethnic Groups," *The Annals,* 353 (May 1964), 27–39.

61. This is most obviously true of the large cities of the West Coast: San Francisco (44 percent foreign stock in 1960), Los Angeles (33 percent), and Seattle (31 percent). These cities are equally or more ethnic than eastern and midwestern cities characterized by machine politics, e.g., Chicago (36 percent), Philadelphia (29 percent), and St. Louis (14 percent).

62. See the works by Frank J. Sorauf cited in notes 39 and 65 and Duane Lockard, *New England State Politics* (Princeton: Princeton University Press, 1959), 245–251.

63. Several studies show major regional or subregional variations in political preferences that cannot be accounted for by varying demographic characteristics. See, e.g., Irving Crespi, "The Structural Basis for Right-Wing Conservatism: The Goldwater Case," *Public Opinion Quarterly,* 29 (Winter 1965), 523–543; James W. Prothro and Charles M. Grigg, "Fundamental Principles of Democracy: Bases of Agreement and Disagreement," *Journal of Politics,* 22 (Spring 1960), 276–294; and Raymond E. Wolfinger and Fred I. Greenstein, "Comparing Political Regions: The Case of California," *American Political Science Review,* 63 (March 1969), 74–86.

64. McNeill, *Democratic Campaign Financing,* 39.

65. Fenton, *Midwest Politics,* 7. For an account of public acceptance of patronage in bucolic, native-stock Centre County, Pennsylvania, see Frank J. Sorauf, "Chairman and Superintendent," in *Cases in State and Local Government,* ed. by Richard T. Frost (Englewood Cliffs, N. J.: Prentice-Hall, Inc., 1961), 109–119.

66. *San Francisco Chronicle,* December 17, 1962, 10; and *CDC Newsletter,* December 1962.

67. The study of regional variations in American political perspectives is still in its infancy. For a general discussion and survey of the literature see Samuel C. Patterson, "The Political Cultures of the American States," *Journal of Politics,* 30 (February 1968), 187–209.

For an interesting typology of three American political value systems that encompasses the regional differences concerning machine politics discussed here see Daniel J. Elazar, *American Federalism: A View from the States* (New York: Thomas Y. Crowell Company, 1966).

Machine Politics–Old and New

THEODORE J. LOWI

The political machine is an institution peculiar to American cities. Like the militant party elsewhere, the American machine as a classic type is centralized, integrated, and relatively ruthless. But there the similarity ends.

Machines have been integrated from within, as fraternities; they do not arise out of opposition to the state or to a hostile class. The power of the machine rested upon being integrated in a dispersed, permissive, and unmobilized society. Integrated, however, in a special American way.

The most militant parties of Europe have depended upon homogeneity—enforced if necessary. Machines have developed ingenious techniques for capitalizing upon ethnic and racial heterogeneity. Militant parties have typically been based on common ends at the center, holding the periphery together by fear. The machines were based upon a congeries of people with uncommon ends, held together at the center by logrolling and at the periphery by *fraternité, egalité*, and ignorance.

As to the significance of the machine for the development of the American city, the returns are still not in. Typically, it was the European observers who were the first to appreciate this unusual, American phenomenon. Ostrogorski, Bryce, Weber, Michels, Schumpeter, and Duverger each in his own way made an outstanding effort to appreciate the peculiarities of urban democracy in America. Harold F. Gosnell, in *Machine Politics: Chicago Model* (1937), was one of the very first Americans to join that distinguished company with anything approaching a systematic treatment of the subject. (By this standard, the muckrakers do not count.)

However, Gosnell was limited by the fact that there was in his time, insufficient experience with alternative forms of big city politics. Too few big cities in the United States had been "reformed" in sufficient degree to provide any basis for comparison.

In the 1960's, sufficient time has passed. The machine is nearly dead, and we have experienced lengthy periods of Reform government. We can now see the machine in perspective.

How does it shape up?

CHICAGO AND NEW YORK

We can begin to introduce perspective by immediately setting aside Gosnell's claim that the Chicago experience on which his book was based is representative. It is the very uniqueness of Chicago's experience with the machine that gives his study such value. It is New York that is the representative big city, not Chicago. Its representativeness derives from the fact that it has experienced Reform in a way that Chicago has not. In 1967, political power in Chicago still has an extremely strong machine base; political power in New York has an entirely new and different base. As New York was being revolutionized by the New Deal and its successors, the structure of Chicago politics was being reaffirmed. When New York was losing its last machine and entering into a new era of permanent Reform, Chicago's political machine was just beginning to consolidate. New York became a loose, multi-party system with wide-open processes of nomination, election, and participation; Chicago became a tight, one-party system. New York sought to strengthen a weak mayor who already operated under a strong-mayor government; Chicago has had the opposite problem of an already strong mayor in a weak-mayor government.

To evaluate the machine we must ask whether, by surviving, machine politics in Chicago in any way distorted that city's growth and development. How much change would there have been in Chicago's history if the nationalization of politics had made possible in Chicago, as it did in virtually every other big American city, ways of "licking the ward boss" and altering precinct organization, means of loosening the hold of the county organization on city hall, power for liberating the personnel and policies of the professional agencies of government? We cannot answer these questions for Chicago because the basis of machine strength still exists there, and the conditions for its continuity might well continue through the remainder of the century. However, we may be able to answer them, at least better than before, by looking at Chicago from the vantage point of New York's experience.

POPULISM AND EFFICIENCY

New York city government, like government in almost all large American cities except Chicago, is a product of Reform. It is difficult to understand these cities without understanding the two strains of ideology that guided local Reform movements throughout the past three-quarters of a century. *Populism* and *efficiency*, once the foundation of most local insurgency, are now almost universally triumphant. These two tenets are now the orthodoxy in local practice.

Populism was originally a statement of the evils of every form of bigness in the city, including big business, big churches, big labor, as well as big political organizations. Decentralization was an ultimate goal. In modern form, it has tended to come down to the aim of eliminating political parties, partisanship, and if possible "politics" itself.

Efficiency provided the positive program to replace that which is excised by populist surgery. The doctrine calls essentially for the centralization and rationalization of government activities and services to accompany the decentralization of power. Some Reformers assumed that services do not constitute power. Others assumed the problem away altogether by positing a neutral civil servant who would not abuse centralized government but who could use it professionally to reap the economies effected by rationalization and by specialization. That was the secret of the business system; and, after all, the city is rather like a business. ("There is no Republican or Democratic way to clean a street.")

While there are many inconsistent assumptions and goals between the doctrines of populism and efficiency, they lived well together. Their coexistence was supported by the fact that different wings of the large, progressive movement they generated were responsible for each. Populism was largely the province of the working class, "progressive" wing. Doctrines of efficiency were very much the responsibility of the upper class wing. Populism resided with the politician-activists. Efficiency was developed by the intellectuals, including several distinguished university presidents, such as Seth Low, Andrew Dickson White, Harold Dodd, and, pre-eminently, Woodrow Wilson, who, while still a professor of political science, wrote a classic essay proclaiming the virtues of applying Prussian principles of administration in the United States.

These two great ideas were, by a strange and wonderful chemistry, combined into a movement whose influence forms a major chapter of American history. Charters and laws have been enacted that consistently insulate city government from politics, meaning party politics. It has become increasingly necessary, with each passing decade, to grant each bureaucratic agency autonomy to do the job as each commissioner saw fit, as increasingly appointments were made of professionals in each agency's fields.

On into the 1960's, the merit system extends itself "upward, outward, and downward," to use the Reformers' own rhetoric. Recruitment to the top posts is more and more frequent from the ranks of those who have made careers in their agencies, party backgrounds increasingly being a mark of automatic disqualification. Reform has succeeded in raising public demand for political morality and in making "politics" a dirty word. A "good press" for mayors results from their determination to avoid intervening in the affairs of one department after another. The typical modern mayor is all the more eager to co-operate because this provides an opportunity to delegate responsibility. Absolution-before-the-fact for government agencies has become part of the mayoral swearing-in ceremony.

Reform has triumphed and the cities are better run than ever before. But that is, unfortunately, not the end of the story, nor would it have been the end of the story even had there been no Negro revolution. The triumph of Reform really ends in paradox: *Cities like New York became well-run but ungoverned*.

THE NEW MACHINES

Politics under Reform are not abolished. Only their form is altered. *The legacy of Reform is the bureaucratic city-state*. Destruction of the party foundation of the mayoralty cleaned up many cities but also destroyed the basis for sustained, central, popularly-based action. This capacity, with all its faults, was replaced by the power of professionalized agencies. But this has meant creation of new bases of power. Bureaucratic agencies are not neutral; they are only independent.

Modernization and Reform in New York and other cities has meant replacement of Old Machines with New Machines. The bureaucracies—that is, the professionally organized, autonomous career agencies—are the New Machines.

Sociologically, the Old Machine was a combination of rational goals and fraternal loyalty. The cement of the organization was trust and discipline created out of long years of service, probation, and testing, slow promotion through the ranks, and centralized control over the means of reward. Its power in the community was based upon services rendered to the community.

Sociologically, the New Machine is almost exactly the same sort of an organization. But there are also significant differences. The New Machines are more numerous, in any given city. They are functional rather then geographic in their scope. They rely on formal authority rather than upon majority acquiescence. And they probably work with a minimum of graft and corruption. But these differences do not alter their definition; they only help to explain why the New Machine is such a successful form of organization.

The New Machines are machines because they are relatively irresponsible structures of power. That is, each agency shapes important public policies, yet the leadership of each is relatively self-perpetuating and not readily subject to the controls of any higher authority.

The New Machines are machines in that the power of each, while resting ultimately upon services rendered to the community, depends upon its cohesiveness as a small minority in the midst of the vast dispersion of the multitude.

The modern city has become well-run but ungoverned because it has, according to Wallace Sayre and Herbert Kaufman, become comprised of "islands of functional power" before which the modern mayor stands denuded of authority. No mayor of a modern city has predictable means of determining whether the bosses of the New Machines—the bureau chiefs and the career commissioners—will be loyal to anything but their agency, its work, and related professional norms. Our modern mayor has been turned into the likes of a French Fourth Republic Premier facing an array of intransigent parties in the National Assembly. These modern machines, more monolithic by far than their ancient brethren, are entrenched by law, and are supported by tradition, the slavish loyalty of the newspapers, the educated masses, the dedicated civic groups, and, most of all, by the organized clientele groups enjoying access under existing arrangements.

ORGANIZED DECENTRALIZATION

The Reform response to the possibility of an inconsistency between running a city and governing it has been to assume the existence of the Neutral Specialist, the bureaucratic equivalent to law's Rational Man. The assumption is that, if men know their own specialties well enough, they are capable of reasoning out solutions to problems they share with men of equal but different technical competencies. That is a very shaky assumption indeed. Charles Frankel's analysis of such an assumption in Europe provides an appropriate setting for a closer look at it in modern New York; ". . . different [technical] elites disagree with each other; the questions with which specialists deal spill over into areas where they are *not* specialists, and they must either hazard amateur opinions or ignore such larger issues, which is no better . . ."

During the 1950's, government experts began to recognize that, despite vast increases in efficiency flowing from the defeat of the Old Machine, New York city government was somehow lacking. These concerns culminated in the 1961 Charter, in which the Office of Mayor was strengthened in many impressive ways. But it was quickly discovered that no amount of formal centralization could definitively overcome the real decentralization around the Mayor. It was an organized disorganization, which made a mockery of the new Charter. The following examples, although drawn from New York, are of virtually universal application:

(1) Welfare problems always involve several of any city's largest agencies, including Health, Welfare, Hospitals, etc. Yet during more than 40 years, successive mayors of New York failed to reorient the Department of Health away from a "regulative" toward a "service" concept of organization. And many new aspects of welfare must be set up in new agencies if they are to be set up at all. The new poverty programs were set up very slowly in all the big cities—except Chicago.

(2) Water pollution control has been "shared" by such city agencies as the Departments of Health, Parks, Public Works, Sanitation, Water Supply, and so on. No large city, least of all New York, has an effective program to combat even the local contributions to pollution. The same is true of air pollution control, although for some years New York has had a separate Department for this purpose.

(3) Land-use patterns are influenced one way or another by a large variety of highly professional agencies. It has proven virtually impossible in any city for one of these agencies to impose its criteria on the others. In New York, the opening of Staten Island by the Narrows Bridge, in what may be the last large urban frontier, found the city with no plan for the revolution that is taking place in property values and land uses in that borough.

(4) Transportation is also the province of agencies too numerous to list. Strong mayors throughout the country have been unable to prevent each from going its separate way. To take just one example: New York pursued a vast off-street parking program, at a cost of nearly $4,000 per parking space, at the very moment when local rail lines were going bankrupt.

(5) Enforcement of civil rights is imposed upon almost all city agencies by virtue of Federal, state, and local legislation. But efforts to set up public, then City Council, review of police processes in New York have been successfully opposed by professional police officials. Efforts to try pairing and busing on a very marginal, experimental basis have failed. The police commissioner resigned at the very suggestion that values other than professional police values be imposed upon the Department, even when the imposition came via the respected tradition of "legislative oversight." The Superintendent of Education, an "outsider," was forced out; he was replaced by a career administrator. One education journalist at that time said: "Often . . . a policy proclaimed by the Board [of Education], without the advice and consent of the professionals, is quickly turned into mere paper policy . . . The veto power through passive resistance by professional administrators is virtually unbeatable. . . ."

The decentralization of city government toward its career bureaucracies has resulted in great efficiency for the activities around which each bureaucracy was organized. The city is indeed well-run. But what of those activities around which bureaucracies are not organized, or those which fall between or among agencies' jurisdictions? For these, as suggested by the cases above, the cities are suffering either stalemate or elephantiasis—an affliction whereby a particular activity, say, urban renewal or parkways, gets pushed to its ultimate "success" totally without regard to its importance compared to the missions of other agencies. In these as well as in other senses, the cities are ungoverned.

THE 1961 ELECTION

Mayors have tried a variety of strategies to cope with these situations. But the 1961 mayoralty election in New York was the ultimate dramatization of the mayor's plight. This election was a confirmation of the New York system, and will some day be seen as one of the most significant in American urban history. For New York, it was the culmination of many long-run developments. For the country, it may be the first of many to usher in the bureaucratic state.

The primary significance of the election can be found in the spectacle of a mayor attempting to establish a base of power for himself in the bureaucracies. The Mayor's running mate for President of the City Council had been Commissioner of Sanitation, a position which culminated virtually a lifetime career of the holder in the Department of Sanitation. He had an impressive following among the sanitation men—who, it should be added, are organized along precinct lines. The Mayor's running mate for Comptroller had been for many years the city Budget Director. As Budget Director, he had survived several Administrations and two vicious primaries that pitted factions of the Democratic Party against one another. Before becoming Director he had served for a number of years as a professional employee in the Bureau. The leaders of the campaign organization included a former, very popular Fire Commissioner who retired from his commissionership to accept campaign leadership and later to serve as Deputy Mayor; and a former Police Commissioner who had enjoyed a strong following among professional cops as well as in the local Reform movement. Added to this was a new and vigorous party, the Brotherhood Party, which was composed in large part of unions with broad bases of membership among city employees. Before the end of the election, most of the larger city bureaucracies had political representation in the inner core of the new Administration.

For the 1961 election, Mayor Wagner had put his ticket and his organization together just as the bosses of old had done. In the old days, the problem was to mobilize all the clubhouses, districts, and counties in the city by putting together a balanced ticket about which all adherents could be enthusiastic. The same seems true for 1961, except that by then the clubhouses and districts had been replaced almost altogether by new types of units.

The main point is that destruction of the machine did not, in New York or elsewhere, eliminate the need for political power. It simply altered what one had to do to get it. In the aftermath of twenty or more years of "modern" government, it is beginning to appear that the lack of power can corrupt city hall almost as much as the possession of power. Bureaucracy is, in the United States, a relatively new basis for collective action. As yet, none of us knows quite how to cope with it.

WHAT IF . . . ?

These observations and cases are not brought forward to indict Reform cities and acquit Chicago. They are intended only to put Chicago in a proper light and to provide some means of assessing the functions of the machine form of collective action.

Review of Reform government shows simply and unfortunately that the problems of cities, and the irrational and ineffectual ways city fathers go about their business, seem to obtain universally, without regard to form of government or type of power base. All cities have traffic congestion, crime, juvenile delinquency, galloping pollution, ghettos, ugliness, deterioration, and degeneracy. All cities seem to be suffering about equally from the quite recent problem of the weakening legitimacy of public institutions, resulting in collective violence and pressures for direct solution to problems. All cities seem equally hemmed in by their suburbs and equally prevented from getting at the roots of many of their most fundamental problems. Nonpartisan approaches, even the approaches of New York's Republican mayor to Republican suburbs and a Republican governor, have failed to prevent rail bankruptcy in the vast Eastern megalopolis, to abate air or water pollution, to reduce automobile pressure, or to ease the pain of the middle-class Negro in search of escape from his ghetto.

The problems of the city seem to go beyond any of the known arrangements for self-government. However, low public morality and lack of what Banfield and Wilson call "public-regardingness" may be a function simply of poor education and ethnic maladjustment. The Old Machine and its abuses may just have been another reflection of the same phenomena. If that is so, then passage of more time, and the mounting of one socio-cultural improvement after another, might have reformed the machines into public-regarding organs, if they had been permitted to survive.

Are there any strong reasons to believe that real reform could have come without paying the price of eliminating the popular base of political action? Intimations can be found in the last of the machine-recruited leaders of Tammany, Carmine DeSapio and Edward Costikyan. Each was progressively more public-regarding than any of his predecessors. Indeed, Costikyan was a model of political responsibility for whom the new New York had no particular use. However, for this question the best answers may lie in looking afresh at Gosnell's Chicago. With a scientific rigor superior to most political analysis of the 1960's, his book goes further than any other single work to capture what political behavior was like under Old Machine conditions. The sum total of his findings, despite Gosnell's own sentiments, does not constitute a very damning indictment of the Chicago machine—if contemporary experience is kept clearly in mind.

CHICAGO IN PERSPECTIVE

Even amidst the most urgent of depression conditions, the machine in Chicago does not seem to have interfered with the modest degree of rationality distributed throughout the United States. Take for instance the case of voting behavior on referendum proposals, the most issue-laden situation an electorate ever faces. Gosnell criticized the referendum as generally subject to fraud and other types of abuse, and most particularly so in Chicago during the 1920's and '30s. But even so, his figures show that the electorate, despite the machine, did not behave indiscriminately. The theory that universal suffrage provides no check against the irresponsible acceptance of financing schemes which pass the real burden on to future generations is simply not borne out in Chicago. Conservative appeals by the propertied were effective. Over a twelve-year period, including six fat years and six lean years, 66 local bond issues were approved and 48 were rejected. Those rejected included some major bond issues offered for agencies whose leaders had become discredited. Other types of issues show responsiveness to appeals other than local precinct or county organizations. As the antiprohibition campaign began to grow, so did the vote on the prohibition repealer. Clear irrationalities tended to be associated primarily with highly technical proposals involving judicial procedure or taxation; but this is true everywhere, and to much the same degree.

In a bold stroke, Gosnell also tried to assess the influence of the newspapers, the best source of rational—at least nonmachine—voting decisions. For this particular purpose Gosnell's data were weak, but fortunately he was not deterred from asking important questions merely for lack of specially designed data. Factor analysis helped Gosnell tease out of census tract data and newspaper subscription patterns a fairly realistic and balanced sense of the role of the local newspapers. Gosnell was led to conclude that the influence of news media is limited, but that this was a limitation imposed far less by the machine than by the extent to which newspapers were regularly read. Newspaper influence on issues was measurably apparent wherever daily readership was widely established—the machine notwithstanding. Here again is suggested the possibility that real machine domination rested upon a level of education and civic training that was, at the very time of Gosnell's research, undergoing a great deal of change.

Taking all the various findings together, and even allowing for abuses that were always more frequent in cities than towns, and probably more frequent in Gosnell's Chicago than other cities, we can come away from Gosnell's analysis with a picture not at all at odds with V. O. Key's notion of the "responsible electorate."

Gosnell felt his book to be an indictment of machine politics. But today, looking at the Chicago experience from the vantage point of New York's, one feels less able to be so sure.

PART 2

Power in Communities

An important aspect of urban politics is the issue of who wields power and who makes decisions; i.e., who governs and what difference does it make? Controversy over this issue was stirred initially by Floyd Hunter in 1953 in his book about Atlanta's politics, *Community Power Structure*. Hunter found that a small, cohesive group of businessmen and wealthy families exercised influence over most of the major decisions made by the city.

This research was generally criticized by political scientists and answered by Robert Dahl in his classic *Who Governs?* Dahl's methods and conclusions differed substantially from Hunter's. Dahl found that *different* people and groups exercised decisive influence on *different* issues. Thus, even though Dahl also discovered that a relatively small number of people played a determinative role in local decisions, he claimed that his findings supported a pluralistic model of community power.

Dahl's interpretation of urban politics as a complex decision-making system is supported by Norton Long in his essay "The Local Community as an Ecology of Games." Long describes the community as an unplanned system of interaction between specialized games. Each activity taking place in the community is viewed as a game; there is a banking game, a political game, a newspaper game, and so forth.

Long contends that there is no overall game providing coordination of the individual games being played in the community. This means, if an unusual problem or a crisis needs to be resolved, the response to it will be in a piecemeal fashion as players of different games will view the problem in terms of their own interests.

Long implies that community power cannot be characterized by an elitist model. Rather it can only be conceived as people acting to achieve the goals of their own individual games. It is, therefore, useless to try to identify who has power in a community, because no one will have overall power. In reality, Long insists, the policy outputs observed in the community are the result of the unplanned piecemeal response of players and games to challenges presented by crises, analogous to the processes of evolution and natural selection which occur in ecology.

A contrasting approach is presented by Peter Bachrach and Morton S. Baratz in their article "Two Faces of Power." Their criticisms of the pluralist model stem from the fact that only a few concrete decisions are used to determine who has power. Bachrach and Baratz argue this is inadequate because it ignores the other face of power, that is, that power is also exercised when issues are *not* decided upon. Those in power may exert influence by limiting the decision-making agenda to relatively meaningless issues.

To identify those who have power in a community, Bachrach and Baratz advocate a three-step strategy. First, it is necessary to examine the dominant values which have established the "political procedures and rules of the game in a community." Secondly, investigations should be conducted regarding the groups and individuals that benefit or are disadvantaged by the status quo. Thirdly, studies should explore which persons or groups, by exercising influence, limit the scope of actual decision-making; that is, who wields the "restrictive force of power." They argue that by using this approach as a research foundation it is possible to analyze participation in direct and indirect decisions or "nondecisions."

Another approach to the analysis of community power is offered by Harvey Molotch in his article, "The City as a Growth Machine: Toward a Political Economy of Place." Molotch states that the basic value structure underlying city politics is a *growth ideology*. He also observes: "The people who participate with their energies and fortunes in local affairs have the most to gain or lose in land-use decisions." Molotch argues, therefore, that a growth-oriented local government is neither representative of the interests of most residents in the community nor necessarily beneficial to most citizens.

Molotch asserts that the increasing realization of the high costs of growth is leading to the development of an antigrowth movement in some communities. As this change takes place, different types of people may become involved in local government and different issues may come to dominate the local political agenda.

The final article in this section looks at community power through the lens of race and ethnic relations. The article by Hahn, Klingman, and Pachon, "Cleavages, Coalitions, and the Black Candidate: The Los Angeles Mayoralty Elections of 1969 and 1973," explores the linkages between racial cleavages, urban voting patterns, mayoral leadership, and community power. Typically, victories by black mayoral candidates are attributed to the presence of a large cohesive black electorate. Hahn, Klingman, and Pachon, however, examine the election of a black mayor in a city with a relatively small black population.

The elections studied are the 1969 and 1973 elections for mayor in Los Angeles involving Sam Yorty and Tom Bradley. The most significant difference between the 1969 and 1973 campaigns involved the issues. The inability of Bradley to form a black-white coalition contributed to his defeat in 1969. By contrast, in 1973, Bradley was able to defuse racial issues and attract white voters by emphasizing overarching programs which he promised would benefit the entire community.

Bradley's experience has several important implications for minority candidates in other cities. Even without the injection of racial issues, any black-white coalition is extremely fragile, easily broken by other controversies, and vulnerable to a set of values which seeks to deemphasize the similarities in the political interests of the urban poor, regardless of their racial or ethnic backgrounds.

The Local Community as an Ecology of Games

NORTON E. LONG

The local community whether viewed as a polity, an economy, or a society presents itself as an order in which expectations are met and functions performed. In some cases, as in a new, company-planned mining town, the order is the willed product of centralized control, but for the most part the order is the product of a history rather than the imposed effect of any central nervous system of the community. For historic reasons we readily conceive the massive task of feeding New York to be achieved through the unplanned, historically developed cooperation of thousands of actors largely unconscious of their collaboration to this individually unsought end. The efficiency of this system is attested to by the extraordinary difficulties of the War Production Board and Service of Supply in accomplishing similar logistical objectives through an explicit system of orders and directives. Insofar as conscious rationality plays a role, it is a function of the parts rather than the whole. Particular structures working for their own ends within the whole may provide their members with goals, strategies, and roles that support rational action. The results of the interaction of the rational strivings after particular ends are in part collectively functional if unplanned. All this is the well-worn doctrine of Adam Smith, though one need accept no more of the doctrine of beneficence than that an unplanned economy can function.

While such a view is accepted for the economy, it is generally rejected for the polity. Without a sovereign, Leviathan is generally supposed to disintegrate and fall apart. Even if Locke's more hopeful view of the naturalness of the social order is taken, the polity seems more of a contrived artifact than the economy. Furthermore, there is both the hangover of Austinian sovereignty and the Greek view of ethical primacy to make political institutions seem different in kind and ultimately inclusive in purpose and for this reason to give them an over-all social directive end. To see political institutions as the same kind of thing as other institutions in society rather than as different, superior, and inclusive (both in the sense of being sovereign and ethically more significant) is a form of relativistic pluralism that is difficult to entertain. At the local level, however, it is easier to look at the municipal government, its departments, and the agencies of state and national government as so many institutions, resembling banks, newspapers, trade unions, chambers of commerce, churches, etc., occupying a territorial field and interacting with one another. This interaction can be conceptualized as a system without reducing the interacting institutions and

This paper is largely based on a year of field study in the Boston Metropolitan area made possible by grants from the Stern Family Foundation and the Social Science Research Council. The opinions and conclusion expressed are those of the author alone.

individuals to membership in any single comprehensive group. It is psychologically tempting to envision the local territorial system as a group with a governing "they." This is certainly an existential possibility and one to be investigated. However, frequently, it seems likely, systems are confused with groups, and our primitive need to explain thunder with a theology or a demonology results in the hypostatizing of an angelic or demonic hierarchy. The executive committee of the bourgeoisie and the power elite make the world more comfortable for modern social scientists as the Olympians did for the ancients. At least the latter-day hypothesis, being terrestrial, is in principle researchable though in practice its metaphysical statement may render it equally immune to mundane inquiry.

Observation of certain local communities makes it appear that inclusive over-all organization for many general purposes is weak or non-existent. Much of what occurs seems to just happen with accidental trends becoming cumulative over time and producing results intended by nobody. A great deal of the communities' activities consist of undirected co-operation of particular social structures, each seeking particular goals and, in doing so, meshing with others. While much of this might be explained in Adam Smith's terms, much of it could not be explained with a rational, atomistic model of calculating individuals. For certain purposes the individual is a useful way of looking at people; for many others the role-playing member of a particular group is more helpful. Here we deal with the essence of predictability in social affairs. If we know the game being played is baseball and that X is a third baseman, by knowing his position and the game being played we can tell more about X's activities on the field than we could if we examined X as a psychologist or a psychiatrist. If such were not the case, X would belong in the mental ward rather than in a ball park. The behavior of X is not some disembodied rationality but, rather, behavior within an organized group activity that has goals, norms strategies, and roles that give the very field and ground for rationality. Baseball structures the situation.

It is the contention of this paper that the structured group activities that coexist in a particular territorial system can be looked at as games. These games provide the players with a set of goals that give them a sense of success or failure. They provide them determinate roles and calculable strategies and tactics. In addition, they provide the players with an elite and general public that is in varying degrees able to tell the score. There is a good deal of evidence to be found in common parlance that many participants in contemporary group structures regard their occupations as at least analogous to games. And, at least in the American culture, and not only since Eisenhower, the conception of being on a "team" has been fairly widespread.

Unfortunately, the effectiveness of the term "game" for the purposes of this paper is vitiated by, first, the general sense that games are trivial occupations and, second, by the pre-emption of the term for the application of a calculus of probability to choice or decision in a determinate game situation. Far from regarding games as trivial, the writer's position would be that man is both a game-playing and a game-creating animal, that his capacity to create and play games and take them deadly seriously is of the essence, and that it is through games or activities analogous to game-playing that he achieves a satisfactory sense of significance and a meaningful role.

While the calculability of the game situation is important, of equal or greater importance is the capacity of the game to provide a sense of purpose and a role. The organizations of society and polity produce satisfactions with both their products and their processes. The two are not unrelated, but, while the production of the product may in the larger sense enable players and onlookers to keep score, the satisfaction in the process is the satisfaction of playing the game and the sense in which any activity can be grasped as a game.

Looked at this way, in the territorial system there is a political game, a banking game, a contracting game, a newspaper game, a civic organization game, an ecclesiastical game, and many others. Within each game there is a well-established set of goals whose achievement indicates success or failure for the participants, a set of socialized roles making participant behavior highly predictable, a set of strategies and tactics handed down through experience and occasionally subject to improvement and change, an elite public whose approbation is appreciated, and, finally, a general public which has some appreciation for the standing of the players. Within the game the players can be rational in the varying degrees that the structure permits. At the very least, they know how to behave, and they know the score.

Individuals may play in a number of games, but, for the most part, their major preoccupation is with one, and their sense of major achievement is through success in one. Transfer from one game to another is, of course, possible, and the simultaneous playing of roles in two or more games is an important manner of linking separate games.

Sharing a common territorial field and collaborating for different and particular ends in the achievement of over-all social functions, the players in one game make use of the players in another and are, in turn, made use of by them. Thus the banker makes use of the newspaperman, the politician, the contractor, the ecclesiastic, the labor leader, the civic leader—all to further his success in the banking game—but, reciprocally, he is used to further the others' success in the newspaper, political, contracting, ecclesiastical, labor, and civic games. Each is a piece in the chess game of the other, sometimes a willing piece, but, to the extent that the games are different, with a different end in view.

Thus a particular highway grid may be the result of a bureaucratic department of public works game in which are combined, though separate, a professional highway engineer game with its purposes and critical elite onlookers; a departmental bureaucracy; a set of contending politicians seeking to use the highways for political capital, patronage, and the like; a banking game concerned with bonds, taxes, and the effect of the highways on real estate; newspapermen interested in headlines, scoops, and the effect of highways on the papers' circulation; contractors eager to make money by building roads; ecclesiastics concerned with the effect of highways on their parishes and on the fortunes of the contractors who support their churchly ambitions; labor leaders interested in union contracts and their status as community influentials with a right to be consulted; and civic leaders who must justify the contributions of their bureaus of municipal research or chambers of commerce to the social activity. Each game is in play in the complicated pulling and hauling of siting and constructing the highway grid. A wide variety of purposes is subserved by the activity, and no single over-all directive authority controls it. However, the interrelation of the groups in constructing a highway has been developed over time, and there are general expectations as to the interaction. There are also generalized expectations as to how politicians, contractors, newspapermen, bankers, and the like will utilize the highway situation in playing their particular games. In fact, the knowledge that a banker will play like a banker and a newspaperman like a newspaperman is an important part of what makes the situation calculable and permits the players to estimate its possibilities for their own action in their particular game.

While it might seem that the engineers of the department of public works were the appropriate protagonists for the highway grid, as a general activity it presents opportunities and threats to a wide range of other players who see in the situation consequences and possibilities undreamed of by the engineers. Some general public expectation of the limits of the conduct of the players and of a desirable outcome does provide bounds to the scramble. This public expectation is, of course, made active through the interested solicitation of newspapers, politicians, civic leaders, and others who see in it material for accomplishing their particular purposes and whose structured roles in fact require the mobilization of broad publics. In a sense the group struggle that Arthur Bentley described in his *Process of Government* is a drama that local publics have been taught to view with a not uncritical taste. The instruction of this taste has been the vocation and business of some of the contending parties. The existence of some kind of over-all public puts general restraints on gamesmanship beyond the norms of the particular games. However, for the players these are to all intents as much a part of the "facts of life" of the game as the sun and the wind.

It is perhaps the existence of some kind of a general public, however rudimentary, that most clearly differentiates the local territorial system from a natural ecology. The five-acre woodlot in which the owls and the field mice, the oaks and the acorns, and other flora and fauna have evolved a balanced system has no public opinion, however rudimentary. The co-operation is an unconscious affair. For much of what goes on in the local territorial system co-operation is equally unconscious and perhaps, but for the occasional social scientist, unnoticed. This unconscious co-operation, however, like that of the five-acre woodlot, produces results. The ecology of games in the local territorial system accomplishes unplanned but largely functional results. The games and their players mesh in their particular pursuits to bring about over-all results; the territorial system is fed and ordered. Its inhabitants are rational within limited areas and, pursuing the ends of these areas, accomplish socially functional ends.

While the historical development of largely unconscious co-operation between the special games in the territorial system gets certain routine, over-all functions performed, the problem of novelty and breakdown must be dealt with. Here it would seem that, as in the natural ecology, random adjustment and piecemeal innovation are the normal methods of response. The need or cramp in the system presents itself to the players of the games as an opportunity for them to exploit or a menace to be overcome. Thus a transportation crisis in, say, the threatened abandonment of commuter trains by a railroad will bring forth the players of a wide range of games who will see in the situation opportunity for gain or loss in the outcome. While over-all considerations will appear in the discussion, the frame of reference and the interpretation of the event will be largely determined by the game the interested parties are principally involved in. Thus a telephone executive who is president of the local chamber of commerce will be playing a civic association, general business game with concern for the principal dues-payers of the chamber but with a constant awareness of how his handling of this crisis will advance him in his particular league. The politicians, who might be expected to be protagonists of the general interest, may indeed be so, but the sphere of their activity and the glasses through which they see the problem will be determined in great part by the way they see the issue affecting their political game. The generality of this game is to a great extent that of the politician's calculus of votes and interests important to his and his side's success. To be sure, some of what Walter Lippmann has called "the public philosophy" affects both politicians and other game-players. This indicates the existence of roles and norms of a larger, vaguer game with a relevant audience that has some sense of cricket. This potentially mobilizable audience is not utterly without importance, but it provides no sure or adequate basis for support in the particular game that the politician or anyone else is playing. Instead of a set of norms to structure enduring role-playing, this audience provides a cross-pressure for momentary aberrancy from gamesmanship or constitutes just another hazard to be calculated in one's play.

In many cases the territorial system is impressive in the degree of intensity of its particular games, its banks, its newspapers, its downtown stores, its manufacturing companies, its contractors, its churches, its politicians, and its other differentiated, structured, goal-oriented activities. Games go on within the territory, occasionally extending beyond it, though centered in it. But, while the particular games show clarity of goals and intensity, few, if any, treat the territory as their proper object. The protagonists of things in particular are well organized and know what they are about; the protagonists of things in general are few, vague, and weak. Immense staff work will go into the development of a Lincoln Square project, but the twenty-two counties of metropolitan New York have few spokesmen for their over-all common interest and not enough staff work to give these spokesmen more substance than that required for a "do-gooding" newspaper editorial. The Port of New York Authority exhibits a disciplined self-interest and a vigorous drive along the lines of its developed historic role. However, the attitude of the Port Authority toward the general problems of the metropolitan area is scarcely different than that of any private corporation. It confines its corporate good citizenship to the contribution of funds for surveys and studies and avoids acceptance of broader responsibility. In fact, spokesmen for the Port vigorously reject the need for any superior level of structured representation of metropolitan interests. The common interest, if such there be, is to be realized through institutional interactions rather than through the self-conscious rationality of a determinate group charged with its formulation and attainment. Apart from the newspaper editorial, the occasional politician, and a few civic leaders the general business of the metropolitan area is scarcely anybody's business, and, except for a few, those who concern themselves with the general problems are pursuing hobbies and causes rather than their own business.

The lack of over-all institutions in the territorial system and the weakness of those that exist insure that co-ordination is largely ecological rather than a matter of conscious rational contriving. In the metropolitan area in most cases there are no over-all economic or social institutions. People are playing particular games, and their playgrounds are less or more than the metropolitan area. But even in a city where the municipal corporation provides an apparent over-all government, the appearance is deceptive. The politicians who hold the offices do not regard themselves as governors of the municipal territory but largely as mediators or players in a particular game that makes use of the other inhabitants.

Their roles, as they conceive them, do not approach those of the directors of a TVA developing a territory. The ideology of local government is a highly limited affair in which the office-holders respond to demands and mediate conflicts. They play politics, and politics is vastly different from government if the latter is conceived as the rational, responsible ordering of the community. In part, this is due to the general belief that little government is necessary or that government is a congery of services only different from others because it is paid for by taxes and provided for by civil servants. In part, the separation of economics from politics eviscerates the formal theory of government of most of the substance of social action. Intervention in the really important economic order is by way of piecemeal exception and in deviation from the supposed norm of the separation of politics and economics. This ideal of separation has blocked the development of a theory of significant government action and reduced the politician to the role of registerer of pressure rather than responsible governor of a local political economy. The politics of the community becomes a different affair from its government, and its government is so structured as to provide the effective actors in it neither a sense of general responsibility nor the roles calling for such behavior.

The community vaguely senses that there ought to be a government. This is evidenced in the nomination by newspapers and others of particular individuals as members of a top leadership, a "they" who are periodically called upon to solve community problems and meet community crises. Significantly, the "they" usually are made up of people holding private, not public, office. The pluralism of the society has separated political, ecclesiastical, economic, and social hierarchies from one another so that the ancient union of lords spiritual and temporal is disrupted. In consequence, there is a marked distinction between the status of the holders of political office and the status of the "they" of the newspapers and the power elite of a C. Wright Mills or a Floyd Hunter. The politicians have the formal governmental office that might give them responsible governing roles. However, their lack of status makes it both absurd and presumptuous that they should take themselves so seriously. Who are they to act as lords of creation? Public expectation neither empowers nor demands that they should assume any such confident pose as top community leaders. The latter position is reserved for a rather varying group (in some communities well defined and clear-cut, in others vague and amorphous) of holders for the most part of positions of private power, economic, social, and ecclesiastical. This group, regarded as the top leadership of the community, and analogous to the top management of a corporation, provides both a sense that there are gods in the heavens whose will, if they exercise it, will take care of the community's problems and a set of demons whose misrule accounts for the evil in the world. The "they" fill an office left vacant by the dethronement of absolutism and aristocracy. Unlike the politicians in that "they" are only partially visible and of untested powers, the top leadership provides a convenient rationale for explaining what goes on or does not go on in the community. It is comforting to think that the executive committee of the bourgoisie is exploiting the community or that the beneficent social and economic leaders are wearying themselves and their digestions with civic luncheons in order to bring parking to a congested city.

Usually the question is raised as to whether *de facto* there is a set of informal power-holders running things. A related question is whether community folklore holds that there is, that there should be, and what these informal power-holders should do. Certainly, most newspapermen and other professional "inside dopesters" hold that there is a "they." In fact, these people operate largely as court chroniclers of the doings of the "they." The "they," because they are "they," are newsworthy and fit into a ready-made theory of social causation that is vulgarized widely. However, the same newspaperman who could knowingly open his "bird book" and give you a run-down on the local "Who's Who" would probably with equal and blasphemous candor tell you that "they" were not doing a thing about the city and that "they" were greatly to be blamed for sitting around talking instead of getting things done. Thus, as with most primitive tribes, the idols are both worshiped and beaten, at least verbally. Public and reporters alike are relieved to believe both that there is a "they" to make civic life explicable and also to be held responsible for what occurs. This belief in part creates the role of top leadership and demands that it somehow be filled. It seems likely that there is a social-psychological table of organization of a community that must be filled in order to remove anxieties. Gordon Childe has remarked that man seems to need as much to adjust to an unseen, socially created spiritual environment as to the matter-of-fact world of the senses.

The community needs to believe that there are spiritual fathers, bad or good, who can deal with the dark: in the Middle Ages the peasants combated a plague of locusts by a high Mass and a procession of the clergy who damned the grasshoppers with bell, book, and candle. The Hopi Indians do a rain dance to overcome a drought. The harassed citizens of the American city mobilize their influentials at a civic luncheon to perform the equivalent and exorcise slums, smog, or unemployment. We smile at the medievals and the Hopi, but our own practices may be equally magical. It is interesting to ask under what circumstances one resorts to DDT and irrigation and why. To some extent it is clear that the ancient and modern practice of civic magic ritual is functional—functional in the same sense as the medicinal placebo. Much of human illness is benign; if the sufferer will bide his time, it will pass. Much of civic ills also cure themselves if only people can be kept from tearing each other apart in the stress of their anxieties. The locusts and the drought will pass. They almost always have.

While ritual activities are tranquilizing anxieties, the process of experimentation and adaptation in the social ecology goes on. The piecemeal responses of the players and the games to the challenges presented by crises provide the social counterpart to the process of evolution and natural selection. However, unlike the random mutation of the animal kingdom, much of the behavior of the players responding within the perspectives of their games is self-conscious and rational, given their ends in view. It is from the over-all perspective of the unintended contribution of their actions to the forming of a new or the restoration of the old ecological balance of the social system that their actions appear almost as random and lacking in purposive plan as the adaptive behavior of the natural ecology.

Within the general area of unplanned, unconscious social process technological areas emerge that are so structured as to promote rational, goal-oriented behavior and meaningful experience rather than mere happenstance. In these areas group activity may result in cumulative knowledge and self-corrective behavior. Thus problem-solving in the field of public health and sanitation may be at a stage far removed from the older dependence on piecemeal adjustment and random functional innovation. In this sense there are areas in which society, as Julian Huxley suggests in his *The Meaning of Evolution*, has gone beyond evolution. However, these are as yet isolated areas in a world still swayed by magic and, for the most part, carried forward by the logic of unplanned, undirected historical process.

It is not surprising that the members of the "top leadership" of the territorial system should seem to be largely confined to ritual and ceremonial roles. "Top leadership" is usually conceived in terms of status position rather than specifiable roles in social action. The role of a top leader is ill defined and to a large degree unstructured. It is in most cases a secondary role derived from a primary role as corporation executive, wealthy man, powerful ecclesiastic, holder of high social position, and the like. The top-leadership role is derivative from the other and is in most cases a result rather than a cause of status. The primary job is bank president, or president of Standard Oil; as such, one is naturally picked, nominated, and recognized as a member of the top leadership. One seldom forgets that one's primary role, obligation, and source of rational conduct is in terms of one's business. In fact, while one is on the whole pleased at the recognition that membership in the top leadership implies—much as one's wife would be pleased to be included among the ten best-dressed women—he is somewhat concerned about just what the role requires in the expenditure of time and funds. Furthermore, one has a suspicion that he may not know how to dance and could make a fool of himself before known elite and unknown, more general publics. All things considered, however, it is probably a good thing for the business, the contacts are important, and the recognition will be helpful back home, in both senses. In any event, if one's committee service or whatever concrete activity "top leadership" implies proves wearing or unsatisfactory, or if it interferes with business, one can always withdraw.

A fair gauge of the significance of top-leadership roles is the time put into them by the players and the institutionalized support represented by staff. Again and again the interviewer is told that the president of such-and-such an organization is doing a terrific job and literally knocking himself out for such-and-such a program. On investigation a "terrific job" turns out to be a few telephone calls and, possibly, three luncheons a month. The standard of "terrific job" obviously varies widely from what would be required in the business role.

In the matter of staffing, while the corporation, the church, and the government are often equipped in depth, the top-leadership job of port promotion may have little more than a secretary and an agile newspaperman equipped to ghost-write speeches for the boss. While there are cases where people in top-leadership positions make use of staff from their own businesses and from the legal mill with which they do business, this seems largely confined to those top-leadership undertakings that have a direct connection with their business. In general, top-leadership roles seem to involve minor investments of time, staff, and money by territorial elites. The absence of staff and the emphasis on publicity limit the capacity of top leadership for sustained rational action.

Where the top leaderships have become well staffed, the process seems as much or more the result of external pressures than of its own volition. Of all the functions of top leadership, that of welfare is best staffed. Much of this is the result of the pressure of the professional social worker to organize a concentration of economic and social power sufficient to permit him to do a job. It is true, of course, that the price of organizing top leadership and making it manageable by the social workers facilitated a reverse control of themselves—a control of whose galling nature Hunter gives evidence. An amusing sidelight on the organization of the "executive committee of the bourgeoisie" is the case of the Cleveland Fifty Club. This club, supposedly, is made up of the fifty most important men in Cleveland. Most middling and even upper executives long for the prestige recognition that membership confers. Reputedly, the Fifty Club was organized by Brooks Emery, while he was director of the Cleveland Council on World Affairs, to facilitate the taxation of business to support that organization. The lead time required to get the august members of the Fifty Club together and their incohesiveness have severely limited its possibilities as a power elite. Members who have tried to turn it to such a purpose report fairly consistent failure.

The example of the Cleveland Fifty Club, while somewhat extreme, points to the need on the part of certain activities in the territorial system for a top leadership under whose auspices they can function. A wide variety of civic undertakings need to organize top prestige support both to finance and to legitimate their activities. The staff man of a bureau of municipal research or the Red Feather Agency cannot proceed on his own; he must have the legitimatizing sponsorship of top influentials. His task may be self-assigned, his perception of the problem and its solution may be his own, but he cannot gain acceptance without mobilizing the influentials. For the success of his game he must assist in creating the game of top leadership. The staff man in the civic field is the typical protagonist of things in general—a kind of entrepeneur of ideas. He fulfils the same role in his area as the stock promoter of the twenties or the Zeckendorfs of urban redevelopment. Lacking both status and a confining organizational basis, he has a socially valuable mobility between the specialized games and hierarchies in the territorial system. His success in the negotiation of a port authority not only provides a plus for his taxpayers federation or his world trade council but may provide a secure and lucrative job for himself.

Civic staff men, ranging from chamber of commerce personnel to college professors and newspapermen, are in varying degrees interchangeable and provide an important network of communication. The staff men in the civic agencies play similar roles to the Cohens and Corcorans in Washington. In each case a set of telephone numbers provides special information and an effective lower-echelon interaction. Consensus among interested professionals at the lower level can result in action programs from below that are bucked up to the prestige level of legitimitization. As the Cohens and Corcorans played perhaps the most general and inclusive game in the Washington bureaucracy, so their counterparts in the local territorial system are engaged in the most general action game in their area. Just as the Cohens and Corcorans had to mobilize an effective concentration of top brass to move a program into the action stage, so their counterparts have to mobilize concentrations of power sufficient for their purposes on the local scene.

In this connection it is interesting to note that foundation grants are being used to hire displaced New Deal bureaucrats and college professors in an attempt to organize the influentials of metropolitan areas into self-conscious governing groups. Professional chamber of commerce executives, immobilized by their orthodox ideology, are aghast to see their members study under the planners and heretics from the dogmas of free-enterprise fundamentalism. The attempt to transform the metropolitan appearance of disorder into a tidy territory is a built-in predisposition for the self-constituted staff of the embryonic top metropolitan management. The major disorder that has to be overcome before all others is the lack of order and organization among the "power elite." As in the case of the social workers, there is a thrust from below to organize a "power elite" as a necessary instrument to accomplish the purposes of civic staff men. This is in many ways nothing but a part of the general groping after a territorial government capable of dealing with a range of problems that the existing feudal disintegration of power cannot. The nomination of a top leadership by newspapers and public and the attempt to create such a leadership in fact by civic technicians are due to a recognition that there is a need for a leadership with the status, capacity, and role to attend to the general problems of the territory and give substance to a public philosophy. This involves major changes in the script of the top-leadership game and the self-image of its participants. In fact, the insecurity and the situational limitations of their positions in corporations or other institutions that provide the primary roles for top leaders make it difficult to give more substance to what has been a secondary role. Many members of present top leaderships are genuinely reluctant, fearful, and even morally shocked at their positions' becoming that of a recognized territorial government. While there is a general supposition that power is almost instinctively craved, there seems considerable evidence that at least in many of our territorial cultures responsibility is not. Machiavellian *virtu* is an even scarcer commodity among the merchant princes of the present than among their Renaissance predecessors. In addition, the educational systems of school and business do not provide top leaders with the inspiration or the know-how to do more than raise funds and man committees. Politics is frequently regarded with the same disgust as military service by the ancient educated Chinese.

It is possible to translate a check pretty directly into effective power in a chamber of commerce or a welfare agency. However, to translate economic power into more general social or political power, there must be an organized purchasable structure. Where such structures exist, they may be controlled or, as in the case of *condottieri*, gangsters, and politicians, their hire may be uncertain, and the hired force retains its independence. Where businessmen are unwilling or unable to organize their own political machines, they must pay those who do. Sometimes the paymaster rules; at other times he bargains with equals or superiors.

A major protagonist of things in general in the territorial system is the newspaper. Along with the welfare worker, museum director, civic technician, etc., the newspaper has an interest in terms of its broad reading public in agitating general issues and projects. As the chronicler of the great, both in its general news columns and in its special features devoted to society and business, it provides an organizing medium for elites in the territory and provides them with most of their information about things in general and not a little of inside tidbits about how individual elite members are doing. In a sense, the newspaper is the prime mover in setting the territorial agenda. It has a great part in determining what most people will be talking about, what most people will think the facts are, and what most people will regard as the way problems are to be dealt with. While the conventions of how a newspaper is to be run, and the compelling force of some events limit the complete freedom of a paper to select what events and what people its public will attend to, it has great leeway. However, the newspaper is a business and a specialized game even when its reporters are idealists and its publisher rejoices in the title "Mr. Cleveland." The paper does not accept the responsibility of a governing role in its territory. It is a power but only a partially responsible one. The span of attention of its audience and the conventions of what constitute a story give it a crusading role at most for particular projects. Nonetheless, to a large extent it sets the civic agenda.

The story is told of the mayor of a large eastern metropolis who, having visited the three capital cities of his constituents—Rome, Dublin, and Tel Aviv—had proceeded home via Paris and Le Havre. Since his staff had neglected to meet the boat before the press, he was badgered by reporters to say what he had learned on his trip. The unfortunate mayor could not say that he had been on a junket for a good time. Luckily, he remembered that in Paris they had been having an antinoise campaign. Off the hook at last, he told the press that he thought this campaign was a good thing. This gave the newsmen something to write about. The mayor hoped this was the end of it. But a major paper felt in need of a crusade to sponsor and began to harass the mayor about the start of the local anti-noise campaign. Other newspapers took up the cry, and the mayor told his staff they were for it—there had to be an antinoise campaign. In short order, businessmen's committees, psychiatrists, and college professors were mobilized to press forward on a broad front the suppression of needless noise. In vindication of administrative rationality it appeared that an antinoise campaign was on a staff list of possibilities for the mayor's agenda but had been discarded by him as politically unfeasible.

The civic technicians and the newspapers have somewhat the same relationship as congressional committee staff and the press. Many members of congressional committee staffs complain bitterly that their professional consciences are seared by the insistent pressure to seek publicity. But they contend that their committee sponsors are only impressed with research that is newsworthy. Congressional committee members point out that committees that do not get publicity are likely to go out of business or funds. The civic agency head all too frequently communicates most effectively with his board through his success in getting newspaper publicity. Many a civic ghost-writer has found his top leader converted to the cause by reading the ghosted speech he delivered at the civic luncheon reported with photographs and editorials in the press. This is even the case where the story appears in the top leader's own paper. The need of the reporters for news and of the civic technicians for publicity brings the participants of these two games together. As in the case of the congressional committee, there is a tendency to equate accomplishment with publicity. For top influentials on civic boards the news clips are an important way of keeping score. This symbiotic relation of newsmen and civic staff helps explain the heavy emphasis on ritual luncheons, committees, and news releases. The nature of the newspapers' concern with a story about people and the working of marvels and miracles puts a heavy pressure for the kind of story that the press likes to carry. It is not surprising that civic staff men should begin to equate accomplishment with their score measured in newspaper victories or that they should succumb to the temptation to impress their sponsors with publicity, salting it to their taste by flattering newspaper tributes to the sponsors themselves. Despite the built-in incapacity of newspapers to exercise a serious governing responsibility in their territories, they are for the most part the only institutions with a long-term general territorial interest. In default of a territorial political party or other institution that accepts responsibility for the formulation of a general civic agenda the newspaper is the one game that by virtue of its public and its conventions partly fills the vacuum.

A final game that does in a significant way integrate all the games in the territorial system is the social game. Success in each of the games can in varying degrees be cashed in for social acceptance. The custodians of the symbols of top social standing provide goals that in a sense give all the individual games some common denominator of achievement. While the holders of top social prestige do not necessarily hold either top political or economic power, they do provide meaningful goals for the rest. One of the most serious criticisms of a Yankee aristocracy made by a Catholic bishop was that, in losing faith in their own social values, they were undermining the faith in the whole system of final clubs. It would be a cruel joke if, just as the hard-working upwardly mobile had worked their way to entrance, the progeny of the founders lost interest. The decay of the Union League Club in *By Love Possessed* is a tragedy for more than its members. A common game shared even by the excluded spectators gave a purpose that was functional in its time and must be replaced— hopefully, by a better one. A major motivation for seeking membership in and playing the top-leadership game is the value of the status it confers as a counter in the social game.

Neither the civic leadership game nor the social game makes the territorial ecology over into a structured government. They do, however, provide important ways of linking the individual games and make possible cooperative action on projects. Finally, the social game, in Ruth Benedict's sense, in a general way patterns the culture of the teritorial ecology and gives all the players a set of vaguely shared aspirations and common goals.

Two Faces of Power[1]

PETER BACHRACH and MORTON S. BARATZ

The concept of power remains elusive despite the recent and prolific outpourings of case studies on community power. Its elusiveness is dramatically demonstrated by the regularity of disagreement as to the locus of community power between the sociologists and the political scientists. Sociologically oriented researchers have consistently found that power is highly centralized, while scholars trained in political science have just as regularly concluded that in "their" communities power is widely diffused.[2] Presumably, this explains why the latter group styles itself "pluralist," its counterpart "elitist."

There seems no room for doubt that the sharply divergent findings of the two groups are the product, not of sheer coincidence, but of fundamental differences in both their underlying assumptions and research methodology. The political scientists have contended that these differences in findings can be explained by the faulty approach and presuppositions of the sociologists. We contend in this paper that the pluralists themselves have not grasped the whole truth of the matter; that while their criticisms of the elitists are sound, they, like the elitists, utilize an approach and assumptions which predetermine their conclusions. Our argument is cast within the frame of our central thesis: that there are two faces of power, neither of which the sociologists see and only one of which the political scientists see.

I

Against the elitist approach to power several criticisms may be, and have been levelled.[3] One has to do with its basic premise that in every human institution there is an ordered system of power, a "power structure" which is an integral part and the mirror image of the organization's stratification. This postulate the pluralists emphatically—and, to our mind, correctly—reject, on the ground that

> nothing categorical can be assumed about power in any community. . . . If anything, there seems to be an unspoken notion among pluralist researchers that at bottom *nobody* dominates in a town, so that their first question is not likely to be, "Who runs this community?," but rather, "Does anyone at all run this community?" The first query is somewhat like, "Have you stopped beating your wife?," in that virtually any response short of total unwillingness to answer will supply the researchers with a "power elite" along the lines presupposed by the stratification theory.[4]

Equally objectionable to the pluralists—and to us—is the sociologists' hypothesis that the power structure tends to be stable over time.

> Pluralists hold that power may be tied to issues, and issues can be fleeting or persistent, provoking coalitions among interested groups and citizens, ranging in their duration from momentary to semi-permanent. . . . To presume that the set of coalitions which exists in the community at any given time is a timelessly stable aspect of social structure is to introduce systematic inaccuracies into one's description of social reality.[5]

A third criticism of the elitist model is that it wrongly equates reputed with actual power:

> If a man's major life work is banking, the pluralist presumes he will spend his time at the bank, and not in manipulating community decisions. This presumption holds until the banker's activities and participations indicate otherwise. . . . If we presume that the banker is "really" engaged in running the community, there is practically no way of disconfirming this notion, even if it is totally erroneous. On the other hand, it is easy to spot the banker who really *does* run community affairs when we presume he does not, because his activities will make this fact apparent.[6]

This is not an exhaustive bill of particulars; there are flaws other than these in the sociological model and methodology[7]—including some which the pluralists themselves have not noticed. But to go into this would not materially serve our current purposes. Suffice it simply to observe that whatever the merits of their own approach to power, the pluralists have effectively exposed the main weaknesses of the elitist model.

As the foregoing quotations make clear, the pluralists concentrate their attention, not upon the sources of power, but its exercise. Power to them means "participation in decision-making"[8] and can be analyzed only after "careful examination of a series of concrete decisions."[9] As a result, the pluralist researcher is uninterested in the reputedly powerful. His concerns instead are to (a) select for study a number of "key" as opposed to "routine" political decisions, (b) identify the people who took an active part in the decision-making process, (c) obtain a full account of their actual behavior while the policy conflict was being resolved, and (d) determine and analyze the specific outcome of the conflict.

The advantages of this approach, relative to the elitist alternative, need no further exposition. The same may not be said, however, about its defects—two of which seem to us to be of fundamental importance. One is that the model takes no account of the fact that power may be, and often is, exercised by confining the scope of decision-making to relatively "safe" issues. The other is that the model provides no *objective* criteria for distinguishing between "important" and "unimportant" issues arising in the political arena.

II

There is no gainsaying that an analysis grounded entirely upon what is specific and visible to the outside observer is more "scientific" than one based upon pure speculation. To put it another way,

> If we can get our social life stated in terms of activity, and of nothing else, we have not indeed succeeded in measuring it, but we have at least reached a foundation upon which a coherent system of measurements can be built up. . . . We shall cease to be blocked by the intervention of unmeasurable elements, which claim to be themselves the real causes of all that is happening, and which by their spook-like arbitrariness make impossible any progress toward dependable knowledge.[10]

The question is, however, how can one be certain in any given situation that the "unmeasurable elements" are inconsequential, are not of decisive importance? Cast in slightly different terms, can a sound concept of power be predicated on the assumption that power is totally embodied and fully reflected in "concrete decisions" or in activity bearing directly upon their making?

We think not. Of course power is exercised when A participates in the making of decisions that affect B. But power is also exercised when A devotes his energies to creating or reinforcing social and political values and institutional practices that limit the scope of the political process to public consideration of only those issues which are comparatively innocuous to A. To the extent that A succeeds in doing this, B is prevented, for all practical purposes, from bringing to the fore any issues that might in their resolution be seriously detrimental to A's set of preferences.[11]

Situations of this kind are common. Consider, for example, the case—surely not unfamiliar to this audience of the discontented faculty member in an academic institution headed by a tradition-bound executive. Aggrieved about a long-standing policy around which a strong vested interest has developed, the professor resolves in the privacy of his office to launch an attack upon the policy at the next faculty meeting. But, when the moment of truth is at hand, he sits frozen in silence. Why? Among the many possible reasons, one or more of these could have been of crucial importance: (a) the professor was fearful that his intended action would be interpreted as an expression of his disloyalty to the institution; or (b) he decided that, given the beliefs and attitudes of his colleagues on the faculty, he would almost certainly constitute on this issue a minority of one; or (c) he concluded that, given the nature of the law-making process in the institution, his proposed remedies would be pigeonholed permanently. But whatever the case, the central point to be made is the same: to the extent that a person or group—consciously or unconsciously—creates or reinforces barriers to the public airing of policy conflicts, that person or group has power. Or, as Professor Schattschneider has so admirably put it:

> All forms of political organization have a bias in favor of the exploitation of some kinds of conflict and the suppression of others because *organization is the mobilization of bias*. Some issues are organized into politics while others are organized out.[12]

Is such bias not relevant to the study of power? Should not the student be continuously alert to its possible existence in the human institution that he studies, and be ever prepared to examine the forces which brought it into being and sustain it? Can he safely ignore the possibility, for instance, that an individual or group in a community participates more vigorously in supporting the *nondecision-making* process than in participating in actual decisions within the process? Stated differently, can the researcher overlook the chance that some person or association could limit decision-making to relatively non-controversial matters, by influencing community values and political procedures and rituals, notwithstanding that there are in the community serious but latent power conflicts?[13] To do so is, in our judgment, to overlook the less apparent, but nonetheless extremely important, face of power.

III

In his critique of the "ruling-elite model," Professor Dahl argues that "the hypothesis of the existence of a ruling elite can be strictly tested only if . . . [t] here is a fair sample of cases involving key political decisions in which the preferences of the hypothetical ruling elite run counter to those of any other likely group that might be suggested."[14] With this assertion we have two complaints. One we have already discussed, viz., in erroneously assuming that power is solely reflected in concrete decisions, Dahl thereby excludes the possibility that in the community in question there is a group capable of preventing contests from arising on issues of importance to it. Beyond that, however, by ignoring the less apparent face of power Dahl and those who accept his pluralist approach are unable adequately to differentiate between a "key" and a "routine" political decision.

Nelson Polsby, for example, proposes that "by pre-selecting as issues for study those which are generally agreed to be significant, pluralist researchers can test stratification theory."[15] He is silent, however, on how the researcher is to determine *what* issues are "generally agreed to be significant," and on how the researcher is to appraise the reliability of the agreement. In fact, Polsby is guilty here of the same fault he himself has found with elitist methodology: by presupposing that in any community there are significant issues in the political arena, he takes for granted the very question which is in doubt. He accepts as issues what are reputed to be issues. As a result, his findings are fore-ordained. For even if there is no "truly" significant issue in the community under study, there is every likelihood that Polsby (or any like-minded researcher) will find one or some and, after careful study, reach the appropriate pluralistic conclusions.[16]

Dahl's definition of "key political issues" in his essay on the ruling-elite model is open to the same criticism. He states that it is "a necessary although possibly not a sufficient condition that the [key] issue should involve actual disagreement in preferences among two or more groups." [17] In our view, this is an inadequate characterization of a "key political issue," simply because groups can have disagreements in preferences on unimportant as well as on important issues. Elite preferences which border on the indifferent are certainly not significant in determining whether a monolithic or polylithic distribution of power prevails in a given community. Using Dahl's definition of "key political issues," the researcher would have little difficulty in finding such in practically any community; and it would not be surprising then if he ultimately concluded that power in the community was widely diffused.

The distinction between important and unimportant issues, we believe, cannot be made intelligently in the absence of an analysis of the "mobilization of bias" in the community; of the dominant values and the political myths, rituals, and institutions which tend to favor the vested interests of one or more groups, relative to others. Armed with this knowledge, one could conclude that any challenge to the predominant values or to the established "rules of the game" would constitute an "important" issue; all else, unimportant. To be sure, judgements of this kind cannot be entirely objective. But to avoid making them in a study of power is both to neglect a highly significant aspect of power and thereby to undermine the only sound basis for discriminating between "key" and "routine" decisions. In effect, we contend, the pluralists have made each of these mistakes; that is to say, they have done just that for which Kaufman and Jones so severely taxed Floyd Hunter: they have begun "their structure at the mezzanine without showing us a lobby or foundation," [18] *i.e.,* they have begun by studying the issues rather than the values and biases that are built into the political system and that, for the student of power, give real meaning to those issues which do enter the political arena.

IV

There is no better fulcrum for our critique of the pluralist model than Dahl's recent study of power in New Haven. [19]

At the outset it may be observed that Dahl does not attempt in this work to define his concept, "key political decision." In asking whether the "Notables" of New Haven are "influential overtly or covertly in the making of government decisions," he simply states that he will examine "three different 'issue-areas' in which important public decisions are made: nominations by the two political parties, urban redevelopment, and public education." These choices are justified on the grounds that "nominations determine which persons will hold public office. The New Haven redevelopment program measured by its cost—present and potential—is the largest in the country. Public education, aside from its intrinsic importance, is the costliest item in the city's budget." Therefore, Dahl concludes, "It is reasonable to expect . . . that the relative influence over public officials wielded by the . . . Notables would be revealed by an examination of their participation in these three areas of activity." [20]

The difficulty with this latter statement is that it is evident from Dahl's own account that the Notables are in fact uninterested in two of the three "key" decisions he has chosen. In regard to the public school issue, for example, Dahl points out that many of the Notables live in the suburbs and that those who do live in New Haven choose in the main to send their children to private schools. "As a consequence," he writes, "their interest in the public schools is ordinarily rather slight."[21] Nominations by the two political parties as an important "issue-area," is somewhat analogous to the public schools, in that the apparent lack of interest among the Notables in this issue is partially accounted for by their suburban residence—because of which they are disqualified from holding public office in New Haven. Indeed, Dahl himself concedes that with respect to both these issues the Notables are largely indifferent: "Business leaders might ignore the public schools or the political parties without any sharp awareness that their indifference would hurt their pocketbooks . . ." He goes on, however, to say that

> the prospect of profound changes [as a result of the urban-redevelopment program] in ownership, physical layout, and usage of property in the downtown area and the effects of these changes on the commercial and industrial prosperity of New Haven were all related in an obvious way to the daily concerns of businessmen.[22]

Thus, if one believes as Professor Dahl did when he wrote his critique of the ruling-elite model that an issue, to be considered as important, "should involve actual disagreement in preferences among two or more groups,"[23] then clearly he has now for all practical purposes written off public education and party nominations as key "issue-areas." But this point aside, it appears somewhat dubious at best that "the relative influence over public officials wielded by the Social Notables" can be revealed by an examination of their nonparticipation in areas in which they were not interested.

Furthermore, we would not rule out the possibility that even on those issues to which they appear indifferent, the Notables may have a significant degree of *indirect* influence. We would suggest, for example, that although they send their children to private schools, the Notables do recognize that public school expenditures have a direct bearing upon their own tax liabilities. This being so, and given their strong representation on the New Haven Board of Finance,[24] the expectation must be that it is in their direct interest to play an active role in fiscal policy-making, in the establishment of the educational budget in particular. But as to this, Dahl is silent: he inquires not at all into either the decisions made by the Board of Finance with respect to education nor into their impact upon the public schools.[25] Let it be understood clearly that in making these points we are not attempting to refute Dahl's contention that the Notables lack power in New Haven. What we *are* saying, however, is that this conclusion is not adequately supported by his analysis of the "issue-areas" of public education and party nominations.

The same may not be said of redevelopment. This issue is by any reasonable standard important for purposes of determining whether New Haven is ruled by "the hidden hand of an economic elite."[26] For the Economic Notables have taken an active interest in the program and, beyond that, the socio-economic implications of it are not necessarily in harmony with the basic interests and values of businesses and businessmen.

In an effort to assure that the redevelopment program would be acceptable to what he dubbed "the biggest muscles" in New Haven, Mayor Lee created the Citizens Action

Commission (CAC) and appointed to it primarily representatives of the economic elite. It was given the function of overseeing the work of the mayor and other officials involved in redevelopment, and, as well, the responsibility for organizing and encouraging citizens' participation in the program through an extensive committee system.

In order to weigh the relative influence of the mayor, other key officials, and the members of the CAC, Dahl reconstructs "all the *important* decisions on redevelopment and renewal between 1950–58 . . . [to] determine which individuals most often initiated the proposals that were finally adopted or most often successfully vetoed the proposals of the others."[27] The results of this test indicate that the mayor and his development administrator were by far the most influential, and that the "muscles" on the Commission, excepting in a few trivial instances, "never directly initiated, opposed, vetoed, or altered any proposal brought before them. . . ."[28]

This finding is, in our view, unreliable, not so much because Dahl was compelled to make a subjective selection of what constituted *important* decisions within what he felt to be an *important* "issue-area," as because the finding was based upon an excessively narrow test of influence. To measure relative influence solely in terms of the ability to initiate and veto proposals is to ignore the possible exercise of influence or power in limiting the scope of initiation. How, that is to say, can a judgment be made as to the relative influence of Mayor Lee and the CAC without knowing (through prior study of the political and social views of all concerned) the proposals that Lee did *not* make because he anticipated that they would provoke strenuous opposition and, perhaps, sanctions on the part of the CAC?[29]

In sum, since he does not recognize *both* faces of power, Dahl is in no position to evaluate the relative influence or power of the initiator and decision-maker, on the one hand, and of those persons, on the other, who may have been indirectly instrumental in preventing potentially dangerous issues from being raised.[30] As a result, he unduly emphasizes the importance of initiating, deciding, and vetoing, and in the process casts the pluralist conclusions of his study into serious doubt.

V

We have contended in this paper that a fresh approach to the study of power is called for, an approach based upon a recognition of the two faces of power. Under this approach the researcher would begin—not, as does the sociologist who asks, "Who rules?" nor as does the pluralist who asks, "Does anyone have power?"—but by investigating the particular "mobilization of bias" in the institution under scrutiny. Then, having analyzed the dominant values, the myths and the established political procedures and rules of the game, he would make a careful inquiry into which persons or groups, if any, gain from the existing bias and which, if any, are handicapped by it. Next, he would investigate the dynamics of *nondecision-making;* that is, he would examine the extent to which and the manner in which the *status quo* oriented persons and groups influence those community values and those political institutions (as, *e.g.*, the unanimity "rule" of New York City's Board of Estimate[31]) which tend to limit the scope of actual decision-making to "safe" issues.

Finally, using his knowledge of the restrictive face of power as a foundation for analysis and as a standard for distinguishing between "key" and "routine" political decisions, the researcher would, after the manner of the pluralists, analyze participation in decision-making of concrete issues.

We reject in advance as unimpressive the possible criticism that this approach to the study of power is likely to prove fruitless because it goes beyond an investigation of what is objectively measurable. In reacting against the subjective aspects of the sociological model of power, the pluralists have, we believe, made the mistake of discarding "unmeasurable elements" as unreal. It is ironical that, by so doing, they have exposed themselves to the same fundamental criticism they have so forcefully levelled against the elitists: their approach to and assumptions about power predetermine their findings and conclusions.

 NOTES

1. This paper is an outgrowth of a seminar in Problems of Power in Contemporary Society, conducted jointly by the authors for graduate students and undergraduate majors in political science and economics.

2. Compare, for example, the sociological studies of Floyd Hunter, *Community Power Structure* (Chapel Hill, 1953); Roland Pellegrini and Charles H. Coates, "Absentee-Owned Corporations and Community Power Structure," *American Journal of Sociology,* Vol. 61 (March 1956), pp. 413–19; and Robert O. Schulze, "Economic Dominants and Community Power Structure," *American Sociological Review*, Vol. 23 (February 1958), pp. 3–9; with political science studies of Wallace S. Sayre and Herbert Kaufman, *Governing New York City* (New York, 1960); Robert A. Dahl, *Who Governs?* (New Haven, 1961); and Norton E. Long and George Belknap, "A Research Program on Leadership and Decision-Making in Metropolitan Areas" (New York, Governmental Affairs Institute, 1956). See also Nelson W. Polsby, "How to Study Community Power: The Pluralist Alternative," *Journal of Politics,* Vol. 22 (August, 1960), pp. 474–84.

3. See especially N. W. Polsby, *op. cit.*, p. 475f.

4. *Ibid.*, pp. 476.

5. *Ibid.*, pp. 478–79.

6. *Ibid.*, pp. 480–81.

7. See especially Robert A. Dahl, "A Critique of the Ruling-Elite Model," this *American Political Science Review*, Vol. 52 (June 1958), pp. 463–69; and Lawrence J. R. Herson, "In the Footsteps of Community Power," this *American Political Science Review*, Vol. 55 (December, 1961), pp. 817–31.

8. This definition originated with Harold D. Lasswell and Abraham Kaplan, *Power and Society* (New Haven, 1950), p. 75.

9. Robert A. Dahl, "A Critique of the Ruling-Elite Model," *loc. cit.*, p. 466.

10. Arthur Bentley, *The Process of Government* (Chicago, 1908), p. 202, quoted in Polsby, *op. cit.,* p. 481n.

11. As is perhaps self-evident, there are similarities in both faces of power. In each, A participates in decisions and thereby adversely affects B. But there is an important difference between the two: in the one case, A openly participates; in the other, he participates only in the sense that he works to sustain those values and rules of procedure that help him keep certain issues out of the public domain. True enough, participation of the second kind may at times be overt; that is the case, for instance, in cloture fights in the Congress. But the point is that it need not be. In fact, when the maneuver is most successfully executed, it neither involves nor can be identified with decisions arrived at on specific issues.

12. E. E. Schattschneider, *The Semi-Sovereign People* (New York, 1960), p. 71.

13. Dahl *partially* concedes this point when he observes ("A Critique of the Ruling-Elite Model," pp. 468–69) that "one could argue that even in a society like ours a ruling elite might be so influential over ideas, attitudes, and opinions that a kind of false consensus will exist—not the phony consensus of a terroristic totalitarian dictatorship but the manipulated and superficially self-imposed adherence to the norms and goals of the elite by broad sections of a community. . . . This objection points to the need to be circumspect in interpreting the evidence." But that he largely misses our point is clear from the succeeding sentence: "Yet here, too, it seems to me that the hypothesis cannot be satisfactorily confirmed without something equivalent to the test I have proposed," and that is "by an examination of a series of concrete cases where key decisions are made. . . ."

14. *Op. cit.,* p. 466.

15. *Op. cit.,* p. 478.

16. As he points out, the expectations of the pluralist researchers "have seldom been disappointed." (*Ibid.,* p. 477).

17. *Op. cit.,* p. 467.

18. Herbert Kaufman and Victor Jones, "The Mystery of Power," *Public Administration Review,* Vol. 14 (Summer 1954), p. 207.

19. Robert A. Dahl, *Who Governs?* (New Haven, 1961).

20. *Ibid.,* p. 64.

21. *Ibid.,* p. 70.

22. *Ibid.,* p. 71.

23. *Op. cit.,* p. 467.

24. *Who Governs?*, p. 82. Dahl points out that "the main policy thrust of the Economic Notables is to oppose tax increases; this leads them to oppose expenditures for anything more than minimal traditional city services. In this effort their two most effective weapons ordinarily are the mayor and the Board of Finance. The policies of the Notables are most easily achieved under a strong mayor if his policies coincide with theirs or under a weak mayor if they have the support of the Board of Finance. . . . New Haven mayors have continued to find it expedient to create confidence in their financial policies among businessmen by appointing them to the Board." (pp. 81–2)

25. Dahl does discuss in general terms (pp. 79–84) changes in the level of tax rates and assessments in past years, but not actual decisions of the Board of Finance or their effects on the public school system.

26. *Ibid.*, p. 124.

27. *Ibid.* "A rough test of a person's overt or covert influence," Dahl states in the first section of the book, "is the frequency with which he successfully initiates an important policy over the opposition of others, or vetoes policies initiated by others, or initiates a policy where no opposition appears." (*Ibid.*, p. 66)

28. *Ibid.*, p. 131.

29. Dahl is, of course, aware of the "law of anticipated reactions." In the case of the mayor's relationship with the CAC, Dahl notes that Lee was "particularly skillful in estimating what the CAC could be expected to support or reject." (p. 137). However, Dahl was not interested in analyzing or appraising to what extent the CAC limited Lee's freedom of action. Because of his restricted concept of power, Dahl did not consider that the CAC might in this respect have exercised power. That the CAC did not initiate or veto actual proposals by the mayor was to Dahl evidence enough that the CAC was virtually powerless; it might as plausibly be evidence that the CAC was (in itself or in what it represented) so powerful that Lee ventured nothing it would find worth quarreling with.

30. The fact that the initiator of decisions also refrains—because he anticipates adverse reactions—from initiating other proposals does not obviously lessen the power of the agent who limited his initiative powers. Dahl missed this point: "It is," he writes, "all the more improbable, then, that a secret cabal of Notables dominates the public life of New Haven through means so clandestine that not one of the fifty prominent citizens interviewed in the course of this study—citizens who had participated extensively in various decisions—hinted at the existence of such a cabal . . ." (p. 185).

In conceiving of elite domination exclusively in the form of a conscious cabal exercising the power of decision-making and vetoing, he overlooks a more subtle form of domination; one in which those who actually dominate are not conscious of it themselves, simply because their position of dominance has never seriously been challenged.

31. Sayre and Kaufman, *op. cit.*, p. 640. For perceptive study of the "mobilization of bias" in a rural American community, see Arthur Vidich and Joseph Bensman, *Small Town in Mass Society* (Princeton, 1958).

The City as a Growth Machine: Toward a Political Economy of Place[1]

HARVEY MOLOTCH

A city and, more generally, any locality, is conceived as the areal expression of the interests of some land-based elite. Such an elite is seen to profit through the increasing intensification of the land use of the area in which its members hold a common interest. An elite competes with other land-based elites in an effort to have growth-inducing resources invested within its own area as opposed to that of another. Governmental authority, at the local and nonlocal levels, is utilized to assist in achieving this growth at the expense of competing localities. Conditions of community life are largely a consequence of the social, economic, and political forces embodied in this growth machine. The relevance of growth to the interests of various social groups is examined in this context, particularly with reference to the issue of unemployment. Recent social trends in opposition to growth are described and their potential consequences evaluated.

Conventional definitions of "city," "urban place," or "metropolis" have led to conventional analyses of urban systems and urban-based social problems. Usually traceable to Wirth's classic and highly plausible formulation of "numbers, density and heterogeneity" (1938), there has been a continuing tendency, even in more recent formulations (e.g., Davis 1965), to conceive of place quite apart from a crucial dimension of social structure: power and social class hierarchy. Consequently, sociological research based on the traditional definitions of what an urban place is has had very little relevance to the actual, day-to-day activities of those at the top of local power structure whose priorities set the limits within which decisions affecting land use, the public budget, and urban social life come to be made. It has not been very apparent from the scholarship of urban social science that land, the basic stuff of place, is a market commodity providing wealth and power, and that some very important people consequently take a keen interest in it. Thus, although there are extensive literatures on community power as well as on how to define and conceptualize a city or urban place, there are few notions available to link the two issues coherently, focusing on the urban settlement as a political economy.

This paper aims toward filling this need. I speculate that the political and economic essence of virtually any given locality, in the present American context, is *growth*. I further argue that the desire for growth provides the key operative motivation toward consensus for members of politically mobilized local elites, however split they might be on other issues, and that a common interest in growth is the overriding commonality among important people in a given locale—at least insofar as they have any important local goals at all.

Further, this growth imperative is the most important constraint upon available options for local initiative in social and economic reform. It is thus that I argue that the very essence of a locality is its operation as a growth machine.

The clearest indication of success at growth is a constantly rising urban-area population—a symptom of a pattern ordinarily comprising an initial expansion of basic industries followed by an expanded labor force, a rising scale of retail and wholesale commerce, more far-flung and increasingly intensive land development, higher population density, and increased levels of financial activity. Although throughout this paper I index growth by the variable population growth, it is this entire syndrome of associated events that is meant by the general term "growth."[2] I argue that the means of achieving this growth, of setting off this chain of phenomena, constitute the central issue for those serious people who care about their locality and who have the resources to make their caring felt as a political force. The city is, for those who count, a growth machine.

THE HUMAN ECOLOGY: MAPS AS INTEREST MOSAICS

I have argued elsewhere (Molotch 1967, 1973) that any given parcel of land represents an interest and that any given locality is thus an aggregate of land-based interests. That is, each landowner (or person who otherwise has some interest in the prospective use of a given piece of land) has in mind a certain future for that parcel which is linked somehow with his or her own well-being. If there is a simple ownership, the relationship is straightforward: to the degree to which the land's profit potential is enhanced, one's own wealth is increased. In other cases, the relationship may be more subtle: one has interest in an adjacent parcel, and if a noxious use should appear, one's own parcel may be harmed. More subtle still is the emergence of concern for an aggregate of parcels: one sees that one's future is bound to the future of a larger area, that the future enjoyment of financial benefit flowing from a given parcel will derive from the general future of the proximate aggregate of parcels. When this occurs, there is that "we feeling" (McKenzie 1922) which bespeaks of community. We need to see each geographical map—whether of a small group of land parcels, a whole city, a region, or a nation—not merely as a demarcation of legal, political, or topographical features, but as a mosaic of competing land interests capable of strategic coalition and action.

Each unit of a community strives, at the expense of the others, to enhance the land-use potential of the parcels with which it is associated. Thus, for example, shopkeepers at both ends of a block may compete with one another to determine in front of which building the bus stop will be placed. Or, hotel owners on the north side of a city may compete with those on the south to get a convention center built nearby (see Banfield 1961). Likewise, area units fight over highway routes, airport locations, campus developments, defense contracts, traffic lights, one-way street designations, and park developments. The intensity of group consciousness and activity waxes and wanes as opportunities for and challenges to the collective good rise and fall; but when these coalitions are of sufficiently enduring quality, they constitute identifiable, ongoing communities. Each member of a community is simultaneously the member of a number of others; hence, communities exist in a nested fashion (e.g., neighborhood within city within region), with salience of community level varying both over time and circumstance. Because of this nested nature of communities, subunits which are competitive with one another at one level (e.g., in an interblock dispute over where the bus stop should go) will be in coalition at a higher level (e.g., in an intercity rivalry over where the new port should go). Obviously, the anticipation of potential coalition acts to constrain the intensity of conflict at more local loci of growth competition.

Hence, to the degree to which otherwise competing land-interest groups collude to achieve a common land-enhancement scheme, there is community—whether at the level of a residential block club, a neighborhood association, a city or metropolitan chamber of commerce, a state development agency, or a regional association. Such aggregates, whether constituted formally or informally, whether governmental political institutions or voluntary associations, typically operate in the following way: an attempt is made to use government to gain those resources which will enhance the growth potential of the area unit in question. Often, the governmental level where action is needed is at least one level higher than the community from which the activism springs. Thus, individual landowners aggregate to extract neighborhood gains from the city government; a cluster of cities may coalesce to have an effective impact on the state government, etc. Each locality, in striving to make these gains, is in competition with other localities because the degree of growth, at least at any given moment, is finite. The scarcity of developmental resources means that government becomes the arena in which land-use interest groups compete for public money and attempt to mold those decisions which will determine the land-use outcomes. Localities thus compete with one another to gain the *preconditions* of growth. Historically, U.S. cities were created and sustained largely through this process;[3] it continues to be the significant dynamic of contemporary local political economy and is critical to the allocation of public resources and the ordering of local issue agendas.

Government decisions are not the only kinds of social activities which affect local growth chances; decisions made by private corporations also have major impact. When a national corporation decides to locate a branch plant in a given locale, it sets the conditions for the surrounding land-use pattern. But even here, government decisions are involved: plant-location decisions are made with reference to such issues as labor costs, tax rates, and the costs of obtaining raw materials and transporting goods to markets. It is government decisions (at whatever level) that help determine the cost of access to markets and raw materials. This is especially so in the present era of raw material subsidies (e.g., the mineral depletion allowance) and reliance on government approved or subsidized air transport, highways, railways, pipelines, and port developments. Government decisions influence the cost of overhead expenses (e.g., pollution abatement requirements, employee safety standards), and government decisions affect the costs of labor through indirect manipulation of unemployment rates, through the use of police to constrain or enhance union organizing, and through the legislation and administration of welfare laws (see Piven and Cloward 1972).

Localities are generally mindful of these governmental powers and, in addition to creating the sorts of physical conditions which can best serve industrial growth, also attempt to maintain the kind of "business climate" that attracts industry: for example, favorable taxation, vocational training, law enforcement, and "good" labor relations. To promote growth, taxes should be "reasonable," the police force should be oriented toward protection of property, and overt social conflict should be minimized (see Rubin 1972, p. 123; Agger, Goldrich, and Swanson 1964, p. 649).[4] Increased utility and government costs caused by new development should be borne (and they usually are—see e.g., Ann Arbor City Planning Department [1972]) by the public at large, rather than by those responsible for the "excess" demand on the urban infrastructure. Virtually any issue of a major business magazine is replete with ads from localities of all types (including whole countries) trumpeting their virtues in just these terms to prospective industrial settlers.[5] In addition, a key role of elected and appointed officials becomes that of "ambassador" to industry, to communicate, usually with appropriate ceremony, these advantages to potential investors (see Wyner 1967).[6]

I aim to make the extreme statement that this organized effort to affect the outcome of growth distribution is the essence of local government as a dynamic political force. It is not the only function of government, but it is the key one and, ironically, the one most ignored. Growth is not, in the present analysis, merely one among a number of equally important concerns of political process (cf. Adrian and Williams 1963). Among contemporary social scientists, perhaps only Murray Edelman (1964) has provided appropriate conceptual preparation for viewing government in such terms. Edelman contrasts two kinds of politics. First there is the "symbolic" politics which comprises the "big issues" of public morality and the symbolic reforms featured in the headlines and editorials of the daily press. The other politics is the process through which goods and services actually come to be distributed in the society. Largely unseen, and relegated to negotiations within committees (when it occurs at all within a formal government body), this is the politics which determines who, *in material terms*, gets what, where, and how (Lasswell 1936). This is the kind of politics we must talk about at the local level: it is the politics of distribution, and land is the crucial (but not the only) variable in this system.

The people who participate with their energies, and particularly their fortunes, in local affairs are the sort of persons who—at least in vast disproportion to their representation in the population—have the most to gain or lose in land-use decisions. Prominent in terms of numbers have long been the local businessmen (see Walton 1970),[7] particularly property owners and investors in locally oriented financial institutions (see, e.g., Spaulding 1951; Mumford 1961, p. 536), who *need* local government in their daily money-making routines. Also prominent are lawyers, syndicators, and realtors (see Bouma 1962) who need to put themselves in situations where they can be most useful to those with the land and property resources.[8] Finally, there are those who, although not directly involved in land use, have their futures tied to growth of the metropolis as a whole. At least, when the local market becomes saturated one of the few possible avenues for business expansion is sometimes the expansion of the surrounding community itself (see Adrian and Williams 1963, p. 24).[9]

This is the general outline of the coalition that actively generates the community "we feeling" (or perhaps more aptly, the "our feeling")[10] that comes to be an influence in the politics of a given locality. It becomes manifest through a wide variety of techniques. Government funds support "boosterism" of various sorts: the Chamber of Commerce, locality-promotion ads in business journals and travel publications, city-sponsored parade floats, and stadia and other forms of support for professional sports teams carrying the locality name. The athletic teams in particular are an extraordinary mechanism for instilling a spirit of civic jingoism regarding the "progress" of the locality. A stadium filled with thousands (joined by thousands more at home before the TV) screaming for Cleveland or Baltimore (or whatever) is a scene difficult to fashion otherwise. This enthusiasm can be drawn upon, with a glossy claim of creating a "greater Cleveland," "greater Baltimore," etc., in order to gain general acceptance for local growth-oriented programs. Similarly, public school curricula, children's essay contests, soapbox derbies, spelling contests, beauty pageants, etc., help build an ideological base for local boosterism and the acceptance of growth. My conception of the territorial bond among humans differs from those cast in terms of primordial instincts: instead, I see this bond as socially organized and sustained, at least in part, by those who have a use for it (cf. Suttles 1972, pp. 111–39). I do not claim that there are no other sources of civic jingoism and growth enthusiasm in American communities, only that the growth-machine coalition mobilizes what is there, legitimizes and sustains it, and channels it as a political force into particular kinds of policy decisions.

The local institution which seems to take prime responsibility for the sustenance of these civic resources—the metropolitan newspaper—is also the most important example of a business which has its interest anchored in the aggregate growth of the locality. Increasingly, American cities are one-newspaper (metropolitan daily) towns (or one-newspaper-company towns), and the newspaper business seems to be one kind of enterprise for which expansion to other locales is especially difficult. The financial loss suffered by the *New York Times* in its futile effort to establish a California edition is an important case in point. A paper's financial status (and that of other media to a lesser extent) tends to be wed to the size of the locality.[11] As the metropolis expands, a larger number of ad lines can be sold on the basis of the increasing circulation base. The local newspaper thus tends to occupy a rather unique position: like many other local businesses, it has an interest in growth, but unlike most, its critical interest is not in the specific geographical pattern of that growth. That is, the crucial matter to a newspaper is not whether the additional population comes to reside on the north side or south side, or whether the money is made through a new convention center or a new olive factory. The newspaper has no axe to grind, except the one axe which holds the community elite together: growth. It is for this reason that the newspaper tends to achieve a statesman-like attitude in the community and is deferred to as something other than a special interest by the special interests. Competing interests often regard the publisher or editor as a general community leader, as an ombudsman and arbiter of internal bickering and, at times, as an enlightened third party who can restrain the short-term profiteers in the interest of more stable, long-term, and properly planned growth.[12] The paper becomes the reformist influence, the "voice of the community," restraining the competing subunits, especially the small-scale, arriviste "fast-buck artists" among them. The papers are variously successful in their continuous battle with the targeted special interests.[13] The media attempt to attain these goals not only through the kind of coverage they develop and editorials they write but also through the kinds of candidates they support for local office. The present point is not that the papers control the politics of the city, but rather that one of the sources of their special influence is their commitment to growth per se, and growth is a goal around which all important groups can rally.

Thus it is that, although newspaper editorialists have typically been in the forefront expressing sentiment in favor of "the ecology," they tend nevertheless to support growth-inducing investments for their regions. The *New York Times* likes office towers and additional industrial installations in the city even more than it loves the environment. The *Los Angeles Times* editorializes against narrow-minded profiteering at the expense of the environment but has also favored the development of the supersonic transport because of the "jobs" it would lure to Southern California. The papers do tend to support "good planning principles" in some form because such good planning is a long-term force that makes for even more potential future growth. If the roads are not planned wide enough, their narrowness will eventually strangle the increasingly intense uses to which the land will be put. It just makes good sense to plan, and good planning for "sound growth" thus is the key "environmental policy" of the nation's local media and their statesmen allies. Such policies of "good planning" should not be confused with limited growth or conservation: they more typically represent the opposite sort of goal.

Often leaders of public or quasi-public agencies (e.g., universities, utilities) achieve a role similar to that of the newspaper publisher: they become growth "statesmen" rather than advocates for a certain type or intralocal distribution of growth. A university may require an increase in the local urban population pool to sustain its own expansion plans and, in addition, it may be induced to defer to others in the growth machine (bankers, newspapers) upon whom it depends for the favorable financial and public-opinion environment necessary for institutional enhancement.

There are certain persons, ordinarily conceived of as members of the elite, who have much less, if any, interest in local growth. Thus, for example, there are branch executives of corporations headquartered elsewhere who, although perhaps emotionally sympathetic with progrowth outlooks, work for corporations which have no vested interest in the growth of the locality in question. Their indirect interest is perhaps in the existence of the growth ideology rather than growth itself. It is that ideology which in fact helps make them revered people in the area (social worth is often defined in terms of number of people one employs) and which provides the rationale for the kind of local governmental policies most consistent with low business operating costs. Nonetheless, this interest is not nearly as strong as the direct growth interests of developers, mortgage bankers, etc., and thus we find, as Schulze (1961) has observed, that there is a tendency for such executives to play a lesser local role than the parochial, home-grown businessmen whom they often replace.

Thus, because the city is a growth machine, it draws a special sort of person into its politics. These people—whether acting on their own or on behalf of the constituency which financed their rise to power—tend to be businessmen and, among businessmen, the more parochial sort. Typically, they come to politics not to save or destroy the environment, not to repress or liberate the blacks, not to eliminate civil liberties or enhance them. They may end up doing any or all of these things once they have achieved access to authority, perhaps as an inadvertent consequence of making decisions in other realms. But these types of symbolic positions are derived from the fact of having power—they are typically not the dynamics which bring people to power in the first place. Thus, people often become "involved" in government, especially in the local party structure and fund raising, for reasons of land business and related processes of resource distribution. Some are "states-men" who think in terms of the growth of the whole community rather than that of a more narrow geographical delimitation. But they are there to wheel and deal to affect resource distribution through local government. As a result of their position, and in part to develop the symbolic issues which will enable them (in lieu of one of their opponents or colleagues) to maintain that position of power, they get interested in such things as welfare cheating, busing, street crime, and the price of meat. This interest in the symbolic issues (see Edelman 1964) is thus substantially an aftereffect of a need for power for other purposes. This is not to say that such people don't "feel strongly" about these matters—they do sometimes. It is also the case that certain moral zealots and "concerned citizens" go into politics to right symbolic wrongs; but the money and other supports which make them viable as politicians is usually nonsymbolic money.

Those who come to the forefront of local government (and those to whom they are directly responsive), therefore, are not statistically representative of the local population as a whole, nor even representative of the social classes which produce them. The issues they introduce into public discourse are not representative either. As noted by Edelman, the distributive issues, the matters which bring people to power, are more or less deliberately dropped from public discourse (see Schattschneider 1960). The issues which are allowed to be discussed and the positions which the politicians take on them derive from the world views of those who come from certain sectors of the business and professional class and the need which they have to whip up public sentiment without allowing distributive issues to become part of public discussion. It follows that any political change which succeeded in replacing the land business as the key determinant of the local political dynamic would simultaneously weaken the power of one of the more reactionary political forces in the society, thereby affecting outcomes with respect to those other symbolic issues which manage to gain so much attention. Thus, should such a change occur, there would likely be more progressive positions taken on civil liberties, and less harassment of welfare recipients, social "deviants," and other defenseless victims.

LIABILITIES OF THE GROWTH MACHINE

Emerging trends are tending to enervate the locality growth machines. First is the increasing suspicion that in many areas, at many historical moments, growth benefits only a small proportion of local residents. Growth almost always brings with it the obvious problems of increased air and water pollution, traffic congestion, and overtaxing of natural amenities. These dysfunctions become increasingly important and visible as increased consumer income fulfills people's other needs and as the natural cleansing capacities of the environment are progressively overcome with deleterious material. While it is by no means certain that growth and increased density inevitably bring about social pathologies (see Fischer, Baldassare, and Ofshe 1974), growth does make such pathologies more difficult to deal with. For example, the larger the jurisdiction, the more difficult it becomes to achieve the goal of school integration without massive busing schemes. As increasing experience with busing makes clear, small towns can more easily have interracial schools, whether fortuitously through spatial proximity or through managed programs.

In addition, the weight of research evidence is that growth often costs existing residents more money. Evidently, at various population levels, points of diminishing returns are crossed such that additional increments lead to net revenue losses. A 1970 study for the city of Palo Alto, California, indicated that it was substantially cheaper for that city to acquire at full market value its foothill open space than to allow it to become an "addition" to the tax base (Livingston and Blayney 1971). A study of Santa Barbara, California, demonstrated that additional population growth would require higher property taxes, as well as higher utility costs (Appelbaum et al. 1974). Similar results on the costs of growth have been obtained in studies of Boulder, Colorado (cited in Finkler 1972), and Ann Arbor, Michigan (Ann Arbor City Planning Department 1972).[14] Systematic analyses of government costs as a function of city size and growth have been carried out under a number of methodologies, but the use of the units of analysis most appropriate for comparison (urban areas) yields the finding that the cost is directly related both to size of place and rate of growth, at least for middle-size cities (see Follett 1976; Appelbaum 1976). Especially significant are per capita police costs, which virtually all studies show to be positively related to both city size and rate of growth (see Appelbaum et al. 1974; Appelbaum 1976).

Although damage to the physical environment and costs of utilities and governmental services may rise with size of settlement, "optimal" size is obviously determined by the sorts of values which are to be maximized (see Duncan 1957). It may indeed be necessary to sacrifice clean air to accumulate a population base large enough to support a major opera company. But the essential point remains that growth is certainly less of a financial advantage to the taxpayer than is conventionally depicted, and that most people's values are, according to the survey evidence (Hoch 1972, p. 280; Finkler 1972, pp. 2, 23; Parke and Westoff 1972; Mazie and Rowlings 1973; Appelbaum et al. 1974, pp. 4.2–4.6) more consistent with small places than large. Indeed, it is rather clear that some substantial portion of the migrations to the great metropolitan areas of the last decade has been more in spite of people's values than because of them. In the recent words of Sundquist: "The notion commonly expressed that Americans have 'voted with their feet' in favor of the great cities is, on the basis of every available sampling, so much nonsense. . . . What is called 'freedom of choice' is, in sum, freedom of employer choice or, more precisely, freedom of choice for that segment of the corporate world that operates mobile enterprises. The real question, then, is whether freedom of corporate choice should be automatically honored by government policy at the expense of freedom of individual choice where those conflict" (1975, p. 258).

Taking all the evidence together, it is certainly a rather conservative statement to make that under many circumstances growth is a liability financially and in quality of life for the majority of local residents. Under such circumstances, local growth is a transfer of quality of life and wealth from the local general public to a certain segment of the local elite. To raise the question of wisdom of growth in regard to any specific locality is hence potentially to threaten such a wealth transfer and the interests of those who profit by it.

THE PROBLEMS OF JOBS

Perhaps the key ideological prop for the growth machine, especially in terms of sustaining support from the working-class majority (Levison 1974), is the claim that growth "makes jobs". This claim is aggressively promulgated by developers, builders, and chambers of commerce; it becomes a part of the statesman talk of editorialists and political officials. Such people do not speak of growth as useful to profits—rather, they speak of it as necessary for making jobs. But local growth does not, of course, make jobs: it distributes jobs. The United States will see next year the construction of a certain number of new factories, office units, and highways—regardless of where they are put. Similarly, a given number of automobiles, missiles, and lampshades will be made, regardless of where they are manufactured. Thus, the number of jobs in this society, whether in the building trades or any other economic sector, will be determined by rates of investment return, federal decisions affecting the money supply, and other factors having very little to do with local decision making. All that a locality can do is to attempt to guarantee that a certain proportion of newly created jobs will be in the locality in question. Aggregate employment is thus unaffected by the outcome of this competition among localities to "make" jobs.

The labor force is essentially a single national pool; workers are mobile and generally capable of taking advantage of employment opportunities emerging at geographically distant points.[15] As jobs develop in a fast-growing area, the unemployed will be attracted from other areas in sufficient numbers not only to fill those developing vacancies but also to form a work-force sector that is continuously unemployed. Thus, just as local growth does not affect aggregate employment, it likely has very little long-term impact upon the local rate of unemployment. Again, the systematic evidence fails to show any advantage to growth: there is no tendency for either larger places or more rapidly growing ones to have lower unemployment rates than other kinds of urban areas. In fact, the tendency is for rapid growth to be associated with higher rates of unemployment (for general documentation, see Follett 1976; Appelbaum 1976; Hadden and Borgatta 1965, p. 108; Samuelson 1942; Sierra Club of San Diego 1973).[16]

This pattern of findings is vividly illustrated through inspection of relevant data on the most extreme cases of urban growth: Those SMSAs which experienced the most rapid rates of population increase over the last two intercensus decades. Tables 1 and 2 show a comparison of population growth and unemployment rates in the 25 areas which grew fastest during the 1950–60 and 1960–70 periods. In the case of both decade comparisons, half of the urban areas had unemployment rates above the national figure for all SMSAs.

Even the 25 slowest-growing (1960–70) SMSAs failed to experience particularly high rates of unemployment. Table 3 reveals that although all were places of net migration loss less than half of the SMSAs of this group had unemployment rates above the national mean at the decade's end.

Just as striking is the comparison of growth and unemployment rates for all SMSAs in California during the 1960–66 period—a time of general boom in the state. Table 4 reveals that among all California metropolitan areas there is no significant relationship ($r = -17$, $z = .569$) between 1960–66 growth rates and the 1966 unemployment rate. Table 4 is also instructive (and consistent with other tables) in revealing that while there is a wide divergence in growth rates across metropolitan areas, there is no comparable variation in the unemployment rates, all of which cluster within the relatively narrow range of 4.3%–6.5%. Consistent with my previous argument, I take this as evidence that the mobility of labor tends to flatten out cross-SMSA unemployment rates, regardless of widely diverging rates of locality growth. Taken together, the data indicate that local population growth is no solution to the problem of local unemployment.

It remains possible that for some reason certain specific rates of growth may be peculiarly related to lower rates of unemployment and that the measures used in this and cited studies are insensitive to these patterns.

TABLE 1

Growth and Unemployment Rates for 25 Fastest-Growing SMSAs, 1950–60
(%)

Metropolitan Area	Rate of Growth	Unemployment Rate, 1960
1. Ft. Lauderdale-Hollywood, Fla.	297.9	4.7
2. Anaheim-Santa Ana-Garden Grove, Calif.	225.6	4.6
3. Las Vegas, Nev.	163.0	6.7*
4. Midland, Tex.	162.6	4.9
5. Orlando, Fla.	124.6	5.1
6. San Jose, Calif.	121.1	7.0*
7. Odessa, Tex.	116.1	5.6*
8. Phoenix, Ariz.	100.0	4.7
9. W. Palm Beach, Fla.	98.9	4.8
10. Colorado Springs, Colo.	92.9	6.1*
11. Miami, Fla.	88.9	7.3*
12. Tampa-St. Petersburg, Fla.	88.8	5.1
13. Tucson, Ariz.	88.1	5.9*
14. Albuquerque, N. Mex.	80.0	4.5
15. San Bernadino-Riverside-Ontario, Calif.	79.3	6.7*
16. Sacramento, Calif.	74.0	6.1*
17. Albany, Ga.	73.5	4.4
18. Santa Barbara, Calif.	72.0	3.6
19. Amarillo, Tex.	71.6	3.3
20. Reno, Nev.	68.8	6.1*
21. Lawton, Okla.	64.6	5.5*
22. Lake Charles, La.	62.3	7.8*
23. El Paso, Tex.	61.1	6.4*
24. Pensacola, Fla.	54.9	5.3*
25. Lubbock, Tex.	54.7	3.9
Total U.S.	18.5	5.2

Source—U.S. Bureau of the Census 1962, tables 33, 154.
*Unemployment rate above SMSA national mean.

Similarly, growth in certain types of industries may be more likely than growth in others to stimulate employment without attracting migrants. It may also be possible that certain population groups, by reason of cultural milieu, are less responsive to mobility options than others and thus provide bases for exceptions to the general argument I am advancing. The present analysis does not preclude such future findings but does assert, minimally, that the argument that growth makes jobs is contradicted by the weight of evidence that is available.[17]

I conclude that for the average worker in a fast-growing region job security has much the same status as for a worker in a slower-growing region: there is a surplus of workers over jobs, generating continuous anxiety over unemployment[18] and the effective depressant on wages which any lumpenproletariat of unemployed and marginally employed tends to exact (see, e.g., Bonacich 1975). Indigenous workers likely receive little benefit from the growth machine in terms of jobs; their "native" status gives them little edge over the "foreign" migrants seeking the additional jobs which may develop. Instead, they are interchangeable parts of the labor pool, and the degree of their job insecurity is expressed in the local unemployment rate, just as is the case for the nonnative worker. Ironically, it is probably

TABLE 2

Growth and Unemployment Rates of the 25 Fastest-Growing SMSAs, 1960–70
(%)

Metropolitan Area	Rate of Growth	Unemployment Rate, 1970
1. Las Vegas, Nev.	115.2	5.2*
2. Anaheim-Santa Ana-Garden Grove, Calif.	101.8	5.4*
3. Oxnard-Ventura, Calif.	89.0	5.9*
4. Ft. Lauderdale-Hollywood, Fla.	85.7	3.4
5. San Jose, Calif.	65.8	5.8*
6. Colorado Springs, Colo.	64.2	5.5*
7. Santa Barbara, Calif.	56.4	6.4*
8. W. Palm Beach, Fla.	52.9	3.0
9. Nashua, N.H.	47.8	2.8
10. Huntsville, Ala.	46.6	4.4
11. Columbia, Mo.	45.8	2.4
12. Phoenix, Ariz.	45.8	3.9
13. Danbury, Conn.	44.3	4.2
14. Fayetteville, Ark.	42.9	5.2*
15. Reno, Nev.	42.9	6.2*
16. San Bernadino-Riverside-Ontario, Calif.	41.2	5.9*
17. Houston, Tex.	40.0	3.0
18. Austin, Tex.	39.3	3.1
19. Dallas, Tex.	39.0	3.0
20. Santa Rosa, Calif.	39.0	7.3*
21. Tallahassee, Fla.	38.8	3.0
22. Washington, D.C.	37.8	2.7
23. Atlanta, Ga.	36.7	3.0
24. Ann Arbor, Mich.	35.8	5.0*
25. Miami, Fla.	35.6	3.7
Total U.S.	16.6	4.3

Source—U.S. Bureau of the Census 1972, table 3, SMSAs.
*Unemployment rate above the SMSA national mean.

this very anxiety which often leads workers, or at least their union spokespeople, to support enthusiastically employers' preferred policies of growth. It is the case that an actual decline in local job opportunities, or economic growth not in proportion to natural increase, might induce the hardship of migration. But this price is not the same as, and is less severe than, the price of simple unemployment. It could also rather easily be compensated through a relocation subsidy for mobile workers, as is now commonly provided for high-salaried executives by private corporations and in a limited way generally by the federal tax deduction for job-related moving expenses.

TABLE 3

Growth, Unemployment, and Net Migration Rates for the 25 Slowest-Growing SMSAs, 1960–70
(%)

SMSA	Rate of Growth	Net Migration	Unemployment 1970
1. Abilene, Tex.	−5.3	−19.7	3.6
2. Altoona, Pa.	−1.4	− 6.6	3.5
3. Amarillo, Tex.	−3.4	−19.5	3.4
4. Brownsville-Harlingen-San Benito, Tex.	−7.1	−32.1	6.6*
5. Charleston, W. Va.	−9.3	−19.0	4.1
6. Duluth-Superior, Minn.-Wis.	−4.1	−10.9	7.3*
7. Gadsden, Ala.	−2.9	−12.4	7.3*
8. Huntington-Ashland, W. Va.–Ky.–Ohio	−0.4	− 9.7	5.1*
9. Jersey City, N.J.	−0.5	− 7.5	4.7*
10. Johnstown, Pa.	−6.4	−11.8	4.9*
11. McAllen-Pharr-Edinburgh, Tex.	−0.3	−25.4	5.9*
12. Midland, Tex.	3.4	−19.1	3.5
13. Montgomery, Ala.	0.9	−11.1	3.8
14. Odessa, Tex.	0.9	−16.7	4.3
15. Pittsburgh, Pa.	−0.2	− 7.0	4.3
16. Pueblo, Colo.	−0.4	−12.3	5.9*
17. St. Joseph, Mo.	−4.0	− 9.2	3.9
18. Savannah, Ga.	−0.3	−13.3	4.3
19. Scranton, Pa.	−0.2	− 1.8	5.2*
20. Sioux City, Iowa	−3.2	−13.5	4.4*
21. Steubenville-Weirton, Ohio–W. Va.	−1.3	− 8.9	3.7
22. Utica-Rome, N.Y.	−1.7	−11.2	5.7*
23. Wheeling, W. Va.–Ohio	−4.0	− 8.3	4.2
24. Wichita Falls, Tex.	−2.6	−15.1	4.0
25. Wilkes-Barre-Hazleton, Pa.	−1.3	− 3.5	4.0
Total U.S.	16.6	...	4.3

Source—U.S. Bureau of the Census 1972, table 3, SMSAs.
*Unemployment rate above SMSA national mean.

TABLE 4

Growth and Unemployment Rates for All California SMSAs, 1960–66

(%)

SMSA	Rate of Growth, 1960–66	Average Annual Change	Unemployment Rate, 1966
Anaheim-Santa Ana-Garden Grove	65.0	8.3	4.3
Bakersfield	11.1	1.7	5.2
Fresno	12.3	1.9	6.5
Los Angeles-Long Beach	11.9	1.9	4.5
Modesto	...	...	...
Oxnard-Ventura	68.8	8.7	6.0
Sacramento	20.0	3.0	5.2
Salinas-Monterey	15.9	2.4	6.1
San Bernadino-Riverside	27.9	4.0	6.2
San Diego	14.0	2.1	5.1
San Francisco-Oakland	11.1	1.7	4.4
San Jose	44.8	6.1	4.8
Santa Barbara	48.7	6.6	4.5
Santa Rosa	...	...	...
Stockton	12.5	1.9	6.3
Vallejo-Napa	20.6	3.0	4.4
California mean	27.47	3.80	5.25

Sources—For average annual change and rate of growth, U.S. Bureau of the Census 1969, table 2; for unemployment rate, 1966, State of California 1970, table C-10.

Workers' anxiety and its ideological consequences emerge from the larger fact that the United States is a society of constant substantial joblessness, with unemployment rates conservatively estimated by the Department of Commerce at 4%–8% of that portion of the work force defined as ordinarily active. There is thus a game of musical chairs being played at all times, with workers circulating around the country, hoping to land in an empty chair at the moment the music stops. Increasing the stock of jobs in any one place neither causes the music to stop more frequently nor increases the number of chairs relative to the number of players. The only way effectively to ameliorate this circumstance is to create a full-employment economy, a comprehensive system of drastically increased unemployment insurance, or some other device which breaks the connection between a person's having a livelihood and the remote decisions of corporate executives. Without such a development, the fear of unemployment acts to make workers politically passive (if not downright supportive) with respect to land-use policies, taxation programs, and antipollution nonenforcement schemes which, in effect, represent income transfers from the general public to various sectors of the elite (see Whitt 1975). Thus, for many reasons, workers and their leaders should organize their political might more consistently not as part of the growth coalitions of the localities in which they are situated, but rather as part of national movements which aim to provide full employment, income security, and programs for taxation, land use, and the environment which benefit the vast majority of the population. They tend not to be doing this at present.

THE PROBLEM OF NATURAL INCREASE

Localities grow in population not simply as a function of migration but also because of the fecundity of the existing population. Some means are obviously needed to provide jobs and housing to accommodate such growth—either in the immediate area or at some distant location. There are ways of handling this without compounding the environmental and budgetary problems of existing settlements. First, there are some localities which are, by many criteria, not overpopulated. Their atmospheres are clean, water supplies plentiful, and traffic congestion nonexistent. In fact, in certain places increased increments of population may spread the costs of existing road and sewer systems over a larger number of citizens or bring an increase in quality of public education by making rudimentary specialization possible. In the state of California, for example, the great bulk of the population lives on a narrow coastal belt in the southern two-thirds of the state. Thus the northern third of the state consists of a large unpopulated region rich in natural resources, including electric power and potable water. The option chosen in California, as evidenced by the state aqueduct, was to move the water from the uncrowded north to the dense, semiarid south, thus lowering the environmental qualities of both regions, and at a substantial long-term cost to the public budget. The opposite course of action was clearly an option.

The point is that there are relatively underpopulated areas in this country which do not have "natural," problems of inaccessibility, ugliness, or lack of population-support resources. Indeed, the nation's most severely depopulated areas, the towns of Appalachia, are in locales of sufficient resources and are widely regarded as aesthetically appealing; population out-migration likely decreased the aesthetic resources of both the migrants to and residents of Chicago and Detroit, while resulting in the desertion of a housing stock and utility infrastructure designed to serve a larger population. Following from my more general perspective, I see lack of population in a given area as resulting from the political economic decisions made to populate other areas instead. If the process were rendered more rational, the same investments in roads, airports, defense plants, etc., could be made to effect a very different land-use outcome. Indeed, utilization of such deliberate planning strategies is the practice in some other societies and shows some evidence of success (see Sundquist 1975); perhaps it could be made to work in the United States as well.

As a long-term problem, natural increase may well be phased out. American birth rates have been steadily decreasing for the last several years, and we are on the verge of a rate providing for zero population growth. If a stable population actually is achieved, a continuation of the present interlocal competitive system will result in the proliferation of ghost towns and unused capital stocks as the price paid for the growth of the successful competing units. This will be an even more clearly preposterous situation than the current one, which is given to produce ghost towns only on occasion.

THE EMERGING COUNTERCOALITION

Although growth has been the dominant ideology in most localities in the United States, there has always been a subversive thread of resistance. Treated as romantic, or as somehow irrational (see White and White 1962), this minority long was ignored, even in the face of accumulating journalistic portrayals of the evils of bigness. But certainly it was an easy observation to make that increased size was related to high levels of pollution, traffic congestion, and other disadvantages. Similarly, it was easy enough to observe that tax rates in large places were not generally less than those in small places; although it received little attention, evidence that per capita government costs rise with population size was provided a generation ago (see Hawley 1951). But few took note, though the very rich, somehow sensing these facts to be the case, managed to reserve for themselves small, exclusive meccas of low density by tightly imposing population ceilings (e.g., Beverly Hills, Sands Point, West Palm Beach, Lake Forest).

In recent years, however, the base of the antigrowth movement has become much broader and in some localities has reached sufficient strength to achieve at least toeholds of political power. The most prominent cases seem to be certain university cities (Palo Alto, Santa Barbara, Boulder, Ann Arbor), all of which have sponsored impact studies documenting the costs of additional growth. Other localities which have imposed growth controls tend also to be places of high amenity value (e.g., Ramapo, N.Y.; Petaluma, Calif.; Boca Raton, Fla.). The antigrowth sentiment has become an important part of the politics of a few large cities (e.g., San Diego) and has been the basis of important political careers at the state level (including the governorship) in Oregon, Colorado, and Vermont. Given the objective importance of the issue and the evidence on the general costs of growth, there is nothing to prevent antigrowth coalitions from similarly gaining power elsewhere—including those areas of the country which are generally considered to possess lower levels of amenity. Nor is there any reason, based on the facts of the matter, for these coalitions not to further broaden their base to include the great majority of the working class in the localities in which they appear.

But, like all political movements which attempt to rely upon volunteer labor to supplant political powers institutionalized through a system of vested economic interest, antigrowth movements are probably more likely to succeed in those places where volunteer reform movements have a realistic constituency—a leisured and sophisticated middle class with a tradition of broad-based activism, free from an entrenched machine. At least, this appears to be an accurate profile of those places in which the antigrowth coalitions have already matured.

Systematic studies of the social make up of the antigrowth activists are only now in progress (e.g., Fitts 1976), but it seems that the emerging countercoalition is rooted in the recent environmental movements and relies on a mixture of young activists (some are veterans of the peace and civil rights movements), middle-class professionals, and workers, all of whom see their own tax rates as well as life-styles in conflict with growth. Important in leadership roles are government employees and those who work for organizations not dependent on local expansion for profit, either directly or indirectly. In the Santa Barbara antigrowth movements, for example, much support is provided by professionals from research and electronics firms, as well as branch managers of small "high-technology" corporations. Cosmopolitan in outlook and pecuniary interest, they use the local community only as a setting for life and work, rather than as an exploitable resource. Related to this constituency are certain very wealthy people (particularly those whose wealth derives from the exploitation of nonlocal environments) who continue a tradition (with some modifications) of aristocratic conservation.[19]

Should it occur, the changes which the death of the growth machine will bring seem clear enough with respect to land-use policy. Local governmnents will establish holding capacities for their regions and then legislate, directly or indirectly, to limit population to those levels. The direction of any future development will tend to be planned to minimize negative environmental impacts. The so-called natural process (see Burgess 1925; Hoyt 1939) of land development which has given American cities their present shape will end as the political and economic foundations of such processes are undermined. Perhaps most important, industrial and business land users and their representatives will lose, at least to some extent, the effectiveness of their threat to locate elsewhere should public policies endanger the profitability they desire. As the growth machine is destroyed in many places, increasingly it will be the business interests who will be forced to make do with local policies, rather than the local populations having to bow to business wishes. New options for taxation, creative land-use programs, and new forms of urban services may thus emerge as city government comes to resemble an agency which asks what it can do for its people rather than what it can do to attract more people. More specifically, a given industrial project will perhaps be evaluated in terms of its social utility—the usefulness of the product manufactured—either to the locality or to the society at large. Production, merely for the sake of local expansion, will be less likely to occur. Hence, there will be some pressure to increase the use value of the country's production apparatus and for external costs of production to be borne internally.

When growth ceases to be an issue, some of the investments made in the political system to influence and enhance growth will no longer make sense, thus changing the basis upon which people get involved in government. We can expect that the local business elites—led by land developers and other growth-coalition forces—will tend to withdraw from local politics. This vacuum may then be filled by a more representative and, likely, less reactionary activist constituency. It is noteworthy that where antigrowth forces have established beachheads of power, their programs and policies have tended to be more progressive than their predecessors'—on all issues, not just on growth. In Colorado, for example, the environmentalist who led the successful fight against the Winter Olympics also successfully sponsored abortion reform and other important progressive causes. The environmentally based Santa Barbara "Citizens Coalition" (with city government majority control) represents a fusion of the city's traditional left and counterculture with other environmental activists. The result of the no-growth influence in localities may thus be a tendency for an increasing progressiveness in local politics. To whatever degree local politics is the bedrock upon which the national political structure rests (and there is much debate here), there may follow reforms at the national level as well. Perhaps it will then become possible to utilize national institutions to effect other policies which both solidify the death of the growth machine at the local level and create national priorities consistent with the new opportunities for urban civic life. These are speculations based upon the questionable thesis that a reform-oriented, issue-based citizens' politics can be sustained over a long period. The historical record is not consistent with this thesis; it is only emerging political trends in the most affected localities and the general irrationality of the present urban system that suggest the alternative possibility is an authentic future.

REFERENCES

Adrian, Charles R., and O. P. Williams. 1963. *Four Cities: A Study in Comparative Policy Making*. Philadelphia: University of Pennsylvania Press.

Agelasto, Michael A., II, and Patricia R. Perry. Undated. "The No Growth Controversy." Exchange Bibliography no. 519. Mimeographed. Box 229, Monticello, Ill.: Council of Planning Libraries.

Agger, Robert, Daniel Goldrich, and Bert E. Swanson. 1964. *The Rulers and the Ruled: Political Power and Impotence in American Communities*. New York: Wiley.

Alonso, William. 1964. "Location Theory." Pp. 79–81 in *Regional Development and Planning*, edited by John Friedman and William Alonso. Cambridge, Mass.: M.I.T. Press.

Ann Arbor City Planning Department. 1972. *The Ann Arbor Growth Study*. Ann Arbor, Mich.: City Planning Department.

Appelbaum, Richard. 1976. "City Size and Urban Life: A Preliminary Inquiry into Some Consequences of Growth in American Cities." *Urban Affairs Quarterly*.

Appelbaum, Richard, Jennifer Bigelow, Henry Kramer, Harvey Molotch, and Paul Relis. 1974. *Santa Barbara: The Impacts of Growth: A Report of the Santa Barbara Planning Task Force to the City of Santa Barbara*. Santa Barbara, Calif.: Office of the City Clerk. Forthcoming in abridged form as *The Effects of Urban Growth: A Population Impact Analysis:* New York: Praeger.

Banfield, Edward. 1961. *Political Influence*. New York: Macmillan.

Bartell, Ted. 1974. "Compositional Change and Attitude Change among Sierra Club Members." Mimeographed. Los Angeles: UCLA Survey Research Center.

Bonacich, Edna. 1975. "Advanced Capitalism and Black/White Race Relations in the U.S." Mimeographed. Riverside: Department of Sociology, University of California.

Bouma, Donald. 1962. "Analysis of the Social Power Position of a Real Estate Board." *Social Problems* 10 (Fall): 121–32.

Brown, Douglas. 1974. *Introduction to Urban Economics*. New York: Academic Press.

Burgess, Ernest W. 1925. *The Growth of the City: An Introduction to a Research Project*. Chicago: University of Chicago Press.

Davis, Kingsley. 1965. "The Urbanization of the Human Population." *Scientific American* 212 (September): 41–53.

Duncan, Otis Dudley. 1957. "Optimum Size of Cities." Pp. 759–72 in *Cities and Societies*, edited by Paul Hatt and Albert Reiss, Jr. New York: Free Press.

Dunlap, Riley E., and Richard P. Gale. 1972. "Politics and Ecology: A Political Profile of Student Eco-Activists." *Youth and Society* 3 (June): 379–97.

Durr, Fred. 1971. *The Urban Economy*. Scranton, Pa.: Intext.

Edelman, Murray. 1964. *The Symbolic Uses of Politics*. Urbana: University of Illinois Press.

Fagen, Richard R., and William S. Tuohy. 1972. *Politics and Privilege in a Mexican City*. Stanford, Calif.: Stanford University Press.

Faich, Ronald G., and Richard Gale. 1971. "Environmental Movement: From Recreation to Politics." *Pacific Sociological Review* 14 (July): 270–87.

Finkler, Earl. 1972. "No-Growth as a Planning Alternative." *Planning Advisory Report No. 283*. Chicago: American Society of Planning Officials.

Fischer, Claud, Mark Baldassare, and Richard J. Ofshe. 1974. "Crowding Studies and Urban Life: A Critical Review." Working Paper no. 242, Institute of Urban and Regional Development, University of California, Berkeley.

Fitts, Amelia. 1976. "No-Growth as a Political Issue." Ph.D. dissertation, University of California, Los Angeles.

Follett, Ross. 1976, "Social Consequences of Urban Size and Growth: An Analysis of Middle-Size U.S. Urban Areas." Ph.D. dissertation, Department of Sociology, University of California, Santa Barbara.

Gruen and Gruen Associates. 1972. *Impacts of Growth: An Analytical Framework and Fiscal Examples*. Berkeley: California Better Housing Foundation.

Hadden, Jeffrey K., and Edgar F. Borgatta. 1965. *American Cities: Their Social Characteristics*. Chicago: Rand-McNally.

Harris, Carl V. 1976. *Political Power in Birmingham, 1871–1921*. Memphis: University of Tennessee Press.

Hawley, Amos. 1951. "Metropolitan Population and Municipal Government Expenditures in Central Cities." *Journal of Social Issues* 7 (January): 100–108.

Hoch, Irving. 1972. "Urban Scale and Environmental Quality." Pp. 231–84 in *Population, Resources and the Environment*. U.S. Commission on Population Growth and the American Future Research Reports, edited by Ronald Ridker, vol. 3. Washington, D.C.: Government Printing Office.

Hoyt, Homer. 1939. *The Structure and Growth of Residential Neighborhoods in American Cities*. Washington, D.C.: Federal Housing Administration.

Lasswell, Harold. 1936. *Politics: Who Gets What, When, How*. New York: McGraw-Hill.

Leven, Charles. 1964. "Regional and Interregional Accounts in Perspective." *Papers, Regional Science Association* 13: 140–44.

Levison, Andrew. 1974. *The Working Class Majority*. New York: Coward, McCann & Geoghgan.

Levy, Steven, and Robert K. Arnold. 1972. "An Evaluation of Four Growth Alternatives in the City of Milpitas, 1972–1977." Technical Memorandum Report. Palo Alto, Calif.: Institute of Regional and Urban Studies.

Livingston, Laurence, and John A. Blayney. 1971. "Foothill Environmental Design Study: Open Space vs. Development." Final Report to the City of Palo Alto. San Francisco: Livingston & Blayney.

McConnell, Grant. 1966. *Private Power and American Democracy*. New York: Knopf.

McKenzie, R. D. 1922. "The Neighborhood: A Study of Local Life in the City of Columbus, Ohio—*Conclusion*." *American Journal of Sociology* 27 (May): 780–99.

Makielski, S. J., Jr. 1966. *The Politics of Zoning: The New York Experience*. New York: Columbia University Press.

Mazie, Sara Mills, and Steve Rowlings. 1973. "Public Attitude toward Population Distribution Issues." Pp. 603–15 in *Population Distribution and Policy*, edited by Sara Mazie. Washington, D.C.: Commission on Population Growth and the American Future.

Molotch, Harvey L. 1967. "Toward a More Human Ecology." *Land Economics* 43 (August): 336–41.

————. 1973. *Managed Integration: Dilemmas of Doing Good in the City*. Berkeley: University of California Press.

Mumford, Lewis. 1961. *The City in History*. New York: Harcourt Brace Jovanovich.

Nash, Roderick. 1967. *Wilderness and the American Mind*. New Haven, Conn.: Yale University Press.

Parke, Robert, Jr., and Charles Westoff, eds. 1972. "Aspects of Population Growth Policy." Report of the U.S. Commission on Population Growth and the American Future. Vol. 6. Washington, D.C.: Commission on Population Growth and the American Future.

Piven, Francis Fox, and Richard Cloward. 1972. *Regulating the Poor*. New York: Random House.

Reilly, William K., ed. 1973. *The Use of Land: A Citizens' Policy Guide to Urban Growth*. New York: Crowell.

Rubin, Lillian. 1972. *Busing and Backlash*. Berkeley: University of California Press.

Samuelson, Paul. 1942. "The Business Cycle and Urban Development." Pp. 6–17 in *The Problem of the Cities and Towns*, edited by Guy Greer. Cambridge, Mass.: Harvard University Press.

Schattschneider, E. E. 1960. *The Semisovereign People*. New York: Holt, Rinehart and Winston.

Schulze, Robert O. 1961. "The Bifurcation of Power in a Satellite City." Pp. 19–80 in *Community Political Systems*, edited by Morris Janowitz. New York: Macmillan.

Sierra Club of San Diego. 1973. "Economy, Ecology, and Rapid Population Growth." Mimeographed. San Diego: Sierra Club.

Spaulding, Charles. 1951. "Occupational Affiliations of Councilmen in Small Cities." *Sociology and Social Research* 35 (3): 194–200.

State of California. 1970. *California Statistical Abstract, 1970*. Sacramento: State of California.

Sundquist, James. 1975. *Dispersing Population: What America Can Learn from Europe*. Washington, D.C.: Brookings.

Suttles, Gerald. 1972. *The Social Construction of Communities*. Chicago: University of Chicago Press.

Tolchin, Martin, and Susan Tolchin. 1971. *To the Victor*. New York: Random House.

U.S. Bureau of the Census. 1962. *Census of Population*. Vol. 1, pt. 1. Washington, D.C.: Government Printing Office.

————. 1969. *Current Population Reports, Population Estimates and Projections*. Series P–25, no. 427 (July 31). Washington, D.C.: Government Printing Office.

————. 1972. *County and City Data Book*. Washington, D.C.: Government Printing Office.

Wade, Richard. 1969. *The Urban Frontier: The Rise of Western Cities*. Cambridge, Mass.: Harvard University Press.

Walton, John. 1970. "A Systematic Survey of Community Power Research." Pp. 443–64 in *The Structure of Community Power*, edited by Michael Aiken and Paul Mott. New York: Random House.

White, Morton, and Lucie White. 1962. *The Intellectual versus the City*. Cambridge, Mass.: Harvard and M.I.T. Press.

Whitt, J. Allen. 1975. "Means of Movement: The Politics of Modern Transportation Systems." Ph.D. dissertation, Department of Sociology, University of California, Santa Barbara.

Wirth, Louis. 1938. "Urbanism as a Way of Life." *American Journal of Sociology* 44 (July): 1–14.

Wyner, Allen. 1967. "Governor—Salesman." *National Civic Review* 61 (February): 81–86.

=== **NOTES**

1. I have had the benefit of critical comments and assistance from Richard Appelbaum, Richard Baisden, Norman Bowers, Norton Long, Howard Newby, Anthony Shih, Tony Pepitone, Gerald Suttles, Gaye Tuchman, and Al Wyner.

2. This association of related phenomena is the common conceptualization which students of the economic development of cities ordinarily utilize in their analyses (see, e.g., Alonso 1964, pp. 79–81; Leven 1964, pp. 140–44; Brown 1974, pp. 48–51; and Durr 1971, pp. 174–80). As Sunquist remarks in the context of his study of population policies in Western Europe, "The key to population distribution is, of course, job availability. A few persons—retired, notably, and some independent professionals such as artists, writers and inventors—may be free to live in any locality they choose but, for the rest, people are compelled to distribute themselves in whatever pattern is dictated by the distribution of employment opportunities. Some investors may locate their investment in areas of surplus labour voluntarily, and so check the migration flow, and others may be induced by government assistance to do so. But if neither of these happens—if the jobs do not go where the workers are—the workers must go to the jobs, if they are not to accept welfare as a way of life. When population distribution is an end, then, job distribution is inevitably the means" (1975, p. 13).

3. For accounts of how "boosterism" worked in this manner, see Wade (1969) and Harris (1976).

4. Agger et al. remark, on the basis of their comparative study of four U.S. cities: "[Members of the local elites] value highly harmony and unity—'pulling together.' They regard local community affairs as essentially nonpolitical, and tend to associate controversy with 'politics.' An additional factor reinforcing the value of harmony in many communities . . . is the nationwide competition among communities for new industries. Conflict is thought to create a highly unfavourable image to outsiders, an image that might well repel any prospective industry" (1964, p. 649).

5. See, e.g., the May 19, 1974, issue of *Forbes,* which had the following ad placed by the State of Pennsylvania: "Q: [banner headline] What state could possibly cut taxes at a time like this? A: Pennsylvania [same large type]. Pennsylvania intends to keep showing businessmen that it means business. Pennsylvania. Where business has a lot growing for it.

. . ." The state of Maryland ran this ad in the same issue: "Maryland Finances the Training. . . . In short, we can finance practically everything you need to establish a manufacturing plant. . . ."

6. The city of Los Angeles maintains an office, headed by a former key business executive, with this "liaison" role as its specific task (see "L.A.'s Business Envoy Speaks Softly and Sits at a Big Desk," *Los Angeles Times* [August 26, 1974]).

7. The literature on community power is vast and controversial but has been summarized by Walton: he indicates, on the basis of 39 studies of 61 communities, that "the proportion of businessmen found in the leadership group is high irrespective of the type of power structure found" (1970, p. 446). It is my argument, of course, that this high level of participation does indeed indicate the exercise of power on behalf of at least a portion of the elite. My analysis does not assume that this portion of the elite is necessarily always united with others of high status on the concrete issues of local land use and the uses of local government.

8. Descriptions of some tactics typically employed in land-use politics are contained in McConnell (1966). Tolchin and Tolchin (1971), and Makielski (1966), but a sophisticated relevant body of literature does not yet exist.

9. Thus the stance taken by civic business groups toward growth and land-use matters affecting growth is consistently positive, although the *intensity* of commitment to that goal varies. In his study of New York City zoning, Makielski indicates that "the general business groups . . . approached zoning from an economic viewpoint, although this often led them to share the Reformer's ideology. Their economic interest in the city gave them a stake in a 'healthy,' 'growing community' where tax rates were not prohibitive, where city government was 'efficient,' and where some of the problems of the urban environment—a constricting labour force, congestion, and lack of space—were being attacked" (1966, p. 141). A similar dynamic has been observed in a medium-size Mexican city: "Despite many other differences, basic agreement on the primacy of stability and growth provides a basis for a dialogue between government and business" (Fagen and Tuohy 1972, p. 56).

10. Bruce Pringle suggested the latter phrase to me.

11. Papers can expand into other industries, such as book publishing and wood harvesting. The point is that, compared with most other industries, they cannot easily replicate themselves across geographical boundaries through chains, branch plants, and franchises.

12. In some cities (e.g., Chicago) it is the political machine that performs this function and thus can "get things done." Political scientists (e.g., Edward Banfield) often identify success in performing this function as evidence of effective local government.

13. In his study of the history of zoning in New York City, Makielski remarks: "While the newspapers in the city are large landholders, the role of the press was not quite like that of any of the other nongovernmental actors. The press was in part one of the referees of the rules of the game, especially the informal rules—calling attention to what it considered violations" (1966, p. 189).

14. A useful bibliography of growth evaluation studies is Agelasto and Perry (undated). A study with findings contrary to those reported here (Gruen and Gruen Associates 1972) limits cost evaluation to only three municipal services and was carried out in a city which

had already made major capital expenditures that provided it with huge unused capacities in water, schools, and sewage.

15. I am not arguing that the labor force is perfectly mobile, as indeed there is strong evidence that mobility is limited by imperfect information, skill limitations, and cultural and family ties. The argument is rather that the essential mobility of the labor force is sufficiently pronounced to make programs of local job creation largely irrelevant to long-term rates of unemployment.

16. This lack of relationship between local population change and unemployment has led others to conclusions similar to my own: "Economists unanimously have agreed that the only jurisdiction that should be concerned with the effects of its policies on the level of employment is the Federal government. Small jurisdictions do not have the power to effect significant changes in the level of unemployment" (Levy and Arnold 1972, p. 95).

17. It is also true that this evidence is based on federal data, accumulated through the work of socially and geographically disparate persons who had purposes at hand different from mine. This important reservation can only be dealt with by noting that the findings were consistent with the author's theoretical expectations, rather than antecedents of them. At a minimum, the results throw the burden of proof on those who would argue the opposite hypothesis.

18. For an insightful treatment of joblessness with respect to the majority of the American work force, see Levison (1974).

19. Descriptions of the social makeup of American environmentalists (who coincide as a group only roughly with the no-growth activists) and of their increasing militancy are contained in Nash (1967), Bartell (1974), Dunlap and Gale (1972), Faich and Gale (1971). For a journalistic survey of no-growth activities, see Robert Cahn, "Mr. Developer, Someone is Watching You" (*Christian Science Monitor* [May 21, 1973], p. 9). A more comprehensive description is contained in Reilly (1973).

Cleavages, Coalitions, and the Black Candidate: The Los Angeles Mayoralty Elections of 1969 and 1973

HARLAN HAHN, DAVID KLINGMAN, and HARRY PACHON

One of the most significant emerging trends in electoral politics is the increased appearance of minority candidates for public office, especially at the local level. Between 1965 and 1975, representatives of many disadvantaged groups including blacks, chicanos, women, Asian- and native-Americans have arisen as nominees for major elective positions. Although attempts to compare these movements with prior ethnic or nationality groups have produced some controversy,[1] perhaps even more important has been electoral reaction to the growth of minority and black political influence in American cities.

Mounting efforts to achieve major political goals for black Americans have probably been most clearly reflected in the increasing number of black candidates for leadership positions in urban areas. In 1969, when Thomas Bradley first sought the office of Mayor of Los Angeles, there were only 29 black mayors in the United States; and only 2, Carl Stokes and Richard Hatcher, served in large cities.[2] By 1974, however, there were 107 black mayors, including Bradley; and several of them were elected in big cities like Los Angeles, Atlanta, Detroit, and Newark, as well as in smaller communities such as Raleigh, North Carolina; Dayton, Ohio; Pontiac, Michigan; East St. Louis, Illinois; and East Orange, New Jersey.[3] Within another decade or two, it is likely that a majority of the mayors in the nation's largest cities will be black.

Yet, the emergence of black mayors can be attributed more to the growth of the black population in cities[4] than to the approval or receptivity of white voters. In 1967, when Stokes and Hatcher were victorious, they received only 19 and 15 percent of the white vote in Cleveland and Gary, respectively. Although subsequently Stokes managed to increase his margin in the white community by 4 percent, and Hatcher by 7 percent, both candidates were running as Democratic nominees in predominantly Democratic cities.[5] Similarly, in Detroit, black mayoralty candidate Richard Austin received only 18 or 19 percent of the white vote in 1969;[6] and his counterpart, Coleman Young, may have drawn an even smaller vote among whites when he won in 1973.[7] In the same year, Maynard Jackson, successful black candidate for mayor of Atlanta, polled only 23 percent of the white vote in that city.[8] Perhaps most notably, Kenneth Gibson, the winning black candidate for mayor of Newark in 1970, drew only 16 or 17 percent of the white vote against incumbent Hugh Addonizio, who was under federal indictment for extortion and income tax evasion.[9] In each of the cities, the victory of black candidates could be attributed to the large black percentage of the population, which ranged from approximately 37 percent in Cleveland to 48 percent in Newark; to intensive black voter registration drives; to high turnout in the black community; and to the cohesion of black voters, who cast from 88 to 97 percent of their ballots for black candidates in these elections. White voters did not contribute significantly to the support of any of these black mayors. In fact, "in most cases, black candidates have been unable to capture more than 25 percent of the white vote."[10]

Both the growing importance of black politics in urban areas and the racial polarization reflected in these votes, therefore, provide the Los Angeles mayoralty elections of 1969 and 1973 with special theoretical and political significance. Unlike the other cities, black residents comprise only 15 to 18 percent of the population of Los Angeles. Yet, in both elections, black city councilman Thomas Bradley was a major contender for mayor. The election of Bradley in 1973 constituted the first victory of a black candidate for mayor in a predominantly white city in the United States.

The candidacy of a black leader for the highest office in the nation's third largest city had a far-reaching effect upon the nature of political conflict in many other cities. Bradley's quest stirred the ambitions of black leaders elsewhere; and many of them were no longer content to cast their support to white candidates or to accept the leadership of white politicians. Illustrative of the impact which Bradley's first nomination had upon other cities is the observation of former Atlanta mayor Ivan Allen, Jr., who presided for many years over a progressive alliance of white business interests and black voters:

> Ironically, events clear across the country—in Los Angeles—soon were to tear the roof off Atlanta's black community. In the mayoralty primary there, a black ex-policeman named Tom Bradley ran very strongly against incumbent Sam Yorty. This, regardless of what anyone says, changed the entire attitude of the black electorate in Atlanta. Bradley's strong showing caused Atlanta's black leaders to feel they had made a mistake this time in wanting to work hand-in-hand as they always had with the "white power structure." . . . If a Negro can make a showing like that in Los Angeles, they began to say to themselves, a Negro can be elected mayor of Atlanta. It was at this point that negotiations broke down between me and the black leadership of the city.[11]

Perhaps even more important than Bradley's showing in the first elections was his victory at the polls four years later, which appeared to prove that a black candidate could entertain some hopes of political success even in a white constituency. Although California voters have elected black leaders to such major offices as State Superintendent of Schools and Lieutenant Governor, both before and since the 1973 vote, Bradley's election as mayor seemed to symbolize the promise of a solution to persistent urban problems. For many, his win raised the hope that polarization had subsided and that racial integration and harmony could be brought to American cities.

The elections in Los Angeles also have major theoretical significance for social scientists. They appear to demonstrate that a black candidate could attract the support of substantial segments of the white electorate. Perhaps even more importantly, they raise the possibility of an informal electoral coalition between black and white voters. Obviously, in an overwhelmingly white city, black politicians cannot expect to gain a majority solely on the strength of the black vote. In addition to the united support of the black community, they require at least minimal assistance from major sectors of the white electorate. Hence, the election returns from Los Angeles can be examined in an effort to determine, in various circumstances, which segments of the white community might form a coalition with minority voters in behalf of black candidates for high elective office.

In an earlier study based upon three cities in the South, Holloway identified three major types of alliances between black and white voters.[12] The "conservative coalition" was the linkage between the black community and powerful white business and financial interests in Atlanta, which may have collapsed under the weight of Bradley's candidacy in Los Angeles.[13] A technique entailing "independent power politics" developed in Memphis in which concessions were sought in exchange for a cohesive black vote.[14] Although this approach might amount to a coalition when it results in the delivery of a large bloc of black votes to a white politician, it also may be used as a truly independent basis of black political strength when white votes are either unnecessary to secure a majority or seemingly impossible to obtain.[15] Finally, in Houston, a "liberal coalition" has emerged in an attempt to unite black voters with low-income whites, labor unions, chicanos, and white or Anglo liberals from the business and professional world.[16] Although the "independent power politics" strategy seems to be based essentially upon social cleavages, both the "conservative" and "liberal" coalitions reflect some important and contrasting implications concerning the association between social attitudes and socioeconomic status among whites.

Prior research on social class and racial prejudice or attitudes toward black candidates frequently has failed to yield clear or consistent results.[17] Although some studies have indicated that racial prejudice tends to decline as socioeconomic status increases,[18] later research has sharply challenged that conclusion.[19] Relatively low-status whites of equivalent education may be less likely to endorse discriminatory practices than middle- or upper-middle-class whites;[20] and low-income white neighborhoods often have given less support to segregationist politicians such as George Wallace than have upper-class areas.[21] In general, measures of racial prejudice seem to be closely related to voting for black candidates.[22] Yet, one survey of white attitudes toward the candidacy of Senator Edward W. Brooke in Massachusetts concluded that "the 'most prejudiced' were distributed relatively evenly throughout all important demographic groups, suggesting that racial prejudice is a phenomenon that is determined only in part by socioeconomic status."[23] In fact, the prior study of voting in the 1969 Los Angeles election failed to show a strong direct relationship between median income or education and support for Bradley, when the proportion of non-white residents was controlled.[24] When this control was introduced, the association between those variables was very weak, although slightly positive. It should be noted that this correlation is different from the inverse relationship which was printed in the prior article about the 1969 election due to a technical error; namely, a data card placed out of order in the original computer run. (See "The First Bradley-Yorty Election: A Reanalysis of a Reconsideration," pp. 645–46 of this issue.) Hence, the interpretation offered in the prior article, based on an inverse correlation, is not supported by the reanalysis of those data, which are reported in this study. However, this discrepancy does not substantially affect the analysis of the direction of change in voting patterns between the 1969 and 1973 elections.

The association between socioeconomic status and support for black candidates has crucial implications both for the type of coalition that black voters might attempt to form with segments of the white community and for the political strategies that black candidates might employ in seeking to gain election in a predominantly white constituency. The necessity of an "independent power politics" strategy would be demonstrated by a perfect correlation, unaffected by control variables, between social characteristics and the vote for a black candidate. A simple and direct association between support for a black candidate and increasing socioeconomic status among whites could provide strong evidence of the feasibility of a "conservative coalition" between black voters and high status white business interests. On the other hand, there are at least three different electoral patterns that might be involved in a "liberal coalition." Initially, a strong inverse association between measures of social class and the vote for a black candidate could imply a need to solicit support among low-income whites. Secondly, a significant direct association between votes for a black candidate and the proportion of other minority groups in the population may indicate the desirability of concentrating attention on the development of alliances with those minorities. Third, a weak positive or essentially nonexistent association between social status and voting for a black candidate, with the effects of race removed, may indicate relatively undifferentiated support for such candidates among white voters, regardless of socioeconomic distinctions. Finally, the discovery of a direct and moderate association between support for a black candidate and social status among whites might suggest the existence of an alignment between black voters and white liberals from the business and professional classes.

Each of these possibilities for a coalition also seems both to imply and to depend upon the strategy adopted by black aspirants for public office. Black candidates who have dismissed or renounced potential white support by pursuing a strategy of "independent power politics," for example, might be expected to portray themselves as the sole and exclusive champions of the black community. By contrast, the hope of being coopted by white economic interests may be the most feasible strategy for black politicans seeking advancement through a "conservative coalition." However, there are also four optional tactics that might be followed by black leaders who attempt to mold a "liberal coalition." Black candidates could attempt to attract support from low-income whites by launching a crusade of "have-nots" who seek some of the advantages enjoyed by privileged sectors of society. This type of coalition could be promoted by the advocacy of so-called "redistributive" policies that aim to improve the position of persons at the bottom of the socioeconomic hierarchy at the expense of those who have been the traditional beneficiaries of public as well as private economic programs. However, it also entails certain political risks, not only in the possible alienation of relatively high-status liberals, but also in the potential loss of campaign contributions. Alternatively, black candidates may seek to join in a common cause with other ethnic minorities that have felt the sting of discrimination imposed by dominant white groups; but the success of this approach could depend both upon the numerical size or voting strength of other minorities in the population and upon their willingness to link their political fortunes to the goals of the black community.

Third, black aspirants for public office could attempt to dismiss racial overtones in a campaign by de-emphasizing or ignoring issues that would fan the flames of prejudice. Finally, black leaders might appeal to white liberal allies by advancing overarching programs that would benefit the entire community and by depicting themselves as legitimate and viable challengers to the persons they are opposing.

In many respects, the electoral response to black candidates probably is determined by the strategies that they pursue, the nature of the constituency in which they are running, and the particular circumstances of a specific election. Unlike other politicians who may not face the threat of a polarized electorate, black leaders are constantly confronted by the dilemma of presenting themselves as candidates who merely happen to be black or as representatives and spokesman for the black community. In many situations, their ability to play either role might be shaped both by their own actions and by the behavior of their opponents. Fundamentally, however, the strategies that they employ, especially in seeking white votes, as well as their reactions to campaign issues and events, could determine not only their prospects at the polls but also the long-term possibilities of an electoral coalition between white and black segments of the community.

The purpose of this research, therefore, is to explore the nature of electoral coalitions reflected by voting behavior in two elections which involved a prominent black candidate for mayor in a predominantly white city. No attempt is made in this study to test various theories of ethnic politics[25] or to determine the precise impact of specific campaign issues upon the changing preferences of Los Angeles voters. Instead, attention is focused upon voting patterns that might denote conflicts or alignments among various segments of the electorate. By investigating the lines of cleavage that divided the city, it is possible to make some general assessments of the informal and unorganized alliances that emerged in the 1969 and 1973 elections involving Mayor Tom Bradley.

THE LOS ANGELES MAYORALTY ELECTIONS OF 1969 AND 1973

Data for this study were obtained from two sources. First, 1973 election returns from 3,168 precincts were derived from a report tape available from the Los Angeles City Clerk. Second, socioeconomic data on census tracts were derived from the 1970 Census, Fourth Count Summary Tape. The precincts were matched with, and their data aggregated for, the corresponding census tracts.[26] Although aggregate data do not permit inferences about individual behavior,[27] they can be used to develop generalizations about the voting behavior of *electorates* with identifiable characteristics.[28] As noted in the prior study of the vote for Bradley in his first mayoralty campaign, "Since cities generally contain relatively clear residential divisions by social status as well as by ethnicity or race, this method permitted the investigation of voter reactions to candidates . . . in various *segments of the community*."[29] Moreover, this analysis allows a comprehensive examination of voting patterns or cleavages throughout the city. Both the data and the methods employed in this research, therefore, were designed to ensure comparability with the earlier study and to facilitate the comparative examination of the 1969 and 1973 mayoralty elections in Los Angeles.

The opportunity for comparison also was enhanced by the fact that, in both elections, black city councilman Tom Bradley was pitted against white incumbent Mayor Sam Yorty. In many respects, however, this was where the similarities between the two election years ended. In the 1969 primary, Los Angeles voters rejected three educational measures, including a $289 million school bond issue, a proposed $1.55 raise in the school tax rate, and a planned 10 percent increase in the tax rate to support local junior colleges. By contrast, in the primary four years later, city voters approved a plan for low-rent housing for the elderly and a $28 million junior college bond issue. Furthermore, in 1969, two self-styled "conservative" candidates, Richard Ferraro and Dr. Donald Newman, defeated two incumbent "liberal" school board members, Dr. Ralph Richardson, a white educator, and the Rev. James Jones, a black minister, respectively. A third "liberal" candidate, Dr. Robert Doctor, won a slim victory over his "conservative" challenger. In 1973, Dr. Doctor easily outpolled five candidates in the primary. But, in the 1973 "run-off" election, the two "conservatives," Ferraro and Newman, won reelection over black candidates Diane Watson and Arnett Hartsfield, respectively. At the same time, Burt Pines upset incumbent city attorney Roger Arnebergh.

Similarly, the mayor's race revealed extensive change in electoral choices both between the April primary and May "run-off" of the first election and between the 1969 and the 1973 elections. In the 1969 primary, Councilman Bradley amassed an impressive 42 percent of the city vote to lead fifteen other mayoralty candidates. A month later, he saw his margin vanish as Mayor Yorty, who had received 26 percent of the total vote in the primary, won reelection with 53 percent of the total vote in the "run-off" election. Perhaps the principal event that intervened between the two votes was Yorty's injection of the issue of race into the campaign. As public opinion polls showed him trailing badly, Yorty unleashed a series of strong attacks in which he accused Bradley of being "anti-police," of conducting a "racist" appeal for black votes, of retaining a former Communist on his staff, and of receiving the support of "militant" and "extremist" groups.[30] As a result, a social scientist who conducted surveys during this period concluded, "A detailed analysis of our post-runoff interviews reveals that many of the whites who initially favored Bradley were in fact more anti-Yorty than pro-Bradley. The election placed them in a harsh avoidance-avoidance conflict between a Mayor they did not like and a challenger whose race presented a threat."[31] The effects of Yorty's charges were evident in the difference in the mean percentage of the vote between the 1969 primary and "run-off" elections in predominantly white and chicano sections of the city. While the mean vote for Bradley increased by only 5 percent in both areas, Yorty scored a gain of 26 percentage points in chicano neighborhoods and an increase of 31 percentage points in white areas.[32]

By contrast, in the 1973 primary, Bradley again led all mayoral candidates with 35 percent of the vote, followed by Yorty with 28 percent. This campaign, however, was not marked by the racist campaign accusations that had characterized the prior election. Bradley moved to victory over Yorty by capturing 54 percent of the vote in the general election of 1973.

Between 1969 and 1973, however, some relatively gradual shifts had occurred within the Los Angeles electorate which indicated the nature of the electoral coalitions that were emerging. Table 1 presents the mean percentage of the vote for Bradley among major ethnic or racial segments of the community[33] in the general elections of 1969 and 1973.

As the mean percentages indicate, Bradley was able to obtain an almost completely unified and cohesive vote in the black community of Los Angeles in both elections. By avoiding intraracial divisions or defections, he satisfied the requirement of black solidarity, which is probably a prerequisite for any black politician who aspires to high elective office in an interracial constituency. On the other hand, the data seem to suggest the futility of any attempts, at least in these elections, to form a coalition based solely upon the votes of blacks and other minorities. Although Bradley managed to increase his margin in chicano neighborhoods by 8 percentage points and eventually to achieve a slight majority there, the vote in predominantly chicano areas of the city did not appear to be sufficiently strong or cohesive to provide a firm foundation for a united assault by minority groups upon the highest office in Los Angeles. Perhaps most importantly, however, the data indicate that a black candidate could attract substantial support among segments of the white community. Between 1969 and 1973, Bradley not only increased his proportion of the vote in white tracts by an average of 9 percentage points, but he also came within striking distance of securing a majority of that vote. Unlike other cities in which black mayoralty candidates have not been able to gain more than one-quarter of the white vote, Los Angeles seemed to provide an environment in which voters in predominantly white areas might be willing to assist black politicians in their quest for major elective positions.

TABLE 1

Mean Percentage of the Vote for Thomas Bradley for Mayor of Los Angeles by Major Ethnic or Racial Groups, 1969 and 1973

	1969	1973
Black	89%	91%
Chicano	43	51
White	37	46

Source—See n. 33.

Bradley was apparently not the only beneficiary of the combination of strong support in predominantly black areas and support from other segments of the community. In the election of the city attorney, challenger Burt Pines received an average of 68 percent of the vote in black areas, 51 percent of the vote in chicano areas, and 50 percent of the vote in white areas. Superficially, at least, it appeared that support from white neighborhoods may have provided the margin of victory for Bradley, while the vote in the black community may have been the "balance of power" in the race for city attorney which tipped that election to Pines.

VOTING PATTERNS IN THE ELECTORATE

Despite these alignments, however, an examination of the demographic correlates of the vote seems to suggest a high degree of similarity, not only between the mayoralty elections of 1969 and 1973, but also between the vote for Bradley and the vote for Pines.[34] To permit meaningful comparisons, Table 2 contains the coefficients of correlation between selected socioeconomic and ethnic characteristics and the vote for mayor in 1969 and 1973.

In both the 1969 and the 1973 elections, the demographic correlates of the vote for mayor were remarkably similar. Support for Bradley in both elections not only was directly related to the non-white proportion of the population, but it was also inversely associated with increasing social status of neighborhoods. In the two elections, neither the signs nor the magnitude of the correlations seemed to change appreciably. Perhaps the most notable feature of both analyses was the strong and direct association between the vote for Bradley and the non-white proportion of the population, which appeared to overshadow the other variables. As the percentage of non-white residents of an area increased, the vote for Bradley also increased. Furthermore, this association was not affected by socioeconomic characteristics such as income or education. As the prior study of the 1969 election noted, "The partial coefficient of correlation between the proportion of non-white persons and vote for Bradley, with income (+.83) and education (+.82) controlled, remained strong."[35] Similarly in 1973, the partial correlations between the non-white variable and the vote for Bradley, controlling on median education and median income, were both +.86. The data, therefore, did not corroborate the frequently expressed fear that the electoral choices of the middle- or upper-middle-class black areas might diverge from the voting patterns of working-class black areas, or that they might provide reduced support for black candidates. Moreover, the same pattern was evident in the 1973 vote for Pines. The partial coefficients of correlation between the percentage of non-white residents of an area and the vote for Pines, controlling for education and income, were +.71 and +.68, respectively. The strong and cohesive vote secured by Bradley among relatively high-status as well as low-income segments of the black community apparently afforded him an independent base of political strength which was transferred, in part, to Pines.

TABLE 2

Coefficients of Correlation Between Selected Socioeconomic
and Ethnic Characteristics and the Vote for Mayor of Los
Angeles, 1969 and 1973

	Percent for Bradley	
	1969	1973
Percent non-white	+.84	+.86
Percent Spanish	−.03	−.19
Median education	−.36	−.20
Median family income	−.32	−.27
Percent professional or managerial	−.34	−.31
Percent clerical or sales	−.22	−.28
Percent craftsmen or foremen	+.03	+.08
Percent laborers or service workers	+.48	+.57
Median house value	−.33	−.23

Source—See n. 33.

On the other hand, the data demonstrate little evidence of the emergence of an electoral coalition between blacks and other minorities in Los Angeles. The association between the vote for Bradley and the percentage of Spanish ethnicity not only was inverse, but this negative correlation was increased in the second election.[36] Apparently, as the proportion of chicano residents in an area increased, the percentage of the vote for Bradley declined. Unlike the vote in the black community, the analysis also suggested some indications of disunity among chicano voters. The partial coefficients of correlation between the percentage of Spanish ethnicity and the vote for Bradley, controlling on median education and income, were −.41 and −.31, respectively. Thus, when education and income were introduced as control variables, the inverse association between percent Spanish and the vote for Bradley was strengthened slightly. Similarly, the partial coefficients of correlation between percent Spanish and the vote for Pines, controlling on education, were −.35 and −.31, respectively. In predominantly chicano areas, as income and education increased, the vote for both Pines and Bradley seemed to decline. The analysis, therefore, provided some substantiation for the proposition that the principal support for Bradley and Pines in chicano areas was provided by low-income rather than by relatively high-status segments of that community.

By contrast, the simple coefficients of correlation between the vote for Bradley and various measures of socioeconomic status appeared to indicate some possibilities for the development of an alignment between low-status white and black areas. In both the 1969 and 1973 elections, increases in the indices of high social status, such as education, income, house value, and the percentage of professional, managerial, clerical, and sales personnel, were associated with declining support for Bradley. On the other hand, the percentage of laborers and service workers, which is generally regarded as an indication of low social status, was related to an increasing vote in favor of Bradley. Throughout the city, as socioeconomic status in neighborhoods increased, the vote for Bradley decreased, and vice versa.

Yet, those associations also may be influenced by the fact that blacks occupy a disproportionate share of the positions at the bottom end of the socioeconomic spectrum. In order to disentangle these factors, it is also necessary to examine the association between measures of socioeconomic status and voting, independent of the effects of the non-white percentage of the population. Table 3 reports these partial correlations for the 1969 and 1973 mayoralty elections. The findings of both analyses are compatible with the conclusions of other studies. The very weak association between measures of social status and the vote for Bradley in 1969, which were disclosed by the partial correlations, does not contradict the results of several surveys of portions of Los Angeles, including one which noted that "the blue-collar environment does not seem to be a massive source of . . . support for Yorty."[37] Similarly, the moderate direct association between increasing socioeconomic status and the vote for Bradley among whites, uncovered by the partial correlations in the examination of the 1973 mayoralty contest, is generally congruent with the findings of a limited study of voting patterns in selected precincts in the latter election.[38]

The reanalysis of the 1969 data revealed a slight, direct correlation between income or education and the Bradley vote, controlling for percent non-white. Removing the effects of race thus greatly reduced the strength of the relationship, although the direction of associa-

TABLE 3

Partial Coefficients of Correlation* Between Selected
Socioeconomic Characteristics and the Vote for Mayor of Los
Angeles, 1969 and 1973

	Percent for Bradley	
	1969	1973
Median education	+.08	+.16
Median family income	+.13	+.26

*Controlling on percent non-white
Source—See n. 33.

tion was changed. By contrast, in the 1973 election, the use of the non-white percentage as a control variable changed the signs or the direction of the associations between education and income and the vote for Bradley; but it did not appreciably change the magnitude of the correlations.[39] Although most of these statistics, and almost all others reported in this study, were significant at the .001 level, the partial correlations between income or education and the vote for Bradley in 1973 were twice as large as the equivalent measures from the 1969 vote.

Significantly, the electoral trends evident in this analysis of the vote for Bradley did not appear in the vote for Pines. The partial coefficients of correlation between median education and income and the vote for Pines, controlling on the non-white variable, were +.14 and +.05, respectively. While Pines seemed to receive approval from the same segments of the black and chicano communities that favored Bradley, the vote for Pines appeared to be relatively unrelated to the socioeconomic sources of support that contributed to the vote for Bradley when the intervening effects of race were removed. Although Bradley did succeed in amassing a large and cohesive vote in the black community, the evidence provided few indications of the emergence of an "independent power politics" strategy in which he would have sought election either without the aid of votes in white areas or with the assistance and collaboration of other white candidates in a biracial exchange of support.

Yet, the results also contained some interesting implications concerning the possible formation of electoral coalitions between white and black electorates. In 1969, in white areas of the city Bradley appeared to draw relatively undifferentiated support that was only marginally related to social status. In 1973, however, this association was enhanced markedly as he became an increasingly legitimate and viable challenger to the incumbent mayor. The findings, therefore, raise some interesting and important questions regarding the shifting nature of electoral alignments and strategies. Although attempts to answer these questions must remain somewhat speculative, some observations can be made in an effort to provide a more comprehensive interpretation of the results of this research.

THE INTERPRETATION OF THE VOTE

Perhaps the most important difference between the two campaigns in Los Angeles involved the nature of the issues presented by the candidates. The effectiveness of the racial issues injected into the 1969 campaign seemed to be related not only to the aggressiveness of Yorty's accusations, but also to Bradley's response. As Maulin noted,

> In essence, Tom Bradley contributed to the backlash sentiment by being black in a de facto segregated society, by espousing liberal political views easily interpreted as being soft on militant protestors and in any case less relevant to the immediate interests of potential allies and by employing a person whose Communist party connection seemed to back up Yorty's claim that Bradley was in league with campus and radical militants.[40]

By contrast, in 1973, Yorty seemingly sought to prevent embarrassment or criticism by avoiding at least the overt presentation of racial charges and by asserting that the principal campaign issue was his retention in office. At the same time, Bradley attempted to avert the question of race and to emphasize issues such as environmental concerns and transportation that might have a wide appeal to the entire Los Angeles electorate.[41] As Carl Stokes, the former mayor of Cleveland, concluded,

> In 1973, Bradley conducted a low-key campaign in which he did not use any black leaders from outside Los Angeles—as I had counseled him in 1969. When Bobby Seales, fresh from his defeat for the mayoralty of Oakland, gratuitously endorsed Bradley's candidacy, Bradley quickly moved to publicly reject Seales' endorsement. He didn't want to do it. But he had to if he wanted to keep those white voters whose fears he had so carefully allayed over the four years.[42]

Since Bradley had designed his campaign to calm the anxieties and to advocate policies favored by relatively high-status white liberals, the empirical findings indicating support from that segment of the electorate might not have been unexpected.

Although the findings reported in this study do not reveal the origins of the shifts in the electorate or the impact of specific issues upon the voters, some interpretations of possible trends and changes between the two elections might be extrapolated from the only available panel survey data on this subject, which was conducted during the 1969 elections.[43] In these surveys, Los Angeles voters were asked to report for whom they had voted in the primary election, their preference in the general election, and later the candidate they had actually supported in the "run-off." Respondents were classified, on the basis of their rankings on self-anchoring scales, into those that were satisfied with their gains in relation to both their own and other social and economic groups; those who felt deprived in relation to the group with which they identified, but who were content with their progress in relation to other groups; those who believed other groups had surpassed them, but who felt secure in comparison with their own group; and those who perceived deprivation in reference to both standards.[44] The results revealed that the greatest defections between the intention to vote for Bradley and the actual ballot cast in the 1969 "run-off" election occurred among those voters who were content with their personal progress in comparison with both their own and other groups. The second largest group of Bradley defectors emerged among those who were satisfied with their progress in relation to their own group, but who felt deprived when the standards of an external group were applied.[45] Since the injection of the racial issue by Yorty was the principal event that occurred between the two surveys, the presumption that those voters may have been responding to racist appeals seems plausible. Apparently the groups which felt the greatest anxiety and who were most threatened by a black candidate consisted of white voters who were satisfied with their progress in life and who may have been anxious to preserve the gains that they had made as well as those who feared that another group was outstripping them. Although these findings do not reflect direct measures of social class, they suggest some interesting inferences concerning both the socioeconomic correlates of voting for a black candidate and the formation of electoral alliances between black and white voters.

As the results of this research indicate, there were changes in the electoral cleavages and alignments between the two Los Angeles elections involving Tom Bradley and Sam Yorty. In the 1969 election, which was marked by extensive racial innuendos and accusations, measures of social status were only very weakly related to the vote for black candidates, when the intervening effects of the non-white proportion of the population were removed. By contrast, in 1973, when racist charges and appeals were notably subdued or lacking in the campaign, the partial correlations between the Bradley vote and income or education, controlling on the non-white percentage of the population, doubled. In the absence of the issue of racism and in a campaign that emphasized overarching programs which would supposedly benefit the entire community, Bradley apparently was able to attract a sufficient number of votes among middle- and upper-middle-class sectors of the white community to forge a winning coalition. The electoral trends in the second election, therefore, indicated the possibilities of an electoral alliance between the black community and relatively high-status white liberals.

IMPLICATIONS FOR OTHER CITIES

Although the results of this analysis include some important implications for elections in other cities, they also may have been influenced by particular or unique features of the election campaigns in Los Angeles. Despite the smoldering reservoir of black discontent that erupted in dramatic violence in Watts in 1965, Los Angeles has not been characterized by extreme degrees of racial polarization and bitterness that have afflicted many other cities. The surveys conducted during the 1969 campaigns, for example, disclosed that

> respondents in Los Angeles did not typically evince the more blatant forms of racism; thus, they overwhelmingly rejected notions of biological inferiority, of sanctioned racial discrimination and segregation, and of the fairness of treat-

ment of Negroes in America today. But the somewhat more subtle and symbolic forms of racism—"most Negroes who receive welfare . . . could get along without it if they tried"—is reflected in our Los Angeles data and does differentiate between Bradley and Yorty supporters.[46]

Perhaps the relative lack of crude and overt racial prejudice in Los Angeles did assist Bradley in polling a larger proportion of the white vote than did black mayoralty candidates in any other city. Moreover, the 1973 campaigns were conducted in a period of less racial tension than were the 1969 elections. In the wake of violence, protests, and demonstrations throughout the country, many voters may have experienced greater anxiety about the prospect of a black mayor in 1969 than they did four years later. Finally, in both elections, Bradley confronted a mayor whose popularity had been steadily declining throughout the city. Although available data do not permit an assessment of the proposition, a great deal of the support that Bradley received may have been as much an "anti-Yorty" vote as it was a vote for a black candidate.[47]

Perhaps most important, however, was the nature of the issues presented to the electorate. In the first campaign, typified by claims of racism and extremism, this research indicated that Bradley received only slightly less support among white voters in working-class areas than in high-income white neighborhoods. It was primarily during a campaign in which the racial issue was effectively removed from public discussion that the partial correlations revealed a moderate tendency for the Bradley vote to increase as the socioeconomic status of the areas increased. Although many attempts have been made to form a coalition between the black community and relatively high-status white liberals, the results of this research do not indicate that such an alliance will necessarily comprise a universal, stable, or enduring partnership.

The findings have some far-reaching implications. Initially, they suggest the extent to which candidates can affect voting patterns and the electoral responses that they receive from their constituents by the nature of the issues that they present to voters.[48] Additionally, and perhaps more importantly, they indicate the vulnerability of black politicians. As this research implies, the elimination of racial issues from a campaign obviously may offer some advantages to black candidates. But black political leaders are constantly exposed to the threat that their opponents might inject such issues into an election, with potentially devastating consequences for their prospects of victory. Finally, this study indicates the extreme flexibility and fragility of any electoral coalition between black and white electorates. As circumstances and issues changed in the separate mayoralty elections in Los Angeles, electoral cleavages and alignments also appeared to shift significantly.

Perhaps of even greater significance than the changes in the white electorate, however, are the patterns which may emerge in the black community. As many commentators have observed, the rise of black political strength, especially in cities, has been marked by a mounting demand for changes in the allocation of governmental benefits.[49] This movement has been accompanied not only by the growth of separatist tendencies, but also by two corresponding trends. Increasingly, there has been a shift from "indivisible" public policies, which allegedly benefit the entire city, to "divisible" programs, in which rewards can be allocated to different segments of the community;[50] and from "distributive" politics, in which benefits are dispensed incrementally to reflect the existing configuration of local power and resources, to "redistributive" politics, in which advantages can be granted to new groups *only at the expense of* those who have traditionally enjoyed the perquisites of political influence.[51] Although some politicians have been able to retain the support of high-income groups by focusing the attention of voters upon "indivisible" and "distributive" programs, both the pressing needs and the growing militancy of minority groups eventually may compel politicians to devote increasing effort to the development of "divisible" and "redistributive" policies. As a result, America might witness the emergence of a new breed of leadership, which could inflict deep-seated cleavages and divisions within both white and black segments of the electorate. The outcome of this conflict could have a decisive impact upon the future of urban areas.

NOTES

1. See, for example, Edgar Litt, *Ethnic Politics in America* (New York: Scott, Foresman, 1970); and Raymond E. Wolfinger, *The Politics of Progress* (Englewood Cliffs: Prentice-Hall, 1974), Chapter 3, especially pp. 71–73.

2. For an insightful account of the election of Stokes in Cleveland, Ohio, and of Hatcher in Gary, Indiana, see Jeffrey K. Hadden, Louis Masotti, and Victor Thiessen, "The Making of the Negro Mayors, 1974," *Trans-Action* 5 (January-February 1968): 21–30.

3. Charles H. Levine, *Racial Conflict and the American Mayor* (Lexington, Mass.: Heath, 1974), p. 116.

4. For an earlier discussion that recognized the political implications of this trend, see Oscar Glanty, "The Negro Voter in Northern Industrial Cities," *Western Political Quarterly* 13 (December 1960): 999–1010.

5. Thomas F. Pettigrew, "When a Black Candidate Runs for Mayor: Race and Voting Behavior," in Harlan Hahn, ed., *People and Politics in Urban Society*, Urban Affairs Annual Review, 6 (Beverly Hills: Sage Publications, 1972) pp. 100, 106.

6. *New York Times*, November 6, 1969, p. 38; Denise J. Lewis, "Victory and Defeat for Black Candidates," *Black Politician* 2 (April 1971), p. 67.

7. Robert L. Pisor, "Strength of Black Vote Gave Young His Historic Victory," *Detroit News*, November 7, 1973, pp. 1, 10.

8. Tom Linthicum, "Jackson Wins Over Massell," *Atlanta Constitution*, October 17, 1973, pp. 1, 22; "Integrating Atlanta's Power Elite," *Business Week*, November 24, 1973, p. 64.

9. Pettigrew, "When a Black Candidate Runs for Mayor," p. 104.

10. Levine, *Racial Conflict*, p. 117.

11. Ivan Allen, Jr., with Paul Hemphill, *Mayor: Notes on the Sixties* (New York: Simon and Schuster, 1971), p. 222.

12. Harry Holloway, "Negro Political Strategy: Coalition or Independent Power Politics?" *Social Science Quarterly* 49 (December 1968): 534–47.

13. Despite its potential weaknesses, this type of coalition continued to attract favorable comments from social scientists for many years. In addition to Holloway, ibid., see James Q. Wilson, "The Negro in Politics," *Daedalus* 94 (Fall 1965): 968. For an analysis of electoral patterns in this coalition, see Jack Walker, "Negro Voting in Atlanta, 1953–1961," *Phylon* 24 (Winter 1963): 379–87.

14. William E. Wright, *Memphis Politics: A Study in Racial Bloc Voting*, Eagleton Institute Case Studies in Practical Politics (New York: McGraw-Hall, 1962).

15. An independent black variant of this strategy has seemed to develop in such Northern cities as Gary and Cleveland in which black voters constitute a near-majority or a sufficient electoral base to justify the prospect of unaided victory. In such localities, black mayors, despairing any hope of attracting significant white support, may focus their energies almost exclusively upon efforts to secure benefits for the black community, presumably in part to solidify their leadership in that constituency. See Levine, *Racial Conflict*, pp. 53–67, 69–84, 109–125; Charles H. Levine and Clifford Kaufman, "Urban Conflict as a Constraint on Mayoral Leadership: Lessons from Gary and Cleveland," *American Politics Quarterly* 2 (January 1974): 78–106.

16. For another interesting and insightful analysis of the Houston coalition, see Chandler Davidson, *Biracial Politics* (Baton Rouge: Louisiana State University Press, 1972).

17. Robin M. Williams, Jr., *Strangers Next Door* (Englewood Cliffs: Prentice-Hall, 1964), pp. 50–56; Bruno Bettleheim and Morris Janowitz, *Social Change and Prejudice* (Glencoe: Free Press, 1964), p. 22.

18. See, for example, Seymour M. Lipset, *Political Man* (Garden City: Doubleday, 1960); Melvin Tumin, *Desegregation: Resistance and Readiness* (Princeton: Princeton University Press, 1958).

19. Richard F. Hamilton, *Class and Politics in the United States* (New York: Wiley, 1972), especially pp. 401–34.

20. Charles H. Stember, *Education and Attitude Change* (New York: Institute of Human Relations Press, 1961).

21. Michael Rogin, "Wallace and the Middle Class: The White Backlash," *Public Opinion Quarterly* 30 (Spring 1966): 98–108; M. Margaret Conway, "The White Backlash Reexamined: Wallace and the 1964 Primaries," *Social Science Quarterly* 49 (December 1968): 710–19.

22. John F. Becker and Eugene E. Heaton, Jr., "The Election of Senator Edward W. Brooke," *Public Opinion Quarterly* 31 (Fall 1967): 346–58; Joel D. Aberbach and Jack L. Walker, *Race in the City* (Boston: Little, Brown, 1973), p. 171.

23. Becker and Heaton, "The Election of Senator Edward W. Brooke," p. 354. For another survey indicating that low-income whites might be more apt to support a black candidate than their higher-status counterparts, see Nathan Glazer and Daniel P. Moynihan, *Beyond the Melting Pot* (Cambridge: M.I.T. Press, 1963), p. 307.

24. Harlan Hahn and Timothy Almy, "Ethnic Politics and Racial Issues: Voting in Los Angeles," *Western Political Quarterly* 24 (December 1971): pp. 719–30.

25. See Raymond Wolfinger, "The Development and Persistence of Ethnic Voting,"

American Political Science Review 59 (December 1965): 896–908; Michael Parenti, "Ethnic Politics and the Persistence of Ethnic Identification," *American Political Science Review* 61 (September 1967): 717–26; Peter Y. Medding, "The Persistence of Ethnic Political Preferences: Factors Influencing the Voting Behavior of Jews in Australia," *Jewish Journal of Sociology* 13 (June 1971): 17–39. Abraham Miller, "Ethnicity and Political Behavior: A Review of Theories and an Attempt at Reformulation," *Western Political Quarterly* 24 (September 1971): 483–500; Richard A. Gabriel, "A New Theory of Ethnic Voting," *Polity* 4 (September 1972): 405–28. Richard A. Gabriel, *The Ethnic Factor in the Urban Polity* (New York: MSS Information Corporation, 1973).

26. For a description of the procedures employed in matching precinct and census tract data, see Harlan Hahn, "Ethos and Social Class Referenda in Canadian Cities," *Polity* 2 (December 1969): 295–315. The authors wish to acknowledge the assistance of Ms. Susan Astarita, and of Mr. Charles Hubay of the Population Research Laboratory and the Program for Data Research at the University of Southern California.

27. W. S. Robinson, "Ecological Correlations and the Behavior of Individuals," *American Sociological Review* 15 (June 1950): 351–57.

28. Austin Ranney, "The Utility and Limitations of Aggregate Data in the Study of Electoral Behavior," in Austin Ranney, ed., *Essays on the Behavioral Study of Politics* (Urbana: University of Illinois Press, 1962), pp. 99–100. For a general discussion of the problems and the advantages of the analysis of aggregate data, see Harlan Hahn, "Ecological Data and Structural Characteristics: Some Notes on the Homogeneity of Precincts and Census Tracts," unpublished paper presented at the annual meeting of the Western Political Science Association, Albuquerque, New Mexico, April 8–10, 1971.

29. Hahn and Almy, "Ethnic Politics and Racial Issues," p. 722.

30. John C. Bollens and Grant B. Geyer, *Yorty: Politics of a Constant Candidate* (Los Angeles: Palisades Publishers, 1973), pp. 166–72.

31. Pettigrew, "When a Black Candidate Runs for Mayor," p. 103.

32. Hahn and Almy, "Ethnic Politics and Racial Issues," p. 723.

33. Ibid. The same procedure used in the study of the 1969 election was employed to define and to classify census tracts. Predominantly black areas were defined as tracts in which 50 percent or more of the population was non-white; tracts in which 50 percent or more of the population was counted as Spanish in the 1970 census were classified as predominantly chicano; and white areas were identified as those having a white population of 60 percent or more. While the 1969 data were based upon the 1960 census, the 1973 data were based upon the 1970 census. The 1969 statistics reported in Tables 1, 2, and 3 are based upon a reanalysis of the 1969 data, discussed earlier in this article. These figures replace those reported in ibid. The authors wish to acknowledge the assistance of Mr. Rodger Madison in the reanalysis.

34. In general, there was a close association between electoral patterns in the contest for city attorney and the mayoralty election of 1973. Not only was the vote for Pines highly related to the non-white percentage of the population (+.71); but it was also inversely associated with the percentage of Spanish ethnicity (−.18), median education (−.13), median family income (−.29), the percentage of professional and managerial employees (−.30),

the percentage of clerical and sales personnel (− .14) and median house value (− .18). On the other hand, support for Pines was directly related to the percentage of craftsmen and foreman (+ .12) and the percentage of laborers or service workers (+ .44). Since the vote for Pines and the vote for Bradley were highly interrelated (+ .88), the data seem to suggest the possibility that some type of "independent power politics" strategy, based either upon Bradley's strength in the black community, or upon an exchange of support between Bradley and Pines, may have emerged in Los Angeles which contributed to the election of both candidates.

35. Hahn and Almy, "Ethnic Politics and Racial Issues," p. 727.

36. Readers should not be disturbed by the fact that the association between the percentage of Spanish ethnicity and the vote for Bradley was inverse, even though the mean vote for Bradley in predominantly chicano tracts reflected a narrow majority. While the latter measure examines predominantly chicano neighborhoods, the former variable reflects the distribution of chicanos in all areas of the city.

37. Vincent Jeffries and H. Edward Ransford, "Ideology, Social Structure, and the Yorty-Bradley Mayoral Election." *Social Problems* 19 (Winter 1972): 369. See also Pettigrew, "When a Black Candidate Runs for Mayor."

38. Robert Mott Halley, "An Analysis of Ethnic Voting Patterns in the 1973 Los Angeles Municipal Elections" (M.A. thesis, University of Southern California, Los Angeles, California, 1974).

39. In 1973, the partial coefficients of correlation between median income and education, controlling on both the percentage of non-white residents and the percentage of Spanish ethnicity, were + .23 and + .11, respectively.

40. Richard L. Maulin, "Los Angeles Liberalism," *Trans-Action* 8 (May 1971): 51.

41. These statements are based upon observations of the election campaign and upon interviews conducted by Mr. Larry Eastland, of the University of Southern California, with the campaign officials of both candidates four days prior to the election.

42. Carl B. Stokes, *Promises of Power* (New York: Simon and Schuster, 1973), pp. 271–72.

43. Pettigrew, "When a Black Candidate Runs for Mayor."

44. This classification is based upon the social-psychological research of W. G. Runciman, *Relative Deprivation and Social Justice* (London: Routledge and Kegan Paul, 1966).

45. Pettigrew, "When a Black Candidate Runs for Mayor," p. 116.

46. Ibid., pp. 103–4.

47. The fact that the "anti-Arnebergh" sentiment appeared to be not as strong may in part explain the differences between the voting patterns for Bradley and Pines in 1973.

48. For a discussion of issue voting, see the special issue of the *American Politics Quarterly* 3, July 1975.

49. Litt, *Ethnic Politics*, p. 150; Hahn and Almy, "Ethnic Politics and Racial Issues," p. 728.

50. Levine, *Racial Conflict*, pp. 19–23.

51. Harlan Hahn, "The American Mayor: Retrospect and Prospect," *Urban Affairs Quarterly* 11, No. 2 (December 1975): 276–88.

PART 3

Urban Services

The delivery of services is a major function of local governments. Because most urban services are personal, direct, specific, and highly divisible, they can be distributed differently to various areas and groups of citizens. The politics of service delivery—who gets what, where, when, and how—highlights how political power can be converted into tangible rewards for groups, neighborhoods, communities, *and* service delivery bureaucracies. The importance of urban services has been underscored in recent years by conflicts between groups, bureaucracies, and segments of the metropolitan population which have demonstrated the crucial relationship between the financial and administrative performance of city governments and the quality of life for local residents.

The conflict surrounding the differential delivery of services is framed in the article by Robert L. Lineberry, "Mandating Urban Equality: The Distribution of Municipal Public Services." Lineberry's study focuses on the services provided to urban areas inhabited by the poor and minority groups. It is Lineberry's contention that urban service delivery patterns are important elements shaping urban growth and the distribution of persons into clusters that are unequal in terms of living conditions. Lineberry identifies zoning and land-use regulation as the two most important policies affecting growth and service delivery patterns. The outcomes of most policy decisions in these two areas, he argues, produce patterns of racial and income separation, with disparities between service needs and resources.

Problems exist, however, when attempts are made to determine service inequities. Since perfect equality is impossible to achieve, a distinction must be made between trivial and substantial inequality. When the concept of equality is used as a standard for distributing public services, the focus is generally on *input equality*. Input tests usually are concerned with only one type of measure such as levels of expenditure. This is a poor index of the quality of public services; and it ignores other critical dimensions such as the relationship between bureaucracies and clients. If *output equality* is used, however, the focus shifts to a concern for results. This form of evaluation, Lineberry argues, is closer to the assessment a citizen makes in determining service equity.

Given the difficulties involved in using equality as a basis for policy-making decisions, Lineberry argues that a better strategy would involve the adoption of a rationality standard based upon agency goals. The rationality standard would require that agency activity be relevant to the attainment of agency goals shaped by citizen preferences.

169

The issue of service distribution inequity is also treated in Oliver Williams' article, "Life-Style Values and Political Decentralization in Metropolitan Areas." Williams argues that inequalities in urban services often are produced by the tendency of individuals to seek locations in metropolitan areas where their *preferences* can be maximized by local governments. He explains why these differences in the distribution of services result in political conflict. Williams views the city as a "special receptacle for storing and transmitting messages." People and firms choose locations which enable them to satisfy their interests and desires.

A related motive for choosing a particular location is expressed by the values held by businesses and households. Many people, for example, tend to value characteristics like good schools, convenient shopping, or recreational facilities. These features of urban living are what Williams terms "life-style values." These values, Williams contends, explain why different locations in metropolitan areas offer specialized and differentiated packages of services. Since proposed changes in the distribution of services threaten to alter the advantage of certain locations, Williams concludes that the process of reducing inequalities *could* threaten life-style values and produce unrest.

The conflict surrounding urban services must inevitably focus on the arm of urban government which citizens usually associate with service delivery; i.e., the street-level bureaucrat. The problems involved in the relationships between street-level bureaucrats and their clients is the concern of the article by Michael Lipsky, "Street-Level Bureaucracy and the Analysis of Urban Reform."

Lipsky argues that the work life of street-level bureaucrats is filled with *stress*. Street-level bureaucrats—police, teachers, community workers, and so forth—cope with this stress by stereotyping (which allows problems to be simplified and decisions to be made quickly) and by employing a variety of defense mechanisms. Eventually, Lipsky concludes that one solution to the problems confronted by street-level bureaucrats might be provided by proposals for radical decentralization and neighborhood control. Decentralization, he argues, would ". . . increase the homogeneity of district populations permitting greater uniformity and responsiveness in designing policies directed toward neighborhoods."

The observation that services are not distributed equally over a metropolitan area is extended by Jones, Greenberg, Kaufman, and Drew in their article "Service Delivery Rules and the Distribution of Local Government Services." Rather than simply document service inequities, Jones et al. attempt to discover and explain the causes for the unequal distribution of local government services. The authors examine the two dominant methods of conceptualizing urban services: the economic model and the political model. They argue that both of these models have problems. The economic model totally ignores the distribution of services produced, and the political model, while considering service distribution, offers an incomplete explanation for why distribution patterns emerge as they do.

The authors contend that the key to understanding observable patterns of service distribution can be found in the manner in which bureaucracies behave. The major operating characteristics of bureaucracies involve the development of professional rules which rationally relate service delivery to the goals of agency productivity. But rational bureaucratic activity has unintended distributional consequences. Thus, to determine why specific agencies produce distinct distributional patterns, it is necessary to examine the nature of these "professional" rules.

The authors examine three service agencies in Detroit: the Environmental Enforcement Division, the Sanitation Department, and the Parks and Recreation Department.

What Jones et al. demonstrate is that routine "professional" rules significantly influence service distribution and that the awareness of bureaucrats of the distributional impact of these rules varies between service agencies. The implication of this finding is that effective policy decisions concerning services must consider the existence and nature of established decisions rules if citizen satisfaction with city services is to be improved.

Most of the literature on service delivery assumes a constant or expanding availability of government resources. The recent financial crises of a number of cities, however, have raised serious questions about what happens to the delivery of urban services when a city is forced to implement a program of retrenchment. This dilemma is vividly illustrated in Martin Shefter's article, "New York City's Fiscal Crisis: The Politics of Inflation and Retrenchment."

Shefter compares New York's fiscal crisis of 1975 to similar events in 1871 and 1933. He concludes that, in each case, the fiscal collapse was preceded by the rise to power of a new political coalition consisting of elements of the city's business community and emerging ethnic groups. The coalitions were maintained by providing increased public employment for members of the victorious ethnic groups to the public payroll and by sponsoring public projects favored by the business community. As the debts from these projects mounted, they forced a takeover of city government by business leaders who sought to forestall bankruptcy by pressuring the city government to implement a program of retrenchment that was harmful to the newly incorporated ethnic groups.

Shefter indicates, however, that retrenchment policies are vulnerable to many destabilizing influences. For retrenchment policies to work, unions must accept contracts with reduced benefits. If union leaders are unable to convince rank and file union members to accept reduced benefits, they may refuse wage freezes and force the city into bankruptcy and receivership. Similarly, deprived groups must remain quiescent. If they become mobilized, they could also upset retrenchment. Furthermore, electoral campaigns could also cause instability and polarization by becoming the forum for addressing the question of who should bear the burden of retrenchment, with campaigning officials seeking election by committing themselves to protect various programs and groups from budget cutbacks.

Shefter indicates that bankers and major creditors as well as elected officials are aware of these potential threats to the orderliness of the retrenchment process. As a result, they have attempted to introduce constraints which would deprive elected officials of the authority to determine how some tax revenues are to be spent. Eventually, Shefter argues, New York City's citizens may be left with no direct control of how they are governed, where their taxes are to be spent, or of the level and quality of public services.

Mandating Urban Equality: The Distribution of Municipal Public Services

ROBERT L. LINEBERRY

Many years ago Lasswell defined politics as "who gets what, when, how."[1] A Lasswellian perspective is equally appropriate to the distribution of municipal public services, an increasingly significant issue in political science, economics, and the law. Exploration of the complex constitutional, administrative, and judicial considerations involved in public service allocation can benefit from the evidence produced by social research.

Urban public services such as police and fire protection, parks, libraries, snow removal, sanitation, public health, and sewerage constitute a form of the "new property"[2] of government largesse. However massive the federal budget, most government activities immediately affecting the lives and sacred fortunes of citizens are provided at the local level. In fact, if defense costs are excluded, state and local governments greatly outspend the federal government.[3] American cities in 1970–1971 spent approximately $32 billion on public services.[4] The services procured through those expenditures ranged from life-and-death matters of police and fire protection to services that provided convenience and comfort—the city of San Antonio in 1972 spent half a million dollars on neighborhood brush removal.[5] Services represent indirect transfer payments, increasing a household's income through service excellence or diminishing it through service denials. Public services, therefore, constitute a "hidden multiplier" of income.[6]

Although it is virtually impossible to estimate the value (as opposed to the cost) of urban goods and services, clearly they touch directly upon life (police, public health, sanitation, and fire protection), liberty (law enforcement and the courts), property (zoning and taxation), and public enlightenment (schools and libraries).[7] Among both scholars and the general public there is a widespread belief, and some scattered evidence to support it, that all citizens do not share equally in the distribution of these public services. Largely anecdotal proof abounds,[8] but little systematic evidence has been compiled.[9] Conventional wisdom holds that suburban residents enjoy superior bundles of services at lower tax rates than central city dwellers and that poorer neighborhoods within the city receive inferior services. The choice of location within the metropolis is at least a partial response to perceived differences in quality and cost of schools, sewers, streets, and sanitation.[10] The suburbanization of the urban population is undoubtedly hastened by the desire to better one's service environment.

One source of the recent demand for "community control" in urban minority neighborhoods is the belief that services are not administered in accordance with citizens' needs and desires.[11] The Kerner Commission concluded that a principal cause of racial disorders of the 1960's was dissatisfaction with municipal governments and their services.[12] The variations, real or imagined, in municipal outputs rub the rawest nerves of urban conflict.

In the leading challenge to municipal disparities in service outputs, *Hawkins v. Town of Shaw*,[13] Judge Tuttle, speaking for the Fifth Circuit majority, wrote:

> Referring to a portion of a town or a segment of society as being "on the other side of the tracks" has for too long been a familiar expression to most Americans. . . . While there may be many reasons why such areas exist in nearly all of our cities, one reason that cannot be accepted is the discriminatory provision of municipal services based on race.[14]

The relationship between the urban public sector and "the other side of the tracks" is the concern here. Urban services are not merely responses to urban growth, but an important causal element shaping that growth. The urban area is conceptualized as a complex mosaic of sociospatial groupings to which services may be differentially delivered. The differences in output among delivery networks raise both common law and constitutional issues of equality, but, as will be developed, there are limitations on the concept of equality as a standard for measuring service distribution.

I. PUBLIC SERVICES: NEGLECT AND EMERGENCE

A. The Metropolitan Turf

Americans have become a metropolitan people. In 1971 about seventy percent of the population lived in metropolitan areas;[15] in fact, "population growth *is* metropolitan growth in contemporary United States."[16] While it is important to understand the growth *of* metropolitan areas, it is equally crucial to explore growth *within* them. Banfield identifies three "imperatives"—demographic, technological, and economic—that exert a strong influence on metropolitan growth patterns.[17] While these may fall short of being imperatives, they are undoubtedly valid as tendencies. The first fact of urban life is that persons of varying social, ethnic, and economic attributes are not scattered randomly about the metropolitan landscape; one of the most evident consequences of urban growth patterns is the sifting of persons and production into clusters in a limited spatial plane.

Thus, the metropolis can be conceptualized, at least metaphorically, as a large sociospatial plane in which groups compete for dominance of their "turf" in much the same manner as the teenage gang, which is "the primitive urban political formation."[18] The desire for areal dominance analogizes metropolitan political conflict to the urban gang; a "territorial imperative" is as applicable to urban political life as to human behavior in general.[19] In the mature adult political system of urban areas, violence as a tool of control is replaced by rules, by legitimate and authoritative use of political power, and by the formation of coalitions. Force gives way to public policy as a device for securing and maintaining locational advantages.

B. Public Policy, Public Services, and the Problem of Urban Growth

The demographic explanation of urban growth, typified by Banfield's three imperatives, is useful, but fails to take sufficient account of the role of public policy in shaping urban locational patterns. Demographic patterns are not merely accidental byproducts of unfettered market choices, but are intentionally manipulated by governmental decisions. Zoning policy, selection of highway routes, location of urban renewal and housing projects, the quality and quantity of urban services, the levels of local taxes, and a myriad of other public choices affect the location decisions of persons and production. These policy decisions are made by the 20,000 governmental units in this country's politically fragmented metropolitan areas, most of which possess taxing, regulatory, and spending authority.

Perhaps the most important, as well as the most thoroughly explored, of these policies are zoning and land use regulation. Exclusionary zoning has become the principal target of liberals and civil rights groups who want to open the suburbs to all racial and economic groups. To the challengers of "snob" zoning, it operates like the "wall of iron" in Jehovah's advice to Ezekiel.[20] In some suburbs at least, zoning undoubtedly has functioned to keep out low income groups, minorities, households with children, and other "undesirables."[21] Quite possibly, then, zoning and land use regulation have significantly distorted patterns of urban growth and locational choice of both families and businesses.

Tax rate and service level variations also combine to attract or repel certain types of sociospatial clusterings. In some central city areas, taxes are now so high that increases provide no real additional yield, for they drive out those who can afford to move.[22] To the degree that the governmentally fragmented metropolitan area can be conceptualized as a "marketplace" of service-producers offering different packages of goods and services at varying costs, the citizen-consumer may pick the government that best satisfies his preference for public goods. For example, millions of ex-urbanites have carefully selected a suburb in partial response to the character of the public school system.

The dynamics of metropolitan growth, reinforced by zoning, regulation, and other policy decisions made by fragmented governmental units, have produced the well-known configuration of service need and resource disparities.[23] Far too often, the level of a community's public service demands is inversely related to its ability to meet those demands.[24] Typically, this relationship is most evident in a comparison of central cities (high need, low resources) with their suburbs (low demand, high resources), although such disparities among suburbs are not uncommon. Based on most indicia of economic vitality—housing quality, tax base, median family income, and so forth—central cities fare worse than their suburbs.[25]

The location and delivery of conventional urban services have been particularly important in producing and fortifying patterns of racial separation in American cities. The location choices of American minority groups have not been made in a free and open market of residential options. American cities in all areas of the country exhibit a high and stable degree of racial segregation.[26] Private forces such as housing market discrimination have played a major role in producing these patterns,[27] but public policy decisions have also contributed to the separation. The United States Civil Rights Commission, for example, has documented the practice of locating schools in the core of ghetto neighborhoods rather than on the peripheries where they would facilitate integrated attendance patterns.[28] Similarly, public housing projects have been located in solidly black neighborhoods, thus enhancing segregated patterns.[29]

When segregation was the dominant moral, social, and legal principle of racial relations, it was essential for minorities to cluster together in order to enjoy the benefits of public facilities. The case of Austin, Texas, is instructive.[30] As the city developed in the latter half of the nineteenth century, it contained several pockets of black settlement in different quadrants of the city. The early years of the twentieth century marked the beginnings of development of publicly operated sewers, streets, water mains, parks, and street lighting systems. The city's growth prompted the municipal government in 1927 to hire a private planning firm to develop systematic plans for the extension of public service facilities. Regarding the issue of race and public services, the consultants concluded that the "race segregation problem" could not legally be solved by zoning. As an alternative measure, they offered the following:

> In our studies in Austin we have found that the negroes are present in small numbers in practically all sections of the city, excepting the . . . ["East Austin" area]. This area seems to be all negro population. It is our recommendation that *the nearest approach to the solution of the race segregation problem will be the recommendation of this district as a negro district; and that all the facilities and conveniences be provided the negroes in this district, as an incentive to draw the negro population to this area.* This will eliminate the necessity of duplicates of white and black schools, white and black parks, and other duplicate facilities.[31]

In effect, the consulting engineers recommended a plan—adopted *in toto* by the city and even reprinted in the 1957 city plan—that would have used city services as a magnet to attract blacks to one area and, by their denial to other areas, to repel location choices outside the segregated neighborhoods. If black families intended to enjoy sewers and paved streets, or convenient schools and parks, they would have had to locate in a particular neighborhood of the city. Two years after adoption of the plan, the city parks board purchased its first "colored playground" in the heart of "East Austin." They did not seriously consider any other area of the city. Because historians have been relatively inattentive to the racial implications of the development of urban services, it is not known whether this pattern is typical of other southern (and northern) cities. It does suggest that marketplace discrimination is not the sole explanation for racial isolation within the city. Service delivery patterns also play a role.

C. Elevating Urban Services to a Constitutional Issue: A Bang or a Whimper?

More than forty years after the implementation of the consultant's plan in Austin, Texas, the town of Shaw, Mississippi (population: 1500 blacks, 1000 whites) became the object of the most noteworthy of the "service equalization" cases. In *Hawkins v. Town of Shaw* [32] the Fifth Circuit found a racially motivated denial of equal protection in the provision of street lighting and paving, water main size, sanitary sewers, storm sewers, and other public services. The evidence established that nearly ninety-eight percent of homes fronting on unpaved streets were black-occupied; ninety-seven percent of homes not served by sanitary sewers were in black neighborhoods; all the city's new mercury vapor street lights were in white neighborhoods.[33] The court ordered the town to submit a plan to rectify the legacy of service discrimination. When the Fifth Circuit's ruling was announced, *Shaw* was hailed in the press as a "pioneering decision" that could be as significant in the field of public services as *Brown v. Board of Education*[34] was in public education.[35] *Time* magazine predicted that "*Shaw* could force big as well as small cities across the U.S. to reallocate everything from police patrols to garbage pick-ups and parkspace."[36] The decision prompted a large volume of legal commentary and was touted as a "landmark decision" that could "prompt a genuine crusade by municipalities to rectify policies of providing unequal services."[37]

The *Shaw* decision has also, however, been labeled "a small leap for minorities, but a giant leap for commentators,"[38] and has thus far failed to satisfy expectations. While a number of equalization suits have been filed (on behalf of poor blacks, whites, Mexican Americans, Puerto Ricans, Chinese Americans, and Sioux Indians), most have challenged discrimination in rural or semi-rural communities. Only a handful of suits have been brought in major cities. Two of those—one involving San Francisco, the other New York—were quite limited in scope, concerned only with parks and recreation facilities in a particular neighborhood; both were resolved, from the plaintiff's point of view, unsuccessfully.[39] A third, much more ambitious suit filed on behalf of the predominantly black residents of the Anacostia area of Washington, D.C., has yet to be tried.[40]

Municipal corporations have long been subject to common law rules concerning the equitable distribution of public services. While they are not required to undertake, except as state statute might dictate, any particular service, once undertaken a service must be extended on a nondiscriminatory basis to all citizen-consumers.[41] While the common law approach may offer remedies for blatant discrepancies such as the utter absence of a service in a particular neighborhood, to mandate "equal and adequate services" is not to define such services. The *Shaw* approach thus represents an effort to elevate the problem of service discrepancies to a constitutional equal protection issue.

The equal protection clause has been a restless constitutional giant.[42] The Warren Court used the clause to strike down many discriminatory state practices, including school segregation,[43] malapportionment of state legislatures,[44] and residency requirements for welfare recipients.[45] Holding firmly to the line that racial classifications are "constitutionally suspect,"[46] the Warren Court flirted with the notion that classifications based on wealth are also suspect. In *McDonald v. Board of Election Commissioners*[47] the Court observed that "a careful examination . . . is especially warranted where lines are drawn on the basis of wealth or race, . . . two factors which would *independently* render a classification highly suspect and thereby demand a more exacting judicial scrutiny."[48] As with racial discrimination, the purposefulness of discrimination based on wealth is irrelevant; the issue is the differential impact of public policy on identifiable groupings, either an insular minority or the poor.[49] Still, the Warren Court was some distance from full elevation of the wealth criterion to coequal constitutional status with the racial criterion. And new courts and new justices can always turn back the clock.

Unquestionably, the thrust of the *Shaw* decision and related attacks has been more consistent with a Warren than a Burger interpretation of the equal protection clause. The new court has virtually slammed shut the door on wealth as a suspect classification. In *San Antonio Independent School District v. Rodriguez*,[50] the school financing decision, the enormous resource disparities produced by the Texas school financing scheme were held not to violate the equal protection clause. No general challenge to the distribution of urban services has ever reached the Court. But the legal questions surrounding urban service distribution are no more a dead issue than those concerning public school financing. If anything, in future years challenges to service allocations are likely to grow with the increasing political sophistication of minority groups and the deepening fiscal problems of major cities. When resource levels become constricted, there is likely to be more intense competition over the distribution of existing resources. Those conflicts are virtually certain to spill over into the legal arena.

It is unfortunate that *Shaw* has been the dominant case in the area. The blatancy of the inequalities—while making *Shaw* an ideal plaintiff's case—is more reminiscent of the Jim Crow era than representative of the intricate, subtle, and difficult-to-measure patterns of service delivery in a large, complex urban system. Virtually no measurement issues are raised by the case; it is a clear example of the dictum that "figures speak and when they do, Courts listen."[51] Furthermore, the case fails, in its simplicity, to raise any questions concerning the varying conceptions of equality in the context of urban public policy. Whether *Shaw* is relevant to the problems of Syracuse, San Francisco, and San Antonio remains a very open question.

II.   THE MEASUREMENT OF SERVICE DISTRIBUTION

A.   The Measurement Problem

The most obvious, although not the most serious, problem in the measurement of urban service distribution is that of data availability. The census provides data on some neighborhood attributes, including items ranging from income levels to appliance ownership, but includes virtually nothing on the delivery of public services. Public records are also less than satisfactory; bureaucracies are notoriously inconstant record keepers. Records are maintained for internal purposes that may not always coincide with the interests of the service analyst. Typically they focus on narrow problems of cost-efficiency and not upon the larger issues of delivery to various sociospatial groupings.[52]

One thing is clear about the measurement of service outputs: money expended is a poor guide. High public service expenditures may reflect, *inter alia*, (1) purchases of high quality goods, services, and personnel; (2) diseconomies of scale; (3) waste and inefficiency; or (4) high labor and material costs. Higher costs necessitated by spiraling inefficiency do not provide an appropriate measure of service quality. In fact, the dimensions of service outputs are numerous. Table 1 . . . provides a sampling of possible service measures.[53] Not all of

TABLE 1

Public Service Indicia

Dimension of Service	Sample Indicia
1. Cost per service unit	Library expenditures per books circulated; cost of garbage collection per number of collection units
2. Location of service facilities	Proximity of parks, libraries, fire stations
3. Promptness of service	Fire response time; police response time
4. Frequency of service	Number of garbage collections per week; frequency of police patrols
5. Condition and quality of facilities	Attractiveness of parks, libraries; space in parks, libraries; number of library books
6. Quality of service personnel	Training and background of personnel; demeanor of personnel
7. Personnel—client ratio	Pupil-teacher ratio; welfare personnel—client ratio; number of police personnel per 1000 population
8. Consumption of services	Library circulation per 1000 books; ratio of park acreage to park users

these are germane to any particular policy decision. It matters little, for example, where a police station is located (dimension 2) if response time (dimension 3) is high; crowding (dimension 8) may be relevant to some services such as parks and libraries but not to others. Some indicia are most appropriate when used in conjunction with others. Expenditures, for example, are most meaningful when related to indicators of services purchased.

B. A Case Study

Examination of an actual case in point will demonstrate not merely the opportunities and possibilities of intra-municipal service distribution analysis, but also the problems and limitations.[54] The analysis is specific to San Antonio, Texas, and the services examined are fire protection and public libraries. For fire protection, only a single dimension of service output—location of public facilities—is measured; for libraries, data on both location and service quality is presented. San Antonio is not offered as a "typical" American city; in fact, it is an interesting subject of analysis in part because it is atypical. San Antonio is unusual in at least four respects. First, the city constitutes a very large proportion (73.7 percent) of its Standard Metropolitan Statistical Area (SMSA);[55] only seven SMSA's over 200,000 outrank San Antonio in the proportion of the total SMSA covered by the central city.[56] There is thus a wide range of racial and income groups within the city itself. This mixture is useful for present purposes since it renders the complications of central city-suburban discrepancies less troublesome. Second, San Antonio is extremely poor. It scores very low on nearly every measure of personal wealth. Third, the city is heavily ethnic, although its ethnicity is Chicano rather than black. In 1970, 52.1 percent of the population was Mexican American, 7.6 percent was black, and 40.2 percent was "Anglo."[57] Finally, San Antonio has a distinctive pattern of political power. The Good Government League has dominated the city's politics since 1954. As is typical of many cities, successful candidates are drawn from the more affluent sectors of the population and, as is often the case with the at-large system of local elections, do not come proportionately from all areas of the city.[38]

The census tract was the chosen unit of analysis. Using the 1970 census, 113 census tracts lie entirely within the boundaries of San Antonio. Data was accumulated on various social, economic, and ethnic attributes of those tracts. Use of the independent variables listed in table 2 . . . should make possible a test of the following hypotheses about public service distribution: (1) the higher the levels of ethnicity in a tract, the lower the quality and/or quantity of public services delivered to that tract; (2) the higher the socioeconomic status of the tract, the higher the quality and/or quantity of public services delivered to that tract; and (3) the older and more densely settled the tract, the lower the quality and/or quantity of public services delivered to that tract.

The service measures selected focus on the proximity dimension of service delivery and, in case of public libraries, on a measure of service quality. These, too, are listed in table 2. The proximity of urban services is a particularly important attribute of their quality. In the

TABLE 2

Variables for Analysis of Urban Public Service Distribution in San Antonio

Variable	Definition and Measurement
Independent Variables	
I. Ethnicity	
A. % Negro	% of census tract population that is non-white
B. % Spanish heritage	% of census tract population defined by Census Bureau as "Spanish heritage"
C. % minority	Sum for census tract of A and B
II. Socioeconomic status	
A. Median family income	Median income for census tract of families and unrelated individuals
B. % white collar	% of work force in census tract in white collar occupations
C. Median school years	Median years of schooling of adult population in census tract
III. Ecological	
A. % houses built before 1949	% of houses in census tract built before 1949
B. Population per acre	Density of population, measured by number of persons per acre in census tract
Dependent Variables	
I. Fire distance	Mean distance from random points in census tract to closest fire station
II. Library distance	Mean distance from random points in census tract to closest public library
III. Library volumes per capita	Ratio of number of volumes in library to total population of census tracts closest to library

case of fire protection, it is obvious that long distances will impair the ability of fire-fighting units to respond promptly and increase the probability of damage to lives and property. The accessibility of public libraries is an important determinant of their quality and use. Studies of public libraries have found a relationship between library usage and the proximity of the facility, with a majority of users living relatively close to the library.[59] The use of public facilities like libraries or parks can be conceptualized as a function of the interdependent relationship between accessibility and motivation; beyond a certain distance, motivation must be extremely high to encourage usage.

There are a number of ways to measure proximity to public facilities. The method chosen here was the creation of a "service area" for each fire station and public library in San Antonio, composed of the census tracts closest to that facility. Thus, for the nine public libraries in the city, nine service areas were constructed. For each census tract in the service area, six points were chosen randomly and measured linearly to the library. Averaging these distances provided a score on the proximity measure for each tract. The same procedure was followed for measurement of proximity to fire stations. In addition to the proximity measure, each census tract can be scored on the quality attributes of the nearest library. This permits a determination that census tracts with certain racial or other attributes are served by libraries with large or small collections, few or many professional staff, high or low increases over time in collection size, and so forth.

1. Proximity of Service Facilities. The coefficients reported in table 3 . . . show the

TABLE 3

Pearsonian Correlations Between Ethnic, Socioeconomic, and Ecological Attributes of San Antonio Census Tracts (N = 113) and Linear Distance to Nearest Fire Station and Library[a]

Census Tract Attribute	Distance to Nearest Fire Station		Distance to Nearest Public Library	
	r	signifi-cance	r	signifi-cance
I. Ethnicity				
A. % Negro	−.127	NS[b]	−.057	NS
B. % Spanish heritage	−.208	.01	−.232	.01
C. % minority	−.282	.01	−.258	.01
II. Socioeconomic status				
A. Median family income	.440	.01	.353	.01
B. % white collar	.313	.01	.257	.01
C. Median school years	.265	.01	.278	.01
III. Ecological				
A. % houses built before 1949	−.619	.01	−.552	.01
B. Population per acre	−.532	.01	−.494	.01

[a] A Pearsonian correlation, symbolized by the letter "r," estimates the degree to which two variables co-vary. The maximum range of the r is ± 1.00. An r of 1.00 indicates perfect association in a positive direction, *i.e.*, whenever the value for one variable increases the other increases proportionately. An r of −1.00 indicates a perfect association in a negative direction, *i.e.*, whenever one variable increases the other decreases proportionately. Note that positive correlations in this table indicate *greater* distances to the service facility.

[b] "NS" means "not significant" at the .01 level of confidence.

correlations between mean linear distances of census tracts to the nearest fire station or library and the ethnic, socioeconomic, and ecological attributes of each tract. Distance to the service facility increases with the value of the correlation coefficient. It is clear from the data that none of the three hypotheses suggested above can be sustained by the evidence. In fact, relationships opposite those predicted are evident: (1) the more heavily ethnic the census tract, the closer it is to libraries and fire stations; (2) the higher the socioeconomic status of the census tract, the farther it is from service facilities; and (3) the older and more densely settled it is, the closer a census tract is to fire stations and library facilities.

The explanation for these conclusions lies in the extremely high correlations associated with the ecological attributes of tracts. The newest areas of the city—exhibiting recency of home construction and scattered, low-density population patterns—are farthest from libraries and fire stations. Urban growth, in San Antonio and elsewhere, is concentrated at the city's periphery, and newly settled areas are largely composed of Anglo, higher income, better educated, and more professional households. Understandably, construction of public facilities lags behind suburban tract development. It would be a foolish use of public resources to construct a new library each time an outlying development opened and a few families moved in. This finding again demonstrates the important nexus between urban growth patterns and public service delivery. It also cautions against generalizing from a single case. San Antonio, unlike Boston, Cleveland, San Francisco, and many other large cities, still has large areas of undeveloped land, whose development inevitably creates lags in the provision of service facilities. Whether studies of other urban areas would result in similar findings is uncertain.

2. The "Quality" of Public Services. Because of the inverse relationship between measures of ethnicity and socioeconomic status on the one hand, and proximity to service facilities on the other, it is possible that disadvantaged groups live closest to service facilities, but that the facilities serving them are the poorest in quality. This would be consistent with a number of studies showing poorer quality library facilities servicing poor and minority neighborhoods.[60] Measuring the quality of any public service is a difficult undertaking, but it is not unreasonable to assume in the case of libraries that such indicia as number and training of professional personnel, size of collection, expenditures, expansions and contractions in collection size, and physical attributes of facilities (for example, space and aesthetic appeal) constitute an appropriate point of departure. Although data were collected on several of these aspects of library service,[61] for purposes of brevity and simplicity the results on only one—volumes per capita—are reported here. The measure of volumes per capita was computed by taking the total population of the service area (that is, the census tracts closest to the particular library) and dividing collection size by population served. This count can then be related to the socioeconomic, ethnic, and ecological attributes of the service area for each library. Table 4 . . . shows the results of this analysis. The quality of the library, measured by volumes per capita, improves moving from left to right on the table, with the largest collection (over nine volumes per capita) in the main library. If the urban lower class is served by the poorest libraries, one would expect to find systematic increases from left to right in such attributes as median family income and decreases from left to right in such attributes as percent minority. In fact, however, there are few patterned increases or decreases of any kind in the table. Although the library collections are certainly not equal in terms of population served, the inequalities correlate poorly with the

TABLE 4

Mean Values of Ethnic, Socioeconomic, and Ecological Attributes of Census Tracts (N = 113) by Library Volumes Per Capita

Census Tract Attributes	Library Volumes Per Capita[a]								
	All	.34 (13[b])	.37 (17)	.50 (35)	.51 (19)	.64 (9)	1.04 (8)	1.56 (5)	9.03 (7)
I. Ethnicity									
A. % Negro	8.45	48.17	4.40	.40	8.52	.48	5.83	4.20	.81
B. % Spanish heritage	50.99	33.52	85.69	49.22	35.85	13.34	72.89	39.42	80.71
C. % minority	60.36	82.63	91.07	50.59	45.03	14.49	80.06	44.62	82.60
II. Socioeconomic status									
A. Median family income	$7786	$5964	$6061	$9134	$7792	$12,074	$5578	$8437	$5149
B. % white collar	47.72	34.80	26.61	55.29	48.88	75.74	40.04	63.90	35.87
C. Median school years	9.85	9.79	7.39	10.61	10.52	13.00	8.78	12.02	7.67
III. Ecological									
A. % houses built before 1949	46.60	65.97	37.21	32.46	47.68	9.01	82.56	73.54	89.20
B. Population per acre	8.22	8.90	10.74	7.31	6.19	3.46	12.61	10.08	11.60

[a] Although San Antonio has nine libraries—one main and eight branches—only eight library scores appear. Two libraries had identical scores on the number of volumes per capita.

[b] Number of census tracts.

attributes of the neighborhoods. The library serving the wealthiest tracts has a collection size of 0.64 books per capita, while the library serving the poorest tracts is the main library with the largest collection. Even if the main library, which presumably is intended to service more than the immediate neighborhood, is disregarded, the table shows that the library serving the next poorest tracts has a collection size of 1.04 books per capita. Overall, however, one is hard-pressed to discover patterned relationships in the data. The results suggest that library collections vary considerably as a ratio of population served, but that those inequalities are only randomly correlated to socioeconomic, racial, or ecological aspects of the census tracts served.

Caution must be used in interpreting these findings, in part because they differ both from conventional wisdom and from other studies of library service to the poor. The findings may result from idiosyncrasies of the measures employed, from the unique attributes of San Antonio itself, or from other factors. They do suggest, however, that categorical assumptions about the relationship of public services to the urban poor should be resisted.

These and similar analyses assume that the most appropriate test of urban service distribution is one of equality, or more precisely, per capita equality. According to this view, differential delivery of services to various sociospatial areas is suspect, at least when the areas may be identified by distinctive racial or economic traits. Whether this assumption is accurate has been addressed with limited data on a single large city. Whether it is warranted is the focus of the next section.

III. THE LIMITS OF EQUALITY: A CRITIQUE OF PER CAPITA EQUALITY AS A TEST

A. The Paradoxical Concept of Equality

Despite its centrality to the social sciences, philosophy, and constitutional law, the concept of equality is both complex and fundamentally paradoxical. It remains "a word so wide and vague as to be by itself almost nonmeaning."[62] There has, nonetheless, been a recent escalation in public debate about equality, its meaning, and its implications.[63] Although few ideas have ramifications for as many issues—from race to reapportionment, from schooling to suffrage, and from income distribution to political power—equality is almost never taken literally as a guide to public policy. No egalitarian envisions the obliteration of distinctions among persons. "To make equality a synonym for the absence of all distinctions," contends Lakoff, "is not to define any of the real proposals of equality but only to prepare an attack on absurd caricatures of them all."[64] Promoters of equality do not advocate literal equality of condition—precisely equal incomes for everyone, identical school expenditures for every pupil—but rather attack extreme inequalities. This negative aspect of the concept is consistent with the fourteenth amendment's equal protection clause, which does not require the states to guarantee equal protection of the laws, but forbids them to deny it.

Equality is a complex and uncertain guide to public policy, not only because its objects are as numerous as its proponents, but also because, paradoxically, equality in one realm may promote inequality elsewhere and vice versa. This is the paradox of equal treatment so eloquently expressed by Anatole France in his observation that "[t]he law, in its majestic equality, forbids the rich as well as the poor to sleep under bridges, to beg in the streets, and to steal bread."[65] A public sector that ignores the inequalities of the private sector formulates its policy in a vacuum. Inequality in one realm can sometimes be warranted because it tends to reduce inequality in another.[66] This paradox received its most explicit consideration by the Supreme Court in the case of *Griffin v. Illinois*,[67] where the Court required the state, in effect, to eliminate the effects of a private sector inequality, poverty, by substituting a public sector inequality, free court transcripts for the indigent on appeal. Seeing perhaps more clearly than his majority colleagues the full implications of the ruling, Justice Harlan feared that it "imposes on the States an affirmative duty to lift the handicaps flowing from differences in economic circumstances."[68]

Apart from the various meanings and objects attached to the concept of equality, several specific problems inhere in its use as a test of the distribution of urban services. Four of these are identified here: the problem of choosing the appropriate units of analysis, the issue of the permissible range of variation, the necessity for tradeoffs between equality and other socially valued criteria, and the confusion of input with output equality.

B. Equal to Whom? The Units of Analysis Problem and the Ecological Fallacy

Proponents of urban service equalization recognize that services cannot literally be provided equally to every citizen. One who insists on equal educational programs would not demand that all pupils have identical books, teachers, curricula, and laboratories. Rather, the argument favors a rough equivalence of schools in various neighborhoods, and the school becomes the unit of analysis. With respect to parks and libraries, it is obviously impossible to provide equally accessible facilities to every individual unless the city locates a park or library on every doorstep. Hence, some neighborhood or sociospatial area becomes the unit of analysis. Not even the most ardent advocate of equal services expects police patrols to be as frequent on the quiet residential cul-de-sac as on a major boulevard. The object, rather, is to secure proportional or equivalent patrol practices among various neighborhoods. The goal in each case, then, is the equalization of public service deliveries to areal units, rather than to individuals. But the fourteenth amendment makes the individual the only unit of analysis for constitutional purposes; equal protection is provided "between persons as such rather than between areas."[69]

In *Norwalk CORE v. Norwalk Board of Education*[70] a federal district court faced the unit of analysis problem directly:

> Although *people* are equal and governmental classification by race will not be tolerated, *neighborhoods* are not. . . . [W]hile neighborhoods theoretically may be created equal, as a practical matter they do not remain equal and the law does not command that they be treated equally . . . [I]t is doubtful that residents of one neighborhood appropriately may claim the benefits of circumstances similar to those of another, where a neighborhood classification has been made.[71]

This is a thorny thicket indeed, doubly so because of the implication that the whole (the neighborhood) may not be equal to the sum of its parts (the individuals within it). It does raise the question whether denials of equal protection in the delivery of municipal services must be demonstrated and rectified on an individual basis or on the basis of some larger aggregate; and, if the latter, at what aggregate level. Other courts have been more sanguine about the application of equal protection to aggregate units. In *Shaw*, for example, the Fifth Circuit resorted to an areal focus in its holding of service discrimination, and, in a challenge to the administration of the District of Columbia schools, the court ordered equalization to the individual school plant, not to the individual student.[72]

Assuming, then, that some aggregate larger than the individual is an appropriate unit of analysis in service equalization issues, what aggregate is appropriate? Shall we insist on service equality at the level of the block, the census tract, the neighborhood, or the "side of town"? Because of the "ecological fallacy," this is not merely an idle or academic question. Some years ago the demographer W. S. Robinson demonstrated that inferences drawn from data based on a particular aggregate, whether a census tract, precinct, city, state, or any other areal base, do not necessarily describe the traits of individuals within those aggregates.[73] For example, the finding that divorce rates correlate positively by census tract with the percentage of whites in the population does not mean that white marriages are more likely to end in divorce. Even more troubling is the fact that a relationship identified at one level of analysis (for example, the individual level) may be reversed based on data from another unit of analysis. It is well known, for example, that electoral participation is positively related to educational levels.[74] Yet when mean participation rates by city are related to the mean educational level of the population, the correlation is negative.[75]

The unit of analysis problem poses two practical difficulties for the service equalization issue. First, because aggregated data is nearly always required to demonstrate service inequalities, the danger of the ecological fallacy is omnipresent. In fact, one reason the Court majority gave for rejecting the *Rodriguez* petition for school finance equalization was in effect an argument based on the ecological fallacy. Citing an elaborate statistical analysis,[76] the Court observed that poor families do not necessarily live in poor school districts.[77] Although apparently unfamiliar with the ecological fallacy concept, the Court argued that what was true at an aggregate level—the school district—was not necessarily true of the individuals within it.

A second problem may be posed in the form of a dilemma. Selection of a very small unit of analysis may make it impossible to guarantee equality of services. It would be enormously expensive, because of the diseconomies of scale involved, to require equalization of parks, libraries, and fire and police protection to the block or perhaps even to the census tract. But the larger the unit chosen, the more the ecological fallacy may obscure the real correlations between the attributes of individuals and the services they receive. Moreover, the progressive enlargement of the unit raises the problem of where to stop. If equality is mandated among census tracts, then why not among cities themselves? The logical extension of the equal protection mandate would require equal services from the smallest unit chosen to the state border.[78]

C. The Permissible Range of Variation

As with most test cases, *Shaw* focused on painfully evident inequalities; the notion of "have and have not" with respect to public services was almost literally true. Yet no study of the distribution of public services in a large city—even when finding clear evidence of discrimination against minority neighborhoods—has unearthed such extreme differences.[79]

Assuming the standard of per capita equality for the distribution of municipal services, how unequally must services be allocated before they violate the test? Because the price of perfect equality in any public service must surely be prohibitive, not every demonstration of inequality, however trivial, suffices to violate the per capita test. The issue of permissible variances is crucial both to the determination of the flagrancy of the deviation from the standard and to the fashioning of a remedy. If the test of equality is applied too literally, it becomes not merely impossible of attainment, but an absurdity. As Glazer has commented, "[J]ust as there is no point at which the sea of misery is finally drained, so, too, there is no point at which the equality revolution can come to an end, if only because as it proceeds we become ever more sensitive to smaller and smaller degrees of inequality."[80] This is a road that, if followed to its end, can lead only to the obfuscation of real inequalities by the incessant identification of trivial ones.

D. Tradeoffs Between Equality and Contending Standards for the Delivery of Urban Services

The tradeoff concept in economic analysis recognizes the impossibility of maximizing two contending values simultaneously. With relatively fixed resources, one cannot maximize both guns and butter. With respect to service delivery criteria, the relentless pursuit of equality as a social and judicial policy entails tradeoffs with other important values. Chief among these are efficiency, citizen preference, and need.

1. Equality vs. Efficiency. Equal distribution does not guarantee efficient distribution. Stated most simply, efficiency is securing the most output with the smallest amount of input. For example, suppose the output goal of a police department is the minimization of crime.[81] Wherever patterns of crime are identified, the police department clusters its resources to prevent crime and apprehend criminals. Such husbanding of resources in high-crime areas is justified on the ground that concentration of resources is the most efficient way to minimize crime within the city. According to the efficiency principle, resource equalization in each neighborhood, regardless of the crime rate, would be irrational. Many violations in a high-crime neighborhood would go unchecked, while "overkill" would result in low-crime areas. Partly because of the inherent difficulties in determining "efficient" uses of resources, courts have traditionally granted a wide discretionary latitude to municipal bureaucracies in determining service allocation patterns.[82] The historical rationale of those decisions has been that administrators are in a better position than courts to determine the efficient allocation of resources.[83] In any event, it is clear that efficiency and equality are contending principles, both of which are legitimate objects of public policy.

2. Equality vs. Consumer Preference. The notion that citizen preferences should determine the distribution of government benefits is one that will unite many citizens, especially democratic theorists and economists. While the public sector by definition is not a free market with consumer sovereignty, there is no a priori justification for government to operate in total disregard of consumer priorities; citzens' tastes are not identical, and in a democratic polity it is reasonable to honor preferences to the extent possible.[84] A narrow insistence on per capita equality as a test of all service distributions will not promote, and might possibly hinder, government's capacity to satisfy varying preference patterns for public goods and services. In a larger sense, one might conceptualize equality as an equal opportunity to have one's tastes transformed into public policy. This is a very different meaning than is implied in the traditional service equalization concept, which emphasizes a per capita test.

3. Equality vs. Need. The concept of "need" is a slippery one that, like beauty, tends to exist in the eyes of the beholder. All political issues are rhetorically wrapped in the raiment of "need," which typically correlates with the advocate's self-interest. No doubt in part because of the ambiguity surrounding the notion of need, the Supreme Court refused to review a holding that a challenge based on the failure to meet educational needs of pupils does not present a judiciable standard.[85] There is, however, a sense in which public policy may be a function of the needs of various groups and areas. Few would dispute the proposition that high density areas of old, frame houses need more fire protection than areas of new, all-brick construction, or that some areas need more TB clinics, mosquito eradication, or traffic control devices. An insistence on per capita equality of service outputs would ignore variations in need.

Determination of needs becomes more complex, however, when it is paired with the demands of consumer preferences. It could be argued that better educated areas of the community "need" more library facilities because their residents read more.[86] Equally persuasive, however, is the contention that poorer and less well-educated sectors of the population "need" more libraries because their inhabitants cannot afford private reading materials. Arguably, low income families clustered in poorer neighborhoods have more "need" for public parks and recreational facilities because they are unable to secure the leisure opportunities (spacious backyards, time and money for travel) afforded the more affluent classes by the private sector. At such points, the contending standards of needs, preferences, and equality meet directly, and tradeoffs must be made as a matter of social policy.

E.   The Confusion of Input and Output Equality

Virtually all service equalization challenges have focused narrowly on "input equality" rather than on the more significant issue of "output equality."[87] Demands for input equality focus on such things as resources and expenditures, facilities, personnel, and equipment— in other words, the raw materials required to produce some valued output. Output equality, on the other hand, focuses not on which resources go in, but rather on what product results.[88] Applying an incipient output equality concept to education, Coleman argued, on the basis of an extensive government-sponsored survey,[89] that

> [T]he schools are successful only insofar as they reduce the dependence of a child's opportunities upon his social origins. . . . *Thus equality of educational opportunity implies not merely equal schools, but equally effective schools,* whose influences will overcome the differences in starting points of children from different social groups.[90]

Although there are difficulties associated with the application of the output equality test, that test does demonstrate two dangers in the exclusive use of input tests of service equality. First, input tests may focus on a single dimension of inputs, particularly expenditures, as a satisfactory test of service equality. Yet expenditures may be a poor index of both the equality and quality of public services. An increasing volume of evidence has accumulated, in the realms of education and other services, to show that expenditures are a most doubtful measure of services actually rendered.[91] Expenditure differences are a function of a number of factors—price and wage differentials, vandalism, inefficiency—unrelated to the quality of service outputs.[92]

The second danger is that inputs, however measured, may have only a weak relationship to outputs. From the consumer's perspective, the inputs that combine to produce a product are relatively unimportant, so long as the output is satisfactory in price and quality. Similarly, concern about public services is most appropriately directed at their outputs. In law enforcement the number of suspects apprehended is far more important than the number of policemen; in fire protection the dollars of fire loss is a more important indicator of success than the condition of equipment; in education the knowledge acquired is more important than the pupil-teacher ratio.

The primary reliance on input tests of service equality, therefore, obscures the more important nexus between public policy and citizens by focusing on the elements of production rather than on the outcomes of production. Output equality, although ultimately a more realistic standard, is also far more difficult to measure. Over the long run, production functions in various areas of public services must be developed.[93] The present state of knowledge in the social sciences probably cannot support a challenge to service inequalities based on the output concept. If input equality concerns the equalization of resources, then output equality involves the equalization of results. Output equality as a test consequently requires the specification and measurement of agency goals, objectives, or "results," and the capacity of public agencies to assure the achievement of those results.

Specification of a public agency's objectives is always difficult.[94] The official objectives of a service agency are often vague and ambiguous; even when clearly stated, they tend to be so broad in scope ("to improve the quality of people's lives through reading," "to give people recreational opportunities") as to defy precise measurement. Furthermore, agencies simultaneously serve a multitude of objectives, some of which may conflict with others.[95] Agencies are expected to provide employment opportunities for minority groups, to meet unofficial, "political" objectives, and to comply with other demands unrelated to achievement of their officially defined objectives.[96]

While the difficulties in defining service objectives are frustrating, they are susceptible to measurement in some cases.[97] Far more serious is the problem of assuring results. The activities of a given service agency seldom, if ever, are the sole determinants of the degree to which the agency's goal of a certain environmental state (a secure community, an educated citizenry, etc.) prevails. Rather, the existence of this "goal state" depends on a host of factors, only some of which are within the purview of the agency's capabilities.[98] For example, the goal of police work is a secure community. But police activity, while important, is rarely, if ever, the sole contributor to community security.[99] The ultimately limited capacity of the police to prevent (let alone equalize) crime is illustrated in the following comments of the President's Commission on Law Enforcement and the Administration of Justice:

> The police did not start and cannot stop the convulsive social changes that are taking place in America. They do not enact the laws they are trying to enforce, nor do they dispose of the criminals they arrest. The police are only one part of the criminal justice system; the criminal justice system is only one part of the government; and the government is only one part of society.[100]

Assuring equal output (for example, equivalence of crime rates, educational results, fire loss rates) is simply beyond the present capacity of most public authorities in the United States.

IV. PUBLIC POLICY, THE COURTS, AND CONVENTIONAL URBAN SERVICES

The standard of equality is a complex one, and the input or per capita equality test in particular exhibits numerous problems in its application to conventional urban services. These are even more acute when the input equality test is narrowed to the single dimension of expenditures.[101] The problems identified, including those of measurement, units of analysis, tradeoffs, and the confusion of input and output equality, demonstrate that any simple application of an egalitarian test to urban services involves serious dilemmas. Obviously, the time has long passed when courts may content themselves with the observation that "statistics often tell much, and Courts listen."[102] Figures do not speak for themselves; they speak only through the mouths and pages of their discoverers, analysts, and interpreters. The evidence on service distribution will invariably be statistical, and data alone provide no warrant for action without some decisional principle. Few demonstrations of service discrimination are likely to be as blatant and unambiguous as in *Shaw*.

Caught between the inherent limitations of a per capita equality standard on the one hand and the virtual impossibility of guaranteeing output equality on the other, policymakers and courts may either abandon the quest for service equalization or seek higher (or middle) ground. Abandonment will consign disadvantaged citizens to the mercy of the electoral process, where the nexus between citizen participation and policy change is not clearly established.[103] Whether the electoral process would have aided the citizens of Shaw, Mississippi, is by no means certain.

Alternatively, middle ground can be secured through the vehicle of the rationality standard.[104] Like equality itself, various formulations of the rationality concept permeate the law, philosophy, and the social sciences. All public policy is—or more precisely, should be—goal-directed, and goal-oriented behavior is exactly what the canon of rationality entails. In a strict sense, rational policymaking requires successive means-end analyses, in which any number of possible means to the accomplishment of a posited goal are compared with respect to their relative costs and benefits, and the one with the most favorable ratio is selected. Such a stringent standard of rationality, however, would be prohibitively expensive in terms of the amount of time, money, and information required, and in fact is incompatible with present computational capabilities.[105] Because of these limitations, "rationality-striving" can at best be a crude approximation of the best choice; therefore, what is required is not the maximum payoff, but simply a satisfactory one.[106] Even with this loosening of the standard, rationality is still conceptualized essentially as choosing a reasonable alternative, and thus is concerned with goal-directed behavior.[107]

Every public service agency attempts to achieve some goals however inchoate their formulation and difficult their specification.[108] Fire departments attempt to reduce fire loss, police departments to reduce crime and facilitate traffic movement, health departments to minimize epidemic potential, etc. The rationality standard as a decisional principle requires that the means chosen to effectuate agency objectives be purposive and based on relevant criteria. This approach would be more stringent than the familiar rational basis test, "which requires only that the State's system be shown to bear some rational relationship to legitimate state purposes."[109] As enunciated by Professor Yudof in the context of school financing,

> The rationality standard requires that the state may not discriminate . . . in the allocation of public funds . . . without a substantial and rational justification. The criteria for distributing the resources must relate to the characteristics of the beneficiaries of the service . . . or to the costs of the programs required to meet their needs as the state perceives them.[110]

A number of possible arrangements of resources might bear a relationship to agency purposes sufficient to pass muster under the rationality standard. With respect to the objectives of crime control, for example, there are numerous ways in which police department resources might be intelligently allocated. Departments might cluster police protection in high-crime areas to achieve the goal of crime minimization. The criterion employed—crime rates—to determine allocation of the resource would be relevant to the beneficiaries' needs and to the attainment of the goal. Similarly, departments might equalize services among neighborhoods so that each citizen receives an equal opportunity to enjoy the fruits of law enforcement. Even though one approach maximizes the goal of crime *minimization*, and the other the goal of service *equalization*, the criteria employed in each case are relevant to perceived citizen needs, and both distributions bear a sufficient relation to the objective of urban law enforcement.[111] On the other hand, a distributional pattern that clusters police resources in low-crime, high-wealth areas would fail under the rationality standard. A wealth criterion alone is inapposite to the need for police services; while crime rates are relevant, the concentration of resources in low-crime areas would not be rationally related to maximizing agency objectives.

The rationality standard does not, of course, provide courts a mathematical formula for the resolution of municipal services distribution challenges. Several issues that are beyond the scope of the present discussion remain; certain criteria may be relevant to the achievement of one objective but not another, and the determination of relevancy will not always be clear. Nevertheless, the rationality standard—unlike the tests of input and output equality, need, efficiency, and the like—does not overreach judicial capacity.[112] Courts are not required to substitute judicial opinion for administrative discretion on a day-to-day basis. Instead, the rationality standard requires the court to determine solely whether a particular means is grounded on relevant criteria and is appropriate to a public service agency's stated end. The necessity for ascertaining means-ends relationships with respect to urban public policy should not unduly burden the courts. Indeed, some states now require courts to determine whether public services provided to an annexed area of a municipality are commensurate with services provided to previously incorporated areas.[113] The judiciary has undertaken this task with great care and sophistication.[114] Surely courts capable of judging variations in services between old and new areas of a city can assess rational patterns of service delivery in the city as a whole. Inevitably, legal challenges to the distribution of municipal public services will continue. The rationality standard provides the courts a workable decisional principle with which to resolve these conflicts.

NOTES

1. H. Lasswell, *Politics: Who Gets What When How* (1938)
2. Reich, "The New Property," 73 *Yale L J*. 733 (1964).
3. In fiscal 1971, state and local government expenditures totaled $171 billion; federal expenditures for the same period totaled $199 billion, U.S. Bureau of the Census, *Statistical Abstract of the United States* 410 (1973) [hereinafter cited as *Statistical Abstract*], with $77.7 billion of that amount going for defense, *id*. at 390.
4. *Id*. at 431.
5. City of San Antonio, Annual Budget: Aug. 1, 1971—July 31, 1972, at 276.
6. S. Miller & P. Roby, *The Future of Inequality*, ch. 5 (1970).
7. One commentator illustrated the importance of urban public services in a citizen's life cycle as follows:

Modern urban man is born in a publicly financed hospital, receives his education in a publicly supported school and university, spends a good part of his time travelling on publicly built transportation facilities, communicates through the post office or the quasi-public telephone system, drinks his public water, diposes of his garbage through the public removal system, reads his public library books, picnics in his public parks, and is protected by public police, fire, and health systems; eventually he dies, again in a hospital, and may even be buried in a public cemetary [*sic*]. Ideological conservatives notwithstanding, his everyday life is inextricably bound up with government decisions on these and numerous other local public services.

Teitz, "Toward a Theory of Urban Public Facility Location," 21 Regional Sci. Ass'n Papers 35, 36 (1968).
8. Claude Brown, speaking of his early years in Harlem, writes: "Harlem was [ignored] by everybody, the politicians, the police, the businessmen, everybody. . . . We'd laugh

about how when the big snowstorms came, they'd have the snowplows out downtown as soon as it stopped, but they'd let it pile up for weeks in Harlem." C. Brown, *Manchild in the Promised Land* 190 (1965). A witness told the United States Civil Rights Commission, "In the section of Roxbury in which I live we have been fighting for street lights for quite some time. But they have completely ignored us. . . . I feel it is because this area is predominatly Negro. If it was any other area they would have gotten action." U.S. Comm'n on Civil Rights, *A Time to Listen—A Time to Act* 18–19 (1967). Similar minority group sentiments abound.

9. Logue, *Prospects for the Metropolis*, in *Thinking about Cities* 127, 128 (A. Pascal ed. 1970); Lowry, *Housing*, in *Cities in Trouble: An Agenda for Urban Research* 20, 22 (A. Pascal ed. 1968).

10. Several economists have developed a theoretical model of residential locational choice among municipalities within the metropolitan area that assumes that location decisions are a function of citizen evaluation of packages of taxes and services offered by various communities. Tiebout suggests the following:

Consider . . . the case of the city resident about to move to the suburbs. What variables will influence his choice of a municipality? If he has children, a high level of expenditure on schools may be important. Another person may prefer a community with a municipal golf course. The availability and quality of such facilities as beaches, parks, police protection, roads, and parking facilities will enter into the decision-making process. . . .

The consumer voter may be viewed as picking that community which best satisfies his preference pattern for public goods.

Tiebout, "A Pure Theory of Local Expenditures," in *The New Urbanization* 355, 358 (1968). *See also* Warren, "A Municipal Services Market of Metropolitan Organization," 30 Am. Inst. of Planners J. 193 (1964). This "rational economic man" approach to urban residential mobility is criticized in W. Thompson, *A Preface to Urban Economics* 259–63 (1965).

11. For a discussion of the move toward community control, see A. Altshuler, *Community Control* (1970); M. Kotler, *Neighborhood Government* (1969).

12. It ranked police practices, inadequate education, poor recreation facilities and programs, and inadequacy of municipal services (the latter apparently a catchall category) as first, fourth, fifth, and tenth among riot area residents' twelve major grievances. *National Advisory Comm'n on Civil Disorders*, Report 81–83 (1968).

13. 437 F.2d 1286 (5th Cir. 1971). The issues of unequal burdens and benefits in the realm of public school financing were crystallized in Serrano *v*. Priest, 5 Cal. 3d 584, 487 P.2d 1241, 96 Cal. Rptr. 601 (1971), and San Antonio Indep. School Dist. *v*. Rodriguez, 411 U.S. 1 (1973). Both cases involved challenges to inter-district differences in educational expenditures. The problem of service distribution is analogous but not identical, for it focuses on intra-, rather than inter-municipal inequities.

14. 437 F.2d at 1287.

15. *Statistical Abstract, supra* note 3, at 17.

16. Commission on Population Growth and the American Future, Population and the American Future 25 (1972) (emphasis in original).

17. E. Banfield, *The Unheavenly City* 23 (1970). The author suggests that the demographic imperative dictates that a city expand in response to population growth; the technological imperative determines whether that expansion will be in a horizontal or a vertical plane; and the economic imperative controls which group, the "well-off" or the "not well-off," will occupy the periphery of the city.

18. O. Williams, *Metropolitan Political Analysis* 43 (1971). Williams compares the urban gang and the adult coalition as follows:

The membership is well defined, the norms of the group quite real, albeit far from explicit, and the boundaries of the turf specific in the minds of the gang members. Gangs follow a variety of strategies, which approximate the practices of adult urban coalitions. They defend their turf against incursions by nonmembers; they build the reputation of the gang by its activities . . .; and they purify by trying to drive out incompatible persons.

Id.

19. See generally R. Ardrey, *The Territorial Imperative* (1966).

20. "[L]ay siege against it, and build a fort against it, and cast a mount against it; set the camp also against it, and set battering rams against it round about. Moreover take thou unto thee an iron pan, and set it for a wall of iron between thee and the city. . . ." *Ezekiel* 4:2–3 (King James version).

21. On exlusionary zoning see Aloi & Goldberg, "Racial and Economic Exclusionary Zoning: The Beginning of the End," 1971 *Urban L. Ann.* 9; Davidoff & Gold, "Exclusionary Zoning," *Yale Rev. L. & Soc. Action*, Winter 1970, at 56; Sager, "Tight Little Islands: Exclusionary Zoning, Equal Protection, and the Indigent," *21 Stan. L. Rev.* 767 (1969); Note, "Exclusionary Zoning and Equal Protection," 84 *Harv. L. Rev.* 1645 (1971). For an empirical assessment of the effects of zoning, which found qualified support for some of the assumptions of the exclusionary zoning model, see Branfman, Cohen & Trubek, "Measuring the Invisible Wall: Land Use Controls and the Residential Patterns of the Poor," 82 *Yale L.J.* 483 (1973).

22. Newark, New Jersey, an often prototypical example of urban problems, provides a case in point. Taxes "are confiscatory. Homeowners pay property tax of 9.63 dollars per 100 dollars of assessed valuation. Since homes in the city are assessed at close to 100 percent of their real worth, a homeowner with a home valued at $20,000 must pay almost $2000 in taxes. And it may get far worse." *Wash. Post*, Dec. 2, 1972, at 10, col. 1.

23. On metropolitan governmental fragmentation and its socioeconomic consequences, see Sacks & Callahan, "Central City Suburban Fiscal Disparity," in *Advisory Comm'n on Intergovernmental Relations, City Financial Emergencies: The Intergovernmental Dimension* 91 (1973); 2 Advisory Comm'n on Intergovernmental Relations, *Fiscal Balance in the American Federal System* (1967); Lineberry, "Reforming Metropolitan Governance: Requiem or Reality," 58 *Geo. L.J.* 675, 676–78 (1970).

24. Sacks & Callahan, *supra* note 23, at 92.

25. *Id.*

26. Taeuber and Taeuber constructed a "segregation index," which varies from 100 (complete segregation with no whites in black areas) to 0 (complete integration with random distribution by race). In their studies of 109 American cities from 1940 through 1960, high

and stable patterns of segregation were discovered, with mean scores for all cities of 85.2 in 1940, 87.3 in 1950, and 86.1 in 1960. K. Taeuber & A. Taeuber, *Negroes in Cities* 44 (1965). Evidence from special censuses between 1960 and 1970 confirm these patterns. Farley and Taeuber, "Population Trends and Residential Segregation since 1960," 159 *Science* 953 (1968). There is, however, scattered evidence of a weakening of the segregated pattern in the most recent years. See Poston & Passell, "Racial Residential Segregation in Cities," 46 *Tex. Bus. Rev.* 142 (1972). Whether such findings would be typical of communities in the rest of the nation awaits additional research.

27. *See* R. Helper, *Racial Policies & Practices of Real Estate Boards* (1969); Taeuber, "Residential Segregation," 213 *Sci. Am.* 12, 18 (1965).

28. U.S. Comm'n on Civil Rights, *Racial Isolation in the Public Schools* 62 (1967).

29. *See* Gautreaux *v.* Chicago Housing Auth., 304 F. Supp. 736 (N.D. Ill. 1969) (injunction against locating projects in predominantly minority areas of Chicago).

30. For an extensive analysis of the Austin case, from which the textual synopsis is taken, see S. Kraus, "Water, Sewers, and Streets: The Acquisition of Public Utilities" in Austin, Texas, 1875–1930 (unpublished thesis in University of Texas Library, May 1973).

31. *Quoted in id.* at 151 (emphasis added).

32. 437 F.2d 1286 (5th Cir. 1971).

33. *Id.* at 1288.

34. 347 U.S. 483 (1954).

35. Rosenthal, "Appeals Court Bids Town Give Races Equal Service," N.Y. Times, Feb. 2, 1971, at 1, col. 2.

36. *Time*, Feb. 22, 1971, at 59.

37. Comment, "Equal Municipal Services for the Other Side of the Tracks," 43 *Miss. L.J.* 67, 89 (1972). On the issues surrounding the *Shaw* decision see Fessler & Forrester, "The Case for the Immediate Environment" (pts. 1 & 2), 4 *Clearinghouse Rev.* 1, 49 (1970); Fessler & Haar, "Beyond the Wrong Side of the Tracks," 6 *Harv. Civ. Rights-Civ. Lib. L. Rev.* 441 (1971); Graham & Kravitt, "The Evolution of Equal Protection—Education, Municipal Services, and Wealth," 7 *Harv. Civ. Rights-Civ. Lib L. Rev.* 103 (1972); Note, "Equalization of Municipal Services: The Economics of Serrano and Shaw," 82 *Yale L.J.* 89 (1972).

38. Comment, Hawkins v. Town of Shaw—"Equal Protection and Municipal Services: A Small Leap for Minorities but a Giant Leap for the Commentators," 1971 *Utah L. Rev.* 397 (1971).

39. In the San Francisco suit, Woo v. Alioto, Civil No. 52,100 (N.D. Cal., filed Oct. 17, 1969), plaintiffs, impoverished residents of Chinatown, claimed that proportionately fewer recreational facilities and services were available in their area than in other sections of the city. They were eventually forced, however, to accept an unfavorable out-of-court settlement when 1970 census results failed to substantiate population projections upon which much of the factual portion of their case was based. Letter from E. H. Steinman, plaintiffs' attorney, to the author, July 13, 1972. In the New York City case, Beal v. Lindsay, 468 F.2d 287 (2d Cir. 1972), black and Puerto Rican residents of the Bronx alleged that a park located in their neighborhood was not being maintained by the city in a condition comparable to that of parks in predominantly white areas of the borough. City officials did not dispute

plaintiffs' allegations concerning the park's deplorable condition, but contended that this condition resulted from a high degree of vandalism, not a deficient city maintenance effort. Judge Friendly, while sympathizing with plaintiffs' complaint, ruled for the court that the city had satisfied its constitutional obligations by making an equal effort to provide all citizens with the same level of service, even though, because of conditions for which it was not responsible, it did not achieve equal results.

40. Burner v. Washington, Civil No. 242–71 (D.D.C., filed Jan. 28, 1971). This suit alleged discrimination in zoning practices, in the administration of housing programs, and in the provision of "essential" municipal services, including police and fire protection, refuse collection, public transportation, education, recreation facilities, and sidewalks.

41. *See, e.g.,* Veach v. City of Phoenix, 102 Ariz. 195, 427 P. 2d 335 (1967) (fire protection); Travaini v. Maricopa Co., 9 Ariz. App. 228, 229, 450 P. 2d 1021, 1022 (1969) (public) sewers); Bair *v.* Mayor & City Council, 243 Md. 494, 498–99, 221 A.2d 643, 645 (1966) (water service); 3 J. Dillon, *Municipal Corporations* § 1298 (5th ed. 1911.)

42. On the development and concept of equal protection, see Tussman & tenBroek, "The Equal Protection of the Laws," 37 *Calif. L. Rev.* 341 (1949). For subsequent development under the Warren Court, see "Developments in the Law: Equal Protection," 82 *Harv. L. Rev.* 1065 (1969).

43. Brown v. Board of Educ., 347 U.S. 483 (1954).

44. Reynolds v. Sims, 377 U.S. 533 (1964).

45. Shapiro v. Thompson, 394 U.S. 618 (1969).

46. *See, e.g.,* Hunter v. Erickson, 393 U.S. 385 (1969); Loving v. Virginia, 388 U.S. 1 (1967); McLaughlin v. Florida, 379 U.S. 184 (1964).

47. 394 U.S. 802 (1969).

48. *Id.* at 807 (emphasis added).

49. In Serrano v. Priest, 5 Cal. 3d 584, 487 P.2d 1241, 96 Cal. Rptr. 601 (1971), the California Supreme Court noted that "none of the wealth classfications previously invalidated by the United States Supreme Court or this court has been the product of purposeful discrimination. Instead, these prior decisions have involved unintentional classifications whose impact simply fell more heavily upon the poor." *Id.* at 602, 487, P.2d at 1253, 96 Cal. Rptr. at 613.

50. 411 U.S. 1 (1973)

51. Brooks v. Beto, 366 F. 2d 1, 9 (5th Cir. 1966).

52. Hirsch, "The Supply of Urban Public Services," in *Issues in Urban Economics* 477, 519 (H. Perloff & L. Wingo eds. 1968).

53. For a more inclusive listing of indicia for the measurment of urban public service performance, see Lineberry & Welch, "Who Gets What: Measuring the Distribution of Urban Public Services," 54 *Soc. Sci. Q.* 700 (1974).

54. The research reported in this section was conducted with the assistance of a grant from the National Science Foundation, which, of course, bears no responsibility for the interpretations or analysis.

55. *Statistical Abstract, supra* note 3, at 891.

56. *See id.* at 851, 871.

57. U.S. Bureau of the Census, 1970, *Census of Population and Housing: San Antonio, Texas SMSA*, at P–1 (1972); *see id.* at P–18.

58. From 1955 through 1971, 88 of the city's 113 census tracts had no councilmen elected from them. In general, the represented census tracts exhibited the usual traits of an upper-middle class population, such as higher incomes, fewer minorities, higher educational attainments, and higher home values.

On the tendency of at-large elections to produce fewer minority and nonaffluent council members, see Sloan, "Good Government and the Politics of Race," 17 *Soc. Prob.* 161 (1969); Note "Ghetto Voting and At-Large Elections: A Subtle Infringement upon Minority Rights," 58 *Geo. LJ.* 989 (1970).

59. *E.g.*, B. Berelson, *The Library's Public* 43–44 (1949).

60. *E.g.*, American Library Ass'n, *Access to Public Libraries* (1963); L. Martin, *Library Response to Urban Change* (1969).

61. The following were included: number of professional personnel, age of the library building, number of new books added annually, circulation, and space.

62. J. Stephen, *Liberty Equality and Fraternity* 201 (1873).

63. *See, e.g.*, H. Gans, *More Equality* (1973); C. Jencks, *Inequality* (1972); Bell, Moynihan & Lipset, "Symposium on Equality," *Pub. Interest*, Fall 1972, at 29.

64. S. Lakoff, *Equality in Political Philosophy* 6 (1964).

65. *Quoted in* J. Cournos, *Modern Plutarch* 27 (1928).

66. Compensatory education is certainly not equal education, even though equality is its defense. Rawls suggests that "the idea is to redress the bias of contingencies in the direction of equality. In pursuit of this principle greater resources might be spent on the education of the less rather than the more intelligent, at least over a certain time of life, say the earlier years of school." J. Rawls, *A Theory of Justice* 100–01 (1971).

67. 351 U.S. 12 (1956).

68. *Id.* at 34 (dissenting opinion).

69. Salsburg v. Maryland, 346 U.S. 545, 551 (1954).

70. 298 F. Supp. 213 (D. Conn. 1969).

71. *Id.* at 222–23 (emphasis in original).

72. Hobson v. Hansen, 269 F. Supp. 401, 514–18 (D.D.C. 1967), *aff'd sub nom.* Smuck v. Hobson, 408 F.2d 175 (D.C. Cir. 1969).

73. Robinson, "Ecological Correlations and the Behavior of Individuals," 15 *Am. Soc. Rev.* 351 (1950).

74. *E.g.*, L. Milbrath, *Political Participation* 122 (1965).

75. Alford & Lee, "Voting Turnout in American Cities," 62 *Am. Pol. Sci. Rev.* 796, 803 (1968).

76. Note, "A Statistical Analysis of the School Finance Decisions: On Winning Battles and Losing Wars," 81 *Yale LJ.* 1303 (1972).

77. 411 U.S. at 23. The statement came partly in response to evidence purporting to show that poor people are concentrated in the poorest districts. *See id.* at 15 n.38. Justice Marshall noted in dissent that

> [I]t cannot be ignored that the data introduced by appellees went unchallenged in the District Court. The majority's willingness to permit appellants to litigate the correctness of that data for the first time before this tribunal—where effective response by appellees is impossible—is both unfair and judicially unsound.

Id. at 95–96 n.56.

78. The reading of *Shaw* and *Serrano* together might effectively require the equalization

of municipal services on both an intra-municipal and an inter-municipal level, hence from the neighborhood to the state border. Comment, "The Evolution of Equal Protection: Education, Municipal Services, and Wealth," 7 *Harv. Civ. Rights-Civ. Lib. L. Rev.* 105, 157 n.227 (1972).

79. For example, one study of school expenditures in Chicago found that predominantly black schools received an average of $391 per pupil in 1969–70, while white schools received $423, a $32 differential. Berk, Mack & McKnight, Race and Class Differences in Per Pupil Staffing Expenditures in Chicago Elementary Schools, 1969–70, at 1–2 (Northwestern University Center for Urban Affairs). Such differences do not compare in magnitude with those observed in *Shaw*.

For a review of studies of municipal service allocation, see Lineberry, "Equality of Urban Services and the Quality of Urban Life," in *Politics and the Quality of Urban Life* (W. Hanna ed. 1975).

80. Glazer, "The Limits of Social Policy," *Commentary*, Sept. 1971, at 51–53.

81. On the implications of various definitions of efficiency in the distribution of police protection, see Shoup, "Standards for Distributing a Free Governmental Service: Crime Prevention," 19 *Pub. Fin.* 383 (1964); Thurow, "Equity versus Efficiency in Law Enforcement," 18 *Pub. Policy* 451 (1970).

82. *See, e.g.,* Gowan v. Smith, 157 Mich. 443, 473, 122 N.W. 286, 297 (1909); Riss v. City of New York, 22 N.Y.2d 579, 240 N.E.2d 860, 293 N.Y.S.2d 897 (1968); 2 E. McQuillin, *The Law of Municipal Corporations* § 10.33 (3d ed. rev. vol. 1966).

83. At the same time, however, it is worth noting that administrative discretion does not assure intelligent policy. One study of police patrol practices in Kansas City, Missouri, experimentally divided the city into matched neighborhoods and varied police patrol practices within the neighborhoods for one year. At the conclusion of the test, changes in the crime rate among neighborhoods with extraordinary police patrolling did not significantly differ from those in areas with no regular patrols, thus calling into question the principal crime-control technique in virtually every urban police department. N.Y. Times, Nov. 11, 1973, at 1, col. 5. Moreover, administrative discretion itself is a constant source of inequality in the public sector. As Madison observed, "[I]n every political institution, a power to advance the public happiness involves a discretion which may be misapplied and abused." *The Federalist* No. 41, at 275 (Bourne ed. 1937). For a critical analysis of administrative discretion see K. Davis, *Discretionary Justice* (1969).

84. That citizen tastes do vary is illustrated by the data compiled in a study of spending priorities among three ethnic groups in Denver, Colorado. Lovrich, "Differing Priorities in an Urban Electorate: Service Preferences Among Anglo, Black, and Mexican-American Voters," 55 *Soc. Sci. Q.*—(1974). Ranking eight services according to preference, Anglos listed pollution control, public protection, and public transportation as their top priorities, while both blacks and Mexican-Americans rated health and hospitals, urban renewal, and public protection as most important. Anglos gave welfare services the lowest priority, blacks accorded pollution control the lowest preference rating, and Mexican-Americans chose city planning and management.

85. McInnis v. Ogilvie, 394 U.S. 322, *aff'g* McInnis v. Shapiro, 293 F. Supp. 327 (1969). *See also* Doe v. San Francisco Unified School Dist., Civil No. 653–312 (Super. Ct. San

Francisco, Dec. 3, 1974) (plaintiff demanded damages for school authorities' alleged failure to provide a high school graduate with basic educational skills; case dismissed for plaintiff's failure to amend after demurrer sustained).

86. A study of library services offered by Baltimore's Enoch Pratt Library indicates that level of education correlates highly with number of books read. L. Martin, *Baltimore Reaches Out: Library Services to the Disadvantaged* 29–31 (1967).

87. For an evaluation of input and output equality as standards of public service distribution, see Lineberry & Welch, *supra* note 53, at 708–11.

88. *See generally* Coleman, "The Concept of Equality of Educational Opportunity," 38 *Harv. Educ. Rev.* 7 (1968).

89. J. Coleman, E. Campbell, C. Hobson, J. McPartland, A. Mood, F. Weinfeld & R. York, *Equality of Educational Opportunity* (1966) [hereinafter cited as Coleman Report].

90. Coleman, "Equal Schools or Equal Students," *The Pub. Interests*, Summer 1966, at 70, 72 (emphasis added).

91. *E.g.,* C. Jencks, *supra* note 63, at 93–96; Sharkansky, "Government Expenditures and Public Services in the American States," 61 *Am. Pol. Sci. Rev.* 1066 (1967). *See generally* Coleman Report, *supra* note 89.

92. *See* Sharkansky, *supra* note 91, at 1074–75.

93. Katzman argues that specification of educational production functions is the sine qua non of effective evaluation of school services. M. Katzman, *The Political Economy of Urban Schools* 45 (1971).

94. As Ridley and Simon observed over thirty years ago, "[T]his task of defining objectives constitutes one of the most difficult tasks in the whole field of measurement." C. Ridley & H. Simon, *Measuring Municipal Activities* 2 (1938).

95. *See generally* Weiss, "A Treeful of Owls," in *Evaluating Action Programs* (C. Weiss ed. 1972).

96. *See* Riecken, Memorandum on Program Evaluation," in *id*. at 87–93.

97. For a discussion of strategies in identifying service goals, see C. Weiss, *Evaluation Research* 28–29 (1972).

98. In part for this reason, the Second Circuit explicitly rejected as inappropriate the criterion of output equality in an action alleging unequal park facilities in New York City. Beal v. Lindsay, 468 F.2d 287 (2d Cir. 1972); *see* note 39 *supra*.

99. Ostrom, "On the Meaning and Measurement of Output and Efficiency in the Provision of Urban Police Services," 1 *J. Crim. Justice* 93, 97 (1973).

100. *President's Comm'n on Law Enforcement and the Administration of Justice, Task Force Report: The Police* 1 (1967).

101. *See* text accompanying notes 52–53 *supra*.

102. Alabama v. United States, 304 F.2d 583, 586 (5th Cir.), *aff'd per curiam*, 371 U.S. 37 (1962).

103. Despite President Johnson's characterization of the vote as "the most powerful instrument ever devised by man for breaking down injustice and destroying the terrible walls which imprison men because they are different from other men," 1 *Weekly Compilation of Presidential Documents* 63 (1965), political scientists have shown that the vote is a much more limited resource. W. Keech, *The Impact of Negro Voting* (1968).

104. For a discussion of the appropriateness of the rationality standard in the realm of school finance, see Yudof, "Equal Educational Opportunity and the Courts," 51 *Texas L. Rev.* 411, 491–97 (1973).

105. Simon, "A Behavioral Model of Rational Choice," 69 *Q J. Econ.* 99 (1955).

106. *Id.* at 101, 108.

107. *Id.* at 99.

108. Indeed, insistence on a rationality standard could have the beneficial spin-off effect of making public service agencies provide more explicit, realistic, and manageable statements of objectives.

109. San Antonio Indep. School Dist. v. Rodriguez, 411 U.S. 1, 40 (1973).

110. Yudof, *supra* note 104, at 491. Yudof suggests, however, that "[t]he most serious drawback of the rationality approach is that it draws no clear distinction between education and other municipal services." *Id.* at 493. This raises an old, and probably unresolvable, argument about the most "important" or "fundamental" public services. It is relatively easy to make a case for one's favorite service over any other: however income-enhancing and life-expanding education may be, police and fire protection are more directly related to life, liberty, and property; libraries provide enlightenment while parks provide only recreation. Many unspecified assumptions are involved, not the least of which is that the importance of any public service at a given time is a function of its context. Guns and butter may both be of value, but guns will almost surely be preferred when invasion is imminent, and butter in time of tranquility. Water pressure, when too low for use in household chores, is an annoyance; when too low to fight fires, it is a serious problem. Examples of the contextual influence could be multiplied endlessly, and hence there is probably no categorical answer to the problem of identifying a hierarchy of municipal services. *But cf. id.* at 493–94.

111. For an analysis of the tensions between the minimization and the equalization standards with respect to police protection services, see Shoup, *supra* note 81.

112. *See* Yudof, *supra* note 104, at 492.

113. In Texas an annexing municipality must provide services "the standard and scope of which are substantially equivalent to the standard and scope of services furnished by such city in other areas of such city which have characteristics of topography, patterns of land utilization, and population density similar to that of the particular area annexed." *Tex. Rev. Civ. Stat. Ann.* art. 970a § 10A (1963).

114. For one court's effort, see City of Cape Girardeau v. Armstrong, 417 S.W.2d 661 (Mo. Ct. App. 1967).

Life-Style Values and Political Decentralization in Metropolitan Areas

OLIVER P. WILLIAMS

[Essentially three models—international relations, power structure, and service marketing—have been developed to explain the proliferation of governments and inter-governmental relations in metropolitan areas. Building on the latter of these, an alternative model stressing municipal life styles is proposed. This model emphasizes the specialized nature and differentiated character of municipalities in the metropolitan milieu.]

Through the second quarter of this century many political scientists were writing on why metropolitan areas needed to be politically integrated through local government consolidation. Thus far, in the third quarter, a major theme has been to document how thoroughly this advice is rejected by the American people. Assuming that the present decentralized metropolitan political structures are durable, rather than transitory, phenomena, it is useful to develop models which enable us to understand them as well as to evaluate their social consequences. A substantial beginning has been made with respect to both of these concerns. This paper seeks to improve on existing analytical models of metropolitan politics as a step toward guiding empirical research and sharpening our perceptions of the social values served by the new metropolitan urban form.

EXISTING MODELS AND THEIR SHORTCOMINGS

There are essentially three models which have been developed to explain the proliferation of governments and the relationships among them in metropolitan areas. These three—international relations, the market place, and power structure—will be briefly reviewed, and then an alternative will be suggested. The eclectic approaches which list separate sets of "political" considerations to explain events in each metropolitan area will be ignored here. It is assumed that theories which promise a higher level of generality should be explored before we resign ourselves to *ad hoc* explanations.

The international relations model was probably first suggested by Victor Jones,[1] then restated by Matthew Holden[2] and given an operational test by James V. Toscano.[3] The

An earlier version of this paper was delivered at the Conference on Comparative Research in Community Politics at Athens, Georgia, November 16–19, 1966, under the sponsorship of the National Science Foundation and the University of Georgia.

201

model relies primarily upon analogies between the relationships among nation states and those among municipalities in a metropolitan area. Parallels are seen between alliances and special districts, international organizations and councils of governmental officials (such as the Association of Bay Area Governments), and imperialism and annexation. The problem of any analogy is that it glosses over dissimilarities. For example, one of the old saws of international relations is that economic integration precedes political integration among nations. But metropolitan areas are economically integrated; that is what gives them their identity. Furthermore, most metropolitan areas were once more fully politically integrated than they are now. Despite economic integration, metropolitan areas have become politically decentralized.

The real test of the usefulness of international relations analogies lies, however, in concrete analysis. One such attempt was made by Toscano,[4] who employed several transaction flow theories, taken from the literature on integration among nations. One hypothesis he tested was derived from spill-over theory. According to this theory, if municipalities learn to agree in one area, they are likely to agree in others. Thus, the experience of successful cooperation will have cumulative effect, and the areas of cooperation will have a cumulative effect, and the areas of cooperation will be extended. Toscano's findings did not substantiate this hypothesis, for the substantive content of the service in question, rather than the experience of interacting, appeared to be the controlling variable.[5] Communication, as such, was not the key.

The market place model treats each municipality as an enterprise in the business of supplying services.[6] The core city, suburbs, and satellite cities each offer a different bundle of services which attract a different type of customer. Thus, families seeking good schools for their children go to suburbs that offer quality school services. Resistance to consolidations is an expression of a desire to preserve a particular service mix. However, all services cannot be provided on a small area basis. This problem is covered by the concept of "packageability" of Ostrom et al.[7] Special districts emerge when the municipalities prove too small to comprehend a problem. Air pollution control needs a different size "package" from police service.

The market place model does have certain attractive features which will be developed later. The fact remains, however, that there is a surprising incongruity between actual service areas and the technically required service area, such as, for example, in controlling pollution in most metropolitan areas. In addition there is some question as to whether the model conceives the time sequence properly. Which comes first, the specialized suburb or its specialized services?

The third model, power structure, raises the question of whether services, which are integrated on an area wide basis, coincide with the interest of a metropolitan wide political elite. Is there an elite which integrates those functions in which it has a particular stake and then ignores all others, which remain decentralized? The power structure approach was first suggested by Floyd Hunter,[8] who defined the Regional City political community in metropolitan dimensions. A specific effort was made to verify this model in the Syracuse study,[9] which concluded that no over-all elite existed and that political leadership varied from one functional service area to another. A more extreme statement rejecting the power structure model was made by Norton Long,[10] who saw the relationships among the metropolitan political structures as ecological in nature. He viewed the metropolitan governmental service pattern as resulting from unplanned and uncoordinated actions.

The shortcoming of all three models, as valuable as some of their insights are, is the failure to perceive the characteristic differences between the services which are centralized and those which are decentralized, or to misconstrue the basis of the distinction where it is perceived. It is the thesis of this paper that a distinction does exist and that it can be identified in terms of values. Models which restrict their attention to economics, technology, or communications will fail to be sufficiently comprehensive, despite the relevance of each of these variables to a theory of metropolitan politics.

THE DEVELOPMENT OF MUNICIPAL LIFE STYLES

While the service–market place theory represents a sound observation, it starts too late in the process of metropolitan development. It is necessary to begin earlier and ask about the way the new metropolitan form emerged. This subject must be dealt with in a brief and suggestive manner here. Economic location theory and cultural ecology will be used as points of departure.

Locational theory endeavors to explain the urban land use pattern in terms of space friction costs and rent.[11] Every economic unit seeks that place in the urban environment where the cost of overcoming space friction is minimized. Space friction exists because of each unit's need for other units to carry out its own purposes. For example, a firm must assemble a labor force, obtain supplies, and deliver its product to customers. As more than one economic unit attempts to occupy the same site in their efforts to minimize the cost of overcoming space friction, rent becomes the determining factor in deciding site occupation. The unit which can exploit a given location most profitably will occupy it through paying higher rent. As similar units seek similar locations, certain homogeneous groupings emerge (such as, industrial areas, the CBD).

An attempt to explain the location of homesites in the same fashion, after scant analysis makes it abundantly clear that the family is not simply an economic unit. Urban ecologists discovered years ago that social values contribute to homesite selection.[12] More recent surveys find families moving to suburbs for a syndrome of child-rearing reasons. Despite the influence of social values, rent also acts as a constraining factor. Thus both the theories of land economics and cultural ecology must be used in explaining urban location decisions.

The use of a slightly different perspective can bring together the statements of the economic location theorists and the cultural ecologists, allowing discussion of all locational decisions with one set of references, minimizing confusion in our discussion. Lewis Mumford has characterized a city as a "special receptacle for storing and transmitting messages."[13] That is to say, a city is a device for overcoming space friction for a social purpose. The content of these messages and the relative importance of particular types of messages vary over time and from city to city. Economic message exchanges are very important in our contemporary cities, but they are not the only ones. Middle class families choose suburban locations with lots of grass, but more important, these locations are where the variety of home-related message exchanges are compatible with middle class values.

These considerations are usually more social and educational than economic. Locational choices are made not only to increase the ease of exchanging rewarding messages, but also to minimize unrewarding and unwanted messages. This situation is particularly true of our homesite selection illustration. A middle class family chooses a suburb which will also reduce unpleasant message exchanges from lower class persons in the form of muggings, fistfights, and uncouth syntax.

Strategic locations, which afford the favorable message exchange arrangement, once acquired, must be safeguarded. The location requires protection, for the curse of urbanism is the instability of site advantages. A variety of social institutions, of which the municipality is one, help to protect the place of advantage for its constituents and to slow down the forces of change. Strategic locations can be maintained, in part, by policies which regulate who will occupy adjacent locations. The values of one household are affected by the values of adjacent ones, particularly if there are children, for modes of child-rearing become an issue. Viewed in these terms, zoning is a device for maximizing rewarding message exchanges and minimizing unpleasant ones, through assuring the spatial contiguity of compatible message generating units. This language may be a bit overwhelming for describing "neighboring," but it permits us to refer to such different social institutions as factories and homes with a common set of concepts.

The political unit in metropolitan analysis is a social unit which has a spatially definable domicile. These units (which will be called *socio-spatial* units) include households, factories, stores, churches, clubs, offices, and the like. Each one of these socio-spatial units possesses a hierarchy of values. For example, businesses generally wish to maximize profits, but the profit value subsumes intermediate values, such as a desire for expansion room, accessibility to a high class labor force, protection from pilfering, and so forth. Households may seek quality education, convenient shopping, pleasant neighbors, and a short trip to work. These sets of values may be called the unit's *life style values*. The realization of some of these life style values are enhanced by the locational choices of the unit; some require the support of local services for their realization. Those life style values which depend upon location for their realization are the major sources of metropolitan politics. Local government, in its various manifestations, is the governmental level which has primary control over the immediate physical and social environment of any given socio-spatial unit. The physical environment includes such factors as highway access patterns, parks, the location of facilities, and other mapable and physically describable appurtenances. The social environment includes the proximate social processes and institutions.

One of the important strategies commonly pursued by socio-spatial units in maximizing their possibilities for realizing life style values is homogeneous and complementary groupings. Jane Jacobs' importunings to the contrary notwithstanding, this remains a cardinal principle of most city planning.[14] Subdivisions, industrial parks, and shopping centers are the norm. Following the logic of this strategy, a decentralized (suburbanized) metropolitan governmental pattern appears to be superior to a centralized (consolidation) mode for the enhancement of life style values. Under the former arrangement, diverse groups need not constantly compete in the same political arena, a situation characteristic of heterogeneous units, such as the core city (particularly as it has existed traditionally). The more nearly the suburb specializes, the easier it is, politically, to maintain the primacy of the values prized by the dominant type of socio-spatial unit. This point brings up the question of why any specialized suburb would ever voluntarily consent to amalgamate with another whose life style was different.

The above analysis is not incompatible with the market place model; it is simply more inclusive. Location choices are made in relationship to many factors, of which municipal services is one—how important a one, we do not know. It is certainly the case that once established, suburbs offer specialized service packages. Some offer good schools, large lot zoning, and a county squire physical setting. Some may be more predisposed to fitting parochial schools into the service set. A list of a few of the exotic types might include the suburb that caters to industries only, where night watchmen supply the required population to establish a voting citizenry; the vice suburb that services a metropolitan area in illicit entertainment by selective police enforcement policies. California even has its dairy farm suburbs, sort of anti-urban islands in an urban sea. These places all have their specialized service packages, which do act as advertisements saying, in effect, "all those who like the kind of life symbolized by these services come and join us, if you can afford it."

THE INTERDEPENDENCE OF SPECIALIZED MUNICIPALITIES

What has been said thus far will enable one to understand much of metropolitan politics, but it covers only half of the situation. It is the other half that leads to many of the intense political battles. The municipalities of the metropolitan area are specialized and, consequently, interdependent. One specialized area can only exist if its complement in specialization exists elsewhere. If there is an industrial suburb, there must also be a residential one; if there is a rich man's suburb, there must also be one for the poor. The fact of interrelatedness is dramatized twice daily by glutted commuter arteries, leading not only to the core city, but criss-crossing in every direction, through any major metropolitan area.

If it were not for this interdependence, each little specialized suburb could have its political cake and eat it too. All local policies could be conceived in terms of self images. But the dynamics of the metropolis will not let that occur. These dynamics are expressed through the need to create integrating mechanisms which, though they maintain the over-all system of specialized areas, often transform the nature and character of individual municipalities in the process.

The *system maintenance* mechanisms of the metropolis may be classified into two principal categories, the communications and utility systems. Here, communication system is intended to include what is traditionally called transportation, as well as communications. Mumford's messages, so to speak, take physical as well as symbolic forms. Highways, airports, mass transit, telephone, telegraph, radio, television, delivery services, mail, and water transport facilities comprise the principal communications system. Each of these systems must have a jurisdiction larger than any single municipality, for it is their function to integrate the specialized municipalities into an operating whole.

The utility networks supply power, water, and waste disposal services which enable the technological appurtenances of each socio-spatial unit to carry on. For technological and financial, rather than functional, reasons, the utilities are usually operated as large area networks, which supply services to more than one municipality. But strictly speaking, none of the utilities has to be larger than a given municipality in order to be functionally operative. Miniaturization of these services can take place in the form of on-site facilities and small package plants.

There is, in addition, a third set which might be considered system maintenance mechanisms—the central facilities. These are the major service facilities in urban areas which sustain and support urban life. These exist in both the private and public sectors. In the more public sector, every metropolitan area requires the presence of one or more university, museum, stadium, arena, library, hospital, and the like. These services are most often handled through *ad hoc* and semi-public arrangements which infrequently demand intergovernmental cooperation for their creation. For those that are revenue-producing, a single government, often the core city, will act as an entrepreneur in providing the service. Generally, central facilities are not major sources of political friction.

The system maintenance functions do just what those words imply: they maintain the over-all system, and in the process, insure that particular life style values are preserved or enhanced. In this sense, they are instrumental services. However, these services not only bind the specialized areas into an over-all social and economic system; they also profoundly affect the spatial distribution of specialized areas. Strategic locations are, in large part, defined in relationship to the system maintenance functions. This is particularly the case with the communications systems, of which the ground transportation arteries are the most important. Utility networks play a similar role, but to a much lesser extent, and their role varies more radically from place to place. The existence of central facilities makes the truncated service complements of small suburbs possible.

It is the central argument of this paper that the socio-spatial units resist integration of what I have called life style services, but accept, and at times encourage, integration of system maintenance services. More accurately, the response is such when the issues are perceived correctly. The consequences of structural changes in service arrangements are subject to numerous interpretations. Campaigns can be obfuscating, and adroit publicity in the context of a metropolitan referendum can at times place issues in a light which does not foretell their likely consequences. However, only occasionally will the campaign techniques alone control outcomes. The proposition about decentralized life style services and centralized system maintenance service generally holds true.

Metropolitan politics can be further understood by realizing that various systems maintenance services have quite different impacts in the course of their creation or expansion. The most essential difference lies in their feedback effect on locational advantages. Several illustrations will help to clarify this point.

The differential effects stemming from the expansion of an intra-urban expressway and a telephone system in a metropolitan area will now be considered. When a new highway is built, it alters the whole pattern of accessibility among points within the metropolis. Areas which were previously too remote for commuter homes suddenly become accessible in a time-of-travel sense. New interchanges in places which previously had no attractions for these uses, become desirable locations for shopping centers and warehouses. A new expressway causes many incongruities between social and economic values attached to locations and the existing zoning ordinances. The established life style of communities becomes threatened by the invasion of socio-spatial units whose values are at variance with those already existing in the community.

Contrast this situation with the impact of the extension of a telephone system. Within certain limits, there are no spatially strategic access points in a telephone system. Aside from a few esthetic objections to new utility poles, telephone system expansion does not disturb the ecological balance of areal specialization. This, indeed, may explain why highways are publicly owned and telephones are not.

The highway problem warrants a closer look. If highways do not comprise some semblance of a network, they are not even highways, because they are supposed to go to places where travelers want to go. To be integrated, they must be planned, not simply added to by each suburban increment to the metropolis. Therefore, there is a tacit consent that area wide governmental agencies have control of highways (usually the state, and now, more and more, the federal government). At the same time, highway construction is the most volatile metropolitan policy area. Every new expressway is fought vehemently; yet it is built! The battle is so intense and bitter because the life style of some areas must be sacrificed to maintain the life styles of most other areas. There is a wrenching conflict between the benefited and the disrupted. Frequently, the problem is solved by building highways through areas with the fewest political resources for obstructionism, or through areas that may acquire actual benefits, such as an industrial or a commercial area. Highway politics cannot be explained in any economic gains and losses fashion. Communities in which land values will be enhanced by highway construction often still oppose it.

Thus it can be seen that the integration and centralization of system maintenance functions does not always proceed with ease or without conflict. But the process does continue, though interrupted by occasional reversals. Strategies may have to be changed, but in the long run, the pattern does not.

While it is possible conceptually to classify municipal services into life style and system maintenance policies, it is more likely that the variable is continuous, rather than dichotomous. The scale on the life style side refers to the importance of the service in maintaining preferred values. Probably the most critical policy is land use regulation, with education a close second. Both of these policy areas have great potential for affecting the rate of rewarding or disruptive message exchanges. Along the continuum, such policies as housing, urban renewal, recreation, libraries, police, and parks follow in approximately that order of importance. Certain health and welfare functions may be effectively neutral, along with such minor administrative matters as joint purchasing and police radio networks.

A similar continuum exists on the system maintenance side, which is related to the importance of the service to the continued existence of specialized areas. Here, central facilities are least important, utilities next, with the communication services most vital. In addition, different socio-spatial units have different value hierarchies. It follows, therefore, that one suburb might bitterly oppose the integration of a certain service, while another would remain neutral on the issue.

INTERVENING VARIABLES

This life style theory involves an ideal type; no metropolitan area behaves exactly as the theory predicts. However, if it is correct, deviations must be explained in terms of intervening variables. Alternatively, to the extent that an actual metropolitan area approaches the ideal type, its politics will conform to that predicted. This can be stated in the form of propositions: for example, *the more specialized the political sub-units of a metropolitan area, the more political behavior in the area will conform to that predicted*. The factors which influence the development of municipal specialization are key areas for investigation.

Specialization should be considered an indicator, for it is only the precondition for a set of social actions. Specialization is the basis for a sense of community solidarity and identity which in turn leads to a protective posture. What can match the political fervor of a Grosse Point on a zoning issue or Cicero on civil rights?

The identification of the politically relevant kinds of specialization has not been developed. Some preliminary investigations have been performed by the author and associates[15] in relating demographic characteristics and policy variations among suburbs. This analysis was based largely on census and fiscal data, both of which are rather blunt instruments. However, positive relationships were established. Work needs to proceed, both in developing indicators of specialization and in establishing the critical breaking points.

Specialization has been chosen as the appropriate descriptive term over homogeneity because even the most suburban municipal units embrace a certain variety and range of socio-spatial units. There are some extremely homogeneous suburbs, but they remain as examples of specialization fully developed. Normally, municipal boundaries do not operate as sharp demographic breakpoints. Any municipality can absorb a certain degree of internal diversity and still maintain a dominant style. In fact, a certain degree of internal diversity is often required for the maintenance of daily activities. However, a scanning of the range of mean values describing any municipal characteristic in a metropolitan area will quickly establish that real diversity (specialization) exists.

If the degree of specialization is a key to the decisions made in a metropolitan area, those factors which influence the degree of specialization become relevant intervening variables. Three conditions are likely to influence the degree of specialization.

(1) *The larger the metropolitan area, the more specialized are the municipal units*. Suburban specialization in a small metropolitan area is likely to be confined to the "good" and the "other" side of town, in a rudimentary Hoyt sector fashion. Larger metropolitan areas are likely to contain the many gradations of status, class residential suburbs, as well as highly specialized industrial, commercial and other types of suburbs. It is probably also the case that specialization is somewhat related to the size of the municipality, with smaller places being more specialized.

(2) *The older the metropolitan area, the more specialized its municipal units*. The assumption here is that place identities become crystallized over time. Moves are made with a greater awareness of the life style of each place. In the burgeoning newer metropolitan areas, growth may take place so rapidly that the visibility of the life style remains low and

the local political structures are not sufficiently stable to employ effective screening policies for entering socio-spatial units.

(3) *The more permissive state incorporation laws are for local self-determination, the more specialized the municipal units.* This postulated metropolitan behavior should be most fully realized when the metropolitan citizens have free choice in drawing their municipal boundaries. In fact, the opportunities for doing so vary greatly from state to state. Some states, such as Michigan and California, for years gave suburban residents wide latitude in fringe incorporation decisions. In the East, suburban boundaries are largely predetermined by traditional town and township lines. In still other states, such as Texas, the core city has had the initiative with respect to annexing fringe areas. However, even under this circumstance a vigorous outcropping of fringe area incorporations has taken place.[16]

Metropolitan area politics is a function not only of internal circumstances, but also of outside influences emanating from state and federal governments. The theory is formulated with reference to indigenous forces. There remains the possibility that accommodations within the metropolitan areas can be amended by higher levels of government. This appears not to be the case to any great extent, as higher levels seem to respect, rather than disrupt, the metropolitan settlement. Interventions from the federal government are most forceful in the system-maintenance areas. The only substantial area in which the federal government is willing to require authoritative metropolitan wide planning as a condition for receiving grants-in-aid is in the interstate highway program. Contrast its policies here with those in housing and urban renewal, where federal policy operates fully within the metropolitan framework of decentralizing decisions on life style policies.

The policies of state governments do not vary radically from those of the federal government. Mandatory county assumption of services is likely to be confined to the more neutral or low conflict service areas such as the distribution of categorical welfare payments or health benefits. In both of these areas, benefits are distributed to individuals and the policies have little effect on the life style of any community. (The county services which antedate metropolitan development may be exceptions to these observations.) In fact, state grant-in-aid programs financially underwrite the whole decentralized pattern of metropolitan areas. Particularly school aid provides a fiscal flow enabling poor suburbs to maintain autonomous school districts. This takes some of the pressure off the consolidation movement. Although there may be some states which are exceptions to the above generalizations, with reapportionment placing more power in the hands of the suburbs, future development is likely to follow the predicted course.

SOCIAL CONSEQUENCES OF SPECIALIZATION

At the outset, it was stated that at present there is neither an adequate analytical model of metropolitan area politics nor a proper appreciation of the social significance of what is occurring. If the life style theory presented here describes the present state, and, more important, the future course of metropolitan development, its probable social consequences are worthy of serious consideration.

Metropolitan areas, as presently constituted, will eventually find solutions for system maintenance services. Many writers point to this trend as a proof of the ability to muddle through using present governmental structures. In the short run, it is often more of a muddle than muddling through, as some of the system maintenance services are expanded only after protracted and costly delays. A twenty year gap between need and construction of a given facility is not uncommon. Even if we accept this course of decision-making as normal, the decentralization of life style policies promises to remain a durable arrangement. It is easy to dismiss this problem. People are happier in living where they have compatible neighbors; certain forms of specialization are highly efficient. But, is the new metropolitan form the best of all possible urban political structures? There remain a number of concerns.

Little research has been done in the United States on life in a specialized community. The English sociologists have shown greater interest in this subject partly because of the new towns policies. Peter Willmott reports on life in a large, homogeneous, and mature working class suburb of London.[17] Homogeneity has removed much conflict from the lives of its inhabitants and contentment is the norm. But there were other consequences of this specialized life style. The school system was miserable. Upward mobility was positively discouraged by the culture of the community. We are now developing our working class suburbs, and the school situations are similar. What does the new metropolitan form mean for the future of social mobility?

The metropolitan form, as it is now emerging, is an ecological heaven for whites only. The most disturbing instances of racial violence in the North are not in the core cities, but in the suburbs. In the core cities, the police force must maintain some semblance of neutrality; at least there is political recourse when it does not. In the specialized suburbs, the whole power of law, police, and social institutions is likely to be arrayed on one side of the conflict, and this assures that the possibility for racial residential mobility will be narrowly circumscribed.

In every major metropolitan area, there are developing obsolete suburbs and satellite cities that are as dysfunctional, in terms of locational and physical requirements for contemporary urban life, as are the old prairie, wheat belt service towns. As the suburbs spiral down, they have an accumulation of tax, service, and leadership woes. Unlike the heterogeneous and diversely composed core cities, which mobilize strengths and resources from viable areas in order to cope with problem areas, the deteriorating suburb cannot employ this urban renewal strategy. When a suburb goes down, people just move away and normally there is no unit of local government that can or will assume responsibility for what happens.

There are other possible consequences of the new metropolitan form. Are we creating unemployment by decentralizing manufacturing, yet excluding low wage persons from access to jobs because of the absence of suitable housing? Few suburbs will permit public or low cost housing to be built near the very factories they seek to alleviate property tax problems. Public health departments tend to exist more in the high status suburbs than in the low status ones. Libraries, recreational programs, and government financed social services exhibit a similar pattern.

In brief, while national attention is focused on the problems of core cities as dumping grounds for the unfortunate metropolitan citizens, the country may be creating a new system, which, in the long run, will have even more unfortunate consequences for the distribution of opportunities. At least the core city has high visibility; consequently, its problems are politically salient at the state and national levels. What is emerging in the new metropolitan form may be more easily overlooked. Thus, even if the study of municipal specialization falls short of explicating metropolitan intergovernmental relations, though I believe it will not, this subject is worthy of our attention for other reasons.

NOTES

1. "The Organization of a Metropolitan Region," *University of Pennsylvania Law Review*, 105 (February, 1957), 538–552.

2. "The Governance of the Metropolis as a Problem in Diplomacy," *Journal of Politics*, 26 (August 1964), 627–647.

3. Philip E. Jacob and James V. Toscano, eds., *The Integration of Political Communities* (Philadelphia: J. B. Lippincott Co., 1963), Chapter IV.

4. *Ibid*.

5. See also Oliver P. Williams, Harold Herman, Charles S. Liebman, and Thomas R. Dye, *Suburban Differences and Metropolitan Policies*, (Philadelphia: University of Pennsylvania Press, 1965), Chapter IX.

6. Wilbur R. Thompson, *A Preface to Urban Economics*, (Baltimore: The Johns Hopkins Press, 1965), Chapter VII.

7. Vincent Ostrom, Charles M. Tiebout, and Roland L. Warren, "The Organization of Government in the Metropolitan Area: A Theoretical Inquiry," *American Political Science Review*, 55 (December 1961), 835–837. The "polycentric" model presented in this article is not strictly an economic one.

8. *Community Power Structure* (Chapel Hill: University of North Carolina Press, 1953).

9. Roscoe C. Martin, Frank Munger, *et al., Decisions in Syracuse*, (Bloomington: Indiana University Press, 1961).

10. "The Local Community as an Ecology of Games," *American Journal of Sociology*, 64 (November 1958), 251–266.

11. A classic statement upon which many subsequent elaborations rest is R. M. Haig, *Major Economic Factors in Metropolitan Growth and Arrangements*. (New York: The Regional Plan of New York and Its Environs, 1928).

12. Pioneering work in this area was contributed by Walter Firey. See his "Sentiment and Symbolism as Ecological Variables," *American Sociological Review*. (April, 1945), 140–148.

13. *The City in History* (New York: Harcourt, Brace & World, 1961), p. 99.

14. *The Death and Life of Great American Cities* (New York: Random House, 1961). Mrs. Jacobs advocates a mixed land use pattern and feels that zoning as presently practiced leads to undesirable blocks of single usage land development patterns.

15. Williams, *et al., op. cit.*

16. Richard L. Stauber, *New Cities in America* (Lawrence: Government Research Bureau, the University of Kansas, 1965). The largest number of SMSA incorporations of any state in the decade 1950–60 was in Texas (83).

17. *The Evolution of a Community* (London: Routledge and Kegan Paul, 1963).

Street-Level Bureaucracy and the Analysis of Urban Reform

MICHAEL LIPSKY

In American cities today, policemen, teachers, and welfare workers are under siege. Their critics variously charge them with being insensitive, unprepared to work with ghetto residents, incompetent, resistant to change, and racist. These accusations, directed toward individuals, are transferred to the bureaucracies in which they work.[1]

STREET-LEVEL BUREAUCRACY

Men and women in these bureaucratic roles deny the validity of these criticisms. They insist that they are free of racism, and that they perform with professional competence under very difficult conditions. They argue that current procedures are well designed and that it is only the lack of resources and of public support and understanding which prevents successful performance of their jobs. Hence bureaucrats stress the need for higher budgets, better equipment, and higher salaries to help them do even better what they are now doing well, under the circumstances.

How are these diametrically opposed views to be reconciled? Do both sides project positions for advantage alone, or is it possible that both views may be valid from the perspective of the policy contestants? Paradoxically, is it possible that critics of urban bureaucracy may correctly allege bias and ineffectiveness of service, at the same time that urban bureaucrats may correctly defend themselves as unbiased in motivation and objectively responsible to bureaucratic necessities?

What is particularly ominous about this confrontation is that these "street-level bureaucrats," as I call them, "represent" American government to its citizens. They are the people citizens encounter when they seek help from, or are controlled by, the American political system. While, in a sense, the Federal Reserve Board has a greater impact on the lives of the poor than, say, individual welfare workers (because of the Board's influence on inflation and employment trends), it nonetheless remains that citizens *perceive* these public employees as most influential in shaping their lives. As ambassadors of government to the American people, and as ambassadors with particularly significant impacts upon the lives of the poor and of relatively powerless minorities, how capable are these urban bureaucrats in providing high levels of service and responding objectively to individual grievances and needs?

This essay was prepared for a Conference on New Public Administration and Neighborhood Control held in Boulder, Colorado, in May 1970, and sponsored by the Center for Governmental Studies in Washington, D.C.

213

It is one conclusion of this paper that both perspectives have some validity. Their simultaneous validity, reflecting differences in perspective and resulting from the responses of street-level bureaucrats to problems encountered in their jobs, focuses attention on one aspect of the institutional racism with which the Kerner Commission charged American society.

In analyzing the contemporary crisis in bureaucracy, and the conflicting claims of urban bureaucrats and their nonvoluntary clients, I will focus on those urban bureaucrats whose impact on citizens' lives is both frequent and significant. Hence the concentration on street-level bureaucrats—those government workers who directly interact with citizens in the regular course of their jobs; whose work within the bureaucratic structure permits them wide latitude in job performance; and whose impact on the lives of citizens is extensive. Thus, the analysis would include the patrolman on the beat, the classroom teacher, and the welfare investigator. It would be less relevant to the public school principal, who deals primarily with subordinates rather than with pupils, or to the traffic cop, whose latitude in job performance is relatively restricted.

Further, I want to concentrate on ways in which street-level bureaucrats respond to conditions of stress imposed by their work environment, where such stress is relatively severe. Analytically, three kinds of stress may be readily observed in urban bureaucracies today.

(1) Inadequate Resources. Street-level bureaucracies are widely thought to lack sufficient organizational resources to accomplish their jobs. Classrooms are overcrowded. Large welfare caseloads prevent investigators from providing all but cursory service. The lower courts are so overburdened that judges may spend their days adjourning but never trying cases. Police forces are perpetually understaffed, particularly as perceptions of crime and demands for civic order increase (Silver, 1967).

Insufficiency of organizational resources increases the pressures on street-level bureaucrats to make quick decisions about clients and process cases with inadequate information and too little time to dispose of problems on their merits. While this may be said about bureaucratic decision-making in general, it is particularly salient to problems of street-level bureaucracy because of the importance of individual bureaucratic outcomes to citizens subject to the influence of urban institutions. The stakes are often high—both to citizen and to bureaucrat.

(2) Threat and Challenge to Authority. The conditions under which street-level bureaucrats work often include distinct physical and psychological threats. Policemen are constantly alert to danger, as are other street-level bureaucrats who function in neighborhoods which are alien to them, are generally considered dangerous, or are characterized by high crime rates. Curiously, it may make little difference whether or not the probabilities of encountering harm are actually high, so long as people think that their jobs are risky.

Even if actual physical harm is somewhat remote, street-level bureaucrats experience threat by their inability to control the work-related encounter. Teachers especially fear the results of loss of classroom discipline or their ability to manage a classroom. Policemen have been widely observed to ensure the deference of a suspect by anticipatory invocation of authority.

(3) Contradictory or Ambiguous Job Expectations. Confronted with resource in-

adequacies and threats which increase the salience of work-related results, street-level bureaucrats often find their difficulties exacerbated by uncertainties concerning expectations of performance. Briefly, role expectations may be framed by peers, by bureaucratic reference groups, or by public expectations in general (Sarbin and Allen, 1968). Consider the rookie patrolman who, in addition to responding to his own conceptions of the police role, must accommodate the demands placed upon him by

1. fellow officers in the station house, who teach him how to get along and try to "correct" the teachings of his police academy instructors;
2. his immediate superiors, who may strive for efficiency at the expense of current practices;
3. police executives, who communicate expectations contradictory to station-house mores; and
4. the general public, which in American cities today is likely to be divided along both class and racial lines in its expectations of police practices and behavior.

One way street-level bureaucrats may resolve job-related problems without internal conflict is to drift to a position consistent with dominant role expectations. This resolution is denied bureaucrats working under conflicting role expectations.

Controversies over schools, police behavior, or welfare practices exacerbate these stress conditions, since they place in the spotlight of public scrutiny behavior which might otherwise remain in the shadows. These stresses result in the development of psychological and behavioral reactions which seem to widen the already existing differences between street-level bureaucrats and spokesmen for the nonvoluntary clienteles. Three such developments may be mentioned here.

First, it is a common feature of organizational behavior that individuals in organizations need to develop simplifications, or some kind of "shorthand," by which they can make decisions quickly and expeditiously. A policeman develops simplifications which suggest to him that crimes are in the process of being committed. Teachers develop simplifications to allow them to determine which pupils are "good" students and which are "troublemakers."

This is a cliche of organizational behavior (see, for example, Downs, 1967: 2–3, 75–78). But it is portentous, and not trivial, when we recognize the conditions under which these simplifications tend to be developed in stereotypic ways with racist orientations. When a black man driving through a white neighborhood is stopped by a policeman merely because he is black and therefore (according to the policeman's mode of simplification) suspiciously out of place, he has been stopped for good reason by the policeman, but for racist reasons, according to this aggrieved citizen. Teachers may select students for special attention or criticism because of their manners of speech, modes of dress, behavior in class, parental backgrounds, or other characteristics unrelated to their ability. Policemen, judges, and welfare investigators may be significantly influenced by symbols of deference or defiance to themselves or their authority. These signs may be related to general and generational responses to the enforced passivity of the past, and unrelated to the bureaucracies or bureaucrats themselves.

Race-oriented simplifications are particularly explosive even if only a few street-level bureaucrats engage in racist name calling. The objects of bureaucratic abuse understandably engage in the same kind of simplifying of the world that bureaucrats do. Thus, it takes only a few racist incidents to develop and sustain the impression that overall police behavior toward blacks is discriminatory. We are truly in a crisis because greater black community solidarity and greater willingness to object to police behavior create the very conditions under which race-oriented simplifications are increasingly invoked, leading to an escalation of tension and hostility. The greater the tensions and the images of conflict in the minds of street-level bureaucrats, the more likely they will be to invoke the simplifications they think provide them with a measure of protection in their work. This increase in discrimination under tension occurs above and beyond the more overtly discriminatory attitudes that are sanctioned by the larger community and society.

The second development heightening the existing bureaucratic crises is the tendency on the part of street-level bureaucrats to develop defense mechanisms, in order to reach accommodation and resolution of stress tendencies, that result in a distortion of the perceived reality.[2]

One such reaction is the tendency to segment psychologically, or fragment conceptually, the population which the bureaucrat considers his clientele. Some police bureaucracies have regularly dealt with Negro crime through this technique (Wilson, 1968: 157). If one can think of black people as "outside" the community, then one can perform according to "community standards" without experiencing the stresses exerted by diverse community elements. The police riots during the 1968 Chicago Democratic Convention, and more recently in various university communities, can only be understood by assuming that long-haired, white college students, some of whom are verbally abusive, are thought by the police to be "outside" the community which can expect to be protected by norms of due process (Walker, 1968).

Similarly, teachers reduce their own sense of stress by defining some students as uneducable or marginally educable. Early selection of some students for higher education, based upon such characteristics as the ability to speak English and class background, permits the educators to perform in their expected roles according to a more limited definition of the population to be served. As Nathan Glazer (1969: 46) has suggested, tensions in city schools and over police practices in ghetto neighborhoods are not only a function of the apparent "foreignness" of teachers and policemen to blacks. The process of determining "foreignness" did not begin yesterday with black people. If nothing else, black labeling of whites as "foreigners" has been reinforced, if not inspired, by bureaucratic processes of categorizing nonvoluntary clients.

The development of tracking systems in public schools illustrates the development of *institutional* mechanisms for segmenting the population to be served so as to better ensure teacher success through population redefinition.[3] This is the latent function of tracking systems. It should be noted that population redefinition, as I have described it, must find support in general community attitudes, or else cross-pressures would emerge to inhibit this development. The growing cleavage in American cities between whites and blacks may never result in actual apartheid, as threatened by the Kerner Commission. But the subtle psychological apartheid resulting from redefinitions of the populations served by public programs and institutions is equally ominous and may be already accomplished.

A third development in the bureaucratic crisis is the way in which the kind of behavior described here may work to create the very reality which people either fear or want to overcome. For example, in categorizing students as low or high achievers—in a sense predicting their capacities to achieve—teachers may create validity for the very simplifications concerning student potential in which they engage. Recently, evidence has been presented to demonstrate that on the whole, students will perform better in school if teachers think they are bright, regardless of whether or not they are (Rosenthal and Jacobson, 1968). Similarly, the propensity to arrest black youngsters for petty crimes, the increasing professionalization of police forces (resulting in the recording of more minor offenses), and society's concern for clean arrest records as criteria for employment may create a population inclined toward further illegal activity per force if not by choice. The society's penal institutions have been characterized as schools for criminal behavior rather than for rehabilitation. Thus we create a class of criminal types by providing them with informal vocational training.

Not only individual teachers, but schools themselves communicate expectations to students. Increasingly, educators of disadvantaged minorities are convinced that student high school achievement is directly related to the extent to which schools communicate expectations of high potential to their students. Various street academies which have grown up in New York, Newark, and other cities, the Upward Bound program, and other experimental programs for poor and ghettoized youth, are premised on the assumption that if educators behave as if they think college—and hence upward mobility—is a realistic possibility for their students, high school dropouts and potential dropouts will respond by developing motivation currently unsuspected by high school personnel.

In their need to routinize and simplify in order to process work assignments, teachers, policemen, and welfare workers may be viewed as bureaucrats. Significantly, however, the workload of street-level bureaucrats consists of *people*, who in turn are reactive to the bureaucratic process. Street-level bureaucrats, confronted with inadequate resources, threat and challenge to authority, and contradictory or ambiguous role expectations, must develop mechanisms for reducing job-related stresses. It is suggested here that these mechanisms, with their considerable impact on clients' futures, deserve increasing attention from students of urban affairs.

PUBLIC POLICY REFORM IN STREET-LEVEL BUREAUCRACIES

Although much more could be said about the stresses placed on street-level bureaucrats, the remainder of this paper will focus on the implications for public policy and for public perceptions of urban bureaucracy, of an analysis of the ways street-level bureaucrats react to problems related to specified work conditions. Where does this kind of analysis lead?

First, it may help bridge the gap between, on the one hand, allegations that street-level bureaucrats are racist and, on the other hand, insistence by individuals working in these bureaucracies that they are free from racism. Development of perceptual simplifications and subtle redefinitions of the population to be served—both group psychological phenomena—may be undetected by bureaucracies and clientele groups. These phenomena will significantly affect both the perception of the bureaucrats and the reactions of clienteles to the bureaucracies. Perceptual modes which assist bureaucrats in processing work and which, though not developed to achieve discriminatory goals, result in discriminatory bias may be considered a manifestation of institutional as opposed to individual racism. So there must be a distinction between institutional routinized procedures which result in bias and personal prejudice.

Second, we may see the development of human relations councils, citizen review boards, special equal opportunity units, and other "community relations" bureaus for what they are. They may provide citizens with increased marginal access to the system, but, equally important, they inhibit institutional change by permitting street-level bureaucrats to persist in behavioral patterns because special units to handle "human relations problems" have been created. These institutional developments do not fundamentally affect general bureaucratic performance. Instead, they insulate bureaucracies from having to confront behavioral factors affecting what appears to be racist work performance. These observations particularly obtain when, as is often the case, these units lack the power to impose on the bureaucracy decisions favorable to aggrieved citizens.

Third, tracking systems, vocational schools with basically custodial functions, and other institutionalized mechanisms for predicting capacities should be recognized as also serving to ease the bureaucratic burden at the expense of equal treatment and opportunity.

Fourth, the inherent limitation of "human relations" (sensitivity training, T-group training) training for street-level bureaucrats should be recognized as inadequate to the fundamental behavioral needs of street-level bureaucrats. Basic bureaucratic attitudes toward clients appear to be a function of workers' background and of socialization on the job. Training designed to improve relationships with black communities must be directed toward helping bureaucrats improve performance, not toward classroom lessons on equality which are soon forgotten (McNamara, 1967). The psychological forces which lead to the kinds of biased simplifications and discriminatory behavior mentioned earlier, appear sufficiently powerful to suggest skepticism over the potential for changing behavior patterns through human relations training efforts.

Fifth, just as training should be encouraged which relates to job performance needs, incentives should be developed which reward successful performance-utilizing indicators of clientele assistance. While performance standards can be trivialized, avoided, or distorted through selective use of statistics, their potential utility has hardly been explored. For example, it would be entirely appropriate to develop indices for teacher success and to develop appropriate merit rewards, based upon adequately assessed performance indicators. For teachers, pay raises and promotions might be based upon average reading score improvements in relation to the school or citywide average for that grade level. In some ghetto schools, this index might initially reward those teachers who minimize the extent to which their students fall behind citywide averages. Public employee unions, of course, would oppose such proposals vigorously. There is every reason to think such proposals would be strongly endorsed in experimental educational units.

To improve public bureaucracies, the American political system has moved from public service as patronage to public service recruitment through merit examination. But in American cities today, administrators are frustrated because of the great difficulty in bringing talented individuals into government at high levels and introducing innovation at lower levels. Mobility in the civil service is based too little on merit. "Dead wood" is built into the systems, where the least talented public employees remain in public service.

These conditions have prevailed for some time. What is new to the discussion is that black educators and critics of police forces now argue that (a) merit examinations do not test abilities for certain kinds of tasks that must be performed in ghetto teaching and ghetto police surveillance; and (b) on the basis of the records of ghetto schools and ghetto law enforcement practices, in many cases, civil service protection cannot be justified. The society cannot afford to continue to protect civil servants, or the natural allies of the bureaucracies, at the expense of their clienteles.[4] The criticism and reevaluation of bureaucratic standards that have accompanied demands for community control are supportive of these proposals.

Sixth, this analysis is more generally supportive of proposals for radical decentralization and neighborhood control. Advocacy of neighborhood control has recently revolved around five kinds of possible rewards resulting from a change in present organizational arrangements. It has been variously held that neighborhood control would

1. increase loyalty to the political system by providing relatively powerless groups with access to governmental influence;
2. increase citizens' sense of well-being as a result of greater participation;
3. provide greater administrative efficiency for overly extended administrative systems;
4. increase the political responsibility and accountability of bureaucracies currently remote from popular influence; and
5. improve bureaucratic performance by altering the assumptions under which services are dispensed (Altshuler, 1970; Kotler, 1969).

The analysis of street-level bureaucracy presented here has been supportive of that strand of neighborhood control advocacy which focuses on the creation of standards by which to judge improved bureaucratic performance. Specifically, it has been proposed, among other things, that the performance of policemen, teachers, and other street-level bureaucrats is significantly affected by the availability of personal resources in the job situation, the sense of threat which is experienced, the ambiguity of role expectations, and the diversity of potential clientele groups. Most community control proposals are addressed to these considerations.

Recommendations for decentralization of police forces provide an opportunity to demonstrate the applicability of these ideas. For example, it has been proposed that the police function be divided into order maintenance (such as traffic control, breaking up domestic quarrels, parade duty, and so on), and crime fighting. The first is said to be a function that could easily be performed at the neighborhood level, whereas the crime fighting function, requiring both weaponry and greater technical training, might continue to be a citywide function. This kind of task redefinition would restore the cop to the beat, would replace city policemen with neighborhood residents more sensitive to community mores, and would relieve the city police of some of the duties they regard as least rewarding and most aggravating (see, e.g., Waskow, 1969; Wilson, 1968). Such reorganization might reduce the stresses resulting from the variety of duties policemen are currently asked to perform, as well as increase the resources available to individuals in police duties.

Radical decentralization is also commended by this analysis because the increased homogeneity of district populations would permit greater uniformity and responsiveness in designing policies directed toward neighborhood clienteles. The range represented by the new clientele would be narrower and could be planned for with greater confidence. The system would not be so constrained by competing definitions of appropriate bureaucratic methods or by competing demands on the conceptualization of service. Citywide performance standards and appropriate regulations concerning nondiscriminatory behavior could be maintained with the expectation that they would be no *less* honored than currently.

This analysis is further supportive of proposals for radical decentralization to the extent that minority group employment under community control would be increased through changes in recruitment methods and greater attraction (for some) of civic employment. Increasing minority group employment in these street-level bureaucratic roles is not suggested here for the symbolism of minority group inclusion or for the sake of increasing minority groups opportunities (although these reasons are entirely justified). Rather, this analysis suggests that such people will be less likely to structure task performance simplifications in stereotypic ways.

Potential clients might also have greater confidence and trust in individuals with whom they can relate, and who they can assume have greater understanding of their needs. However, it is not clear to what extent such predictions are reliable. Black recruits to police bureaucracies as currently designed would undoubtedly continue to be governed by the incentive systems and job perceptions of the current force. Black patrolmen today may even be the objects of increased community hostility. But in systems encouraging increased community sensitivity, black patrolmen might thrive. The benefits of community control, perhaps like most political arrangements, may ultimately depend upon the development of political consciousness and arousal. Voter turnout is low when community participation is introduced through elections in which people have previously developed little stake or involvement (such as elections for Community Action Agency boards and the recent school elections in New York City).[5] Similarly, the potential for greater rapport between street-level bureaucrats and clients may ultimately depend upon the extent to which community involvement in the issues of community control precedes transfer of power. Without such prior arousal, community control may only provide unrealized structural *opportunities* for increased community participation and greater bureaucracy-client rapport should community groups seek to influence public policy in the future.

These comments are made in full recognition that they are supportive of structural and institutional changes of considerable magnitude. If the analysis developed here is at all persuasive, then it may be said that the bureaucratic crises I have described are built into the very structure of organizational bureaucratic life. Only structural alterations, made in response to a comprehensive analysis of the bureaucratic crisis, may be expected to be effective.

CONCLUSION

Let me conclude and summarize by indicating why the current situation, and this analysis, point to a continuing crisis in city politics. It is not only that bureaucracy-client antagonisms will continue to deepen or that black separatism will continue to place stress on street-level bureaucracies which they are poorly equipped to accommodate. In addition to these factors, we face a continuing crisis because certain modes of bureaucratic behavior effectively act to shield the bureaucracies from the nature of their own shortcomings.

Street-level bureaucrats, perceiving their clients as fully responsible for their actions—as do some policemen, mental hospital workers, and welfare workers—may thereby absolve themselves from contributing to the perpetuation of problems. Police attribution of riots to the riff-raff of the ghetto provides just one illustration of this tendency (see Rossi et al., 1968: 110–113).

On the other hand, attributing clients' performance to cultural or societal factors beyond the scope of human intervention also works to absolve bureaucrats from responsibility for clients' futures (Rossi et al., 1968: 136). While there may be some validity to both modes of perception, the truth (as it often does) lies somewhere in between. Meanwhile both modes of perception function to trivialize the bureaucrat-client interaction, at the expense of responsibility.

Changing role expectations provides another mechanism which may shield street-level bureaucrats from recognizing the impact of their actions. This may take at least two forms. Bureaucrats may try to influence public expectations of their jobs, so as to convince the public of their good intentions under difficult conditions. Or they may seek role redefinition in such a way as to permit job performance according to role expectations *in some limited way*. The teacher who explains that "I can't teach them all, so I will try to teach the bright ones," is attempting to foster an image of fulfilling role expectations in a limited way. While this may be one way to utilize scarce resources and deserves some sympathy, it should be recognized that such tendencies deflect pressures *away* from providing for more adequate *routine* treatment of clients.

But perhaps most significantly, it is difficult for street-level bureaucrats to acknowledge the impact of their behavior toward clients because their very ability to function in bureaucratic roles depends upon routines, simplifications, and other psychological mechanisms to reduce stress. Under such circumstances, attacks upon the substance or content of these reactions to job stress may be interpreted as criticisms of the basic requirements of job performance. As such, the criticisms are interpreted as ignorant or inaccurate.

Even if street-level bureaucrats are prepared to accept the substance of criticisms, they are likely to view them as utopian in view of the difficulties of the job. They may respond by affirming the justice of criticism in theory, but reject the criticism as inapplicable in the real world. Because they (and we) cannot imagine a world in which bureaucratic simplifications do not take place, they reject the criticism entirely.

This inability to recognize or deal with substantive criticism is reinforced by the fact that street-level bureaucrats find the validity of their simplifications and routines confirmed by selective perception of the evidence. Not only do the self-fulfilling prophecies mentioned earlier confirm these operations, but street-level bureaucrats also affirm their judgments because they depend upon the routines that offer a measure of security and because they are unfamiliar with alternative procedures which might free them to act differently. That street-level bureaucrats are in some sense shielded from awareness of the impact to their job-related behavior ensures that the crisis between street-level bureaucrats and their clients will continue; even while administrators in these bureaucracies loudly proclaim the initiation of various programs to improve community relations, reduce tensions among clientele groups, and provide token measures of representation for clientele groups on lower-level policy-making boards.

The shelter from criticism may contribute to conservative tendencies in street-level bureaucracies, widely commented upon in studies of bureaucracy generally. For our purposes they may help to explain the recourse of community groups to proposals for radical change, and the recognition that only relatively radical alternatives are likely to break the circle of on-the-job socialization, job stress, and reaction formation.

An illustration of relatively drastic changes may be available in the recent recruitment of idealistic college students into the police and teaching professions.[6] These individuals are not only better educated, but are presumed to approach their new jobs with attitudes toward ghetto clients quite different from those of other recruits. What higher salaries, better working conditions, and professionalization were unable to accomplish is being achieved on a modest level by the selective service system, the war in Vietnam, and the unavailability of alternative outlets for constructive participation in reforming American society. Higher salaries (which go mostly to the kinds of people who would have become policemen and teachers anyway) have not previously resulted in recruitment of significantly more sensitive or skillful people in these bureaucracies, although this has been the (somewhat self-serving) recommendation for bureaucratic improvement for many years. On the contrary, the recruitment of college students whose career expectations in the past did not include this kind of public service orientation may accomplish the task of introducing people with the desired backgrounds to street-level bureaucratic work independent (or even in spite) of increased salaries, professionalization, seniority benefits, and the like.

It is obviously too early to evaluate these developments. The new breed of street-level bureaucrat has yet to be tested in on-the-job effectiveness, ability to withstand peer group pressures and resentments, or staying power. But their example does illustrate the importance of changing basic aspects of the bureaucratic systems fundamentally, instead of at the margin. If the arguments made here are at all persuasive, then those who would analyze the service performance of street-level bureaucracies should concentrate attention on components of the work profile. Those components discussed here—resource inadequacy, physical and psychological threat, ambiguity of role expectations, and the ways in which policemen, teachers, and other street-level bureaucrats react to problems stemming from these job-related difficulties—appear to deserve particular attention.

NOTES

1. This paper draws heavily upon and extends two recent papers (Lipsky, 1969a, 1969b). For a more detailed analysis of street-level bureaucrats and the factors affecting their performance, see the latter.

   The reader will recognize the tentative nature of some of the conclusions and analyses which follow. The analysis of street-level bureaucracy thus far has consisted of trying to discover characteristics common to a certain set of urban bureaucrats which obtain beyond the narrow contexts of individual bureaucracies such as the police or teachers. The latter half of this paper is similarly a tentative attempt to relate the analysis to issues of current public policy.

2. For a general discussion of psychological reaction to stress, see Lazarus (1966: esp. ch. 1, pp. 266–318). This work is particularly useful in providing conceptual distinctions for various phenomena related to the coping process.

3. See the decision of Judge Skelly Wright in Hobson *v.* Hanson, June 19, 1967, 269F Supp. 401 (1967); also see Clark (1965: 128); also see Rosenthal and Jacobson (1968: 116–118).

4. For example, the requirements for becoming a building department inspector in New York City have virtually assured the building trade unions of public employment for their members.

5. A number of writers have commented on the low turnout for elections to CAP and Model Cities boards. See, e.g., Altshuler (1970: 138–139). On decentralized school board elections, see the issues of the *New York Times* dated from February 19 to March 22, 1970.

6. See, for example, the *New York Times* of February 13, 1970.

REFERENCES

Altshuler, A. (1970) *Community Control: The Black Demand for Participation in American Cities*. New York: Western.

Becker, H. (1957) "Social Class and Teacher-Pupil Relationships," in B. Mercer and E. Carr (eds.) *Education and the Social Order*. New York: Holt, Rinehart and Winston.

Bordua, D. [ed.] (1967) *The Police: Six Sociological Essays*. New York: John Wiley.

Clark, K. (1965) *Dark Ghetto*. New York: Harper & Row.

Downs, A. (1967) *Inside Bureaucracy*. Boston: Little, Brown.

Gittell, M. and A. G. Hevesi [eds.] (1969) *The Politics of Urban Education*. New York: Praeger.

Glazer, N. (1969) "For White and Black Community Control Is the Issue." New York Times Magazine (April 27).

Goffman, E. (1969) *Asylums*. Chicago: Aldine.

Kotler, M. (1969) *Neighborhood Government*. Indianapolis: Bobbs-Merrill.

Lazarus, R. (1966) *Psychological Stress and the Coping Process*. New York: McGraw-Hill.

Lipsky, M. (1969a) "Is a Hard Rain Gonna Fall: Issues of Planning and Administration in the Urban World of the 1970's." Prepared for delivery at the Annual Meetings of the American Society of Public Administration, Miami Beach, May 21.

——— (1969b) "Toward a Theory of Street-Level Bureaucracy." Prepared for delivery at the Annual Meetings of the American Political Science Association, New York, September 20.

McNamara, J. (1967) "Uncertainties in Police Work: the Relevance of Police Recruits' Background and Training," in D. Bordua (ed.) *The Police: Six Sociological Essays*. New York: John Wiley.

Niederhoffer, A. (1967) *Behind the Blue Shield*. New York: Doubleday.

Rogers, D. (1968) *110 Livingston Street*. New York: Random House.

Rosenthal, R. and L. Jacobson (1968) *Pygmalion in the Classroom*. New York: Holt, Rinehart and Winston.

Rossi, P. et al. (1968) "Between White and Black, the Faces of American Institutions in the Ghetto." Supplemental Studies for the National Advisory Commission on Civil Disorders. Washington, D.C.

Sarbin, T. and V. Allen (1968) "Role Theory," in G. Lindzey and E. Aronson (eds.) *The Handbook of Social Psychology*. Reading, Mass.: Addison-Wesley.

Silver, A. (1967) "The Demand for Order in Civil Society," in D. Bordua (ed.) *The Police: Six Sociological Essays*. New York: John Wiley.

Skolnick, J. (1967) *Justice Without Trial*. New York: John Wiley.

Walker, D. (1968) *Rights in Conflict*. New York: Bantam.

Waskow, A. (1969) "Community Control of the Police." *Trans-action* (December).

Wilson, J. Q. (1968) *Varieties of Police Behavior*. Cambridge, Mass.: Harvard Univ. Press.

Service Delivery Rules and the Distribution of Local Government Services: Three Detroit Bureaucracies

BRYAN D. JONES, SAADIA R. GREENBERG, CLIFFORD KAUFMAN, and JOSEPH DREW

In the decentralized tradition of American government structures, autonomous local jurisdictions have responsibility for the provision of a wide range of services essential for the well-being of the public. Such services include both those which are universally accepted to be in the domain of state power (e.g., law enforcement) as well as those which could in principle be provided privately, but for historical or other reasons are often not (e.g., education, sanitation).

One may isolate two general approaches to the study of municipal public services. In the first, government is viewed as a productive organization, producing public services from resources in the same manner that a private factory transforms raw materials into consumer goods. The removal of municipal services from the market pricing system makes it difficult to ascertain the *value* (as distinct from the costs) of these services to the consuming citizenry. This approach to the study of municipal public services has dealt with the problem of valuation of urban public services and the related problem of the efficiency of the service delivery organization.

A second approach to the study of municipal services is more recent in origin. It focuses on the levels of municipal services provided to different groups in the metropolis. Rooted in the academic tradition of Harold Lasswell's definition of politics, the attention to "who gets what" in public services is termed the study of service distribution. This concern with the distribution of services to definable demographic groups also may be called the *political* approach to the study of municipal services, while the study of the valuation of services, which emphasizes the nature of the governmental product and the efficiency of the producing organization, might be termed the *economic* approach.

The thesis of this paper is that the economic model has political consequences. Local government officials in most American metropolitan areas have adopted a model stressing productivity in their conceptualization of the delivery of the services for which they are responsible. Local government bureaucracies more or less explicitly accept the goal of implementing rational criteria for the delivery of services to citizens, even though com-

Revised version of a paper presented at the 1975 meeting of the American Political Science Association, San Francisco, California, September 2–5, 1975. Data analysis was facilitated by grants from Wayne State's Computer and Data Processing Center and Department of Political Science.

promises may have to be made in the establishment of these criteria. These production oriented criteria give rise to *service delivery rules*, regularized procedures for the delivery of services, which are attempts to codify the productivity goals of urban service bureaucracies. These rules have distinct, definable distributional consequences which often go unrecognized. That is, the decisions of governments to adopt rational service delivery rules can (and usually do) differentially benefit citizens.

In order to shed some empirical light on the ideas outlined in the above paragraph, we have assembled extensive data from three City of Detroit bureaucracies: the Environmental Enforcement Division of the (now) Environmental Protection and Maintenance Department, the Sanitation Division of the same department, and the Department of Parks and Recreation. Data from these service organizations have been supplemented by data from the U.S. Census and from other sources in order to assess the demographic characteristics of citizens to whom services are made available. These bureaucracies are useful for this study for several reasons. First, by being less visible than, say, police and fire departments, they may give a freer range to the operation of service rules, less constrained by the operation of macro-politics at the City Council or Mayor's Office. Second, these bureaucracies are those most intimately concerned with the city's environment, a major topic of concern in an older, northern industrial city such as Detroit which has been deeply affected by suburban migration and expanding blight. Third, the service rules employed are substantially different for each of these bureaucracies. Our strategy will be first to examine the two approaches outlined above in more detail and then to trace the distributional impacts of service rules in the three bureaucracies.

THE ECONOMIC OR PRODUCTIVITY APPROACH

Academic concern with the problem of the measurement and efficient production of municipal outputs can be traced back at least as far as a monograph by Ridley and Simon, published in 1938.[1] Then, as now, services were conceptualized as the product of governmental activity, with the private firm as an explicit or implicit analogy. Input factors are transformed into the service, the output or product of the operation.[2] In the ideal model of the private firm, outputs are evaluated by the consumer through his willingness to purchase the product. Efficiency of the firm may be measured as a ratio of input to output, in physical units or in dollars.[3] However, because the market pricing mechanism is not generally involved when government produces services, it becomes quite difficult to measure the value of those products, the efficiency of the producing organization, or even to specify an output unit. The problem of defining an output unit also exists in the private service sector but creates less of a problem because of the existence of market pricing. As the economist Werner Hirsch has indicated, "Inquiries into these matters require information on government service demand and cost functions which are usually difficult to determine because of the economist's inability to find readily quantifiable output units and quality characteristics."[4]

Whatever the problems of defining governmental output, it is clear that the service product must be tied directly to the goals of the producing agency. Output units can be defined as contributions to a desired goal state, usually conceived as communitywide conditions. The activities of police, for example, contribute more or less to the goal of community security.[5] This model of government activity rests on a conception of government as a rational actor which attempts to affect social conditions in a community, rather than a passive object of extra-governmental actors competing for valuable public policy benefits.

Studies emphasizing the production of urban services stem from two sources. First, there is the classic concern of organizational analysis with goal attainment and the rational application or efficient utilization of administrative resources. Given the development of much of organizational theory in the context of the private firm, this typically means meeting production schedules. The union of organization theory and microeconomics provided a method which, in principle at least, could be applied to problems of government service provision. The second source also encourages the application of such economic analysis: the desire of municipal reformers to implement "businesslike" practices in local governments. The watchwords became cost efficiency in the production of services by professionally-managed and effective bureaucracies divorced from local politics.[6]

In the production model, the delivery of services, defined as getting the service product to citizen consumers, is generally treated as secondary, if it is treated at all. The focus on production severs product production from product delivery; the latter can be routinized subject only to efficiency considerations. Citizen preferences or needs may be incorporated in the formulation of the original goal, but delivery is not generally considered relevant to goal setting. Delivery is, rather, the technical problem of getting the product to a location in a manner that maximizes the impact on the goal.

The literature on service as product is partly analytical and partly normative, so that the degree to which a particular government service organization has adopted a productivity orientation is an empirical question. There may be discernable prior causes associated with the adoption of this style of delivery: city size, region of the country, nature of the goal of the service organization, etc. At any rate, it is clear that the production model has significantly influenced many local service delivery networks; for example, Detroit, in company with other large cities, has established a Productivity Center to coordinate departmental productivity programs.[7]

THE POLITICAL OR DISTRIBUTIONAL APPROACH

It is one of the truisms of politics that, to quote the authors of a popular introductory textbook, "Government decisions have differential impact on citizens."[8] In countless analyses and case studies, political scientists have tried to assess the benefits and costs of governmental decisions, policies and routine procedures and their effects on groups of citizens who are identifiable by their demographic characteristics or economic interests. The differential assignment of the benefits of local public services, as Lineberry notes, ". . . represent(s) indirect transfer payments, increasing a household's income through service excellence or diminishing it through service denials."[9]

Two systematic approaches have been employed to study the distribution of local services. One, utilizing survey research, has examined the perceptions of citizens of the absolute and relative adequacy of the city services they receive.[10] A second has studied government records of service delivery, associating them with demographic data on neighborhoods from the United States Census or other sources.[11] The attempt to ascertain the level of services which a demographically definable area of a city receives according to governmental records provides an objective mapping of the distribution of services, while the survey research approach offers a perceptual mapping of the incidence of those same service efforts. Both approaches suffer defects. Perceptions of service quality are not adequate indicators of the actual level consumed, although dissatisfaction with the current level may be more adequately assessed. The "objective" approach is limited by the character of government records, and, more significantly, by the lack of satisfactory knowledge concerning the impacts of the services delivered to a geographic area of a city. None the less, this approach offers us, in principle, a method of examining the effort which a local government makes in attempting to achieve a goal state in a neighborhood.[12]

The findings emerging from this line of inquiry are complex and not easily summarized. However, several aspects of these studies are noteworthy. First, service delivery systems in large cities, at least cities in the Southwest, the West, and the North, are not identical to those found in some small Southern towns. The crude racial discrimination of the city fathers in Shaw, Mississippi[13] is not matched in Berkeley,[14] San Antonio,[15] Houston,[16] Oakland,[17] and Detroit.[18] In those large cities, no clear, cumulative pattern of service distribution emerges. The particular pattern of service distribution observed seems to depend on the service studied and the service indicator employed. One reasonably conclusive result which does appear, however, is strong evidence against what Lineberry terms the "underclass hypothesis," the hypothesis that the poor, the black, and the powerless consistently receive less than an equal share of the benefits of city services.[19] At times they do receive less; at other times they get more. The question of whether the governmental effort is "enough" or "equitable" is not answered by this research; all we can say is that the lower classes do not consistently receive the lowest level of services. The literature is conclusive on one more point: services are virtually never distributed equally. Variation in service level from neighborhood to neighborhood is the general rule.

THE NATURE OF SERVICE DELIVERY RULES

As one may surmise from the above discussion, the productivity model fails to consider systematically the distribution of the services produced. The distributional approach has begun the mapping of the distributional patterns of service levels, but it has been weak in specifying *why* patterns emerge as they do.

One of the keys to understanding service distribution lies in the internal structure of the organization responsible for the delivery of services. In many public bureaucracies, service delivery rules, routinized procedures for accomplishing the purposes of the organization, heavily influence distributional patterns. These rules are formulated, consciously or unconsciously, in an environment which favors the view of service as product and discourages inquiry into the distribution consequences of the rules. That is, while rules may be relevant to the production of a product or achieving a goal at community level, distributional consequences are generally not considered, unless elements outside the service delivery organization, such as the mayor, the city council, or irate, organized citizens, impinge on the bureaucratic routine.

Cyert and March have discussed at some length the propensity of private firms to adopt *task performance rules* which have the effect of reducing uncertainty and encouraging coordination:

> Task performance rules exist in considerable detail at many different levels in the organization. . . . In most of the firms we have studied, price and output decisions were almost as routinized as production line decisions. Although the procedures changed over time and the rules were frequently contingent on external feedback, price and output were fixed by recourse to a number of simple operating rules.[20]

Similar rules emerge in structuring the task of public delivery. But while distribution to consumers is of minimal interest to the theory of the firm, it is of critical concern to the theory of public bureaucracies. These rules, ". . . like many 'neutral' decision rules, are not neutral."[21] They affect not only the success of individuals within the organization, but they also influence the amount of the service product which different citizens receive. The unintended distributional consequences of bureaucratic activity have been termed *resultants* by Levy, Meltsner, and Wildavsky.[22]

Task performance rules in public and private organizations can arise internally or externally, either through learning within the organization or through the values of the individuals recruited into the organization. Cyert and March observe that ". . . through recruitment and selection, many employees come to a firm with established task performance rules."[23]

When service delivery rules are rationally related to the goals of the service delivery organization, they are termed *professional*. Professional standards have come to dominate political considerations in service delivery; that is, a focus on overall goals rather than attention to dividing up governmental resources to various groups is viewed by most service deliverers as legitimate. "Precisely who gets how much of these products is not normally a professional concern."[24] Professionalizing, however, will not make the distributional problem disappear, although it may screen it from public view. Service delivery rules, professional or not, invariably have distributional consequences.

Professional public administrators often focus on services as products which are subject to quality control standards, rather than on services as scarce commodities to be divided up by groups who disagree, at least implicitly, about who ought to receive what level of service. From the professional viewpoint, intrusion into the routine of service delivery by citizens or by the elected elements of local government is a bother, since there is generally a "fair rule" for the delivery of services, on which all reasonable men would agree. The rule is a good one, from the productivity standpoint, if it is *effective* in contributing to the goal of the service organization at the community level (e.g. reducing the overall crime rate) and if it is reasonably *efficient* in allocating organizational resources. Citizen input often plays a role in the productivity approach to the service delivery process, but not in questioning the rule. Citizen complaints are "legitimate" to the professional when they point out a failure in the operation of the service rule ("My garbage was not picked up on my collection day."), or when the rule is to rely on citizen calls as indicative of need for the service, as is clearly the case with fire service. Citizen complaints may be viewed much less benevolently when they question the distributional aspects of the rule used to deliver a service.

THE ROLE OF SERVICE DELIVERY RULES IN SERVICE DISTRIBUTION: EMPIRICAL ANALYSES

In the remainder of this paper we trace the distributional consequences of service delivery rules, using data from three Detroit city bureaucracies. To the degree possible, this is done quantitatively, by interposing the service delivery rule between the demographic character of the city neighborhoods and the service outputs they receive. Our evidence concerning the consequences of such rules will be firmer than that on the origin of the rules, although we try to indicate likely sources for them. The basic unit of analysis is the census tract; we have been able to assign service indicators to the tract level for each bureaucracy studied. We make no claim that a tract represents a neighborhood in any meaningful sense of that term. The tract is a geographic unit on which much demographic data has been assembled, and which is relatively homogeneous with regard to many social and economic characteristics. Further, in Detroit there is a good deal of variability among tracts. Average family income, for example, had a mean of $10,607 and a standard deviation of $3455 in 1970; more graphically, the range was from $2655 to $47,000. This later tract is fully $20,000 above its closest competitor; nevertheless, even an industrial, somewhat decaying, Northern city surrounded by rapidly expanding suburbs contains sufficient socio-economic variation in the composition of its population to make a study of service distribution a worthwhile enterprise.

The census tract seems a sound choice for another reason. We have chosen to keep the unit of analysis constant for different service areas, for the sake of comparison. It has often been necessary to disaggregate service data collected to the tract. To disaggregate to the block level would have done too much violence to the data; moreover, census data on tracts is much more complete than on blocks.

THE ENVIRONMENTAL ENFORCEMENT DIVISION: THE EFFICACY OF CITIZEN CONTACTS

The Environmental Enforcement Division of what is now the Environmental Protection and Maintenance Department is responsible for enforcing the City of Detroit environmental ordinances. As such, the Division possesses quasi-police powers, employing about forty or so fulltime inspectors who issue violation notices for problems of debris and overgrowth. The Division also supervises the City's rodent control program. Each inspector is assigned an area of the city for which he is responsible; these areas are based on the Sanitation Division's districts. Inspectors are sent to each area on the day before garbage is collected because it is believed that more violations will be in evidence on that day; consequently, the activities of the inspectors will have maximum impact.

Theoretically, inspectors follow a relatively rigid set of procedures in their field activities. Violations come to the attention of the organization through two mechanisms. Citizens may contact the bureaucracy, complaining of possible violations, or the inspector may spot a potential violation in his travels in the field. Upon investigation, the inspector may decide to issue a violation notice or determine that no action is warranted. If he decides the former, he reinspects the situation when he is next in the field, generally five working days from the date of the issuance of the violation notice. At this point, the inspector again has three choices: abate the violation notice if the situation, in his mind, has been corrected; let the violation notice stand and hope for compliance; or issue a court notice. The Division files these notices with the Traffic and Ordinance Division of Recorder's Court. At this point, enforcement is now in the hands of another agency (the court) which, in the eyes of Division personnel, has been notoriously lenient with violators. Actually, very few court notices are indeed served, both because of an unwillingness to place further strain on the over-burdened courts dockets and a realization that violators often receive light punishment. In July of 1973, for example, there were 3,129 citizen complaints, 1,417 field pickups of violations, 7,395 reinvestigations, 4,846 abatements, 261 court notices served and 194 court notices filed. The process is diagrammed in Figure 1.

FIGURE 1

Pattern of Governmental Activity: Environmental Enforcement Division

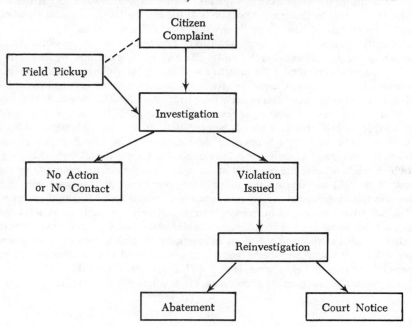

The data that we have used to explore the distributional impact of this set of delivery rules was collected for July and October 1973 from the summary sheets of the investigators active during that period. Each work day of each inspector was apportioned to census tracts. Since there are 420 tracts in Detroit, and about 200 distinct areas which inspectors cover, there is some overlap in assignment of service level to tracts. We have 200 independent pieces of information on each service variable, but 420 units of analysis. In what follows, the primary statistical technique used is regression analysis. Since the independence assumption is not involved in the derivation of the statistical estimators of regression parameters, our findings will not be biased because of this source. However, independence is assumed in the derivation for the standard errors of the estimators, and these may be mis-stated in our results. The effects are not likely to be drastic, however, because the independence assumption is violated only marginally in practice.[25]

If the service delivery procedures outlined above are followed without bias, service contacts will accrue disproportionately to those neighborhoods with a higher propensity to initiate contacts. The first question related to the distribution of benefits thus involves which neighborhoods generate contacts. For reasons we have detailed elsewhere,[26] citizen-initiated contacts with the EED come from all over the city, but are disproportionately concentrated in neighborhoods at the middle ranges of social well-being. These neighborhoods, neither the best nor the worst in terms of housing condition, income, and other measures of social well-being, are located spatially in a semi-circle about halfway between the central business district and the city's boundaries. Inspection of the data reveals that the environmental inspectors virtually always respond to those citizen contacts which are referred to them. If the inspectors always investigate citizen complaints, as our evidence indicates, then it will be those neighborhoods at the middle levels of social well-being that will benefit most, rather than the city's worst or best neighborhoods.

The Environmental Enforcement Division, however, has a possible equalization mechanism in the procedure whereby violations may be "picked up" by inspectors in the field. The inspectors could take the initiative and search for violations in areas where they have observed numerous violations but from which they receive few complaints. On the other hand, the agency may behave according to "Adam Smith" rules: let the requesting customer dictate where organization resources are to go.[27] Inspectors who follow this market allocation principle will simply spot violations as they investigate citizen complaints. If this is in fact what happens, field pickups will be concentrated in just those census tracts from which citizen complaints originate. To test these contradictory propositions (which really involve the question of the aggressiveness of the agency), we regressed the number of field pickups on the number of complaints, the average age of housing structures in the census tract (an inverse measure of social well-being that correlates $-.93$ with distance from the central business district), and percent black. In general, when we regress a service variable on demographic variables, we employ only one indicator of social well-being or social status, and one of racial composition. This allows the assessment of the separate effects of social well-being and race, which could not be done if "redundant" measures of social well-being were included.[28] Logarithms are taken when the service variable is "count" data (number of contacts, etc.), which served to bring "outliers" closer to the main body of data, allowing them less impact on the results than they would otherwise have. Table 1 presents the results of these regressions, for July and October 1973.

The results presented in Table 1 support the model of the passive bureaucracy. The number of complaints originating from tracts is significantly related to the number of field pickups in both July and October, with complaints being more efficacious in generating field pickups in July than in October. Racial composition is not significantly related to field pickups, but housing age is inversely related to them, which indicates that there are more residual field pickups (pickups after controlling for citizen complaints) in the better-off areas of the city.

For the first investigation by inspectors of a possible violation, those areas which complain more frequently receive more service contacts, both directly as a consequence of the complaint and as a result of the lack of aggressiveness of the investigators in seeking out violators in other areas. The newer parts of the city are residually benefited in that they receive some investigations which are unrelated to the number of citizen complaints generated. This is probably a consequence of the fact that EED bases its activities on Sanitation Division districts. Sanitation routes are adjusted to the amount of garbage generated, and more garbage is generated in the newer areas of the city. The apportionment of EED districts and through this the apportionment of the inspectors' time is not directly linked to demand for environmental enforcement service (as indicated by citizen complaints) or to an objective determination of service needed (which is likely to be greater in the worse-off part of the city). The work load for inspectors should be lighter in the newer areas of the city, where neither need nor demand is particularly high. Therefore, they are likely to conduct extra inspections in the newer areas because they have the time to do so.

TABLE 1

Field Pickups, Environmental Enforcement Division[a]

LN (OFP) = 0.6082 + 0.2824 LN (OCOM) − 0.0039 HSEAGE + 0.0048 BLACK				
Std. error:	(0.098)	(0.049)	(0.002)	(0.062)
t:	6.20	5.75	−2.04	0.07
R = .316				
N = 341				
LN (JFP) = 0.3616 + 0.6085 LN (JCOM) − 0.0086 HSEAGE + 0.0478 BLACK				
Std. error:	(0.098)	(0.048)	(0.002)	(0.065)
t:	3.98	12.61	−4.62	0.74
R = .584				
N = 379				

[a]The variables employed are as follows: OFP = October field pickups, JFP = July field pickups, OCOM = October citizen contacts, JCOM = July citizen contacts, HSEAGE = Average age of housing structure, BLACK = Percent black.

Assessing the distribution of government-to-citizen contacts is not enough; what the inspectors do at the site of the potential violation is also important. The number of actual violations issued should naturally be a function of complaints from citizens and field pick-ups, but the demography of the neighborhood may influence the number of violations issued. Table 2 indicates that the number of violations is a function of the number of citizen complaints and the number of field pickups, as expected. The (inverse) measure of social well-being, average age of housing structure, enters significantly into the equation for violations in both months, but the direction of influence is different for the two months. Racial composition is consistent in direction, but is significant only for October. We conclude that demography does not directly affect the number of violations issued, but does affect them through the association of citizen complaints and field pickups with the demographic characteristics of neighborhoods. To summarize at this point: citizens living in neighborhoods at middle levels of social well-being have a greater propensity to complain about environmental problems in their neighborhoods. Environmental enforcement inspectors are most likely to pick up violations en route to the site of the citizen complaint. As Table 2 indicates, violations are actually written as a consequence of citizen complaints. Citizen-to-government contacts are efficacious in getting violations issued to the neighbors of complaining citizens.

The established procedures of the Environmental Enforcement Division diagrammed in Figure 1 may be traced further with respect to distributional impact. Table 3 represents regression equations for the number of reinvestigations as a function of the number of violations issued and our two familiar demographic variables, housing age and percentage black. Not unexpectedly, the results show that violations generate reinvestigations. Coefficients for housing age in equations for both months indicate that there are more reinvestigations in the less well-off areas of the city. This may indicate special compliance problems here, perhaps as a consequence of the number of absentee landlords in these parts of the

TABLE 2

Violation Notices Issued, Environmental Enforcement Division[a]

LN (OVIL) = 0.3381	+ 0.6085 LN (OCOM)	+ 0.5002 LN (OFP)	− 0.0069 HSEAGE	+ 0.1607 BLACK	
Std. error:	(0.077)	(0.038)	(0.041)	(0.001)	(0.047)
t:	4.38	15.87	12.32	−4.79	3.42
R = .813					
N = 341					
LN (JVIL) = − 0.0764	+ 0.3630 LN (JCOM)	+ 0.6501 LN (JFP)	+ 0.0067 HSEAGE	+ 0.0738 BLACK	
Std. error:	(0.085)	(0.053)	(0.047)	(0.002)	(0.059)
t:	7.46	6.86	13.70	3.79	1.24
R = .768					
N = 379					

[a]OVIL = Number of violations issued, October, JVIL = Number of violations issued, July. Other variables are defined in Table 1.

city. One note of caution should be mentioned with regard to Table 3. Reinvestigations generally take place five working days after the first investigation, so the reinvestigation for, say, the first week in July will be in response to violation notices from the last week in June. However, the areas of the city from which complaints originate are reasonably stable: the logarithm of the number of complaints correlate .42 between July and October; a similar stability existed with respect to the logarithms of the number of field pickups (.54 between months) and the number of reinvestigations (.48). Because of the stability of the environmental enforcement process, it is not likely that the one week misadjustment affected the results presented here.

Tables 4 and 5 indicate that abating violation notices and serving court notices are primarily explained by the number of reinvestigations an inspector makes. However, the reasonably tight relationship observed thus far in the chain representing the service delivery rules of the organization drops off somewhat for court notices served, probably as a result of the low number of notices inspectors serve. Demographic variables do not enter consistently in the equations for abatements nor for those for court notices. Demography still seems to have its primary effect indirectly, through the entry points of citizen complaints and field pick-ups.

Because of the operation of the service delivery rules in the Environmental Enforcement Division, whatever mechanisms are responsible for the generation of citizen complaints about environmental problems heavily influence the distributional pattern observed. Citizen contacts are efficacious because the enforcement contacts made by the inspectors are triggered by such citizen complaints about environmental violations. Citizens do not have power over EED inspectors because they can prod government into action in this instance. Inspectors come on call because they have a set of task performance rules which explain the behavior of individual members of the service organization. Control of the rule implies control over the distribution of the benefits which the organization provides to citizens.

TABLE 3

Reinvestigations, Environmental Enforcement Division[a]

LN (OREN) = -0.0172 + 1.1098 LN (OVIL) + 0.0101 HSEAGE + 0.0105 BLACK

Std. error:	(0.101)	(0.0408)	(0.002)	(0.071)
t:	-0.16	27.19	4.90	0.15

R = .817
N = 412

LN (JREN) = 0.0207 + 0.4793 LN (JVIL) + 0.0086 HSEAGE + 0.3561 BLACK

Std. error:	(0.136)	(0.057)	(0.003)	(0.098)
t:	0.15	8.35	3.00	3.63

R = .515
N = 379

[a]OREN = Number of reinvestigations in October, JREN = Number of reinvestigations in July. Other variables are as in Table 2.

TABLE 4

Abatements, Environmental Enforcement Division[a]

LN (OABT) = 0.0661 + 0.6873 LN (OREN) − 0.0012 HSEAGE − 0.0293 BLACK

Std. error:	(0.048)	(0.014)	(0.001)	(0.029)
t:	1.37	47.62	−1.20	−0.86

R = .924
N = 411

LN (JABT) = −0.1619 + 0.4661 LN (JREN) + 0.0101 HSEAGE + 0.0382 BLACK

Std. error:	(0.062)	(0.022)	(0.001)	(0.046)
t:	−2.61	20.86	7.38	0.82

R = .802
N = 379

[a]OABT = Number of abatements in October, JABT = Number of abatements in July.

SANITATION: ONCE A WEEK, EVERY WEEK

The primary service delivery rule in Detroit's Sanitation Division is an egalitarian one: pick up garbage from each residence once a week, every week. Prior to 1972, this was essentially the only formal delivery rule operative in the Division. No formal rules governed the allocation of resources, such as the size of routes, at Division headquarters; the process was essentially a decentralized one worked out by route foremen and district supervisors. (A route is the area covered by one crew, i.e., one garbage truck, in one day. A section is the area covered by the crew in one week. There are about 260 sections in the City of Detroit, and 1300 routes.) One would expect some within-section adjustment according to work loads, but, again, this was not formalized at central headquarters. Then, in the summer of 1972, disaster struck. The inefficient distribution of input resources designed to bring about organizational goals quickly became a severe liability. "The city's refuse

TABLE 5

Court Notices Served, Environmental Enforcement Division[a]

LN (OCTS) = 0.0309 + 0.0973 LN (OREN) − 0.0014 HSEAGE + 0.0354 BLACK

Std. error:	(0.031)	(0.009)	(0.001)	(0.02)
t:	0.99	10.4	−1.62	1.61

R = .485
N = 412

LN (JCTS) = −0.0060 + 0.0635 LN (JREN) + 0.1740 HSEAGE − 0.0027 BLACK

Std. error:	(0.036)	(0.013)	(0.001)	(0.003)
t:	−0.18	4.80	2.14	−0.10

R = .301
N = 379

[a]OCTS = Number of court notices served, October, JCTS = Number of court notices served, July.

collection was two to three weeks behind schedule, with both complaints and costs soaring."[29] At this point the Division began a restructuring of the routes across the entire city in the name of efficiency. The adjustment of routes began in October 1972 and the implementation took place from December 1972 to April of 1973.

The route restructuring was primarily the work of Andrew A. Giovanetti, an industrial engineer working on a Ph.D. from the University of Detroit. In a massive data collection effort, he assembled the information necessary for the implementation of a new, explicit service delivery rule: assign routes on the basis of the amount of garbage collected. This "weight" figure was highly related to the time required to pick up the waste, according to Giovanetti; thus basing routes on weight seemed to be an efficient way of allocating organizational resources. With the new restructuring, it was less likely that some crews would have trouble finishing their routes, while others reported in early. The implemented delivery rule was a rational one which would seem to contribute to the productivity of the Division.

In the Sanitation Division, then, one delivery rule is explicitly distributional, and the rule attempts to equalize results. If the garbage generated by each city neighborhood is adequately collected, then the resulting condition of the neighborhood should be similar. But in attempting to achieve equal results, it is necessary to allocate the resources of the organization unequally, according to the weight of the garbage discarded by neighborhoods. It is important, though, that the division did not conceive of its institution of the "weight rule" explicitly in distributional terms. Rather the justification for the rule was that it was efficient and productive.

We collected data on the operation of the Sanitation Division during October and November of 1973, about six months after the full implementation of the new route structure, although minor adjustments were still going on at the time. Most of the data presented below are weekly averages from these two months; however, some data were collected during a single week in June during which garbagemen engaged in a work "slowdown" in a labor dispute. Since this slowdown caused some problems with uncompleted routes, it could have had distributional consequences, and we wanted to examine these. The data from the 1300 sanitation routes were converted into data on the 420 census tracts of Detroit. Such an operation gave us the opportunity to study the distributional effects of the sanitation delivery structure.

The success of the "weight rule" may be easily evaluated. The correlation between the pounds of residential garbage collected per person and the proportion of a route assigned to each one thousand persons is .842. This second measure was obtained by assigning routes and route segments to census tracts, dividing through by the population of the tract, and multiplying by 1,000 to make the resulting figure more manageable. Another measure of resource allocation, the number of paid man-hours per one thousand occupied units, correlates .699 with pounds of garbage collected. The two resource allocation variables themselves intercorrelated .849.

That resource allocation correlates with the weight of the collected garbage is not conclusive evidence that the garbage produced by citizens caused the observed resource allocation. Clearly directionality could be reversed; perhaps the way in which routes are adjusted affects the amount of garbage crews can pick up. Doubtless this is somewhat the case. But the key piece of information in explaining the observed association is the explicit "weight rule" institutionalized in an attempt to equalize work loads among crews. Such a rule, properly instituted, would have the effect of causing a high correlation between garbage collected per person and resource allocation.

Does the delivery rule have distributional effects? The rule benefits some citizens at the expense of others if the Division expends more resources in collecting garbage in some areas of the city. Even if results are equal, the expenditure of more resources to bring about such results means that there are distributional consequences to the resource allocation process. But the consequences are trivial unless definable categories of citizens are differentially treated, and these categories are more rooted in the social structure than just the amount of garbage they generate.

Can, then, the amount of garbage a citizen produces be related to his class, race, or social well-being? Table 6 indicates that this is the case. More garbage per person is produced in neighborhoods characterized by a higher degree of social well-being (as measured by the distance of their residences from the central business district) and by higher proportions of white residents. Further, these variables have independent effects, as can be seen by examining the regression equations.

It is of some interest that the man primarily responsible for the "weight rule," Andrew Giovanetti, explains the correlations reported above in terms of the density of the living situation. "Given two equal income groups, one living in a three block area with 1700 people, the other living in a ten block area with 900 people, the 900 people will generate the same amount of garbage as the 1700 people." The problem, as he sees it, is that individuals living in a high density situation have less room to accumulate possessions that they later throw away. With smaller yards, there are also smaller amounts of lawn and shrub clippings to be discarded seasonally. In Detroit, lower density living is highly related to distance from the central city. Even if one ignores apartment structures, single family houses and two family flats are built closer together as one travels toward the central business district from any part of the outer city. Income, racial composition, and general social well-being are correlated with low density living.[30] Whether Giovanetti is correct or not, conceptualizing the problem as one of living styles removes the problem of allocation from the sphere of distribution, or politics, and allows a more comfortable, professional, productivity conception of the problem to dominate.

We conclude, then, that the "weight rule" has distributional consequences. But this may not be the whole story. Demography may affect the distribution of resources inde-

TABLE 6

Demography and Garbage[a]

$$\text{GRB/Per} = 12.177 + 0.3999 \text{ DISTANCE} - 2.418 \text{ BLACK}$$

Std. error:	(0.81)	(0.098)	(0.70)
t:	15.03	4.06	−3.45

R = .335
N = 412

[a]GRB/Per = pounds of garbage collected per person.

pendently of the "weight rule." The Division is aware of special problems in the center city, and believes that these problems are the result of "alley pickup," a collection system in which crews move through the city's alleys removing citizens' garbage from containers. In the areas of the city which were built up later, alleys behind dwellings often were discontinued, and "front pickup" is generally the case. The Division management believes that crews do a poorer job in the alleys than in the streets, and consequently claims to have allocated extra resources to the center city. Or, as James Watts, the Director of the Environmental Protection and Maintenance Department (the former Department of Public Works, including the Sanitation Division and the Environmental Enforcement Division), told an aggressive center city resident at a community meeting on decentralization, "You get more bang for the buck in the center city."

To test management's claims we need to examine the distribution of resources after the influence of the "weight rule" is accounted for. Table 7 presents regressions of two measures of resource allocation, routes per 1,000 persons and man hours per 1,000 persons separately, on garbage per person, distance from the central business district, and percent black. Percent black is not significant, but distance is significantly related to resource level allocated in both equations. The influence is negative in direction, indicating that resource allocation is higher in the worse-off areas of Detroit when the influence of the "weight rule" is controlled. If we first regress the resource variable (man-hours) on garbage per person, then examine the residuals of that regression as a function of distance, we obtain a correlation coefficient of $-.378$. More interestingly, it is evident from a scatterplot of these two variables that the assumption of linearity inherent in the correlation coefficient *under* accesses the relationship. As is evident in Figure 3, there is a relatively constant function relating the two variables until one gets quite close to the center city, where there occurs a substantial jump in resource allocation (with the weight rule controlled). (See Figure 2.)

In Detroit's Sanitation Division, then, three service delivery rules determine the distribution of services to citizens. The first rule is clearly most determinative: collect the garbage once a week, each week. The second rule, to allocate resources according to the

TABLE 7

Resource Distribution, Sanitation Division[a]

$$\text{RT/KP} = 0.1281 + 0.0525 \, \text{GBG/Per} - 0.0254 \, \text{DISTANCE} + 0.0176 \, \text{BLACK}$$

Std. error:	(0.030) (0.001)	(0.003)	(0.021)
t:	4.30 36.01	−8.57	0.83

R = .875
N = 412

$$\text{MANHOUR} = 43.477 + 3.698 \, \text{GBG/Per} - 2.028 \, \text{DISTANCE} + 4.321 \, \text{BLACK}$$

Std. error:	(4.21) (0.162)	(0.373)	(2.40)
t:	3.18 22.79	−5.43	1.80

R = .756
N = 406

[a] RT/KP = Number of Routes per 1,000 persons, MANHOUR = Paid man hours per 1,000 occupied units. All other variables as in Table 6.

FIGURE 2

Paid Manhours Versus Distance from the Central Business District, Corrected for the Weight Rule

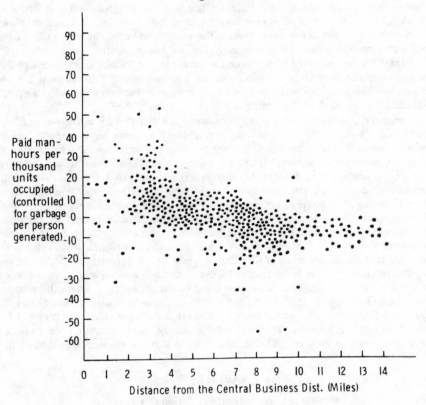

amount of garbage neighborhoods generate, benefits the better-off areas of the city disproportionately. The third rule, to allocate more resources to the center city than they would receive according to the first two rules, benefits those less well-off disproportionately. In contrast to the Environmental Enforcement Division, where services were distributed in an n-shaped curve, sanitation services follow a u-shaped curve, where social well-being corresponds to the abscissa, service level to the ordinate of the hypothetical graph. Figure 3 summarizes our findings on the delivery of services in the Sanitation Division.

PARK ACCESS: DISTRIBUTIONAL UNCONTROLLABLES

The third bureaucracy which we examine is the Department of Parks and Recreation. Recreation services differ from environmental enforcement and sanitation services in that they are delivered from fixed sites rather than to the citizen's residence. As such, there are two dimensions of recreation service quality: the accessibility of the facility in question, and the particular facilities and programs available at the park or recreation center. In this paper we analyze only the location of parklands in Detroit, although our larger study examines facilities made available at the parks.

Public budget analysts have isolated large segments of public budgets which are extremely difficult to control. Expenditures are mandated by statute, and are uncontrollable in the appropriations process.[31] Uncontrollables exist in distribution of services as well as in the spending for them. Once a service delivery pattern is established, it [is] more or less amenable to change, depending on a number of factors, the most important of which is the cost of altering the existing arrangement. We have already documented the changes in service delivery rules in the Sanitation Division, changes which have distributional effects. The distribution of recreational opportunities, however, is much more resistant to change, or at least change by public authorities. So long as a city continues to operate the facilities it has acquired over the years, the distributional pattern of recreational opportunities must change only gradually. Indeed, the movement of populations will likely have a greater

FIGURE 3
The Process of Resource Distribution in the Sanitation Division

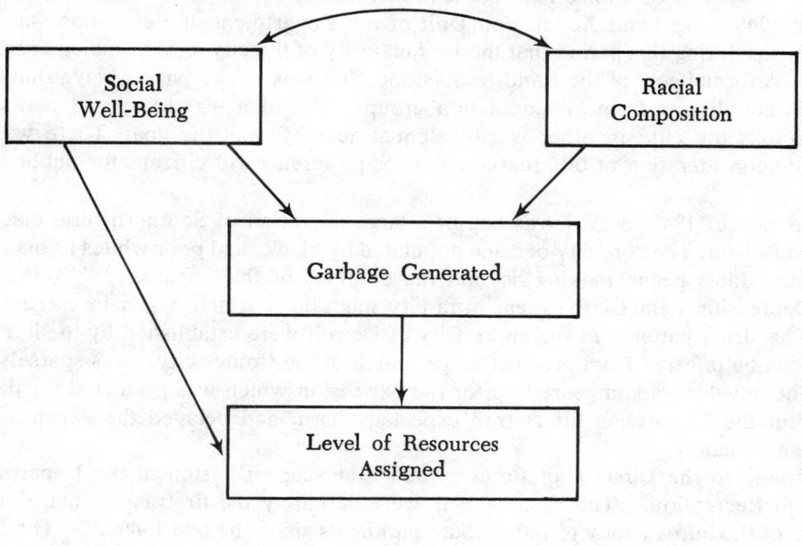

effect on the distributional pattern than the activities of public authorities, especially in an era of limited budgetary expansion, during which the acquisition of large land units is virtually precluded. Distributional patterns which are beyond the short run control of policy makers we term *distributional uncontrollables*. The distributional pattern will change only incrementally, since the existing pattern is more a function of past decisions than of present ones. Distributional incrementalism will hold so long as the city continues to operate the facilities it has acquired over the years. This will normally be done, since to surrender parks or other recreational facilities will reduce the total recreational product.

A clear trade-off exists: to change the distributional pattern of recreational access radically, one would have to reduce the quantity of recreational opportunities offered. Continuing operation of existing facilities is a primary service delivery rule in bureaucracies whose services are tied to costly capital developments or land units. This rule results in a relatively uncontrollable distributional pattern, which can change only incrementally.[32]

In acquiring parklands, the City of Detroit has used three different rules for deciding where parks should be established. The City's "major parks," each consisting of over 200 acres, were ceded to the City in the era of the 1890s. Palmer Park, for example, was given to Detroit by Senator Thomas W. Palmer in 1893. At the date of the cessation, the park, directly north of the central business district, was so far out in the country that citizens had to take a streetcar ride out to the Highland Park Electric Railway, and ride the train for three-and-a-half miles. From the terminus of that line one needed a horse and buggy to get to the park.[33] All of the major parks involved cessations along the outer edge of the city, since by the time it became fashionable to worry about urban recreation, the central area of the city had little land available for park development. At any rate, if any was left, it was probably too valuable for any citizen to think of giving it away. The first rule in acquiring parks, then, was, "Don't look a gift horse in the mouth."

In the 1940s, the Land Acquisition Unit of the Department of Recreation was established. It was during this period that the vast majority of the city's "non-major" parks was acquired. A formal goal of the Land Acquisition Unit was to site parks, playgrounds, and playfields equidistant from all population groups. The idea was to spread parks fairly evenly across the city; in other words, "equal access" was the goal. There was little systematic consideration of differential needs or preferences of citizens for public recreation.

The period of 1940 to 1967 was one of a large migration of Southern rural blacks and whites to Detroit. The core city became populated by blacks and poor whites as many more well-to-do whites began moving beyond the confines of the "near city." Actually, the Great Depression delayed the great intra-city migrations which began in earnest in the 1940s. The street patterns of the entire City of Detroit were established by the late 1920s, but, as can be inferred from precinct maps, much of the "outer city" was sparsely populated. The developers had geared up for the expansion which was predicted for the early 1930s. But the Depression hit Detroit especially hard, and delayed the expansion by a decade and a half.

According to the Director of Forestry and Landscape Division of the Department of Parks and Recreation, "The riots of 1967 were definitely the first and primary cause of attempts of the bureaucracy to redistribute parklands since the late 1940s."[34] The Department became acutely aware of the lack of a major park in downtown Detroit. By the 1960s, however, there was little flexibility in the options for park acquisition. Large parcels of land in the center city (or, for that matter, anywhere in the city) were unavailable. Relocating citizens or tax-paying industries to make such land available was an expensive and politically sensitive proposition. Specifically, the Federal Urban Relocation Act operated as a constraint because it required municipalities to relocate citizens who had been displaced as a result of urban renewal. Finally, given the problems of acquiring new parkland once land use patterns have been determined, the City decided to utilize federally provided Urban Beautification funds for the refurbishing of its older existing parks, rather than the establishing of new Parks. This left the Department of Parks and Recreation only one option: the development of lot-sized playlots in the inner city.

The rules governing parkland acquisition thus correspond to historical periods. Most of the parkland, in acres, was acquired around the turn of the century. The City simply accepted the gifts of wealthy citizens who had spare farmland. By the 1940s, the Land Acquisition Unit had been established, and the only period of what might be called aggressive land acquisition took place. The rule of acquisition was egalitarian: make the distance each person had to travel to a park equal to that of all other citizens. Finally, the post riot policy had been to try to do something for the dwellers of the inner city. However, the impact of past policies is so heavy that there is little flexibility left.

The Department categorizes its parkland holdings into four groupings, which are related to land use. Parks are multifunctional, generally allowing picnicking, strolling, and a variety of activities, such as ball playing. Other facilities and programs available depend on the park. Playfields are large open areas, averaging eighteen acres, with little facility or program development. Playgrounds, averaging a little under three acres, generally provide facilities for the young. Playlots, most of which were developed since the 1967 riots, consist of less than half an acre, on average, and are generally placed where a vacant housing structure is demolished in an otherwise viable neighborhood. A final category includes land at schools, owned by the Board of Education, but supervised by the Department of Parks and Recreation. Table 8 gives number and acreage figures for the parkland owned by the City of Detroit.

In our study of access to parks, we have adopted the Department's classification, with two exceptions. For obvious reasons, we have examined Detroit's major parks separately.

TABLE 8

Parklands in Detroit

Category of Park	Number	Total Acreage	Proportion of Total Parklands
Parks	59	3,820.72	.765
Playfields	43	796.67	.159
Playgrounds	116	335.48	.067
Playlots	101	42.06	.008
Total	319	4,994.93	.999

We have also examined access to municipally owned golf courses, which are generally associated with parks. One course, Rackham, is actually two miles north of the city limits; we have not studied that facility in this paper.

Our measure of park access is a distance measure. We measure the distance from the center of a census tract to the nearest boundary of a park, and this measurement is assumed to be an inverse indicator of access. Measurements are repeated for each category of parkland. In all, almost three thousand separate measurements were required. Actually the measure would seem to be a measure of *ease* of access, and really gives no indication of use patterns. But it does adequately assess the effects of the City's past acquisition rules on the present population groupings, rules which, at least since the 1940s, have been implicitly based on proximity to parkland.

Table 9 presents separate regression equations for distance to each category of parkland on distance from the census tract to the central business district (CBD) and percent black in the tract. Distance to major parks and golf courses is inversely related to distance to the CBD, a direct measure of social well-being, indicating that the better-off neighborhoods are closer to major parks and golf courses than are those in less favorable circumstances. Percent black is also significantly related to access to major parks and golf courses, but it is inversely related, indicating that neighborhoods with large proportions of black residences are closer to major parks than are neighborhoods with high proportions of white residents, with social well-being controlled. In this one case, at least, race and class bear opposite relationships to public service delivery.

If one considers *all* parks, the direction of the relationship reverses itself for distance to the CBD. It is now poorer, inner city neighborhoods which are closer to parks. Percent black does not enter the equation significantly. The policy of equalizing access seems to have been effective.

The multiple correlations for playgrounds and playfields are quite low. For playgrounds, there is an approximately equal distribution in regard to social well-being, although majority black neighborhoods are again somewhat advantaged relative to park access. For playfields, better-off outer city neighborhoods are very marginally benefited, but there is no relationship for neighborhood racial composition. Access to school facilities is better for both poorer and blacker neighborhoods; distance to the CBD is directly related to park distance, while percent black is negatively related. Distance to playlots is inversely related to social well-being, and the relationship is fairly strong. This indicates the impact of the Department's post 1967 policy of playlot placement.

What can one say about the distribution of park benefits? First, even in regard to access, the measure we have employed involves some difficulties. One strategically placed small park can drastically cut down distance for many individuals, especially where density is high (and, consequently, census tracts are comparatively small in area). One example illustrates this problem. Russell Woods Park, a small park of just over three acres, is the closest park for over 102,400 Detroit residents. Rouge Park, the largest of Detroit's parks, is an eleven-hundred acre giant which alone accounts for one-quarter of all Detroit parklands and is the closest park for less than 58,100 individuals. If tiny Russell Woods Park were abolished tomorrow, one wonders if the recreational opportunities of the people for whom this is the closest park would be drastically affected. In our future studies, we plan to incorporate quality variables such as acreage, facilities, and programs available at parks.

Our data indicate that all types of parklands are closer to the poor in the City of Detroit, with the exceptions of major parks and golf courses. However, because the major parks are not only extensive, but replete with facilities and programs, we believe that proximity to a major park is so much more beneficial than access to any other category of parkland that it is the better-off who must be considered the most benefited.

TABLE 9

Regressions of Distances to Various Types of
Park Land Units on Distance to the
CBD and Percent Black

Major Park = 4.814 − 0.260 Distance − 1.050 Black
Std. error: (0.342) (0.042)   (0.302)
      t: 14.06   −6.20   −3.47
  R = .293
  N = 420

Golf Course = 6.402 − 0.431 Distance − 1.453 Black
Std. error: (0.379) (0.046)   (0.335)
      t: 16.87   −9.27   −4.33
  R = .413
  N = 420

Any Park = 0.604 + 0.594 Distance + 0.579 Black
Std. error: (0.090) (0.011)   (0.080)
      t: 6.66   5.36   0.72
  R = .267
  N = 420

Playground = 0.628 − 0.010 Distance − 0.136 Black
Std. error: (0.044) (0.005)   (0.039)
      t: 14.35   −1.87   −3.51
  R = .170
  N = 420

Playfield = 1.001 − 0.018 Distance + 0.025 Black
Std. error: (0.073) (0.009)   (0.065)
      t: 13.66   −2.02   (0.384)
  R = .170
  N = 420

Playlot = 0.302 + 0.085 Distance − 0.087 Black
Std. error:(0.067) (0.008)   (−0.59)
      t: 4.52   10.34   −1.47
  R = .517
  N = 420

School Facility = 0.526 + 0.014 Distance − 0.177 Black
Std. error: (0.048) (0.005)   (0.043)
      t: 10.89   2.36   −4.13
  R = .292
  N = 420

Whatever the distribution of benefits, those benefits are clearly influenced by past service rules. Acquiring the major parks along the city's rim caused a moderate positive relationship between proximity to those parks and social well-being. The equalization policies of the 1940s resulted in a reversal of the sign of this relationship when all parks are considered. There is almost no relationship between proximity to playfields and playlots, also a likely consequence of this policy. Playlot proximity is inversely related to social well-being, as a result of recent Department policy. The rule of never disposing of parkland once acquired solidifies the pattern of benefits which was determined in the past, but conscious public policy action can alter the distribution at the margins.

Of the bureaucracies we have studied, we rate the Department of Parks and Recreation as most sensitive to the distributional aspects of its service delivery rules. The policy change as a consequence of the 1967 disturbances is indicative. Further, in interviews with Department personnel there was expressed concern about the activities of local interest groups, ad hoc or otherwise. Most "professionals" in the Department do not care for the intrusion of citizen groups, which often demand that the Department acquire a particular parcel of land and transform it into a recreational facility. Recently, one citizens' group demanded that a playfield be established where an old school was demolished. Within two blocks of this site exist a playground, playfield, and recreation center, according to a Department bureaucrat. "It makes no rational sense to locate a new facility at this location, but I'll bet my life that they get something. It may not be a playfield, but it'll be something. And once they get that, they'll be back to demand the rest of what they asked for originally."

CONCLUSIONS

We have argued that service delivery rules (i.e., routinized procedures governing the delivery of local public services) influence the observed distribution of services to citizens. These rules are generally born of productivity considerations, of applying economic criteria to the public service sector. In the three bureaucracies we have studied, these delivery rules do have distributional or political consequences, although the nature of the impact and the characteristics of the resulting distributional patterns vary. The consciousness of the distributional nature of the delivery rule also varies from agency to agency. Of those agencies we studied, the Department of Parks and Recreation seems most conscious of distributional impacts, while the Environmental Enforcement Division seems least conscious. These facts are probably the results of the relative politization of the arena within which recreation services are delivered. Only in this area do local groups of citizens become regularly active. None the less, middle and upper level personnel at the Department of Parks and Recreation resent citizen intrusion where it is not part of the delivery rule as much as managers in the other two agencies, which experience less such ad hoc citizen input. Ironically, of the services studied, the distributional pattern of recreational opportunities is the least controllable by policy-makers.

Although we have emphasized the impact of internal bureaucratic operating rules on distributional patterns, one ought not conclude that service distribution and conscious policy decisions are divorced altogether. The Sanitation Division employs an explicitly distributional rule to supplement its weight rule: it dictates special effort in the inner city. The Department of Parks and Recreation clearly attempts, albeit incrementally, to affect the distribution of recreational opportunities. The Environmental Enforcement Division stands alone as a pure example of complete inattention to distributional considerations.

What is true is that routine delivery rules can heavily influence service distribution, and the impacts of these rules may be traced quantitatively. Each service bureaucracy uses service rules which are affected by the nature of the delivery task. EED keys service delivery to citizen request; the Sanitation Division adjusts its delivery system to actual use; Parks and Recreation maintains facilities acquired in the past, so that its distributional pattern is more a reflection of past action than current policy. Each set of rules yields different service distribution patterns. Resultants are quite complex, but generally EED allocates disproportionate effort to neighborhoods at middle levels of well-being, while the Sanitation Division distributes more resources to poorer and wealthier neighborhoods than to middle-city districts. Detroit's major parks are more accessible to better-off neighborhoods, but minor parks and playlots are close to poorer and blacker inner city areas.

The influence of service rules indicates the necessity of studying the internal structures and processes of service bureaucracies in attempting to understand local public policy. Conscious policy decisions can be effective, but they take place in an established milieu of organizational rules and procedures which have their own independent impacts.

NOTES

1. Clarence Ridley and Herbert Simon, *Measuring Municipal Outputs* (Chicago: International City Managers Association, 1938).

2. See Elinor Ostrom, "On the Meaning and Measurement of Output and Efficiency in the Provision of Urban Police Services," *Journal of Criminal Justice*, 1 (1973), 93–112; Martin T. Katzman, *The Political Economy of Urban Schools* (Cambridge, Massachusetts: Harvard University Press, 1971); Werner Z. Hirsch, *Urban Economic Analysis* (New York: McGraw-Hill, 1973), Chapters 10–12.

3. Ostrom, "On the Meaning . . .," 95–96.

4. Werner Z. Hirsch, "Cost Functions of the Urban Government Service: Refuse Collection," *Review of Economics and Statistics*, 47 (February, 1965), 87.

5. Ostrom, "On the Meaning . . .," and Robert L. Lineberry and Robert Welch, "Who Gets What: Measuring the Distribution of Urban Services," *Social Science Quarterly*, 54 (March, 1974), 691–99. Clearly service delivery agencies may have vague, incommensurate or even incompatible goals; such states of affairs will create difficulties for the productivity approach in practice.

6. A history of the municipal reform movement is contained in *The Emergence of Met-*

ropolitan America: 1915–1916 (New Brunswick: Rutgers University Press, 1968), by Blake McKelvey.

7. See Andrew A. Giovanetti, "Make Productivity Programs Work," *The American City* (July, 1975), 31–33.

8. Kenneth Prewitt and Sidney Verba, *An Introduction to American Government* (New York: Harper & Row, 1974), 7.

9. Robert L. Lineberry, "Mandating Urban Equality: The Distribution of Municipal Public Services," *Texas Law Review*, 53 (December, 1974), 26.

10. See Joel Aberbach and Jack Walker, *Race in the City* (Boston: Little, Brown, 1973), 48–55; Howard Schuman and Barry Greenberg, "Dissatisfaction with City Services: Is Race an Important Factor?" in *People and Politics in Urban Society*, Harlan Hahn, ed. (Beverly Hills, California: Sage, 1972): Herbert Jacob, "Contact with Government Agencies: A Preliminary Analysis of the Distribution of Government Services," *Midwest Journal of Political Science* 16 (February, 1972), 123–146; Thomas Anton and Bruce Bowen, "Toward a Clarification of Citizen 'Satisfaction' with Metropolitan Public Services," paper presented at the 1976 meeting of the American Political Science Association, Chicago, Illinois, September 2–6, 1976.

11. See the studies cited in footnotes 13 through 18.

12. For a further discussion, see Bryan D. Jones and Clifford Kaufman, "The Distribution of Urban Public Services: A Preliminary Model." *Administration and Society*, 6 (November, 1974), 337–360.

13. *Hawkins v. Town of Shaw, Mississippi*, 437 F. 2d 1286 (5th Cir. 1971).

14. Charles S. Benson and Peter B. Lund, *Neighborhood Distribution of Local Public Services* (Institute of Government Studies, University of California, Berkeley, 1969).

15. Robert Welch and Truett Chance, "The Distribution of Urban Public Services: Some Conceptual Considerations and a Preliminary Analysis," paper presented at the annual meeting of the Southwest Political Science Association, San Antonio, Texas, March 30–April 1, 1972; Robert Welch, "Who Gets What and Why: The Distribution of Street Lights in San Antonio," paper presented at the annual meeting of the Southwest Political Science Association, San Antonio, Texas, March 26–29, 1975; Robert L. Lineberry, "Equality, Public Policy, and Public Services: The Underclass Hypothesis and the Limits to Equality," *Politics and Policy*, 4 (December, 1975), 67–84; Robert L. Lineberry, *Equality and Public Policy: The Distribution of Municipal Public Services* (Beverly Hills, California; Sage, 1977).

16. Kenneth R. Mladenka, "Citizen Demand and Bureaucratic Response: Direct Dialing Democracy in a Major American City," *Urban Affairs Quarterly*, 12 (March, 1977), 273–290; George E. Antunes and John P. Plumlee, "The Distribution of an Urban Public Service: Ethnicity, Socioeconomic Status, and Bureaucracy as Determinants of Neighborhood Streets," *Urban Affairs Quarterly* 12 (March, 1977), 313–332; Kenneth R. Mladenka and Kim Q. Hill, "The Distribution of Urban Police Services," *Journal of Politics* (1978); Kenneth R. Mladenka and Kim Quaile Hill, "The Distribution of Benefits in an Urban Environment: Parks and Libraries in Houston," *Urban Affairs Quarterly* 13 (September 1977), 73–95.

17. Frank Levy, Arnold J. Meltsner, and Aaron Wildavsky, *Urban Outcomes* (Berkeley: University of California Press, 1974).

18. Bryan D. Jones, Saadia R. Greenberg, Clifford Kaufman, and Joseph Drew, "Bureaucratic Response to Citizen Initiated Contacts: Environmental Enforcement in Detroit," *American Political Science Review* 71 (March, 1977), 148–165; Bryan D. Jones, "Distributional Considerations in Models of Government Services Provision," *Urban Affairs Quarterly*, 12 (March, 1977), 291–312; Steven D. Gold, "The Distribution of Government Services in Theory and Practice: The Case of Recreation in Detroit," *Public Finance Quarterly*, 2 (January, 1974), 107–129.

19. Lineberry, "The Underclass Hypothesis."

20. Richard M. Cyert and James G. March, *A Behavioral Theory of the Firm* (Englewood Cliffs, New Jersey: Prentice-Hall, 1963), 104–105.

21. Levy, Meltsner, and Wildavsky, *Urban Outcomes*, 232.

22. *Ibid.*, 224.

23. Cyert and March, *Behavioral Theory*, 105.

24. Levy, Meltsner, and Wildavsky, *Urban Outcomes*, 228.

25. This problem is part of a more general one termed *spatial autocorrelation*, a two-dimensional analogue to the more familiar problem of temporal autocorrelation. Both may be solved by using generalized least squares estimators rather than the more familiar ordinary least squares estimators. The spatial GLS estimators, however, require careful specification of the error structure, and seem to be quite sensitive to mis-specification. See Alexander Lebanon and Howard Rosenthal, "Least Squares Estimation for Models of Cross-Sectional Correlation," *Political Methodology*, 2 (May, 1975), 221–244. For these reasons, we employ the familiar OLS estimators in this paper.

26. Jones, et. al., "Bureaucratic Response."

27. Levy, Meltsner, and Wildavsky, *Urban Outcomes*, 229.

28. See R. A. Gordon, "Issues in Multiple Regression," *American Journal of Sociology*, 73 (March, 1968), 592–616; and Richard B. Darlington, "Multiple Regression in Psychological Research and Practice," *Psychological Bulletin*, 69 (No. 3, 1968), 161–182. For a discussion and justification of the measures of social well-being we use, see Jones, et. al., "Bureaucratic Response," 153–154. For Detroit, we have found distance from the central business district and average age of housing structures to be most satisfactory.

29. Giovanetti, "Productivity Programs," 31.

30. The correlations with distance from the C.B.D. are −.46 for percent black, .53 with housing value, .71 with average rent, and .44 with per capita income.

31. On budget uncontrollables, see Murray L. Weidenbaum, Institutional Obstacles to Reallocating Government Expenditures," in *Public Expenditures and Policy Analysis*, ed. Robert H. Haveman and Julius Margolis (Chicago: Markham, 1970), 232–245. An excellent recent study is Marth Derthick, *Uncontrollable Spending for Social Service Grants* (Washington, D.C.: The Brookings Institution, 1975).

32. Clearly, services vary in their relative distributional uncontrollability. This is also true of budgets. See Derthick, *Uncontrollable Spending*, 107.

33. See Beulah P. Groehn, "The Palmer Log Cabin," *Detroit Historical Society Bulletin*, (April, 1965).

34. The *Report of the National Advisory Commission on Civil Disorders* (New York: Bantam, 1968), 149, suggests that poor recreation facilities were a major grievance of ghetto dwellers nation-wide.

New York City's Fiscal Crisis: The Politics of Inflation and Retrenchment

MARTIN SHEFTER

The current New York City fiscal crisis is above all a political crisis. Its origins lie in a set of political changes the city experienced in the 1960's, which led municipal expenditures and indebtedness to grow at an explosive pace. And the eruption of the crisis has produced a further transformation in the structure of the city's politics.

This is not to deny that changes in the city's demographic and economic base over the past three decades have contributed to the problems the municipal government faces. The migration of more than a million poor blacks and Puerto Ricans to New York since World War II has placed pressure on the municipal budget at the same time that the movement of business firms and middle-class whites to the suburbs has reduced the city's capacity to finance new expenditures. But these developments, which are commonly cited to explain the city's difficulties, cannot in themselves account for the crisis; unemployed men and fatherless children do not, after all, have the authority to appropriate public monies or float municipal bonds. To account for the rapid growth of the municipal budget and debt, one must explain why public officials responded as they did to these changes in the city's demographic and economic base—an explanation to be found in the transformation of New York City politics in the 1960's.

During that decade, the regime that had formerly governed New York City collapsed, and a new coalition of political forces attempted to seize control. This initiated a pattern of political activity that has characteristically led to rising public expenditures and indebtedness, financial collapse, and ultimately budgetary retrenchment and a reorganization of politics, shifting the balance of power to the owners of the public debt. This pattern of political and fiscal change is not unique to New York City in the 1960's and 1970's; it has appeared both in other places and in earlier periods of the city's history.

TWO ROUTES TO RETRENCHMENT

The political conditions that lead city governments to increase municipal expenditures at a rapid rate and accumulate large deficits are similar to those which encourage national governments to pursue highly inflationary fiscal and monetary policies. Such policies are likely to be adopted in the following combination of circumstances: 1) A social group that has recently gained political power begins to assert claims upon the government for greater public benefits or a larger slice of the national income; 2) the government responds to these claims either because it is allied with the group in question or because it cannot withstand

251

its opposition; and 3) the government is too weak politically to finance these new claims by reducing the flow of benefits to other groups, or by raising taxes. To cover the difference between expenditures and revenues, both municipal and national governments can borrow money. In addition, national governments can print money—in large quantities, if necessary—to finance their deficits, and hence deficit financing on the national level can generate rampant price inflation.

These political conditions have prevailed, as the historian Charles Maier has noted, during the major episodes of national inflation in this century. The hyperinflations in Central Europe in 1919–1922, for example, followed the creation of democratic regimes in Germany and Austria, which for the first time granted representation in the government to working-class parties. These regimes, however, were threatened by anti-democratic forces on the Right and dared not alienate the nation's industrialists. The only economic policies compatible with the maintenance of a tacit coalition between labor and industry were highly inflationary: The industrialists would not tolerate any new taxes on corporate or personal incomes, and the government thus increasingly financed its operations by resorting to the printing presses. Similarly, in Latin America, periods of severe inflation characteristically occur after the rise of regimes that speak for the urban or rural lower classes, but—because of political weakness, administrative incapacity, or corruption—cannot collect taxes from the middle and upper classes, or prevent the wealthy from sending their money abroad, or foster economic development. The Peronist regime in Argentina, for example, sponsored the organization and political incorporation of labor, but failed to industrialize the nation and generate the wealth necessary to pay for the benefits provided its supporters. Consequently, claims to the national income that the government granted exceeded the national income, and inflation followed.

The European nations now experiencing the highest levels of inflation—Portugal and Italy—are characterized by politics most closely approximating the pattern outlined above. The Italian case is too complex to describe here, but the Portuguese situation is quite straightforward. Following the revolution of 1974, which granted the Portuguese political rights they had been unable to exercise freely for 50 years, a succession of weak governments (six in two years) either encouraged, or found it impossible to resist, the demands of the army for an immediate withdrawal from Portugal's colonies, of agricultural laborers for land, of workers and civil servants for wage increases, and of unions for greater control over factories and offices. The result was a rise in the nation's wage bill, a decline of labor and military discipline, the influx of more than half a million refugees from Angola who had to be housed and fed by the government, a rise in government deficits, and consequently an inflation rate in 1975 of 46 per cent.

The conditions fostering very high levels of inflation are inherently unstable. Double- or triple-digit inflation can lead to a credit or liquidity crisis, to balance-of-payments difficulties, and ultimately to a recession. When this occurs, industrialists become less willing to accept inflationary policies. Middle-class *rentiers,* who generally are the most seriously injured by inflation, and who find it difficult under normal circumstances to assert themselves politically against better-organized groups, can erupt into an angry political force when inflation threatens to wipe out the fruits of a lifetime of thrift. And the banks, which are in a position to extend the necessary loans for stabilizing the nation's currency and refinancing its international debt, gain enormous political leverage by their ability to attach conditions to their aid. If all these interests coalesce, they can overturn the government that fostered inflation, and install a government that will implement a program of retrenchment.

Retrenchment involves eliminating nonessential public expenditures. What this commonly means in practice is that those groups that have only recently gained a measure of power will be deprived of whatever benefits they won by being incorporated into the political system. For the purposes of retrenchment, these groups must either be driven off the political stage, or compelled to accept a more modest role.

Historically, the first of these alternatives is probably the more common: Retrenchment often occurs at the expense of democracy. In 1922, for example, the Austrian government received a stabilization loan from the League of Nations by agreeing in the Geneva Protocols to abrogate parliamentary authority over all financial matters for a period of two years. And the agreements that brought stability to Weimar Germany involved the overthrow of the last coalition government in which a working-class party had representation. In Latin America, typically only military governments can carry out the retrenchment policies that international lending agencies insist upon. Argentina—and Chile—provide stark examples of what the implementation of a retrenchment program can entail.

The alternative route to retrenchment involves a system of discipline imposed upon the new political group not by an alliance of domestic conservatives and foreign bankers, but rather by the leadership of the group in question. And this can lead to harsh measures. The halt to the leftward drift of Portugal's revolution and the rise to power of the moderate Socialist government of Mario Soares came only after many offices of the Portuguese Communist Party were firebombed, leftist groups in the military were smashed, the army was purged by a stern disciplinarian, General Ramilho Eanes, and the Socialists allied themselves with the two most conservative parties behind his presidential candidacy. And the success of Italy's current retrenchment program ironically depends upon the ability of a Leninist party—the Italian Communist Party—to impose its new line (the "historic compromise") upon restive party militants and compel the unions affiliated with the Communist labor federation to limit their wage demands.

BOSS TWEED AND TAMMANY HALL

New York City's budget rises and falls in response to a political logic similar to the one outlined above. Periods of increased public expenditures and indebtedness follow upon the rise to power of new but loosely organized political coalitions, and periods of retrenchment are associated with the expulsion of these new forces from the political arena, or their subjugation to tighter political discipline.

In New York City, these new political forces have generally been coalitions of elements of the city's business community and members of ethnic groups that had previously been politically weak. Such political coalitions have traditionally been pieced together by machine politicians, who placed new ethnic groups on the public payroll to win their votes, and at the same time sponsored the public projects favored by their allies in the business community. This method of purchasing political support can be costly. On three occasions in the city's history—in 1871, 1933, and 1975—it has led to a fiscal crisis that enabled the banks owning the city's debt to insist that municipal expenditures be drastically reduced as part of a bail-out plan. The politicians in office when the city amassed its debt are then discredited by their responsibility for the city's difficulties, and weakened by the retrenchment program; this in turn permits the political agents of the bankers to call themselves reformers and win the next election. This experience chastens the defeated political forces, and enables a more sober leadership to emerge among them. It also gives the new leaders an incentive to organize their followers more tightly, and upon returning to power they can be less generous in dealing with their rank-and-file supporters, and more accommodating in dealing with their erstwhile opponents.

The rise and fall of the Tweed Ring illustrates this process quite clearly. Boss Tweed was allied with businessmen who operated chiefly in local markets—building contractors, real-estate men, street-railway promoters, savings bank owners, and manufacturers, who benefited from Tweed's ambitious program of opening up new streets and transit lines in the northern sections of the city. Uptown development had previously proceeded slowly; city officials had been more responsive to the elite merchants and bankers operating in national and international markets—interests that were oriented to the downtown district and the port, and that regarded as utterly profligate uptown development on the scale proposed by Tweed.

Tweed also sponsored the political incorporation of the immigrant Irish. In the three weeks prior to the election of 1868, the judges allied with the Tweed Ring naturalized several thousand new citizens, and expanded the number of registered voters in the city by more than 30 per cent. The attachment of these new voters to the Tammany organization was reinforced through placing many on the public payroll, and through a public-welfare program that bore some marked similarities to the poverty programs of the 1960's. (The poverty programs funneled public monies into community groups and Baptist churches in black neighborhoods; Boss Tweed's public-welfare program channeled public funds into charitable institutions and Catholic churches in Irish neighborhoods.)

The cost of bringing the local businesses and the immigrants into the political system was high. The budget of the Streets Department, for example, quadrupled in Tweed's first years as Deputy Commissioner. It was especially high because the Ring was structurally weak. Tweed was unable to command the obedience of other politicians; instead, he was compelled to purchase with cash bribes the support of state legislators, county supervisors, and even his immediate associates. To finance its operations, the Ring levied a surcharge on all city contracts. And because the Ring was weak, Tweed hesitated to raise taxes sufficiently to meet the city's current expenses, let alone to cover the costs of the capital improvements he sponsored. Just as Mayors Lindsay and Beame were to do a century later, Tweed funded short-term revenue notes into long-term bonds. In the last four years of Ring rule in New York the city's outstanding indebtedness tripled.

The Ring was brought down by the city's creditors, who were driven to act by two events that destroyed their tolerance for a regime based upon the two groups from which Tweed drew his support. The first was the Orange Riot of July 1871, sparked by a parade of Irish Protestants celebrating the Catholic defeat at the Battle of the Boyne. Catholic spectators threw stones at the troops protecting the marchers, and the troops responded with a volley of gunfire that killed 37 spectators. The press blamed the city government for provoking the disturbance, and respectable elements in New York concluded from the incident that a municipal government dependent upon the political support of the Irish could not preserve public order. The second event that led the city's financial elite to move against the Ring was the suspension of trading in New York City bonds on the Berlin Stock Exchange, and the refusal of bankers in London, Paris, and Frankfurt to extend any more loans to the city, after a series of exposés in the press revealed the extent of municipal corruption and the size of the city's debt. The collapse of the city's credit threatened the solvency of all the New York banks owning municipal securities. To protect itself, the city's financial community felt it imperative that the Ring be overthrown. This was accomplished, in the words of a contemporary pamphlet, through an "insurrection of the capitalists": A group of the city's most prominent businessmen, the Committee of 70, organized a tax strike, and a thousand property owners refused to pay their municipal taxes until the city's accounts were audited. In addition, the city's bankers refused to lend the municipal government the money needed to meet the city payroll and cover debt-service payments until a reformer, Andrew Haswell Green, was appointed Deputy Comptroller with absolute authority over the city's finances. The *coup de grâce* was given the Tweed Ring when the Committee of 70 entered a slate of candidates in the 1871 municipal elections and won control of the city government.

The collapse of the Tweed Ring enabled "Honest John" Kelly, in alliance with a group of wealthy, nationally oriented Democrats, to seize control of Tammany Hall. Kelly inferred from the Tweed episode that Tammany could not survive if all elements of the business community united against it, and that to avoid such opposition it must shed its reputation for corruption and profligacy. He accomplished this by purging Tammany of its more disreputable elements and by centralizing and strengthening the party organization. (It has been said that Kelly "found Tammany a horde and left it an army.") Kelly then used this organization to elect a succession of respectable merchants to the mayoralty, discipline lower-level Tammany officials engaged in the grosser forms of curruption, and make himself Comptroller, in which position he pursued an extremely tight-fisted policy of retrenchment.

By creating the modern Tammany machine, Kelly and his successors, Richard Croker and Charles Murphy, established a mechanism for incorporating immigrants into the city's political system in a way that was tolerable to, if not entirely to the liking of, the city's propertied elite. This involved extruding from the political system competing contenders for control over the city's immigrant masses. Kelly's victory represented the triumph of a respectable lower-middle-class leadership group among the Irish (Kelly himself was married to a niece of Cardinal McCloskey), and the maintenance of this group's control entailed the defeat of both the lower-class gangs that had formerly played an important role within Tammany, and the trade-union and socialist movements that at various times (most notably the 1880's and the 1910's) had attempted to assume political leadership of the working classes.

The preservation of Tammany's hegemony, however, required that the machine's subordinate functionaries be tightly disciplined, and that new ethnic groups be given a share of the spoils. When the hold of the machine's central leadership weakened, as it increasingly did after Murphy's death in 1925, Tammany officials were free to enrich themselves without limit, and to freeze out newcomers. The bacchanalia of corruption during the administration of Jimmy Walker, and the inability of Tammany's fragmented leadership to face up to, or impose upon their subordinates, the stringencies that the Depression required, set the stage for the New York fiscal crisis of 1933, and the triumph in the municipal election that year of a coalition of reformers, businessmen, Italians, and Jews, under the leadership of Fiorello LaGuardia.

FROM ACCOMMODATION TO COMMUNITY PARTICIPATION

The last political leaders in New York to successfully pursue Kelly's strategy were Carmine DeSapio, Alex Rose, and Robert Wagner. These leaders won a secure position for Italians and Jews in New York politics by helping to expel from the political system those elements of their ethnic constituency who were least acceptable to other groups in the city. DeSapio consolidated his hold over the Democratic Party by purging Tammany of its gangster element, which was primarily Italian, but included Jewish district leaders such as Sidney Moses and Harry Brickman. Rose established the influence of the Liberal Party by destroying the Communist-dominated American Labor Party, which was heavily Jewish, although its most prominent ally was the Italian-American Congressman Vito Marcantonio. Both DeSapio and Rose created tightly centralized party organizations, and when they united behind the same candidates, municipal elections involved as little competition as they had during the heyday of machine rule in the 1920's. In the mayoral race of 1957, Robert Wagner, who had the support of both organizations, won 72 per cent of the vote and defeated his Republican opponent by almost one million votes.

The politicians who governed the city during the 1950's defused opposition by accommodating its major organized interests. The downtown business community was satisfied because control over the development programs that were of prime interest to them was placed in the hands of Robert Moses and/or various public authorities responsible only to their bondholders. Municipal civil servants and the prestigious civic associations were granted substantial influence over the city's major service-delivery agencies. And in making revenue and expenditure decisions, elected officials paid special heed to the views of the city's tax-conscious lower-middle-class homeowners. Consequently, during Mayor Wagner's first two terms, the city government did little that aroused controversy, and its expense budget increased at an average annual rate of only 6.6 per cent between 1953 and 1960.

This political calm was shattered in the late 1950's and early 1960's by the emergence of three new political groups in New York—the Democratic reform movement, the school-integration movement, and the movement to unionize city employees. The effort of politicians to gain power in the city by allying with these movements destroyed the regime constructed by DeSapio, Rose, and Wagner, and initiated the present era of budgetary inflation.

The first of these to gather force was the reform movement in the Democratic Party. In the face of its threat, Mayor Wagner undertook to salvage his career in 1961 by turning on his political mentor, DeSapio, and seeking renomination with the support of the reformers and the municipal civil service. The steps Wagner took to win their backing—especially his sponsorship of a new city charter—weakened the regular party organizations, loosened some of the restraints upon budgetary inflation in New York, and made him more dependent politically upon groups demanding services. Consequently, municipal expenditures increased during Wagner's third term at an average annual rate of 8.9 per cent. Significantly, in 1961 the city's expense budget fell into deficit for the first time since the Depression, and it continued to do so during each year of Wagner's third term.

In 1965, the reformers and liberals abandoned their former allies in the municipal labor movement, and supported the mayoral candidacy of John Lindsay. The political forces backing Lindsay sought to drive the civil-service unions from power and seize control of the municipal bureaucracy themselves. Lindsay centered his 1965 campaign around an attack upon the "power brokers" (i.e., the civil-service union leaders); he undertook to reorganize the municipal bureaucracy into 10 super-agencies, which would be responsive to his leadership; and he regularly contracted with outside institutions (such as the RAND Corporation, the Ford Foundation, and various universities) to perform tasks formerly conducted by municipal civil servants. To gain political support, the Lindsay administration allied itself with the third new political movement of the 1960's, the black civil-rights movement. Blacks were useful allies because they could be used to legitimize the administration's efforts to seize control of the bureaucracy, which was criticized for its failure to adopt "innovative" programs that were "responsive" to the needs of the black community. And the alliance Lindsay cultivated with blacks provided the administration with shock troops to attack the bureaucracy from below, a function served by the mechanisms of community participation established by the administration.

New York City's budget during the early Lindsay years reflected this political strategy and the political constituency of the administration. The three major municipal programs in which expenditures rose the most rapidly during the period 1966–1971 were higher education (251 per cent), welfare (225 per cent), and hospitals (123 per cent). The clientele of two of these programs (welfare and public hospitals) is predominantly black, and the explosion in expenditures for the third (higher education) occurred after the enactment of an open-admissions program that tripled black enrollments at the City University. Moreover, the staff providing services in each of these programs (whose salaries account for much of the increase in expenditures) is composed of large numbers of highly educated and well-paid professionals. To be sure, federal and state assistance under Aid to Families with Dependent Children and Medicaid helped the city pay for some of these new expenditures. But even as far as the city's own funds (so-called tax-levy expenditures) were concerned, welfare and higher education were by far the fastest-growing budgetary categories during the first five years of the Lindsay administration.

The Lindsay administration was not in a position to finance the benefits it provided to its constituency by reducing, or even holding the line on, expenditures for other municipal programs, because Lindsay's victory in the mayoral election of 1965 did not destroy the influence of the unions that represented the employees of the more traditional municipal agencies. After Lindsay's election, the city-employee unions might no longer have had an ally in the mayor's office, but they retained their capacity to strike, to lobby before the state legislature, and to support or oppose candidates in future municipal elections. By the end of his first term, the mayor discovered how vulnerable he was to each of these maneuvers. He initially attempted to break the power of the unions by refusing to enter into the give-and-take of labor negotiations, by inviting strikes, and by then seeking to mobilize public opinion (and, in one instance, the national guard) against the unions. These efforts repeatedly failed, and Lindsay eventually learned that he could not govern the city without the cooperation of the unions. In addition to the wage increases they obtained by striking, the unions were able to secure very lucrative retirement benefits from the state legislature during the Lindsay years, because as the regular party organizations in New York grew weaker, many state assemblymen and senators from the city found the civil-service unions to be their most effective source of campaign assistance.

Finally, Lindsay himself was desperately in need of such assistance in his campaign for reelection in 1969. To win union support and to pay off his campaign debt, he gave the unions everything they demanded during the 1969–70 round of contract negotiations. In these ways, the civil-service unions were able to secure substantial salary and benefit increases for city employees during his tenure, thereby compelling the mayor to increase expenditures for the agencies employing their members. During the period 1966–1971, the budgets of the traditional municipal departments—Police, Fire, Sanitation, the Board of Education—did not double or triple, as expenditures did for welfare, hospitals, and higher education, but they nonetheless did increase on the average by 66 per cent.

SETTING THE STAGE FOR FINANCIAL RUIN

The Lindsay administration did not find it politically possible to obtain either enough additional state aid or enough additional taxing authority to finance all these expenditure increases. Although state aid payments to the city did rise substantially during the Lindsay years, there were limits to the willingness of upstate and suburban legislators to tax their constituents for the benefit of New York City. And the state legislature, when it considered New York City financial legislation, followed a set of informal procedures that enabled political forces unfriendly to Lindsay to block some of his proposals for tax increases, and that favored the passage of legislation authorizing the city to borrow money to close its annual budget gap.

The Republican and Democratic leaders in the Assembly and Senate would round up the votes necessary to pass New York City financial legislation only if every single assemblyman and senator from the city voted in favor of the bills in question. In practice, this informal requirement for unanimous consent meant that these bills had to meet with the approval of each of the major interests enjoying access to the city's legislative delegation, the legislative leaders, and the governor. One such group was the lower-middle-income homeowners, who were unable to defeat Lindsay in mayoral elections, but did send Republican assemblymen and senators to Albany to defend their interests. These legislators found it politically difficult to vote for tax increases, and to avoid losing their votes, the mayor and governor found it necessary to substitute bond and note issues. The city's major banks, whose views were represented in such deliberations by the governor, were quite happy to endorse deficit financing, because bond and note issues provided them with healthy commissions and good investment opportunities. Moreover, so long as the office boom of the 1960's continued—assisted by capital projects the city and state constructed with borrowed funds—it appeared that rising municipal tax receipts would enable the city to cover its debt-service payments.

The Lindsay administration was ultimately compelled to abandon its efforts to break the power of the public-employee unions, to seize control of the municipal bureaucracy, and to use the authority of the city government for new purposes. These efforts suffered a number of serious setbacks at the end of the mayor's first term and the beginning of his second. Lindsay's efforts to decentralize the city school system precipitated a bitter controversy and a teachers' strike—the Ocean Hill strike of 1968—and the settlement of the controversy was something of a defeat for the most militant advocates of community control. The upper-middle-class liberals and blacks who comprised the core of the Lindsay coalition were unable on their own to provide him with the votes he needed to win reelection in 1969, and Lindsay was consequently compelled to come to terms with the civil-service unions. And the administration's plans to place a large, low-income housing project in the middle-class neighborhood of Forest Hills in 1971 generated intense local opposition, and had to be drastically scaled down.

The defeat at Forest Hills chastened Lindsay, and the growth rate of the city's budget slowed considerably. From 1966 through 1971, operating expenditures had increased at an average annual rate of 16.5 per cent. In 1972, the growth rate of the city's budget declined to 8.6 per cent; in 1973 it was 9.3 per cent. Moreover, much of this budgetary growth resulted from rising prices, and the deceleration of the city's budget after the Lindsay administration had received its political chastening is thus particularly dramatic when measured in constant dollars: Annual expenditure increases in constant dollars averaged 11.5 per cent from 1966 through 1971; they averaged 3.7 per cent in the next two years. Abe Beame's election as mayor in 1973 simply confirmed that a new political and fiscal plateau had been reached. Mayor Beame's budgets, again measured in constant dollars, grew at an average annual rate of only 2.8 per cent.

This new political and fiscal plateau did not involve a return to the *status quo ante* of 1965. The new players in the political game, who had been ushered onto the field by John Lindsay, were not expelled—apart from a few unruly ones who had attempted to drive out some of the older players. And the claims of these new players to a share of the gate were recognized. Consequently, as Mayor Lindsay left office and Mayor Beame came in, the city's budget was more than three times as large as it had been at the close of the Wagner administration.

In the mid-1970's, however, it was far more difficult than it had been in the late 1960's for New York City to honor the claims upon its budget granted during the Lindsay administration. Inflation drove up the cost of providing a fixed bundle of municipal services, and the failure of the city's economy to recover from the recession of the early 1970's made it increasingly difficult for New York to cover these rising costs. Moreover, by the mid-1970's there was an explosion in the costs of the retirement benefits that the municipal government and the state legislature had granted to city employees during the previous decade. In 1965, the city's retirement costs had been $364 million; by 1974, they had risen to $1.121 billion, and in 1976 they were $1.480 billion. In 1965, the city's annual debt-service payments had been $470 million; by 1974, they had risen to $1.269 billion, and in two more years they reached $2.304 billion. In order to close the gap between current expenditures and current revenues, and refinance the short-term debt as it fell due, the city resorted ever more heavily to borrowing. By 1975, the city's cumulative short-term debt had risen to $5.3 billion. The budget Mayor Beame initially presented to the state legislature for fiscal year 1976 anticipated a further deficit of $460 million, and had the city been able to borrow all that it wanted in 1975, its short-term debt might have amounted to as much as 33 per cent of the entire outstanding short-term municipal debt in the United States! The city's request for huge grants and additional taxing authority from the state legislature, and its enormous demands upon the municipal-securities market for additional loans, set the stage for the New York fiscal crisis of 1975.

THE RISE OF THE BANKS

The fiscal crisis of 1975 was precipitated by a combination of events resembling the taxpayers' strike and bondholders' coup that had brought down Tweed a century earlier. The Republican state senators from New York City banded together in May 1975, and agreed to present a common front against the pressure from their party leaders and colleagues to vote for legislation granting additional taxing authority to the city. The refusal of these spokesmen for the city's taxpayers to consent to any new taxes increased the city's demand for credit, and thereby weakened the market for New York City securities. Later that month, the major New York banks refused to underwrite or purchase any more New York City notes and bonds, and thereby drove the city to the verge of bankruptcy.

There is little reason to believe that the Republican legislators and the New York bankers foresaw the enormous consequences their actions would have, or that in precipitating the crisis they were motivated by anything beyond the desire to protect the short-run economic interests of the groups they represented and their own short-run political and institutional interests. As for the Republican state legislators, they were heavily dependent upon the support of small-property owners, who were being squeezed by the combination of inflation, recession, high levels of taxation, and rent control in New York, and were increasingly voting on the Conservative Party line. Moreover, in 1975 the governor's office was occupied by a Democrat for the first time in 16 years and hence Republican legislators no longer had a compelling reason to support a tax package hammered out in negotiations between the governor and the mayor.

As for the major New York banks, there were a number of strictly economic reasons why they were becoming increasingly reluctant to purchase the city's securities. Other more lucrative investment opportunities (foreign loans, leasing, consumer financing) had recently been developed by the banks, or had been made available to them by amendments to the Bank Holding Company Act, and the failure of the Real Estate Investment Trusts had created liquidity problems for many of them. But most importantly, as the city's short-term debt began to skyrocket, it was becoming increasingly clear to outsiders as well as insiders that the city was engaged in a great ponzi game: It was financing current expenditures by borrowing, and paying off old debt by issuing new debt. So long as dealing in New York municipal securities had been a high-profit, low-risk venture for the city's banks, they had been quite happy to participate without asking too many embarrassing questions of city officials. But when the 11 major New York banks realized in the spring of 1975 that the outside world would shortly be able to figure out what the municipal government had been doing, they unloaded $2.7 billion in New York City securities that they owned. With the banks flooding the market with old New York bonds at the same time the city was seeking to sell additional hundreds of millions in new municipal notes and bonds, the market in the city's securities collapsed.

This collapse confronted the banks with immediate and grave dangers. Unless the city could borrow additional money, it could not redeem its old notes and bonds as they fell due, and if the city defaulted on these obligations, the value of New York securities remaining in the banks' portfolios would plummet. If this occurred, not only would the banks suffer a direct loss, they also could be sued by the clients whose money they had invested in New York notes and bonds. Thus the major New York banks sought desperately to keep the city from defaulting: They pleaded with out-of-town banks to purchase New York securities; when that failed, they pleaded with the federal government to guarantee the city's bonds. Indeed, the very desperation of the banks made it possible for the architects of the plan that bailed out New York to squeeze additional loans out of the banks to shore up the city's finances.

In addition to these short-run economic dangers, the fiscal crisis presented the banks with long-run political opportunities. It has enabled the banks (and, more generally, the city's corporate elite) to gain a dominant voice in municipal affairs. Some of this influence rests upon the ability of the banks to extract concessions from the city government in return for lending it money. But the banks have actually lent the city less money than either the municipal-employee pension funds or the federal government. The major reason the banks have become so influential lies instead in the following combination of circumstances. First, the city must be able to regain access to the municipal credit market, unless some other means of managing its cash flow, financing capital projects, and discharging its outstanding debts becomes available. Second, the city has no chance whatever of regaining access unless its most prominent bankers and business leaders are prepared to assert that they are satisfied it is managing its affairs in a prudent and economical fashion. Third, public officials at the municipal, state, and national levels have accepted the banks' claim that if the business community's retrenchment program is adopted, the market *will* reopen to the city—in other words, that enactment of the retrenchment program is sufficient, as well as necessary, for the city to regain access to the market. This claim is, to say the least, highly conjectural.

In the name of making New York bonds marketable, the banks have managed to extract enormous concessions from the city. In the process, the local business elite has come to play a larger and larger role in governing the city, and the conduct of public policy in New York has increasingly come to reflect the priorities of the business community. The state initially created a Stabilization Reserve Corporation (SRC) to market a new series of bonds for the city, and it specifically set aside the proceeds of certain city taxes to cover the debt-service payments on these bonds. When these bonds failed to sell, a new state-appointed board, the Municipal Assistance Corporation (MAC), was created to replace SRC. In addition to being granted the authority to issue bonds and use municipal tax revenues for debt service on these securities, MAC was given the power to revamp New York City's accounting system. When the MAC bonds also failed to sell, the state, at the urging of the banks, passed a statute requiring the city to balance its budget within three years and limit its annual expenditure increases to not more than two per cent during that period, and creating an Emergency Financial Control Board (EFCB) empowered to freeze the wages of city employees, approve all city contracts, and supervise city finances.

The EFCB is composed of two state officials (the governor and state comptroller), two city officials (the mayor and city comptroller), and three private citizens appointed by the governor. The governor resisted pressure to appoint a labor and a minority representative, and selected instead the top executives of the New York Telephone Company, American Airlines, and Colt Industries. In addition, the mayor—at the urging of the business community—established the Mayor's Committee on Management Survey, chaired by the president of the Metropolitan Life Insurance Company, to reorganize the municipal bureaucracy along business lines. And in response to pressure from the banks, the mayor fired one of his oldest associates as First Deputy Mayor, and appointed prominent business executives to three of the most important financial and managerial positions in the city government: Deputy Mayor for City Finances, Budget Director, and Director of Operations. Just as the New York banks in 1871 were able to install their man, Andrew H. Green, as Deputy Comptroller, thereby gaining control of the city's finances, the leaders of the New York financial and business community over the last two years have been able to install their representatives in key positions, thereby gaining effective control over the city government today.

These spokesmen for the city's business community have argued, with considerable justification, that New York has little alternative but to close the gap between expenditures and revenues by reducing expenditures. Tax increases would encourage more employers and taxpayers to leave the city, thus exacerbating New York's economic and fiscal problems. Among the city's expenditures, however, two categories have been the particular targets of New York's fiscal overseers. The first are labor costs. In response to pressure from MAC and the EFCB, the city instituted a wage freeze and eliminated 56,000 employees from its payroll. This represents a 19-percent reduction in the city's labor force. The second are programs with predominantly black clienteles—youth services, addiction services, compensatory higher education—which have suffered disproportionately severe budget and personnel cutbacks. Moreover, personnel have been fired in disproportionate numbers from job categories—clerical, paraprofessional, and maintenance—heavily staffed by blacks and Puerto Ricans. Consequently, between July 1974 and February 1976, the number of Hispanics employed by mayoral agencies declined by 51 per cent, and the number of black males declined by 40 per cent. What retrenchment has meant in practice is that the city has curtailed the benefits it provides to two of the groups—civil servants and blacks—that had gained a measure of political power in the 1960's.

THE FALL OF THE BLACKS AND THE UNIONS

Squeezing out the blacks has been a rather simple matter. Black leaders had mobilized their constituency in the 1960's by relying upon the resources provided by federal and local agencies, and by drawing upon the publicity and support of the press, national foundations, and universities. In the early 1970's, however, the Nixon Administration turned sharply to the right, and federal expenditures for community organization were cut drastically. At about the same time, the Lindsay administration abandoned its mobilization strategy, and the various institutions in the not-for-profit sector committed wholeheartedly to social activism in the 1960's felt the pinch of a declining stock market and reduced federal social expenditures and became far less aggressive politically. Finally, upper-middle-class youths, who had provided much of the manpower for community organization drives in the 1960's, turned to other causes in the following decade: environmentalism, consumerism, feminism, or simply careerism. The New York fiscal crisis represents the culmination of this trend: Blacks have simply been abandoned by their erstwhile supporters. It appears that the upper-middle classes, who in the flush 1960's saw blacks as useful allies in the drive to extend their influence over municipal government, have concluded in the harsher climate of the 1970's that their political interests can better be served by entering into an alliance with the banks. The *New York Times*, for example, has uncritically accepted the most questionable assumption underlying the retrenchment program advocated by the city's business leadership—the notion that retrenchment will restore the city's access to the capital market—and it now attacks the civil service not in the name of responsiveness and innovation, but rather in the name of economy and productivity.

It has been a far more troublesome problem to deprive the city employees of the gains they achieved in the late 1960's and early 1970's, because city employees are far better organized than blacks, and their power is less dependent upon the steadfastness of their allies. Nonetheless, the civil-service unions have been compelled to accept a wage freeze, layoffs, longer hours, and heavier workloads. In addition, they have been induced to invest (or to commit themselves to invest) some $3.7 billion of their pension-fund assets in New York City and MAC bonds. Indeed, since the onset of the fiscal crisis, the tables have been entirely turned in municipal labor relations. No longer do the unions and the city bargain to determine which of the unions' demands the city will accede to; now the question has become which of the city's demands the unions will accede to. How has this been accomplished?

In an immediate sense, the tables were turned by the state's Financial Emergency Act, which granted the EFCB the power to review—and to reject—municipal labor contracts. But one must ask why the unions have agreed to play by these new rules, instead of striking to obtain higher wages. The most direct explanation for the unions' meekness is that strikes would almost certainly fail. New York City's creditors and potential creditors regard the wage freeze as the acid test of whether public officials in New York are prepared to mend their ways. Were city and state officials to bow to the demands of a striking union, the city's present and future sources of credit would dry up. If the unions were to strike nonetheless—in an effort to compel the mayor and governor to choose between losing access to credit once the city's current cash balance was depleted, and an immediate and total disruption of municipal services—the mayor and governor would probably take the latter. The success of a strike ultimately depends upon public tolerance—or more concretely, whether the public will countenance the use of the national guard to perform the functions of striking workers. Mayor Lindsay floated the idea of using the national guard during the 1968 sanitation strike, and quickly discovered that it was totally outside the realm of political possibility at that time. It is a measure of how dramatically New York politics have been transformed since the fiscal crisis that the municipal unions dare not tempt the mayor to make such a proposal today.

Another reason for the remarkable restraint of the unions during the crisis is that they have an enormous stake in the city's fiscal viability. Bankruptcy would cause the value of the New York City and MAC bonds owned by the union pension funds to plummet. More importantly still, bankruptcy would throw the city into the hands of a receiver with the unilateral authority to abrogate union contracts, slash wages, order wholesale firing, and reduce pension benefits. This would mean the end of collective bargaining and would threaten the very existence of the unions. To avoid these dangers, municipal union leaders have undertaken the task of selling the retrenchment program to their members, convincing them that they have no alternative but to bear with it. And by doing this, they have made it unnecessary for the bankers and business leaders to rely upon harsher measures to implement the program. In this respect, since the fiscal crisis the municipal labor leaders have played a role in New York politics similar to that played by John Kelly after the overthrow of Tweed: They have assumed the job of disciplining the municipal labor force, just as Kelly imposed a system of discipline upon the ward heelers, in Tammany. In praising Victor Gottbaum for being "responsible" in urging his members to bear with the wage freeze, the editorial writers for the *New York Times* were saying in 1975 precisely what the editor of the *Commercial Advertiser* said a century ago of Kelly, in somewhat more forthright terms: "Kelly has ruled the fierce Democracy in such a manner that life and property are comparatively safe . . . It requires a great man to stand between the City Treasury and this most dangerous mass . . . Dethrone Kelly and where is the man to succeed him?"

SOURCES OF INSTABILITY

There are, then, some striking similarities between the financial and political developments in New York since the fiscal crisis of 1975, and those in the aftermath of Tweed's downfall a century ago. In each case, municipal expenditures exceeded municipal revenues, and the city was compelled to bring the two into line by reducing its expenditures. Retrenchment has involved a reduction in the flow of benefits to groups that had recently acquired political power, which in turn means that the members of these groups must endure a new and more stringent fiscal and political order. This process of financial and political contraction has been accomplished, in part at least, with the cooperation of leaders from the very groups that are being compelled to lower their sights and accept the harsher discipline of the new order.

The parallel is not perfect, however. The most obvious difference is that blacks and

Puerto Ricans have thus far been less successful in defending their economic and political gains than the Irish were under Kelly, or for that matter, than the civil-service unions have been during the present crisis. Another difference is that the regime currently governing the city is less tightly organized, centralized, and broadly based than the Tammany of Kelly, Croker, and Murphy. Consequently, no single organization today is capable of subjecting both the electorate and public officials to its discipline. And for these reasons, the *modus vivendi* that has emerged among the major actors in New York politics in the present crisis is not entirely stable.

The structural weakness of the present New York regime, and the substantial exclusion of blacks from it, could lead to the collapse of the entire set of accommodations sustaining the retrenchment program so far. One potential threat to the success of the current retrenchment program arises from the weakness and lack of discipline of some of the city's public-employee unions. If the leaders of a union are to risk negotiating a contract that reduces their members' benefits, they must be politically secure; if they are to get their members to approve such a contract, the union must be organizationally strong. Victor Gottbaum and the union organization he leads (the State, County, and Municipal Employees) may well be strong enough to impose discipline upon its rank-and-file, but some of his colleagues in the municipal labor movement are not so well situated. The leadership of the Patrolman's Benevolent Association (PBA), in particular, is very insecure, and the union itself is highly factionalized and quite weak. It is not surprising, therefore, that two successive PBA presidents, Ken McFeely and Douglas Weaving, refused to agree to the wage freeze, and were reluctant to negotiate a contract that—in the city's judgment, at least—stayed within the EFCB's guidelines. When Weaving finally did hammer out an agreement with the city's negotiators, it was rejected by the union's delegate assembly, and bands of policemen, encouraged by Weaving's political opponents within the union, staged a series of protests and demonstrations. Unable to mediate successfully between his members and the EFCB, Weaving resigned, as McFeely had before him. The refusal or inability of any one union to accept wage restraints, of course, makes it more difficult for the other unions to do so.

The very fact that New York City employees are represented by a number of independent unions is another potential source of instability: Each union can attempt to exploit its peculiar advantages, and pass the burdens of moderation on to the other unions. On a number of occasions the United Federation of Teachers (UFT) has sought to do exactly this. The UFT is probably the most politically powerful of the city-employee unions, because it can both draw upon its own resources and count on other groups to rally to the cause of education. Thus the UFT relied on its strength in the state legislature to secure passage of the Stavinsky-Goodman bill in the spring of 1976, which directed the mayor to restore $150 million of the funds he had cut from the Board of Education's budget. And the UFT has been the only civil-service union to stage a strike during the first two years of the financial crisis. The contract settlement that ended the brief teachers' strike in September 1975 provided salary increases for senior teachers, which the Board of Education financed by reducing the length of the school day and by failing to rehire any of the teachers laid off earlier. In all probability, when the UFT and the Board agreed to this contract, they anticipated that they would be able, with the support of aroused parents' groups, to pressure the mayor into giving the schools enough money to rehire teachers and restore the full school day.

The Stavisky-Goodman bill and the 1975 UFT contract indicate other tensions that can undermine the retrenchment program—those between the handful of officials in New York directly responsible for the city's finances and the hundreds of officials in legislative and administrative positions without such a responsibility. The overriding concern of the mayor and comptroller of New York City, and the governor and comptroller of New York State, is what might be termed the "cash-flow imperative." The city simply must have cash on hand to pay its bills when they fall due—especially to meet its payroll and debt-service obligations—if the government of the city is not to grind to a halt. The cash-flow imperative is the central preoccupation of these four officials, because they bear the ultimate responsibility for the day-to-day administration of the city's affairs, and for obtaining the loans the city needs to continue operating. This is a less immediate concern to city and state legislators, and to administrative officials who are only responsible for spending money but not raising it. And because politicians in New York today (in contrast to the situation during the heyday of Tammany rule) are independent political operators who are not subject to the discipline of a common party organization, the mayor and governor have found it difficult to compel other officials to pay heed to the imperatives imposed upon the city by the capital market.

The inability of the mayor and the governor to control other politicians provides groups demanding services with the opportunity to get their way by mobilizing other public officials against them. The Stavisky-Goodman bill, for example, was strenuously opposed in the name of fiscal responsibility by Mayor Beame and Governor Carey—both of whom, it should be noted, are moderately liberal Democrats. Nonetheless, the UFT and its allies were able to secure overwhelming majorities in the State Assembly and Senate to pass the bill—even though the governor had vetoed it, the legislature had not overridden a gubernatorial veto in more than 100 years, and one house of the legislature was controlled by moderately conservative Republicans. The UFT was also able to pressure the EFCB into approving its labor contract, although questions had been raised by the EFCB staff about whether the contract was consistent with the wage freeze, by getting the two United States Senators from New York to urge ratification in public testimony before the Board. Likewise, the Board of Higher Education and the Health and Hospitals Corporation, which as quasi-independent agencies have somewhat more leeway to maneuver politically than regular city departments, have attempted to resist budget cuts by getting various elected officials to support their cause. In this way, they hope to isolate and pressure the mayor and governor.

THE ELECTORAL THREAT

The final difference between the regime governing New York today and the regime Kelly and his successors constructed involves perhaps the most serious threat to the retrenchment program. The Tammany machine in the days of Kelly, Croker, and Murphy rested on a very broad and tightly controlled electoral base. The structure of electoral politics in New York today is quite different. A substantial proportion of the city's electorate—particularly its potential black and Puerto Rican electorate—does not vote. And many of the groups that do vote, but have acquiesced in the retrenchment process so far, are capable of acting independently in the electoral arena to protect themselves from the full rigors of retrenchment. The potential thus exists for elections to disrupt the retrenchment process. If black leaders were to mobilize a broader electoral base now than in the past—and they now have a stronger incentive to do so—public officials would not find it so easy to slash expenditures on programs with a black clientele. And if various groups that have acquiesced thus far to retrenchment were to adopt a new stance and enter into a new set of electoral alliances, public officials might find it politically impossible to heed the imperatives imposed upon the city by the capital market.

In short, the structure of electoral politics in New York today is such that political campaigns can generate serious strains within the retrenchment coalition, and can result in the election of public officials committed to opposing aspects of the retrenchment program. Just how real this possibility is can be seen by examining the potential electoral resources commanded by blacks, homeowners, liberals, and city employees, and by considering the various ways candidates might construct coalitions among these groups in their efforts to win municipal elections.

Blacks and Puerto Ricans participate in elections in far smaller proportions than other major groups in the city. (During the first round of the 1973 Democratic mayoral primary election, for example, a total of 3,828 votes was cast in the predominantly black 54th Assembly District in Brooklyn, while 23,080 votes were cast in the predominantly Jewish 45th Assembly District a few miles to the south.) This is a consequence, at least in part, of the peculiar role blacks and Puerto Ricans played in the city's politics in the 1960's—one that contrasts sharply with the role the Irish played in New York politics a century before. While the political leaders of the Irish were rewarded in direct proportion to the number of votes they commanded, for the most part black leaders in the 1960's were not rewarded on this basis, because their support was valued less for the number of votes they could swing in municipal elections, than for the legitimacy they were able to confer upon public officials or public programs in the eyes of federal grant-givers, national opinion leaders, and the most ardent supporters of these officials and programs. To the extent that black leaders were able to obtain administrative appointments, influence over policy-making, access to the mass media, federal or foundation grants for their organizations, or election to public office in predominantly black constituencies, all without a large mass following, they had no compelling incentive to undertake the effort involved in mobilizing such a following.

The legitimacy that black leaders can confer on the officials or programs they support has been a far less valuable political commodity in the mid-1970's than it was in the late 1960's, and blacks have consequently suffered heavily from retrenchment. The immediate reason why blacks have borne the brunt of the recent wave of firings, of course, is that the city removes workers from the municipal payroll in reverse order of seniority. Black leaders have predictably denounced this practice as "racist" and "anti-black." The city has adhered to it nonetheless, because any alternative would be denounced with equal vehemence by the civil-service unions, and the mayor is less willing to arouse their ire than that of the black leadership. If it were the case, however, that blacks and Puerto Ricans cast as large a proportion of the vote in the Democratic primary as their proportion of the city's population (roughly one third), rather than voting at less than half that rate, it is likely that the mayor would have taken greater pains to protect blacks from the full force of the "last-hired, first-fired" rule. He might, for example, have cut more deeply into job categories occupied predominantly by whites, rather than by blacks.

Such political lessons are not likely to be lost on black politicians. To the extent that black leaders in the future will only be rewarded in proportion to the help they are able to give their friends at the polls, or the harm they are able to inflict on their enemies, they will have a stronger incentive than they had in the 1960's to mobilize the enormous pool of black non-voters. At the same time, retrenchment will provide black politicians with the inducement to adopt a new leadership style, and it may well spark leadership struggles within the black community. The skills involved in organizing large blocs of voters and forging coalitions in the electoral arena are not the same as the ones rewarded and hence encouraged by the city's political system in the 1960's. In this way, the current fiscal crisis may well foster leadership changes within the black community akin to those among the Irish a century ago, which favored the respectable and taciturn John Kelly over both the fiery Irish nationalist O'Donovan Roosa and the disreputable gambler John Morrissey. Such leadership is by no means alien to blacks: It is the style of the black labor leader (e.g., Bayard Rustin or Lillian Roberts) rather than the black preacher. There are some indications that such a transformation may in fact be taking place today. In announcing his candidacy for the 1977 Democratic mayoral nomination, for example, Percy Sutton ignored racial issues and focused his remarks solely on the problem of crime, an issue around which he clearly hopes to mobilize a biracial electoral majority. Over the long run, then, the fiscal crisis may do for blacks what the overthrow of Tweed did for the Irish: It may facilitate their incorporation into the political system under a chastened and more sober political leadership.

Whatever its long-run consequences, however, in the short run the incorporation of the enormous reserve of black non-voters into the electoral arena can only upset the current retrenchment program. The success of this program is contingent upon the political feasibility of firing a large fraction of the city's minority-group employees, and cutting heavily into the budgets of municipal agencies providing services to blacks and Puerto Ricans. No black leader could hold onto his following while tolerating a retrenchment program whose burdens fall so disproportionately on his constituency. (Although his general strategy entails avoiding racially divisive issues as much as possible, even Percy Sutton rose to the defense of John L. S. Holloman, the black director of the New York City Health and Hospitals Corporation, whose removal from office was engineered by the EFCB and Mayor Beame because he resisted cutting the budget of the public hospital system, most of whose patients and a majority of whose nonprofessional personnel are black and Puerto Rican.) The entry of thousands of blacks into the electorate would give black politicians the bargaining power to back up their demand that the burdens of retrenchment be redistributed. Any such changes would of course be resisted by the groups that would be disadvantaged, and elected officials might well find it impossible, within the constraints imposed upon the city by the municipal-bond market, to arrange a new set of fiscal and political accommodations acceptable to the city's unions, taxpayers, business interests, liberals, and blacks.

WHO SHOULD BEAR THE BURDEN?

The civil-service unions are also in a position to use their electoral influence to improve their bargaining power in the retrenchment process. The unions can deploy manpower and money in political campaigns, and public employees and their spouses constitute a substantial voting bloc, especially influential in primary elections. A natural strategy for a candidate would be to court the support of the unions and middle-class Jews (the group whose turnout rate is the highest in the city's electorate) by casting himself as the defender of the city's traditional public programs, especially its public schools and colleges, and its subsidized middle-income housing program and rent-control program. The two chief sponsors of the Stavisky-Goodman bill, one of whom had his eye on the presidency of the city council and the other on the mayoralty, were clearly laying the groundwork for such a campaign appeal when they introduced the bill in the state legislature.

Elections and political campaigns can also lead to changes in the relative influence of the two groups most strongly committed to budgetary cutbacks—the city's downtown business elite and its homeowning population—and might thereby disrupt the retrenchment coalition. Since the eruption of the fiscal crisis, bankers and corporate executives have wielded enormous power in their role as mediators between the city and the capital market. They are able to exercise far less leverage in electoral politics, however, because apart from the Republican organization in Manhattan, they have no organizational presence. On the other hand, representatives of the city's homeowners have played little direct role in governing the city since the onset of the fiscal crisis (no spokesman for this group sits on the EFCB or MAC), but they are an important force in the city's electoral politics. Tax-conscious homeowners are a major bloc in the city's electorate, and their representatives play a considerable role in municipal elections through the regular Democratic and Republican organizations in Brooklyn, Queens, and the Bronx, and through the Conservative Party.

The question of who speaks for retrenchment in the governmental and electoral arenas is quite significant because the politicians who represent the city's homeowners are likely to cultivate alliances that differ considerably from the ones the bankers have struck. It would be natural for a candidate seeking the votes of the homeowners (who are chiefly lower-middle-class Catholics) to advocate that the municipal bureaucracies that employ and serve them (the Police and Fire Departments) be spared drastic budget cuts, and that reductions be made instead in programs (especially welfare) that have a black clientele and employ middle- or upper-middle-class personnel. Nothing could be more calculated to alienate the reformers and liberals, who have been happy to join a retrenchment coalition led by men of their own class or a higher social class (like Felix Rohatyn), and would find it hard enough anyway to overcome cultural and ethnic antipathies sufficiently to collaborate with politicians speaking for lower-middle-class Irish and Italians.

Finally, reformers and liberals may come to play a different role in the city's politics during and after an election campaign than they have since the eruption of the fiscal crisis. Since 1975, reformers and liberals have followed the political leadership of the banks. In electoral politics, however, they have the ability to act independently, and they command a number of important resources—organizational skills, money, talent, energy, and a committed mass following. During an election campaign, these resources could be deployed in one (or both) of two ways. One alternative, which might be called the West Side option, would be for liberals to recultivate an alliance with blacks, oppose budgetary cutbacks, attack the banks, and—apart from calling for increased federal aid—ignore the issue of how the city is to pay its bills. The second, the East Side option, would be for liberals to maintain their current alliance with the banks, insist that the city has no choice but to cut its budget, attack the politicians and union leaders (the power brokers?) responsible for getting the city into its present mess, and—apart from opposing appeals to racism—ignore the blacks.

Campaigns can thus open the question of who should bear the burden of retrenchment, and elections can compel public officials to commit themselves to protect various municipal programs from budgetary cutbacks. When this source of strain is considered along with the other tensions besetting the retrenchment coalition, it is little wonder that New York City's creditors and potential creditors are reluctant to trust their fate to democratic politics.

THE LOGIC OF POLITICAL CONTRACTION

There are, as I noted above, two fundamental routes to retrenchment. One, the path of political organization and internally imposed discipline, preserves at least the forms of democracy. The other, the path of political contraction and externally imposed discipline, does not. Any particular retrenchment program may of course involve elements of both self-discipline and political contraction. Although New York City recovered from the fiscal crisis of 1871 by pursuing for the most part the path of self-discipline, there were aspects of the post-Tweed regime that could scarcely be considered democratic. For example, the reform charter under which the city operated from 1873 through 1897 included provisions for "minority representation" guaranteeing the anti-Tammany forces at least one third of the seats on the Board of Alderman. And Tammany relied, at least in part, upon its control of the police to deal with opponents who challenged its hegemony over the working classes: The police commonly intervened against unions in labor disputes, and dealt rather harshly with anarchists, socialists, and communists.

These qualifications aside, New York City recovered from its 1871 fiscal crisis without abandoning the forms of democracy, because John Kelly and his successors discovered a way, in a city where the ownership of property was not widespread, to reconcile mass political participation with the security of private property. They accomplished this by constructing a political machine that exchanged patronage for votes, and had both a broad base and a centralized structure and was therefore able to subject voters, public officials, and public employees to its discipline.

No such political organization exists in New York today. This is why the process of retrenchment in New York is currently beset by so many tensions, and why political campaigns and elections could so easily upset the retrenchment program. And it is for this reason that legal and institutional reforms that would sharply limit the scope of local democracy are being seriously considered in New York today.

New York City's creditors are well aware of the dangers threatening the retrenchment process. This explains the character of the proposals that the banks have advanced, and that public officials themselves have supported, in an effort to make the city's bonds marketable. For example, at the insistence of the banks, the statute creating the Municipal Assistance Corporation diverted the revenues of the stock-transfer tax and sales tax from the city's general fund, and earmarked them for debt-service payments on MAC bonds. And in February 1977, Mayor Beame proposed that revenues from the city's property tax be set aside in a fund under the State Comptroller for the purpose of meeting debt-service payments on New York City bonds and notes. Together, these reforms would deprive locally elected officials in New York City of the authority to determine how the monies raised by the city's most productive taxes are to be spent. (An analogous reform on the federal level would be a constitutional amendment depriving Congress of its authority over the $150 billion raised by the federal income tax, declaring that this money must be spent for national defense, and placing it in a fund controlled by the Joint Chiefs of Staff.)

In a similar vein, Governor Carey proposed that a "health czar" be jointly appointed by the mayor and governor to exercise all the authority of the city and state governments over hospitals and health care in New York City. This would permit both the mayor and governor to disclaim responsibility for the health czar's actions, and would thus give him enough freedom from popular pressures to accomplish what officials subject to such pressures find impossible to do—order the closing of hospitals.

Finally, in March 1977, the banks proposed that a state-appointed Budget Review Board be established as a long-term successor to the EFCB. The Review Board would have the power to review the city's budget before it was adopted, to reject it if—in the Board's judgment—it was not legitimately balanced, and to approve or disapprove all subsequent budgetary changes and all city borrowing. If city officials refused to obey the orders of the Review Board, it would have the authority to assume total control over the city's finances, and even to prefer criminal changes against municipal officials. The banks also proposed that restrictions be placed upon the city's ability to issue short-term debt, that a fund be created to cover revenue shortfalls and expenditure overruns, and that city officials be required to observe various reporting requirements and internal budgetary controls.

As these proposals indicate, a process of political contraction is well under way in New York. And the logic behind that process seems to be inexorable. If New York City is to manage its cash flow, finance capital projects, and pay off its accumulated deficit, it must enjoy access to credit. It will obtain such access only if its creditors are convinced that the city is able to repay the money it borrows. The city can only pay its debts if its current expenditures do not (as they presently do) exceed its revenues. Since the city's ability to increase its revenues through additional taxation is reaching the point of diminishing returns, it has no alternative but to reduce its expenditures. If elected officials find it politically impossible to reduce municipal expenditures, then the city can obtain the loans it requires only if outsiders are empowered to do the job for them, or if their authority to do otherwise is restricted by law.

In the absence of a political leadership with the power that John Kelly had to impose restraints upon public officials, New York City's creditors have searched for other means to insure that their loans will be repaid. And in an effort to provide such guarantees, the city has been driven down the second route to retrenchment—that of political contraction. To be sure, New York City is not the Weimar Republic or Argentina. David Rockefeller is not in a position to organize bands of black-shirted thugs to beat up municipal union leaders and break up meetings of West Side reformers, nor is Felix Rohatyn likely to propose that welfare recipients be disqualified from voting in municipal elections. The process of political contraction, however, can proceed not only by direct assaults upon the rights of newly powerful groups, but also by removing authority from the hands of elected officials amenable to the influence of these groups and transferring it to officials insulated from popular pressures. Moreover, statutes can be enacted and standards placed in the covenants of 20-year municipal bonds that limit the freedom of elected officials within the domain where they do retain some authority. And, as Boss Tweed learned, the criminal law can be used to keep profligate politicians in line. Just such reforms have been enacted or are being proposed in New York in an effort to make the city's bonds marketable. Whatever may be the long-run consequences of the city's fiscal crisis, as a result of these reforms, the citizens of New York may be left over the next decade with very little control over how they are governed.

PART 4

Intergovernmental Politics

Cities are increasingly enmeshed in a network of politics involving other governments. The articles in this section analyze intergovernmental relations by exploring in detail the complex linkages and interactions that occur among local governments and between local governments and other levels of political authority.

The article by Deil Wright, "Intergovernmental Relations: An Analytical Overview," presents the concept of Intergovernmental Relations (IGR) as an alternative to the concept of federalism (formal national-state relations) for viewing the American political system. Wright points out that federalism is primarily concerned with the formal structure of relationships between different levels of government, whereas "IGR consists of the continuous day-to-day pattern of contacts, knowledge, and evaluations of government officials including both their formal and informal interaction." By focusing on the role of elected and appointed officials in the policy process, IGR acknowledges the growing importance of public bureaucracies as well as popularly elected representatives in American government.

Wright describes American IGR by outlining five phases IGR has gone through from the Depression to the present: the conflict period (pre-1937), the cooperation period (1933–1953), the concentrated period (1945–1960), the creative period (1958–1968), and the competitive period (1965–present). For each phase, Wright sets forth the main problems which dominated the public agenda, the perceptions held by the main participants in the administration of policy, and the mechanisms and techniques used to implement intergovernmental programs.

During the 50-year period of this transition, patterns of interaction between governmental units have reflected a gradual change in relationships from adversarial and antagonistic to cooperative and, most recently, to competitive and tension-ridden. Wright argues that the latest period, "the competitive period," has been characterized by "picket-fence-federalism" in which competition and tension have prevailed between elected policy generalists and program professionals as well as between functional program areas. Each program area has become a vertical alliance of professionals from all levels of governmental units. The horizontal isolation of programs from one another has caused local governments to become battlegrounds among program professionals for clients and resources, a situation which has often produced ineffective service delivery and local political instability.

Many of these themes are supported in the article by David Walker, "The New System of Intergovernmental Relations: Fiscal Relief and More Governmental Intrusions." Walker argues that increased federal and state financial aid for local governments without systematically dealing with the functional and fiscal defects of local government has created problems of accountability, administrative effectiveness, and economic efficiency, which "pose a challenge to how the ideal of strong local government can be made a reality in the years ahead." At the heart of this problem are many uncoordinated changes taking place throughout the federal system in the assignment of functions and in funding arrangements. These changes have both increased and strained the interdependence of levels and units and government on one another and have created what Walker calls an "intergovernmentalized system" of service provision.

The article by the Advisory Commission on Intergovernmental Relations (ACIR) "Governmental Processes and Functions, Local and Area-Wide," argues that the present system of assigning functions to governments is plagued by endless variations because there is no existing uniformity between states concerning the type or level of government which is responsible for a particular function. Rationalizing these arrangements is difficult because there are structural and procedural constraints in most state-local governmental systems which impede attempts at reorganization.

These difficulties stem from an assignment system that is constantly centralizing and decentralizing without considering the *appropriate* level of government for the nature of the service or good being provided. The ACIR offers four factors or criteria to provide a base for an assignment system: economic efficiency, fiscal equity, political accountability, and administrative effectiveness. In other words, functional assignments should be made to jurisdictions that can supply the service at the lowest cost, finance the function with the greatest fiscal equalization, provide the service with adequate popular political control, and administer the function in an authoritative, technically proficient and cooperative fashion.

The study by Elinor Ostrom, "Metropolitan Reform: Propositions Derived from Two Traditions," addresses the functional assignment issue from a theoretical perspective. Ostrom examines two competing theories of metropolitan organization—the reform tradition and the political economy approach. Her purpose is to develop a scheme for the organization of urban services which is efficient as a means of delivering services and for meeting the needs and preferences of the citizens who are served.

To compare these two theories, Ostrom first formalizes the theory underlying the metropolitan reform tradition. Ostrom argues that this theory is not empirically verified; instead she sets forth a set of alternative propositions based upon a political economy (or public choice) approach. She argues that increasing the size of governmental units, reducing the number of public agencies, and increasing the reliance upon hierarchy may not result in increased output per capita, efficient provision of services, and equal distribution of costs to beneficiaries.

The key to Ostrom's argument is the intervening variable—the type of public good or service involved. Ostrom asserts that the optimum scale for production is not the same for all public goods and services. Therefore, one large centralized metropolitan unit would not be able to provide all goods and services most efficiently. For some public goods and services, competition among many local governments acting as producers of public services may cause public officials to be more responsive to citizens' needs and desires, and may result in more efficient, lower cost, and more responsive service provision.

Intergovernmental Relations: An Analytical Overview

DEIL S. WRIGHT

William Anderson, one of the intellectual parents of the intergovernmental relations field, once claimed that "intergovernmental relations is, I believe, a term indigenous to the United States, of a relatively recent origin, and still not widely used or understood." [1] Since Anderson's assertion in 1960, the phrase intergovernmental relations (IGR) has experienced wider usage, but whether the term is clearly or adequately understood remains questionable. Brief attention to the definition and features of IGR is therefore appropriate if not mandatory.

GAINING FORCE BY UNUSUALNESS: THE DISTINCTIVE FEATURES OF IGR

We need look no further than the author quoted above for a starting point in clarifying IGR. Professor Anderson says that IGR is a term intended "to designate an important body of activities or interactions occurring between governmental units of all types and levels within the [United States] federal system." [2] It is possible to use his general definition as a starting point to elaborate the concept of IGR.

First and foremost, IGR occurs within the federal system. American federalism is the context, not the totality, of IGR. IGR encompasses more than is usually conveyed by the concept of federalism, where the emphasis is chiefly on national-state relationships with occasional attention to interstate relationships. IGR recognizes not only national-state and interstate relations, but also national-local, state-local, national-state-local, and interlocal relations. In short, IGR includes as proper objects of study all the permutations and combinations of relations among the units of government in the American system.

Anderson also assists us in making a second important point about IGR. "It is human beings clothed with office who are the real determiners of what the relations between units of government will be. Consequently the concept of intergovernmental relations necessarily has to be formulated largely in terms of human relations and human behavior . . ." [3] Strictly speaking, then, there are no intergovernmental relations, there are only relations among officials in different governing units. Individual interactions among public officials is at the core of IGR. In this sense it could be argued that federalism deals with the anatomy of the system, whereas IGR treats its physiology.

275

A third notion implicit in IGR is that relations are not one-time, occasional occurrences, formally ratified in agreements, or rigidly fixed by statutes or court decisions. Rather, IGR is the continuous, day-to-day pattern of contacts, knowledge, and evaluations of government officials. A major concern is with the informal as well as with the formal, the practices as well as the principles, pursued in both competitive and cooperative interjurisdictional patterns. This third facet of IGR reads into the concept those activities—as well as research studies—that have previously gone under the title of cooperative federalism, which the late E. S. Corwin defined as one in which governmental units "are regarded as mutually complementary parts of a single governmental mechanism all of whose powers are intended to realize the current purposes of government according to their applicability to the problem at hand."[4] These words from a constitutional law scholar provide the desirable emphasis on the working, problem-oriented informalities of IGR and at the same time are a reminder of the formal, legal, institutional context within which those relationships originate and flourish.

It has been shown that IGR recognizes multiple unit relationships, that it respects the primacy of public officials acting in an interjurisdictional context, and that it is concerned with informal working relationships in institutional contexts. A fourth distinguishing characteristic of IGR is its awareness of the role played by all public officials. Automatically assumed as integral and important to IGR are mayors, councilmen, governors, state legislators, members of Congress and others. But in recent years more attention has been paid to the actions, attitudes and roles of appointed administrators. The increased focus on administrators as relevant IGR participants is a natural outgrowth of the increasingly important role played by public bureaucracies in government. The concern for the administrative aspects of IGR also arises, however, from attention to informal working relationships and from the academic leanings of most of the writers who have staked out claims to the IGR field. A majority of these persons have been oriented toward public administration and have also held a strong interest in state and local government.

A fifth and final distinctive feature of IGR is its policy component. Federalism has, to a large extent, translated questions of policy into questions of law and relied upon the courts for their resolution. Economic and political complexities, combined with rapid rates of social and technological change, have greatly reduced the capacity of courts—and legislatures—to deal with continuous pressures for policy change. The secular shift from regulatory politics to distributive and redistributive politics signaled new power relationships and configurations to which the term federalism could be applied only with awkward and ambiguous modifiers, such as direct, private, functional, economic. From its origins in the 1930s, IGR was recognized as anchored in politics and suffused with policy. It retains those features in the 1970s.

IGR cut its teeth on the massive political and policy issues that remained following the Supreme Court decisions on the social welfare legislation of the New Deal. It reached early adolescence in grappling with federal aid to education, urban development and civil rights. It is now attempting to claim maturity on issues related to citizen participation and effective services delivery systems. Near the policy core of IGR have been fiscal issues. These have been dominated by allocational issues: Who shall raise what amounts by what method from which citizens, and who shall spend how much for whose benefit with what results? This "fiscal fixation" has sometimes skewed diagnoses of and prescriptions for IGR problems, but the main point stands: IGR is centrally concerned with policy. As the Kestnbaum Commission noted in 1955, "The crucial questions now are questions of policy: What level ought to move? Or should both?"[5] These questions, the commission added, are ones on which the criteria for judgment "are chiefly political, economic, and administrative rather than legal."[6]

The five distinctive features of IGR are summarized in table 1. These characteristics combine and interact to produce new directions, vectors, and results in the conduct of public affairs in the United States. A new term or phrase to describe these special features therefore seems amply justified. The term IGR alerts one to the multiple, behavioral, continuous and dynamic exchanges occurring between various officials in the political system. It may be compared to a different, novel and visual filter or concept that can be laid on the American political landscape. It permits one to observe, classify and cumulate knowledge without obscuring other relevant data which prior political concepts have provided.

TABLE 1

Distinctive Features of Intergovernmental Relations

1. All Units (Multiple Entities)

National	Municipalities
States	Special districts
Counties	School districts

2. Interactions of Officials (Informal)

Behavior	Perceptions
Beliefs	Preferences

3. Continuous and Cumulative (Regularities)
   Day-to-day contacts
   Working relationships
   Cumulative patterns

4. All Public Officials (Administrators)
   Elected officials
   a. legislators
   b. executives
   c. judges
   Appointed administrators
   a. generalists
   b. functional specialists or
      program professionals

5. Policy Emphasis (Fiscal Focus)
   Financial issues
   Anchored in politics
   Suffused with policy

PHASES OF IGR

"To follow still the changes of the moon." Shakespeare

To say that the American political system has evolved and changed is trite. The significant questions in dealing with change are ones centering on the frequency, mechanisms, direction, and effects of change. It is possible, for example, to understand aspects of the solar system by studying carefully the phases of the moon. Similarly, a better grasp of the American political system may hopefully be gained by identifying and analyzing five phases of IGR.

In each of the five IGR phases, three main components are considered. First, what were the main problems dominating the public agenda during each phase? Second, what were the perceptions held by the main participants that seemed to guide or direct their behavior in each phase? Third, what mechanisms and techniques were used to implement intergovernmental actions and objectives during each period? Additional elements will help describe each phase, orient the reader, and reveal the effects of changing intergovernmental behavior patterns. These elements are a one-word descriptor, a metaphoric or graphic characterization, and an indication of the approximate dates in which each IGR phase peaked or climaxed.

The five phase descriptors employed here, together with rough date designations are: (1) conflict (pre–1937); (2) cooperative (1933–1953); (3) concentrated (1945–1960); (4) creative (1958–1968); and (5) competitive (1965–?). A condensed and summary chart of the successive phases is offered in table 2. Added to that overview are verbal and graphic expositions of the phases with important caveats. The phases are clearly indicated as successive ones with some overlapping of dates among the periods. While the dates have been selected with deliberateness, they are not sharp and arbitrary cutting points. Forces and tendencies bringing one or another phase to its climax were present or had antecedents in prior periods. Also caution is necessary on terminal dates. None of the phases ends in any exact or literal sense. Each phase produces carryover effects beyond the years designated in table 2. Indeed, it is probably most accurate to think of the current state of intergovernmental affairs as resulting from overlaps of the cumulative and successive effects of each IGR phase.

Conflict (pre–1937)

The chief concern of the conflict phase of IGR was the effort to identify and implement "proper" spheres of governmental jurisdiction and neatly defined boundaries for officials' actions. This emphasis operated at the state-local level as well as between national and state governments. Dillon's rule, as a principle for interpreting narrowly the powers of local governments, was not only an assertion of state supremacy but also a consequence of the search for the exact limits of local power. Guiding this search was an expectation of exclusive powers. Public officials' perceptions reflected these adversary and antagonistic patterns of interaction.

TABLE 2

Phases of Intergovernmental Relations (IGR)

Phase Descriptor	Main Problems	Participants Perceptions	IGR Mechanisms	Federalism Metaphor	Approximate Climax Period
Conflict	Defining boundaries Proper spheres	Antagonistic Adversary Controversy Exclusivity	Statutes Courts Regulations	Layer cake federalism	pre–1937
Cooperative	Economic stress International threat	Collaboration Complementary Mutuality Supportive	Policy planning Broad formula grants Open-ended grants Tax credit	Marble cake federalism	1933–1953
Concentrated	Program needs Capital works	Professionalism Objectivity Neutrality Functionalism	Categorical grants Service standards	Focused or channelled federalism (water taps)	1945–1960
Creative	Urban-metropolitan Disadvantaged clients	National goals Great society Grantsmanship	Program planning Project grants Participation	Fused-foliated federalism (proliferated)	1958–1968
Competitive	Coordination Program effectiveness Delivery systems Citizen access	Disagreement Tension Rivalry	Revenue sharing Reorganization Regionalization Grant consolidation	Picket fence federalism (fragmented)	1965– ?

These conceptions and attitudinal postures by participants were anchored in deeper societal values of competition, corporate organizational forms, profit and efficiency. Residual elements of this phase remain today on the urban-metropolitan scene in the so-called market models of metropolitanism and in the search for the political jurisdiction to perform most efficiently a particular function—for example, should an activity be assigned to a city or to an areawide body?

The manner in which problems of jurisdiction were resolved in the conflict model of IGR was through statutes and the courts. Growing social and economic complexity subsequently brought regulatory agencies and commissions into being to referee jurisdictional boundary disputes. The Interstate Commerce Act of 1887 created the first of the great regulatory commissions and was a major breach in the century-old "administrative settlement" between the national government and the states.[7] It broke the long-standing presumption against the creation and growth of a national administrative establishment. Attempts to locate the scope of federal regulatory power under the commerce clause and other authority have persisted to the point that under a recent court ruling *all* electric generating and transmission companies fall under the rate-making authority of the Federal Power Commission.

Other illustrations of the continued adversary, conflict-oriented pattern of national-state relations abound. Environmental and health concerns recently precipitated a jurisdictional dispute over the spheres of national and state power to regulate the safety levels of a nuclear generating plant in Minnesota. National standards set by the Atomic Energy Commission (AEC) specified one level of allowable millirems of radiation escaping from the reactor into the atmosphere. The Minnesota Pollution Control Agency set the permissible level of millirems at only two percent of that sanctioned by the AEC. The Northern States Power Company brought suit in the federal court challenging the state standards and requesting permission to construct the nuclear power plant without regard for the Minnesota regulations. At issue in the case was the application and intent of federal statutes dealing with atomic energy. The court ruled in favor of the exclusive jurisdiction of the national government and invalidated the more restrictive state regulations.[8]

These recent court decisions probably come as close to reflecting current economic realities, social interdependencies, and technological necessity as pre–1937 courts and legislatures thought they were reflecting economic, social and technological separatism. That supposed separatism—however limited, qualified or restricted in practice—gave credence to the metaphor of "layer cake federalism" as a crude means of describing national, state and local disconnectedness.

Cooperation (1933–1953)

Several authors have ably argued and amply demonstrated that intergovernmental collaboration in the United States existed throughout the 19th and 20th centuries.[9] That such collaboration was of major significance or the dominant fact of our political history is less clear. It does seem possible, however, to point to one period in which complementary and supportive relationships were most prominent and had high political significance. That period is the cooperative phase from 1933–1953. The prime elements of national concern during those two decades were the alleviation of widespread economic distress and response to international threats. It seems logical and natural that internal and external challenges to national survival would bring us closer together.

The means by which increased collaboration occurred were several and varied. Most pertinent for our concerns were such approaches as national policy planning, tax credits, and categorical grants-in-aid. Most of the dozen or so grant programs enacted during the depression period were broad formula grants, with a few being open-ended. Special emergency funding arrangements were instituted during the depression years and repeated in selected federally-impacted areas in wartime. As one observer noted in 1943:

> Cooperative government by federal-state-local authorities has become a byword in the prodigious effort to administer civilian defense, rationing, and other war-time programs. . . . Intergovernmental administration, while it is a part of all levels of government, is turning into something quite distinct from them all.[10]

The IGR collaboration that persisted during these years was present on such unusual occasions as the 1952 steel seizure confrontation; prior to his seizure effort, President Truman polled state governors for their views.

The prime IGR mechanism, as well as the major legacy of this cooperative period, was fiscal. Substantial and significant fiscal links were firmly established. These established conduits were harbingers of more to come. They also served as important illustrations of a new and differently textured model of intergovernmental patterns, the well-publicized "marble cake" metaphor. The marble cake characterization appears to have been coined by Professor Joseph McLean of Princeton University in the early 1940s for the visual or contrast effect with the layer cake conception. Professor Morton Grodzins probably had the greatest impact in popularizing and elaborating the marble cake concept.

Concentrated (1945–1960)

The descriptor employed for this IGR phase stands for the specific, functional, highly focused nature of intergovernmental interaction that evolved and dominated the Truman-Eisenhower years. From 1946 to 1960, twenty-nine major new grant-in-aid programs were established, a number that doubled the total number of programs enacted before and during the depression and wartime eras. The expanded use of categorical grant programs was accompanied by increased attention to service standards and program measurement.

Guiding this growing functional emphasis were corps of program professionals in each of the specialized grant fields, such as airport construction, hospital construction, slum clearance and urban renewal, urban planning, waste treatment facilities, library construction, and so on. The pervasiveness of professionalism enhanced the service standards emphasis by covering the domain with a cloak of objectivity and neutrality. These fit comfortably into Professor Herbert Kaufman's conception of the autonomy accompanying "neutral competence" in public administration contrasted with the control over policy by a strong executive leader.[11] The professionalism, specialized grants and growing insulation also coincided neatly in time, as well as thematically, with Professor Frederick Mosher's view that the 1950s confirmed the triumph of the "professional state" in the public service.[12]

What aims or ends guided and provided the rationale for this surge of activity? Two appear to be most prominent. One was a capital works, public construction push. Between 1946 and 1960, state and local capital outlays increased twelvefold while current operating expenses rose by a multiple of four. Federal grants for highways, hospitals, sewage plants, and airports underwrote much of the state-local effort to meet deferred wartime needs and respond to changing technology and population configurations, especially its suburbanization.

A second motive force propelling intergovernmental action in this period was the political realization that government generally, and IGR especially, was capable of responding to

FIGURE 1
Public Expenditures by Type and by Level of Government and the Intergovernmental Flow of Funds, Fiscal Year 1950
(in Billions of Dollars)

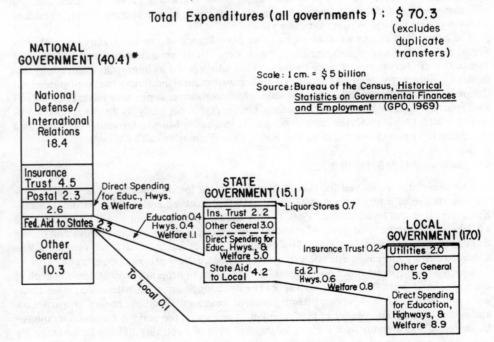

Total Expenditures (all governments) : $ 70.3
(excludes duplicate transfers)

* Excludes interest on the national debt ($ 4.4 billion)

particularistic middle class needs. The New Deal may have had its most telling political effect in making the American middle class acutely aware of the positive and program-specific capabilities of governmental action. Effective political action based on this awareness came after World War II and was reinforced by several conditions.

One condition already mentioned was suburbanization. It constituted the urban frontier and reinforced the myth of Jeffersonian ward republics. Another was the predisposition for using intergovernmental mechanisms because they also meshed with the historical political tradition of localism. In addition, IGR techniques fitted middle class values of professionalism, objectivity and neutrality. It appeared that objective program needs rather than politics were being served. Like reform at the turn of the century, IGR appeared to take a program out of politics.

Those political values coincided with an important structural change at the national level: the legislative reorganization of Congress in 1946. The most significant result of this event for IGR was the creation and stabilization of standing committees with an explicit program emphasis. These congressional committee patterns soon became the leverage points and channels through which influence on program-specific grants flowed. Furthermore, the committees developed their own cadre of professional staff members with functional and programmatic inclinations.

The flow of influence combined with the concentrated or focused flow of funds in the 1946–1960 period prompts one to employ a hydraulic metaphor in depicting this phase of IGR. The national government had become an established reservoir of fiscal resources to which a rapidly increasing number of water taps were being connected. The functional flows of funds could be facilitated by those knowledgeable at turning on the numerous spigots, that is, the program professionals. Cooperation was prominent during this period, but it occurred in more concentrated and selectively channeled ways.

A crude effort to express the water tap phase of IGR is made in figure 1. The intergovernmental flow of funds for 1950 is shown by the lines connecting the national-state and state-local spending sectors. This phase of IGR confirmed the interconnected and interdependent nature of national-state-local relations.

Creative (1958–1968)

The foundations for the creative phase of IGR were formed and filled in the cooperative and concentrated periods. The dates delimiting this phase are again somewhat arbitrary, but they mark a decade of moves toward decisiveness rather than drift in American politics and public policy. The election of a heavily Democratic Congress in 1958 and the 1964 presidential results were the political pegs to which this phase of IGR was attached. An added input that contributed to direction and cohesiveness, if not decisiveness, was the report of the Eisenhower-appointed President's Commission on National Goals. The commission, appointed partially in response to the Russian challenge of Sputnik, was created in 1959 and reported in 1961.[13]

The term Creative Federalism is applied to this decade because of presidential usage and because of the novel and numerous initiatives in IGR during the period. Three mechanisms are prominent: (1) program planning, (2) project grants, and (3) popular participation. The sheer number of grant programs alone is sufficient to set this decade apart from the preceding periods. In 1961 the Advisory Commission on Intergovernmental Relations (ACIR) identified approximately 40 major grant programs in existence that had been enacted prior to 1958. By 1969 there were an estimated 160 major programs, 500 specific legislative authorizations, and 1,315 different federal assistance activities, for which money figures, application deadlines, agency contacts, and use restrictions could be identified. Federal grants jumped in dollar magnitude from $4.9 billion in 1958 to $23.9 billion in 1970. At the state-local level, state aid to local governments rose from $8.0 billion to $28.9 billion over the 1958–1970 span.

Numbers and dollars alone are insufficient to distinguish the creative phase. Planning requirements, for example, were attached to 61 of the new grant programs enacted between 1961 and 1966. The tremendous growth in project grants as contrasted with formula grants increased the diversity of activities supported by federal funds and increased further the autonomy and discretion of program professionals. Project grant authorizations grew from 107 to 280 between 1962 and 1967, while formula grants rose from 53 to 99 in the same period. Finally, the public participation requirements tied to some grants increased the complexity, the calculations, and occasionally the chagrin of officials charged with grant allocation choices.

To what ends or aims were these federal initiatives directed? What were the chief problems addressed by this activism? At the risk of great oversimplification, two major policy themes are identified: (1) an urban-metropolitan emphasis and (2) attention to disadvantaged persons in the society through the anti-poverty programs and aid to education funds. The latter problem needs little documentation. Only one supporting item is mentioned for the former. Between 1961 and 1969 the percentage of all federal aid that went to urban areas increased from 55 percent to 70 percent, as total dollar amount so allocated went from $3.9 billion to $14.0 billion.[14]

Supporting the urban and disadvantaged emphases of this phase were selective but significant views held by important actors. President Johnson's speech first mentioning Creative Federalism also contained a phrase of larger and more popular political importance, that is, "The Great Society." As one observer has noted: "The Great Society was, by definition, one society; the phrase was singular, not plural."[15] How much this consensus politics push owed to the popularity of national goals efforts in the late 1950s and early 1960s is unknown. The unitary emphasis was evident, however. The president's preference on the need for centralized objective-setting made his 1965 moves toward planning-programming-budgeting a natural offshoot of views which held that our governmental system was a single system. Indeed, the basis for such revisionary thinking had been spelled out in a 1961 speech by Senator Joseph Clark entitled "Toward National Federalism."[16]

Accompanying these national and unitary sets of participants' perspectives was a subsidiary theme. It grew out of the expansion and proliferation of federal grants. This was the grantsmanship perspective that formed around the poverty and project grant programs. Playing the federal grant game became a well-known but time-consuming activity for mayors, managers, governors, universities, and of course, for the program professionals.

This creative phase of IGR contains a paradox. Federal grants expanded massively in number, scope, and dollar magnitudes. The diversity that accentuated grantsmanship tendencies, however, moved from political and policy assumptions that were common—if not unitary—in their conception about the aims of society. The paradox is one of proliferation, participation, and pluralism amid convergence, consent, and concord. The prominence of the latter set suggests that "fused" is an appropriate metaphor by which this IGR phase can be characterized. An effort to show visually the coalesced character of IGR at the end of the creative period is provided in figure 2. The ties between national-state and state-local sectors are broad and weld the segments into a closely linked system. The visual contrast between figures 1 and 2 helps confirm the shift from a focused to a fused model of the IGR system.

The contrasting component present in this creative phase has not yet been noted. Figure 2 conveys the impression of intense interconnectedness and interdependence. What it does not convey is the diversity, proliferation, and fragmentation of the national-state fiscal links. There may be a superficial appearance of fusion, but the scores of specific and discrete categorical grants require additional adjectives to describe this period, such as the fused-foliated or proliferated phase.

Other, more crude metaphors that could be used are flowering federalism and spaghetti federalism. Both terms attempt to capture the elaborate, complex, and intricate features of IGR that developed in this phase.

Competitive (1965–?)

The proliferation of grants, the clash between professional and participation-minded clients, the gap between program promises and proven performance, plus the intractability of domestic urban and international problems, formed a malaise in which IGR entered a new phase.

A different statement of central problems emerged when the administrative consequences of prior legislative whirlwinds became the center of attention. Issues associated with bureaucratic behavior and competence came to the forefront. One talisman earnestly sought was coordination. Others in close association were program accomplishment, effective service delivery systems and citizen access. Attention shifted to administrative performance and to organizational structures and relationships that either hindered or helped the effective delivery of public goods and services.

A sharply different tack was taken regarding appropriate IGR mechanisms. Pressure grew to alter and even reverse previous grant trends. Grant consolidation and revenue sharing were mentioned, popularized, and ultimately proposed by a Republican president on the basis of both program effectiveness and strengthening state and local governments. Some progress was made in the grant consolidation sphere, but as of 1973 the ACIR reported 69 formula grants and 312 project grants in existence. On the federal administrative scene, moves were made toward regionalization and reorganization. With the strong support of mayors, governors and county officials, general revenue sharing slipped through a divided Congress.

A flood of other developments in the late 1960s and early 1970s underscored the competition present in the system and also signaled efforts to reduce it. Perhaps the more visible

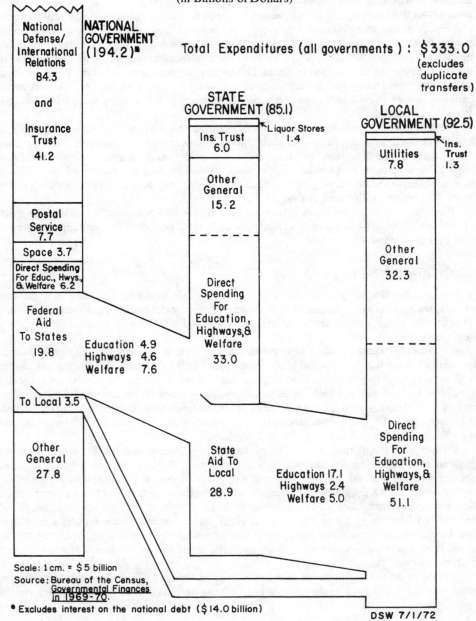

FIGURE 2
Public Expenditures by Type and by Level of Government and the Intergovernmental Flow
of Funds, FY1970
(in Billions of Dollars)

National
Defense/
International
Relations
84.3

and

Insurance
Trust
41.2

NATIONAL
GOVERNMENT
(194.2)*

Postal
Service
7.7

Space 3.7

Direct Spending
For Educ., Hwys.,
& Welfare 6.2

Federal
Aid
To States
19.8

Education 4.9
Highways 4.6
Welfare 7.6

To Local 3.5

Other
General
27.8

Total Expenditures (all governments): $333.0
(excludes
duplicate
transfers)

STATE
GOVERNMENT (85.1)

Ins. Trust
6.0

Liquor Stores
1.4

Other
General
15.2

Direct
Spending
For
Education,
Highways,&
Welfare
33.0

State
Aid To
Local
28.9

Education 17.1
Highways 2.4
Welfare 5.0

LOCAL
GOVERNMENT (92.5)

Utilities
7.8

Ins.
Trust
1.3

Other
General
32.3

Direct
Spending
For
Education,
Highways,&
Welfare
51.1

Scale: 1 cm. = $5 billion
Source: Bureau of the Census,
Governmental Finances
in 1969-70.

* Excludes interest on the national debt ($14.0 billion)

DSW 7/1/72

actions and initiatives came at the national level, but in numerical terms and potential significance, important policy shifts occurred at the state and local levels. It is impossible to compress the numerous trends that were competition-inducing and to acknowledge some that eased competitive tendencies. Only three policy patterns will be mentioned as illustrations of tension-promoting developments: (1) economic opportunity programs and their chief implementation mechanisms—community action agencies; (2) "white flight" and the polarization of central city-suburban relationships, especially along racial lines; and (3) elimination or funding reductions in several grant programs by the Nixon administration in 1973—some of which were achieved by the impounding of funds.

Countervailing tendencies in the direction of reduced tensions and increased cooperation appeared during this competition-dominated phase. At the local level, prompted and supported by national action, councils of governments sprang into existence in large numbers. One major aim was to foster metropolitan and regional coordination, especially through the A–95 grant review process. At the state level, herculean tax efforts were made to: (1) expand state services, (2) greatly increase state aid to local governments, and (3) meet the enlarged state-level funding requirements to match the vastly expanded federal grant monies.[17] Tension-reducing aims can also be attributed to such national-level actions as new departures with interstate compacts, the Partnership for Health Act (P.L.89–749), the Intergovernmental Cooperation Act of 1968 (P.L.90–577) and the Intergovernmental Personnel Act of 1970 (P.L.91–648).

The developments noted above reflected contrasting sets of perspectives that old as well as new participants brought to IGR. A statement by Senator Edmund Muskie—Democrat, Maine—in 1966 will serve as one example: "The picture, then, is one of too much tension and conflict rather than coordination and cooperation all along the line of administration—from top Federal policymakers and administrators to the state and local professional administrators and elected officials."[18] Similar views about the unwarranted degree of disagreement, tension, and rivalry among and between officials prompt the use of "competitive" for this phase of IGR.

The competition, however, is different in degree, emphasis, and configuration from the interlevel conflict of the older, layer cake phase. It is more modulated, and it acknowledges the lessons learned from the intervening periods of cooperation, concentration and creativity. For example, the current competitive phase appears reasonably realistic about the interdependencies within the system and the inability to turn the clock back in IGR. The three statutory enactments cited above bear witness to reasoned and reality-oriented approaches to IGR.

The nature of the competition in the present IGR phase is indicated in part by Senator Muskie's remarks. He mentions professional program administrators and state-local elected officials. It is the tension between the policy generalist, whether elected or appointed, and the program-professional-specialists that currently produces great static and friction in IGR. This cleavage is another reason for describing this phase of IGR as competitive. A visual representation of the fractures and rivalry characterizing this phase is offered in figure 3. The metaphor of the picket fence, referred to in former Governor Sanford's book, *Storm Over the States*,[19] was the original stimulus for this formulation. The seven public interest groups, often called the Big Seven, have parted ways from the functional specialists. Their common interest in revenue sharing, grant consolidation and similar proposals represents a reassertion of the executive leadership doctrine and a challenge to the program professionals' doctrine of neutral competence.

A second type of competition can also be discerned from figure 3: the competition between the several functional program areas. Each vertical picket represents an alliance among like-minded program specialists or professionals, regardless of the level of government in which they serve. As early as the mid-1950s these interlevel linkages of loyalties were identified and criticized as "vertical functional autocracies."[20] Other epithets used against these patterns are: balkanized bureaucracies, feudal federalisms and autonomous autocracies. These terms emphasize not only the degree of autonomy that the program specialists have from policy control by political generalists, but also the separateness and independence that one program area has from another. This lack of horizontal linkage prompts interprogram, interprofessional and interagency competition. The cross-program competition combined with the generalist-specialist split helps confirm the contention that the competition depicted by the picket fence model best describes the current and most recent phase of IGR.

Both competitive patterns were captured in the words of local officials as quoted by James Sundquist. Speaking in the late 1960s, the director of a local model cities program contended that "Our city is a battleground among federal Cabinet agencies."[21] Similar sentiments came from mayors and city managers whose limited control and coordination powers over federal programs caused them to feel like spectators of the governmental process in their own cities. If, in fact, this competitive model is applicable to IGR today, then a recognition of these tensions and cleavages would seem to be the first-order task of those seeking changes and improvements in IGR.

CONCLUDING COMMENT

IGR has become a distinctive dimension of activities in the American political system. It refers to a significant domain of political, policy and administrative actions by public officials. An acknowledged emphasis was made in this discussion on the meaning, features and trends in IGR (as a term or phrase). Concept explication and clarification have their uses; but they also have limits. There is much more to be said about the realities, practices and problems of IGR. Subsequent articles are appropriately addressed to these types of concerns.

One concluding comment on this exposition is offered in anticipation of the analyses that follow. This is an era when the *management* of IGR is a matter of major moment. James Sundquist observes that "The federal system is too important to be left to chance."[22] His book can be seen as an effort to critique and reconstruct the organizational philosophy undergirding effective intergovernmental action. Sundquist's treatment and the mood of this essay move toward a similar conclusion: intergovernmental achievements hinge on coping successfully with complexity. Complexity is an inherent and persistent characteristic of the several features of IGR. Accomplishments in the intergovernmental arena therefore depend on the successful management of complexity.

FIGURE 3
Picket Fence Federalism: A Schematic Representation

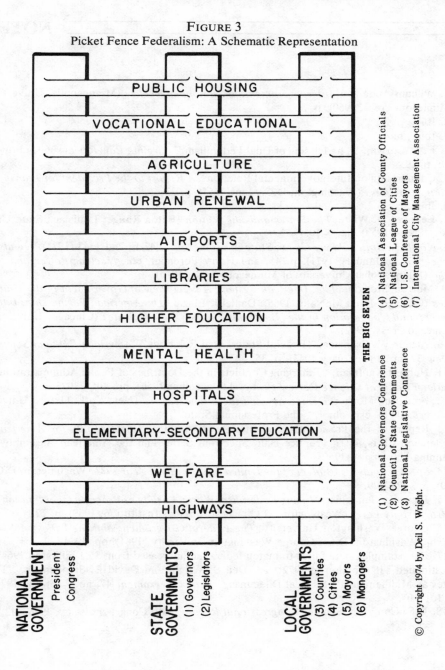

NOTES

1. William Anderson, *Intergovernmental Relations in Review* (Minneapolis: University of Minnesota Press, 1960), p. 3.

2. Ibid., p. 3.

3. Ibid., p. 4.

4. E. S. Corwin, "The Passing of Dual Federalism," *Virginia Law Review* 36 (February 1950), p. 19.

5. Commission on Intergovernmental Relations, *A Report to the President for Transmittal to the Congress* (Washington, D.C., June 1955), p. 33.

6. Ibid., p. 33.

7. Leonard D. White, *The States and The Nation* (Baton Rouge: Louisiana State University Press, 1953), pp. 9–10.

8. *Northern States Power Co.* v. *State of Minnesota,* 447 F. 2nd 1143 (1971); *see also, Science* 171 (8 January 1971), p. 45, and Harry Foreman, ed., *Nuclear Power and the Public* (Minneapolis: University of Minnesota Press, 1970).

9. Morton Grodzins, *The American System: A New View of Government in the United States* (Chicago: Rand McNally, 1966); Daniel J. Elazar, *The American Partnership: Intergovernmental Cooperation in the Nineteenth Century United States* (Chicago: University of Chicago Press, 1962).

10. Arthur W. Bromage, "Federal-State-Local Relations," *American Political Science Review* 37, no. 1 (February 1943), p. 35.

11. Herbert Kaufman, "Emerging Conflicts in the Doctrines of Public Administration," *American Political Science Review* 50, no. 4 (December 1956), pp. 1057–1073.

12. Frederick Mosher, *Democracy and the Public Service* (New York: Oxford University Press, 1968), esp. ch. 4, "The Professional State."

13. Report of the President's Commission on National Goals, *Goals for Americans* (Englewood Cliffs, N.J.: Prentice-Hall, Spectrum Series and the American Assembly of Columbia University, 1960).

14. *Special Analyses, Budget of the United States, Fiscal Year 1971* (Washington, D.C., 1970), pp. 228–229.

15. James L. Sundquist, *Making Federalism Work: A Study of Program Coordination at the Community Level* (Washington, D.C.: The Brookings Institution, 1969), p. 12.

16. George Washington University, *The Federal Government and the Cities: A Symposium* (Washington, D.C.: George Washington University, 1961), pp. 39–49.

17. For example, state funds to match federal aid increased from $5.1 billion in 1964 to an estimated $18.4 billion in 1972; *see,* Deil S. Wright and David E. Stephenson, "The States as Middlemen: Five Fiscal Dilemmas," *State Government* 47, no. 2 (Spring 1974), pp. 101–107.

18. U.S. Congress, Senate, *Congressional Record*, 89th Cong., 2nd sess., 1966, 112, p. 6834.

19. Terry Sanford, *Storm Over the States* (New York: McGraw-Hill, 1967), p. 80.

20. Advisory Committee on Local Government, *An Advisory Committee Report on Local Government* (submitted to the Commission on Intergovernmental Relations, Washington, D.C., June 1955), p. 7.

21. Sundquist, *Making Federalism Work,* p. 27.

22. Ibid., p. 31.

The New System of Intergovernmental Relations: Fiscal Relief and More Governmental Intrusions

DAVID WALKER

INTRODUCTION

The pattern of governance below the state level in the American federal system has experienced significant fiscal, functional, administrative and institutional changes during the past decade and a half. The dominant themes that emerge from even a cursory comparison of the condition of American localities in the early sixties with that in the late seventies include:

—continuing local jurisdictional fragmentation and only a handful of formal reorganizations, but also steady federal and, to a lesser extent, state efforts to establish coordinative planning and development units at the multi-county level;

—significant, but unsystematic, shifts in servicing arrangements with both upward and downward assignments occurring;

—continuing socio-economic and fiscal disparities between a majority of the central cities and their respective suburbs, with growing contrasts between central cities as well as their metropolitan areas in the northeast and Great Lakes regions and those elsewhere; and

—rising fiscal pressures on local governments generally and on those in the northeast quadrant especially, coupled with a dramatic hike in intergovernmental fiscal transfers—particularly from the federal government—as the primary response to these pressures.

These are the basic recent trends in local government and in the system as a whole. They suggest basic changes on certain fronts, significant continuity on others and above all they combine to confront American federalism with some fundamental structural challenges. The system, after all, has never been as "intergovernmentalized" (marbelized, if you will) as it is now.

THE PRIMACY OF THE FISCAL CHALLENGE AND RESPONSES TO IT

Significant shifts as well as some continuing changes are reflected in jurisdictional developments, the pattern of local functional assignments (and reassignments), and inter-local disparities, and most of these underscore the mounting pressures to which local public finances have been subjected over the past decade and a half. This, in turn, has produced various intergovernmental fiscal initiatives and these have been the prime response of the system to the plight of the localities.

293

ON THE FISCAL FRONT

The fundamental problem here is that the chief revenue source historically of American local governments has been the property tax and that this levy, generally, has been incapable—for a variety of fiscal, administrative and political reasons—of meeting the mounting demands for more and better local services.

Beginning in the late sixties and the growing realization that dual federalism was an inappropriate principle to apply to state-local finances, various shifts began to transpire. One was a series of efforts to reform the property tax. Over one-third the states reorganized or strengthened their property tax supervisory units over the past decade. Four states joined Hawaii in centralizing assessment; 15 established or beefed up assessor-training programs; 14 launched or revamped their assessment ratio studies; and more than a dozen adopted full disclosure policies regarding the average level of assessment in a community.

Another move was enactment of various property tax relief measures. Between 1970 and 1975, the number of state-financed relief enactments jumped from 12 to 33. Twenty-five of these were of the "circuit breaker" type, which like its counterpart in an electrical system cuts in when there is an "overload;" i.e., when the property tax reaches a percent of individual income that the state deems oppressive.

Still other changes are reflected in the growing reliance on interlocal contracting and servicing shifts and in the increasing tendency of some states to assume direct responsibility for certain heretofore exclusively or shared local functions.

A fourth trend in this broad effort to reduce the dependency on the local property tax was some increase in the number of states authorizing some or all of their cities and/or counties to levy nonproperty taxes. As of 1976, 26 states had taken such action in the local sales tax and 11 in the local income tax areas. One state—Minnesota—had sanctioned a modest "share the growth" regional tax arrangement for the seven-county "Twin Cities" region.

Of far greater fiscal significance than any of the above, however, has been the expansion of intergovernmental fiscal transfers. State and federal aid more than tripled between 1967 and 1975 (see Table I). And, this drastic downward, vertical fiscal response with all of its attendant by-products has served as the primary conditioner of the super-intergovernmentalized system that presently prevails at the local level.

The cumulative effect of these various fiscal or fiscally related developments, however, has been the emergence of a much more diversified, and some would say, "balanced" local revenue system. As a proportion of both local and state-local revenue systems, the property tax has declined significantly (to 33 percent of the former and 18 percent of the latter, as of 1976). The lesser share in the overall state-local revenue pie, of course, relates directly to the fact that since 1970 the states have assumed the senior partner role in this system, thanks to the fact that 37 states now have broad sales and income taxes (and only one has neither). (See Figure 1.)

Above and beyond the growing state role here is that of the federal government. Despite a gradual decline in the federal share of own source general revenues (see Figure 2), federal

TABLE 1

Local Governments Are Moving Toward More Balanced Revenue Systems, Selected Years 1942–1975

Fiscal Year	All Local Governments		Percent Distribution by Type of Government			
	Amount[1] (millions)	Percent Distribution by Source	Cities	School Districts	Counties	Townships and Special Districts
Total General Revenue (Local Revenue and Federal-State Aid)						
1942	$7,071	100.0%	37.0%	33.7%	22.0%	7.3%
1952	16,952	100.0	32.0	38.4	20.7	8.9
1957	25,916	100.0	30.3	41.9	19.5	8.3
1967	59,383	100.0	26.8	47.0	17.8	8.5
1971	93,868	100.0	27.1	46.4	18.4	8.2
1974	133,994	100.0	28.2	43.5	19.3	9.0
1975 est.	147,700	100.0	28.4	42.9	19.5	9.1
Intergovernmental Revenue (Federal and State Aid)						
1942	1,785	25.2	24.0	43.8	27.8	4.5
1952	5,281	31.2	18.7	49.9	26.2	5.2
1957	8,049	31.1	17.6	53.6	23.5	5.3
1967	21,338	35.9	17.7	58.2	18.5	5.5
1971	36,375	38.8	21.1	55.1	18.6	5.2
1974	57,253	42.7	24.0	49.6	19.6	6.7
1975 est.	64,000	43.3	24.2	49.0	18.9	7.0
General Revenue *From Local Sources* (Taxes and Charges)						
1942	5,286	74.8	41.4	30.3	20.0	8.3
1952	11,671	68.8	38.0	33.3	18.3	10.5
1957	17,866	68.9	36.1	36.6	17.7	9.6
1967	38,045	64.1	32.0	40.5	17.4	10.1
1971	57,491	61.2	30.9	40.8	18.2	10.1
1974	76,742	57.3	31.3	38.9	19.1	10.8
1975 est.	83,700	56.7	31.6	38.3	19.3	10.8
Local Property Taxes						
1942	4,344	61.4	39.0	32.9	20.1	8.0
1952	8,282	48.9	32.7	39.2	19.8	8.3
1957	12,385	47.8	29.7	42.8	19.2	8.3
1967	25,186	42.4	24.8	48.9	18.5	7.8
1971	36,726	39.1	23.3	50.3	18.3	8.0
1974	46,452	34.7	23.0	50.0	18.4	8.6
1975 est.	49,220	33.3	22.7	50.1	18.5	8.7

ACIR Staff Tabulation

FIGURE 1

Number of States with General Sales and Broad-Based Personal Income Taxes, as of January 1, 1950, 1960 and 1977

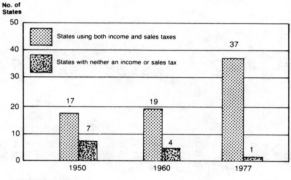

ACIR Staff Compilations

domestic expenditures have soared during this decade. Most of these outlays have gone for aid programs to state and local governments (see Figure 3). Moreover, since 1966 with the advent of the first block grant, the Partnership for Health Program, a tripartite federal aid package has emerged with categorical grants accounting for 79 percent of the 1977 total, five block grants for 12 percent and general revenue sharing for nine percent. Finally, over 30 percent of the 1977 aid package ($78 billion) was channeled directly to local governments, not through or to states—a marked hike over the 10 percent (of $11 billion) that bypassed the states at the beginning of the Johnson Administration.

In general, most of these general trends would seem to bode well for the condition of local public finances. Yet, these fairly salutory cumulative statistics tend to conceal many differences, difficulties and defects. They focus, after all, too heavily on fiscal figures.

Turning first to the states, their aid packages, overall, more than doubled between 1969 and 1975 (reaching the $50.5 billion mark). Yet, these packages reflect wide interstate variations and are channeled chiefly into four functional areas (education, welfare, highways and health-hospitals, accounting for 87 percent of the total aid outlays in 1972). The bulk of these conditional aids, then, goes to school districts and counties, not to cities. Ten percent of total state assistance in any recent fiscal year is allocated for general support payments and this usually favors cities. Yet, only eight states utilize formulas here that reflect any real attempt at equalization. Regarding revenue efforts, seven states in 1975 still were junior partners to their localities. Moreover, only a little more than one-fifth (11) of the fifty are making fairly "heavy" use of the income tax, while 13 are exerting a "moderate" effort and 19 a "low" one (with nine making no effort at all). In supervising local financial management practices—a matter of more than a little concern of late—only about eight states can be given a good to excellent rating. Overall, then, the state fiscal role, while markedly better than that of a decade ago, still falls short of the normative role many would prefer them to assume.

FIGURE 2
The Relative Growth in Federal Taxes Lags the State-Local Sector, Selected Years
1948–1976.
(Federal, State and Local Taxes as a Percent of GNP)

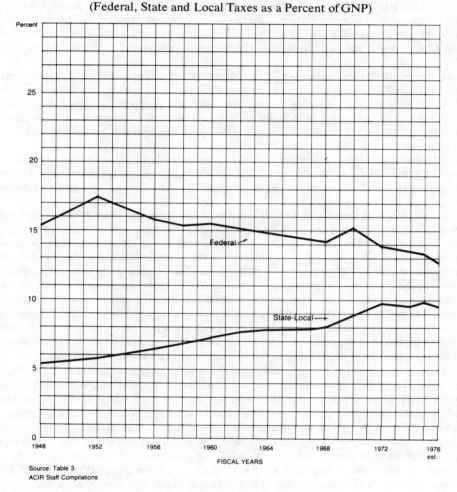

Source: Table 3.
ACIR Staff Compilations

With the quadrupling of federal aid amounts between 1968 and FY 1978, the nearly 50 percent hike in the number of programs and the extraordinary increase in the variety of aid programs, more federal dollars have been provided, but several problems have arisen:

—In terms of participation, practically all local jurisdictions, as well as the 50 states, are direct recipients, thanks to general revenue sharing, CETA and CDBG—to mention only the more obvious new programs of the early seventies;

—Accompanying the heavy bypassing of state governments, local governmental lobbies have assumed a more powerful stance in Washington, raising basic questions about the future of the states as authoritative middlemen in the system;

—With the growing reliance on allocating grant funds by formula (up to 75 percent of the total, compared to 66 percent in the mid-sixties), a new form of grantsmanship (and conflict among the public interest groups) has emerged that focuses not on administrators as much as on Congress and the need to fashion the formulas (and eligibility provisions) to their liking;

—In terms of services aided, all of the big efforts of intergovernmental and national import (like welfare, health, hospitals, transportation and education) are federally aided with social programs experiencing the greatest dollar and proportionate gains since 1965, but so are a range of activities that not so long ago were deemed wholly state-local responsibilities (like rural fire protection, libraries, jelly fish control, police and historical preservation);

—The forms of federal assistance, at least outwardly, have changed drastically since 1966, but with all the traditional types of categorical grants (project, project/formula, formula and open ended) still in use, along with at least five block grants and general revenue sharing;

—Conditions now are attached to all forms of federal aid; the procedural strings (civil rights, citizen participation and auditing requirements) that were added to GRS in 1976 and the hybrid nature of most of the block grants along with the tendency to pick up program and other constraints over time, render inaccurate the older description of these two forms of aid as essentially "no strings" and "few strings" assistance programs, respectively. Moreover, the emergence of a range of across-the-board requirements in the environmental, equal access, equal rights, relocation, historic preservation and personnel areas only underscores the fact that the conditions now attached to practically all federal assistance are infinitely more complex, more controversial (with more judicial decision-making), more pervasive (in terms of the focus of some on the internal operations of whole governmental jurisdictions) than their largely program-oriented predecessors of the mid-sixties.

—Despite the above, the form of aid can make a difference. Recipient discretion still is greater with general revenue sharing than with the other forms, and insofar as block grants cover a fairly wide portion of the functional turf and are adequately funded, they, too, confer greater discretion than do the categoricals. Moreover, certain ostensible categoricals in practice become block grants due to a range of factors that can produce lax federal agency oversight. Above all, perhaps, the servicing and fiscal discretion that comes as a consequence of receiving a number of federal grants—whether categorical, block or GRS—must not be discounted at this point in time. Put differently, and relating this discretionary theme with the previous one, increasing conditions characterize the recent evolution of all federal assistance and some of these conditions are more intrusive in a procedural and systemic sense than the old style categorical strings, but the practical effect now on those localities that receive a large and mixed package of federal aid is potentially, if not actually, to expand their fiscal and program options.

—Paralleling the above, the fiscal impact of federal aid is more difficult to gauge now than ever before. Earlier studies tended to agree that its impact was chiefly stimulative of greater state and/or local outlays, either in the aided area or aggregatively. Random evi-

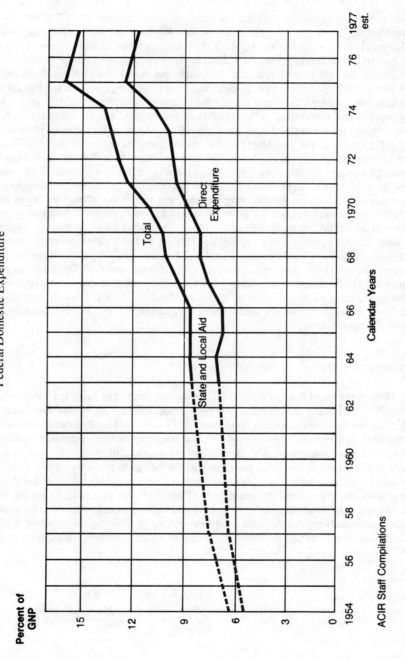

FIGURE 3

Government Domestic Expenditures as a Percentage of Gross National Product. Selected Years 1954-1977

(The Dominant Federal Role in the Domestic Public Sector)

Federal Domestic Expenditure

dence and impressions, along with a Brookings' assessment of CETA and an unpublished Treasury study of the impact of aid on certain hard pressed cities suggests more of an additive, if not a substitutive, effect. This seems to be especially true with the newer forms of aid and with larger urban jurisdictions that participate in several big money, federal programs. In this connection, the no-match feature of the community development and manpower programs (as well as general revenue sharing, of course) should not be overlooked. And, while "maintenance of effort" and other nonsubstitutive provisions are cited by some as real constraints, others feel they are merely "paper" conditions. A forthcoming GAO report on the subject may shed more light on the real character of their impact; .

—Finally, with the enactment of the countercyclical programs in 1976–77, direct federal aid to cities soared, with the figure for those of more than 500,000 in population zooming from 28 percent of their own-source revenues in 1976 to an estimated 50 percent in 1978; few can argue the need here, but some have questioned the growing degree of fiscal dependence that these figures suggest; the real long-term effects of these recent federal efforts, of course, depend on how "permanent" the programs become (the prospective renewal of CETA, though with many more conditions and constraints, suggests a partial answer to this question), the aggregative impact of these diverse asssistance undertakings on the very diverse localities that partake of them (a subject yet to be researched authoritatively) and what the essential nature of dependency really is. Dependency, after all, has more than fiscal connotations to it; administrative, political and even psychological factors also come into play and each of these combine in differing ways in each of the many recipient cities and counties. Needless to say, this topic, too, has received meager attention from the researchers.

CONCLUSION

The recent rapid hike in federal and state aid, then, has been the basic response to the manifold challenges confronting America's localities. Yet, it has not been an unmixed blessing for the cities, counties and towns of the nation. Heavily intergovernmentalized local programs, budgets and bureaucracies raise major questions regarding accountability, administrative effectiveness, not to mention economic efficiency. They pose a challenge to how the ideal of strong local government can be made a reality in the years ahead. This growing tendency to focus almost exclusively on intergovernmental fiscal transfers as a means of resolving local governmental difficulties and generally to ignore the fiscal and functional defects of present local institutional arrangements suggests the need for a much more balanced approach—one that recognizes the linkages between and among the functional, institutional, and fiscal factors that shape America's local governments.

Governmental Functions and Processes:
Local and Areawide

ADVISORY COMMISSION ON
INTERGOVERNMENTAL RELATIONS

Every level of government in a federal system has exclusive or shared responsibility for providing a wide variety of public services. However, the actual sorting out of functional tasks among different levels and types of government is a perennial source of tension and uncertainty in American federalism. The question continually arises: who should do what?

Since its 1963 report *Performance of Urban Functions: Local and Areawide*, this Commission has recommended various specific functional assignment policies that would result in a more manageable set of service responsibilities for national, State, areawide, and local governments. This report, though broader in scope, continues in that tradition. It discusses deficiencies in the existing apportionment of service responsibilities, suggests the characteristics of an ideal functional assignment policy, and offers recommendations as to how Federal, State, and local governments might reorder their respective functional responsibilities.

PRESENT ASSIGNMENT POLICIES

Endless Variation

Who does what? That is a question with innumerable answers in the American federal system. There is little uniformity among and within States as to what level and type of government has responsibility for a particular function or any of its components.

The 50 State-local governmental systems all differ in their functional assignment policies. Education is provided through county-dependent districts in parts of the South, by municipalities and townships in New England, and by independent non-coterminous school districts elsewhere. Corrections is almost exclusively a State function in Connecticut, Delaware, Rhode Island, and Vermont; it displays significant county dimensions in California, Michigan, and Texas; municipalities have considerable responsibilities in New York, Missouri, and Pennsylvania. Similarly, highways are an exclusive State function in Virginia, but primarily a county-municipal function in Wisconsin. Variations of this sort occur in almost every State-local governmental service (see Table 1).

Even within a service there are different allocation patterns. For example, municipal governments are often the primary providers of basic police services, but councils of government may provide communications services while a State government may have responsibility for training and criminal laboratory services. Land-use controls are basically a local function although comprehensive land-use planning occurs at the regional level and States sometimes assume direct control of critical environmental areas or promulgate land-use regulations that affect local actions.

Varying patterns of service allocation reflect State-local reliance on different service providers. Counties are of minimal or no functional significance in New England while they are major service providers in California, Maryland, New York, and Virginia. Townships have extensive service responsibilities in 11 Northeast and Midwest States, are limited-purpose governments in another ten States, and do not exist in another 29. Special districts have considerable duties in Florida, Georgia, Illinois, and Washington, but are virtually unused in Alaska, Hawaii, Montana, Rhode Island, and Vermont. Similarly, substate districts have gained increasing prominence in States like Texas, Georgia, and Virginia, but are not used in Wyoming, Hawaii, Delaware, Alaska, and Rhode Island.

The distribution of service responsibilities also varies among jurisdictions within a State. Home-rule counties, for example, assume more urban and regional service responsibilities than their non-home-rule counterparts (see Table 2). Large, independent, multi-county special districts have more than doubled in the last ten years, but they are mainly concentrated in metropolitan areas. On the other hand, State governments usually assume more direct and contractual service responsibilities in rural areas. Moreover, regional councils of local governments usually have quite different functional planning duties in urban and rural areas.

Functional assignments, then, differ among and within functions and also among and within the 50 State-local governmental systems. This variation in service allocation patterns makes it almost impossible to ascertain what the general service roles of State, regional, county, special district, and municipal governments are. The proliferation of assignment patterns, in turn, makes it difficult to determine whether functions are being effectively allocated to different levels and units of State and local government.

Structural and Procedural Hurdles

Frequently, the variation of service allocation patterns reflects structural and procedural traits of many State-local governmental systems that hinder a reordering of service assignments. The main obstacles to more effective functional assignment include:

1. the voluntary but selective character of most intergovernmental service agreements and functional transfers and consolidations;
2. the unwillingness to use Federal grant-in-aid management procedures such as the A–95 project notification and review system to sort out eligible areawide and local service providers;
3. the lack of authoritative and generalist substate districts and regional councils generally that can provide various areawide services;
4. the continued proliferation of independent, unifunctional, areawide and local special districts that do not coordinate their services with established local governments;
5. the slow pace of county modernization and the resultant inability or unwillingness of

counties to assume various local and regional service responsibilities;

6. the continued defeat of most local government reorganization proposals that would involve a clearer sorting out of local and areawide service responsibilities; and

7. the lack of decentralization of State-administered services and the inability of most State-local governmental systems to devolve service responsibilities from county or regional to municipal and neighborhood sub-units of government.

The most prominent obstacle to more effective service assignment involves the lack of authoritative regional service mechanisms. The need for stronger county government highlights this barrier. Only 16 States now grant functional home rule to counties and only 4 percent of eligible jurisdictions now are home-rule entities. Most counties also face stringent restrictions affecting city-county and multi-county consolidation. The various strictures on county organization and powers and State reliance on these bodies to deliver State-mandated services have combined to help prevent them from assuming more urban and regional services. Thus, over 70 percent of 160 surveyed non-home-rule metropolitan counties did not perform such urban or regional functions as fire protection, refuse collection, urban renewal, mass transit, solid waste disposal, water supply, or air and water pollution control (see Table 2).

Other regional service mechanisms are even less authoritative. Federally and State-encouraged substate districts and regional councils generally have only planning and grant management responsibilities and rarely deliver areawide services. The weak financial base of these jurisdictions, their often tenuous relationships with established local governments, and their competition with other separate regional planning organizations, in many cases have reduced even their supportive planning capabilities. Combined with this is the reluctance of most local officials to vest these instrumentalities with direct operational responsibilities. All these factors now make many of these mechanisms relatively weak actors on the substate scene.

The paucity of generalist regional bodies in turn has encouraged the proliferation of independent regional special districts with substantial regional service responsibilities. Over half of the countywide or multicounty special districts in the 72 largest metropolitan areas in 1970 were responsible for more than 40 percent of metropolitan expenditures in their respective functions. In 15 cases, they were responsible for 80 percent or more of their respective functional outlays. Health and hospital, sewerage, and utility districts were most prominent in this regard (see Table 3). These instrumentalities generally perform only one service, and their organizational and fiscal independence often prompts them to perform their assignments with little or no regard for the interrelated responsibilities of other local or areawide bodies. While a few States have authorized regional multiservice corporations and a few others have brought these special districts under the central control of a regional council, these independent entities still are the main regional service devices in most substate areas.

Another conspicuous structural problem affecting functional assignment has been the failure of most major governmental reorganizations. Most proposals have been defeated in popular referenda; those that have succeeded continue to face the problem of providing services on both areawide and local bases. Miami-Dade County and Indianapolis-Marion

County, for example, have experienced pressures to reinvigorate local administrative or governmental units so that the upper-tier or areawide government can better attend to pressing regional service needs.

Certain procedural problems adversely affect functional assignments as well. Intergovernmental service agreements often occur in relatively noncontroversial functions or in the supportive aspects of a service (see Table 4). Some governments, especially smaller rural municipalities and some larger central cities, sometimes are not involved in interlocal agreements even though they could benefit by them. On the other hand, functional transfers and consolidations, often a more durable way of changing functional assignments, sometimes result in the unnecessary centralization of local services or the decentralization of areawide ones.

The existing ad hoc approach to functional assignment, then, reflects certain basic structural and procedural features of most State-local governmental systems. In only a few instances have procedures been instituted to handle functional assignments in a systematic and balanced fashion.

Tensions in the Assignment System

The present, piecemeal system of functional assignment tends to produce continuing pressures for the centralization or decentralization of various services.

These strains take four main forms. First, there is concern about service efficiency. Present assignment patterns often result in service inefficiencies when local or areawide governments perform services which could be less expensively provided by another level or unit of government for reasons of economies of scale. Inefficiencies also can result when jurisdictions do not use interlocal contracts or pricing policies to provide services at the lowest possible cost.

A second pressure stems from service inequities. These occur when a functional assignment imposes uncompensated costs or benefits on another jurisdiction. For example, local governments often engage in exclusionary or fiscal zoning practices which create severe fiscal disparities and patterns of racial and economic segregation. Such practices burden some jurisdictions far more than others. Other inequities result when local governments have to perform redistributive services requiring regional or State fiscal equalization.

A third source of servicing stress is ineffective delivery. This occurs when functions are assigned to jurisdictions that do not have the management expertise, breadth of functional responsibilities, geographic scale, or legal authority to perform the service adequately. Thus, non-home-rule counties assume fewer urban and regional functions than home-rule jurisdictions. Unifunctional special districts generally do not coordinate their services with related local governmental units. Very large or very small governments often do not have a well-defined management expertise for considering different program strategies that might best meet their assigned functional responsibilities.

Finally, present assignments frequently neglect the need for citizen access, control, and participation in the delivery of services. Regional special districts are often State-imposed and have faulty working relationships with general local governments. Some federally encouraged substate districts have extensive systems of citizen participation while others

TABLE 1

Dominant Direct Service Provider* by Type of Government and Selected Function, the Fifty States: 1967

Function	Type of Dominant Service Provider						Total Number of States
	State	County	Munici-pality Township	School District	Special District	More than One Main Provider	
Education	1	3	4	40	0	2	50
Highways	46	0	0	0	0	4	50
Public Welfare	35	11	3	0	0	1	50
Hospitals	28	10	2	0	4	6	50
Health	29	2	4	0	0	15	50
Police	1	0	47	0	0	2	50
Fire	0	0	50	0	0	0	50
Sewage	0	0	41	0	3	6	50
Refuse Collection	0	0	49	0	0	1	50
Parks & Recreation	0	2	44	0	2	2	50
Natural Resources	48	1	0	0	0	1	50
Housing/Renewal	2	0	22	0	22	4	50
Airports	5	8	29	0	6	2	50
Water Transport**	12	0	21	0	11	1	45
Parking	0	0	48	0	1	1	50
Corrections	46	1	1	0	0	2	50
Libraries	1	14	30	0	3	2	50
General Control	5	28	6	0	0	11	50
General Public Buildings	3	29	16	0	0	12	50
Water Supply	0	0	45	0	2	3	50

*A dominant service provider is one that accounts for more than 55 percent of the direct general expenditure in a particular function.

**Only 45 State-local systems exhibit this function; consequently, dominant producers total only 45 whereas in all other functions they total 50 for the 50 State-local systems under consideration.

Source: Derived from U.S. Bureau of the Census, *Compendium of Government Finances Volume 5, 1967 Census of Governments* (Washington: U.S. Government Printing Office, 1969), Tables 46, 48.

TABLE 2

Performance of Selected Urban, Regional, and Traditional Services by Selected Types of Metropolitan Counties: 1971

	Type of Metropolitan County			
	Home-Rule	Unicounty	Central County	Suburban Fringe
		Percent Performing Function		
Function	(N=28)	(N=59)	(N=76)	(N=31)
URBAN				
Fire	43%	27%	22%	19%
Refuse Collection	39	10	13	23
Libraries	68	34	37	42
Parks & Recreation	75	32	34	45
Hospitals	64	18	22	45
Urban Renewal	25	5	9	6
REGIONAL				
Mass Transit	14	0	3	0
Airports	36	17	17	35
Junior Colleges	39	3	17	13
Solid Waste Disposal	61	22	31	29
Sewage Disposal	61	12	26	19
Air Pollution	57	21	22	13
Water Pollution	57	16	25	6
Water Supply	39	4	17	22
TRADITIONAL				
Police	79	73	63	64
Coroner's Office	82	76	78	71
Jails	86	80	92	64
Probation/Parole	71	75	71	68
General Assistance	61	68	75	64
Medical Assistance	54	61	64	58
Roads & Highways	79	58	72	61
Public Health	86	70	70	68
Mental Health	79	73	70	48
Tax Assessment/Coll.	75	64	77	61
Courts	79	77	66	61
Prosecution	79	61	74	58
Public Defender	54	61	71	42

Source: ACIR tabulation of questionnaires from the 1971 ACIR-ICMA-NACO county survey.

TABLE 3

Regional Special District Share of Selected Metropolitan Functional Expenditures in the 72 Largest SMSA's: 1970

Function	Percent of Metropolitan Functional Expenditure					Total # of Cases
	0–20	21–40	41–60	61–80	81–100	
Education	1	0	0	0	0	1
Highways	1	1	0	0	1	3
Health/Hospital	2	1	1	4	0	8
Sewerage	5	1	7	1	1	15
Parks/Recreation	8	1	0	0	0	9
Natural Resources	4	1	2	0	1	8
Housing/Urban Renewal	1	4	0	2	1	8
Water Transport	1	0	1	1	4	7
Library	0	0	0	0	2	2
Utility	5	3	4	4	1	17
TOTAL	28	12	15	12	11	78
% of Distribution	36	15	19	15	15	100

Source—ACIR Tabulation.

do not. Regional councils are not governed usually on a one-man, one-vote basis. A–95 agencies generally do not refer their grant notifications to interested non-governmental agencies, and both cities and counties have been pressured by various types of Federally encouraged districts to increase their citizen participation efforts.

What are the ramifications of these imbalances in the present assignment system? Inefficient assignments raise the cost and reduce the quality and scope of a service. Inequitable assignments result in an unfair distribution of service costs and benefits. Ineffective assignments yield illogical and uncoordinated patterns of service delivery; unaccountable assignments produce popular political alienation with all levels of government. All these costs arise, to a greater or lesser degree, from the present, ad hoc approach to distributing service responsibilities. A more ordered and reasoned assignment policy could certainly avoid many of these costs.

Summary

The present functional assignment system produces little consistency as to the servicing roles of State, area-wide, or local governments. The structural and procedural deficiencies of most State-local governmental systems prevent a wholesale sorting out of functional responsibilities among different levels and units of government. This, in turn, has created an assignment system that is continuously and precipitously centralizing or decentralizing functions without any real thought being given to the appropriate servicing roles of various governmental levels and units. Consequently, most services are not delivered in as efficient, effective, equitable, and accountable fashion as they might be if there were a systematic functional assignment policy.

TABLE 4

Function or Activity Ranked by Prevalence of Interlocal Cooperation: 1972

Percent of Service Agreements	Activities (Supportive)				Functions		
	Data	Legal	Fiscal	Personnel	Areawide	Shared	Local
301+	Crime Lab			Police Training	Sewage Disposal Solid Waste	Jails Libraries	Street Lighting Refuse Collection Animal Control
201–300	Police Comm. Planning Engineering Service Crime Identification	Legal Services	Assessing		Water Supply Electric Supply Civil Defense	Ambulance Public Health	Schools Fire Services
101–200	Fire Comm.		Tax Collection Utility Billing Payroll	Fire Training	Air Pollution Abatement Hospitals Mosquito Control Flood Control Water Pollution Abatement Nursing Services Soil Conservation	Police Mental Health Housing Juvenile Delinq. Welfare Probation	Street Construction Water Dist. Parks Mapping Plumbing Sewer Lines Alcohol Rehab. Traffic Control
0–100	Civil Defense Comm. Microfilm Services Public Relations Record Maintenance	Licensing	Treasury	Civil Defense Training Personnel Services Transportation Management Services	Service Trans. Museums Irrigation	Zoning Urban Renewal Noise Pollution General Develop. Work Release	Cemeteries School Guards Police Patrol Building Inspection Snow Removal

Source—ACIR Tabulation from 1972 ACIR/ICMA survey on intergovernmental service agreements (2,248 municipalities over 5,000 population were surveyed).

A NORMATIVE APPROACH TO FUNCTIONAL ASSIGNMENT

Four Assignment Factors

This report probes four basic characteristics that an ideal assignment system should reflect: economic efficiency, fiscal equity, political accountability, and administrative effectiveness. Taken together these characteristics suggest that functional assignments should be made to jurisdictions that can (1) supply a service at the lowest possible cost; (2) finance a function with the greatest possible fiscal equalization; (3) provide a service with adequate popular political control; and (4) administer a function in an authoritative, technically proficient, and cooperative fashion. In more specific terms, these factors include:

1. *Economic Efficiency*: Functions should be assigned to jurisdictions
   (a) that are large enough to realize economies of scale and small enough not to incur diseconomies of scale [economies of scale]
   (b) that are willing to provide alternative service offerings to their citizens and specific services within a price range and level of effectiveness acceptable to local citizenry; [service competition] and
   (c) that adopt pricing policies for their functions whenever possible. [public pricing]

2. *Fiscal Equity*: Appropriate functions should be assigned to jurisdictions
   (a) that are large enough to encompass the cost and benefits of a function or that are willing to compensate other jurisdictions for the service costs imposed or for benefits received by them; [economic externalities] and
   (b) that have adequate fiscal capacity to finance their public service responsibilities and that are willing to implement measures that insure interpersonal and inter-jurisdictional fiscal equity in the performance of a function. [fiscal equalization]

3. *Political Accountability*: Functions should be assigned to jurisdictions
   (a) that are controllable by, accessible to, and accountable to their residents in the performance of their public service responsibilities; [access and control] and
   (b) that maximize the conditions and opportunities for active and productive citizen participation in the performance of a function. [citizen participation]

4. *Administrative Effectiveness*: Functions should be assigned to jurisdictions
   (a) that are responsible for a wide variety of functions and that can balance competing functional interests; [general-purpose character]
   (b) that encompass a geographic area adequate for effective performance of a function; [geographic adequacy]
   (c) that explicitly determine the goals of and means of discharging public service responsibilities and that periodically reassess program goals in light of performance standards; [management capability]
   (d) that are willing to pursue intergovernmental policies for promoting inter-local

functional cooperation and reducing inter-local functional conflict; [intergovernmental flexibility] and

(e) that have adequate legal authority to perform a function and rely on it in administering the function. [legal adequacy]

Criteria and Service Assignment

How do these four criteria and their subcomponents actually relate to service assignment? In general, they focus on either the level or type of government to which a function is to be assigned. Thus, some of the criteria argue for regional or State provision of a function and others for local provision of a service. Still other criteria argue for certain types of governmental units to perform the service at a regional or local level. Figure 1 indicates the relationship of the various criteria subcomponents to the assignment question.

Criteria subcomponents that generally call for regional or State assumption of a function include economies of scale, fiscal equalization, economic externalities, and geographic adequacy. These suggest that a jurisdiction should be large enough to provide services at a relatively low unit cost, have enough resources to provide redistributive services, or have enough area to administer services which should be uniformly delivered over a wide area (i.e., transportation and water resources management) to avoid imposing costs on neighboring jurisdictions.

Criteria subcomponents that favor local provision of a function are service competition, citizen access and control, and citizen participation. These factors suggest that services which depend on continuous political control or popular participation for satisfactory performance should be assigned locally. Moreover, where public choice about service quantity or quality is especially significant, local administration can lead to wider service choices and better evaluation of service delivery.

Other criteria subcomponents underscore the type of governmental unit that should be assigned a function. Public pricing and management capability argue for a technically proficient jurisdiction. Legal adequacy and general purpose character suggest that an authoritative jurisdiction (both in its powers and the number of functions that it has responsibility for) should administer a regional or local service. Finally, intergovernmental flexibility means that cooperative units of government are best suited to administer areawide or local functions, especially those having inter-level or inter-local ramifications.

In practice, these criteria argue for the assignment of certain activities regionally and others locally (see Table 5). But since many functions have subcomponents that are of an areawide or local nature, they frequently argue for local or areawide assignment of these subcomponents (see Table 6). In short, functions and parts of functions can be assigned to local, areawide, and State units of government on the basis of these ideal assignment criteria.

At the same time, however, application of these assignment criteria is not an easy task. These standards are not always mutually compatible or easily ordered. Many functions (i.e., social services and land-use control) have differing elements of political accountability and fiscal equity, for example. The first criterion would argue for local assignment of the service; the latter for regional or State assignment. It is not always completely clear, then, which level of government should be accorded the responsibility for the service. Much depends, then, on how important each criteria is in a particular service.

FIGURE 1

Assignment Criteria and Their Relationship to the Level and Form of Government
to Which a Function Should Be Assigned

Criteria Subcomponent	Level of Government To Which Function Is Assigned	Type of Government
ECONOMIC EFFICIENCY—Economies of Scale	Areawide or State	
FISCAL EQUITY—Economic Externalities	Areawide or State	
FISCAL EQUITY—Fiscal Equalization	Areawide or State	
ADMINISTRATIVE EFFECTIVENESS—Geographic Adequacy	Areawide or State	
POLITICAL ACCOUNTABILITY—Access and Control	Local	
POLITICAL ACCOUNTABILITY—Citizen Participation	Local	
ECONOMIC EFFICIENCY—Service Competition	Local	
ECONOMIC EFFICIENCY—Public Pricing	Local	
ADMINISTRATIVE EFFECTIVENESS—Management Capability		Technically Proficient
ADMINISTRATIVE EFFECTIVENESS—Legal Adequacy		Technically Proficient
ADMINISTRATIVE EFFECTIVENESS—General Purpose Character		Authoritative
ADMINISTRATIVE EFFECTIVENESS—Intergovernmental Flexibility		Authoritative / Cooperative

Alternative Assignment Systems

While the different assignment criteria indicate, in general terms, what level and type of government should perform a particular function, what governmental systems can accommodate these assignment criteria? Chapters V and VI of this report indicate three alternative governmental systems that theoretically can balance these criteria and apportion service responsibilities among State, areawide, and local jurisdictions.

The first governmental system for assigning services is a polycentric one. This has both local and regional jurisdictions, but the regional units have no formally delegated functional responsibilities. Rather they assume functions that are transferred to them by underlying local governments or that they perform for constituent units by contract. Consequently, the polycentric method for assigning services involves the market method of allocating functions to different levels of government. Functions—local, areawide, and State—are provided only by the governments that choose or are sought out to perform them.

A second method of distributing service responsibilities involves essentially a two-tier governmental set-up. This system apportions legal responsibilities between the general purpose governments at the two levels. The upper or areawide tier performs generally those functions that involve regulation or redistribution or economies of scale, mediates interlocal functional conflict, and coordinates local decisions having an areawide impact. Local governments and counties in a multi-county setting perform all those functions not specifically delegated to the higher level of government. The State provides services that neither the areawide or local levels can administer effectively. Moreover, local units of government are sometimes but not always represented in the upper-tier units.

A third approach places all regional and local functions under a single consolidated unit of government. In this fashion, a unified government directly performs area-wide services throughout its jurisdiction and administers local services through decentralized local service districts. The State, again, performs those functions that the consolidated unit cannot manageably administer.

Each of these three governmental arrangements for administering local and areawide services exists in one form or the other in one or more metropolitan area, with the first being the most prevalent. All three obviously reflect different political preference for the assignment of local and areawide services. And all three models, to a greater or lesser degree, meet some of the ideal assignment criteria already enumerated.

Summary

Functional assignment criteria offer a normative guide to more effective allocation of service responsibilities among State, areawide, and local jurisdictions. Moreover, they are reflected partially in the polycentric, two-tier, and consolidated governmental arrangements that exist in substate areas. Considerations of economic efficiency, fiscal equity, political accountability, and administrative effectiveness continue also to be prominent issues in various functional assignment debates. Simultaneously, the urgency of the service allocation issue is highlighted by numerous pressures: local fiscal disparities; nationally sponsored areawide programs in environmental control, transportation, and economic development; the emergence of stronger State bureaucracies; and continued emphasis on human resource service decentralization, especially in larger cities. A systematic assignment policy and process involving Federal, State, and local government is clearly needed. Such a policy would permit a more reasoned and manageable apportionment of service responsibilities among State, areawide and local governments.

TABLE 5

Activities Which Can and Cannot Be Handled Locally

Functions	10,000 Population	Local Activities Which Can Be Handled by a Locality of 25,000 or More	Area-wide Activities Which Cannot Be Handled Locally
Police	Patrol Routine investigation Traffic control	Same	Crime laboratory Special investigation Training Communications
Fire	Fire company (minimal)	Fire companies (better)	Training Communications Special investigation
Streets and Highways	Local streets, sidewalks, alleys: Repairs, cleaning, snow removal, lighting, trees	Same	Expressways Major arteries
Transportation			Mass transit Airport Port Terminals
Refuse	Collection	Same	Disposal
Water and Sewer	Local mains	Same	Treatment plants Trunk lines
Parks and Recreation	Local parks Playgrounds Recreation centers Tot-lots Swimming pool (25 m.)	Same plus Community center Skating rink Swimming pool (50 m.)	Large parks, zoo Museum Concert hall Stadium Golf courses
Libraries	Branch (small)	Branch (larger)	Central reference
Education	Elementary	Elementary Secondary	Community colleges Vocational schools
Welfare	Social services	Same	Assistance payments
Health		Public health services Health center	Hospital
Environmental Protection		Environmental sanitation	Air pollution control
Land Use and Development	Local planning Zoning Urban renewal	Same plus Housing and building code enforcement	Broad planning Building and housing standards
Housing	Public housing management	Public housing management & construction	Housing subsidy allocation

Source—Adapted from Howard Hallman, *Government by Neighborhoods* (Washington, D.C.: Center for Governmental Studies, 1973), p. 24.

TABLE 6

Hypothetical Assignment for Components of Functional Activities

Activity/Component	Areawide	Shared	Local
PLANNING			
Intelligence	x		
Forecasting	x		
Plan Formulation		x	
Operations Review		x	
Liaison/Coordination	x		
FINANCING			
Revenue Raising		x	
Revenue Distribution	x		
Fiscal Control		x	
Budgeting			x
STAFFING			
Selection			x
Recruitment		x	
Training	x		
Appointment/Removal			x
ADMINISTRATION			
Supervision	x		
Management Analysis		x	
Productivity Analysis		x	
Technical Assistance	x		
STANDARD SETTING			
Formulation of Rules		x	
Rule Interpretation	x		
Rule Adjudication	x		
Rule Evaluation		x	
Rule Amendment		x	
Rule Enforcement			x
ENFORCEMENT			
Investigation	x		
Inspection	x		
Licensing	x		
Certification	x		
SERVICE DELIVERY			
Operations			x
Construction			x
INFORMATION			
Record Keeping		x	
Communication		x	
Data Collection		x	
Reporting			x
Public Relations			x
EVALUATION			
Fact-Finding	x		
Public Hearings		x	
Testing/Analysis	x		
Consultation		x	

Source—ACIR Tabulation.

Metropolitan Reform: Propositions Derived from Two Traditions[1]

ELINOR OSTROM

Cries for reform and change are frequently heard concerning problems occurring in American urban areas. While the existence of grave problems tells us that reform is needed, it does not tell us what kind of reform will lead to amelioration of problems. Reforms can make things worse as well as making them better.[2] One purpose of this essay is to attempt to isolate the theoretical structure implicit in the traditional metropolitan reform movement so that empirical research can be organized to examine the warrantability of the propositions contained therein. A second purpose of the essay is to pose an alternative theoretical structure derived from the work of political economists.

The elucidation of alternative theoretical structures may help guide future research efforts toward ascertaining which of these theoretical structures (or possibly others) provides a better explanation for the relationship among variables such as the size of governmental units and their multiplicity in a metropolitan area, and variables such as output, efficiency, equal distribution of costs, responsibility of public officials, and citizen participation. With a warrantable explanation for changes in these variables, reforms can be devised which will produce desired, rather than undesired, outcomes.[3] In addition to the above, this essay will also (1) discuss the need for developing agreed-upon definitions of terms and their operationalizations, and (2) present findings from a few studies which challenge the empirical warrantability of some of the propositions elucidated in the first section.

THE TRADITIONAL CONCEPTION OF "THE" URBAN PROBLEM

For more than a half century, most political scientists, urban planners, and many other social scientists writing about urban areas have agreed that *"the"* urban problem is the existence of a large number of independent public jurisdictions within a single metropolitan area. A metropolitan region has been viewed as one large community tied together by many economic and social relationships but artificially divided by imposed governmental units.[4] The basic textbook on American city government during the 1940's and 1950's describes the development of local governments as being woven ". . . piecemeal and without general plan by local groups to meet transient needs; the web of local boundaries spreads unevenly and most chaotically over the land."[5] In a report released in February of 1970, the Committee for Economic Development argued that:

. . . the present arrangement of overlapping local units is not serving the people well. Citizens in metropolitan areas are confronted by a confusing maze of many—possibly a dozen—jurisdictions, each with its own bureaucratic labyrinth. This baffling array of local units had made it difficult for citizens— the disadvantaged particularly—to gain access to public services and to acquire a voice in decision making.[6]

Since the turn of the century, many scholars have participated in a reform movement which has attempted to build a different type of governmental structure in large metropolitan areas. Participants in this tradition have not always agreed on all aspects of their description of and prescriptions for "the" metropolitan problem (i.e. too many governmental units). However, enough consistency in their recommendations for change exists to talk about a single tradition.[7] In their attempts to reform institutional arrangements so as to achieve their objectives, metropolitan reformers also share a relatively consistent, although implicit, underlying theoretical structure. In a discussion of the efforts of one team of social scientists to prepare a reform proposal for the greater St. Louis area, Scott Greer summarizes the working hypotheses of that group. In his words:

It was . . . hypothesized that this congery of heterogeneous and overlapping governmental units would produce these results:
1) great variation in output, or service levels, among the different units,
2) great variations in the efficiency, or cost benefit ratio, among the units,
3) a generally low level of some services throughout the area, due to the deleterious effects of poor services in one governmental unit upon the services in other, interdependent units. . . .
Finally, it was hypothesized that size of governmental units would have no relationship to the vitality of the local political process. . . .[8]

Greer indicates that the propositions sketched in above "were not initially stated as hypotheses; *their validity was assumed, for they were part of the over-all ideology of the movement to save the cities.*"[9]

Based upon similar working hypotheses, proponents of the metropolitan reform tradition have consistently recommended basic institutional changes in metropolitan areas. Most metropolitan reformers have recommended that:

. . . as far as possible in each major urban area *there should be only one local government.* . . .
A second point upon which agreement is almost complete is that *the voters should elect only the important, policy-making officers* and that these should be few in number. . . .
Most reformers are also anxious to see *the complete abolition* of the separation of powers in local government. . . .
At the same time, however, . . . the functions of legislation and control on

the one hand are so distinct from that of administration . . . that *those who do the work of administration should* be a separate group of men and women, especially trained and adequately compensated for their work. . . .

Furthermore, the *administration should be organized as a single integrated system* upon the hierarchial principle, tapering upward and culminating in a single chief executive officer. . . .[10]

Another theme of considerable importance in the work of metropolitan reformers is a concern for a more equal distribution of the costs of urban services throughout a metropolitan area. Jurisdictional lines are considered to be arbitrary boundaries which protect rich suburban residents from the necessity of paying for the costs of services provided by the center city. Since residents of suburban communities surrounding a center city live in the metropolitan area, it is assumed that services provided by the center city spill over and benefit all who live within the area. Consequently, reformers have argued that all residents in the metropolitan area should bear an equal share of these costs.[11]

Thousands of books, reports, and articles have been written in this tradition. Specific proposals for metropolitan "reform" by consolidation or similar means have been placed before the voters in city after city.[12] When presented to the residents of an area, such proposals have usually met a rousing defeat at the polls.[13] The number of local units in metropolitan areas has, in fact, been increasing. "Metropolitan areas are leading the rest of the country in municipal incorporations and establishment of special districts, and lagging behind in the reduction of school districts."[14]

The lack of success at the polls has not reduced the reformers' zeal. Rather, votes have been blamed for their inconsistency[15] or for being ". . . influenced more by arguments promising to keep the tax rate low and the government close to the people and free of corruption than by arguments stressing the correction of service inadequacies and the economical and efficient provisions of services."[16]

Another possible explanation for these failures is that the metropolitan reform proposals have been based upon theoretical presumptions which are not warranted in light of experience. The theory underlying the major reform proposals is a collection of implicit presuppositions which are largely unsupported by specific research designed to ascertain their warrantability. The basic working hypotheses of the metropolitan reform proposals have rarely been clearly formulated and subjected to empirical research by those who recommend drastic change.[17] The changes recommended are presumed to lead to the postulated consequences without need for empirical investigation of the relationships involved. Without empirical examination of the postulated relationships implicit in the reform tradition, it is possible that different consequences than those predicted flow from adopting the recommendations made by metropolitan reform advocates. If this is the case, voters may have had a better intuitive understanding of the relationship among structural variables in metropolitan areas than the social scientists who have consistently made, and are still making, the same recommendations. Empirical research investigating the warrantability of the postulated relationships may be long overdue.

PROPOSITIONS DERIVED FROM THE METROPOLITAN REFORM TRADITION

A first step in the process of ascertaining the warrantability of the theoretical structure implicit in the metropolitan reform movement is to make the structure explicit and organize it in propositional form. An attempt to do this is presented in this section. A set of seven propositions are stated which have been derived from the literature cited above. This is not a complete listing of all the logical statements which could be derived from the reform tradition. Rather, it represents a beginning effort directed at isolating the most general theoretical structure implicit in the work of the metropolitan reformers. Further effort will be needed to extend these propositions in order to complete a description of the theoretical structure of the metropolitan reform tradition.

P_1 Increasing the size of urban governmental units will be associated with higher output per capita, more efficient provision of services, more equal distribution of costs to beneficiaries, increased responsibility of local officials and increased participation by citizens.[18]

P_2 Increasing the size of urban governmental units will be associated with more professionalization of the public service and a greater reliance upon hierarchy as an organizing principle.

P_3 Reducing the number of public agencies within a metropolitan area will be associated with more output per capita, more efficient provision of services, more equal distribution of costs to beneficiaries, more responsibility of local officials and more participation by citizens.

P_4 Reducing the number of public agencies within a metropolitan area will increase the reliance upon hierarchy as an organizing principle and will decrease the number of locally elected public officials within the metropolitan area.

P_5 Increasing the professionalization of public employees will be associated with a higher level of output per capita, more efficient provision of services and increased responsibility of local officials.

P_6 Increasing the reliance upon hierarchy as an organizing principle within a metropolitan area will be associated with higher output per capita, more efficient provision of services, more equal distribution of costs to beneficiaries, and increased responsibility of local officials.

P_7 Increasing the number of locally elected officials within a metropolitan area will be associated with less responsibility on the part of public officials and less participation by citizens.

The theoretical structure outlined above contains two independent variables: size of urban governmental units and multiplicity of agencies within a metropolitan area. Three intervening variables are also posited: professionalization, reliance upon hierarchy and number of elected officials. Five dependent variables are included in the system: output per capita, efficient provision of services, equal distribution of costs to beneficiaries, responsibility of local officials and participation by citizens. The posited relationships among this set of variables are represented schematically in Figure 1.

AN ALTERNATIVE CONCEPTION OF URBAN PROBLEMS

While political scientists, urban planners, and other social scientists associated with the traditional reform movement have repeatedly reaffirmed propositions similar to the set specified above, a group of political economists have analyzed urban problems from a different perspective. Little communication has occurred between these two groups. Political economists have studied urban problems rather than *the* urban problem. The conclusions of political economists differ radically from the traditional "reform" oriented scholars. The extent of the difference in approach can be seen from the following conclusion reached by Stigler:

> If we give each governmental activity *to the smallest governmental unit* which can efficiently perform it, there will be a vast resurgence and revitalization of local government in America. A vast reservoir of ability and imagination can be found in the increasing leisure time of the population, and both public functions and private citizens would benefit from the increased participation of citizens in political life. An eminent and powerful structure of local government is a basic ingredient of a society which seeks to give to the individual the fullest possible freedom and responsibility.[19]

FIGURE 1

Posited Relations among Variables in the Metropolitan Reform Tradition

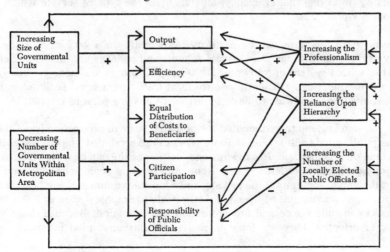

How can conclusions be so different? They differ, in part, because working assumptions of the two schools of thought vary significantly.[20] Most political economists begin with an assumption that the individual is the basic unit of analysis. Next, they assume that any individual, if given full information, will make decisions so as to maximize his own welfare. Third, they assume that some goods and services are most efficiently produced and distributed through the workings of private market arrangements. Fourth, they assume that some other goods and services, once provided, generate extensive spillovers beyond those individuals who are directly involved in a transaction. Sometimes these spillovers are of benefit to others affected and are referred to as external economies; otherwise, spillovers are costly to those affected and are called external diseconomies.[21] Goods which involve either extensive external economies or diseconomies may need to be provided by public agencies of some form. Most urban public goods and services, public health, and education would be included in this group. A fifth assumption is frequently made that the provision of goods involving extensive externalities affects a clearly delineated group or area. Such a group or area ". . . can be as large as the entire population of the earth, or as small as the population of the smallest community."[22]

Analysts of metropolitan problems who have been trained in political economy are quite familiar with the analysis of complex private industries involving many hundreds or thousands of enterprises, large and small, interacting in such a way as to produce and distribute vast quantities of goods in a reasonably efficient way. Consequently, the large number of public enterprises operating in a metropolitan area does not seem unusual. Stigler, for example, has noted that the student of industrial organization is surprised by repeated references to a presumed optimum scale of performance by large units of government. He comments that he is "accustomed to finding that the activity in an industry with a complex technology is usually efficiently conducted by a firm smaller by almost any measure than the government of a town of 25,000."[23] He goes on to ask: "Is there some special characteristic of governmental functions that makes large units necessary to efficiency?" He responds by observing that efficiency depends upon the type of service which a governmental agency produces.

> Some of these functions can be performed efficiently on a very small scale. Many of the most distinguished private schools and colleges are much smaller than the school system of a town of 5,000 people. Others are more varied. A police department can efficiently control local traffic on a small scale; in one sense it must be worldwide to have an efficient "missing persons bureau."[24]

Political economists tend to assume that the optimum scale of production is not the same for all urban public goods and services. Some services are produced "more efficiently on a large scale than on a small scale. In a few instances the opposite can be true, while in others scale of operation is unimportant."[25] It is frequently felt that scale economies are not as prevalent in the public sector as in the private, since most governmental goods and services are "user oriented" and cannot be "rendered efficiently over large distances."[26] Examples of such services include police and fire protection and education. Because these are services and user oriented, they are labor intensive rather than capital intensive. Normal economies of scale accrue when a capital intensive firm can spread the high cost of a capital over a large number of customers. Political economists will usually agree that major economies of scale are likely to occur in the production of the following services: air pollution control, sewage disposal, public transportation, power production and distribution, water supply, public health services, hospitals and public works planning.

In addition to examining the effect of scale economies for a single agency, political economists are also interested in the efficiencies that can result from the exchange and utilization by one enterprise of goods and services produced by other agencies. Stigler has noted that:

> Every enterprise must use goods and services, or produce goods and services, which must be produced or sold on a much wider scale than the enterprise itself can undertake. Even a huge department store is not large enough to make its own delivery trucks, or to print the newspapers in which it advertises. Just as cooperation in these matters is brought about by the price system, so cooperation among governmental units has been developed—and could be carried much further—to avoid the determination and execution of all public functions by the governmental unit which is most efficient in conducting the functions with the largest scale of operation.[27]

The existence of multiple agencies with some overlap may enable some aspects of services to be performed at a small scale while other aspects can be performed at a large scale. If there were no overlap between municipal, county, state and national police agencies, for example, all aspects of police service would have to be performed by one agency alone even though some aspects of police services can be provided efficiently on a small scale while other aspects require a much larger scale for efficient provision.[28]

The recognition that most private enterprises purchase many of the goods and services which they need from other enterprises leads the political economist to consider the *production* (physical rendering) of urban government services separately from the *provision* of such services (i.e., the decision to provide, and possibly the billing and/or other financing).[29] Thus, questions such as scale and efficiency, concerned mainly with production, can be considered separately from questions of the distribution of the costs of such services. In their normative analysis, most political economists will use as a first maxim that those individuals who receive services should pay for them. Whenever the boundaries of political jurisdictions correspond to the group of individuals receiving benefits from their provision, and all costs are borne by the residents, this maxim is followed. Whenever a political jurisdiction is larger than the group receiving benefits, some individuals may pay for benefits which they do not receive. On the other hand, whenever a political jurisdiction is smaller than the group receiving benefits, some individuals may receive benefits and not pay. Either of the last two situations can occur easily in a metropolitan area particularly if restrictions are placed on the number and size of political jurisdictions which may be established within the area. When the most efficient scale of production is a large political unit, then the establishment of a large jurisdiction in the area will have the dual effect of providing goods at least cost and forcing individuals who receive benefits to pay for them.

However, if the most efficient scale of production is small, but there are spill-overs to other jurisdictions, the political economist as policy analyst would recommend that production be undertaken by small units and that larger units of government provide grants-in-aid to cover the marginal cost of the production which benefits the larger units. If the policy concern is primarily that of redistribution, the political economist is apt to recommend that grants-in-aid be provided by larger units of government to smaller units of government without concern to marginal cost.[30] With such a program, one gains a redistribution of resources from a large economic base to help support service levels in poorer areas. Thus, the posited relationships between the size of governmental units and the number of governmental units within an area on the distribution of costs within the area is a far more complex relationship for the political economist than for the metropolitan reformer.

To further understand the differences between these two approaches, it is necessary to examine the political economist's orientation toward competition. In the political economist's view, competition among numerous producers and sellers of goods and services enables the market to be an efficient decision structure for producing and distributing goods not subject to externalities. Consequently, when political economists turn to the analysis of non-market decision structures, they do not assume *a priori* that competition among public agencies is necessarily inefficient.[31] Competition among public agencies within an urban area does *not* take the same form as market competition and would not always be beneficial. The presence of multiple producers within the same geographic region may have an effect on the relationship between citizens and public agencies as well as on the relationship between elected and appointed public officials and the producers of public services. The presence of more than a single producer of urban public goods within a metropolitan area may enable citizens to make more effective choices about the mix of services they prefer to receive than reliance upon voting mechanisms and a single producer. Multiple governments existing within a metropolitan area enable citzens to "vote with their feet."[32] The presence of multiple producers within one metropolitan area may also reduce the cost for citizens of comparing the levels of output provided by different jurisdictions. Public officials who are representing one constituency in a bargaining process with other public officials over cooperative arrangements (such as contracting for services to be performed) may be able to bargain more effectively if alternative public producers are present in the area.[33] However, it is also possible that multiple producers of some urban public goods may nullify each other's actions and lead to a reduction in the net output of urban public goods. The political economist will consider the effect of competition among public agencies as an empirical question. The effect may be positive or negative depending upon the type of urban public good being considered.

To political economists, the market is an efficient decision-making structure for some purposes and grossly inefficient for others. Likewise, hierarchy is considered to be a potentially efficient decision structure for some purposes and inefficient for others. However, political economists are apt to argue that most large bureaucracies are less efficient in solving problems than either smaller bureaucracies or a multiplicity of independent agencies coordinating their efforts through competition or bargaining.[34] Tullock has argued that a significant loss of information and control occurs between those at the bottom of a large hierarchy and those at the top.[35] Schlesinger has posited that "large organizations find it hard to anticipate, to recognize, or to adjust to change."[36] McKean and Anshen have suggested that large centralized public agencies frequently neglect the variety of choices available and may underestimate the degree of uncertainty involved in a problem.[37]

PROPOSITIONS DERIVED FROM THE POLITICAL ECONOMIST'S TRADITION

In an attempt to compare the theoretical structure underlying the work of those associated with the metropolitan reform movement and those associated with the political economy tradition, a group of alternative propositions derived from the work of political economists is presented below. No attempt has been made to present the complete theoretical structure of the political economists. Rather, an attempt has been made to examine posited relationships among the same variables utilized in the propositions derived from the work of the metropolitan reform tradition. This is possible for the two independent variables and the five dependent variables posited above. However, the intervening variables of professionalization and number of locally elected officials are rarely considered in the political economy tradition and have consequently been omitted from the following propositions. A new intervening variable, type of public good or service, has been included in the following propositions.

Alternative P_{1A} Whether increasing the size of urban governmental units will be associated with a higher output per capita, more efficient provision of services, more equal distribution of costs to beneficiaries depends upon the type of public good or service being considered.

Alternative P_{1B} Increasing the size of urban governmental units will be associated with decreased responsibility of local officials and decreased participation by citizens.[38]

Alternative P_2 Increasing the size of urban governmental units will be associated with a greater utilization of hierarchy as an organizing principle.

Alternative P_{3A} Whether reducing the number of public agencies within a metropolitan area will be associated with more output per capita, more efficient provision of service and more equal distribution of costs to beneficiaries depends upon the type of public good or service being considered.

Alternative P_{3B} Reducing the number of public agencies within a metropolitan area will be associated with less responsibility of public officials.

Alternative P_4 Reducing the number of public agencies within a metropolitan area will increase the reliance upon hierarchy as an organizing principle within the metropolitan area.

Alternative P_{6A} Whether increasing the reliance upon hierarchy as an organizing principle within a metropolitan area will be associated with higher output per capita and more efficient provision of services depends upon the type of public good or service being considered.

Alternative P_{6B} Increasing the reliance upon hierarchy as an organizing principle within a metropolitan area will be associated with decreased participation by citizens and decreased responsibility of local officials.

The posited relationships among this set of variables are represented schematically in Figure 2.

THE NEED FOR RESEARCH TO EXAMINE ALTERNATIVE THEORETICAL STRUCTURES

Utilizing one or the other of the theoretical structures outlined above as the foundation for recommending reform of the institutions serving metropolitan areas leads to drastically different types of proposals.[39] Given the different recommendations for reform which would be derived from these two traditions, considerable need exists for research to increase the warrantability of one or the other approach. Until a warrantable explanation has been established, recommendations for reform may produce more harm than good.

FIGURE 2
Posited Relations among Variables in the Political Economy Tradition

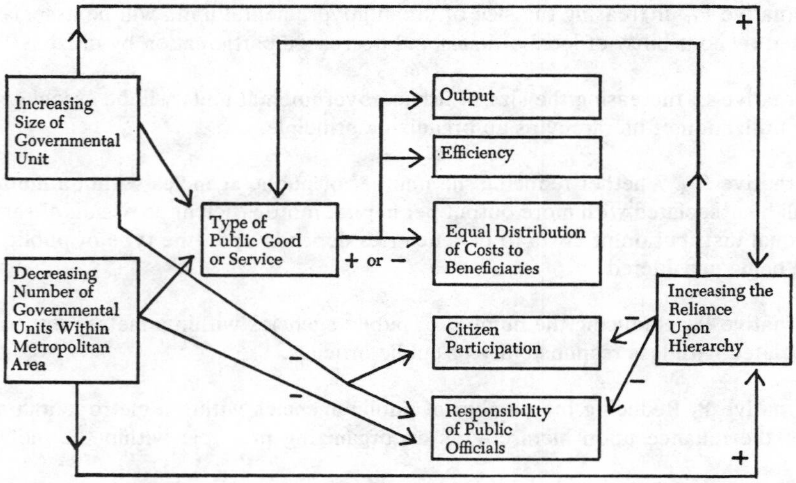

The development of an explanation will also require the careful and consistent definition of all concepts included in the theoretical structures. Frequently, terms used in one tradition do not quite mean the same as when used in another tradition. For example, the term "efficiency" is used as a dependent variable in both of the theoretical structures posed above. However, as used by the metropolitan reformers, the term "efficiency" is usually conceptualized as a ratio of benefits *produced* to the cost of *producing* them.[40] Social costs are rarely included within this definition of efficiency. In analyzing the efficiency of public agencies, political economists are apt to define efficiency so as to include the social costs or the resources required to produce and consume the public good valued in terms of alternative uses foregone.[41] Social costs "may not equal the costs borne by the urban government that provides the service."[42] That portion of the total costs represented in the budget of a government agency may be called "agency costs." But, in addition, other parties, both public and private, may incur costs that are not explicitly charged to the agency in question, nor considered in that agency's efficiency and financial deliberations.[43]

Equally perplexing problems exist with such concepts as "output," "equal distribution of costs," "responsibility of local leaders" and "citizen participation." Not only will scholars define these concepts differently, but the indicators which are utilized for operationalizing variables are frequently open to serious questions of validity. One of the most perplexing problems facing those interested in quantitative, comparative urban research is the development of valid measures of output. Many of the pioneering efforts have relied upon expenditure figures (input or "effort" measures) as indicators of output.[44] However, since the amount expended by a government may not always be transformed on a one-to-one basis into benefits for the citizens of the jurisdiction, we need to be developing other measures of output which indicate the level of output received by citizens.

SOME EVIDENCE RELATED TO ALTERNATIVE PROPOSITIONS

The primary purpose of this essay is to elucidate alternate theoretical structures and not to evaluate the warrantability of either. However, since so many reform proposals are based on the metropolitan reform structure and its *warrantability is assumed to be established* by so many scholars, it is important to briefly present findings from a few studies which raise questions about the warrantability of this theoretical structure.

A number of studies have examined the effect of the size of the governmental agency on its output and are consequently of relevance to P_1 and Alternative P_{1A}. A summary of the results of these studies adapted from the work of Werner Hirsch is presented in Table 1.[45] Hirsch has interpreted the results of these studies in terms of the Average Unit Cost (AUC) of providing a service. The conclusion one would reach based upon the series of studies reviewed by Hirsch is that economies of scale are *not* uniformly presented in the public sector. The output of public agencies does not appear from these studies to be positively associated with the size of an agency. Consistent with this finding is a recent bulletin issued by the A.C.I.R. which concluded that:

Size does not seem to matter in cities of 25,000 to 250,000—neither economies nor diseconomies of scale were of significant number. But in cities over 250,000 population, size *does* make a difference—the law of diminishing returns sets in and there are significant *diseconomies* of scale.[46]

Kirkpatrick and Morgan recently interviewed 87 public officials in 21 cities in the Oklahoma City metropolitan area. Each official was asked to evaluate the services performed by his city. The authors expected city size and growth rate to affect these evaluations since ". . . larger cities are often thought to provide better services. . . ."[47] However, they found no such relationship. These officials were also asked to rank services according to

TABLE 1

Empirical Studies of the Effect of Scale of Production on Average Unit Cost

Name of Investigator Year of Study	Type of Urban Public Service	Type of Data Used[a]	Result[b]
Riew (1966)	Secondary Education	S	AUC is U-shaped with a trough at about 1,700 pupils.
Kiesling (1966)	Primary & Secondary Education	S	AUC is about horizontal.
Hirsch (1959)	Primary & Secondary Education	S	AUC is about horizontal.
Schmandt-Stevens (1960)	Police Protection	S&Q	AUC is about horizontal.
Hirsch (1960)	Police Protection	S&Q	AUC is about horizontal.
Will (1965)	Fire Protection	E	AUC is declining with major economies reached at 300,000 population.
Hirsch (1959)	Fire Protection	S	AUC is U-shaped with trough at about 110,000 population.
Hirsch (1965)	Refuse Collection	S	AUC is about horizontal.
Hirsch (1959)	School Administration	S	AUC is U-shaped with trough at about 44,000 pupils.
Nerlove (1961)	Electricity	S	AUC is declining.
Isard-Coughlin (1957)	Sewage Plants	S	AUC is declining.
Lomax (1951)	Gas	S	AUC is declining.
Johnston (1960)	Electricity	S	AUC is declining.

[a] S = statistical data; Q = questionnaire data; E = engineering data.

[b] AUC = average unit cost.

whether they favored their provision on an area-wide basis. Officials most supported the provision of services including health, libraries, transportation/traffic planning, water, refuse and parks/recreation on an area-wide basis. They least supported area-wide provision of planning/zoning, fire, urban renewal, education and police.[48]

Several research projects have been initiated at Indiana University to examine the empirical warrantability of P_1 and Alternative P_{1A} concerning the effect of size of governmental agencies on their output. In the first study, a most similar systems research design was utilized to compare the output on one large and three small police departments serving very similar neighborhoods within the Indianapolis metropolitan area.[49] Using citizen-reported experiences with the police and their evaluations as measures of output, we concluded from this study that the smaller departments were consistently providing higher levels of output. A study similar to the one undertaken in Indianapolis has examined the comparative output of three small departments and one large department in the Grand Rapids, Michigan metropolitan area with findings consistent with those in Indianapolis.[50] A comparative study of the output of small and poor police forces serving two independent black communities and the Chicago police force serving similar black neighborhoods found the smaller forces performing at least as well as the Chicago force even though the difference in cost of the services were extreme.[51] A major study of police forces in the St. Louis metropolitan area has now been initiated and preliminary data analysis seems to indicate that small to medium sized departments have higher levels of output than the largest police forces serving the area. The findings from a variety of studies, thus, seem to reduce the warrantability of P_1.

Hawkins and Dye have reported findings which relate to P_3 and Alternative P_{3A}. In particular, they were interested in examining "one of the assumptions of the reform literature on metropolitan 'problems' [which] is that fragmentation adversely affects the level of governmental services. Fragmentation is said to increase the costs of municipal services and lower the quality and/or quantity of services provided."[52] Hawkins and Dye computed the simple correlation coefficients for 212 metropolitan areas in 1962 between the number of governments within the areas and per capita expenditures. They found that fragmentation did ". . . *not* appear to increase or decrease government spending for municipal services."[53] They interpret their findings to mean that the ". . . dollar consequences of metropolitan governmental fragmentation have probably been over-emphasized in the reform literature."

Some recent studies by Aiken and Alford and by Clark provide empirical evidence regarding the relation between centralization of authority (or hierarchy as an organizing principle) and the output of public agencies. Both studies are related to Proposition P_6 and Alternative P_{6A}. Aiken and Alford examined three types of policy outputs (public housing, urban renewal and the War on Poverty) for approximately 600 cities with a population of 25,000 or more in 1960.[54] In the course of their study, they tested a number of alternative hypotheses for explaining the variance in levels of output (measured in number of units constructed per 100,000 population since 1933 for public housing and per capita expenditure figures for the other two policy areas). One set of hypotheses related to the concentration of formal political structure. Aiken and Alford's data lead them to conclude that communities with high outputs are not the most centralized and hierarchically organized communities. Rather, communities with exactly the opposite characteristics from those of centralization and integration seem to have the highest levels of output.[55] Consequently, they pose the need for a different theory of community output from that frequently presented. The beginning proposition in such a theory, they argue, should be that "successful performance in such programs is more frequently attained in decentralized, heterogeneous and probably fragmented community systems."[56] They pose a further hypothesis that "the greater the number of centers of power in a community and the (more) pervasive and encompassing are the interfaces in the community system, the higher the probability that a community innovation in a given issue will occur."[57] They reason that the "more choice among units in the system . . . and the greater the state of information about organizational actors, the higher the probability that a coalition sufficient to make a decision will occur."[58] The number of cities included in their study and the methodological rigor of their analysis seriously challenges the warrantability of the relationship between reliance on hierarchy and higher output posited in P_6.

An intensive study of 51 communities recently undertaken by Clark provides further evidence related to P_6.[59] Clark's indicators of output were general municipal expenditure figures and urban renewal expenditure figures in the cities studied. One of the hypotheses examined was "the more centralized the decision-making structure, the higher the levels of output."[60] Clark measured the centralization or decentralization of the decision-making structure by asking a small group of key respondents for the names of those who had been involved in policy making related to four specific policy areas. Cities in which a large number of names were mentioned were coded as having a more decentralized decision-making structure than those in which a few names were mentioned. Using these indicators, Clark's findings were similar to Aiken and Alford's and, thus, ". . . were precisely the opposite of those predicted by this proposition."[61] Since earlier empirical work had provided some support for the proposition relating centralization of decision-making structure to higher output,[62] Clark argued that the type of decision being made may affect whether the proposition is empirically true or not—a working hypothesis which is somewhat related to Alternative P_{6A}. Clark characterized decision areas as "fragile" versus "non-fragile"—a distinction which appears somewhat ambiguous. However, in a recent article Clark introduces the concept of public goods as an intervening variable between the centralization of decision-making structures and the level of outputs.[63] Given these findings P_6 would seem seem to have been seriously challenged.

CONCLUSION

Two theoretical structures have been derived which postulate relationships among independent variables including the size of governmental units and their multiplicity in a metropolitan area and the dependent variables of output, efficiency, responsibility of local officials and citizen participation. Recommendations for reforming the organization of governmental units in metropolitan areas would vary dramatically depending upon which theoretical structure provided the foundations for analysis. Recent empirical evidence challenges several of the propositions derived from the metropolitan reform movement and tends to increase the warrantability of several of the propositions derived from the political economy tradition. However, considerable further research is needed before a firm explanation for the relationships among these variables can be established. It is to be expected that a warrantable explanation may be a far more complex structure than the alternative structures posed in this essay.

NOTES

1. Revision of a paper presented at the annual meeting of the Society for the Study of Social Problems, August, 1971. The author gratefully acknowledges support from the National Science Foundation, Grant No. GS–27383 and from the Center for Studies of Metropolitan Problems of the National Institute of Mental Health, Grant No. 5 ROI MH19911. I am deeply appreciative of the comments and suggestions made by William Baugh, Vincent Ostrom, Nancy Neubert, Roger Parks, Dennis Smith and Gordon Whitaker.

2. See Elinor Ostrom, "Institutional Arrangements and the Measurement of Policy Consequences in Urban Areas," *Urban Affairs Quarterly*, 6 (June, 1971), pp. 447–476. Vincent Ostrom will also raise questions whether reforms have not in some instances done more harm than good in *The Intellectual Crisis in American Public Administration* (University: University of Alabama Press, 1973).

3. The term explanation is being used here to mean ". . . an instrument that generates anticipations about the environment, and makes possible control over events in the environment, by linking changes in the values of two or more variables according to the rules." Eugene J. Meehan, *The Foundations of Political Analysis: Empirical and Normative* (Homewood, Ill.: The Dorsey Press, 1971).

4. See for example Amos H. Hawley and Basil G. Zimmer, *The Metropolitan Community. Its People and Government* (Beverly Hills, Cal.: Sage Publications, 1970), p. 2, and The Institute for Local Self Government, *Special Districts or Special Dynasties? Democracy Diminished* (Berkeley, Cal.: The Institute for Local Self Government, 1970). See also H. Paul Friesema, "The Metropolis and the Maze of Local Government," *Urban Affairs Quarterly*, 2 (Dec., 1966), p. 69.

5. William Anderson and Edward W. Weidner, *American City Government* (Rev. ed.; New York: Henry Holt and Company, 1950), p. 169.

6. Committee for Economic Development, *Reshaping Government in Metropolitan Areas* (New York: Committee for Economic Development, 1970), p. 10. See also the earlier report of the CED entitled *Modernizing Local Government* (New York: Committee for Economic Development, 1966); National Commission on Urban Problems, *Final Report* Part IV (Washington, D.C.: U.S. Government Printing Office, 1968); John C. Bollens and Henry J. Schmandt, *The Metropolis. Its People, Politics and Economic Life* (2nd ed.; New York: Harper & Row, 1970), particularly Chap. 11.

7. An early advocate of this tradition was Richard S. Child. The leading advocate in more recent times has been ". . . the Committee for Economic Development composed of 200 prominent businessmen and educators, which maintains there is a great need for a revolutionary restructuring of what is labeled as anachronistic system of local government," Joseph F. Zimmerman, "Metropolitan Reform in the U.S.: An Overview," *Public Administration Review*, 30 (Sept./Oct., 1970), p. 532.

8. Scott Greer, "Dilemmas of Action Research on the Metropolitan Problem" in Morris Janowitz, ed., *Community Political Systems* (Glencoe, Ill.: The Free Press, 1961), p. 193.

9. *Ibid*. (my emphasis).

10. Anderson and Weidner, *American City Government*, pp. 609–610 (their emphasis). While this summary comes from a textbook written originally in 1925, the basic recommendations of metropolitan reformers have remained amazingly stable. Chapter One of Hawley and Zimmer's book, *The Metropolitan Community*, is entitled "The Metropolitan Problem" and restates most of the recommendations made by Anderson and Weidner. See also Daniel R. Grant, "Trends in Urban Government and Administration." *Journal of Law and Contemporary Problems*, 30 (Winter, 1965), pp. 38–56, and Allen D. Marvel, "Interlocal Relations," *Municipal Finance*, 39 (Feb., 1967), pp. 125–130. Charles R. Adrian in "Public Attitudes and Metropolitan Decision Making," in *Politics in the Metropolis* (Columbus, Ohio: Charles E. Merrill, 1967), pp. 454–469 also discusses the stability of the recommendations and the lack of basic research on the underlying logic of the ideology of metropolitan reform.

Many individuals who participated in the metropolitan reform movement were also strong advocates of a related movement to change institutional arrangements *within* cities. Recommended reforms within a city usually included the adoption of a council-manager form of government (or, in the early days, the commission form of government), nonpartisan elections and at-large elections.

11. See Robert L. Lineberry, "Reforming Metropolitan Governance: Requiem or Reality," *The Georgetown Law Journal*, 58 (March–May, 1970), pp. 676–678.

12. Charles Press, "The Cities Within a Great City: A Decentralist Approach to Centralization," *Centennial Review*, 7 (1963), p. 113.

13. See Advisory Commission on Inter-Governmental Relations, *Factors Affecting Voter Reactions to Governmental Reorganization in Metropolitan Areas* (Washington: Advisory Commission on Inter-Governmental Relations, 1962) for a description of the difficulties encountered in attempts at governmental reorganization in 18 metropolitan areas. Robert L. Lineberry, "Reforming Metropolitan Governance," p. 716, presents a list of major reorganization referendums from 1946–1968.

14. Advisory Commission on Inter-Governmental Relations, *Metropolitan America: Challenge to Federalism* (Washington, D.C.: Advisory Commission on Inter-Governmental Relations, 1966), p. 22.

15. Hawley and Zimmer, *The Metropolitan Community*, p. 140.

16. Zimmerman, "Metropolitan Reform in the U.S.," p. 531.

17. However, a number of studies have focused on propositions relating to the socioeconomic correlates of the adoption of reform proposals *within* particular cities or the correlates of the presence of "reform" institutions within a city and tax and expenditure

levels. Indicators of reformed institutions have usually included the council-manager form of government, at-large elections and non-partisan elections. See Edward C. Banfield and James Q. Wilson, *City Politics* (Cambridge: Harvard University Press, 1963); James Q. Wilson and Edward C. Banfield, "Public-Regardingness as a Value Premise in Voting Behavior," *American Political Science Review*, 58 (Dec., 1964), pp. 876–887; Raymond Wolfinger and John Osgood Field, "Political Ethos and the Structure of City Government," *American Political Science Review*, 60 (June, 1966), pp. 306–326; Lewis A. Froman, Jr., "An Analysis of Public Policies in Cities," *Journal of Politics*, 29 (Feb., 1967), pp. 94–108; Robert L. Lineberry and Edmund P. Fowler, "Reformism and Public Policies in American Cities," *American Political Science Review*, 61 (Sept., 1967), pp. 701–716; Terry N. Clark, "Community Structure, Decision-Making, Budget Expenditures, and Urban Renewal in 51 American Communities," *American Sociological Review*, 33 (Aug., 1968), pp. 576–593; Robert R. Alford and Harry M. Scoble, "Political and Socioeconomic Characteristics of American Cities," *Municipal Yearbook 1965* (International City Managers Association, 1965); see also Timothy M. Hennessy, "Problems in Concept Formation: The Ethos 'Theory' and the Comparative Study of Urban Politics," *Midwest Journal of Political Science*, 14 (Nov., 1970), pp. 537–564.

18. It is, of course, assumed that some limits exist on the postulated relationship stated in this series. Such limits would need to be ascertained empirically if the propositions appeared warrantable within some range. Metropolitan reformers had an implicit concept of a limit for some of their variables: i.e., the *a priori* upper limit on size implied in their work was the size of the metropolitan area involved; the *a priori* limit on multiplicity was a single unit for the entire metropolitan area. Richard Childs argued that the "ideal" number of local officials to be elected in an area was five. Limits of professionalization are hard to conceptualize. The *a prior* limit on reliance on hierarchy would be the development in institutional arrangements within a metropolitan area of a perfect pyramid in shape with *no* overlap between superordinate positions for any subordinate position. See Christopher Alexander, "A City is Not a Tree," *Architectural Forum*, 122 (May, 1965), pp. 58–61 for a good analytical description of hierarchy and semi-lattices as alternative forms of organization.

19. George J. Stigler, "The Tenable Range of Functions of Local Government," in Edmund S. Phelps, ed., *Private Wants and Public Needs* (New York: W. W. Norton, 1962), p. 146.

20. It is hard to know exactly what the underlying assumptions are of the metropolitan reform school of thought. While statements concerning the consequences which are predicted to flow from specified reforms are frequently made, the underlying reasons are infrequently given. If one relies on (A) the work of Richard Childs and the other early reformers who were somewhat more apt to state their underlying logic, and (B) the development of a set of assumptions from which the above propositions can logically be derived, then a possible set of underlying assumptions of the reform tradition would be the following: (1) the metropolitan area as a whole is the basic unit of analysis. Actions are judged in light of how they affect the area as a whole; (2) Individual citizens are presumed to be primarily occupied with their own livelihood and have little information about community problems; (3) Urban residents make wise decisions only when they are presented

with limited and simplified alternatives; (4) Most urban problems are metropolitan-wide in scope; and (5) Individuals can be trained to be superior public servants.

21. For an excellent discussion of the effect of externalities on the provision of urban public or "quasi" public goods see David Davies, "Financing Urban Functions," *Law and Contemporary Problems*, 30 (1965), pp. 127–161. See also Albert Breton, "A Theory of the Demand for Public Goods," *Canadian Journal of Economics and Politics*, 32 (Nov., 1966), pp. 455–467; Otto Davis and Andrew Whinston, "On the Distribution Between Public and Private Goods," *American Economic Review*, 57 (May, 1967), pp. 360–373; James M. Buchanan and W. Craig Stubblebine, "Externality," *Economica*, 29 (Nov., 1962), pp. 371–384.

22. Mancur Olson, "The Optimal Allocation of Jurisdictional Responsibility: The Principle of 'Fiscal Equivalence'," in Vol. 1 of *The Analysis and Evaluation of Public Expenditures: The PPB System* (Washington, D.C.: U.S. Congress, Joint Economic Committee, 1969), pp. 321–331.

23. Stigler, "The Tenable Range of Functions of Local Government," pp. 144–145.

24. *Ibid.*, p. 145.

25. Werner Z. Hirsch, "Local Versus Areawide Urban Government Services," *National Tax Journal*, 17 (Dec., 1964), p. 332.

26. *Ibid.* Scale economies refers to enterprises in which the larger the scale of production, the lower the costs of production. If scale diseconomies exist, the larger the scale of production, the higher the cost of production.

27. Stigler, "The Tenable Range of Functions of Local Government," p. 145.

28. See Vincent Ostrom and Elinor Ostrom, "A Behavioral Approach to the Study of Inter-Governmental Relations," *The Annals of the American Academy of Political and Social Science*, 359 (May, 1965), pp. 137–146.

29. Hirsch, "Local Versus Areawide Urban Government Services," p. 332. See also Dick Netzer, "Federal, State and Local Finance," in Harvey S. Perloff and Lowden Wingo, Jr., eds., *Issues in Urban Economics* (Baltimore: Johns Hopkins Press, 1968), pp. 435–476.

30. Mancur Olson, "The Optimal Allocation of Jurisdictional Responsibility," p. 329.

31. See Vincent Ostrom, Charles M. Tiebout, and Robert Warren, "The Organization of Government in Metropolitan Areas: A Theoretical Inquiry," *American Political Science Review*, 55 (Dec., 1961), pp. 831–842, and Robert Bish, *The Public Economy of Metropolitan Areas* (Chicago: Markham Press, 1971).

32. Charles Tiebout, "A Pure Theory of Local Expenditure," *Journal of Political Economy*, 64 (Oct., 1956), pp. 416–435. See also Bryan Ellickson, "Jurisdiction Fragmentation and Residential Choice," *American Economic Review*, 61 (May, 1971), pp. 334–339; and Wallace E. Oates, "The Effects of Property Taxes and Local Spending on Property Values: An Empirical Study of Tax Capitalization and the Tiebout Hypothesis," *Journal of Political Economy*, 77 (Dec., 1969) pp. 957–971.

33. William A. Miskanen, Jr., *Bureaucracy and Representative Government* (Chicago: Aldine-Atherton, 1971), pp. 155–168.

34. For a review of the basic literature in the political economy tradition and its relevance for the study of administration see Vincent Ostrom and Elinor Ostrom, "Public

Choice: A Different Approach to the Study of Public Administration," *Public Administration Review*, 31 (March/April, 1971), pp. 203–216.

35. Gordon Tullock, *The Politics of Bureaucracy* (Washington, D.C.: Public Affairs Press, 1965); see also Oliver G. Williamson, "Hierarchical Control and Optimum Firm Size," *Journal of Political Economy*, 75 (April, 1967), pp. 123–138 for a more formal statement of the same propositions.

36. James Schlesinger, *Organizational Structures and Planning* (Santa Monica: The Rand Corporation, 1966), p. 19.

37. Roland N. McKean and Melvin Anshen, "Limitations, Risks and Problems," in David Novick, ed., *Program Budgeting* (Boston: Harvard University Press, 1965).

38. A very similar proposition is posited by Robert A. Dahl, "The City in the Future of Democracy," *American Political Science Review*, 61 (Dec., 1967), p. 957.

39. The simultaneous existence of two or more underlying models for analyzing social problems is not unique only to variables associated with the organization of government in metropolitan areas. Alternative theoretical structures underlie many areas of social science. Peter Rossi has noted that the existence of more than one model means ". . . that policy making ought to seek to test out the relative worths of alternative models." "No Good Idea Goes Unpunished: Moynihan's Misunderstanding and the Proper Role of Social Science in Policy Making," *Social Science Quarterly*, 50 (Dec., 1969), p. 477.

40. Herbert Simon, *Administrative Behavior* (2nd ed.; New York; The Free Press, 1957), pp. 172–197.

41. See R. H. Coase, "The Problem of Social Cost," *The Journal of Law and Economics*, 3 (Oct., 1960), pp. 1–44.

42. Hirsch, "The Supply of Urban Public Services," p. 493.

43. *Ibid*.

44. See Raymond Gastil, "Social Indicators and the Quality of Life," *Public Administration Review*, 30 (Nov./Dec., 1970), pp. 596–601.

45. Adapted from Table 2 in Werner A. Hirsch, "The Supply of Urban Public Services," in Harry S. Perloff and Lowden Wingo, Jr., eds., *Issues in Urban Economics* (Baltimore: Johns Hopkins Press, 1968), p. 508.

46. Advisory Commission on Intergovernmental Relations, *Information Bulletin No. 70–8* (Washington, D.C.: Advisory Commission on Intergovernmental Relations, Sept. 16, 1970), p. 2.

47. Samuel A. Kirkpatrick and David R. Morgan, "Policy Support and Orientations Toward Metropolitan Political Integration Among Urban Officials," *Social Science Quarterly*, 52 (Dec., 1971), p. 660.

48. *Ibid.*, p. 669.

49. See Elinor Ostrom and Gordon Whitaker, "Does Local Community Control of Police Make a Difference? Some Preliminary Findings," *Midwest Journal of Political Science* (forthcoming, February, 1973); Elinor Ostrom, William Baugh, Richard Guarasci, Roger Parks and Gordon Whitaker, *Community Organization and the Provision of Police Services* (Beverly Hills, Cal.: Sage Publications, 1973) and Elinor Ostrom, Roger B. Parks and Gordon Whitaker, "Do We Really Want to Consolidate Urban Police Forces? A Reappraisal of Some Old Assertions," *Public Administration Review* (1973).

50. Samir Ishak, *Consumers' Perception of Police Performance. Consolidation vs. Deconcentration: The Case of Grand Rapids, Michigan Metropolitan Area* (Ph.D. Thesis, Indiana University, Bloomington, Indiana, 1972).

51. See Elinor Ostrom and Gordon Whitaker, "Black Citizens and the Police: Some Effects of Community Control," paper presented at the Annual Meeting of the American Political Science Association, Chicago, September 7–11, 1971.

52. Brett W. Hawkins and Thomas R. Dye "Metropolitan 'Fragmentation': A Research Note," in Thomas R. Dye and Brett W. Hawkins, eds., *Politics in the Metropolis* (2nd ed.: Columbus, Ohio: Charles E. Merril, 1971), p. 497.

53. *Ibid.*, p. 499.

54. Michael Aiken and Robert R. Alford, "Comparative Urban Research and Community Decision-Making," *The New Atlantis*, 2 (Winter, 1970), pp. 85–110.

55. *Ibid.*, p. 103.

56. *Ibid.*

57. *Ibid.*, p. 105.

58. *Ibid.* See also Michael Aiken and Robert R. Alford, "Community Structure and Innovation: The Case of Urban Renewal," *American Sociological Review*, 35 (Aug., 1970), pp. 650–665, Laura L. Morlock comes to similar conclusions in her study of 91 cities. See her "Business Interests, Countervailing Groups and the Balance of Influence in 91 Cities," paper presented at the Annual Meeting of the Society for the Study of Social Problems, Denver, August, 1971.

59. Terry N. Clark, "Community Structure, Decision-Making, Budget Expenditure and Urban Renewal in 51 American Communities," in Charles M. Bonjean, Terry N. Clark and Robert L. Lineberry, eds., *Community Politics: A Behavioral Approach* (New York: The Free Press, 1971), pp. 293–314.

60. *Ibid.*, p. 306.

61. *Ibid.* See also Terry N. Clark, "Community Structure and Decision Making," in Terry N. Clark, ed., *Community Structure and Decision Making: Comparative Analysis* (San Francisco: Chandler Publishing Co., 1968).

62. Hawley and Zimmer, *The Metropolitan Community*; Donald Rosenthal and Robert L. Crain, "Structure and Values in Local Political Systems: The Case of Flouridation Decisions," *Journal of Politics*, 28 (Feb., 1966), pp. 169–196.

63. See Terry N. Clark "The Structure of Community Influence," in *People and Politics in Urban Society*, Vol. 6, *Urban Affairs Annual Review* (Beverly Hills, Cal.: Sage Publications, 1972).

PART 5

The Future of Urban Politics

This final part presents three visions of the future of politics in urban areas. While all of the articles engage in some speculation, they also are based on an interpretation of trends which have been identified previously in this book. In the study of cities, as in most other areas of human activity, an understanding of the past is a requisite for predicting the future.

The selection by Robert A. Dahl, "The City in the Future of Democracy," is an inquiry into the prospect of finding the optimal size of local government for future democracies. Historically, the ideal unit for a democracy was the autonomous city-state; but, as territories expanded, this jurisdiction was replaced by the nation-state. Since the nation-state is too large for effective participation and the autonomous city-state is no longer feasible, Dahl contends that the most appropriate unit for democracy in the future is the democratic city. Dahl foresees the city of the future as a jurisdiction nested within a series of political units much like a complex of "Chinese boxes," overlapping one another according to function.

To retain its advantages, however, the democratic city must remain at a size below what Dahl terms the "critical threshold for wide participation." This is not a level at which everyone *does* participate; but it is small enough to allow people to *feel* that they are part of the decision-making process. Dahl believes that the optimum size for a city is between 50,000 and 200,000. According to Dahl, therefore, cities within this range should be the primary and most important unit in democratic society.

The article by Douglas Yates, "The Future of Urban Government," examines the factors which may prevent city governments from fulfilling their critical role in the future. Yates asserts that cities cannot be a significant force in democratic societies if they fail to solve urban problems or to survive as healthy political and financial institutions.

Yates does not agree that the inability of urban governments to perform these tasks is caused by a lack of money—what he calls the "empty cupboard" syndrome. Instead, he observes that the primary failure of city government can be attributed to a "leaky sieve," which prevents expenditures from reaching their intended targets.

Yates concludes that urban governance is weak because the urban political system is fragmented to the point of chaos. His solution to the problem blends strategies of centralization and decentralization. Yates favors the decentralization of ordinary urban services as far as possible by using neighborhood institutions to strengthen relationships

337

between street-level bureaucrats and their clients. On the other hand, the mayor and the central administrators would be responsible for controlling and coordinating service policies and expenses. Finally, Yates argues that city administrators must realize they cannot provide every imaginable service; instead, the city should *limit* its mission to basic municipal services such as police, fire, sanitation, education and a limited number of social services. This strategy, which Yates calls the "new politics of less," embodies a limited approach to the future of urban government.

The study by Norman I. Fainstein and Susan S. Fainstein, "The Future of Community Control," examines two ideological approaches to community control with the intent of forecasting which ideology will prevail in the future. The two ideologies presented are the democratic model and the race-conflict model. The democratic model emphasizes neighborhood government as a means of allowing individuals to participate in the determination of public policy at the grass-roots level. The race-conflict model stresses homogeneous black neighborhoods as vehicles for the mobilization of political power through the identification of a geographic community with a racial group.

From a sample of local leaders in New York City, Fainstein and Fainstein found that most of the leaders—black and white—favor some type of community control, and a majority adhered to the democratic model. However, important racial differences were discovered concerning perceived group interests, probable outcomes, and appropriate actions in concrete situations. Fainstein and Fainstein conclude that situational factors—the socioeconomic class of residents, the racial composition of neighborhoods, social divisions within neighborhoods, and the relative power of contending groups—influence the politics of community control and must be considered in making predictions about future support for this type of decentralization.

The City in the Future of Democracy

ROBERT A. DAHL

I need hardly remind this audience that one of the characteristics of our field is the large number of old and quite elemental questions—elemental but by no means elementary—for which we have no compelling answers. I don't mean that we have no answers to these questions. On the contrary, we often have a rich variety of conflicting answers. But no answer compels acceptance in the same way as a proof of a theorem in mathematics, or a very nice fit between a hypothesis and a satisfactory set of data.

Whether the obstacles that prevent us from achieving tight closure on solutions lie in ourselves—our approaches, methods, and theories—or are inherent in the problems is, paradoxically, one of these persistent and elemental questions for which we have a number of conflicting answers. For whatever it may be worth, my private hunch is that the main obstacles to closure are in the problems themselves—in their extraordinary complexity, the number and variety of variables, dimensions, qualities, and relationships, and in the impediments to observation and data-gathering.

However that may be, a question of this sort often lies dormant for decades or even centuries, not because it has been solved but because it seems irrelevant. For even when no satisfactory theoretical answer exists to a very fundamental question, historical circumstances may allow it to be ignored for long periods of time. Even specialists may refuse to take a question seriously that history seems to have shoved into the attic. What seem like fundamental controversies in one age are very likely to be boring historical curiosities in the next. And conversely it is my impression that a great many of the elemental political questions regarded as settled in one age have a way of surfacing later on.

I

One question of this kind is the problem of the appropriate unit for a democratic political system. Some aspects of this problem are, at least to me, quite puzzling. For example, suppose we accept the guiding principle that the people should rule. We are immediately confronted by the question: what people? I don't mean which particular individuals among a collection of people, but rather: what constitutes an appropriate collection of people for purposes of self-rule? Among the vast number of theoretically possible ways of dividing up the inhabitants of this globe into more or less separate political systems, or, if you will, into

Presidential address delivered at the Annual Meeting of the American Political Science Association, Chicago, September 7, 1967.

"peoples," are there any principles that instruct us as to how one ought to bound some particular collection of people, in order that they may rule themselves? Why *this* collection? Why *these* boundaries?

Of course there are answers, like Schumpeter's statement that "a people" must define itself. But answers like these do not take us very far, or else they take us too far toward the simple doctrine that past might makes present right, and hence present might will make future right. A century ago in the United States a Civil War was fought to compel the Southern States by force of arms and military conquest to remain in the Union, a war, it is now painful to recall, that did not have as its official, ostensible, or ideological purpose the noble end of liberating Negroes and incorporating them into American life but, simply, the maintenance of the Federal Union, if necessary at the cost of the Negro. We can understand this easily enough as pure nationalism. But it is more difficult to see that the proclaimed goals of the North were much more than a particular and somewhat arbitrary definition of American nationhood. Do we then conclude that even if the development of a strong and uniform nationhood might be a condition for large-scale representative democracy, the manner and process by which a "people" defines itself—how it becomes a nation—cannot be judged or determined by any criteria derived from democratic theories or principles?

Just in case you may be about to dismiss all the questions I have just raised as irrelevant or uninteresting, let me be deliberately provocative by asking whether it could be wrong for the American South to have seceded in 1861 but right for South Vietnam to do so today. Alternatively, if military conquest of the Southern Confederacy by the North was justified, is military conquest of the South also justified by North Vietnam? If autonomous self-rule was right for Belgium in 1830 is it wrong for the Flemings today? If the independence of Canada from the United States is right, is the independence of Quebec from Canada also right? And if autonomy is right for France is it also right for the Celtic fringe in Brittany? Or in Britain?

I hope I have asked enough questions to persuade you that the problem of what particular and peculiar collections of people can be said to form a proper unit for self-government is relevant. And not only relevant: It is also perhaps just a bit disturbing, quite possibly even a frightening problem. Yet I do not think we are going to be permitted to ignore it in the near future.

Now that the problem of the appropriate unit for a democratic political system has been opened up, I want to skirt around the questions I have just raised in order to focus in the brief time available to me this evening on certain other aspects of the problem. I propose to ask what *kind* of unit is most appropriate for democratic government. Is there a unit within which the policies steadfastly supported by a majority of citizens should prevail against minorities within that unit and against all persons outside that unit? In fact, can we say that any specific unit is more appropriate for popular rule than any other?

Before I proceed, let me clarify what I mean by the kind of unit. Should democracy be based on a territorial unit, like a town, state, or country, or a non-territorial unit, like a labor union, business firm, or industry? How big should the unit be? Small, like a committee or neighborhood, large like a country or world region, or something in between like a state, province or region? Or should it be any and all of these things?

Like the question of what constitutes a people, the question of what constitutes an appropriate unit is very widely regarded as settled. Yet a little reflection shows that it is actually a wide-open question. The approved school-solution is, of course, the nation-state. Yet the bare possibility that the question has not been so much answered by this solution as ignored is hinted at by the troubling recollection of a simple historical fact: accepting the nation-state as the appropriate unit for democracy required the flat negation of an older conventional view that prevailed for some two thousand years.

II

The prior view, as I surely need not remind this audience, held that the appropriate unit for democracy is the city-state. The vision of democracy in the city-state that prevailed, by and large, from the Greeks to Rousseau is surely one of the most seductive ever generated in the Western world. Its millenial appeal draws its force, I think, from the vision of man living in a genuine human community of man-sized proportions. In this vision, the city-state must be small in area and in population. Its dimensions are to be human, not colossal, the dimensions not of an empire but of a town, so that when the youth becomes the man he knows his town, its inhabitants, its countryside about as well as any of us knows his own college or university. Given these human dimensions, at its best citizenship would be close to friendship, close even to a kind of extended family, where human relations are intense rather than bland, and where the eternal human quest for community and solidarity can be wholly satisfied within the visible and comprehensible limits of the *polis*. If the city-state is democratic—and it is this particular vision I have in mind—it would be small enough to insure extensive opportunities for direct participation by all free (male) citizens in the management of the community; and in the best of circumstances policies and decisions would reflect wide discussion and a pervasive consensus. Above all, the city-state would be autonomous, in the sense that no one who is a not a citizen of that community would possess any legitimate right or power to interfere in the management of the affairs of the city.

I cannot think of any better description of this vision than Kitto's lovely account of an imaginary conversation between an Ancient Greek and a present-day member of the Athenaeum Club in London:

The member regrets the lack of political sense shown by the Greeks. The Greek replies, "How many clubs are there in London?" The member, at a guess, says about five hundred. The Greek then says, "Now if all these combined, what splendid premises they would build. They could have a clubhouse as big as Hyde Park." "But," says the member, "that would no longer be a club." "Precisely," says the Greek, "and a polis as big as yours is no longer a polis."[1]

One cannot help wondering how much the geography of Greece helped to stimulate this vision, for that land of mountains, valleys, islands and the sea provided magnificent natural boundaries for each community and such a limited supply of arable land for each valley and island that it is only the barest poetic license to say that nature herself suggested the small, autonomous city state—and with this hint from nature a people to whom Prometheus himself had given the first elements of civilization were bound to elaborate among themselves the ideal form of the harsher and very often uglier reality they knew so intimately.

If the deficiencies of the vision seem obvious to the modern man who prefers the grandeur of the great nations and the glories of great metropolises like New York, London, Tokyo and Calcutta, it is worth recalling that the Greeks, too, understood that a price had to be paid for the small, autonomous city-state. If the city were to maintain its autonomy, and particularly if it were to be truly self-sufficient the price included a frugal and austere standard of daily life, pervasive violence and anarchy in inter-city relationships, and the need to defend one's city against all comers, including the giants. The Athenians, as we know proved unwilling to accept the first and developed an empire; they suffered horribly from the second; and in the end they could not pay the last.

Nonetheless, two thousand years thereafter the vision of democracy in the city-state dominated thought about democratic-republics. Today, that vision may be seen by a few people as a beguiling form of political life; but as a reality and as an ideal it is in no sense fundamental to modern political culture, it is known mainly to specialists, and almost no one seriously proposes that the modern democratic nations be carved up into genuinely autonomous city-states.

What happened is simply this: In the course of the nineteenth century, the nation-state displaced the city-state as the appropriate unit for democracy. The change, when it came, came swiftly. We can bracket the transition quite nicely by comparing Montesquieu and Rousseau, who still see the city-state as the only proper and indeed viable unit for a democratic republic, with John Stuart Mill, who in *Representative Government* dismisses as irrelevant in a single sentence at the end of a chapter, almost as an afterthought, the two-thousand year-old tradition. By Mill's time the nation-state had triumphed, the city-state was for all practical purposes an historical curiosity, and if democratic ideals were to survive they had to survive, it seemed, in the form of representative governments for nation-states and subordinate—but not autonomous—territorial units within nation-states.

In retrospect, the change seems simpler and more complete than it was. Nonetheless, it is almost as if Americans were to go away for a long week-end and come back on Monday morning believing that the Soviet Union represented free enterprise and bourgeois democracy.

We could zero-in even more precisely on this historic cross-roads by looking at the debate in our own Constitutional Convention of 1787, which was to create a constitution for the first of the giant representative democracies. By 1787, the population of the United States was already greater than that of all of Ancient Greece; in area it was immense, and everyone knew that its territory would go on growing. Yet the traditional view that a republic could flourish only in relatively small communities still persisted even among leading members of the Convention. In his famous argument in *Federalist No. 10*, which he originally advanced in the Convention itself, Madison met this prejudice head-on and in a brilliant exercise turned it upside down by arguing that faction, the inevitable and fatal disease of small republics, could be mitigated only in a republic of large size. Extend the bounds of a republic, the old tradition argued, and you destroy it. Narrow the bounds of a republic, Madison argued in rebuttal, and you make it vulnerable to the dread disease of all small republics—factionalism. Extend the bounds of a republic and you help to generate immunity to that disease.

As we all know, the institutional innovation that made it possible to extend the bounds of a republic was representation: an innovation that democrats like Madison, Jefferson, their French contemporary whose work Jefferson so much admired, Destutt de Tracy, and James Mill all regarded as one of the most profound political inventions of all time.

When the years of the American republic grew into decades, its mere existence stood as living proof that a democratic republic need not be as small as the city; thanks to representation it might indeed be gigantic. In the contest for supremacy in Europe the nation-state had long since come to prevail over the city-state; and as democratic ideas spread, they were focussed not on the obsolete and by now largely forgotten city-state but, naturally, on the nation-state. By the middle—and certainly by the end—of the nineteenth century the idea of democracy in the city-state had been entirely displaced by the idea of representative democracy in the nation-state. The triumph was complete.

Although it is often thought that the older view was refuted, it seems to me that it was not so much refuted as rejected. It is not clear, at least to me, that the kind of political life the Greeks thought possible in the small, autonomous, democratic city-state—even if these possibilities were not often fulfilled—is even theoretically possible with representative government in the large nation-state. Perhaps we create needless trouble for ourselves by claiming that the ideals and potentialities of democracy in the city-state are realized, or theoretically capable of being realized, through the institutions of representative government in the nation-state. One may question the value of the city-state ideal, and suspect the extent to which it was ever realized, for practice fell far short of the ideal even in Athens, and the seamy side of the city-state was, if one looks at it unromantically, pretty appalling. Yet however one may feel about these matters, the essential point is that representative government in the nation-state is in many respects so radically—and inescapably—different from democracy in the city-state that it is rather an intellectual handicap to apply the same term, democracy, to both systems, or to believe that in essence they are really the same.

III

In any case it would surely be a sign of *hubris* to assert that the ideals and institutions of democracy have reached or will reach their final destination, and their fulfillment, in the nation-state. For one thing, with each passing day it grows more reasonable to see the nation-state as a transitory historic form, to foresee that the nation-state will some day cease to exist as an autonomous unit, just as the city-state did. I do not mean to rush things. The nation-state is a tough organism, with great capacities for survival; it is still far and away the strongest and most durable political unit we know. In much of the world political leaders are even now struggling desperately to create their own nation-state out of the fragments of traditional societies; or, having achieved a momentary success, they go to bed each night half sick with worry lest they awake next morning and find their fragile nation has fallen into fragments during the night. In many parts of the world, it will be generations before peoples have defined themselves and have arrived at that state of confident nation-hood where it finally becomes possible to imagine, without panic, the decline and supercession of the nation.

Those Western nation-states in which democracy has flourished for some generations are not only tough, but on the whole, I believe, extraordinarily benign units of government. Historically and comparatively, all the alternatives to representative government in the nation-state seem to me, and I imagine to most of us here, markedly inferior by comparison and often malignant, vicious, and anti-human. Nonetheless, straining to peer into the thick murk of the future, it is difficult, at least for me, to see mankind still existing on this globe without larger political orders than the nation-state, without greater displacement of international anarchy by constitutionalism and the rule of law. In the West, the nation-state has already lost some of its autonomy; it will lose more. Unless we political scientists are to be overswept by events, as we usually are; if we try, as Bertrand de Jouvenel keeps urging us, to conjecture about the future, in order to help shape it; if we use the past to help foresee the longer stretch ahead and not merely to dissect yesterday in order to understand a moment in the past and a moment today—then it is not too soon for us to anticipate a future for democracy when the major unit that has prevailed during the past two centuries, the nation-state, has become an integral and subordinate unit in some larger legal and constitutional order.

There is a second and more immediate reason why the nation-state is not an altogether satisfactory fulfillment of the ancient and continuing aspiration for democratic self-government: its immensity—immensity not so much of territory, which becomes less and less important, as immensity of numbers, of population, of citizens.

Unless wholly new evidence turns up, we shall never have anything more than the shakiest estimates of the population of Athens, but there are some reasonable if very rough guesses as to the approximate number of adult male citizens at about the time of Pericles the demos, then, in the Athenian democracy. A quorum in the Assembly was fixed for some purposes at 6,000. There were about 18,000 seats in the Pnyx, where the Assembly met. An estimate of 40,000 adult male citizens may be high; it is surely not too low.[2] And Athens, remember, was the largest of the ancient Greek city-states.

Consider, now, some present-day nation-states. The smallest democratic nation-state, Iceland, has more than twice as many adult citizens as Athens had by our outside estimate. What we ordinarily call small democracies are, in fact, gigantic. The number of adult citizens in New Zealand is around 30 times that of Athens, while the Netherlands has more than 100 times as many adult citizens as Athens had. France has more than 500 times as many, the United States about 2500, and India, the largest representative democracy in the world, five to six thousand times as many. In fact the number of new voters coming of age each year in India would supply a citizen body for more than a hundred city-states the size of Athens.

Fortunately for these giant systems, there are some important ways of participating in the political life of a democracy that are not significantly limited by the size of the citizen body or its territory. One of these, happily, is voting. Because different individuals can vote more or less simultaneously, and in different places, time and space do not limit the size of an electorate. Nor do time and space limit the number of citizens who can engage in various forms of consummatory and symbolic participation, such as reading about politics in the press, listening to the radio, or watching TV.

Some kinds of participation, on the other hand, cannot be performed simultaneously. Instead they have to be carried on sequentially. In these cases, time does impose restraints on size, and particularly on the number of individuals who can participate. For example, time's harsh and inescapable constraints impose severe limits on the size of a group that is intended for full and free discussion—a group, that is, in which every member has an opportunity to present his views to all the other members. I shall come back to these constraints in a moment.

Returning to our question of the appropriate unit for democracy, and keeping in mind time's inexorable constraint, we discover that this simple and elemental limit on human behavior cuts both ways: Whenever the number of citizens grows large, to maximize their equal opportunities to control their government people must resort to representation. They have no alternative. Yet if time's constraint demands this shift from direct democracy to representative government, it also reduces and ultimately eliminates the possibility that every citizen can engage in a discussion that includes the officials who are charged with the authority to decide.

The greater the number of citizens, then, the longer and more indirect must be the channel of communication from the citizen to his top political leaders. But the communication between a citizen and his leaders is not a symmetrical relationship. Even in the Assembly at Athens, Pericles could speak directly and at great length to many more Athenians than could ever hope to speak directly to Pericles. But where the size of Pericles' audience was limited by the range of the unamplified human voice, radio and television have eliminated all constraints on the size of a speaker's audience. As a result, the larger a system grows, the more and more one-sided becomes communication between citizens and top leaders: the President of the United States can, in principle, speak directly to a hundred million potential voters, of whom only an infinitesimally small fraction can ever speak directly to him. If you doubt that the fraction is infinitesimally small, I urge you to try a few simple arithmetical exercises using the most generous calculations as to the President's time and the most severe restrictions on the length of the conversation between citizen and President.

There are, of course, ways of coping with this asymmetry in communications, but it would take me too far afield to explore them here. The essential point is that nothing can overcome the dismal fact that as the number of citizens increases, the proportion who can participate *directly* in discussions with their top leaders must necessarily grow smaller and smaller. The inherent constraint is neither evil men nor evil institutions, nor any other eradicable aspect of human life, but rather a dimension of all existence that is morally neutral, because it is implacable, unswerving, and inescapable—time.

IV

I have a fantasy in which a modern Constitutional Convention assembles a group of 55 men or thereabouts whose commitment to democracy and whose wisdom are neither of them in doubt. Their task is to design democratic institutions suitable for this small planet in the year 2,000. And so they come to the problem of the unit.

Being learned, as well as wise, naturally they recall the city-state. Well, says one, since full civic participation is possible only if the number of citizens is small, let us arrange for a world of small democratic city-states. Let the unit of democracy, then, be the small city.

Ah, says another, you forget that the world of the 21st Century is not ancient Greece. You even forget that ancient Greece was the setting for a highly defective international system. The trouble with the small city in the modern world is that there are too many problems it cannot cope with, because they go beyond its boundaries. Think of some of the problems of American cities: revenues, transportation, air and water pollution, racial segregation, inequality, public health . . . I would make the list longer, but it is already long enough to show that the small city is obviously an inappropriate unit and that we have to locate democracy in a larger unit. I urge that we consider the metropolis.

But, says a third, even the boundaries of the metropolis are smaller than the kinds of problems you mention. The legal boundaries of the metropolis are an obsolete legacy of the past. What we need is metropolitan governments with legal boundaries extending to the limits of the metropolitan area itself, boundaries set not by obsolete patterns of settlement but by present densities.

Your argument is persuasive, says a fourth, but you do not carry it far enough. Demographers and planners now tell us that in the United States, to take one example, there is an uninterrupted urban area on the East Coast extending from Virginia to Maine. Even your metropolitan governments will be too small there. And in the future much of the world will surely be as densely settled as our Eastern seaboard. Consequently, I believe that we must design regional democracies, controlled by democratic governments responsive to the electorate of a whole region.

Well, says a fifth, I notice you have already bypassed such things as states and provinces, which is all to the good, since they are as anachronistic as the small city. But you will have to agree that even if you carve up the world into regional governments big enough, for instance, to cover the Eastern seaboard, you cannot expect these units to be adequate for very long. With the population of the world reaching 6 billion, or 10 billion, most of the United States will soon be a vast, undifferentiated, urban mass. Other countries are headed in the same direction. There is, then, a good deal to be said for the only traditional unit that enjoys consensus and allegiance on a scale commensurate with the problems. I mean, of course, the nation-state. If we were to think of the United States as one city, as we shall have to do in the future, it is obvious that the proper unit to bound our sovereign electorate cannot be smaller than the United States. With minor changes here and there, the nation-state is probably good for another century or so. So let us proceed to make use of it by eliminating the powers of all, only obstacles that permit local groups to frustrate national majorities.

But, objects a sixth, you are still too much the victim of the past to think clearly about the future. Obviously our very existence depends on our capacity to create a government that will subordinate the nation-state to a larger legal order. Just as your villages, towns, cities, metropolises, and regions are too small to cope singlehandedly with their problems, so too is your nation-state, even one as big as the United States, the USSR, or China. The fatal flaw of the nation-state is its inability to eliminate interstate violence; and because of our genius for violence we can now destroy the species. Even prosaic problems are now beyond the control of the nation-state: the efficiencies that come from world markets, monetary problems, the balance of trade, the movement of labor and skills, air and water pollution, the regulation of fishing, the dissemination of nuclear weapons. . . . I know it is bold, but we must plan for a world government, and to us that surely means a democratic world government. The appropriate electorate for the 21st Century is nothing smaller than the human race. The only legitimate majority is the majority of mankind.

At this point there is a tumult of objections and applause. Finally the first speaker gains the floor. Each speaker, he says, has been more persuasive than the last. But, he adds, I simply cannot understand how my learned friend, the last speaker, proposes to govern the world, if he has in mind, as I thought, a single world-wide electorate, a single parliament, a single executive, all attempting to represent that nonexistent monstrosity, a single world-wide majority. I say that even if it would miraculously hold together, which I doubt, a democracy with six billion citizens is no democracy at all. I, for one, do not wish to be only one six-billionth part of any government. One may as well accept a despot and have done with the Big Lie that what we have is a democracy.

Ah, the advocate of a democratic world government now replies, of course I meant that there would be subordinate governments, which would be democracies.

I thank my learned colleague for this important clarification, says the advocate of the small city-state. I now propose that these subordinate governments consist of units about the size of small cities.

Again there is tumult. The speaker who now gains the floor is the one who had earlier spoken in behalf of the metropolis. Hold on, he objects, if we are to have a subordinate unit, surely it must be one large enough to deal with the problems of an urban society. Obviously this unit should be the metropolis. . . .

Suddenly it becomes as clear to everyone at the Constitutional Convention as it has become to you that the argument over the unit has now started all over again, that it has no logical terminus, that it could go on forever. Perhaps that is why we still talk about the city-state.

For the logic seems unassailable. Any unit you choose smaller than the globe itself—and that exception may be temporary—can be shown to be smaller than the boundaries of an urgent problem generated by activities of some people who are outside the particular unit and hence beyond its authority. Rational control over such problems dictates ever larger units, and democratic control implies a larger electorate, a larger majority. Yet the larger the unit, the greater the costs of uniform rules, the larger the minorities who cannot prevail, and the more watered down is the control of the arguments.

For we drop completely the notion so dear to the Greeks and early Romans that to be legitimate a unit of government must be wholly autonomous. With autonomy we also drop the belief that there is a single sovereign unit for democracy, a unit in which majorities are autonomous with respect to all persons outside the unit and authoritative with respect to all persons inside the unit. Instead we begin to think about appropriate units of democracy as an ascending series, a set of Chinese boxes, each larger and more inclusive than the other, each in some sense democratic, though not always in quite the same sense, and each not inherently less nor inherently more legitimate than the other.

Although this may be a discomforting and alien conception in some democratic countries where political tradition has focussed on the over-riding legitimacy, autonomy, and sovereignty of the nation-state and of national majorities, even in these countries the evolution of pluralistic institutions has vastly modified the applicability of monistic conceptions of democracy. And of course in democracies with federal systems, like Switzerland, Canada, and the United States, or in non-federal countries like the Netherlands that inherit a political tradition powerfully shaped by federalism and the legitimacy of pluralist institutions, to see the units of democracy as a set of Chinese boxes is very much easier—though even in these countries it will take some re-thinking and a vast amount of institution-building before any of us can think easily about the nation-state as a Chinese box nested in yet larger ones of equal legitimacy.

Our imaginary Constitutional Convention, and our Chinese boxes do not, of course, bring us much closer to a solution to our original problem of the appropriate unit for democracy. But they do suggest that there is not necessarily a single kind of unit, whether it be city-state or nation-state, in which majorities have some specially sacred quality not granted to majorities in other units, whether smaller or larger, more or less inclusive.

A Frenchman, perhaps even an Englishman, or any strong believer in majority rule will tell me that surely in some of these boxes there must be a majority that is sovereign, or else conflicts between different majorities, one of which may in a larger perspective be only a minority, can never be resolved. I ask, very well, a majority of what unit? And my critic will say, the majority, naturally, of the nation. To which I reply, *why* is this more sacred than the others? Because it is larger? But I can point to still larger majorities in the making in this world. Will you remain faithful to your answer when your nation is a unit in a world polity? Or will you not, instead, revert to federalist conceptions? Anyway, I might add, in a number of federal countries, including some rather old and respectable representative democracies, citizens have grown moderately accustomed to the idea that national majorities—or rather their spokesman—are not necessarily more sacred than majorities or minorities in certain kinds of less inclusive units. This is logically untidy, and it requires endless readjustments as perspectives and levels of interdependence change. But it makes for a better fit with the inevitable pluralistic and decentralizing forces of political life in nation-states with representative governments.

The hitherto unreported debate at our imaginary Convention also suggests that in a world of high population densities, ease of communication, and great interdependence, where autonomy is in fact impossible short of the earth itself, we confront a kind of dilemma that the Greeks could hardly have perceived. Let me suggest it by advancing a series of propositions:

The larger and more inclusive a unit, the more its government can regulate aspects of the environment that its citizens want to regulate, from air and water pollution and racial justice to the dissemination of nuclear weapons.

Yet, the larger and more inclusive a unit with a representative government, and the more complex its tasks, the more participation must be reduced for most people to the single act of voting in an election.

Conversely, the smaller the unit, the greater the opportunity for citizens to participate in the decisions of their government, yet the less of the environment they can control.

Thus for most citizens, participation in very large units becomes minimal and in very small units it becomes trivial. At the extremes, citizens may participate ·in a vast range of complex and crucial decisions by the single act of casting a ballot; or else they have almost unlimited opportunities to participate in decisions over matters of no importance. At the one extreme, then, the people vote but they do not rule; at the other, they rule—but they have nothing to rule over.

These are extreme cases, and if they were all there were, it would be discouraging prospect. But may there not be others in between?

Before we turn to this question, I want you to notice that our hypothetical Constitutional Convention and the Chinese boxes also hint at the possibility that we may need different models of democracy for different kinds of units. By models I mean here both empirical models that would help us to understand the world as it *is* and normative models that would guide us in shaping the world we believe *ought* to be. We need models that approximate reality in the world of history and experience, and models that indicate standards of performance by which we can appraise the achievements of a particular democracy. I see no reason to think that all kinds of units with democratic institutions and practices do, can, or should behave in the same way—no reason, then, why we should [not] expect democracy in a committee, in a city, and in a nation to be markedly different both in fact and in ideal. If we expect that representative government in the nation-state is roughly equivalent to democratic participation in a committee then we are bound to be misled in our understanding of political life, in our hopes, and in our strategies for changing the world from what it is to what it ought to be.

V

Let me rephrase my question. If the nation-state is too immense, and if interdependence and population densities render the autonomous self-governing city-state too costly, are there units powerful enough, autonomous enough, and small enough to permit, and in the right circumstances to encourage, a body of citizens to participate actively and rationally in shaping and forming vital aspects of their lives in common? Is there, in this sense, an optimal unit?

There are a number of candidates for this position. Occasionally, for example, one still runs across a nostalgia for the village—a nostalgia strongest, I suspect, among people who have never lived in small towns. There are also suggestions going back nearly a century that we shift our search for the democratic unit away from the government of the state to the government of non-state institutions, such as the workplace, business firm, corporation, or industry. And lately there has been a resurgence of interest, especially among young political activists, in the old and recurring idea of reconstructing democracy around small units that would offer unlimited opportunities for participation.

Although I cannot possibly do justice to these various alternatives in the brief time available to me here, I would like to venture a few comments on each.

The fragmented and even shattered community in which modern man seems condemned to live tempts one to suppose that the appropriate unit for democratic life might be the village or small town. Only there, it might be thought, could one ever hope to find a center of life small enough so that it permits wide participation, and small enough besides to foster the sense of unity, wholeness, belonging, of membership in an inclusive and solidary community which we sometimes seem to want with such a desperate yearning. Speaking for myself, I doubt whether man can ever recapture his full sense of tribal solidarity. Like childhood itself, there is no returning to the childhood of man. What is more, the attempt to satisfy this craving, if carried far on a densely packed globe, leads not to community but to those hideously destructive forms of tribalism that this century has already seen too much of.

Anyway, I suspect that the village probably never was all that it is cracked up to be. The village, including the pre-industrial village, is less likely to be filled with harmony and solidarity than with the oppressive weight of repressed deviation and dissent which, when they appear, erupt explosively and leave a lasting burden of antagonism and hatred. I have not been able to discover much evidence of the consensual *gemeinschaft* in descriptions of the small town of Springdale in upstate New York, or St. Denis in Quebec, or Peyrane, the village in the Vaucluse, or the small English town of Glossop near Manchester, or the peasant village of Montegrano in South Italy, or the Tanjore village in South India that André Betéille recently described.[3]

Here, for example, is how Horace Miner saw political life in the French Canadian parish of St. Denis thirty years ago:

> Politics is a topic of continual interest and one which reaches fever heat during election time. . . . The whole parish is always divided between the "blues" or Conservatives, and the "reds." Party affiliations follow family lines and family cliques and antagonisms. The long winter *veillées* are attended almost invariably by family groups of similar political belief. Constituents of each party have a genuine dislike for those of other. . . . Election time is one of great tension, of taunts and shouting as parishioners get their evening mail. . . . Insults are common, and many speaking acquaintances are dropped. During the last election the minority candidate had to have one meeting in the parish in secret, another open but under provincial police protection. . . . Campaigns reach their climax with the *assemblée contradictoire*, at which both candidates speak. Characteristically at these meetings there are organized strong-arm tactics, drinking, and attempts to make each candidate's speech inaudible. . . .
>
> The chicanery of politicians is a byword in the parish. Factional strife threatens the life of every organized association. . . . On the whole the associational life of the community is weak. The people are not joiners.[4]

Thus the village democracy before the demos was ruined by industrialization and urbanization!

If the democratic village seems hardly worth seeking in this industrial and post-industrial epoch, the prospect is all the more appealing that democracy might be extended to the place where most adult citizens spend most of their time—their place of work. Professional people with a great deal of autonomy, academics like ourselves who enjoy an extraordinary amount of autonomy and a fair measure of self government in our universities, executives and administrators who see authority relationships from above rather than from below, all are likely to underestimate the consequences for the average citizen in a modern industrial society flowing from the fact that at his place of work he is a rather low-level subordinate in a system of hierarchical relationships. Although the term democracy has been prostituted in the service of employee relationships, the fact is that practically everywhere in the world, the industrial workplace—the factory, industry, or corporation, whether owned privately or publicly—is no democracy in any sense consistent with our usage in the realm of the state. "The idea of a factory, nationalized or privately-owned," it has been said, "is the idea of command."[5] The factory, the enterprise, the industry, the corporation is a hierarchy; it may be an aristocracy, an oligarchy, a monarchy, a despotism, but it is not a democracy. This is as true in socialist economies as in capitalist and mixed economies. A century ago Engels asserted that hierarchy would be necessary in the factory even under socialism, that even in a socialist enterprise the worker would lose his autonomy. Over the entrance to the factory, he said, recalling *The Inferno*, the words should be written:

Lasciate ogni autonomia, voi che entrate![6]

Whether the work-place should be democratized, and if so how and how much, are questions that need to be distinguished from the problem of regulating the enterprise industry, or corporation to insure that it accomplishes the social and public functions that are the only reason the rest of us are willing to grant its vast legal rights, privileges and immunities, and extraordinary power. If democratic states have become immense, so have corporations. There are privately owned corporations that have gross annual revenues greater than the GNP of most countries of the world, that spend annually sums greater than the entire budgets of the governments of most of the nation-states in the world. To insure that these immense resources and powers are used for public purposes is a staggering problem. But internal democracy in the factory, firm, industry or corporation is not necessarily a more effective means of public control than regulating a hierarchically administered firm by competition and the price system, by a regulatory agency, by government ownership, or by various combinations of these and other possibilities. Indeed, even if the modern corporation were internally democratic, no matter whether it were public or private and no matter whether it were to operate in an economy predominantly privately owned or predominantly publicly owned, I do not think we any more than the Soviets or Yugoslavs would want to dispense entirely with such external controls as competition and the price system. In short, no system of *internal* control negates the need for a system of *external* controls that compel or induce those who exercise authority within the enterprise, whether these managers are chosen by and are accountable to stockholders, workers, or the state, to employ their power and resources for jointly beneficial purposes rather than for exploiting consumers.

But even if we can distinguish the problem of internal democracy from that of external control, the problem does not vanish. And even if this problem is extraordinarily difficult—as I think it is—it seems to me too important to be neglected, particularly by political scientists. It is true that in many developed countries with representative governments, trade union power has substituted bargaining for undiluted hierarchy in the control of wages and working conditions. But even where they are most powerful, labor unions have by no means created a democratic factory or industry; moreover, as a result more of apathy than of repression, few unions anywhere have developed a really high degree of internal democracy. Aside from a few scattered instances elsewhere,[7] the most massive, ambitious, and far-reaching experiment in democratizing the workplace has been taking place in Yugoslavia since 1950. Sober studies[8] suggest that while the system of workers' control has problems—some of them, like apathy and Michel's iron law of democratic organizations—it might well prove to be a viable system of internal control. If it does, it will surely stand as an alternative with a very great appeal—at least in the long run—to workers in other industrial nations. If workers can participate in the government of their factories in Yugoslavia, and if these factories prove to be relatively efficient, surely the whole question of internal democracy will come alive in other countries.

Yet even if it should prove to be possible, efficient, and desirable, I do not believe that democracy in the work-place is a substitute for democracy in the state. For one thing, I doubt whether democracy in the work place can be preserved indefinitely unless there is democracy in the state. Moreover, where an opposition party is illegal in the state, opposition in the factory has distinct limits.[9] Finally—and this is the most important point—the work place is not as important as the state and with increasing leisure it may grow less so. To accept as a focus for self-government a type of unit that is and must be concerned with only a small part of the range of colllective concerns would be to trivialize the democratic idea. I find it hard to believe that man's aspiration toward rational control over his environment by joint action with his fellow men will ever be satisfied by democratizing the production of aspirin, cars, and television sets.

As I have already suggested, any form of political participation that cannot be performed more or less simultaneously but must be carried on sequentially runs into the implacable barrier of time. Time's relentless arrow flies directly to the Achilles' heel of all schemes for participatory democracy on a grand scale. It is easy to show that any unit small enough for all the members to participate fully (where each member has the opportunity to present his views and have them discussed) cannot be larger than a working committee. If you doubt this, I ask you to sit down with pencil and paper and do a few exercises with various assumptions as to the time available for decisions and the time required for each participant to make his point or at least present his point of view.[10] You will quickly see how cruel is time's neutral guillotine. Or let me simply evoke your own experience with committees to remind you how quickly a committee grows too large for every member to participate fully. Or consider the experience of legislative committees, cabinets, regulatory commissions, judicial bodies.

Would we not all agree that an effective working committee can have no more than—let us err on the side of generosity—30 to 40 members? Drawing on your own experience, most of you, I imagine, would cut these figures by a half or two-thirds.

Now if the great advantage of a unit the size of a working committee is that it allows full participation by its members, its great drawback, from a democratic point of view, is that unless it is a representative body or an agent of a representative body it ought not be given much public authority. Either the unit, though small, is granted authority because it represents a much larger number of citizens; or else, not being a representative body, it has little authority other than to recommend and advise; or else, if it has much power and is not a representative body, its power is illegitimate. In an interdependent society, any significant power wielded by a body the size of a working committee is bound to have important effects on citizens not sitting on that committee. Consequently either the committee is representative or its power is illegitimate. We can hardly espouse the small, self-governing, fully participatory unit as a normative goal if it is illegitimate. If it is representative, then it is no longer a body in which all citizens can participate fully. We have run into a cul de sac, as you see, and so we must get back to the starting point.

Some of you may regard this as a pessimistic analysis. It is, I admit, a very large fly in the ointment. Like death, it may be a brutal and perhaps even a tragic limit on man's possibilities, but I do not see why this conclusion must lead to pessimism. The idea of democracy would never have gotten off the ground if enthusiastic democrats had not been willing to settle for something a good deal less than complete and equal participation by all citizens in all decisions. It is worth recalling that in Athens, where the opportunities for free male citizens to participate in running the city seem to have been about as great as they have ever been anywhere, citizens were chosen for what was probably the most coveted participation in the life of the polis—a seat on the Council of Five Hundred, the inner council, or the various administrative boards—by lot or, in the case of the Board of Generals, by election, and to that extent these bodies were instances of representative government and not direct democracy. Participation in the Assembly, which met about once a month, was scarcely the fullest flowering of participatory democracy. I have been to enough town meetings myself to know something of their limitations. If you think of a town meeting in which a quorum sometimes required the presence of 6,000 people, where maybe as many as 30–40,000 were eligible to attend, and where perhaps 4–5,000 were frequently present, it is obvious that most Athenian citizens must have lived their lives without once speaking to their fellow citizens in the Assembly. That, one judges from the reports in Thucydides, was a forum that gave preference to orators.

Nonetheless, I doubt—although we shall never know—whether many Athenians felt frustrated because their opportunities to participate were not as unlimited as their skies. Between the working committee and the nation-state there is, I think, a critical threshold of size, below which the opportunities for participation can be so great and so fairly meted out that no one feels left out and everyone feels that his viewpoint has been pretty fairly attended to. Athens was far too large for the democracy of the working committee; de facto it had to employ a certain amount of representation. Yet I suspect that it was below the critical threshold. And even if we now reject as unattainable the ideal of full, equal, and direct participation by all citizens in all collective decisions—the ideal of committee democracy—we can still search for a unit that remains within this critical threshold for widespread participation.

VI

We have travelled a long trail and turned into a number of branching paths in our quest but we have not found a unit that seems optimal for rational self-government. The journey would have been much longer had we taken the time to explore the by-ways as carefully as they deserve. Yet if we keep going, I think that we shall finally end up about at the place where the Greeks left off: somewhere within view of the democratic city.

Yet what we come to is not the Greek city, nor can it be; not the *polis*, then, but a democratic city that would be consistent with the presence of the nation-state, the institutions of representative government, a level of technology beyond anything the Greeks dreamed of, and huge populations densely spread over the face of our shrunken earth.

If ancient Greeks were the first truly modern people, choice shaped by geography and historical accident made them also city people. So, too, choice shaped by demography and technology makes us a city people. But even if the Greeks were a city people and though they were modern in almost every important sense, our cities must differ in fact and in ideal from their actual and ideal cities. For one thing, the proportion of the residents of a modern democratic city eligible to participate in political life will be very much larger—something like half of the population, so that even a city of 100,000 will have around 50,000 adult citizens. Much more quickly than the Greeks, we reach the limits of direct democracy. Moreover, the citizens of a modern city will also be highly mobile. A resident of Athens was a citizen only if his ancestors were Athenians; in any modern city, many citizens are recent arrivals, or are about to move to another city. In 1960 more than one resident out of every six in American cities had moved there within the last five years.[11] As a result of our mobility, socialization into the political life of the modern democratic city is enormously more difficult for us than for the Greeks. Then, too, the Greek city was completely autonomous in ideal and pretty much so in fact. Our cities are not autonomous in fact nor would many of us offer total autonomy as an ideal. Finally, the citizen of a Greek city ordinarily had one inclusive loyalty to the city of his ancestors and to its gods. He invested in his city a kind of engagement in comparison with which patriotism in the nation-state must seem either shallow or strident. But the citizens of our modern cities will have no single loyalty and no single community; they will have multiple loyalties to many associations; and nowhere will they find the all-inclusive community.

If for these reasons a modern city cannot be a *polis*, we can nonetheless reasonably hope one day to achieve great democratic cities. As the optimum unit for democracy in the 21st Century, the city has a greater claim, I think, than any other alternative.

To begin with, from now on into the next century man seems clearly destined to live in cities. If to live in cities is our fate, to live in great cities is our opportunity. Is it not of some significance that of the four great waves of experimentation in the West with popular government, during three of these—the Greek, the Roman, and the medieval communes of North Italy—popular governments managed to construct cities of exceptional and enduring beauty?

Yet during the fourth wave, that of representative democracy in the nation-state, we have so far failed most profoundly in our cities. Is it too much to hope that we might be on the verge of a fifth wave, the age of the democratic city within the democratic nation-state? By we, I mean of course, the whole of the Western democratic world and its off-shoots. But most of all, I mean we here in the United States.

City-building is one of the most obvious incapacities of Americans. We Americans have become an urban people without having developed an urban civilization. Though we live in cities, we do not know how to build cities. Perhaps because we have emerged so swiftly out of an agrarian society, perhaps because so many of us are only a generation or two removed from farm and field, small town and peasant village, we seem to lack the innate grasp of the essential elements of the good city that was all but instinct among Greeks, Romans, and the Italians of the free communes. Our cities are not merely non-cities, they are anti-cities— mean, ugly, gross, banal, inconvenient, hazardous, formless, incoherent, unfit for human living, deserts from which a family flees to the greener hinterlands as soon as job and income permit, yet deserts growing so rapidly outward that the open green space to which the family escapes soon shrinks to an oasis and then it too turns to a desert.

One advantage of the city as a unit for democratic government is, then, that it confronts us with a task worthy of our best efforts because of its urgency, its importance, its challenge, the extent of our failure up to now, and its promise for the good life lived jointly with fellow citizens.

These considerations point to another asset of the city as a democratic unit. While the city is not and cannot be autonomous, the policies of city hall and the totality of city agencies and activities are so important to our lives that to participate in the decisions of the city means, or anyway can mean, participating in shaping not merely the trivial but some of the most vital aspects of our environment. I say shaping and not totally controlling because the city is only one of our Chinese boxes. But it is in the city and with the powers and resources made available to cities that we shall deal with such crucial problems as the education of our children, our housing, the way we travel to and from our place of work, preventive health measures, crime, public order, the cycle of poverty, racial justice and equality—not to mention all those subtle and little understood elements that contribute so heavily to the satisfaction of our desires for friendship, neighborhood, community, and beauty.

Yet if the city and its government are important to us, can the good city today be small enough to remain below that critical threshold for wide participation that I mentioned a moment ago? I do not know any question more important to us as political scientists, nor any that we have so completely ignored. From evidence and analysis that are both all too incomplete, I should like to hazard an answer.

The existence of a few giant metropolises here and there may mislead us as to fact and possibility. Only a modest percentage of the world's population lives even today in the giant metropolis. Indeed, in 1960 only one-fifth of the people of the world lived in cities over 100,000. It is true that in the most urbanized region of the world, North America, in 1960 six out of every ten people lived in cities over 100,000. Yet even in the United States, less than one out of every ten lived in cities over a million.

It will take some doing, but we do not have to end up all jammed together in the asphalt desert of the large metropolis—unless that is really what we want. And Americans pretty clearly do not want to live in the large metropolis but rather in cities of modest dimensions. For example, in a survey by Gallup last year nearly half the respondents living in cities of 500,000 and over said they would like to live somewhere else—suburb, small town, farm; by contrast, few of the people living in suburb or town wanted to move to the big cities. About three out of four respondents are distressed by the prospect that their own community will double in population.[12] Census figures for the past several decades tell us that Americans have been acting out these preferences.

What, then, is the optimum size for a city? Curiously, this question, which so far as I know was first asked by political philosophers in Athens over 2,000 years ago, is no longer a subject of discussion among political scientists. I do not know why this should be so, but I wonder if it is because we have come to take a purely passive and defeatist view: the size of a city, we say, is beyond control, so the best we can do is to adapt political institutions to the facts. I am reminded of Rousseau's comment on Grotius, that his invariable mode of reasoning was always to establish right from fact. One might employ a more logical method, Rousseau remarked, but not one more favorable to tyrants.

If to our own loss we have ignored the question of the optimum size of cities, fortunately it has been examined by scholars in a variety of fields other than our own. It is impossible to do justice to this discussion here but the analysis and the evidence are too important for us to ignore.[13] It is only fair to warn you that this is a controversial area, yet the evidence seems to me to support the conclusion that the all-round optimum size for a contemporary American city is probably somewhere between 50,000 and 200,000, which, even taking the larger figure, may be within the threshold for wide civic participation.

There is, for example, no worthwhile evidence that there are any significant economies of scale in city governments for cities over about 50,000. The few items on which increasing size does lead to decreasing unit costs, such as water and sewerage, are too small a proportion of total city outlays to lead to significant economies; and even these reductions are probably offset by rising costs for other services, such as police protection.[14]

Per capita city expenditures increase with the size of city, at least in the United States. In 1960 the mean expenditure for U.S. cities over 150,000 was $123 per capita compared with $70 per capita for cities in the 25 –50 thousand range. Yet there is no evidence that these higher costs per capita provide residents of large cities with a better life, taking it in the round, than the life enjoyed by residents of smaller cities. If it costs more in a city of a million than in a city of 25,000 to build, maintain, and police a park within walking distance of every citizen, then higher per capita expenditures for parks in big cities hardly signify that their residents have better public services than residents of smaller cities. What is more, the outlays in larger cities are actually less for some key functions than in smaller cities. For example, even though larger cities employ more persons per capita in public administration than smaller cities, per capita employment in education is on the average lower in larger cities than in small cities.[15]

Roads and highways nullify the older economic advantage of the metropolis as a market and a source of specialized labor. A student of urban economics argues, for example, that

> A half-dozen towns of, say, 25,000 population with two or three main industries
> each plus a dozen small one- or two-industry towns of half that size add up to a

300,000 population, extended local labor market, built on the moderately broad base of a couple of dozen separate industries.[16]

The oft-cited cultural advantages of metropolis are also largely illusory. On the basis of his research on American cities, Duncan estimates that the requisite population base for a library of "desirable minimum professional standards" 50,000 –75,000, for an art museum, 100,000, "with a somewhat higher figure for science and historical museums." Yet, even though larger cities have larger libraries, the circulation of library books per capita markedly decreases with size of city. There is also a negative correlation between city size and per capita museum attendance.[17] Moreover, just as smaller cities can retain their collective identities and yet form a larger economic unit, thanks to ease of transportation and communication, so we have barely begun to explore the ways in which small cities by federating together for specific purposes might enjoy all of the cultural advantages of the large city and yet retain their individual identities, the pleasures of living in communities of lower densities and more open spaces,[18] and relatively greater opportunities for political participation.

When we think about the size of a city in which a high culture may flourish, it is instructive to recall that Rome in the Augustan age probably had a population of about 350,000. During the Renaissance the city that produced Machiavelli and, I think it fair to say, an outpouring of great paintings, sculpture, and architecture beyond anything we Americans have yet created, had a population of around a hundred thousand. This was probably about the population of the city of Venice during the Renaissance, and of Rome when Michaelangelo chiseled out his Moses and painted his frescoes in the Sistine Chapel.

Now what is strangely missing from the discussion of the optimum size of cities is the voice of the political scientist. The question is, of course, broader than the problem of what size of city may be optimal for a democratic political life. But political life is not trivial. Surely political criteria have a place among the criteria for the optimum size of cities; and among these political criteria surely one of the most important is whether a city is beyond the threshold for widespread participation. The whole question needs more study than it has had. But it looks to me as if the all-round optimum size for a city—the range, say, from 50 thousand to about 200 thousand—is below this threshold. If this is so, then there is no other unit in the nest of Chinese boxes that is at once so important and so accessible; a unit that can and must be clothed with great powers, if it is to manage its problems, and yet can be small enough so that citizens can participate extensively in determining the ways in which this great power will be used. Only the city, it seems to me, can avoid the extremes we began to confront some time back. For the city need not be so huge that, like the nation-state, it reduces participation to voting, nor so small that its activities are trivial.

The city has at least one more advantage: it has great potentialities as a unit for educating citizens in civic virtue or—if I must use a term that comes more readily to the lips of a contemporary political scientist—for political socialization.

We may be approaching a crisis in the socialization of citizens into the political life of the democratic nation-state, a crisis that the challenges of nation-building, democratization, and overcoming the most blatant evils of industrialism have delayed or obscured. There are signs of malaise among young people, among the very citizens who shortly before the dawn of the 21st Century will have become—to use the word that has now become a mindless cliché—the establishment. If the malaise were only American, one could put it down to television, over-permissive child-rearing, the persistence of an unpopular and ugly war, or other causes more or less specific to the United States; but there are signs of this malaise among youth in almost all the democratic countries.

I am not going to try to explain here a phenomenon too complex for brief analysis. But a part of the phenomenon—I don't know how much it is symptom and how much underlying cause—is a belief that the government of the nation-state is remote, inaccessible, and unresponsive, a government of professionals in which only a few can ever hope to participate actively and a still smaller number can ever gain great influence after years of dedication to political life.

What we need, what they need, and what some of them are trying to create (often with incredible ignorance of elementary political wisdom) is a political unit of more truly human proportions in which a citizen can acquire confidence and mastery of the arts of politics— that is, of the arts required for shaping a good life in common with fellow citizens. What Pericles said of Athens, that the city is in general a school of the Grecians, may be said of every city of moderate size: it is a marvelous school. I have no doubt that a modern city even of moderate size is a good deal more complicated than Athens was. It has a much greater need for highly trained professionals, permanent administrative agencies, full-time leaders. Yet in the main, its problems are, I believe, within reach of the average citizen. And I believe it may be easier for citizens to reason about the good life and the ways to reach it by thinking in the more immediate and palpable context of the city than in the context of the nation-state or international politics. Even if solving the problems of the city is not quite enough for the good life, it is a great, indispensable, and comprehensible prerequisite.

VII

What I have presented is not a program but a perspective, not a prophecy but a prospect. It is not a solution to the problems of the city or of democracy, but a viewpoint from which to look at the problems of democracy and the city. It does not lead directly to the answers, it might nonetheless help one to see the questions.

I have already suggested one implication of this way of looking at things—if popular governments in the modern world are a series of Chinese boxes, then we obviously need different models, theories, and criteria of excellence for each. I may seem to be repeating only what was commonly said nearly two centuries ago as ideas about representative government began to develop, that we cannot judge representative government in the nation-state as if it were or could be democracy in a committee, or, for that matter, a town meeting. Yet it is interesting to me that we have made so little of these palpable and evidently inherent differences in the performance of different kinds of units, all of which we are prone to call democratic.

Yet if the democratic city lies somewhere between democracy in the committee or in the town meeting and representative government in the nation-state, then it would be important to know what the similarities and differences are, and what standards of excellence we can apply to one but not the other. Even the democratic city, I fear, cannot satisfy anyone who has a vision of leaderless and partyless democracy, for at its best the politics of the democratic city will be more like a competitive polyarchy than a committee; organized parties and interest groups are more likely to exist than the free and spontaneous formation and dissolution of groups for every issue; a full-time leader or activist will exert more influence than any of his followers; institutionalized conflict is more likely than uncoerced consensus. Yet these are hunches that do no more than point to new worlds that need exploring.

The perspective I have been describing also bears on the way we think about units of government intermediate between nation-state and city. An American obviously must take the 50 states into account. These are too solidly built to be done away with and I don't propose to break any lances tilting against them. Yet in the perspective I am suggesting the states do not stand out as important institutions of democratic self-government. They are too big to allow for much in the way of civic participation—think of California and New York, each about as large in population as Canada or Yugoslavia and each larger than 80% of the countries of the world. Yet an American state is infinitely less important to citizens of that state than any democratic nation-state is to its citizens. Consequently the average American is bound to be much less concerned about the affairs of his state than of his city or country. Too remote to stimulate much participation by their citizens, and too big to make extensive participation possible anyway, these units intermediate between city and nation are probably destined for a kind of limbo of quasi-democracy. They will be pretty much controlled by the full-time professionals, whether elected or appointed. Moreover, many of the problems that states have to deal with will not fit within state boundaries. It cannot even be said that the states, on the whole, can tap any strong sentiments of loyalty or like-mindedness among their citizens. Doubtless we shall continue to use the states as important intermediate instruments of coordination and control—if for no other reason than the fact that they are going institutions. But whenever we are compelled to choose between city and state, we should always keep in mind, I think, that the city, not the state, is the better instrument of popular government.

This argument also applies to megalopolis, to the city that is *not* a city, to the local government that is *not* a local government. The city of New York, for example, has about the same population as Sweden or Chile. It is twice as large as Norway, three times the size of New Zealand. To regard the government of New York as a local government is to make nonsense of the term. If the Swedes were to rule their whole country from Stockholm with no local governments, I am quite sure that we would begin to question whether the people of Sweden could rightly be called self-governing. Where, we might ask the Swedes, are your local governments? But should we not ask the same thing of New Yorkers: Where are *your* local governments? For purely historical and what to me seem rather irrational reasons, we continue to regard the government of the giant metropolis as if it were a local government, when we might more properly consider it as the equivalent of a state or a provincial government—and hence badly in need of being broken up into smaller units for purposes of local government. If it turns out that the government of a metropolis cannot be decentralized to smaller territorial units, then should we not quite openly declare that the metropolis cannot ever be made into a democratic city? This may be an inconvenient truth, but if it is true, it may be—like much truth—liberating in the end.

Yet I must admit that problems like these involving the metropolis demand more than we now know. The metropolis is a world to be explored, so let us explore it, hoping that we may discover how even it might be turned into a democratic city.

VIII

There are many questions that I shall have to leave unanswered. I could plead lack of time, but the fact is I don't know the answers, nor perhaps does anyone else quite yet.

There is above all the question that now overshadows all else in American life of how we shall solve the problems presented by race, poverty, inequality, discrimination, and centuries of humiliation. No failure in American society has been as enduring, as profound, as visible, as corrosive, as dangerous, and as tragic as our refusal to enable black Americans to share in equal measure with white Americans the realities of the American dream. Now this problem has become central to the whole future of our cities and indeed to the future of the country. I scarcely need to say that unless and until it is solved neither we nor our children nor our grandchildren nor any future generation can have anything like a decent urban life.

There is also the question of how the city can acquire adequate resources, particularly funds, without becoming excessively subordinated to higher levels of government. The bloc grant is a very promising solution, but only if grants are made directly to the cities and not, as is often proposed, exclusively to the states. In the perspective that I have been suggesting, to think of the states as the natural and exclusive recipients of bloc grants is anachronistic; for if the autonomy that is promised by the bloc grant is desirable for states—those barely democratic units in the limbo—autonomy is all the more desirable, and indeed necessary, if citizens are to enjoy the power to shape their cities.

A third question is how to control the size of cities. If there is an optimum size in the broad range from about 50,000 to about 200,000, as I have suggested further inquiry might show, then how can cities be maintained within this range—to say nothing of breaking up the giant metropolis? Typically, the people who influence decisions about the future of cities have acted on the simple-minded axiom: the bigger the better. This is most notably true here in America where the rational prospect of great gain encourages an almost pathological obsession with the virtues of sheer bigness, as if the very bigness of the city, the height of its buildings, and the crowds on its streets must somehow outweigh all squalor and ugliness. There seems to be a fear, too, that the moment we stop growing we start to die, a half truth that overlooks the fact that in nature the mouse and the sparrow have outlasted the brontosaurus and the sabre-toothed tiger. There are, I suspect, all sorts of devices we could use to control the growth of a city when it reaches the optimum range. These need to be explored, but they will be of little use until we decide that this is what we really want to do.

A closely related though much more formidable question is how we can make the legal boundaries of a city coincide more closely with what might be called its sociological boundaries. As I suggested earlier, our view up to now has been passive or defeatist: we say that we must constantly change legal boundaries to it's social boundaries. But as I tried to suggest with my fantasy of a Constitutional Convention, this way lies madness; for the legal boundaries must be extended until they cover the whole globe, which, whatever else it may be, cannot be a complete substitute for smaller territorial units. In general, the political autonomy allowed a territorial unit is likely to be less, the higher the amount of interaction with others outside the legal boundaries. In building nations or international systems, the greater the interaction; and consequently the less "real" the significance of local boundaries, the easier the task. Yet if we are to build democratic cities with enough autonomy to permit their citizens to participate extensively in significant decisions about their environment, we must somehow reverse the tendency for the legal boundaries of the city to lose all social and economic significance. Nor can we simply go on creating separate authorities for each problem. Obviously different problems call for different boundaries, and we may have to live in a network of authorities. Yet the indefinite multiplication of units of government is bound to fragment the control of the ordinary citizen over a broad range of policies.

The problem of fragmented authority touches closely upon another, the problem of decentralization of authority and power within the city. Even in a city in the range from 50,000–200,000 political participation is reduced for most people to nothing more than voting in elections—as it is in the representative government of the nation-state—unless there are smaller units within which citizens can from time to time formulate and express their desires, consult with officials, and in some cases participate even more fully in decisions. Unfortunately, I can only indicate the problem; I have no answers to it. There are a number of proposals floating around for creating smaller participatory units in the city, the oldest and most popular candidate being the neighborhood; and there are even some interesting experiments of this kind going on. So far as I know none of the proposals or experiments triumph over the universal tendency for a few activists to engage in most of the overt activities while the rest participate only sporadically, symbolically, or not at all. Although this limitation seems to me to deflate rather cruelly the most grandiose and utopian claims for citizen participation, and in addition raises serious problems, I do not think it is a reason for rejecting these efforts and experiments out of hand, if we are aiming not for committee democracy but, as I suggested a moment ago, a degree of participation so great and so fairly spread about that no one feels neglected and everyone feels, with justice, that his viewpoint has been pretty fairly attended to. To aim for the point at which practically everyone in the city believes with good reason that his claims ordinarily receive a fair hearing, and decisions, even when adverse to his claims, have been arrived at with understanding and sympathy, is already so distant and so splendid a goal that I am quite content to leave the exploration of what lies beyond it to someone in the 21st Century.

If there were time, I know that one could turn up more questions, more problems, more obstacles. We might even conclude that the fifth high tide of democracy, the age of the democratic city in the democratic republic, is not after all in our destiny.

Or it may be within the possibilities of other countries, but not our own, to achieve in the rest of this century what the Greeks did 2500 years ago, to develop an urban civilization founded on the democratic city, only consistent this time with the imperatives of modern technology, the existence of representative governments ruling over huge populations and territories, and the extension of constitutionalism and the rule of law to vast areas of the earth—ultimately, perhaps, to the globe itself.

Yet even if no one can say whether this will ever come about, or where, for everyone stirred by the prospect of shaping politics now toward the good life in the 21st Century—or at least toward a better life—the opportunities lie all around.

NOTES

1. H. D. F. Kitto, *The Greeks* (Baltimore: Penquin Books, 1951, 1957) p. 79.

2. Various classical scholars have made valiant attempts to guess the population of Athens and its composition—citizens, adult males, metics, slaves—from the most fragmentary bits of evidence. I have not be able to locate any estimate that does not seem to leave great room for error. Kitto suggests "30,000 as a reasonable estimate of the normal number of citizens" in the Fifth Century: *op. cit*, p. 131.

3. Arthur J. Vidich and Joseph Bensman, *Small Town in Mass Society* (Garden City, N.Y.: Anchor Books, 1960); Horace Miner, *St. Denis, A French Canadian Parish* (Chicago: University of Chicago Phoenix Books, 1939, 1963); Laurence Wylie, *Village in the Vaucluse* (New York: Harper Colophon, 1957, 1964); A. H. Birch, *Small-Town Politics, A Study of Political Life in Glossop* (Oxford: Oxford University Press, 1959); Edward C. Banfield, *The Moral Basis of a Backward Society* (New York: The Free Press, 1958); André Betéille, *Caste, Class and Power* (Berkeley: University of California Press, 1966).

4. Miner, *op. cit.*, 58–61.

5. Graham Wooton, *Workers, Unions and the State* (London: Routledge and Kegan Paul, 1966), 36.

6. *Ibid.*, p. 36. The quotation is from Engels' essay "On Authority" in Lewis S. Feuer (ed.), *Marx and Engels: Basic Writings* (New York: Doubleday Anchor, 1959), 481–484.

7. Wooton, *op cit.*, 113–124.

8. Cf. Albert Meister, *Socialisme et Autogestion, L'Expérience Yougoslave* (Paris: Editions du Seuil, 1964); and Jiri Kolaja, *Workers Council: The Jugoslav Experience* (New York and Washington: Frederick A. Praeger, 1966).

9. See the comments of Kolaja, *op. cit.*, pp. 7 and 66ff.; and Meister, *op. cit.*, pp. 240–245, 263–278, 373.

10. Cf. Bertrand de Jouvenel, "The Chairman's Problem," American Political Science Review, 55 (June, 1961), 368–372.

11. In 1960 the percentage of migrants from another country since 1955 for all U.S. cities 25,000 and over was 18.4%. The percentages ran slightly higher (19.7%) in small cities of 25 –50,000 than in cities over 150,000 (15.6%). See Jeffrey K. Hadden and Edgar F. Borgatta, *American Cities, Their Social Characteristics* (Chicago: Rand McNally, 1965), Appendix, Table 1, variable #19, p. 108.

12. American Institute of Public Opinion release, April 24, 1966.

13. The most extensive survey and analysis of the evidence seems to be the work of Otis Dudley Duncan. The findings of his Ph.D. dissertation, *An Examination of the Problem of Optimum City-Size* (University of Chicago, 1949) have been summarized in Otis Dudley Duncan, "Optimum Size of Cities" in Paul Hatt and Albert Reiss (eds.), *Reader in Urban Sociology* (Glencoe, Ill: Free Press, 1951), 632–645; and James Dahir, "What is the Best Size for a City?," *American City* (August, 1951), 104–105. Robert A. Lillibridge, "Urban Size: An Assessment," *Land Economics*, 38 (Nov., 1952), 341–352, summarizes Duncan and others. In addition, see William Fielding Ogburn and Otis Dudley Duncan, "City Size as a Sociological Variable," in Ernest W. Burgess and Donald J. Bogue, eds., *Urban Sociology* (Chicago: The University of Chicago, Phoenix Books) 58–76; Otis Dudley Duncan, "Optimum Size of Cities" in Joseph J. Spengler and Otis Dudley Duncan (eds.), *Demographic Analysis* (Glencoe, The Free Press, 1956), 372–385.

14. I am indebted to Mr. Garry D. Brewer for undertaking an extensive survey of the writings and findings dealing with economies of scale in American cities. The relevant literature is extensive, but the most relevant studies appear to be Amos H. Hawley's seminal article, "Metropolitan Population and Municipal Government Expenditures in Central Cities," *Journal of Social Issues*, 7, nos. 1 and 2 (1951), 100–108; Werner Z. Hirsch, "Expenditures Implications of Metropolitan Growth and Consolidation," *Review of Economics and Statistics*, 41 (August, 1959) 232–241; Harvey E. Brazer, *City Expenditures in the United States*, National Bureau of Economic Research Occasional Paper no. 66 (New York, 1959). See also the analysis of the evidence of these studies in Wilbur R. Thompson, *A Preface to Urban Economics* (Baltimore: Johns Hopkins Press, 1965), Ch. 7, "The Urban Public Economy," 255–292.

15. Data in the paragraph above are from Hadden and Borgatta, *op. cit.*, Appendix, Table 1, p. 110, variables 57, 58, and 65.

16. Thompson, *op. cit.*, p. 34.

17. Duncan, "Optimum Size of Cities," *op. cit.*, p. 381.

18. ". . . museums, professional athletic teams, complete medical facilities, and other accoutrements of modern urban life could be supported collectively. As the federated places grew and prospered the interstices would, of course, begin to fill in, moving the area closer to the large metropolitan area form. But alert action in land planning and zoning could preserve open spaces in a pattern superior to those found in most large urban areas." Thompson, *op. cit.*, p. 36.

The Future of Urban Government

DOUGLAS YATES

It has recently become fashionable to ask whether city government has any future at all. After all, the "urban crisis" spawned, by all accounts, an unsuccessful War on Poverty; and, more recently, as a result of either excessive generosity or profligacy (or both), some city governments have come close to bankruptcy. Seen in this light, the problems of New York City merely underscore the apparent failure of big city governments either to solve problems or remain healthy financial or political institutions.

The trouble is that in reacting to this clear and present failure of city government, we may prescribe solutions for the future based on mistaken evaluations of what went wrong in the past. Even worse than picking a general to fight the last war is picking a general to fight the last war when one does not understand why the last war was lost.

It is obvious to anyone that New York's present problems are the result of fiscal imbalances. But, it is not obvious that the explanation for these problems is found either in the generous interpretation that the city does not have enough money to deal with its real problems or in the harsh judgment that it has lived far beyond its means—has spent money like a drunken sailor.

There is another explanation. It is that the city's problems are not primarily fiscal in character but rather have to do with the basic structure of urban government and politics. The logic of this is that: a) many of the city's major problems cannot be resolved with increased financial resources; and b) to the extent that city government tries to solve them, it will either fail outright or provide a weak and unreliable instrument for applying its financial resources to its problems.

The main difference between those explanations of the failure of city government can be depicted sharply in terms of the following metaphors: Does the city constitute an "empty cupboard" which yawns emptily for new resources to take care of its needy residents or is it a "leaky sieve" which fails to allocate and manage effectively the financial resources that it possesses. In my view, it would be foolish to say that either metaphor is entirely correct, although, of late, there are many commentators who enthusiastically endorse one or the other. Indeed, in deciding which metaphor of the urban dilemma to employ and emphasize, we must make clear what kinds of urban problems we are talking about in the first place.

THE EMPTY CUPBOARD

The empty cupboard metaphor stands for a general class of "resource" problems in city government—problems that could not possibly be addressed or solved without money. For example, there is no way to build housing, highways, parks or new schools without capital investment. And anyone who can think of a way to provide these public goods without spending money should run for mayor on the Alchemist ticket. These resource problems, involving physical construction, have long been dealt with by city government, and, given available resources, cities have managed to build an impressive amount of housing, highways and schools. The competence of the city in handling this type of problem is not an issue here.

There is, however, another kind of resource problem which arises from economic, social and political forces beyond the control of city government. If industry moves to another state, for example, because of tax and locational advantages, city government is not directly responsible for the loss of revenues or the rise in unemployment that may result. If poor blacks migrate to a northern city because of living conditions in the South, the city is suffering from another externality that imposes high costs (for example, in increased welfare payments). Again, in this case, it would be both illogical and mean-spirited to blame the city for having to bear the heavier financial burdens that were placed on it by outside forces. Finally, if the federal government builds a highway system that paves the way to the suburbs or sets up a tax program that redistributes money away from the cities, city government is once again a victim of external forces.

Thus, to a fair-minded observer, the case against city government cannot and should not be based on the city's failure to "solve" this kind of problem. And it is at this point that the call for federal intervention is most compelling.

THE LEAKY SIEVE

I would argue that the primary failing of city government is not one created by an "empty cupboard." Rather the "city problem" is largely an expression of the city as a "leaky sieve" whose financial resources never reach the targets they were aimed at in the first place. Instead, the resources are diverted and lost because urban government is too fragmented and unstable in its policy-making to manage its money and implement its programs coherently. Having said that, it becomes clear that the "city problem" that we are talking about now is not really a resource problem at all (although it has implications for the use of resources); it is instead a problem of weak governance and lack of public control. Furthermore, city government has insisted on treating as resource problems many problems that have other roots and that can only be alleviated by means other than the application of more money. The "leaky sieve" metaphor, understood in this way is reflected in city expenditures for police, education and social-service programs generally, where the launching of a great number of new programs has had hardly any discernible impact on the problems that initially troubled city hall. For, despite all the efforts of city government, street crime, juvenile delinquency, low reading scores, drug addiction and family breakdown have persisted and often worsened.

The truth of the matter is that city government had no idea how to attack its problems, but nevertheless launched policy initiatives on many fronts in the hopes that something would work. Here the failing of governance is at least partly understandable because it is hard to know what a government should do in the face of serious problems when it literally does not know what to do. What is worse, this well-intentioned but blind search for possible solutions to difficult problems clearly led city governments to further fragment their energies and further lose control of the urban service bureaucracies that were running these experimental programs.

REGULATION, CONTROL, TRUST AND STRUCTURE

If not all problems involve getting and using more money, what then are the real problems? In general, all of them are problems of governance and control; however, they fall into four major groups. One is the problem of responsiveness in government—lack of accessibility to citizens; slowness in dealing with legitimate service demands; rigidity in administration; and, the inability to recognize (and respond to) the many variations in service requirements within and between city neighborhoods. Indeed, it was this problem, not the resource problem, that in the last decade stirred demands for administrative decentralization and community control, ombudsmen, little city halls and other devices for creating a closer relationship between government and neighborhood.

The second problem is that of regulation which occurs when city governments are unable to control the conduct of "their" street-level bureaucrats enough to establish desired standards of performance or prevent corruption and abuses of government power. Police brutality and "cooping," sanitationmen not following their routes, neighborhood service centers not rendering the services they were paid to provide as well as teachers and welfare workers ignoring city policies and procedures are all examples of ineffective regulation. Indeed, lack of regulation lies at the heart of the common complaint that something always seems to go wrong at the street level in implementing hopeful, new urban policies.

The third category of problems is a pyschological one which could be called a lack of trust between citizens and public employees. This problem is manifest when urban residents, particularly nonwhites, feel that public servants are ignorant, indifferent or hostile to their particular needs, and it exists in an opposite form when public employees believe that urban residents are indifferent or hostile to them and feel no respect or gratitude for their services.

The final problem is one of structure, and it exists when city government is incapable of planning for and providing critical goods and services because its present structure is inadequate. The structure problem points in two directions: toward the neighborhood and toward the region. City government first of all lacks strong neighborhood structures and policy-planning mechanisms to coordinate its services. Secondly, the city, in its present form, is incapable of implementing policies that extend beyond itself—to the metropolitan area, the state, the region or even the nation.

If these are the problems that frustrate urban policy-making today (and which urban administrators might plausibly be able to handle), it becomes clear that we must look for the source of the "city problem" in city government itself. We cannot look for solutions to the problems of governance and control in resource-expanding or belt-tightening strategies alone. We must instead examine the basic structure of urban government to determine what makes these nonfinancial problems arise in the first place.

THE URBAN JIG-SAW

The problems discussed above pop up because urban policy-making is highly incoherent, unstable and reactive. That is, it is hard to gather power and authority together in the city, hard to focus attention for long on any one problem and hard for city hall to avoid reacting to the latest batch of demands and "crises." But this still is only a description of city government. What explains the city's weak and unstable structure of governance and control and the various nonfinancial problems resulting from that structure?

City governance is weak because the urban political system is fragmented to the point of chaos. Urban government is a jig-saw puzzle that few people are ever able to put together—however hard they try and whatever strategies they employ. The sources of urban fragmentation are several.

First of all, urban government is shaped by the city's historical function—the delivery of ordinary services like police, fire, sanitation and education. These services are direct, routine and tangible. Thus, urban government has always had direct, daily relationships with its citizens and has always been hard-pressed to respond to the demands of different communities. Also, because urban services are often highly personal in character (consider, for example, the relationship between the servers and the served in police and education), city government has always been dependent on the existence of mutual trust and understanding between citizens and public employees. The atomistic nature of citizen demands and the need to spread "service stations" (police precincts, schools, firehouses) across the city to provide direct, daily services in very different neighborhoods has fragmented city government.

City government may never be as "close to the people" as some citizens would like, but compared to higher-level governments, it is very close indeed—right out in the neighborhoods and on the streets. As such, it is a "street-level government," and, more precisely, an aggregation of different street-level governments—the government of police stations, the government of schools, the government of firehouses.

A second source of urban fragmentation lies in the way city bureaucracies are organized. Service bureaucrats are like feudal barons whose loose coalition represents the sum total of urban government. Perhaps more important, urban government is deeply fragmented by the weak control of urban administrators "downtown" over their foot-soliders out on the streets. Of necessity, an unusual number of the important, day-to-day policy and administrative decisions are made by teachers, policemen and welfare workers. And because these "street-level bureaucrats" have unusual discretion and responsibility—because the service relationship is so much in their hands—it is intrinsically hard for central administrators (police and fire chiefs, for example) to monitor the workings of city government at the crucial point of impact in the neighborhood.

But, if central administrators often feel that they have only tenuous control over their foot-soldiers, the foot-soldiers themselves feel that they have little control over urban policy-making—either that made "downtown" or in other service bureaucracies. Many will say, if asked, that city policy is arbitrary and insensitive to the needs of residents in their neighborhoods. In addition, urban foot-soldiers often assert that their own attempts to improve service delivery are constantly frustrated by the uncoordinated or even contradictory policies and programs of other service bureaucracies. So, from the bottom up or the top down, governance and control of service delivery is weakened by fragmentation between different levels of administration and between different urban bureaucracies.

THE FEDERAL AND STATE FACTORS

The fragmentation of city government is also aggravated by the proliferation of federal and state programs and by the resulting competition and conflict between different levels of government over urban services. The New Deal and later the War on Poverty forced city government to perform more and more functions, deliver more and more services at the same time that governance of these services has become increasingly divided and complicated.

Therefore, the mayor is faced with a barrage of problems and demands coming from many different directions—from neighborhoods and community groups, service bureaucracies and various levels of government. As a result, the agenda of urban policy-making is diffuse and unstable and the urban policy-making system itself is greatly overloaded. The mayor and his advisors rush from problem to problem, and from "crisis" to "crisis;" they are continually *reacting* to demands knowing that they have only weak control over "their" service bureaucracies and street-level bureaucrats. Seen in this light, it is no wonder that city hall's attention is unfocused, its actions spasmodic and that its policy-making traces an erratic course through various initiatives, corrections, obstacles and reversals.

Because of this, the urban system often appears anarchic. Urban policy-making could be viewed as a street fight in which a great number of community and governmental contestants fight it out for some benefits of public action. The great debate in political science between those who contend that a centralized power elite controls urban government and those who believe there is a pluralism of political powers operating in the city either ignores or understates the fragmentation of the urban system. We might better speak of street-fighting pluralism to capture the free-for-all quality in urban government.

Having examined the city's problem of governance and control and located its source in the deep-lying patterns of fragmentation and street-fighting pluralism, we can see why the city is a leaky sieve and why its distinctive problems of responsiveness, trust, regulation and structure arise. Most important, we can also see from this analysis why the city seems to have become increasingly ungovernable and why the search for new solutions to the "city problem" has intensifed and become frantic.

CENTRALIZATION VS. DECENTRALIZATION

Before considering certain new urban "solutions" as well as a number of "old"' ones that continually reappear, two features of the "ungovernable" city which I believe must be taken into account by any real solution must be underlined. The first feature, which goes a long way toward explaining why the city is increasingly ungovernable, is that urban government is both too centralized and too decentralized. It is too centralized in the sense that even as a street-level government, the relationship between the servers and the served is not close enough to produce the responsiveness and trust on which the service relationship depends. This failing would appear to call for greater decentralization, for a stronger partnership between citizens and public employees at the street level.

At the same time, city government is too decentralized. The cost of having service bureaucracies act as relatively independent street governments is insufficient regulation by the center to insure that street-level foot-soldiers consistently meet qualitative and quantitative performance standards. More important, there is not enough central control to insure that money gets spent on its intended purposes; that money is spent efficiently; and that expenditures are accounted for in a way that both affirms the basic fiscal responsibilities of city government and also provides a basis for evaluating the relative effectiveness of different programs.

Furthermore, because of fragmentation among the service bureaucracies, policy-makers in city hall lack an overview of the way services are packaged and allocated throughout the city, and they have almost no idea of what the city service profile is in a particular neighborhood or policy area (such as services for the elderly or programs to combat juvenile delinquency.) Thus, a mayor simply does not know what service strategy, if any, he is buying with his expenditures and how the elements of the service strategy fit together. Ask a mayor what his "coverage" is in services to the elderly, what service treatments are emphasized, what overlapping exists between programs, what neighborhoods are receiving disproportionately large expenditures, how many elderly residents are served by a particular program (or programs), what is the comparative cost per client served among different services for the elderly, and how high the administration overhead is as a percentage of spending in any given program—the mayor will surely be unable to answer. Even if he decided to make a study to find out what the city was doing in the area of services for the elderly, he might have a very difficult time finding usable information about how city money was being spent and with what discernible effect. This failing of urban governance and control would appear to call for greater centralization in policy-planning, coordination and evaluation in service delivery.

There is also a second sense in which the city is too decentralized. That is, in dealing with large-scale policy problems such as the migration of people, jobs and industries as well as school finance, welfare, environmental protection and urban growth, the cities are too small as governmental units to provide solutions within the city limits. This is a point that has been made by generations of urban analysts, and it remains no less true today for having been repeated so often in the past. This "failing" of urban governance—which is not really the city's failing at all—would seem to call for far greater centralized planning and financing of a number of "urban" functions by the states and by the federal government.

SIMPLIFYING THE MAYOR'S JOB

In performing its service delivery function, city hall must reduce the barrage of demands on it and its responsibility for managing an unmanageable number of programs as its first priority. I therefore want to make an argument for simplification, for focusing on essential urban services as a way of relieving the mayor and others in city hall from the frustration of coping with an impossible number of demands and functions.

This is, of course, only a principle. It does not tell us in any precise way which programs to cut and which programs to preserve. But it does give us a criterion for assessing the various solutions which have been offered now and in the past to the city and the city's persistent problem of governance and control.

Two solutions have repeatedly been offered for the governance problem, and their own past failings do not prevent them from being offered again today. One solution is that of the scientific manager or "business" efficiency expert who asserts that if only tight managerial controls were imposed on city spending and if business techniques were introduced into the daily administration of city government, the leaky sieve problem would be largely resolved. There is some truth and considerable illusion in this view. With any more rigorous accounting system, sloppy spending practices could and would be reduced—obviously a highly desirable result. However, it is important to note at the same time that the thrust of the "efficiency" solution is essentially negative. That is, the logic of this solution whether in the form of a city manager government or in the Emergency Financial Control Board of New York City (on which prominent businessmen sit) is to *prevent* wasteful spending and to *avoid* corruption. And, as such, the solution does not address the city's problems in any positive way nor does it establish trust between citizens and public employees.

Of course, when city government is on the brink of bankruptcy, the efficiency solution, even if negative, cannot be lightly dismissed. For it is hard to see how city hall can improve its responsiveness and increase trust if it cannot meet the payroll. So the use of an Emergency Financial Control Board in New York is a necessary condition of the survival and future viability of urban government. However, after tough business management techniques have been introduced (and even if they are successful), the task of making city government work *will* still remain, and we must find positive solutions to these problems of responsiveness, trust, regulation and structure.

Moreover, the introduction of business management techniques in city government has had its clear costs as well as its benefits. When an earlier generation of reformers set out to make city government run efficiently, they chose strategies designed to get politics out of the "business" of urban management. One such strategy was the creation of independent boards and commissions which would be divorced from the street-fight of politics and would supposedly operate more rationally and efficiently in the style of those large-scale business organizations so greatly admired by the reformers of the period. A second strategy involved the appointment of a city manager who would be the central administrative officer in the city and who would act not as a politician but as a business manager. The result of these strategies, and particularly of the boards and commissions, was that they made city government less accountable, as democratic control and participation were sacrificed for efficient management. It is not suprising that in the last two decades, movements for decentralization and citizen participation arose in reaction to the perceived bureaucratic rigidity and inaccessibility of these instruments of strongly centralized management.

GOVERNMENT BY PROFESSIONAL

A second solution to the problem of urban governance is that of the professional bureaucrat who contends that if only urban bureaucracies were strongly centralized under the control of professionals and operated according to professional principles and practices, the disorder and inefficiency of street-level service delivery would be remedied. The strategy of professionalism shares with the efficiency-through-business-management solution the guiding desire to remove "politics" from urban administration. But in this case it is the professional policemen, administrators, school superintendents and social workers who are the beneficiaries of strongly centralized administration. There is no doubt that increasing the professionalism of policemen, teachers, firemen and social workers did produce significant benefits for our urban delivery service. At least, that is the indication if one compares the modern day policemen or firemen with the disorganized corps of volunteer firemen or the untrained policemen of the "night-watch." Despite these gains, the strategy of professionalism in service bureaucracies simply has not produced the rational, well-ordered system that its advocates envisioned.

Professionalism, after all, only raised standards of professionalism. It did not and could not provide a complete answer, and it carried with it the same kinds of costs as the business management strategy—without any of its advantages—for professionalism, with its attendant centralization of service created a greater physical and social distance between citizens and urban administrators and produced a costly, cumbersome, centralized bureaucratic structure.

THE UNANSWERED PROBLEM OF CENTRALIZATION

The two strategies discussed above are eminently plausible, and even desirable. (It is hard to be against efficiency and professionalism in principle.) It seems that these strategies should work—at least, they could work better than they have. The question is: what is it about the city that causes these strategies to be less successful than their proponents hoped would be the case? The even trickier question is: should not any city government worth having be one in which these strategies would work?

However, the trouble with both strategies is that while they address the problems created by decentralization, they do not address the equally important problems created by centralization. Such solutions therefore provide only half a loaf. Furthermore, neither strategy is explicitly designed to decrease the overload of demands on city hall, and the strategy of professionalism may indeed increase that load if, as is so often the case, professionals try to expand their own programs.

But the matter goes deeper than that. In the first place, both strategies are based on wishful notions of what city government and politics are like or would be like if only the right policies were pursued. That is, the efficiency strategy makes sense in a world where there are clear goals, rules of conduct and divisions of responsibility and, more important, a reasonable clear understanding of what kinds of inputs (such as manpower) produce what kinds of outputs (such as "better" schooling or police protection). Otherwise, the efficiency strategy inevitably comes down to cost-cutting, and that is a slightly less compelling strategy than one that says city government could be both more efficient and more effective. Unfortunately, the world of city government simply does not conform to the world of the efficiency expert.

Similarly, if we knew that upgrading the training or status of a policeman or paying him a certain amount more would lead to a discernible change in police protection, then the strategy of professionalism could be put on a more solid foundation. Note that it is for these reasons that the use of productivity measures in city government are relatively effective if one is talking simply about the productivity of garbagemen, measured in tons of garbage collected; but the productivity of the teachers, policemen and social workers cannot be measured so easily. And they are even less useful if one really wants to know whether the streets are cleaner or whether the schools are more effective.

A different way of making this point is to say that the city's weak control system reflects not only government failings but also the crucial fact that so many forces and problems impinging on the city are beyond the direct control of city hall. In addition, the mayor and other administrators must always devise policies to deal with these elusive problems while lacking control over the great number of political actors and bureaucratic organizations that operate within thier domain. So the city is an open system—open to problems coming from different sources (some outside the city) and open to the involvement of many would-be policy-makers, most of whom are beyond the direct control of city hall. Because the city as an organization has such weak boundaries, it is not easy to construct simple organizational goals and strategies, and this makes the city an inhospitable environment for both the efficiency expert and the "professional." So many ingredients have been mixed into the melting-pot of urban problems and policy-making that it is virtually impossible to transform the city into the kind of stable, tightly organized, hierarchical organization in which efficiency experts and service professionals could flourish. More important, the solutions we have been considering are frustrated by the fact that the city is not only a management and policy-making system, it is also a democratic institution. As a service-delivery mechanism, "good" management would seem to be the main imperative of city government. But, as that government in the American system closest to its citizens, "good" democratic procedure is also an imperative. I would argue that in the end, good management and democracy must go hand in hand because, given the nature of urban service delivery, it is hard to be responsive to the diverse claims of urban residents if democratic processes are not working to represent the views and complaints of citizens and if there are few opportunities for citizen participation and evaluation in urban administration.

At the same time, it would be naive to believe that there are no conflicts and trade-offs between the goals of good management and democracy. In fact, the strategies of efficient business management and professionalism have pursued the first goal at the expense of the second, producing in the 1960's a strong citizen reaction against centralized bureaucratic control.

A BLENDING OF STRATEGIES

My own "solution" to the problem of urban governance seeks to nurture both good management and democracy by avoiding any all-or-nothing choices between the virtues of centralized control and the virtues of a decentralized street-level service relationships and citizen participation.[1] This solution would blend strategies of centralization and decen-

---

1. There are, of course, a number of other possible solutions to the city's massive problem of governance. Many of them, such as metropolitan government, massive federal intervention, home rule and model-city experiments have proven unsuccessful or unlikely to be adopted. The other obvious solution—revenue-sharing—is still so new that it is difficult to assess its benefits, costs and future promise with any confidence.

tralization. Thus, I would decentralize the delivery of ordinary urban services as far as possible using neighborhood institutions and arrangements of various kinds to strengthen the street-level service relationship. With an ample menu of strategies to choose from, a city government should easily be able to devise different decentralization strategies for different services and even more different neighborhoods.[2]

The role of the mayor and other central administrators primarily becomes one of controlling and coordinating service policies and expenditures. The mayor would greatly increase his policy-planning and project management activities, his capacity for performing economic analysis and his ability to make use of the techniques of rigorous fiscal control presently being imposed on New York City. The central service administrators would also focus on the problem of the regulation of street-level foot-soldiers. They would also be the chief sources of innovation and experimentation. And the states and the federal government should assume responsibility for the planning and financing of those large-scale policy problems that extend beyond the city limits. This may be wishful thinking, but it is at least a coherent strategy for American federalism or one that is already widely urged for the treatment of welfare programs, school finance and environmental planning and protection.

The second main purpose of the strategy is to reduce the overload of policy-making in city hall. There is no way to eliminate completely the reactiveness of urban policy-making. But some steps can be taken. First, if service delivery were decentralized, fewer citizen demands would reach the mayor. Second, if the states and federal government assumed a greater role in crucial areas like welfare and education, the mayor would be freed of both the present conflict between levels of government or the management of these services.

Finally, city government will have to admit that it cannot do everything, that it has gotten into trouble trying to provide every imaginable service and, therefore, will redefine its mission as the provision of basic, historical city services—police, fire, sanitation, education and a limited number of social services. This strategy requires that a mayor be willing to eliminate between a quarter and a third of his present service programs and concentrate on the so-called "essential urban services." It requires also a willingness to say that the city does not know how to solve a great many of its present problems (and is not soon likely to know); therefore, it will concentrate its energies on those functions where either there is an established technology or where, as in education, the city has an historical commitment to service delivery.

I therefore propose for the city what was labeled in the last issue of *New York Affairs* a "new politics of less." This is a conservative strategy in that it calls city government back to its earlier mission. But it is radical in its requirement that city government sharply redefine its goals and get down to essentials—the delivery of ordinary services. It is now clear that city governments, acting alone, cannot solve the nation's problems. Sometimes, when "less" is done better, "less" becomes "more." And delivery of ordinary services is still a challenge of the highest order and one worth the full attention of urban policy-makers.

---

2. There are many different ways to decentralize, and Robert Yin and I have examined a good many of them in our study, *Street Level Governments*.

The Future of Community Control

NORMAN I. FAINSTEIN and SUSAN S. FAINSTEIN

It is now more than a decade since the slogan black power symbolized a radical reorientation in the movement to improve the condition of American minority groups. It is eight years since the clash between black activists in New York City and the United Federation of Teachers (UFT) linked the issue of municipal decentralization with black power under the rubric of community control. The early 'seventies have been a period of reduced militancy, but legacies of the 1960s persist. We now expect that black groups will participate in the pluralist bargaining structure (black power devoid of radical potential), and we continue to experiment with the structure of municipal government in order to make it more responsive to neighborhood-based demands. While race remains a crucial determinant of attitude in the debate over municipal reform, changes in historical circumstances have influenced the ideologies of blacks and whites so that the term community control has taken on more complex meanings and its identification with specifically racial demands has diminished. It is our purpose here to explore the meaning of community control for black and white community leaders in New York City; to investigate the importance of racial background, perceptions of city services, and neighborhood contexts in determining that meaning; and to relate our findings to the political future of urban minorities.

TWO TYPES OF COMMUNITY CONTROL IDEOLOGY

The argument in favor of community control has been made within two related, but distinguishable, ideological frameworks. The first, which we shall refer to as the *democratic model*, presents the demand for vesting governmental authority at the neighborhood level in terms of the liberal democratic tradition. According to this model individuals become alienated from government and society unless they can effectively participate in the determination of public policy as it affects them most directly:

> It is primarily at the neighborhood level that meaningful (i.e., potentially rewarding) opportunities for the exercise of urban citizenship exist. And it is the breakdown of neighborhood controls (neighborhood self-government, if you

The research reported here was conducted as part of the New York City Neighborhood Project at the Bureau of Applied Social Research, Columbia University. The New York City Neighborhood Project was funded by Grant No. GI-32437. Advanced Productivity Research and Technology Division of the Research Applied to National Needs Directorate (RANN), National Science Foundation. Any opinions, findings, conclusions or recommendations expressed are those of the authors and do not necessarily reflect the views of NSF.

We wish to acknowledge the assistance provided by Gary Barrett, Charles L. Bennett, Neil Bomberg, Fran LaSpina, Peter Roggemann, and Mary Jane Wilson.

will) that accounts for the principal concerns of urban citizens. When they can neither take for granted nor influence by their actions and those of their neighbors the standards of conduct within their own neighborhood community, they experience what to them are "urban problems"—problems that arise directly out of the unmanageable consequences of living in close proximity.[1]

Size of the governmental unit is a significant limiting condition on the capacity of citizens for self-government. Large-scale units, although capable of commanding more resources and controlling a broader range of policy than small ones, permit only a minuscule proportion of the population to participate actively in decisionmaking. They submerge even fairly large minorities within a mass of competing interests and produce a majority based on the lowest common denominator. Even if his or her goal is far short of direct democracy, the reformer still must seek to break up vast governing structures if he or she is to realize any degree of citizen participation and responsive administration:

> It must be pretty clear by now that if we want to reduce time's implacable constraints in order to increase opportunities for participation, we shall have to find ways by which citizens can participate more fully in smaller units, units smaller than nation-state or megalopolis. These smaller units must be, I think, neighborhoods and cities of human proportions. This means both preserving and creating. To move in this direction is to transform into terms appropriate to modern life a much older perspective on the human dimensions of an urban policy, a perspective that the explosive and fascinating eruption of megalopolis during the past century has all but buried from view.[2]

The argument for decentralization based on democratic principles has no necessary implications for racial separatism. Kotler, who is perhaps the strongest and most romantic recent proponent of the democratic community, goes so far as to maintain that community control is a universalistic principle which, by protecting the rights of minorities, inhibits separatist drives:

> By gaining legal authority, the neighborhood government participates in the constituted power of the state. This has no value for purposes of separatism. It is not only endangered by such a policy; it is also the best protection against it.[3]

The second paradigm of community control, which we call the *race-conflict model*, stresses the utilization of the homogeneous black neighborhood as a vehicle for the mobilization of political power. As Carmichael and Hamilton wrote, "We must begin to think of the black community as a base of organization to control institutions in the community."[4] While the race-conflict model also emphasizes the importance of citizen participation for both the political education of individuals and the assurance of just outcomes, its principal thrust is the identification of geographic community with racial group. Community control thus becomes the *black* demand for participation in large cities.[5] In general the two models differ according to their preoccupation with different actors in the political system—the democratic construct is concerned with governmental processes as they involve individuals and territorially defined groups; the race-conflict model is oriented towards outcomes for groups defined by their social status.

Both models have a common root in reaction to the urban dialectic of machine and reform.[6] These two structural forms have shaped the ideology and institutions of American cities since the last century, and their clash has provided much of the drama of local politics. Although antagonistic to each other, neither machine nor reform provides a means of representation of locally based policy interests. Despite its ward organization, the machine excluded neighborhood groups interested in public goods; reform, in its achievement of centralized, professionalized city government, virtually eliminated the representational function or urban public institutions altogether. The triumph of reform has meant that in most cities policy is made by functionally organized central bureaucracies, governed by universal norms and insulated from grass-roots pressure.[7]

The democratic and race-conflict models of community control converge in their concern over the powerlessness of bureaucratic clients. They can be distinguished, however, according to the grounds on which they counter the reform values of professionalism, centralization, and universalism. The democratic model attacks the legitimacy of contemporary governmental institutions because they deprive individuals of their right to affect the formulation and implementation of governmental policy. According to the democratic argument, professionalism and centralization prevent responsiveness by public officials to the needs of constituents.

The race-conflict model contends that the reliance on universalism as a legitimating value results in discrimination against the interests of relatively deprived groups.[8] Only the winning of power by groups which have been treated discriminatorily can result in a redress of their grievances. This view is based on an evaluation of government as a zero-sum game and assumes that a redistribution of jobs, contracts, and services in favor of blacks will occur at the expense of previously favored groups. The redistributive argument is, of course, threatening to those who receive income and status from the present system; and it precipitated the acute reaction to community control which created the New York school confrontation. Holders of the race conflict ideology thus do not expect that power will be ceded to them gracefully, but rather that it must be seized through militant, although not necessarily violent, tactics. Built on a colonial analogy,[9] the race conflict model considers the situation of blacks as resulting from exploitation that can be eliminated only through radical changes in the socioeconomic structure.

The empirical dominance of one or the other model of community control has important theoretical and practical consequences. The theoretical question is whether the position of minority groups in America is sufficiently unique to cause them to adopt a radical ideology, or whether, despite their situation as a victimized and isolated stratum, they nonetheless remain adherents of the liberal democratic political formula. If the latter is true, then cultural values could be so strong as to outweigh marked structural differences in shaping group ideologies. While even the more moderate, democratic type of community control ideology is opposed to the status quo, it does not repudiate the concepts of individualism and majority rule that underlie American liberalism. Rather it presses for institutional forms under which those values can be better realized. Adherence to this model by blacks and

Latins would signify that even the least assimilable groups in American society continue to view the world through the framework of an ideology which values individual freedom and mobility above all, and promises participation in a pluralistic society.

In practice, widespread belief in the democratic model would mean that urban political institutions could be made more flexible and responsive without necessarily precipitating hostile outbreaks and increased polarization. Such an outcome may be viewed as either a palliative, representing minor accommodation and coöptation of dissidents, or as evidence of reformism and adaptability. The calm acceptance of Boston's little city halls [10] and New York's Office of Neighborhood Government, [11] the assimilation of many of the poverty and Model Cities programs into the regular political structure, and the willingness of big city mayors to lobby for their continuance—all these seem to point to the prevalance of the reformist rather than the radical ideology. Within that ideological framework, these developments provide evidence of minority group successes and confirm a pluralistic world view. Outside of that framework, they are evidence of coöptation which points to the truth of demystifying, group-conflict ideologies. [12]

Our hypotheses, which we test by examining the orientations toward community control of white and minority community leaders within New York City, are that (1) among both groups the holders of the democratic model of community control far exceed adherents to the race conflict model, but that, (2) because they view their group interests differently, minority leaders are willing to carry the implementation of this democratic model much farther than are most whites. This difference means that the strong racial component which persists in attitudes toward community control is expressed largely through institutional preferences rather than ideological rationales. We further expect to discover that among both white and minority leaders evaluation of the functioning of city services powerfully determines attitudes toward decentralization of authority. Finally, we predict that the institutional preferences of leaders will vary according to the particular situation in which they find themselves, and thus will differ according to the homogeneity and balance of power in any specific community.

ATTITUDES TOWARD COMMUNITY CONTROL OF COMMUNITY LEADERS IN NEW YORK CITY

New York City presents an especially interesting locale in which to examine attitudes toward decentralization and community control. Politics in the city is characterized by a high level of ethnic and racial consciousness. Here, more than in most other American cities, black (and to some extent Hispanic) leaders make explicit ideological appeals to racial solidarity and participate in a politics of group conflict which further heightens minority-white ideological differences. [13] In contrast to a city like Chicago, where intergroup exchanges have been made primarily within the organizational confines of the political machine, New York's weak party structures have long encouraged the public mobilization of ethnic and racial sentiment as a vehicle for enhancing the power of local leaders. As far back as the 'thirties, the efforts of blacks to enter the political process took the form of establishing citywide interest groups which articulated "racial" programs, rather than working strictly within the established structure of the declining Tammany organization. [14]

When agitation on behalf of poor black and Hispanic communities surfaced in northern cities during the 'sixties, New York became a major center of racial conflict and developed ideological demands. In fact, many of the programmatic elements which would later be termed "black power" and "community control" appeared in the city during the early 'sixties in the activities of Mobilization for Youth, an agency sponsored by the Ford Foundation's Gray Areas Program which quickly took a stance of racial militance.[15] Thus, well-developed ideological thinking should be found among New York City leaders, if it is to be found anywhere; and so should positions of racial militance.

For structural reasons, too, New York should be the place where community control ideology and opposition to it, would be most highly developed. In no other American city is the central government so highly bureaucratized and so distant—both politically and geographically—from local communities. The scale of the city means that areas designated "local" or "communities" would constitute sizable cities elsewhere in America. Thus, the official "communities" in New York which have received some increased power over government agencies in the early 'seventies are the Community Planning Districts (CPDs). The CPDs average 125,000 in population, and some have more than 200,000. Analysts of city affairs, as well as most politicians and civic leaders, have recognized for some years the problems of acute bureaucratic insulation, goal displacement, rigidity and lack of responsiveness to the environment which constitute the "bureaucratic phenomenon."[16]

During the late 'sixties, New York was rocked by severe racial conflict resulting from the efforts of some minority group leaders to effect community control over the city's largest bureaucracy, the school system. The association of community control with racial militancy (especially with "black power") was one of the factors which helped to defeat the movement, at least in its more radical form. The open warfare between minority communities and city bureaucracies on the one hand reflected the city's politics of group mobilization and the objective conditions stemming from the bureaucratic phenomenon, but on the other, contributed greatly to minority-white conflict and to the symbolic association of community control with minority solidarity and power. The very term "community control" became a condensation symbol which evoked strong hostility from many whites.

The community control controversies emphasized the need to deal with the problem of the large bureaucracies, and the inadequacy of linkage structures connecting the administrative centers of government with ordinary citizens in their neighborhoods, particularly with minority neighborhoods where citizens were both most dependent upon public services and most dissatisfied with their quality. The low legitimacy of some bureaucratic structures meant that they became centers of popular mobilization, instead of stabilizing instruments of social control.

The end of the decade could, then, be categorized by two ideological currents, an inter-racial split over community control, as well as a collective recognition that some structural changes could benefit all New York communities. The future of community control and decentralization will hinge largely on which tendency becomes dominant. Thus, New York City is a research site where the problems which have produced demands for governmental reform in many large cities are most acute, and where the relatively high degree of ideological concern about community control issues should make analysis of leadership attitudes particularly interesting in pointing to the political solutions which are likely to be adopted.

THE OFFICE OF NEIGHBORHOOD GOVERNMENT

The waning of the movement for community control was associated with continued efforts by the administration of Mayor Lindsay to deal with the bureaucratic phenomenon and the attenuation of mechanisms linking city and public. Some of the city officials who had helped to precipitate the battle for community control of education tried again to reform governmental structures, but this time with much greater caution, and in an historical context less racially charged. After two abortive attempts at establishing new community institutions, the city began an experimental program in the winter of 1971–72 called the Office of Neighborhood Government (ONG).

The Office of Neighborhood Government was aimed at establishing some degree of administrative decentralization and area-based coordination among the dozen or more agencies servicing a community planning district. A district cabinet of agency representatives was chaired by a professional district manager who, with a small staff, attempted to monitor agency performance, determine community (i.e., CPD) priorities, suggest new programs, and link the city bureaucracies with local organizations and civic leaders. In some places, the district managers created neighborhood councils, a step in the direction of community control.

ONGs were initially established in five CPDs.[17] These five experimental districts, and three additional CPDs which were chosen for comparative purposes,[18] constitute the areas from which our data are drawn. On the whole they fall into the second and third quartiles of CPDs in terms of socioeconomic status, social problems, and racial segregation. They range from being about 20 per cent white to 80 per cent white, and are broadly representative of many areas of New York and other large American cities.[19] Information about politics in such typical yet anonymous places, and about the attitudes of their leadership structure, is therefore of interest to the urban political sociologist, particularly given the relative paucity of such data in the literature.

This paper is based upon four primary sources of empirical evidence. First, a closed-ended field survey of a total sample of 368 community leaders chosen through a reputational methodology was carried out during 1972 in four of the five experimental CPDs and in the three control districts. (The survey was pretested in the other ONG district, the Rockaways.) Second, intensive, semi-structured interviews were conducted during 1973 with a sample of 114 community leaders active in three CPDs: Bushwick, Crown Heights, and Wakefield-Edenwald. Both leadership samples included members of community planning boards, police precinct councils, community (anti-poverty) corporation boards, clergymen, officers of a wide range of voluntary organizations (such as PTA's, taxpayers and block or neighborhood improvement groups, tenants councils and race or ethnic organizations), city councilmen, state legislators and party leaders. Third, voluntary organizations, protest groups, quasi-government agencies, and the political clubs and parties were observed directly during 1973 and 1974 in Bushwick, Crown Heights, and Wakefield-Edenwald. Fourth, all city bureaucrats (e.g., police precinct captains, district sanitation supervisors) who sat on the five ONG cabinets were interviewed in 1973. This population consisted of 78 individuals.

The next section of the paper will depend mainly on the first two sources of data, which we will designate, respectively, the *survey* of community leaders and the *interviews* with community leaders. Field observation data are used to illustrate the impact of community types on operational orientations toward community control. Finally, the cabinet interviews are examined in the last section, when we discuss the attitudes of minority-group cadres within city bureaucracies.

(An extensive discussion of sample characteristics and of methodological issues is contained in an appendix to this article which, for reasons of space, could not be printed here. Interested readers may request copies from the authors.)

RACIAL DIFFERENCES IN IDEOLOGICAL AND OPERATIONAL ORIENTATIONS TOWARD COMMUNITY CONTROL

An ideology is a differentiated and logically organized set of beliefs which identifies relevant social and political actors, diagnoses the forces which constrain them, and proposes courses of action which are ethically justifiable and can lead to valued ends. The race-conflict and democratic systems of beliefs are alternative ideologies by this definition, even though they are not complete in the sense that they focus only on particular political questions and problems, and could be fitted into more general typologies of political thought.

Individuals employing the same ideological framework may have different *operational beliefs* about group interests, probable outcomes, and appropriate actions in concrete situations. For example, there is much greater consensus among Americans about the liberal ideological belief in freedom of speech than in the operational belief that communists should be allowed to speak in their communities.[20] Operational beliefs are easier to specify than are the patterns we call ideologies. And because they are more closely tied to immediate situations, they are more readily utilized predictors of behavior than are ideologies.

The survey and interviews provide evidence about both the community control ideologies and the operational beliefs of community leaders. After describing both levels of thought and analyzing some of the factors which explain differences among leaders, we will consider the implications of these findings for the possible future of community control.

Ideologies of Community Control. The overwhelming majority of community leaders favors some form of community control and shares one of the two ideological frameworks supportive of it. When leaders are presented with a list of city services in their CPDs, only 18 per cent of those surveyed oppose any degree of local control over the agency they *least* wish to control, the fire department (Table 1). Opposition to community control averages less than 10 per cent for the entire array of thirteen services. Of the 97 leaders whose beliefs about community control are codable into ideological types, 92 (95 per cent) advance either the race conflict or the democratic supporting ideologies (Table 2). *The evidence is unambiguous in pointing to a positive orientation toward local control over government agencies by the entire community leadership stratum.*

TABLE 1

Orientation of Community Leaders Toward Operationalization of Community Control for Each of Thirteen City Services[a]

Service	Percentage Favoring Decision-Making Powers	Percentage Favoring Advisory Powers	Percentage Opposing Community Control	Percentage Don't Know/ Doesn't Matter
Recreation	61[b]	35	3	1
Drug Addict Treatment Programs	52	40	7	1
Housing Maintenance & Code Enforcement	52	38	9	1
Public Schools	52	39	8	1
Parks	50	42	6	2
Street Repairs	44	46	8	2
Health Services	44	48	8	0
Sanitation	40	52	6	2
Traffic	32	58	8	2
Police Protection	30	56	12	2
Welfare	29	52	16	3
Subway & Bus Lines	27	58	11	4
Fire Protection	20	58	18	4

[a] Services are ranked in decreasing order of percentage favoring decision-making power.

[b] Percentages sum to 100 horizontally. *N*'s vary slightly, but are approximately 350 for each row.

When leaders explain what they mean by community control most invoke a democratic type of ideology. About 14 per cent (see Table 2) employ an ideological framework which can be interpreted as reflecting the race-conflict type. In coding for this type of ideology we accepted rather subtle indicators of racial orientation, because the overt support for black power or racial militancy which was current six or seven years ago is almost completely absent from the interview responses. Here is a typical expression of race-conflict ideology:

> People must be made aware of their potential to influence government policy and education processes. People have to learn how to protect themselves. The crisis is immense, staggering. The biggest problem is to get the poor to participate in government. . . . We have to learn to share [power]. Black politicians should make it clear that they represent the black community. . . .
> We must train our people to do research and gain evidence in their favor. We're going to win. . . .

Missing from this and other race-conflicting arguments are explicit statements concerning racism, the colonial status of minority groups, or the zero-sum nature of politics. Rather, the emphasis is on development of minority communities so that they can act effectively within (rather than against) governmental institutions. Outcomes and institutional processes are linked. Accountability to the community will both help facilitate community development and guarantee an adequate share of services. Nevertheless, adherents to race-conflict ideas do clearly equate "community" with minority-group collectivities, rather than with a geographical area, and their major concern is in improving the situation of racial minorities.

There are several possible explanations for the moderation shown by supporters of the race-conflict position. Minority group respondents may have chosen their words carefully in talking with our white interviewers. This stratum of leaders, however, produced the activists who participated in the urban political movements of the 'sixties, when many of them were willing to get involved in public confrontations with city officials and frequently with the police as well. Methodological factors seem to us of less importance in accounting for the lack of militant rhetoric than do changes which have taken place in the situation of minority groups. First, at the time of the interviews, the political climate nationwide was one of conservatism, declining expectaitons, and political "realism," all of which discouraged racial militancy. Second, minority-group community leaders had better access to governmental institutions and the political process than they did in the mid 'sixties. Whether this was viewed as progress or co-optation, it seemed to have dampened rhetoric considerably, and to have led to efforts to use the system, to work through newly developed channels of communication. Finally, the need for some kind of bureaucratic decentralization and local political input had been recognized as a general problem in New York City, no longer as primarily a racial demand. Minority leaders, while having a greater stake in community control than whites, could frame their demands in terms which did not undermine the possibility of interracial coalition.

Approximately four-fifths of community leaders rationalize support for community control through a democratic-type ideology (Table 2). As the following examples (from five respondents) indicate, however, within a common ideological framework beliefs vary considerably concerning the manner in which local control should be effected and the degree of power local majorities should have over city agencies:

> There's a need for real change, change that would provide a greater voice with power to speak for those who live in the city and are victims of the existing situation. What is needed is an organization to speak for the community.

> We need simultaneously to have community development and administrative decentralization. We need the orderly interpretation of the feelings of the community . . . so the community can have input into city offices. We need to get away from street rhetoric and to have a formal mechanism for input.

> City agencies have become too large. I feel decentralization at this point would help; the community would set the priorities for the agencies. . . .

TABLE 2

Types of Ideology Used by Community Leaders Interviewed
in Bushwick, Crown Heights, and Wakefield-Edenwald as
Rationales for Community Control[a]

	Support Some Form of Community Control		Oppose All Forms of Community Control
	Ideology used to Rationalize Support is:		
	Race-Conflict Type	Democratic Type	
Minority Leaders	20%[b] (11)	80% (45)	0%
White Leaders	7% (3)	81% (33)	12% (5)

[a]Tabulation based on analysis of 97 interviews with community leaders who provided codable responses to the following question: "The Charter Commission is particularly concerned with devising ways of making city institutions more responsive to citizens. What suggestions do you have?" Interviews probed for attitudes about decentralization, citizen participation, decision-making or advisory power for community boards, elective versus appointed boards.

[b]Percentages sum to 100 per cent horizontally. Of the 45 minority leaders, 10 are Hispanic. Three of the Hispanic leaders support Hispanic group power, and 8 of the 48 black leaders support black power. These are roughly comparable percentages. Since minority leaders tend not to focus on black-Hispanic conflict, the aggregation of black and Hispanic leaders into a single minority-group designation seems justifiable for the purpose of this analysis.

I go for decentralization and, of course, citizen participation. I favor neighborhood boards with real power. Advisory power is just the status quo. They should have power over personnel, the budget—so as to give a chance for the community people to participate in city government and to keep city government money here. Part of the problem is that people setting policy don't live in the area they are setting the policy for. It is only a job for them.

To restructure the agencies you should put a member of every board or organization or of the Community Corporation [community action agency] Board into an affiliation with a service agency at a decisional level. . . . that community person should be consulted on services and priorities. If the agency doesn't perform, this liaison should finger the person responsible and report him to higher political officials. These liaisons should report monthly to the local community organization office.

Elected officials should give attention to the needs of their constituency. The Borough President should have more power. The City must eliminate the superagencies and give the Borough President the authority.

This range of responses suggests that the dominance of democratic ideology among community leaders, whatever their racial background, may mask large differences in operational beliefs about community control. Qualitative examination of the interviews confirms two generalizations about these differences: first, that individuals who utilize a race-conflict ideology are certain to want to operationalize community control by giving relatively great power to local communities; but, [second, that] community control (a large plurality of both minority and white leaders) encompass a great range of possible degrees and modes of operationalization. And, as we will show, although racial differences in ideological rationales for community control are fairly small, racial differences in operational beliefs are quite large.

Operational Support for Community Control. The survey provides considerable evidence about the predictors of operational support for community control. The main indicators of operational support derive from the item presented in Table 1. Respondents were asked whether they favored (1) local decision making or (2) local advisory powers over thirteen separate city services, or (3) whether they opposed community control altogether. Since so few people oppose community control, the practical distinction is between those who favor decision-making powers versus all others, and an aggregate indicator of their general support can be provided by the total number of agencies over which they wish to extend local decision-making powers. Using these indicators of operational support for community control, we find that the racial background of community leaders is a significant predictor of degree of operational support, but that income, education, religion, partisan affiliation and extent of organizational activity are not correlated with such support.

If we examine the first column in Table 1, we see considerable range in the percentage of respondents favoring decision-making powers over the various services. The services are ranked according to this percentage, which is greatest for recreation (61 per cent) and least for fire protection (20 per cent). This large range suggests that community leaders judge the particulars of each service separately, rather than having an undifferentiated response set toward community control. Table 3 shows that willingness to operationalize community control seems to depend upon a complex assessment of the conditions affecting a given city service.

With one exception rank order is similar regardless of race, even though a greater percentage of minority than white leaders operationally support community control over every single service.[21] The percentage of minority leaders showing high support is, in general, between 15 and 20 per cent greater than the white percentage. The largest interracial differences are in support for community control of drug addiction programs, housing maintenance, schools, health services, sanitation, and police protection (20 per cent or more in each case; Table 3). For each service, the race of a leader is a statistically significant predictor of the leader's degree of support for community control (i.e. for local *decision-making* power). Gamma correlation coefficients range between .29 and .53, with all significant at better than the .05 level.

TABLE 3

Orientation Toward Community Control of Minority and White Leaders for Each of Thirteen City Services[a]

Service	Percentage of Each Racial Group Favoring Decision-making Powers[b]		Gamma Correlation between Race and Decision-making Powers	Significance of Chi-square with 1 df; P Less Than:
	Minority	White		
Recreation	71	56	.37	.01
Drug Addict Treatment Programs	69	43	.48	.001
Housing Maintenance and Code Enf.	66	45	.44	.001
Public Schools	65	43	.41	.001
Parks	59	46	.28	.05
Street Repairs	57	37	.38	.01
Health Services	58	36	.41	.001
Sanitation	53	33	.39	.01
Traffic	40	28	.29	.05
Police Protection	46	21	.53	.001
Welfare	41	23	.42	.001
Subway & Bus Lines	37	21	.36	.01
Fire Protection	33	14	.51	.001

[a] Services are ranked in decreasing order of percentage of *all* leaders favoring decision-making powers (as in Table 1).

[b] Based on N favoring decision-making powers, advisory powers, or opposing community control for each racial group. N's vary slightly, but are approximately 350 for each row.

TABLE 4

Index of Minority and White Operational Support for Local Decision-Making Power over City Services

Rank		(Range of Scores[a] Included in Rank)	Minority	White	All
Least Support	0	(.00−.08)	17% (21)	31% (74)	26% (95)
	1	(.09−.25)	10% (12)	16% (39)	14% (51)
	2	(.26−.50)	18% (22)	19% (46)	19% (68)
Most	3	(.51−.69)	16% (20)	17% (40)	17% (60)
Support	4	(.70−1.000)	39% (47)	17% (41)	24% (88)
			100% (122)	100% (240)	100% (362)

Gamma = .41
Chi-square = 23.44 with 4 df;
P less than .0001

[a] Index score = number of services over which respondent favored *decision-making* power divided by number of services rated in terms of "decision-making," "advisory," or "opposed to community control." Services for which response was DK or "Doesn't Matter" are excluded from the computation, and respondents with 4 or more such exclusions are eliminated from the tabulation. The resulting scores are essentially the percentage of the thirteen city services over which respondent favored decision-making powers. Almost all respondents in the lowest rank "0" did not favor decision-making powers over any services; while those in the highest rank "4" favored such powers over 10 or more of the thirteen services.

Racial differences in support for community control are presented in a more simplified form by the index described in Table 4. As would be expected from the previous findings, minority leaders score considerably higher on the index than do whites. Only 17 per cent of minority leaders, but 31 per cent of white leaders, fall into the lowest index rank; while 39 per cent of minority leaders and 17 per cent of whites show the highest level of support for community control. The Gamma correlation between race and the five-rank index is .41. *Thus, there are consistently large interracial differences with regard to degree of operational support for community control despite similar ideological rationales and similar overall support for some kind of local citizen participation.*

This apparent anomaly is, in part, explained by the existence of other political beliefs according to which blacks and whites differ. Our data, in fact, point to such an attitudinal correlate of operational support. Using a two-item index of support for citizen militancy, we find considerably greater support for militancy among minority leaders than among whites (Gamma = .62; Table 5). Furthermore, there is a strong correlation between support for militancy and for community control (Gamma = .42; Table 9). A factor, therefore, which accounts for greater minority support for community control is the predisposition of minority leaders toward citizen militancy. Intraracial variation in orientation toward community control can likewise be partially explained by this attitudinal correlate (see Table 9, columns 2 and 3).

General political beliefs offer one explanation for varying attitudes toward operationalizing community control. Another explanation relies on analysis of the overall structural position of minority groups in American cities. Eisinger argues that the social position of individual respondents is less important in accounting for racial differences in support for protest activities than is the structural position of the group with which individuals identify.[22] By this logic minority leaders would support community control more than whites if the interests of minority groups are advanced by community control to a greater extent than those of whites. The process by which community leaders come collectively to represent their racial groups need not be conscious and is, in any event, not accessible to us without additional data.

Race constitutes a dominant and continuously functioning structural force shaping the interests and beliefs of community leaders. Further factors, arising out of the specific political situations in which individuals find themselves, assist in explaining the variations within racial groups. These situationally specific factors include perception of the quality of city agencies, experience with actual instances of decentralization and community input, and the relations among social groups in the community. Stress upon the importance of situationally specific beliefs about the costs and benefits of operationalizing community control should not obscure the importance of race as a discriminating variable. It does, however, point to the complex set of cross-cutting cleavages and interests to which community leaders are sensitive.

SITUATIONAL FACTORS AFFECTING OPERATIONAL SUPPORT FOR COMMUNITY CONTROL

Our evidence suggests three situational factors which influence attitudes toward community control. First, the more dissatisfied leaders are with governmental performance, the more likely they are to favor community control. Second, like the doctors who support Medicaid when they find it in fact raises rather than lowers their incomes, leaders who have had favorable experience of actual programs of decentralization and community control indicate higher levels of operational support for community control. Third, the operational model of community control which leaders desire to see implemented is strongly influenced by the racial composition and political organization of their local districts. These propositions reflect situationally specific interest cleavages which cross-cut the basic interracial divisions among community leaders.

Quality of Agency Performance. Leaders show considerable variation in their evaluations of the performance of different city agencies in their districts. The average evaluation of city services also varies among the districts, and does so in a manner which probably reflects objective reality (see Table 7). While there is an overall correlation between race and rank on an index of service evaluation (Table 6), closer analysis shows that this association is minimal or even reversed in three of the seven CPDs. These data suggest that leaders' perception of the quality of services is tied to factors situationally specific to each agency and to each CPD.

The evaluation of city services is negatively correlated with operational support for community control, and this correlation remains unchanged when minority and white leaders are examined separately. Table 8 shows these relationships most simply by cross-

TABLE 5

Support for Citizen Militancy by Minority and White Community Leaders

Rank on Index of Support for Citizen Militancy[a]	Minority	White	All
Lowest	6% (7)	20% (44)	15% (51)
Intermediate	74% (85)	76% (169)	75% (254)
Highest	20% (23)	4% (9)	10% (32)
Gamma = .62	100% (115)	100% (222)	100% (337)

Chi-square = 29.78 with 2 df; P less than .0001

[a] The index is based on two questions from the survey with which the respondent could strongly agree, agree, disagree, or strongly disagree:
(1) Tenants are justified in organizing a rent strike if the landlord fails to make needed repairs in a building.
(2) Sometimes violence is necessary to bring about important changes in society.
Forty-four per cent strongly agreed with the rent strike item, and 39% agreed; 9% strongly agreed with the violence item, and 27% agreed.
The index was constructed so as to clearly identify individuals at the two extremes of support for militancy. Only respondents who *strongly* agreed with the violence item were labeled "highest supporters." Those who disagreed or strongly disagreed with *both* items were placed in the "lowest support" category. Those who agreed with the violence item and agreed or strongly agreed with the rent strike item were designated as "moderate supporters" of militancy. There were six cases where an individual agreed or strongly agreed with the violence question but disagreed or strongly disagreed with the rent strike question. These cases were designated as "logical errors" and not included in the index.

TABLE 6

Racial Differences in the Evaluation of the Quality of Local City Services

Rank on Index[a]	Minority Leaders	White Leaders	All Leaders
1. Most Positive Evaluation	26%	38%	34%
2. Intermediate	29	35	33
3. Most Negative Evaluation	46	27	33
Gamma = .29	101%	100%	100%
	N = 122	N = 240	N = 362

Chi-square = 13.02 with 2 df; P less than .002

[a] Respondents were asked to rate the quality of each of thirteen city services in their own Community Planning District on a five point scale from excellent to very bad. The services were the same as those in the community control item.
The index is based on a summation (weighted by score) of the number of services each respondent rated "very bad" or "bad" divided by the number of services rated "excellent," "good," "fair," "bad," or "very bad." This index was divided into ranks at the 34th and 67th percentile.

tabulating the variables in dichotomized form. (Table 9 shows similar Gamma correlations for the full indexes.) Within the minority group, there is a 17 percentage point difference in positive support for community control between those with lower and higher rankings on the service index (Gamma = .34); within the white group, the difference is 19 per cent (Gamma = .39). Thus, the overall perception by leaders of the quality of city services apparently influences their willingness to operationalize community control over those services. We have also examined these relationships for individual services, and our findings are identical. The correlation within each social group between an index of service evaluation and community control attitudes is replicated service by service. The more negatively a leader rates a particular service (say, police protection in his CPD), the more likely the leader is to favor local decision-making powers over that service.

Nevertheless, analysis of Table 8 (and examination of service-by-service relationships) also shows that the basic disparity in support for community control *between* racial groups is not eliminated when service evaluation is partialled out. Among the leaders with lower service evaluations, 64 per cent of minority leaders, but only 48 per cent of whites, indicate higher support for community control. This 16 percentage point difference within service-evaluation groupings is comparable to the differences within each racial group when service evaluation is a variable. Computation of correlation coefficients between race and community control for the higher and lower service-evaluation groupings produces Gammas, respectively, of .38 and .33, which are almost identical to those between community control and service evaluation within each racial group. (Table 9 shows similar results using the full indexes for the two variables.) We conclude, therefore, that the structurally rooted factor of race and the situationally specific factor of service evaluation are equally important as predictors of the dependent variable. Jointly, they explain a good deal of the variance in levels of operational support for community control.

Experience with Programs of Decentralization and Community Control. Since 1969 New York City has established a number of programs intended to produce administrative decentralization and mechanisms for local input or community control. The most significant programs involving to some degree both elements of institutional change are the Community School Boards and the Office of Neighborhood Government (ONG). The response of community leaders to each of these programs provides additional evidence about the way situational factors affect the basic racial cleavages in operational support for community control. Each presents leaders with a concrete institutional form and actual experience. In these instances, the operational orientation of leaders need not depend entirely on deductions from general propositions.

In actual practice, community control of schools in New York took a much less radical form than white critics had feared or than minority advocates had desired during the period of major interracial hostility in the 'sixties. The thirty-odd community school boards have been, in general, dominated by groups supportive of educational professionalism. This leads us to expect that, at the least, white opposition to community control of education would be lessened by contact with the new institutional arrangements, although it is not clear what effect these arrangements might have for minority leaders.

Table 10 presents data on support for community control of schools among self-identified specialists in educational problems. White educational specialists indicate much higher approval of community control of education than white non-specialists. Sixty-six per cent of the white specialists, as opposed to 37 per cent of other white leaders, endorse local decision-making powers over schools.[23] This suggests that familiarity with the actual operation of school decentralization has created support for its continuation.[24]

ONG presents a second example of a governmental program which provided a concrete stimulus for leadership attitudes. As we will discuss shortly, ONG constituted only a step toward community control, and the program was introduced in a way least likely to exacer-

TABLE 7

Racial Differences in the Evaluation of the Quality of Local City Services for Leaders from the Same Community Planning Districts

| Community Planning District | Percentage of Each Group of Leaders Falling into the Lowest Rank (Most Negative Evaluation) on the Service Index[a] | | | Racial Differences Within Districts |
	All Leaders from District	Minority (a)	White (b)	(a) minus (b)
East N.Y. (Brooklyn)	46% ($N = 50$)	63%	38%	25%
Bushwick (Brooklyn)	43 ($N = 49$)	59	23	36
Jackson Heights (Queens)	33 ($N = 55$)	47	25	22
Grand Concourse (Bronx)	32 ($N = 56$)	70	24	46
Crown Heights (Brooklyn)	32 ($N = 50$)	27	36	−9
Wakefield-Edenwald (Bronx)	26 ($N = 51$)	32	22	10
Washington Heights (Manhattan)	24 ($N = 51$)	22	24	−2

[a] This index is defined in Table 6. Note that respondents are ranking the services in *their own* Community Planning Districts.

TABLE 8

Racial Differences in the Relation between Support for Community Control and Evaluation of the Quality of Local Services

| | Minority | | White | |
	Lower Service Evaluation[a]	Higher Service Evaluation[b]	Lower Service Evaluation	Higher Service Evaluation
Lower Support for Community Control[c]	36% (20)	53% (35)	52% (34)	71% (125)
Higher Support for Community Control[d]	64% (36)	47% (31)	48% (31)	29% (50)
	100% (56)	100% (66)	100% (65)	100% (175)

Gamma = −.34
Chi-square = 3.94 with 1 df; *P* less than .05.

Gamma = −.39
Chi-square = 7.93 with 1 df; *P* less than .01

[a] Rank 3 on service evaluation index defined in Table 6.

[b] Rank 1 and 2 on service evaluation index.

[c] Ranks 0, 1, and 2 on index of support for community control defined in Table 4.

[d] Ranks 3 and 4 on index of support for community control.

TABLE 9

Summary of Predictors of Operational Support for
Community Control for All Leaders, and for Minority
and White Leaders Examined Separately

Predictor	Gamma Correlations between Rank on Index of Support for Community Control and Specified Variables for:		
	All Leaders	Minority Leaders	White Leaders
Race (Minority Status)	.35*[e]	—	—
Education[a]	−.05	.09	−.02
Income[b]	−.04	−.03	−.03
Index of Support for Militancy[c]	.42*	.31*	.38*
Index of Evaluation of Quality of City Services[d]	−.28*	−.28[f]	−.26*

[a] Four rank index.

[b] Five rank index.

[c] Three rank index using categories specified in Table 5.

[d] Three rank index using categories as specified in Table 6.

[e] All coefficients marked with an asterisk are significant using a Chi-square statistic at .05 level or beyond.

[f] This cross-tabulation has 15 cells (since the community control index has five ranks), and 8 df. Collapsing either or both of the indexes produces a Chi-square significant at better than .05 and a Gamma higher than .28. (See Table 8.)

bate latent racial cleavages. Probably as a result of these specific aspects of the ONG innovation, the response of community leaders in Bushwick, Crown Heights and Wakefield-Edenwald to ONG reflected no racial division.[25] Fifty-eight per cent of minority leaders interviewed expressed positive evaluations of ONG; 18 per cent gave mixed evaluations; and 18 per cent were negative (3 of the 60 minority leaders had uncertain opinions). The white breakdown was virtually identical, with 58 per cent positive, 16 per cent mixed, and 13 per cent negative (4 of 31 white leaders were uncertain). These findings underline once more the complexity of forecasting leadership responses to actual programs. The politics of implementation of community control does not depend on leadership ideologies and general attitudes alone. Predicting the impact of specific programs requires taking into account situational factors, such as the process by which institutional innovation is effected and the particular interests which leaders think are being serviced in the actual instance.

TABLE 10

Orientation toward Community Control of Schools of White and Minority Leaders by Problem Specialization[a]

	Minority		White	
	Educational Specialists	Nonspecialists	Educational Specialists	Nonspecialists
Oppose Community Control of Schools or Favor Only Advisory Powers	33% (8)	35% (34)	34% (13)	63% (126)
Favor Decision-making Powers Over Schools	67% (16)	65% (63)	66% (25)	37% (75)
	100% (24)	100% (97)	100% (38)	100% (201)

Gamma = $-.04$
Chi-square = .03 with 1 df; P less than .80

Gamma = $-.53$
Chi-square = 10.65 with 1 df; P less than .01

[a] Leaders were asked which one of a list of "problems" they had "the most experience dealing with" in their community planning district. Those who identified schools are designated educational specialists.

Types of Communities. Several dimensions are involved in a typology of neighborhoods which would explain variation in the politics of community control. First, the social class of residents should indicate their level of dependence on governmental services and bureaucracies. Second, racial composition is obviously important given what we know about the general correlation between race and operational support for community control. Third, social divisions within a single neighborhood and the relative power of the various groups within the community affect their interests in institutional change. Such dimensions help identify how leaders measure the effects on their constituencies of alternative programs of administrative decentralization and community control.

Brief examinations of the Bushwick, Crown Heights, and Wakefield-Edenwald districts illustrate how community type affects orientations toward local control. Bushwick is the most ethnically pluralistic yet homogeneously poor of the three CPDs. It is divided among a shrinking white population of Italian and German ethnicity (25 per cent of the total), blacks (30 per cent) and Hispanics (45 per cent). Most people in Bushwick are working or lower class. The district had a median income in 1969 of about $6500, or $400 less than the New York City norm. In Bushwick, the primary concern of all groups of leaders seems to be community development, both in an economic and social sense. The relative lack of civic leadership is seriously compounded by the virtual desertion of the district by partisan political organizations. The main centers of community activity and of linkage with city government are the community corporation (originally a community action agency under the federal poverty program) and ONG.

Bushwick leaders emphasize the need to increase public services in the district and see community control as a means for doing this. But control in Bushwick must be advanced in spite of the inactivity of the population. Thus, leaders believe that new institutional structures should not be premised on widespread community participation. Rather, Bushwick needs more professionals who would act as its advocates within the city bureaucratic arena. According to this conception, community control in Bushwick might take a technocratic form, with ONG and community corporation professionals advancing the interests of the Bushwick community through virtual rather than mandated representation of the larger population.

Crown Heights falls between Bushwick and Wakefield-Edenwald in terms of both racial and economic composition. Blacks are in a numerical majority, comprising 75 per cent of the population, with the remainder divided between a small Hispanic group (5 per cent) and whites (20 per cent), most of whom are Jews. The Jewish population is dominated by a tightly knit sectarian community of Hasidim. The 1969 median income was $7,500. Both blacks and whites are divided along economic lines. Many blacks (approximately 50 per cent) are homeowners and thereby rooted in the district, while the Hasidim are also rooted, but for religious and cultural reasons. The politics of Crown Heights is defined by a sharp cleavage between homeowners and renters, which is reflected in splits within the Democratic party leadership. Crown Heights has a high level of civic activity among all social groups. The Hasidim, however, have political power far beyond their numbers in the district, both because they have religious ties with bureaucrats in the central city government, and because they have been able to vote as a disciplined bloc in local elections (something the blacks have not accomplished). As a result of their voting power, the Hasidim have considerable influence in one of the Democratic party clubs and dominate the board of the community corporation. The major vehicle linking the black majority with government agencies is a community board created by ONG. The board represents local civic organizations and is controlled by black groups.

Black leaders in Crown Heights strongly favor community control through the ONG community board. They feel they need a vehicle for resolving conflicts among civic and partisan organizations, so that the "community" can focus its attentions on collective development. They want representation on any local board, however, to reflect the interests of communal groups in proportion to their share of the population. Because the Hasidim dominate popular elections, black leaders prefer to have an appointed board. The Hasidim, for their part, would like to maintain the status quo. They are probably correct in seeing any form of community control as likely to be disadvantageous for themselves since they are a numerical minority in the CPD. In the context of Crown Heights, the politics of community control centers about maintaining unity within a popular majority beset by cleavages, and balancing democratic norms against the power of a unified minority fearful of being overwhelmed at the local level.

Wakefield-Edenwald is a relatively well-off district almost three-quarters white (primarily Italian). Most whites are homeowners as are almost half of the black residents. The district is politically conservative. Homeowners are concerned with maintaining property values and a high level of "hard" services (e.g., sanitation, fire). There are many organizations in the district, with a cohesive structure of civic leaders who tend to be alienated from the relatively active Democratic and Republican clubs. The black lower class (perhaps 10 per cent of the entire population) is segregated into a remote corner of the CPD where a public housing project is located. This part of the black community is politically disorganized. Black homeowners participate in civic organizations, but not in partisan ones;

their interests differ little from those of the white majority, and racial agitation is rarely evident.

In Wakefield, community control is seen as a vehicle for giving this geographically remote CPD a greater share of city resources and a local say over how these will be distributed. The emphasis is on decentralization rather than community power. Few leaders desire the establishment of a local board with decision-making powers, though most would like to see the community consulted by city bureaucrats. The minority of leaders who are active in the political clubs want elected officials to have more power, while the civic leaders are suspicious of politicians and want any structures of local input to be nonpartisan. Wakefield does not suffer from the problems of Bushwick or Crown Heights and neither does it present much of an indigenous force for community control.

These sketches of three very different types of communities suggest the ways in which local situational factors influence the politics of community control. The descriptions of the three CPDs also call attention to the dynamic elements which must be considered in making any predictions about community control. In the next section we further examine these dynamic forces, but this time at a citywide and national level.

COMMUNITY CONTROL: A PROGNOSIS

The future of community control, as an issue and an ideology, will be determined by a combination of factors deriving from broad ideological currents, national and citywide policies, and specific local situations. The continued dominance of the democratic model, and in fact the continuation of community control as a meaningful organizing concept around which to center discussions of local politics, depends on a variety of different inputs, some of them unpredictable. The phrase community control had no particular significance when Banfield and Wilson published their path-breaking text on urban politics in 1963,[26] its disappearance from the urban scene might be just as sudden. In this section we examine the variables at the citywide and national level which affect the debate over community participation in policy making and implementation, and which will determine its longevity as an issue.

Citywide Factors. New York City presents two contrasting cases of the implementation of experiments in community participation and administrative decentralization—one in school decentralization that culminated in a crisis, and the second, the Office of Neighborhood Government (ONG), which was accepted calmly. While a significant factor in differentiating the reactions to the two experiments was the difference in militancy of the times in which they occurred, an important contributing cause also was the strategy pursued by governmental policy-makers. Comparison of the city government's role in these two experiments should help to isolate some of the variables which can make community control into a more or less controversial issue.[27]

In 1967 the New York City Board of Education, in response to great dissatisfaction with the school system expressed by vocal black parents, and at the prompting of the Ford Foundation, set up three demonstration school districts (IS 201, Two Bridges, and Ocean Hill-Brownsville). Their declared purpose was to show the effects of placing limited control over school policy at the community level. The three demonstration districts quickly elected governing boards which interpreted their mandate as going well beyond the planning function visualized by the Board of Education. There was also hostility between the governing boards and professional school employees, eventually resulting in the transfer by the Ocean Hill board of a group of teachers out of the district and the lengthy teachers' strike of 1968. Intense emotion surrounded the conflict, and it came to symbolize a whole range of issues concerning the relationships between clients and public bureaucracies and between the races.

Throughout the school decentralization controversy the city administration played an indecisive role. No central office, either under the Board of Education or the Mayor, coordinated the decentralization effort. A research institute at Queens College provided the fledgling districts with what technical assistance they received. The Board of Education, although the nominal sponsor of the program, quickly lost control of it. The Mayor, while acting as an advocate of the program until the political consequences of doing so became too heavy, had no statutory power over an eduational program. Many of the individuals associated with the experiment, including governing board members and some school personnel, believed that the programs could be meaningful only if their supporters were willing to confront the school bureaucracy directly.

In contrast, the ONG experiment was mounted with great caution. Its promoters, some of whom had been involved in the school dispute, devoted much attention to developing a program that would be politically viable. Thus, while many of them hoped to see considerable power transferred to community boards, their rhetoric concentrated primarily on administrative decentralization rather than community participation, and when they referred to participation it was in terms of democratic rather than race-conflict ideology. The program was set up so that the five experimental districts reported to a central Office of Neighborhood Government, which itself was directly under the Mayor. The Mayor issued a directive to the agencies under his control that ONG was vested with his authority. The director of the central office was diligent in keeping track of the activities of the neighborhood offices and selling the program to the various city bureaucracies. A key role was played by the local district managers who acted as intermediaries between neighborhood groups and the city service agencies. Some of the districts had community boards and others did not; in all cases the district manager worked actively to insure cooperation between community groups and the district service cabinet. He also worked especially hard to see that local elected officials did not regard ONG as usurping their role, and sought to provide staff services to these officials and give them credit for ONG activities.

A second important factor contributing to the nonthreatening nature of the ONG experiment was the composition of the district service cabinets. The establishment of cabinet structures enhanced the authority of district service chiefs, who while only occupying middling positions within their agencies, were at the top from the district perspective. Besides giving their egos a boost, the new structure permitted cabinet members to consult with their counterparts about district matters without going all the way up the agency hierarchy and back down again. As long as forces in the community were not viewed as hostile by the cabinet members, there was little reason for them not to welcome the new structure, and in fact, of 82 cabinet members interviewed, 68 (83 percent) regarded the district cabinet as useful or very useful and only 4 members (5 per cent) evaluated it negatively.[28]

The fact that the cabinet bureaucrats were not seen as enemies by community leaders in the experimental districts results in part from the cautiousness of the ONG program in comparison with the far more ambitious school decentralization experiment. The rhetoric of some of the school decentralizers, including that of the Bundy Commission,[29] proclaimed that the educational system needed a thorough overhaul and that the experiments in community participation were a step in that direction. This overhaul was taken to mean major changes in the civil service rules which had long kept the administrative cadres of the system white and insulated from parental pressures. The goals of the school experiments thus were perceived as a direct threat by the administrative hierarchy and the teachers' and supervisors' unions, while the limited scope of the ONG experiment meant that it provided little threat to established interests.

Another important reason for the serenity surrounding ONG, however, was itself a product of the programs and activism of the 'sixties. One effect of strong pressures for bureaucratic change was minority-group recruitment to agency positions. Thus, 19 of the 82 district service cabinet members, or nearly a quarter, were nonwhite (only one was Puerto Rican). As a result, the client bureaucratic cleavage was no longer so clearly reinforced by a minority-white division. Moreover, the presence of blacks on the cabinets created an ideological force within the bureaucracy supporting community control. This finding is particularly noteworthy since it indicates that blacks who "make it" maintain an ideological commitment different from their white peers (Table 11). The very high relationship between race and attitude toward community control among cabinet members (Gamma = .80) revealed in Table 11 is striking when compared with the relationship shown in Table 3 for community leaders, where Gamma ranges between .28 and .51.

Despite the presence of blacks on the service cabinets, and the preponderance of cabinet members of both races who support at least advisory powers for neighborhood groups, analysis of the cabinet interviews shows that the potential for racially polarized conflict between community activists and bureaucracies over local control has not disappeared. Further inspection of Table 11 indicates that the higher correlation between race and operational support for community control by cabinet members than by community leaders results almost entirely from the more negative attitudes toward community decision-making powers held by white cabinet members as compared with white community leaders. Only 18 per cent of white cabinet members favor decision-making powers for local boards, while above 40 per cent of white leaders favor local decision-making powers over at least some city services. Moreover, as Table 12 indicates, when the white group of cabinet members is examined by type of bureaucratic status, only 5 per cent of the 21 whites in the "hard services" support decision-making powers (just one black cabinet member held a position in the hard services). The implication of this finding is that intrusion by community groups into these service areas could well precipitate hostile reactions.

On the whole, the ONG experience suggests that the two citywide factors which most influence reactions to the introduction of decentralized governmental programs are the strategies followed by the program's sponsors and the responses of the affected bureaucrats. Community control could become an extremely divisive issue once again in New York

TABLE 11

Relationship between Race and Support for Advisory versus
Decision-making Power for Community Boards among
Bureaucrats on District Service Cabinets

	Minority[a]	White
Favor Advisory Powers for Community Boards	33% (5)	82% (32)
Favor Decision-making Powers for Community Boards	67% (10)	18% (7)
	100% (15)[b]	100% (39)[c]

Gamma = .80

Chi-square = 11.92 with 1 df;
P less than .001

[a] One Puerto Rican was included in this group.

[b] Fifteen of the 19 minority members interviewed responded to the probe concerning community boards.

[c] An additional 19 white members did not respond to the probe concerning community boards, and one white member opposed any form of community participation. While it is possible that the exclusion of 19 respondents may bias the results presented here, it is most likely that failure to answer points to a negative attitude toward community participation. In that case the table would understate the correlation between race and attitude.

if it is pressed as a redistributional program, particularly if it is interpreted as an attack on the still white-controlled hard service bureaucracies. In cities where racial integration of the service bureaucracies has proceeded less far than in New York, we would expect that programs for neighborhood participation, when neighborhoods are black and bureaucrats are white, would continue to produce interracial conflict.

National Factors. The policies of city governments will produce wide variations from place to place in the introduction of decentralized programs and the intensity of conflict surrounding them. The parameters, however, will be set by the national situation; urban conflict will be as much affected by federal programs and national currents concerning relations between the races as by particular events in any one city. Whether the federal government chooses revenue-sharing as its method of "returning government to the people" or reverts to the Johnson administration programs of maximum feasible participation will significantly influence not just the kinds of programs offered to city dwellers but also the extent of minority activism and white reaction.

The dismantling of the Office of Economic Opportunity (OEO); the demise of Model Cities, and the insistence that funding of organizations to benefit the poor must be channeled through regular governmental bodies have meant a decline in the resources available to ghetto residents in their battle against the status quo. Although few of these programs directly sponsored militant action,[30] they spawned militant leaders and raised the expectations of large numbers of people, thereby creating highly volatile situations. Reduced

TABLE 12

Relationship between Service Area and Support for
Advisory versus Decision-making Power for Community
Boards among White[a] Bureaucrats on District Service
Cabinets[b]

	Hard Services[c]	Soft Services[d]
Support Advisory Powers for Community Boards	95% (20)	66% (12)
Support Decision-making Powers for Community Boards	5% (1)	34% (6)
	100% (21)	100% (18)

P (Fisher's Exact) = .03

[a] There was only one black cabinet member in a hard service area.

[b] Nineteen white members did not respond to the probe concerning community boards, and one white member opposed any form of community participation.

[c] Hard services are sanitation, police, sewer, fire, water resources, traffic control, highway maintenance, and parks.

[d] Soft services are health, education, planning, human resources, aging, housing, youth, social services, welfare, drug addiction.

prospects of funding, a change in the national mood, and the routinization of organizations serving poor people have all served to reduce volatility. The strength of the counterattack following the urban disorders of the last decade made many black leaders wary of radical strategies. As a result, we have seen a nationwide decline in conflict organizations and militant rhetoric.

This decline, however, has not meant a return to the 1950s. There are a number of legacies of the previous era. Most important are the intermediate structures such as community planning boards, health boards, housing councils, block associations, and community corporations which arose in response to the urban programs of the 'sixties. These provided an arena for the development of a new cadre of civic leaders in areas of the city where, since the decline of the political machine, there had been almost a total absence of representative institutions. While the absolute number of participants in these structures is small and they lack authoritative power, such participants nonetheless act as attentive publics. The existence of a layer of even weak intermediate structures means some access, some patronage, and a reservoir of experienced individuals used to dealing with bureaucratic agencies.

A national Democratic administration would undoubtedly redirect attention toward the cities once again. Whether it would also foment the level of political activism which characterized the last period of Democratic ascendancy is an open question.[31] Fear of intense reaction by whites, and realization that much of the earlier conflict was between deprived groups fighting with each other over limited resources, may make it less likely that minority leaders will again regard widespread mobilization as a useful strategy. J. Q. Wilson's prediction in *Negro Politics*[32] that black leadership would be primarily specialized and bureaucratically oriented is sustained, even though in 1968 it appeared outdated. Although the current dominance of the democratic type of community control ideology over the race-conflict type may diminish, the basis for a rapid shift is not at the moment obvious. Which of the two ideologies is more valid or would produce better tactics from the minority-group point of view is a different question.

As we have seen, within the broad type of the democratic model there is a split, correlated with race, over operational beliefs in community control. Blacks and Hispanics are continuing to push for community decision-making powers based on their position not so much as racial minorities but as a bureaucratic clientele. This pressure, combined with a recognition on the part of even conservative policy makers that too much centralization leads to rigidity and poor areal coordination, means that we will continue to see programs aimed at devolving authority to lower administrative levels and providing channels for citizen input into bureaucracies. These programs, however, have for the last six years been implemented without any large infusion of new resources. While they have created more flexibility and more responsiveness, as well as new neighborhood leaders and new bureaucrats whose social backgrounds more closely resemble those of their clients, they have not produced basic changes in the distribution of social benefits. Nor have they really had much effect on the dominant position of central bureaucratic authorities and unions of service providers.[33]

The various movements for community control and programs for decentralizing urban bureaucracies, then, have provided some new chips for the previously most disadvantaged players in the urban ecology of games.[34] Robert Dahl has commented that

> a central guiding thread of American constitutional development has been the evolution of a political system in which all the active and legitimate groups in the population can make themselves heard at some crucial stage in the process of decision.[35]

Decentralization and the creation of new linkage structures enlarge the number of groups participating in the policy-making process and increase the legitimacy and bargaining power of the relatively deprived. In other words, deprived minorities in many urban areas have now been absorbed into the pluralist bargaining system. Where once their impact on the political marketplace was no more substantial than that of the impoverished consumer on the economic one, they may now participate on a level analogous to the individual with some money to spend but little to invest. The predictable result is compromise, an occasional gain, but no major redistribution across social classes.[36]

The game, moreover, is limited to the municipal level. The greater power of racial minorities to control garbage collections or allocations in the city budget is not reflected in a commensurate ability to influence national priorities. In an era of rapid inflation and high unemployment, achievements at the local level often seem insignificant and diversionary, although there is no compelling logic to show that the energy spent on local causes could be easily redirected to more general issues.

The question of whether community control is a useful strategy for minority groups has been much debated.[37] Its general endorsement by whites as well as blacks, the lessening of its identification as a specifically black cause, despite the willingness of minorities to carry its implementation farther than most whites would, and its framing in democratic rather than group conflict terms, tend to validate the criticism by radicals that it is a moderate and coöptative strategy. Whether to sacrifice the limited but tangible gains that it brings in the hopes of larger redistributive goals is tied up with a number of political and normative judgments. These concern the possibility of radical black-white coalition, the virulence of majority reaction to militant strategies, the capacity of minority groups to constitute a revolutionary class, and the superiority of a direct system of income redistribution to one of service provision. The continued predominance among minority and white urban leaders of an ideology of community control based on the democratic model indicates a general acceptance on their part of the inevitability, although not necessarily the desirability, of the pluralist model of urban politics.

NOTES

1. James Q. Wilson, "The Urban Unease," *The Public Interest*, No. 12 (Summer, 1968), p. 28.

2. Robert Dahl, *After the Revolution?* (New Haven: Yale University Press, 1970), p. 153.

3. Milton Kotler, *Neighborhood Government* (New York: Bobbs-Merrill, 1969), p. 93. Kotler, in this work, presents the argument in favor of neighborhood democracy in its most extreme form, and traces its roots to the origins of the American republic. Yates, however, asserts that while local democracy is often considered characteristic of the American political tradition, it was in fact more myth than history. Douglas Yates, *Neighborhood Democracy* (Lexington, Mass.: D.C. Heath, 1973), p. 12.

4. Stokely Carmichael and Charles V. Hamilton, *Black Power* (New York: Vintage, 1967), p. 166.

5. See Alan Altshuler, *Community Control* (New York: Pegasus, 1970).

6. See Norman I. Fainstein and Susan S. Fainstein, *Urban Political Movements* (Englewood Cliffs, N.J.: Prentice-Hall, 1974), chap. 1; J. David Greenstone and Paul E. Peterson, *Race and Authority in Urban Politics* (New York: Russell Sage Foundation, 1973), chap. 4.

7. While proponents of community control promote values of lay participation, decentralization, and group particularism, they do not see these as requiring the jettisoning of technical expertise and fair treatment of individuals. Rather, they claim that reform principles have been carried out to an extreme where they produce results contrary to their original intentions.

8. See Leonard J. Fein, "Community Schools and Social Theory: The Limits of Univer-

salism," in *Community Control of Schools*, ed., Henry M. Levin (Washington, D.C.: The Brookings Institution, 1970), pp. 76–99.

9. Carmichael and Hamilton, *op. cit.;* Robert Blauner. *Racial Oppression in America* (New York: Harper and Row, 1972), chap. 3; Ira Katznelson, *Black Men, White Cities* (New York: Oxford University Press, 1973), chap. 3.

10. See Eric A. Nordlinger, *Decentralizing the City: A Study of Boston's Little City Halls* (Cambridge: M.I.T. Press, 1972).

11. See Susan S. Fainstein *et al.,* "Community Leadership and the Office of Neighborhood Government in Bushwick, Crown Heights and Wakefield-Edenwald" (New York: Bureau of Applied Social Research, Columbia University, November, 1973), interim report; Susan S. Fainstein and Fran LaSpina, "District Service Cabinets and the Office of Neighborhood Government" (New York: Bureau of Applied Social Research, Columbia University, November, 1973), interim report.

12. See Frances Fox Piven, "The Great Society as Political Strategy," in Richard A. Cloward and Frances Fox Piven, *The Politics of Turmoil* (New York: Pantheon, 1974), pp. 271–83.

13. Greenstone and Peterson, *Race and Authority in Urban Politics*, pp. 39–43.

14. Katznelson, *Black Men, White Cities*, chap. 5.

15. Joseph Helfgot, "Professional Reform Organizations and the Symbolic Representation of the Poor," *American Sociological Review*, 39 (August, 1974), 475–91.

16. Michel Crozier defines the term in *The Bureaucratic Phenomenon* (Chicago: University of Chicago Press, 1967).

17. Brooklyn No. 4 (Bushwick), Brooklyn No. 8 (Crown Heights), Manhattan No. 12 (Washington Heights). Bronx No. 13 (Wakefield-Edenwald), and Queens No. 14 (Rockaways).

18. Brooklyn No. 5 (East New York), Bronx No. 5 (Grand Concourse), and Queens No. 3 (Jackson Heights).

19. More detailed information is provided in Norman Fainstein and Susan Fainstein, "Political Representation and the Urban District," paper presented at the 1975 meeting of the American Sociological Association, and in Nathalie Friedman and Naomi Golding, "Urban Residents and Neighborhood Government: Profile of the Public in Seven Urban Neighborhoods of New York City" (New York: Bureau of Applied Social Research, Columbia University, June 1973).

20. Empirical evidence and a theoretical discussion of the concept of ideology versus operational or procedural beliefs is provided by Herbert McClosky, "Consensus and Ideology in American Politics," *American Political Science Review*, 58 (1964), 361–82.

21. The only service with a ranking that differs significantly depending on the race of leaders is police protection. Presumably this may be explained by minority leaders assigning a much higher priority to controlling the police because of their greater interest in changing current police practices.

22. Peter K. Eisinger, "Racial Differences in Protest Participation," *American Political Science Review*, 68 (June 1974), 592–606.

23. The percentage of white specialists most supportive of community control of schools is identical to the percentage of all minority leaders in this category. There is no difference between minority specialists and other minority leaders, however. From additional

analyses, we also know that white specialists and nonspecialists do not differ from each other in their support for community control over other city services. Moreover, the relationship between specialization and support for community control over the institution with which leaders are most familiar does not hold for other city services.

24. It does not tell us whether our sample of white specialists has increased its level of support from what it was prior to 1969, or whether there has been selective recruitment into the educational arena of whites who favor community control of schools. If viewed with caution, however, the data do seem to describe a cleavage which results from situational experience with, or vested interests in, actual programs.

25. The following data are drawn from Fainstein et al., "Community Leadership and the Office of Neighborhood Government. . . ."

26. Edward C. Banfield and James Q. Wilson, City Politics (Cambridge: Harvard University and M.I.T. Press, 1963).

27. A more extended analysis is provided in Susan S. Fainstein and Norman I. Fainstein. "From the Folks Who Brought You Ocean Hill-Brownsville," New York Affairs 2, No. 2 (1974), 104 –115.

28. Fainstein and LaSpina, "District Service Cabinets and the Office of Neighborhood Government," part II.

29. Mayor's Advisory Panel on Decentralization of the New York City Schools (Bundy Commission), Reconnection for Learning (New York: Praeger, 1967).

30. See Fainstein and Fainstein, Urban Political Movements, pp. 31 –36; Kenneth Clark and Jeanette Hopkins, A Relevant War Against Poverty (New York: Harper and Row, 1969), p. 65; James J. Vanecko, "Community Mobilization and Institutional Change: The Influence of the Community Action Program in Large Cities," in Planned Social Intervention, ed. Louis A. Zurcher (New York: Chandler, 1970), p. 270.

31. Piven argues that coöptation of dissidents, increases in welfare spending, and the lessened political power of the cities vis-à-vis the suburbs all mean that the Democratic party in the future will not feel compelled to pay attention to the black urban masses. Frances Fox Piven, "The Urban Crisis: Who Got What, and Why?" in Cloward and Piven, The Politics of Turmoil, pp. 338 –9. Her premise is that ghetto activism forced responses, rather than government programs creating activism, as Moynihan has argued. Daniel Patrick Moynihan, Maximum Feasible Misunderstanding (New York: Free Press, 1969), pp. 134 –5. An alternative view is that the two factors, programs for the poor and activism by the poor, are interactive and intensify each other, even while coöptative tendencies are also at work. Fainstein and Fainstein, pp. 231 –3.

32. James Q. Wilson, Negro Politics (New York: Free Press, 1960), chap. 8.

33. See Sterling D. Spero and John M. Capozzola. The Urban Community and its Unionized Bureaucracies (New York: Dunellen, 1973); The American Assembly, Public Workers and Public Unions, ed. Sam Zagoria (Englewood Cliffs, N.J.: Prentice-Hall, 1972).

34. Norton E. Long, "The Local Community as an Ecology of Games." American Journal of Sociology, 64 (November 1958), 251 –61.

35. Robert A. Dahl, A Preface to Democratic Theory (Chicago: University of Chicago Press, 1956), p. 137.

36. See Robert Paul Wolff, The Poverty of Liberalism (Boston: Beacon Press, 1968).

37. See Dorothy Buckton James, "The Limits of Liberal Reform"; Ira Katznelson, "Antagonistic Ambiguity: Notes of Reformism and Decentralization"; and Dorothy Buckton James, "Response," *Politics and Society,* 2 (Spring 1972), 309 –36. We provide a policy-oriented analysis in Susan S. Fainstein and Norman I. Fainstein, "Local Control as Social Reform: Planning for Big Cities in the Seventies," *Journal of the American Institute of Planners* (July 1976), 275 –285.